P9-DYZ-441

The Economic Regulation of Business and Industry

STATUTORY HISTORY
OF THE UNITED STATES

Bernard Schwartz, General Editor

Titles in the Series:

Civil Rights (2 volumes)	Bernard Schwartz, Editor
Income Security	Robert B. Stevens, Editor
Labor Organization	Robert F. Koretz, Editor
Economic Regulation of Business and Industry	Bernard Schwartz, Editor
Trusts and Anti-Trusts (forthcoming)	Earl W. Kintner, Editor

Published by Chelsea House Publishers

THE ECONOMIC
REGULATION OF
BUSINESS AND INDUSTRY

A Legislative History
of U.S. Regulatory Agencies

VOLUME IV

Editor

BERNARD SCHWARTZ

Edwin D. Webb Professor of Law
New York University

CHELSEA HOUSE PUBLISHERS
in association with
R. R. BOWKER COMPANY
New York and London
1973

Managing Editor: Karyn G. Browne

Editorial Staff: Jeanette Morrison, Michele Sacks,
                     Jan Schwartz, Ellen Tabak

Published by Chelsea House Publishers in association
with R. R. Bowker Company (A Xerox Education Company)

Copyright © 1973 by Chelsea House Publishers
(A Division of Chelsea House Educational Communications, Inc.)
70 West 40 Street, New York, N.Y. 10018

Library of Congress Cataloging in Publication Data

Schwartz, Bernard, 1923–   comp.
    The economic regulation of business and industry.

    (Statutory history of the United States)
    1. Independent regulatory commissions—United
States. 2. Industrial laws and legislation—United
States. I. Title. II. Series.
KF5407.S34   342'.73'066   73-14862
ISBN 0-8352-0694-7

Contents

Volume I

Volume II

MANN-ELKINS ACT, 1910

TRANSPORTATION ACT, 1920

Volume III

FEDERAL TRADE COMMISSION
FEDERAL TRADE COMMISSION ACT, 1914

THE ORIGINS

THE DEBATE

THE DECISION

FEDERAL POWER COMMISSION
WATER POWER ACT, 1920

THE ORIGINS

WATER POWER ACT, 1930

THE ORIGINS

THE DEBATE

FEDERAL COMMUNICATIONS COMMISSION
RADIO ACT, 1927

THE ORIGINS

Volume IV

COMMUNICATIONS ACT, 1934

SECURITIES AND EXCHANGE COMMISSION
SECURITIES ACT, 1933

THE ORIGINS

THE DEBATE

SECURITIES EXCHANGE ACT, 1934

THE ORIGINS

THE DEBATE

NATIONAL LABOR RELATIONS BOARD
NATIONAL LABOR RELATIONS ACT, 1935

CIVIL AERONAUTICS BOARD
CIVIL AERONAUTICS ACT, 1938

Volume V

FEDERAL AVIATION AGENCY
FEDERAL AVIATION ACT, 1958

DEPARTMENT OF TRANSPORTATION
DEPARTMENT OF TRANSPORTATION ACT, 1966

COMMUNICATIONS ACT
1934

Commentary

The Radio Act of 1927 had set up the Federal Radio Commission on an experimental and temporary footing. The FRC was given full powers as a full-time regulatory agency only for one year; it was then to become a part-time commission with only appellate powers. The FRC's status as a full-time agency was, however, continued on a one-year basis by statutes of the next two years. Then, a law at the end of 1929 provided that the commission was to continue "until otherwise provided by law." But this law did not settle the ultimate future of the Radio Commission, for it still implied existence on other than a permanent basis. In addition, certain powers over radio were left to the Secretary of Commerce, so that there was, in important respects, a division of authority between the commission and the Secretary.

Under the Radio Act the regulatory authority of the commission was limited to the field of radio. Control over the entire field of communications (both wire and wireless) was distributed among the Radio Commission, the Department of Commerce, and the Interstate Commerce Commission (which had been given jurisdiction over telephone and telegraph companies by the Mann-Elkins Act of 1910).

By the Communications Act of 1934, Congress abolished the Radio Commission and set up in its stead the Federal Communications Commission. Control over all forms of communications was consolidated in this single body. It was given the regulatory authority over radio which had been divided between the Radio Commission and the Secretary of Commerce, as well as the powers of the ICC over telephone and telegraph.

Under the 1934 Act, the FCC's regulatory authority falls into two general areas. Over common carriers by wire the commission exercises more or less the same type of regulatory authority that the ICC and the FPC exert over other utilities. Thus, the FCC is given the power, with regard to interstate telephone and telegraph companies, to fix rates, to prohibit improper practices such as unjust discrimination, to issue licenses for the establishment of new lines, and to control accounting practices.

The second broad area of the FCC's competence is in the field of wireless broadcasting. The commission's authority here is essentially based upon the licensing power. It alone determines who is to engage in broadcasting and, as the physical characteristics of broadcasting make it impossible for more than one licensee to use a particular frequency in a given area, licensees from the commission obtain what amount to exclusive franchises for the terms of their licenses.

The Act gives the FCC power to classify broadcast stations; prescribe the nature of the service to be rendered; assign frequency bands; determine the location of stations; regulate interferences between stations; establish areas or zones to be served by a station; regulate network broadcasting; prescribe the qualifications of station operators; suspend or revoke the license of any operator; and inspect transmitting apparatus. These, together with the commission's power to license all broadcast stations, give it all but complete regulatory control over the broadcast industry.

Perhaps the outstanding feature of the Communications Act is the well-nigh unfettered discretion that it vests in the FCC. The field of radio was still new in 1934 and the Congress felt that there had not been enough regulatory experience to include in the law detailed standards to limit the commission's discretion. In granting a broadcast-station license the FCC need only consider "if public convenience, interest, or necessity will be served thereby." And the same test is to govern the commission in the exercise of all its other extensive powers over broadcasting. Thus, Congress has given the commission what amounts to carte blanche. Telling the FCC to act in the public interest is the practical equivalent of saying: "Here is the regulatory problem; deal with it as you will."

The Communications Act represents the high-water mark of congressional abdication of power to the regulatory agency. The only one who touched on the delegation issue during the legislative debate was Congressman Schuyler Merritt [Rep., Conn.] in the House. As a Congressman, he conceded, he knew little about radio and the problems involved in regulating it and other communications. The only solution was to form a commission to gather experience in the field. It was much safer to give the commission powers "than to attempt with what little knowledge we have to lay down a code which will cover all sorts of conditions and all sorts of individual practices." Presumably Congress could later, in the light of actual regulatory experience, enact more detailed standards to guide the regulatory agency. This was the hope expressed at the end of the House debate on the conference report by Congressman Thomas Blanton [Dem., Tex.] (though he was overly optimistic in hoping it would be done in the next Congress). The reality has been otherwise. Congressman Frederick Lehlbach's [Rep., N.J.] response to Mr. Blanton—that a future congressional revision of radio legislation "will be precluded if we enact" the Communications Act—has proved accurate. Despite four decades of regulatory experience, Congress has never enacted legislation making the broadside "public interest" standard more specific. The result is to leave communications regulation in the unfettered discretion of the FCC even today, when the Merritt justification for doing so no longer exists.

The commission's power over broadcasting is made even greater by the fact that station licenses are granted only for a term of three years under the 1934 Act. This means that every licensee must come to the commission seeking renewal of his license every three years. Living under the constant Damocles' sword of the renewal proceeding, he is far more amenable to the authority of the regulatory agency than is the licensee who has received a permanent franchise.

There is another side of the regulatory coin in the communications field. The powers vested in the FCC are so tremendous, giving it virtually uncontrolled life-and-death authority over the broadcast industry, that those engaged in broadcasting simply cannot afford to risk a commission which is hostile to them. The result has been constant efforts on the part of the industry to influence the commission, to ensure that it will not act in a manner adverse to those established in broadcasting. Such attempts on the part of those regulated to control the agency present problems in all of the regulatory commissions, but the FCC has been particularly prone to them.

Although the field of broadcasting has expanded greatly during the past four decades, Congress has not seen fit to make any basic change in the Communications Act. Except for some procedural amendments enacted in 1952, the law remains substantially what it was when passed in 1934. There has, however, been one significant expansion in the FCC's area of authority. This occurred when the commission itself assumed regulatory competence over the new broadcast medium of television. This could be done, despite the fact that the Congress had not thought of television in 1934, because the definition of broadcasting in the Communications Act is broad enough to cover all forms of wireless broadcasting, including television.

The history of the Communications Act starts in 1933 with President Franklin Roosevelt's request to Secretary of Commerce Roper to set up an interdepartmental committee to make a thorough study of the regulation of communications. The interdepartmental committee submitted its report at the beginning of 1934. It emphasized the division of authority which existed over communications and proposed instead a unified system of control, with all regulation of communications vested in a single body. The President sent the report to Congress, together with a special message urging the creation of a new commission to exercise control over all communications by wire and wireless. Bills were introduced in both houses to give effect to the President's recommendation. It was the Senate bill, introduced by Senator Clarence Dill [Dem., Wash.], that became the Communications Act. It is fully explained in the report of the Senate Commerce Committee (*infra* p. 2425), as well as that of the House Commerce Committee (*infra* p. 2436).

The Dill bill was debated only briefly in the Senate, the entire debate taking place on May 15, 1934. The debate started with the speech of Senator Dill introducing the measure. The Dill speech starts by explaining why new legislation, rather than a mere transfer of powers under existing law, was necessary. Dill then gives the background of the bill and a summary of its provisions. He deals with the new commission (of five members in the Senate bill), and the provision for its functioning in two divisions. He discusses the provision for appeals to the courts and explains why such appeals are to be permitted only in the Court of Appeals for the District of Columbia in most cases.

The debate then was occupied with various committee amendments. Next came amendments introduced by other Senators. Among these were the amendment of Senator (later Justice) Black, giving the commission full power to inspect books and records and that of Senator David Walsh [Dem., Mass.] resolving the controversy over exemption from the civil service laws of members of the FCC staff and their salaries. About the only controversy in the debate arose from the Wagner-Hatfield amendment providing for a reallocation of frequencies, with at least 25 percent allotted to educational, religious, and other nonprofit organizations. After Senator Dill explained why the committee had refused to accept the amendment, it was rejected in a roll call vote. The Senate debate concluded with complaints against loading the commission with high salaried employees and the hope that the day had come when no more commissions would be created. The bill was then passed without a roll call.

In the House, the debate was even briefer, being limited to only two hours on June 2, 1934. The shortness of the debate in both houses is most striking, bearing in mind the importance of the bill, which worked a complete transformation in the regulation of communications. In the House, Congressman Louis McFadden [Rep., Penn.], for the minority, objected to the speed with which such a long and important bill was being pushed through: "Just as the President wishes, this House is again signing on the dotted line without crossing a 't' or dotting an 'i'." McFadden also referred to the broadcast monopoly of the two networks and asserted that the Federal Radio Commission had operated as though it were encouraging doing away with the small stations, in accordance with the aim of the networks.

The McFadden complaint could avail nothing in the face of the majority desire and the House adopted the resolution limiting debate to two hours. The debate, in Committee of the Whole House, was introduced by Congressman Sam Rayburn [Dem., Tex.], then Chairman of the Commerce Committee. Rayburn states that the bill only reenacts existing law (an understatement of the bill's effect) and summarizes its provisions. The House committee's provision for a commission of seven (the number in the final Act) is explained.

There was very little opposition to the bill in the House (even the Fish attack [*infra* p. 2506] was not on the merits of the bill). Even Congressman Carl Mapes [Rep., Mich.], the ranking minority committee member, came out in favor. There was the speech of Congressman Harold McGugin [Rep., Kan.] asserting that the licensing power gave the government too great a control over freedom of speech; but he did not really attack the bill. Also of interest is the urging of Congressman Francis Maloney [Dem., Conn.] that the House adopt the Wagner-Hatfield amendment, as well as (on a lesser level) the attempt by Congressman Charles Truax [Dem., Ohio] to amend the bill to give the commission power to investigate the exclusion of Father Coughlin from the air. At the end of the debate, the House voted to substitute the House committee bill for the Senate bill and passed the bill without a roll-call vote.

The differences between the Senate and House bills were ironed out in conference. The conference report is explained in the statement of the House managers (*infra* p. 2514). The minority objected that the conferees had written a new bill, particularly in their express provision for repeal of the 1927 Radio Act. Despite this, the House quickly voted by 158 to 40, on June 9, 1934, to agree to the conference report. On the same day, without debate, the Senate agreed to the report without a roll call. The Communications Act became law on June 19, 1934, when it was signed by the President.

COMMUNICATIONS ACT
June 19, 1934

Be it enacted by the Senate and House of Representatives of the United States of America in Congress assembled,

TITLE I–GENERAL PROVISIONS

Purposes of Act: Creation of Federal Communications Commission

SECTION 1. For the purpose of regulating interstate and foreign commerce in communication by wire and radio so as to make available, so far as possible, to all the people of the United States a rapid, efficient, Nation-wide, and world-wide wire and radio communication service with adequate facilities at reasonable charges, for the purpose of the national defense, and for the purpose of securing a more effective execution of this policy by centralizing authority heretofore granted by law to several agencies and by granting additional authority with respect to interstate and foreign commerce in wire and radio communication, there is hereby created a commission to be known as the "Federal Communications Commission," which shall be constituted as hereinafter provided, and which shall execute and enforce the provisions of this Act.

Application of Act

SEC. 2. (a) The provisions of this Act shall apply to all interstate and foreign communication by wire or radio and all interstate and foreign transmission of energy by radio, which originates and/or is received within the United States, and to all persons engaged within the United States in such communication or such transmission of energy by radio, and to the licensing and regulating of all radio stations as hereinafter provided; but it shall not apply to persons engaged in wire or radio communication or transmission in the Philippine Islands or the Canal Zone, or to wire or radio communication or transmission wholly within the Philippine Islands or the Canal Zone.

(b) Subject to the provisions of section 301, nothing in this Act shall be construed to apply or to give the Commission jurisdiction with respect to (1) charges, classifications, practices, services, facilities, or regulations for or in connection with intrastate communication service of any carrier, or (2) any carrier engaged in interstate or foreign communication solely through physical connection with the facilities of another carrier not directly or indirectly controlling or controlled by, or under direct or indirect common control with, such carrier; except that sections 201 to 205 of this Act, both inclusive, shall, except as otherwise provided therein, apply to carriers described in clause (2).

Definitions

SEC. 3. For the purposes of this Act, unless the context otherwise requires—

(a) "Wire communication" or "communication by wire" means the transmission of writing, signs, signals, pictures, and sounds of all kinds by aid of wire, cable, or other like connection between the points of origin and reception of such transmission, including all instrumentalities, facilities, apparatus, and services (among other things, the receipt, forwarding, and delivery of communications) incidental to such transmission.

(b) "Radio communication" or "communication by radio" means the transmission by radio of writing, signs, signals, pictures, and sounds of all kinds, including all instrumentalities, facilities, apparatus, and services (among other things, the receipt, forwarding, and delivery of communications) incidental to such transmission.

(c) "Licensee" means the holder of a radio station license granted or continued in force under authority of this Act.

(d) "Transmission of energy by radio" or "radio transmission of energy" includes both such transmission and all instrumentalities, facilities, and services incidental to such transmission.

(e) "Interstate communication" or "interstate transmission" means communication or transmission (1) from any State, Territory, or possession of the United States (other than the Philippine Islands and the Canal Zone), or the District of Columbia, to any other State, Territory, or possession of the United States (other than the Philippine Islands and the Canal Zone), or the District of Columbia, (2) from or to the United States to or from the Philippine Islands or the Canal Zone, insofar as such communication or transmission takes place within the United States, or (3) between points within the United States but through a foreign country; but shall not include wire communication between points within the same State, Territory, or possession of the United States, or the District of Columbia, through any place outside thereof, if such communication is regulated by a State commission.

(f) "Foreign communication" of "foreign transmission" means communication or transmission from or to any place in the United States to or from a foreign country, or between a station in the United States and a mobile station located outside the United States.

(g) "United States" means the several States and Territories, the District of Columbia, and the possessions of the United States, but does not include the Philippine Islands or the Canal Zone.

(h) "Common carrier" or "carrier" means any person engaged as a common carrier for hire, in interstate or foreign communication by wire or radio or in interstate or foreign radio transmission of energy, except where reference is made to common carriers not subject to this Act; but a person engaged in radio broadcasting shall not, insofar as such person is so engaged, be deemed a common carrier.

(i) "Person" includes an individual, partnership, association, joint-stock company, trust, or corporation.

(j) "Corporation" includes any corporation, joint-stock company, or association.

(k) "Radio station" or "station" means a station equipped to engage in radio communication or radio transmission of energy.

(l) "Mobile station" means a radio-communication station capable of being moved and which ordinarily does move.

(m) "Land station" means a station, other than a mobile station, used for radio communication with mobile stations.

(n) "Mobile service" means the radio-communication service carried on between mobile stations and land stations, and by mobile stations communicating among themselves.

(o) "Broadcasting" means the dissemination of radio communications intended to be received by the public, directly or by the intermediary of relay stations.

(p) "Chain broadcasting" means simultaneous broadcasting of an identical program by two or more connected stations.

(q) "Amateur station" means a radio station operated by a duly authorized person interested in radio technique solely with a personal aim and without pecuniary interest.

(r) "Telephone exchange service" means service within a telephone exchange, or within a connected system of telephone exchanges within the same exchange area operated to furnish to subscribers intercommunicating service of the character ordinarily furnished by a single exchange, and which is covered by the exchange service charge.

(s) "Telephone toll service" means telephone service between stations in different exchange areas for which there is made a separate charge not included in contracts with subscribers for exchange service.

(t) "State commission" means the commission, board, or official (by whatever name designated) which under the laws of any State has regulatory jurisdiction with respect to intrastate operations of carriers.

(u) "Connecting carrier" means a carrier described in clause (2) of section 2 (b).

(v) "State" includes the District of Columbia and the Territories and possessions.

Provisions Relating to the Commission

SEC. 4. (a) The Federal Communications Commission (in this Act referred to as the "Commission") shall be composed of seven commissioners appointed by the President, by and with the advice and consent of the Senate, one of whom the President shall designate as chairman.

(b) Each member of the Commission shall be a citizen of the United States. No member of the Commission or person in its employ shall be financially interested in the manufacture or sale of radio apparatus or of apparatus for wire or radio communication; in communication by wire or radio or in radio transmission of energy; in any company furnishing services or such apparatus to any company engaged in communication by wire or radio or to any company manufacturing or selling apparatus used for communication by wire or radio; or in any company owning stocks, bonds, or other securities of any such company; nor be in the employ of or hold any official relation to any person subject to any of the provisions of this Act, nor own stocks, bonds, or other securities of any corporation subject to any of the provisions of this Act. Such commissioners shall not engage in any other business, vocation, or employment. Not more than four commissioners shall be members of the same political party.

(c) The commissioners first appointed under this Act shall continue in office for the terms of one, two, three, four, five, six, and seven years, respectively, from the date of the taking effect of this Act, the term of each to be designated by the President, but their successors shall be appointed for terms of seven years; except that any person chosen to fill a vacancy shall be appointed only for the unexpired term of the commissioner whom he succeeds. No vacancy in the Commission shall impair the right of the remaining commissioners to exercise all the powers of the Commission.

(d) Each commissioner shall receive an annual salary of $10,000, payable in monthly installments.

(e) The principal office of the Commission shall be in the District of Columbia, where its general sessions shall be held; but whenever the convenience of the public or of the parties may be promoted or delay or expense prevented thereby, the Commission may hold special sessions in any part of the United States.

(f) Without regard to the civil-service laws or the Classification Act of 1923, as amended, (1) the Commission may appoint and prescribe the duties and fix the salaries of a secretary, a director for each division, a chief engineer and not more than three assistants, a general counsel and not more than three assistants, and temporary counsel designated by the Commission for the performance of special services, and (2) each commissioner may appoint and prescribe the duties of a secretary at an annual salary not to exceed $4,000. The general counsel and the chief engineer shall each receive an annual salary of not to exceed $9,000; the secretary shall receive an annual salary of not to exceed $7,500; the director of each division shall receive an annual salary of not to exceed $7,500; and no assistant shall receive an annual salary in excess of $7,500. The Commission shall have authority, subject to the provisions of the civil-service laws and the Classification Act of 1923, as amended, to appoint such other officers, engineers, inspectors, attorneys, examiners, and other employees as are necessary in the execution of its functions.

(g) The Commission may make such expenditures (including expenditures for rent and personal services at the seat of government and elsewhere, for office supplies law books, periodicals, and books of reference, and for printing and binding) as may be necessary for the execution of the functions vested in the Commission and as from time to time may be appropriated for by Congress. All expenditures of the Commission, including all necessary expenses for transportation incurred by the commissioners or by their employees, under their orders, in making any investigation or upon any official business in any other places than in the city of Washington, shall be allowed and paid on the presentation of itemized vouchers therefor approved by the chairman of the Commission or by such other member or officer thereof as may be designated by the Commission for that purpose.

(h) Four members of the Commission shall constitute a quorum thereof. The Commission shall have an official seal which shall be judicially noticed.

(i) The Commission may perform any and all acts, make such rules and regulations, and issue such orders, not inconsistent with this Act, as may be necessary in the execution of its functions.

(j) The Commission may conduct its proceedings in such manner as will best conduce to the proper dispatch of business and to the ends of justice. No commissioner shall participate in any hearing or proceeding in which he has a pecuniary interest. Any party may appear before the Commission and be heard in person or by attorney. Every vote and official act of the Commission shall be entered of record, and its proceedings shall be public upon the request of any party interested. The Commission is authorized to withhold publication of records or proceedings containing secret information affecting the national defense.

(k) The Commission shall make an annual report to Congress, copies of which shall be distributed as are other reports transmitted to Congress. Such report shall contain such information and data collected by the Commission as may be considered of value in the determination of questions connected with the regulation of interstate and foreign wire and radio communication and radio transmission of energy, together with such recommendations as to additional legislation relating thereto as the Commission may deem necessary: *Provided*, That the Commission shall make a special report not later than February 1, 1935, recommending such amendments to this Act as it deems desirable in the public interest.

(l) All reports of investigations made by the Commission shall be entered of record, and a copy thereof shall be furnished to the party who may have complained, and to any common carrier or licensee that may have been complained of.

(m) The Commission shall provide for the publication of its reports and decisions in such form and manner as may be best adapted for public information and use, and such authorized publications shall be competent evidence of the reports and decisions of the Commission therein contained in all courts of the United States and of the several States without any further proof or authentication thereof.

(n) Rates of compensation of persons appointed under this section shall be subject to the reduction applicable to officers and employees of the Federal Government generally.

Divisions of the Commission

SEC. 5. (a) The Commission is hereby authorized by its order to divide the members thereof into not more than three divisions, each to consist of not less than three members. Any commissioner may be assigned to and may serve upon such division or divisions as the Commission may direct, and each division shall choose its own chairman. In case of a vacancy in any division, or of absence or inability to serve thereon of any commissioner thereto assigned, the chairman of the Commission or any commissioner designated by him for that purpose may temporarily serve on said division until the Commission shall otherwise order.

(b) The Commission may by order direct that any of its work, business, or functions arising under this Act, or under any other Act of Congress, or in respect of any matter which has been or may be referred to the Commission by Congress or by either branch thereof, be assigned or referred to any of said divisions for action thereon, and may by order at any time amend, modify, supplement, or rescind any such direction. All such orders shall take effect forthwith and remain in effect until otherwise ordered by the Commission.

(c) In conformity with and subject to the order or orders of the Commission in the premises, each division so constituted shall have power and authority by a majority thereof to hear and determine, order, certify, report, or otherwise act as to any of said work, business, or functions so assigned or referred to it for action by the Commission, and in respect thereof the division shall have all the jurisdiction and powers now or then conferred by law upon the Commission, and be subject to the same duties and obligations. Any order, decision, or report made or other action taken by any of said divisions in respect of any matters so assigned or referred to it shall have the same force and effect, and may be made, evidenced, and enforced in the same manner as if made, or taken by the Commission, subject to rehearing by the Commission as provided in section 405 of this Act for rehearing cases decided by the Commission. The secretary and seal of the Commission shall be the secretary and seal of each division thereof.

(d) Nothing in this section contained, or done pursuant thereto, shall be deemed to divest the Commission of any of its powers.

(e) The Commission is hereby authorized by its order to assign or refer any portion of its work, business, or functions arising under this or any other Act of Congress or referred to it by Congress, or either branch thereof, to an individual commissioner, or to a board composed of an employee or employees of the Commission, to be designated by such order, for action thereon, and by its order at any time to amend, modify, supplement, or rescind any such assignment or reference: *Provided, however*, That this authority shall not extend to investigations instituted upon the Commission's own motion or, without the consent of the parties thereto, to contested proceedings involving the taking of testimony at public hearings, or to investigations specifically required by this Act. All such orders shall take effect forthwith and remain in effect until otherwise ordered by the Commission. In case of the absence or inability for any other reason to act of any such individual commissioner or employee designated to serve upon any such board, the chairman of the Commission may designate another commissioner or employee, as the case may be, to serve temporarily until the Commission shall otherwise order. In conformity with and subject to the order or orders of the Commission in the premises, any such individual commissioner, or board acting by a majority thereof, shall have power and authority to hear and determine, order, certify, report, or otherwise act as to any of said work, business, or functions so assigned or referred to him or it for action by the Commission and in respect thereof shall have all the jurisdiction and powers now or then conferred by law upon the Commission and be subject to the same duties and obligations. Any order, decision, or report made or other action taken by any such individual commissioner or board in respect of any matters so assigned or referred shall have the same force and effect, and may be made, evidenced, and enforced in the same manner as if made or taken by the Commission. Any party affected by any order, decision, or report of any such individual commissioner or board may file a petition for rehearing by the Commission or a division thereof and every such petition shall be passed upon by the Commission or a division thereof. Any action by a division upon such a petition shall itself be subject to rehearing by the Commission, as provided in section 405 of this Act and in subsection (c). The Commission may make and amend rules for the conduct of proceedings before such individual commissioner or board and for the rehearing of such action before a division of the Commission or the Commission. The secretary and seal of the Commission shall be the secretary and seal of such individual commissioner or board.

TITLE II–COMMON CARRIERS

Service and Charges

SECTION 201. (a) It shall be the duty of every common carrier engaged in interstate or foreign communication by wire or radio to furnish such communication service upon reasonable request therefor; and, in accordance with the orders of the Commission, in cases where the Commission, after opportunity for hearing, finds such action necessary or desirable in the public interest, to establish physical connections with other carriers, to establish through routes and charges applicable thereto and the divisions of such charges, and to establish and provide facilities and regulations for operating such through routes.

(b) All charges, practices, classifications, and regulations for and in connection with such communication service, shall be just and reasonable, and any such charge, practice, classification, or regulation that is unjust or unreasonable is hereby declared to be unlawful: *Provided*, That communications by wire or radio subject to this Act may be classified into day, night, repeated, unrepeated, letter, commercial, press, Government, and such other classes as the Commission may decide to be just and reasonable, and different charges may be made for the different classes of communications: *Provided further*, That nothing in this Act or in any other provision of law shall be construed to prevent a common carrier subject to this Act from entering into or operating under any contract with any common carrier not subject to this Act, for the exchange of their services, if the Commission is of the opinion that such contract is not contrary to the public interest.

Discrimination and Preferences

SEC. 202. (a) It shall be unlawful for any common carrier to make any unjust or unreasonable discrimination in charges, practices, classifications, regulations, facilities, or services for or in connection with like communication service, directly or indirectly, by any means or device, or to make or give any undue or unreasonable preference or advantage to any particular person, class of persons, or locality, or to subject any particular person, class of persons, or locality to any undue or unreasonable prejudice or disadvantage.

(b) Charges or services, whenever referred to in this Act, include charges for, or services in connection with, the use of wires in chain broadcasting or incidental to radio communication of any kind.

(c) Any carrier who knowingly violates the provisions of this section shall forfeit to the United States the sum of $500 for each such offense and $25 for each and every day of the continuance of such offense.

Schedules of Charges

SEC. 203. (a) Every common carrier, except connecting carriers, shall, within such reasonable time as the Commission shall designate, file with the Commission and print and keep open for public inspection schedules showing all charges for itself and its connecting carriers for interstate and foreign wire or radio communication between the different points on its own system, and between points on its own system and points on the system of its connecting carriers or points on the system of any other carrier subject to this Act when a through route has been established, whether such charges are joint or separate, and showing the classifications, practices, and regulations affecting such charges. Such schedules shall contain such other information, and be printed in such form, and be posted and kept open for public inspection in such places, as the Commission may by regulation require, and each such schedule shall give notice of its effective date; and such common carrier shall furnish such schedules to each of its connecting carriers, and such connecting carriers shall keep such schedules open for inspection in such public places as the Commission may require.

(b) No change shall be made in the charges, classifications, regulations or practices which have been so filed and published except after thirty days' notice to the Commission and to the public, which shall be published in such form and contain such information as the Commission may by regulations prescribe; but the Commission may, in its discretion and for good cause shown, modify the requirements made by or under authority of this section in particular instances or by a general order applicable to special circumstances or conditions.

(c) No carrier, unless otherwise provided by or under authority of this Act, shall engage or participate in such communication unless schedules have been filed and published in accordance with the provisions of this Act and with the regulations made thereunder; and no carrier shall (1) charge, demand, collect, or receive a greater or less or different compensation for such communication or for any service in connection therewith, between the points named in any such schedule than the charges specified in the schedule then in effect, or (2) refund or remit by any means or device any portion of the charges so specified, or (3) extend to any person any privileges or facilities in such communication, or employ or enforce any classifications, regulations, or practices affecting such charges, except as specified in such schedule.

(d) The Commission may reject and refuse to file any schedule entered for filing which does not provide and give lawful notice of its effective date. Any schedule so rejected by the Commission shall be void and its use shall be unlawful.

(e) In case of failure or refusal on the part of any carrier to comply with the provisions of this section or of any regulation or order made by the Commission thereunder, such carrier shall forfeit to the United States the sum of $500 for each such offense, and $25 for each and every day of the continuance of such offense.

Hearing as to Lawfulness of New Charges; Suspension

SEC. 204. Whenever there is filed with the Commission any new charge, classification, regulation, or practice, the Commission may either upon complaint or upon its own initiative without complaint, upon reasonable notice, enter upon a hearing concerning the lawfulness thereof; and pending such hearing and the decision thereon the Commission, upon delivering to the carrier or carriers affected thereby a statement in writing of its reasons for such suspension, may suspend the operation of such charge, classification, regulation, or practice, but not for a longer period than three months beyond the time when it would otherwise go into effect; and after full hearing the Commission may make such order with reference thereto as would be proper in a proceeding initiated after it had become effective. If the proceeding has not been concluded and an order made within the period of the suspension, the proposed change of charge, classification, regulation, or practice shall go into effect at the end of such period; but in case of a proposed increased charge, the Commission may by order require the interested carrier or carriers to keep accurate account of all amounts received by reason of such increase, specifying by whom and in whose behalf such amounts are paid, and upon completion of the hearing and decision may by further order require the interested carrier or carriers to refund, with interest, to the persons in whose behalf such amounts were paid, such portion of such increased charges as by its decision shall be found not justified. At any hearing involving a charge increased, or sought to be increased, after the organization of the Commission, the burden of proof to show that the increased charge, or proposed increased charge, is just and reasonable shall be upon the carrier, and the Commission shall give to the hearing and decision of such questions preference over all other questions pending before it and decide the same as speedily as possible.

Commission Authorized to Prescribe Just and Reasonable Charges

SEC. 205. (a) Whenever, after full opportunity for hearing, upon a complaint or under an order for investigation and hearing made by the Commission on its own initiative, the Commission shall be of opinion that any charge, classification, regulation, or practice of any carrier or carriers is or will be in violation of any of the provisions of this Act, the Commission is authorized and empowered to determine and prescribe what will be the just and reasonable charge or the maximum or minimum, or maximum and minimum, charge or charges to be thereafter observed, and what classification, regulation, or practice is or will be just, fair, and reasonable, to be thereafter followed, and to make an order that the carrier or carriers shall cease and desist from such violation to the extent that the Commission finds that the same does or will exist, and shall not thereafter publish, demand, or collect any charge other than the charge so prescribed, or in excess of the maximum or less than the minimum so prescribed, as the case may be, and shall adopt the classification and shall conform to and observe the regulation or practice so prescribed.

(b) Any carrier, any officer, representative, or agent of a carrier, or any receiver, trustee, lesee, or agent of either of them, who knowingly fails or neglects to obey any order made under the provisions of this section shall forfeit to the United States the sum of $1,000 for each offense. Every distinct violation shall be a separate offense, and in case of continuing violation each day shall be deemed a separate offense.

Liability of Carriers for Damages

SEC. 206. In case any common carrier shall do, or cause or permit to be done, any act, matter, or thing in this Act prohibited or declared to be unlawful, or shall omit to do any act, matter, or thing in this Act required to be done, such common carrier shall be liable to the person or persons injured thereby for the full amount of damages sustained in consequence of any such violation of the provisions of this Act, together with a reasonable counsel or attorney's fee, to be fixed by the court in every case of recovery, which attorney's fee shall be taxed and collected as part of the costs in the case.

Recovery of Damages

SEC. 207. Any person claiming to be damaged by any common carrier subject to the provisions of this Act may either make complaint to the Commission as hereinafter provided for, or may bring suit for the recovery of the damages for which such common carrier may be liable under the provisions of this Act, in any district court of the United States of competent jurisdiction; but such person shall not have the right to pursue both such remedies.

Complaints to the Commission

SEC. 208. Any person, any body politic or municipal organization, or State commission, complaining of anything done or omitted to be done by any common carrier subject to this Act, in contravention of the provisions thereof, may apply to said Commission by petition which shall briefly state the facts, whereupon a statement of the complaint thus made shall be forwarded by the Commission to such common carrier, who shall be called upon to satisfy the complaint or to answer the same in writing within a reasonable time to be specified by the Commission. If such common carrier within the time specified shall make reparation for the injury alleged to have been caused, the common carrier shall be relieved of liability to the complainant only for the particular violation of law thus complained of. If such carrier or carriers shall not satisfy the complaint within the time specified or there shall appear to be any reasonable ground for investigating said complaint, it shall be the duty of the Commission to investigate the matters complained of in such manner and by such means as it shall deem proper. No complaint shall at any time be dismissed because of the absence of direct damage to the complainant.

Orders for Payment of Money

SEC. 209. If, after hearing on a complaint, the Commission shall determine that any party complainant is entitled to an award of damages under the provisions of this Act, the Commission shall make an order directing the carrier to pay to the complainant the sum to which he is entitled on or before a day named.

Franks and Passes

SEC. 210. Nothing in this Act or in any other provision of law shall be construed to prohibit common carriers from issuing or giving franks to, or exchanging franks with each other for the use of, their officers, agents, employees, and their families, or, subject to such rules as the Commission may precribe, from issuing, giving, or exchanging franks and passes to or with other common carriers not subject to the provisions of this Act, for the use of their officers, agents, employees, and their families. The term "employees," as used in this section, shall include furloughed, pensioned, and superannuated employees.

Copies of Contracts to Be Filed

SEC. 211. (a) Every carrier subject to this Act shall file with the Commission copies of all contracts, agreements, or arrangements with other carriers, or with common carriers not subject to the provisions of this Act, in relation to any traffic affected by the provisions of this Act to which it may be a party.

(b) The Commission shall have authority to require the filing of any other contracts of any carrier, and shall also have authority to exempt any carrier from submitting copies of such minor contracts as the Commission may determine.

Interlocking Directorates—Officials Dealing in Securities

SEC. 212. After sixty days from the enactment of this Act it shall be unlawful for any person to hold the position of officer or director of more than one carrier subject to this Act, unless such holding shall have been authorized by order of the Commission, upon due showing in form and manner prescribed by the Commission, that neither public nor private interests will be adversely affected thereby. After this section takes effect it shall be unlawful for any officer or director of any such carrier to receive for his own benefit, directly or indirectly, any money or thing of value in respect of negotiation, hypothecation, or sale of any securities issued or to be issued by such carrier, or to share in any of the proceeds thereof, or to participate in the making or paying of any dividends of such carrier from any funds properly included in capital account.

Valuation of Carrier Property

SEC. 213. (a) The Commission may from time to time, as may be necessary for the proper administration of this Act, and after opportunity for hearing, make a valuation of all or of any part of the property owned or used by any carrier subject to this Act, as of such date as the Commission may fix.

(b) The Commission may at any time require any such carrier to file with the Commission an inventory of all or of any part of the property owned or used by said carrier, which inventory shall show the units of said property classified in such detail, and in such manner, as the Commission shall direct, and shall show the estimated cost of reproduction new of said units, and their reproduction cost new less depreciation, as of such date as the Commission may direct; and such carrier shall file such inventory within such reasonable time as the Commission by order shall require.

(c) The Commission may at any time require any such carrier to file with the Commission a statement showing the original cost at the time of dedication to the public use of all or of any part of the property owned or used by said carrier. For the showing of such original cost said property shall be classified, and the original cost shall be defined, in such manner as the Commission may prescribe; and if any part of such cost cannot be determined from accounting or other records, the portion of the property for which such cost cannot be determined shall be reported to the Commission; and, if the Commission shall so direct, the original cost thereof shall be estimated in such manner as the Commission may prescribe. If the carrier owning the property at the time such original cost is reported shall have paid more or less than the original cost to acquire the same, the amount of such cost of acquisition, and any facts which the Commission may require in connection therewith, shall be reported with such original cost. The report made by a carrier under this paragraph shall show the source or sources from which the original cost reported was obtained, and such other information as to the manner in which the report was prepared, as the Commission shall require.

(d) Nothing shall be included in the original cost reported for the property of any carrier under paragraph (c) of this section on account of any easement, license, or franchise granted by the United States or by any State or political subdivision thereof, beyond the reasonable necessary expense lawfully incurred in obtaining such easement, license, or franchise from the public authority aforesaid, which expense shall be reported separately from all other costs in such detail as the Commission may require; and nothing shall be included in any valuation of the property of any carrier made by the Commission on account of any such easement, license, or franchise, beyond such reasonable necessary expense lawfully incurred as aforesaid.

(e) The Commission shall keep itself informed of all new construction, extensions, improvements, retirements, or other changes in the condition, quantity, use, and classification of the property of common carriers, and of the cost of all additions and betterments thereto and of all changes in the investment therein, and may keep itself informed of current changes in costs and values of carrier properties.

(f) For the purposes of enabling the Commission to make a valuation of any of the property of any such carrier, or to find the original cost of such property, or to find any other facts concerning the same which are required for use by the Commission, it shall be the duty of each such carrier to furnish to the Commission, within such reasonable time as the Commission may order, any information with respect thereto which the Commission may by order require, including copies of maps, contracts, reports of engineers, and other data, records, and papers, and to grant to all agents of the Commission free access to its property and its accounts, records, and memoranda whenever and wherever requested by any such duly authorized agent, and to cooperate with and aid the Commission in the work of making any such valuation or finding in such manner and to such extent as the Commission may require and direct, and all rules and regulations made by the Commission for the purpose of administering this section shall have the full force and effect of law. Unless otherwise ordered by the Commission, with the reasons therefor, the records and data of the Commission shall be open to the inspection and examination of the public. The Commission, in making any such valuation, shall be free to adopt any method of valuation which shall be lawful.

(g) Notwithstanding any provision of this Act the Interstate Commerce Commission, if requested to do so by the Commission, shall complete, at the earliest practicable date, such valuations of properties of carriers subject to this Act as are now in progress, and shall thereafter transfer to the Commission the records relating thereto.

(h) Nothing in this section shall impair or diminish the powers of any State commission.

Extension of Lines

SEC. 214. (a) No carrier shall undertake the construction of a new line or of an extension of any line, or shall acquire or operate any line, or extension thereof, or shall engage in transmission over or by means of such additional or extended line, unless and until there shall first have been obtained from the Commission a certificate that the present or future public convenience and necessity require or will require the construction, or operation, or construction and operation, of such additional or extended line: *Provided*, That no such certificate shall be required under this section for the construction, acquisition, operation, or extension of (1) a line within a single State unless said line constitutes part of an interstate line, (2) local, branch, or terminal lines not exceeding ten miles in length, or (3) any lines acquired under section 221 of this Act: *Provided further*, That the Commission may, upon appropriate request being made, authorize temporary or emergency service, or the supplementing of existing facilities, without regard to the provisions of this section.

(b) Upon receipt of an application for any such certificate the Commission shall cause notice thereof to be given to and a copy filed with the Governor of each State in which such additional or extended line is proposed to be constructed or operated, with the right to be heard as provided with respect to the hearing of complaints; and the Commission may require such published notice as it shall determine.

(c) The Commission shall have power to issue such certificate as prayed for, or to refuse to issue it, or to issue it for a portion or portions of a line, or extension thereof, described in the application, or for the partial exercise only of such right or privilege, and may attach to the issuance of the certificate such terms and conditions as in its judgment the public convenience and necessity may require. After issuance of such certificate, and not before, the carrier may, without securing approval other than such certificate, comply with the terms and conditions contained in or attached to the issuance of such certificate and proceed with the construction, acquisition, operation, or extension covered thereby. Any construction, acquisition, operation, or extension contrary to the provisions of this section may be enjoined by any court of competent jurisdiction at the suit of the United States, the Commission, the State commission, any State affected, or any party in interest.

(d) The Commission may, after full opportunity for hearing, in a proceeding upon complaint or upon its own initiative without complaint, authorize or require by order any carrier, party to such proceeding, to provide itself with adequate facilities for performing its service as a common carrier and to extend its line; but no such authorization or order shall be made unless the Commission finds, as to such extension, that it is reasonably required in the interest of public convenience and necessity, or as to such extension or facilities that the expense involved therein will not impair the ability of the carrier to perform its duty to the public. Any carrier which refuses or neglects to comply with any order of the Commission made in pursuance of this paragraph shall forfeit to the United States $100 for each day during which such refusal or neglect continues.

Transactions Relating to Services, Equipment, and So Forth

SEC. 215. (a) The Commission shall examine into transactions entered into by any common carrier which relate to the furnishing of equipment, supplies, research, services, finances, credit, or personnel to such carrier and/or which may affect the charges made or to be made and/or the services rendered or to be rendered by such carrier, in wire or radio communication subject to this Act, and shall report to the Congress whether any such transactions have affected or are likely to affect adversely the ability of the carrier to render adequate service to the public, or may result in any undue or unreasonable increase in charges or in the maintenance of undue or un-reasonable charges for such service; and in order to fully examine into such trans-actions the Commission shall have access to and the right of inspection and examination of all accounts, records, and memoranda, including all documents, papers, and correspondence now or hereafter existing, of persons furnishing such equipment, supplies, research, services, finances, credit, or personnel. The Commission shall include in its report its recommendations for necessary legislation in connection with such transactions, and shall report specifically whether in its opinion legislation should be enacted (1) authorizing the Commission to declare any such transactions void or to permit such transactions to be carried out subject to such modification of their terms and conditions as the Commission shall deem desirable in the public interest; and/or (2) subjecting such transactions to the approval of the Commission where the person furnishing or seeking to furnish the equipment, supplies, research, services, finances, credit, or personnel is a person directly or indirectly controlling or controlled by, or under direct or indirect common control with, such carrier; and/or (3) authorizing the Commission to require that all or any transactions of carriers involving the furnishing of equipment, supplies, research, services, finances, credit, or personnel to such carrier be upon competitive bids on such terms and conditions and subject to such regulations as it shall prescribe as necessary in the public interest.

(b) The Commission shall investigate the methods by which and the extent to which wire telephone companies are furnishing wire telegraph service and wire tele-graph companies are furnishing wire telephone service, and shall report its findings to Congress, together with its recommendations as to whether additional legislation on this subject is desirable.

(c) The Commission shall examine all contracts of common carriers subject to this Act which prevent the other party thereto from dealing with another common carrier subject to this Act, and shall report its findings to Congress, together with its recommendations as to whether additional legislation on this subject is desirable.

Application of Act to Receivers and Trustees

SEC. 216. The provisions of this Act shall apply to all receivers and operating trustees of carriers subject to this Act to the same extent that it applies to carriers.

Liability of Carrier for Acts and Omissions of Agents

SEC. 217. In construing and enforcing the provisions of this Act, the act, omission, or failure of any officer, agent, or other person acting for or employed by any common carrier or user, acting within the scope of his employment, shall in every case be also deemed to be the act, omission, or failure of such carrier or user as well as that of the person.

Inquiries into Management

SEC. 218. The Commission may inquire into the management of the business of all carriers subject to this Act, and shall keep itself informed as to the manner and method in which the same is conducted and as to technical developments and improvements in wire and radio communication and radio transmission of energy to the end that the benefits of new inventions and developments may be made available to the people of the United States. The Commission may obtain from such carriers and from persons directly or indirectly controlling or controlled by, or under direct or indirect common control with, such carriers full and complete information necessary to enable the Commission to perform the duties and carry out the objects for which it was created.

Annual and Other Reports

SEC. 219. (a) The Commission is authorized to require annual reports under oath from all carriers subject to this Act, and from persons directly or indirectly controlling or controlled by, or under direct or indirect common control with, any such carrier, to prescribe the manner in which such reports shall be made, and to require from such persons specific answers to all questions upon which the Commission may need information. Such annual reports shall show in detail the amount of capital stock issued, the amount and privileges of each class of stock, the amounts paid therefor, and the manner of payment for the same; the dividends paid and the surplus fund, if any; the number of stockholders (and the names of the thirty largest holders of each class of stock and the amount held by each); the funded and floating debts and the interest paid thereon; the cost and value of the carrier's property, franchises, and equipments; the number of employees and the salaries paid each class; the names of all officers and directors, and the amount of salary, bonus, and all other compensation paid to each; the amounts expended for improvements each year, how expended, and the character of such improvements; the earnings and receipts from each branch of business and from all sources; the operating and other expenses; the balances of profit and loss; and a complete exhibit of the financial operations of the carrier each year, including an annual balance sheet. Such reports shall also contain such information in relation to charges or regulations concerning charges, or agreements, arrangements, or contracts affecting the same, as the Commission may require.

(b) Such reports shall be for such twelve months' period as the Commission shall designate and shall be filed with the Commission at its office in Washington within three months after the close of the year for which the report is made, unless additional time is granted in any case by the Commission; and if any person subject to the provisions of this section shall fail to make and file said annual reports within the time above specified, or within the time extended by the Commission, for making and filing the same, or shall fail to make specific answer to any question authorized by the provisions of this section within thirty days from the time it is lawfully required so to do, such person shall forfeit to the United States the sum of $100 for each and every day it shall continue to be in default with respect thereto. The Commission may by general or special orders require any such carriers to file monthly reports of earnings and expenses and to file periodical and/or special reports concerning any matters with respect to which the Commission is authorized or required by law to act; and such periodical or special reports shall be under oath whenever the Commission so requires. If any such carrier shall fail to make and file any such periodical or special report within the time fixed by the Commission, it shall be subject to the forfeitures above provided.

Accounts, Records, and Memoranda; Depreciation Charges

SEC. 220. (a) The Commission may, in its discretion, prescribe the forms of any and all accounts, records, and memoranda to be kept by carriers subject to this Act, including the accounts, records, and memoranda of the movement of traffic, as well as of the receipts and expenditures of moneys.

(b) The Commission shall, as soon as practicable, prescribe for such carriers the classes of property for which depreciation charges may be properly included under operating expenses, and the percentages of depreciation which shall be charged with respect to each of such classes of property, classifying the carriers as it may deem proper for this purpose. The Commission may, when it deems necessary, modify the classes and percentages so prescribed. Such carriers shall not, after the Commission has prescribed the clasess[1] of property for which depreciation charges may be included, charge to operating expenses any depreciation charges on classes of property other than those prescribed by the Commission, or, after the Commission has prescribed percentages of depreciation, charge with respect to any class of property a percentage of depreciation other than that prescribed therefor by the Commission. No such carrier shall in any case include in any form under its operating or other expenses any depreciation or other charge or expenditure included elsewhere as a depreciation charge or otherwise under its operating or other expenses.

(c) The Commission shall at all times have access to and the right of inspection and examination of all accounts, records, and memoranda, including all documents, papers, and correspondence now or hereafter existing, and kept or required to be kept by such carriers, and the provisions of this section respecting the preservation and destruction of books, papers, and documents shall apply thereto. The burden of proof to justify every accounting entry questioned by the Commission shall be on the person making,

---

[1] So in original.

authorizing, or requiring such entry and the Commission may suspend a charge or credit pending submission of proof by such person. Any provision of law prohibiting the disclosure of the contents of messages or communications shall not be deemed to prohibit the disclosure of any matter in accordance with the provisions of this section.

(d) In case of failure or refusal on the part of any such carrier to keep such accounts, records, and memoranda on the books and in the manner prescribed by the Commission, or to submit such accounts, records, memoranda, documents, papers, and correspondence as are kept to the inspection of the Commission or any of its authorized agents, such carrier shall forfeit to the United States the sum of $500 for each day of the continuance of each such offense.

(e) Any person who shall willfully make any false entry in the accounts of any book of accounts or in any record or memoranda kept by any such carrier, or who shall willfully destroy, mutilate, alter, or by any other means or device falsify any such account, record, or memoranda, or who shall willfully neglect or fail to make full, true, and correct entries in such accounts, records, or memoranda of all facts and transactions appertaining to the business of the carrier, shall be deemed guilty of a misdemeanor, and shall be subject, upon conviction, to a fine of not less than $1,000 nor more than $5,000 or imprisonment for a term of not less than one year nor more than three years, or both such fine and imprisonment: *Provided*, That the Commission may in its discretion issue orders specifying such operating, accounting, or financial papers, records, books, blanks, or documents which may, after a reasonable time, be destroyed, and prescribing the length of time such books, papers, or documents shall be preserved.

(f) No member, officer, or employee of the Commission shall divulge any fact or information which may come to his knowledge during the course of examination of books or other accounts, as hereinbefore provided, except insofar as he may be directed by the Commission or by a court.

(g) After the Commission has prescribed the forms and manner of keeping of accounts, records, and memoranda to be kept by any person as herein provided, it shall be unlawful for such person to keep any other accounts, records, or memoranda than those so prescribed or such as may be approved by the Commission or to keep the accounts in any other manner than that prescribed or approved by the Commission. Notice of alterations by the Commission in the required manner or form of keeping accounts shall be given to such persons by the Commission at least six months before the same are to take effect.

(h) The Commission may classify carriers subject to this Act and prescribe different requirements under this section for different classes of carriers, and may, if it deems such action consistent with the public interest, except the carriers of any particular class or classes in any State from any of the requirements under this section in cases where such carriers are subject to State commission regulation with respect to matters to which this section relates.

(i) The Commission, before prescribing any requirements as to accounts, records, or memoranda, shall notify each State commission having jurisdiction with respect to any carrier involved, and shall give reasonable opportunity to each such commission to present its views, and shall receive and consider such views and recommendations.

(j) The Commission shall investigate and report to Congress as to the need for legislation to define further or harmonize the powers of the Commission and of State commissions with respect to matters to which this section relates.

Special Provisions Relating to Telephone Companies

SEC. 221. (a) Upon application of one or more telephone companies for authority to consolidate their properties or a part thereof into a single company, or for authority for one or more such companies to acquire the whole or any part of the property of another telephone company or other telephone companies or the control thereof by the purchase of securities or by lease or in any other like manner, when such consolidated company would be subject to this Act, the Commission shall fix a time and place for a public hearing upon such application and shall thereupon give reasonable notice in writing to the Governor of each of the States in which the physical property affected, or any part thereof, is situated, and to the State commission having jurisdiction over telephone companies, and to such other persons as it may deem advisable. After such public hearing, if the Commission finds that the proposed consolidation, acquisition, or control will be of advantage to the persons to whom service is to be rendered and in the public interest, it shall certify to that effect; and thereupon any Act or Acts of Congress making the proposed transaction unlawful shall not apply. Nothing in this subsection shall be construed as in anywise limiting or restricting the powers of the several States to control and regulate telephone companies.

(b) Nothing in this Act shall be construed to apply, or to give the Commission jurisdiction, with respect to charges, classifications, practices, services, facilities, or regulations for or in connection with wire telephone exchange service, even though a portion of such exchange service constitutes interstate or foreign communication, in any case where such matters are subject to regulation by a State commission or by local governmental authority.

(c) For the purpose of administering this Act as to carriers engaged in wire telephone communication, the Commission may classify the property of any such carrier used for wire telephone communication, and determine what property of said carrier shall be considered as used in interstate or foreign telephone toll service. Such classification shall be made after hearing, upon notice to the carrier, the State commission (or the Governor, if the State has no State commission) of any State in which the property of said carrier is located, and such other persons as the Commission may prescribe.

(d) In making a valuation of the property of any wire telephone carrier the Commission, after making the classification authorized in this section, may in its discretion value only that part of the property of such carrier determined to be used in interstate or foreign telephone toll service.

TITLE III–SPECIAL PROVISIONS RELATING TO RADIO

License for Radio Communications or Transmission of Energy

SECTION 301. It is the purpose of this Act, among other things, to maintain the control of the United States over all the channels of interstate and foreign radio transmission; and to provide for the use of such channels, but not the ownership thereof, by persons for limited periods of time, under licenses granted by Federal authority, and no such license shall be construed to create any right, beyond the terms, conditions, and periods of the license. No person shall use or operate any apparatus for the transmission of energy or communications or signals by radio (a) from one place in any Territory or possession of the United States or in the District of Columbia to another place in the same Territory, possession, or District; or (b) from any State, Territory, or possession of the United States, or from the District of Columbia to any other State, Territory, or possession of the United States; or (c) from any place in any State, Territory, or possession of the United States, or in the District of Columbia, to any place in any foreign country or to any vessel; or (d) within any State when the effects of such use extend beyond the borders of said State, or when interference is caused by such use or operation with the transmission of such energy, communications, or signals from within said State to any place beyond its borders, or from any place beyond its borders to any place within said State, or with the transmission or reception of such energy, communications, or signals from and/or to places beyond the borders of said State; or (e) upon any vessel or aircraft of the United States; or (f) upon any other mobile stations within the jurisdiction of the United States, except under and in accordance with this Act and with a license in that behalf granted under the provisions of this Act.

Zones

SEC. 302. (a) For the purposes of this title the United States is divided into five zones, as follows: The first zone shall embrace the States of Maine, New Hampshire, Vermont, Massachusetts, Connecticut, Rhode Island, New York, New Jersey, Delaware, Maryland, and the District of Columbia; the second zone shall embrace the States of Pennsylvania, Virginia, West Virginia, Ohio, Michigan, and Kentucky; the third zone shall embrace the States of North Carolina, South Carolina, Georgia, Florida, Alabama, Tennessee, Mississippi, Arkansas, Louisiana, Texas, and Oklahoma; the fourth zone shall embrace the States of Indiana, Illinois, Wisconsin, Minnesota, North Dakota, South Dakota, Iowa, Nebraska, Kansas, and Missouri; and the fifth zone shall embrace the States of Montana, Idaho, Wyoming, Colorado, New Mexico, Arizona, Utah, Nevada, Washington, Oregon, and California.

(b) The Virgin Islands, Puerto Rico, Alaska, Guam, American Samoa, and the Territory of Hawaii are expressly excluded from the zones herein established.

General Powers of Commission

SEC. 303. Except as otherwise provided in this Act, the Commission from time to time, as public convenience, interest, or necessity requires, shall—

(a) Classify radio stations;

(b) Prescribe the nature of the service to be rendered by each class of licensed stations and each station within any class;

(c) Assign bands of frequencies to the various classes of stations, and assign frequencies for each individual station and determine the power which each station shall use and the time during which it may operate;

(d) Determine the location of classes of stations or individual stations;

(e) Regulate the kind of apparatus to be used with respect to its external effects and the purity and sharpness of the emissions from each station and from the apparatus therein;

(f) Make such regulations not inconsistent with law as it may deem necessary to prevent interference between stations and to carry out the provisions of this Act: *Provided, however,* That changes in the frequencies, authorized power, or in the times of operation of any station, shall not be made without the consent of the station licensee unless, after a public hearing, the Commission shall determine that such changes will promote public convenience or interest or will serve public necessity, or the provisions of this Act will be more fully complied with;

(g) Study new uses for radio, provide for experimental uses of frequencies, and generally encourage the larger and more effective use of radio in the public interest;

(h) Have authority to establish areas or zones to be served by any station;

(i) Have authority to make special regulations applicable to radio stations engaged in chain broadcasting;

(j) Have authority to make general rules and regulations requiring stations to keep such records of programs, transmissions of energy, communications, or signals as it may deem desirable;

(k) Have authority to exclude from the requirements of any regulations in whole or in part any radio station upon railroad rolling stock, or to modify such regulations in its discretion;

(l) Have authority to prescribe the qualifications of station operators, to classify them according to the duties to be performed, to fix the forms of such licenses, and to issue them to such citizens of the United States as the Commission finds qualified;

(m) Have authority to suspend the license of any operator for a period not exceeding two years upon proof sufficient to satisfy the Commission that the licensee (1) has violated any provision of any Act or treaty binding on the United States which the Commission is authorized by this Act to administer or any regulation made by the Commission under any such Act or treaty; or (2) has failed to carry out the lawful orders of the master of the vessel on which he is employed; or (3) has willfully damaged or permitted radio apparatus to be damaged; or (4) has transmitted superfluous radio communications or signals or radio communications containing profane or obscene words or language; or (5) has willfully or maliciously interfered with any other radio communications or signals;

(n) Have authority to inspect all transmitting apparatus to ascertain whether in construction and operation it conforms to the requirements of this Act, the rules and regulations of the Commission, and the license under which it is constructed or operated;

(o) Have authority to designate call letters of all stations;

(p) Have authority to cause to be published such call letters and such other announcements and data as in the judgment of the Commission may be required for the efficient operation of radio stations subject to the jurisdiction of the United States and for the proper enforcement of this Act;

(q) Have authority to require the painting and/or illumination of radio towers if and when in its judgment such towers constitute, or there is a reasonable possiblity that they may constitute, a menace to air navigation.

Waiver by Licensee

SEC. 304. No station license shall be granted by the Commission until the applicant therefor shall have signed a waiver of any claim to the use of any particular frequency or of the ether as against the regulatory power of the United States because of the previous use of the same, whether by license or otherwise.

Government-Owned Stations

SEC. 305. (a) Radio stations belonging to and operated by the United States shall not be subject to the provisions of sections 301 and 303 of this Act. All such Government stations shall use such frequencies as shall be assigned to each or to each class by the President. All such stations, except stations on board naval and other Government vessels while at sea or beyond the limits of the continental United States, when transmitting any radio communication or signal other than a communication or signal relating to Government business, shall conform to such rules and regulations designed to prevent interference with other radio stations and the rights of others as the Commission may prescribe.

(b) Radio stations on board vessels of the United States Shipping Board Bureau or the United States Shipping Board Merchant Fleet Corporation or the Inland and Coastwise Waterways Service shall be subject to the provisions of this title.

(c) All stations owned and operated by the United States, except mobile stations of the Army of the United States, and all other stations on land and sea, shall have special call letters designated by the Commission.

Foreign Ships

SEC. 306. Section 301 of this Act shall not apply to any person sending radio communications or signals on a foreign ship while the same is within the jurisdiction of the United States, but such communications or signals shall be transmitted only in accordance with such regulations designed to prevent interference as may be promulgated under the authority of this Act.

Allocation of Facilities; Term of Licenses

SEC. 307. (a) The Commission, if public convenience, interest, or necessity will be served thereby, subject to the limitations of this Act, shall grant to any applicant therefor a station license provided for by this Act.

(b) It is hereby declared that the people of all the zones established by this title are entitled to equality of radio broadcasting service, both of transmission and of reception, and in order to provide said equality the Commission shall as nearly as possible make and maintain an equal allocation of broadcasting licenses, of bands of frequency, of periods of time for operation, and of station power, to each of said zones when and insofar as there are applications therefor; and shall make a fair and equitable allocation of licenses, frequencies, time for operation, and station power to each of the States and the District of Columbia, within each zone, according to population. The Commission shall carry into effect the equality of broadcasting service hereinbefore directed, whenever necessary or proper, by granting or refusing licenses or renewals of licenses, by changing periods of time for operation, and by increasing or decreasing station power, when applications are made for licenses or renewals of licenses: *Provided*, That if and when there is a lack of applications from any zone for the proportionate share of licenses, frequencies, time of operation, or station power to which such zone is entitled, the Commission may issue licenses for the balance of the proportion not applied for from any zone, to applicants from other zones for a temporary period of ninety days each, and shall specifically designate that said apportionment is only for said temporary period. Allocations shall be charged to the State or District wherein the studio of the station is located and not where the transmitter is located: *Provided further*, That the Commission may also grant applications for additional licenses for stations not exceeding one hundred watts of power if the Commission finds that such stations will serve the public convenience, interest, or necessity, and that their operation will not interfere with the fair and efficient radio service of stations licensed under the provisions of this section.

(c) The Commission shall study the proposal that Congress by statute allocate fixed percentages of radio broadcasting facilities to particular types or kinds of non-profit radio programs or to persons identified with particular types or kinds of non-profit activities, and shall report to Congress, not later than February 1, 1935, its recommendations together with the reasons for the same.

(d) No license granted for the operation of a broadcasting station shall be for a longer term than three years and no license so granted for any other class of station shall be for a longer term than five years, and any license granted may be revoked as hereinafter provided. Upon the expiration of any license, upon application therefor, a renewal of such license may be granted from time to time for a term of not to exceed three years in the case of broadcasting licenses and not to exceed five years in the case of other licenses, but action of the Commission with reference to the granting of such application for the renewal of a license shall be limited to and governed by the same considerations and practices which affect the granting of original application.

(e) No renewal of an existing station license shall be granted more than thirty days prior to the expiration of the original license.

Applications for Licenses; Conditions in License for Foreign Communication

SEC. 308. (a) The Commission may grant licenses, renewal of licenses, and modification of licenses only upon written application therefor received by it: *Provided, however,* That in cases of emergency found by the Commission, licenses, renewals of licenses, and modifications of licenses, for stations on vessels or aircraft of the United States, may be issued under such conditions as the Commission may impose, without such formal application. Such licenses, however, shall in no case be for a longer term than three months: *Provided further,* That the Commission may issue by cable, telegraph, or radio a permit for the operation of a station on a vessel of the United States at sea, effective in lieu of a license until said vessel shall return to a port of the continental United States.

(b) All such applications shall set forth such facts as the Commission by regulation may prescribe as to the citizenship, character, and financial, technical, and other qualifications of the applicant to operate the station; the ownership and location of the proposed station and of the stations, if any, with which it is proposed to communicate; the frequencies and the power desired to be used; the hours of the day or other periods of time during which it is proposed to operate the station; the purposes for which the station is to be used; and such other information as it may require. The Commission, at any time after the filing of such original application and during the term of any such license, may require from an applicant or licensee further written statements of fact to enable it to determine whether such original application should be granted or denied or such license revoked. Such application and/or such statement of fact shall be signed by the applicant and/or licensee under oath or affirmation.

(c) The Commission in granting any license for a station intended or used for commercial communication between the United States or any Territory or possession, continental or insular, subject to the jurisdiction of the United States, and any foreign country, may impose any terms, conditions, or restrictions authorized to be imposed with respect to submarine-cable licenses by section 2 of an Act entitled "An Act relating to the landing and the operation of submarine cables in the United States," approved May 24, 1921.

Hearings on Applications for Licenses; Form of Licenses; Conditions Attached to Licenses

SEC. 309. (a) If upon examination of any application for a station license or for the renewal or modification of a station license the Commission shall determine that public interest, convenience, or necessity would be served by the granting thereof, it shall authorize the issuance, renewal, or modification thereof in accordance with said finding. In the event the Commission upon examination of any such application does not reach such decision with respect thereto, it shall notify the applicant thereof, shall fix and give notice of a time and place for hearing thereon, and shall afford such applicant an opportunity to be heard under such rules and regulations as it may prescribe.

(b) Such station licenses as the Commission may grant shall be in such general form as it may prescribe, but each license shall contain, in addition to other provisions, a statement of the following conditions to which such license shall be subject:

(1) The station license shall not vest in the licensee any right to operate the station nor any right in the use of the frequencies designated in the license beyond the term thereof nor in any other manner than authorized therein.

(2) Neither the license nor the right granted thereunder shall be assigned or otherwise transferred in violation of this Act.

(3) Every license issued under this Act shall be subject in terms to the right of use or control conferred by section 606 hereof.

Limitation on Holding and Transfer of Licenses

SEC. 310. (a) The station license required hereby shall not be granted to or held by—

(1) Any alien or the representative of any alien;

(2) Any foreign government or the representative thereof;

(3) Any corporation organized under the laws of any foreign government;

(4) Any corporation of which any officer or director is an alien or of which more than one-fifth of the capital stock is owned of record or voted by aliens or their representatives or by a foreign government or representative thereof, or by any corporation organized under the laws of a foreign country;

(5) Any corporation directly or indirectly controlled by any other corporation of which any officer or more than one-fourth of the directors are aliens, or of which more than one-fourth of the capital stock is owned of record or voted, after June 1, 1935, by aliens, their representatives, or by a foreign government or representative threeof, or by any corporation organized under the laws of a foreign country, if the Commission finds that the public interest will be served by the refusal or the revocation of such license.

Nothing in this subsection shall prevent the licensing of radio apparatus on board any vessel, aircraft, or other mobile station of the United States when the installation and use of such apparatus is required by Act of Congress or any treaty to which the United States is a party.

(b) The station license required hereby, the frequencies authorized to be used by the licensee, and the rights therein granted shall not be transferred, assigned, or in any manner either voluntarily or involuntarily disposed of, or indirectly by transfer of control of any corporation holding such license, to any person, unless the Commission shall, after securing full information, decide that said transfer is in the public interest, and shall give its consent in writing.

Refusal of Licenses and Permits in Certain Cases

SEC. 311. The Commission is hereby directed to refuse a station license and/or the permit hereinafter required for the construction of a station to any person (or to any person directly or indirectly controlled by such person) whose license has been revoked by a court under section 313, and is hereby authorized to refuse such station license and/or permit to any other person (or to any person directly or indirectly controlled by such person) which has been finally adjudged guilty by a Federal court of unlawfully monopolizing or attempting unlawfully to monopolize, radio communication, directly or indirectly, through the control of the manufacture or sale of radio apparatus, through exclusive traffic arrangements, or by any other means, or to have been using unfair methods of competition. The granting of a license shall not estop the United States or any person aggrieved from proceeding against such person for violating the law against unfair methods of competition or for a violation of the law against unlawful restraints and monopolies and/or combinations, contracts, or agreements in restraint of trade, or from instituting proceedings for the dissolution of such corporation.

Revocation of Licenses

SEC. 312. (a) Any station license may be revoked for false statements either in the application or in the statement of fact which may be required by section 308 hereof, or because of conditions revealed by such statements of fact as may be required from time to time which would warrant the Commission in refusing to grant a license on an original application, or for failure to operate substantially as set forth in the license, or for violation of or failure to observe any of the restrictions and conditions of this Act or of any regulation of the Commission authorized by this Act or by a treaty ratified by the United States: *Provided, however*, That no such order of revocation shall take effect until fifteen days' notice in writing thereof, stating the cause for the proposed revocation, has been given to the licensee. Such licensee may make written application to the Commission at any time within said fifteen days for a hearing upon such order, and upon the filing of such written application said order of revocation shall stand suspended until the conclusion of the hearing conducted under such rules as the Commission may prescribe. Upon the conclusion of said hearing the Commission may affirm, modify, or revoke said order of revocation.

(b) Any station license hereafter granted under the provisions of this Act or the construction permit required hereby and hereafter issued, may be modified by the Commission either for a limited time or for the duration of the term thereof, if in the judgment of the Commission such action will promote the public interest, convenience, and necessity, or the provisions of this Act or of any treaty ratified by the United States will be more fully complied with: *Provided, however*, That no such order of modification shall become final until the holder of such outstanding license or permit shall have been notified in writing of the proposed action and the grounds or reasons therefor and shall have been given reasonable opportunity to show cause why such an order of modification should not issue.

Application of Antitrust Laws

SEC. 313. All laws of the United States relating to unlawful restraints and monopolies and to combinations, contracts, or agreements in restraint of trade are hereby declared to be applicable to the manufacture and sale of and to trade in radio apparatus and devices entering into or affecting interstate or foreign commerce and to interstate or foreign radio communications. Whenever in any suit, action, or proceeding, civil or criminal, brought under the provisions of any of said laws or in any proceedings brought to enforce or to review findings and orders of the Federal Trade Commission or other governmental agency in respect of any matters as to which said Commission or other governmental agency is by law authorized to act, any licensee shall be found guilty of the violation of the provisions of such laws or any of them, the court, in addition to the penalties imposed by said laws, may adjudge, order, and/or decree that the license of such licensee shall, as of the date the decree or judgment becomes finally effective or as of such other date as the said decree shall fix, be revoked and that all rights under such license shall thereupon cease: *Provided, however*, That such licensee shall have the same right of appeal or review as is provided by law in respect of other decrees and judgments of said court.

Preservation of Competition in Commerce

SEC. 314. After the effective date of this Act no person engaged directly, or indirectly through any person directly or indirectly controlling or controlled by, or under direct or indirect common control with, such person, or through an agent, or otherwise, in the business of transmitting and/or receiving for hire energy, communications, or signals by radio in accordance with the terms of the license issued under this Act, shall by purchase, lease, construction, or otherwise, directly or indirectly, acquire, own, control, or operate any cable or wire telegraph or telephone line or system between any place in any State, Territory, or possession of the United States or in the District of Columbia, and any place in any foreign country, or shall acquire, own, or control any part of the stock or other capital share or any interest in the physical property and/or other assets of any such cable, wire, telegraph, or telephone line or system, if in either case the purpose is and/or the effect thereof may be to substantially lessen competition or to restrain commerce between any place in any State, Territory, or possession of the United States, or in the District of Columbia, and any place in any foreign country, or unlawfully to create monopoly in any line of commerce; nor shall any person engaged directly, or indirectly through any person directly or indirectly controlling or controlled by, or under direct or indirect common control with, such person, or through an agent, or otherwise, in the business of transmitting and/or receiving for hire messages by any cable, wire, telegraph, or telephone line or system (a) between any place in any State, Territory, or possession of the United States, or in the District of Columbia, and any place in any other State, Territory, or possession of the United States; or (b) between any place in any State, Territory, or possession of the United States, or the District of Columbia, and any place in any foreign country, by purchase, lease, construction, or otherwise, directly or indirectly acquire, own, control, or operate any station or the apparatus therein, or any system for transmitting and/or receiving radio communications or signals between any place in any State, Territory, or possession of the United States, or in the District of Columbia, and any place in any foreign country, or shall acquire, own, or control any part of the stock or other capital share or any interest in the physical property and/or other assets of any such radio station, apparatus, or system, if in either case the purpose is and/or the effect thereof may be to substantially lessen competition or to restrain commerce between any place in any State, Territory, or possession of the United States, or in the District of Columbia, and any place in any foreign country, or unlawfully to create monopoly in any line of commerce.

Facilities for Candidates for Public Office

SEC. 315. If any licensee shall permit any person who is a legally qualified candidate for any public office to use a broadcasting station, he shall afford equal opportunities to all other such candidates for that office in the use of such broadcasting station, and the Commission shall make rules and regulations to carry this provision into effect: *Provided*, That such licensee shall have no power to censorship over the material broadcast under the provisions of this section. No obligation is hereby imposed upon any licensee to allow the use of its station by any such candidate.

Lotteries and Other Similar Schemes

SEC. 316. No person shall broadcast by means of any radio station for which a license is required by any law of the United States, and no person operating any such station shall knowingly permit the broadcasting of, any advertisement of or information concerning any lottery, gift enterprise, or similar scheme, offering prizes dependent in whole or in part upon lot or chance, or any list of the prizes drawn or awarded by means of any such lottery, gift enterprise, or scheme, whether said list contains any part or all of such prizes. Any person violating any provision of this section shall, upon conviction thereof, be fined not more than $1,000 or imprisoned not more than one year, or both, for each and every day during which such offense occurs.

Announcement that Matter Is Paid For

SEC. 317. All matter broadcast by any radio station for which service, money, or any other valuable consideration is directly or indirectly paid, or promised to or charged or accepted by, the station so broadcasting, from any person, shall, at the time the same is so broadcast, be announced as paid for or furnished, as the case may be, by such person.

Operation of Transmitting Apparatus

SEC. 318. The actual operation of all transmitting apparatus in any radio station for which a station license is required by this Act shall be carried on only by a person holding an operator's license issued hereunder. No person shall operate any such apparatus in such station except under and in accordance with an operator's license issued to him by the Commission.

Construction Permits

SEC. 319. (a) No license shall be issued under the authority of this Act for the operation of any station the construction of which is begun or is continued after this Act takes effect, unless a permit for its construction has been granted by the Commission upon written application therefor. The Commission may grant such permit if public convenience, interest, or necessity will be served by the construction of the station. This application shall set forth such facts as the Commission by regulation may prescribe as to the citizenship, character, and the financial, technical, and other ability of the applicant to construct and operate the station, the ownership and location of the proposed station and of the station or stations with which it is proposed to communicate, the frequencies desired to be used, the hours of the day or other periods of time during which it is proposed to operate the station, the purpose for which the station is to be used, the type of transmitting apparatus to be used, the power to be used, the date upon which the station is expected to be completed and in operation, and such other information as the Commission may require. Such application shall be signed by the applicant under oath or affirmation.

(b) Such permit for construction shall show specifically the earliest and latest dates between which the actual operation of such station is expected to begin, and shall provide that said permit will be automatically forfeited if the station is not ready for operation within the time specified or within such further time as the Commission may allow, unless prevented by causes not under the control of the grantee. The rights under any such permit shall not be assigned or otherwise transferred to any person without the approval of the Commission. A permit for construction shall not be required for Government stations, amateur stations, or stations upon mobile vessels, railroad rolling stock, or aircraft. Upon the completion of any station for the construction of continued construction of which a permit has been granted, and upon it being made to appear to the Commission that all the terms, conditions, and obligations set forth in the application and permit have been fully met, and that no cause or circumstance arising or first coming to the knowledge of the Commission since the granting of the permit would, in the judgment of the Commission, make the operation of such station against the public interest, the Commission shall issue a license to the lawful holder of said permit for the operation of said station. Said license shall conform generally to the terms of said permit.

Designation of Stations Liable to Interfere with Distress Signals

SEC. 320. The Commission is authorized to designate from time to time radio stations the communications or signals of which, in its opinion, are liable to interfere with the transmission or reception of distress signals of ships. Such stations are required to keep a licensed radio operator listening in on the frequencies designated for signals of distress and radio communications relating thereto during the entire period the transmitter of such station is in operation.

Distress Signals and Communications

SEC. 321. (a) Every radio station on shipboard shall be equipped to transmit radio communications or signals of distress on the frequency specified by the Commission, with apparatus capable of transmitting and receiving messages over a distance of at least one hundred miles by day or night. When sending radio communications or signals of distress and radio communications relating thereto the transmitting set may be adjusted in such a manner as to produce a maximum of radiation irrespective of the amount of interference which may thus be caused.

(b) All radio stations, including Government stations and stations on board foreign vessels when within the territorial waters of the United States, shall give absolute priority to radio communications or signals relating to ships in distress; shall cease all sending on frequencies which will interfere with hearing a radio communication or signal of distress, and, except when engaged in answering or aiding the ship in distress, shall refrain from sending any radio communications or signals until there is assurance that no interference will be caused with the radio communications or signals relating thereto, and shall assist the vessel in distress, so far as possible, by complying with its instructions.

Intercommunication in Mobile Service

SEC. 322. Every land station open to general public service between the coast and vessels at sea shall be bound to exchange radio communications or signals with any ship station without distinction as to radio systems or instruments adopted by such stations, respectively, and each station on shipboard shall be bound to exchange radio communications or signals with any other station on shipboard without distinction as to radio systems or instruments adopted by each station.

Interference between Government and Commercial Stations

SEC. 323. (a) At all places where Government and private or commercial radio stations on land operate in such close proximity that interference with the work of Government stations cannot be avoided when they are operating simultaneously, such private or commercial stations as do interfere with the transmission or reception of radio communications or signals by the Government stations concerned shall not use their transmitters during the first fifteen minutes of each hour, local standard time.

(b) The Government stations for which the above-mentioned division of time is established shall transmit radio communications or signals only during the first fifteen minutes of each hour, local standard time, except in case of signals or radio communications relating to vessels in distress and vessel requests for information as to course, location, or compass direction.

Use of Minimum Power

SEC. 324. In all circumstances, except in case of radio communications or signals relating to vessels in distress, all radio stations, including those owned and operated by the United States, shall use the minimum amount of power necessary to carry out the communication desired.

False Distress Signals; Rebroadcasting; Studios of Foreign Stations

SEC. 325. (a) No person within the jurisdiction of the United States shall knowingly utter or transmit, or cause to be uttered or transmitted, any false or fraudulent signal of distress, or communication relating thereto, nor shall any broadcasting station rebroadcast the program or any part thereof of another broadcasting station without the express authority of the originating station.

(b) No person shall be permitted to locate, use, or maintain a radio broadcast studio or other place or apparatus from which or whereby sound waves are converted into electrical energy, or mechanical or physical reproduction of sound waves produced, and caused to be transmitted or delivered to a radio station in a foreign country for the purpose of being broadcast from any radio station there having a power output of sufficient intensity and/or being so located geographically that its emissions may be received consistently in the United States, without first obtaining a permit from the Commission upon proper application therefor.

(c) Such application shall contain such information as the Commission may by regulation prescribe, and the granting or refusal thereof shall be subject to the requirements of section 309 hereof with respect to applications for station licenses or renewal or modification thereof, and the license or permission so granted shall be revocable for false statements in the application so required or when the Commission, after hearings, shall find its continuation no longer in the public interest.

Censorship; Indecent Language

SEC. 326. Nothing in this Act shall be understood or construed to give the Commission the power of censorship over the radio communications or signals transmitted by any radio station, and no regulation or condition shall be promulgated or fixed by the Commission which shall interfere with the right of free speech by means of radio communication. No person within the jurisdiction of the United States shall utter any obscene, indecent, or profane language by means of radio communication.

Use of Naval Stations for Commercial Messages

SEC. 327. The Secretary of the Navy is hereby authorized, unless restrained by international agreement, under the terms and conditions and at rates prescribed by him, which rates shall be just and reasonable, and which, upon complaint, shall be subject to review and revision by the Commisison[2] to use all radio stations and apparatus, wherever located, owned by the United States and under the control of the Navy Department, (a) for the reception and transmission of press messages offered by any newspaper published in the United States, its Territories or possessions, or published by citizens of the United States in foreign countries, or by any press association of the United States, and (b) for the reception and transmission of private commercial messages between ships, between ship and shore, between localities in Alaska and between Alaska and the continental United States: *Provided*, That the rates fixed for the reception and transmission of all such messages, other than press messages between the Pacific coast of the United States, Hawaii, Alaska, Guam, American Samoa, the Philippine Islands, and the Orient, and between the United States and the Virgin Islands, shall not be less than the rates charged by privately owned and operated stations for like messages and service: *Provided further*, That the right to use such stations for any of the purposes named in this section shall terminate

[2] So in original.

and cease as between any countries or localities or between any locality and privately operated ships whenever privately owned and operated stations are capable of meeting the normal communication requirements between such countries or localities or between any locality and privately operated ships, and the Commission shall have notified the Secretary of the Navy thereof.

Special Provision as to Philippine Islands and Canal Zone

SEC. 328. This title shall not apply to the Philippine Islands or to the Canal Zone. In international radio matters the Philippine Islands and the Canal Zone shall be represented by the Secretary of State.

Administration of Radio Laws in Territories and Possessions

SEC. 329. The Commission is authorized to designate any officer or employee of any other department of the Government on duty in any Territory or possession of the United States other than the Philippine Islands and the Canal Zone, to render therein such services in connection with the administration of the radio laws of the United States as the Commission may prescribe: *Provided*, That such designation shall be approved by the head of the department in which such person is employed.

TITLE IV—PROCEDURAL AND ADMINISTRATIVE PROVISIONS

Jurisdiction to Enforce Act and Orders of Commission

SECTION 401. (a) The district courts of the United States shall have jurisdiction, upon application of the Attorney General of the United States at the request of the Commission, alleging a failure to comply with or a violation of any of the provisions of this Act by any person, to issue a writ or writs of mandamus commanding such person to comply with the provisions of this Act.

(b) If any person fails or neglects to obey any order of the Commission other than for the payment of money, while the same is in effect, the Commission or any party injured thereby, or the United States, by its Attorney General, may apply to the appropriate district court of the United States for the enforcement of such order. If, after hearing, that court determines that the order was regularly made and duly served, and that the person is in disobedience of the same, the court shall enforce obedience to such order by a writ of injunction or other proper process, mandatory or otherwise, to restrain such person or the officers, agents, or representatives of such person, from further disobedience of such order, or to enjoin upon it or them obedience to the same.

(c) Upon the request of the Commission it shall be the duty of any district attorney of the United States to whom the Commission may apply to institute in the proper court and to prosecute under the direction of the Attorney General of the United States all necessary proceedings for the enforcement of the provisions of this Act and for the punishment of all violations thereof, and the costs and expenses of such prosecutions shall be paid out of the appropriations for the expenses of the courts of the United States.

(d) The provisions of the Expediting Act, approved February 11, 1903, as amended, and of section 238 (1) of the Judicial Code, as amended, shall be held to apply to any suit in equity arising under Title II of this Act, wherein the United States is complainant.

Proceedings to Enforce or Set Aside the Commission's Orders—Appeal in Certain Cases

SEC. 402. (a) The provisions of the Act of October 22, 1913 (38 Stat. 219), relating to the enforcing or setting aside of the orders of the Interstate Commerce Commission, are hereby made applicable to suits to enforce, enjoin, set aside, annul, or suspend any order of the Commission under this Act (except any order of the Commission granting or refusing an application for a construction permit for a radio station, or for a radio station license, or for renewal of an existing radio station license, or for modification of an existing radio station license), and such suits are hereby authorized to be brought as provided in that Act.

(b) An appeal may be taken, in the manner hereinafter provided, from decisions of the Commission to the Court of Appeals of the District of Columbia in any of the following cases:

(1) By any applicant for a construction permit for a radio station, or for a radio station license, or for renewal of an existing radio station license, or for modification of an existing radio station license, whose application is refused by the Commission.

(2) By any other person aggrieved or whose interests are adversely affected by any decision of the Commission granting or refusing any such application.

(c) Such appeal shall be taken by filing with said court within twenty days after the decision complained of is effective, notice in writing of said appeal and a statement of the reasons therefor, together with proof of service of a true copy of said notice and statement upon the Commission. Unless a later date is specified by the Commission as part of its decision, the decision complained of shall be considered to be effective as of the date on which public announcement of the decision is made at the office of the Commission in the city of Washington. The Commission shall thereupon immediately, and in any event not later than five days from the date of such service upon it, mail or otherwise deliver a copy of said notice of appeal to each person shown by the records of the Commission to be interested in such appeal and to have a right to intervene therein under the provisions of this section, and shall at all times thereafter permit any such person to inspect and make copies of the appellant's statement of reasons for said appeal at the office of the Commission in the city of Washington. Within thirty days after the filing of said appeal the Commission shall file with the court the originals or certified copies of all papers and evidence presented to it upon the application involved, and also a like copy of its decision thereon, and shall within thirty days thereafter file a full statement in writing of the facts and grounds for its decision as found and given by it, and a list of all interested persons to whom it has mailed or otherwise delivered a copy of said notice of appeal.

(d) Within thirty days after the filing of said appeal any interested person may intervene and participate in the proceedings had upon said appeal by filing with the court a notice of intention to intervene and a verified statement showing the nature of the interest of such party, together with proof of service of true copies of said notice and statement, both upon appellant and upon the Commission. Any person who would be aggrieved or whose interests would be adversely affected by a reversal or modification of the decision of the Commission complained of shall be considered an interested party.

(e) At the earliest convenient time the court shall hear and determine the appeal upon the record before it, and shall have power, upon such record, to enter a judgment affirming or reversing the decision of the Commission, and in event the court shall render a decision and enter an order reversing the decision of the Commission, it shall remand the case to the Commission to carry out the judgment of the court: *Provided, however,* That the review by the court shall be limited to questions of law and that findings of fact by the Commission, if supported by substantial evidence, shall be conclusive unless it shall clearly appear that the findings of the Commission are arbitrary or capricious. The court's judgment shall be final, subject, however, to review by the Supreme Court of the United States upon writ of certiorari on petition therefor under section 240 of the Judicial Code, as amended, by appellant, by the Commission, or by any interested party intervening in the appeal.

(f) The court may, in its discretion, enter judgment for costs in favor of or against an appellant, and/or other interested parties intervening in said appeal, but not against the Commission, depending upon the nature of the issues involved upon said appeal and the outcome thereof.

Inquiry by Commission on Its Own Motion

SEC. 403. The Commission shall have full authority and power at any time to institute an inquiry, on its own motion, in any case and as to any matter or thing concerning which complaint is authorized to be made, to or before the Commission by any provision of this Act, or concerning which any question may arise under any of the provisions of this Act, or relating to the enforcement of any of the provisions of this Act. The Commission shall have the same powers and authority to proceed with any inquiry instituted on its own motion as though it had been appealed to by complaint or petition under any of the provisions of this Act, including the power to make and enforce any order or orders in the case, or relating to the matter or thing concerning which the inquiry is had, excepting orders for the payment of money.

Reports of Investigations

SEC. 404. Whenever an investigation shall be made by the Commission it shall be its duty to make a report in writing in respect thereto, which shall state the conclusions of the Commission, together with its decision, order, or requirement in the premises; and in case damages are awarded such report shall include the findings of fact on which the award is made.

Rehearing before Commission

SEC. 405. After a decision, order, or requirement has been made by the Commission in any proceeding, any party thereto may at any time make application for rehearing of the same, or any matter determined therein, and it shall be lawful for the Commission in its discretion to grant such a rehearing if sufficient reason therefor be made to appear: *Provided, however,* That in the case of a decision, order, or requirement made under Title III, the time within which application for rehearing may be made shall be limited to twenty days after the effective date thereof, and such application may be made by any party or any person aggrieved or whose interests are adversely affected thereby. Applications for rehearing shall be governed by such general rules as the Commission may establish. No such application shall excuse any person from complying with or obeying any decision, order, or requirement of the Commission, or operate in any manner to stay or postpone the enforcement thereof, without the special order of the Commission. In case a rehearing is granted, the proceedings thereupon shall conform as nearly as may be to the proceedings in an original hearing, except as the Commission may otherwise direct; and if, in its judgment, after such rehearing and the consideration of all facts, including those arising since the former hearing, it shall appear that the original decision, order, or requirement is in any respect unjust or unwarranted, the Commission may reverse, change, or modify the same accordingly. Any decision, order, or requirement made after such rehearing, reversing, changing, or modifying the original determination, shall be subject to the same provisions as an original order.

Mandamus to Compel Furnishing of Facilities

SEC. 406. The district courts of the United States shall have jurisdiction upon the relation of any person alleging any violation, by a carrier subject to this Act, of any of the provisions of this Act which prevent the relator from receiving service in interstate or foreign communication by wire or radio, or in interstate or foreign transmission of energy by radio, from said carrier at the same charges, or upon terms or conditions as favorable as those given by said carrier for like communication or transmission under similar conditions to any other person, to issue a writ or writs of mandamus against said carrier commanding such carrier to furnish facilities for such communication or transmission to the party applying for the writ: *Provided*, That if any question of fact as to the proper compensation to the carrier for the service to be enforced by the writ is raised by the pleadings, the writ of peremptory mandamus may issue, notwithstanding such question of fact is undetermined, upon such terms as to security, payment of money into the court, or otherwise, as the court may think proper pending the determination of the question of fact: *Provided further*, That the remedy hereby given by writ of mandamus shall be cumulative and shall not be held to exclude or interfere with other remedies provided by this Act.

Petition for Enforcement of Order for Payment of Money

SEC. 407. If a carrier does not comply with an order for the payment of money within the time limit in such order, the complainant, or any person for whose benefit such order was made, may file in the district court of the United States for the district in which he resides or in which is located the principal operating office of the carrier, or through which the line of the carrier runs, or in any State court of general jurisdiction having jurisdiction of the parties, a petition setting forth briefly the causes for which he claims damages, and the order of the Commission in the premises. Such suit in the district court of the United States shall proceed in all respects like other civil suits for damages, except that on the trial of such suits the findings and order of the Commission shall be prima facie evidence of the facts therein stated, except that the petitioner shall not be liable for costs in the district court nor for costs at any subsequent stage of the proceedings unless they accrue upon his appeal. If the petitioner shall finally prevail, he shall be allowed a reasonable attorney's fee, to be taxed and collected as a part of the costs of the suit.

Orders Not for Payment of Money—When Effective

SEC. 408. Except as otherwise provided in this Act, all orders of the Commission, other than orders for the payment of money, shall take effect within such reasonable time, not less than thirty days after service of the order, and shall continue in force until its further order, or for a specified period of time, according as shall be prescribed in the order, unless the same shall be suspended or modified or set aside by the Commission, or be suspended or set aside by a court of competent jurisdiction.

General Provisions Relating to Proceedings—Witnesses
and Depositions

SEC. 409. (a) Any member or examiner of the Commission, or the director of any division, when duly designated by the Commission for such purpose, may hold hearings, sign and issue subpenas, administer oaths, examine witnesses, and receive evidence at any place in the United States designated by the Commission; except that in the administration of Title III an examiner may not be authorized to exercise such powers with respect to a matter involving (1) a change of policy by the Commission, (2) the revocation of a station license, (3) new devices or developments in radio, or (4) a new kind of use of frequencies. In all cases heard by an examiner the Commission shall hear oral arguments on request of either party.

(b) For the purposes of this Act the Commission shall have the power to require by subpena the attendance and testimony of witnesses and the production of all books, papers, schedules of charges, contracts, agreements, and documents relating to any matter under investigation. Witnesses summoned before the Commission shall be paid the same fees and mileage that are paid witnesses in the courts of the United States.

(c) Such attendance of witnesses, and the production of such documentary evidence, may be required from any place in the United States, at any designated place of hearing. And in case of disobedience to a subpena the Commission, or any party to a proceeding before the Commission, may invoke the aid of any court of the United States in requiring the attendance and testimony of witnesses and the production of books, papers, and documents under the provisions of this section.

(d) Any of the district courts of the United States within the jurisdiction of which such inquiry is carried on may, in case of contumacy or refusal to obey a subpena issued to any common carrier or licensee or other person, issue an order requiring such common carrier, licensee, or other person to appear before the Commission (and produce books and papers if so ordered) and give evidence touching the matter in question; and any failure to obey such order of the court may be punished by such court as a contempt thereof.

(e) The testimony of any witness may be taken, at the instance of a party, in any proceeding or investigation pending before the Commission, by deposition, at any time after a cause or proceeding is at issue on petition and answer. The Commission may also order testimony to be taken by deposition in any proceeding or investigation pending before it, at any stage of such proceeding or investigation. Such depositions may be taken before any judge of any court of the United States, or any United States commissioner, or any clerk of a district court, or any chancellor, justice, or judge of a supreme or superior court, mayor, or chief magistrate of a city, judge of a county court, or court of common pleas of any of the United States, or any notary public, not being of counsel or attorney to either of the parties, nor interested in the event of the proceeding or investigation. Reasonable notice must first be given in writing by the party or his attorney proposing to take such deposition to the opposite party or his attorney of record, as either may be nearest, which notice shall state the name of the witness and the time and place of the taking of his deposition. Any person may be compelled to appear and depose, and to produce documentary evidence, in the same manner as witnesses may be compelled to appear and testify and produce documentary evidence before the Commission, as hereinbefore provided.

(f) Every person deposing as herein provided shall be cautioned and sworn (or affirm, if he so request) to testify the whole truth, and shall be carefully examined. His testimony shall be reduced to writing by the magistrate taking the deposition, or under his direction, and shall, after it has been reduced to writing, be subscribed by the deponent.

(g) If a witness whose testimony may be desired to be taken by deposition be in a foreign country, the deposition may be taken before an officer or person designated by the Commission, or agreed upon by the parties by stipulation in writing to be filed with the Commission. All depositions must be promptly filed with the Commission.

(h) Witnesses whose depositions are taken as authorized in this Act, and the magistrate or other officer taking the same, shall severally be entitled to the same fees as are paid for like services in the courts of the United States.

(i) No person shall be excused from attending and testifying or from producing books, papers, schedules of charges, contracts, agreements, and documents before the Commission, or in obedience to the subpena of the Commission, whether such subpena be signed or issued by one or more commissioners, or in any cause or proceeding, criminal or otherwise, based upon or growing out of any alleged violation of this Act, or of any amendments thereto, on the ground or for the reason that the testimony or evidence, documentary or otherwise, required of him may tend to incriminate him or subject him to a penalty or forfeiture; but no individual shall be prosecuted or subjected to any penalty or forfeiture for or on account of any transaction, matter, or thing concerning which he is compelled, after having claimed his privilege against self-incrimination, to testify or produce evidence, documentary or otherwise, except that any individual so testifying shall not be exempt from prosecution and punishment for perjury committed in so testifying.

(j) Any person who shall neglect or refuse to attend and testify, or to answer any lawful inquiry, or to produce books, papers, schedules of charges, contracts, agreements, and documents, if in his power to do so, in obedience to the subpena or lawful requirement of the Commission, shall be guilty of a misdemeanor and upon conviction thereof by a court of competent jurisdiction shall be punished by a fine of not less than $100 nor more than $5,000, or by imprisonment for not more than one year, or by both such fine and imprisonment.

Use of Joint Boards—Cooperation with State Commissions

SEC. 410. (a) The Commission may refer any matter arising in the administration of this Act to a joint board to be composed of a member, or of an equal number of members, as determined by the Commission, from each of the States in which the wire or radio communication affected by or involved in the proceeding takes place or is proposed, and any such board shall be vested with the same powers and be subject to the same duties and liabilities as in the case of a member of the Commission when designated by the Commission to hold a hearing as hereinbefore authorized. The action of a joint board shall have such force and effect and its proceedings shall be conducted in such manner as the Commission shall by regulations prescribe. The joint board member or members for each State shall be nominated by the State commission of the State or by the Governor if there is no State commission, and appointed by the Federal Communications Commission. The Commission shall have discretion to reject any nominee. Joint board members shall receive such allowances for expenses as the Commission shall provide.

(b) The Commission may confer with any State commission having regulatory jurisdiction with respect to carriers, regarding the relationship between rate structures, accounts, charges, practices, classifications, and regulations of carriers subject to the jurisdiction of such State commission and of the Commission; and the Commission is authorized under such rules and regulations as it shall prescribe to hold joint hearings with any State commission in connection with any matter with respect to which the Commission is authorized to act. The Commission is authorized in the administration of this Act to avail itself of such cooperation, services, records, and facilities as may be afforded by any State commission.

Joinder of Parties

SEC. 411. (a) In any proceeding for the enforcement of the provisions of this Act, whether such proceeding be instituted before the Commission or be begun originally in any district court of the United States, it shall be lawful to include as parties, in addition to the carrier, all persons interested in or affected by the charge, regulation, or practice under consideration, and inquiries, investigations, orders, and decrees may be made with reference to and against such additional parties in the same manner, to the same extent, and subject to the same provisions as are or shall be authorized by law with respect to carriers.

(b) In any suit for the enforcement of an order for the payment of money all parties in whose favor the Commission may have made an award for damages by a single order may be joined as plaintiffs, and all of the carriers parties to such order awarding such damages may be joined as defendants, and such suit may be maintained by such joint plaintiffs and against such joint defendants in any district where any one of such joint plaintiffs could maintain such suit against any one of such joint defendants; and service of process against any one of such defendants as may not be found in the district where the suit is brought may be made in any district where such defendant carrier has its principal operating office. In case of such joint suit, the recovery, if any, may be by judgment in favor of any one of such plaintiffs, against the defendant found to be liable to such plaintiff.

Documents Filed to Be Public Records—Use in Proceedings

SEC. 412. The copies of schedules of charges, classifications, and of all contracts, agreements, and arrangements between common carriers filed with the Commission as herein provided, and the statistics, tables, and figures contained in the annual or other reports of carriers and other persons made to the Commission as required under the provisions of this Act shall be preserved as public records in the custody of the secretary of the Commission, and shall be received as prima facie evidence of what they purport to be for the purpose of investigations by the Commission and in all judicial proceedings; and copies of and extracts from any of said schedules, classifications, contracts, agreements, arrangements, or reports, made public records as aforesaid, certified by the secretary, under the Commission's seal, shall be received in evidence with like effect as the originals: *Provided*, That the Commission may, if the public interest will be served thereby, keep confidential any contract, agreement, or arrangement relating to foreign wire or radio communication when the publication of such contract, agreement, or arrangement would place American communication companies at a disadvantage in meeting the competition of foreign communication companies.

Designation of Agent for Service

SEC. 413. It shall be the duty of every carrier subject to this Act, within sixty days after the taking effect of this Act, to designate in writing an agent in the District of Columbia, upon whom service of all notices and process and all orders, decisions, and requirements of the Commission may be made for and on behalf of said carrier in any proceeding or suit pending before the Commission, and to file such designation in the office of the secretary of the Commission, which designation may from time to time be changed by like writing similarly filed; and thereupon service of all notices and process and orders, decisions, and requirements of the Commission may be made upon such carrier by leaving a copy thereof with such designated agent at his office or usual place of residence in the District of Columbia, with like effect as if made personally upon such carrier, and in default of such designation of such agent, service of any notice or other process in any proceeding before said Commission, or of any order, decision, or requirement of the Commission, may be made by posting such notice, process, order, requirement, or decision in the office of the secretary of the Commission.

Remedies in This Act Not Exclusive

SEC. 414. Nothing in this Act contained shall in any way abridge or alter the remedies now existing at common law or by statute, but the provisions of this Act are in addition to such remedies.

Limitations as to Actions

SEC. 415. (a) All actions at law by carriers for recovery of their lawful charges, or any part thereof, shall be begun within one year from the time the cause of action accrues, and not after.

(b) All complaints against carriers for the recovery of damages not based on overcharges shall be filed with the Commission within one year from the time the cause of action accrues, and not after, subject to subsection (d) of this section.

(c) For recovery of overcharges action at law shall be begun or complaint filed with the Commission against carriers within one year from the time the cause of action accrues, and not after, subject to subsection (d) of this section, except that if claim for the overcharge has been presented in writing to the carrier within the one-year period of limitation said period shall be extended to include one year from the time notice in writing is given by the carrier to the claimant of disallowance of the claim, or any part or parts thereof, specified in the notice.

(d) If on or before expiration of the period of limitation in subsection (b) or (c) a carrier begins action under subsection (a) for recovery of lawful charges in respect of the same service, or, without beginning action, collects charges in respect of that service, said period of limitation shall be extended to include ninety days from the time such action is begun or such charges are collected by the carrier.

(e) The cause of action in respect of the transmission of a message shall, for the purposes of this section, be deemed to accrue upon delivery or tender of delivery thereof by the carrier, and not after.

(f) A petition for the enforcement of an order of the Commission for the payment of money shall be filed in the district court or the State court within one year from the date of the order, and not after.

(g) The term "overcharges" as used in this section shall be deemed to mean charges for services in excess of those applicable thereto under the schedules of charges lawfully on file with the Commission.

Provisions Relating to Orders

SEC. 416. (a) Every order of the Commission shall be forthwith served upon the designated agent of the carrier in the city of Washington or in such other manner as may be provided by law.

(b) Except as otherwise provided in this Act, the Commission is hereby authorized to suspend or modify its orders upon such notice and in such manner as it shall deem proper.

(c) It shall be the duty of every person, its agents and employees, and any receiver or trustee thereof, to observe and comply with such orders so long as the same shall remain in effect.

TITLE V—PENAL PROVISIONS—FORFEITURES

General Penalty

SECTION 501. Any person who willfully and knowingly does or causes or suffers to be done any act, matter, or thing, in this Act prohibited or declared to be unlawful, or who willfully and knowingly omits or fails to do any act, matter, or thing in this Act required to be done, or willfully and knowingly causes or suffers such omission or failure, shall, upon conviction thereof, be punished for such offense, for which no penalty (other than a forfeiture) is provided herein, by a fine of not more than $10,000 or by imprisonment for a term of not more than two years, or both.

Violations of Rules, Regulations, and So Forth

SEC. 502. Any person who willfully and knowingly violates any rule, regulation, restriction, or condition made or imposed by the Commission under authority of this Act, or any rule, regulation, restriction, or condition made or imposed by any international radio or wire communications treaty or convention, or regulations annexed thereto, to which the United States is or may hereafter become a party, shall, in addition to any other penalties provided by law, be punished, upon conviction thereof, by a fine of not more than $500 for each and every day during which such offense occurs.

Forfeiture in Cases of Rebates and Offsets

SEC. 503. Any person who shall deliver messages for interstate or foreign transmission to any carrier, or for whom as sender or receiver, any such carrier shall transmit any interstate or foreign wire or radio communication, who shall knowingly by employee, agent, officer, or otherwise, directly or indirectly, by or through any means or device whatsoever, receive or accept from such common carrier any sum of money or any other valuable consideration as a rebate or offset against the regular charges for transmission of such messages as fixed by the schedules of charges provided for in this Act, shall in addition to any other penalty provided by this Act forfeit to the United States a sum of money three times the amount of money so received or accepted and three times the value of any other consideration so received or accepted, to be ascertained by the trial court; and in the trial of said action all such rebates or other considerations so received or accepted for a period of six years prior to the commencement of the action, may be included therein, and the amount recovered shall be three times the total amount of money, or three times the total value of such consideration, so received or accepted, or both, as the case may be.

Provisions Relating to Forfeitures

SEC. 504. The forfeitures provided for in this Act shall be payable into the Treasury of the United States, and shall be recoverable in a civil suit in the name of the United States, brought in the district where the person or carrier has its principal operating office, or in any district through which the line or system of the carrier runs. Such forfeitures shall be in addition to any other general or specific penalties herein provided. It shall be the duty of the various district attorneys, under the direction of the Attorney General of the United States, to prosecute for the recovery of forfeitures under this Act. The costs and expenses of such prosecutions shall be paid from the appropriation for the expenses of the courts of the United States.

Venue of Offenses

SEC. 505. The trial of any offense under this Act shall be in the district in which it is committed; or if the offense is committed upon the high seas, or out of the jurisdiction of any particular State or district, the trial shall be in the district where the offender may be found or into which he shall be first brought. Whenever the offense is begun in one jurisdiction and completed in another it may be dealt with, inquired of, tried, determined, and punished in either jurisdiction in the same manner as if the offense had been actually and wholly committed therein.

TITLE VI—MISCELLANEOUS PROVISIONS

Transfer to Commission of Duties, Powers, and Functions under Existing Law

SECTION 601. (a) All duties, powers, and functions of the Interstate Commerce Commission under the Act of August 7, 1888 (25 Stat. 382), relating to operation of telegraph lines by railroad and telegraph companies granted Government aid in the construction of their lines, are hereby imposed upon and vested in the Commission: *Provided*, That such transfer of duties, powers, and functions shall not be construed to affect the duties, powers, functions, or jurisdiction of the Interstate Commerce Commission under, or to interfere with or prevent the enforcement of, the Interstate Commerce Act and all Acts amendatory thereof or supplemental thereto.

(b) All duties, powers, and functions of the Postmaster General with respect to telegraph companies and telegraph lines under any existing provision of law are hereby imposed upon and vested in the Commission.

Repeals and Amendments

SEC. 602. (a) The Radio Act of 1927, as amended, is hereby repealed.

(b) The provisions of the Interstate Commerce Act, as amended, insofar as they relate to communication by wire or wireless, or to telegraph, telephone, or cable companies operating by wire or wireless, except the last proviso of section 1 (5) and the provisions of section 1 (7), are hereby repealed.

(c) The last sentence of section 2 of the Act entitled "An Act relating to the landing and operation of submarine cables in the United States," approved May 27,

1921, is amended to read as follows: "Nothing herein contained shall be construed to limit the power and jurisdiction of the Federal Communications Commission with respect to the transmission of messages."

(d) The first paragraph of section 11 of the Act entitled "An Act to supplement existing laws against unlawful restraints and monopolies, and for other purposes," approved October 15, 1914, is amended to read as follows:

"SEC. 11. That authority to enforce compliance with sections 2, 3, 7, and 8 of this Act by the persons respectively subject thereto is hereby vested: In the Interstate Commerce Commission where applicable to common carriers subject to the Interstate Commerce Act, as amended; in the Federal Communications Commission where applicable to common carriers engaged in wire or radio communication or radio transmission of energy; in the Federal Reserve Board where applicable to banks, banking associations, and trust companies; and in the Federal Trade Commission where applicable to all other character of commerce, to be exercised as follows:"

Transfer of Employees, Records, Property, and Appropriations

SEC. 603. (a) All officers and employees of the Federal Radio Commission (except the members thereof, whose offices are hereby abolished) whose services in the judgment of the Commission are necessary to the efficient operation of the Commission are hereby transferred to the Commission, without change in classification or compensation; except that the Commission may provide for the adjustment of such classification or compensation to conform to the duties to which such officers and employees may be assigned.

(b) There are hereby transferred to the jurisdiction and control of the Commission (1) all records and property (including office furniture and equipment, and including monitoring radio stations) under the jurisdiction of the Federal Radio Commission, and (2) all records under the jurisdiction of the Interstate Commerce Commission and of the Postmaster General relating to the duties, powers, and functions imposed upon and vested in the Commission by this Act.

(c) All appropriations and unexpended balances of appropriations available for expenditure by the Federal Radio Commission shall be available for expenditure by the Commission for any and all objects of expenditure authorized by this Act in the discretion of the Commission, without regard to the requirement of apportionment under the Antideficiency Act of February 27, 1906.

Effect of Transfers, Repeals, and Amendments

SEC. 604. (a) All orders, determinations, rules, regulations, permits, contracts, licenses, and privileges which have been issued, made, or granted by the Interstate Commerce Commission, the Federal Radio Commission, or the Postmaster General, under any provision of law repealed or amended by this Act or in the exercise of duties, powers, or functions transferred to the Commission by this Act, and which are in effect at the time this section takes effect, shall continue in effect until modified, terminated, superseded, or repealed by the Commission or by operation of law.

(b) Any proceeding, hearing, or investigation commenced or pending before the Federal Radio Commission, the Interstate Commerce Commission, or the Postmaster General, at the time of the organization of the Commission, shall be continued by the Commission in the same manner as though originally commenced before the Commission, if such proceeding, hearing, or investigation (1) involves the administration of duties, powers, and functions transferred to the Commission by this Act, or (2) involves the exercise of jurisdiction similar to that granted to the Commission under the provisions of this Act.

(c) All records transferred to the Commission under this Act shall be available for use by the Commission to the same extent as if such records were originally records of the Commission. All final valuations and determinations of depreciation charges by the Interstate Commerce Commission with respect to common carriers engaged in radio or wire communication, and all orders of the Interstate Commerce Commission with respect to such valuations and determinations, shall have the same force and effect as though made by the Commission under this Act.

(d) The provisions of this Act shall not affect suits commenced prior to the date of the organization of the Commission; and all such suits shall be continued, proceedings therein had, appeals therein taken and judgments therein rendered, in the same manner and with the same effect as if this Act had not been passed. No suit, action, or other proceeding lawfully commenced by or against any agency or officer of the United States, in relation to the discharge of official duties, shall abate by reason of any transfer of authority, power, and duties from such agency or officer to the Commission under the provisions of this Act, but the court, upon motion or supplemental petition filed at any time within twelve months after such transfer, showing the necessity for a survival of such suit, action, or other proceeding to obtain a settlement of the questions involved, may allow the same to be maintained by or against the Commission.

Unauthorized Publication of Communications

SEC. 605. No person receiving or assisting in receiving, or transmitting, or assisting in transmitting, any interstate or foreign communication by wire or radio shall divulge or publish the existence, contents, substance, purport, effect, or meaning thereof, except through authorized channels of transmission or reception, to any person other than the addressee, his agent, or attorney, or to a person employed or authorized to forward such communication to its destination, or to proper accounting or distributing officers of the various communicating centers over which the communication may be passed, or to the master of a ship under whom he is serving, or in response to a subpena issued by a court of competent jurisdiction, or on demand of other lawful authority; and no person not being authorized by the sender shall intercept any communication and divulge or publish the existence, contents, substance, purport, effect, or meaning of such intercepted communication to any person; and no person not being entitled thereto shall receive or assist in receiving any interstate or foreign communication by wire or radio and use the same or any information therein contained for his own benefit or for the benefit of another not entitled thereto; and no person having received such intercepted communication or having become acquainted with the contents, substance, purport, effect, or meaning of the same or any part thereof, knowing that such information was so obtained, shall divulge or publish the existence, contents, substance, purport, effect, or meaning of the same or any part thereof, or use the same or any information therein contained for his own benefit or for the benefit of another not entitled thereto: *Provided*, That this section shall not apply to the receiving, divulging, publishing, or utilizing the contents of any radio communication broadcast, or transmitted by amateurs or others for the use of the general public, or relating to ships in distress.

War Emergency—Powers of President

SEC. 606. (a) During the continuance of a war in which the United States is engaged, the President is authorized, if he finds it necessary for the national defense and security, to direct that such communications as in his judgment may be essential to the national defense and security shall have preference or priority with any carrier subject to this Act. He may give these directions at and for such times as he may determine, and may modify, change, suspend, or annul them and for any such purpose he is hereby authorized to issue orders directly, or through such person or persons as he designates for the purpose, or through the Commission. Any carrier complying with any such order or direction for preference or priority herein authorized shall be exempt from any and all provisions in existing law imposing civil or criminal penalties, obligations, or liabilities upon carriers by reason of giving preference or priority in compliance with such order or direction.

(b) It shall be unlawful for any person during any war in which the United States is engaged to knowingly or willfully, by physical force or intimidation by threats of physical force, obstruct or retard or aid in obstructing or retarding interstate or foreign communication by radio or wire. The President is hereby authorized, whenever in his judgment the public interest requires, to employ the armed forces of the United States to prevent any such obstruction or retardation of communication: *Provided*, That nothing in this section shall be construed to repeal, modify, or affect either section 6 or section 20 of an Act entitled "An Act to supplement existing laws against unlawful restraints and monopolies, and for other purposes," approved October 15, 1914.

(c) Upon proclamation by the President that there exists war or a threat of war or a state of public peril or disaster or other national emergency, or in order to preserve the neutrality of the United States, the President may suspend or amend, for such time as he may see fit, the rules and regulations applicable to any or all stations within the jurisdiction of the United States as prescribed by the Commission, and may cause the closing of any station for radio communication and the removal therefrom of its apparatus and equipment, or he may authorize the use or control of any such station and/or its apparatus and equipment by any department of the Government under such regulations as he may prescribe, upon just compensation to the owners.

(d) The President shall ascertain the just compensation for such use or control and certify the amount ascertained to Congress for appropriation and payment to the person entitled thereto. If the amount so certified is unsatisfactory to the person entitled thereto, such person shall be paid only 75 per centum of the amount and shall be entitled to sue the United States to recover such further sum as added to such payment of 75 per centum will make such amount as will be just compensation for the use and control. Such suit shall be brought in the manner provided by paragraph 20 of section 24, or by section 145, of the Judicial Code, as amended.

Effective Date of Act

SEC. 607. This Act shall take effect upon the organization of the Commission, except that this section and sections 1 and 4 shall take effect July 1, 1934. The Commission shall be deemed to be organized upon such date as four members of the Commission have taken office.

Separability Clause

SEC. 608. If any provision of this Act or the application thereof to any person or circumstance is held invalid, the remainder of the Act and the application of such provision to other persons or circumstances shall not be affected thereby.

Short Title

SEC. 609. This Act may be cited as the "Communications Act of 1934."

Approved, June 19, 1934.

THE ORIGINS

REPORT OF THE SENATE INTERSTATE COMMERCE COMMITTEE
April 17 (calendar day, April 19), 1934

Mr. Dill, from the Committee on Interstate Commerce, submitted the following

REPORT
[To accompany S. 3285]

The Committee on Interstate Commerce, to whom was referred the bill (S. 3285) to provide for the regulation of interstate and foreign communications by wire or radio, and for other purposes, having considered the same, report the same with amendments and, as amended, recommend the bill do pass.

The purpose of this bill is to create a communications commission with regulatory power over all forms of electrical communication, whether by telephone, telegraph, cable, or radio. Under the Radio Act of 1927, the Radio Commission licenses radio stations. Since 1910 the Interstate Commerce Commission has had some jurisdiction over telephone, telegraph, and wireless common carriers. Likewise the Postmaster General has certain jurisdiction over these companies. There is a vital need for one commission with unified jurisdiction over all of these methods of communication.

The original bill (S. 2910) was the subject of extensive public hearings. Following those hearings a subcommittee considered that bill in detail. Attorneys from the Interstate Commerce Commission, the Radio Commission, and the State Department assisted the subcommittee. The subcommittee made many tentative changes. Those changes were written into the new bill, S. 3285. This bill was considered in detail by the full committee and is the subject of this report.

In originally framing the bill two courses were open. One was to prepare a detailed and practicable bill which incorporated all legislation pertinent to the subject. The other was to draft a short bill creating the Commission and delegating to it by reference the powers now vested in the Radio Commission, the Interstate Commerce Commission, and the Postmaster General.

While this latter course would seem at first thought a simpler legislative method, it has many administrative obstacles from the viewpoint of effective regulation by the Commission to be created.

The Interstate Commerce Act has evolved during a period of nearly 50 years with the emphasis primarily on transportation by railroads. The Interstate Commerce Act and legislation supplemental thereto is contained in a publication of 242 pages, plus a 59-page supplement. Congress gave the Interstate Commerce Commission jurisdiction over communications only incidentally beginning in 1910, by a series of amendments of certain provisions of that act.

This bill is so written as to enact the powers which the Interstate Commerce Commission and the Radio Commission now exercise over communications, by means of definite statutory provisions. This is preferable to leaving the Commission in doubt as to its powers by reference to general legislation primarily designed for railroads. There are certain inherent weaknesses in the present Interstate Commerce Act so far as it applies to communication companies, and these weaknesses would continue if this legislation simply transferred the powers of the Interstate Commerce Commission to this Commission. In addition, certain provisions of the Radio Act are no longer applicable to radio regulation.

In this bill many provisions are copied verbatim from the Interstate Commerce Act because they apply directly to communication companies doing a common carrier business, but in some paragraphs the language is simplified and clarified. These variances or departures from the text of the Interstate Commerce Act are made for the purpose of clarification in their application to communications, rather than as a manifestation of congressional intent to attain a different objective.

Under existing provisions of the Interstate Commerce Act the regulation of the telephone monopoly has been practically nil. This vast monopoly which so immediately serves the needs of the people in their daily and social life must be effectively regulated. No Government organization can provide such regulation without a full knowledge of the contractual relations between the parent, subsidiary, and affiliated corporations engaged in the telephone, telegraph, and cable business.

It may be found necessary to give the Commission power to void or modify the contracts between these corporations. For these reasons section 215 of the bill specifically directs the Commission to investigate and report its recommendations to Congress on this subject and also as to the need of legislation to control leased lines.

The bill further expressly directs the Commission to make recommendations for such amendments as it may think desirable to be sent to Congress on or before February 1, 1935. It also expressly directs the Commission to investigate certain important phases of the communications business and report its recommendations to Congress. These investigations are provided for in the following sections:

Section 220. Desirability of permitting State regulation of systems of accounts and rates of depreciation charges; and

Section 307 (c). Study of proposal that Congress by statute allocate a fixed percentage of broadcasting facilities for nonprofit programs, such as educational religious, fraternal, labor, and charitable purposes.

It is believed that a study of these questions and reports to Congress will be quite helpful in framing future legislation directly affecting the regulation of the communication business.

ANALYSIS OF BILL

Title I. General Provisions

Section 1: Declares the policy of Congress, assuring an adequate communication system for this country and creates the Federal Communications Commission.

Section 2: Provides that the act is applicable to the regulation of all radio stations and to interstate and foreign communication, but reserves to the States exclusive jurisdiction over intrastate telephone and telegraph communication.

Section 3: Contains the definitions. Most of these are taken from the Radio Act, the Interstate Commerce Act, and international conventions.

Section 4: Provides for a bipartisan commission of five members with terms of 6 years at an annual salary of $10,000.

Section 5: Divides the Commission into two divisions: The Radio Division, and the Telegraph and Telephone Division. The chairman of the Commission, to be designated by the President, is made a members of both divisions.

One reason for this statutory division is a desire to achieve effective regulation of the telephone and telegraph business. Experience has shown that commercial broadcasting takes the attention of all of the members of the Radio Commission. Railroads and other transportation take most of the attention of the Interstate Commerce Commission. Your committee believes that unless the law provides a clear division of powers, broadcasting problems being so numerous, the Commission would give most of its attention to radio and neglect the problems of telephone and telegraph regulation. The study and regulation of the telephone and telegraph business must be a full-time task if it is to be effective.

The recent preliminary report on communication companies by Commissioner Walter M. W. Splawn, made to the House Committee on Interstate and Foreign Commerce, bears eloquent witness to the need of a most complete study and for real regulation.

Except in certain instances, enumerated in section 5, each division will act independently of the other, nor shall the full Commission review the action of a division. It should be emphasized that for all purposes the action of either division with respect to matters under its jurisdiction is the action of the Commission; in other words, for such purposes the division is the Commission.

Title II. Common Carriers

This title sets forth the duties and obligations of common carriers engaged in communication service and the powers of the Commission relating thereto. For the most part it follows provisions of the Interstate Commerce Act now applicable to communications or adapts some provisions of that act now applicable only to transportation.

Section 201 (a) requires carriers to furnish service upon reasonable request and to establish with other carriers physical connections, through routes, through rates, and divisions of through rates. It is adapted from section 1 (4) of the Interstate Commerce Act.

Section 201 (b) requires reasonable charges, and limits the contracts for exchange of services between carriers to such contracts as the Commission deems "not contrary to the public interest." It is adapted from section 1 (5) and (6) of the Interstate Commerce Act.

Section 202 combines section 2 and 3 (1) of the Interstate Commerce Act, making unjust discrimination and undue preference unlawful. The committee recommends amendments by inserting the word "unjustly" after the word "discriminate" and by changing the words "such communication service" to "like communication service." These amendments will make the language more nearly conform to the Interstate Commerce Act.

Section 203 (a) adapts section 6 (1) and (6) of the Interstate Commerce Act to communications. It requires publication and filing of schedules of charges, classifications, regulations, and practices. Subsections (b), (c), (d), and (e) are all copies from section 6, paragraphs (3), (7), (9), and (10), respectively, of the Interstate Commerce Act.

Section 204 authorizes suspension and investigation of proposed changes in such schedules. It is adapted from section 15 (7) of the Interstate Commerce Act so as to apply to communications.

Section 205 follows sections 15 (1) and 16 (8) of the Interstate Commerce Act, but does not apply to minimum charges of communication companies. It reduces forfeiture from $5,000 for each offense to $1,000 for each offense for violation of the Commission's orders.

Sections 206, 207, 208, and 209 are the present law in sections 8, 9, 13 (1), and (2), and 16 (1) of the Interstate Commerce Act, and deal, respectively, with liability for damages, complaints, reparation, and orders for payment of money.

Section 210 permits railroads and communication companies to continue to exchange services, franks, and passes under rules prescribed by the Commission. It adapts the language of section 1 (7) of the Interstate Commerce Act.

Section 211 requires filing of all contracts between carriers engaged in the communication business and between communication companies and other common carriers not covered by this bill. It changes the language of section 6 (5) of the Interstate Commerce Act to apply to carriers under both acts.

Section 212 follows the text of section 20a (12) of the Interstate Commerce Act and extends the prohibition against interlocking directorates to communication carriers. It also prohibits any officer or director of a carrier from profiting out of the funds of the capital account. The necessity for regulation of these matters is well exemplified by Commissioner Splawn's report previously mentioned in which he states at page XX:

The president of this company (Associated Telephone Investment Co.) before the receivership used his authority as president to (a) make loans, with A.T.I. funds, to outside companies with which he was connected as officer or director; (b) borrow stock from A.T.I. which stock was pledged by himself and a vice president of A.T.U. and A.T.I. as collateral to private loans; and (c) advance A.T.I. funds to a vice president of the company for use in maintaining private brokerage accounts.

Section 213 differs in some respects from the valuation provisions of section 19a of the Interstate Commerce Act. Except with respect to annual reports of improvements and retirements, the bill is permissive whereas the Interstate Commerce Act is mandatory. The bill omits the detailed requirements of the act for ascertainment and report of various elements of value and does not repeat the elaborate procedural provisions of the act relating to determination of tentative and final valuation. The Interstate Commerce Commission shall, upon request of the Communications Commission, complete the valuations now in progress of the property of communication carriers.

Section 214 requires certificates of public convenience and necessity for extension or construction of new interstate lines. It is similar to section 1 (18-22) of the Interstate Commerce Act relating to construction. It provides for certain exceptions and your committee recommends subsection (a) be amended by inserting the words "or the supplementing of existing facilities" so that repairs, replacements, and the stringing of additional wires may be exempted also.

Section 215 authorizes the Commission to investigate and report to Congress regarding the need of legislation to control interservice contracts between holding, subsidiary, and affiliated companies and concerning the need of further legislation relating to leased-wire services.

Section 216 makes the bill applicable to receivers and trustees of carriers. A similar provision is in the Interstate Commerce Act.

Section 217 provides that the carriers shall be liable for the acts and omissions of its agents and is copied from the Elkins Act.

Section 218 is based on section 12 (1) of the Interstate Commerce Act and makes it the duty of the Commission to keep itself informed of the conduct of the carriers' business and also of new developments in the art of communication.

Section 219 is based on section 20 (1) and (2) of the Interstate Commerce Act, but also requires annual reports of affiliates of carriers as well as of carriers and requires that all reports shall include statement of the privileges of each class of stock, the names of all holders of 5 percent or more of any class of stock, and the names of all officers and directors and the amount of salary, bonus, and all other compensation paid to each.

Section 220 (a-g) is taken from section 20 (5-8) of the Interstate Commerce Act dealing with accounts, records, and memoranda. It also adds the new provisions found in subsections (h), (i), and (j). Subsections (h) and (i) reflect the present practice of the Interstate Commerce Commission. Subsection (j) is responsive to the recommendations of the State public utilities commissions, except that it calls for investigation and report to Congress instead of immediately turning over these matters to the State.

Section 221 (a) permits mergers of telephone companies and is copied verbatim from section 5 (18) of the Interstate Commerce Act. Paragraphs (b), (c), and (d) conform to recommendations of the State commissions and will enable those commissions, where authorized to do so, to regulate exchange services in metropolitan areas overlapping State lines.

Title III. Special Provisions Relating to Radio

Title III consists of the Radio Act of 1927 written to bring into a single title the effective provisions of that act and its several amendments. The language has been changed in minor respects to conform to the terms and definitions in the remainder of the bill. Most of the changes from the present Radio Act of 1927 are changes carried in H.R.7716 of the Seventy-second Congress which passed both Houses of Congress, but failed to become a law because of the failure of President Hoover to sign the bill.

Section 301 is the same as section 1 of the Radio Act.

Section 302 (a) is copied from section 2 of the Radio Act.

Section 302 (b) excludes the territories from the zones for purposes of equal division of radio facilities. This was carried in H. R. 7716.

Section 303 (a-e) combines sections 4 and 5 of the Radio Act with the additions herein noted.

Section 303 (f) requires a public hearing before the Commission may make changes in the frequency, authorized power, or times of operation of any station. It was a part of H. R. 7716.

Section 303 (g) directs the Commission to study new uses for radio and to encourage the more effective use of radio in the public interest.

Section 303 (h-p) is copied from sections 4 and 5 of the Radio Act.

Section 303 (q) requires the painting or illumination of radio towers which constitute a menace to air navigation.

Sections 304, 305, and 306 dealing with waivers, Government-owned stations, and foreign ships are copied from sections 5, 6, and 8, respectively, of the Radio Act.

Section 307 (a) and (b) dealing with allocation of facilities and terms of licenses is section 9 of the Radio Act as modified by the Davis amendment of March 28, 1928 (45 Stat. 373).

Section 307 (b) also authorizes additional licenses for stations not exceeding 100 watts of power regardless of other restrictions in the zone when they will not interfere with the efficient service of other licensed stations. This proviso will permit additional broadcasting service in sections of the country now inadequately served without increasing interference. It was contained in H. R. 7716. The committee eliminated the provision which would restrict cleared channels to 2,200 miles because of its unwillingness to set a statutory limit upon the solution of a technical problem.

Section 307 (c) directs the Commission to study the proposal that Congress by statute allocate fixed percentages of broadcasting facilities to particular types of nonprofit programs or to persons identified with particular kinds of activities. There has been an increasing demand that Congress enter upon a partial statutory allocation of broadcasting facilities, particularly for educational and religious broadcasting.

Section 307 (d) modifies section 9 of the Radio Act by reducing the maximum terms of broadcasting licenses from 3 years to 1 year and for other stations, from 5 years to 3 years. The Radio Commission has limited broadcasting licenses to 6 months in the past and commercial station licenses to 1 year. Reduction of the maximum term of licenses will assist the Government in retaining control over these valuable privileges. This was passed by the Senate and House in H. R. 7716.

Section 308 is copied from section 10 of the Radio Act as modified by H. R. 7716, which adds the requirement that modifications and renewals of licenses may be granted only upon written application. This is the present practice of the Radio

Commission. The two provisos permit the Commission to issue temporary licenses in cases of emergency.

Section 309 provides for hearings and is copied from section 11 of the Radio Act.

Section 310, dealing with limitation on foreign holding and transfer of licenses, is adopted from section 12 of the Radio Act as modified by H. R. 7716, with additional limitations as to foreign ownership.

Section 310 (a) (4) modifies the present law by (1) refusing a station license to a company more than one fifth of whose capital stock is owned of record by aliens, and (2) by changing the words "may be voted by aliens" in the present law to "is voted by aliens." The purpose of this is to guard against alien control and not the mere possibility of alien control.

Section 310 (a) (5) seeks to insure the American character of holding companies whose subsidiaries operate under radio licenses granted by the Commission. The provision has been made effective after June 1, 1935, in order to give the companies affected an opportunity to bring their organizations into harmony with the provisions of the paragraph. Whatever apparent objection there might be to one fourth foreign ownership from the standpoint of war or emergency leading to war, becomes less important when it is remembered that the President has full power to seize all radio stations in the United States in case of war or threat of war.

To prohibit a holding company from having any alien representation or ownership whatsoever would probably seriously handicap the operation of those organizations that carry on international communications and have large interests in foreign countries in connection with their international communications. Such a rigid restriction seems unnecessary.

Section 310 (b) is section 12 of the Radio Act as modified by H. R. 7716, requiring the Commission to secure full information before giving its consent to the transfer of a license.

Section 311 is based on section 13 of the radio act but it also modifies the present law in certain respects.

The effect of the alteration is to bring section 311 more closely into harmony with section 313. If the court revokes a license the Commission should not grant an application for another license to the same parties. If, however, the court has adjudged the person guilty, but has not revoked the license, the Commission can determine whether or not public interest will be served by the granting of a license.

Section 312 is adapted from section 14 of the Radio Act and confers upon the Commission the power to suspend radio licenses. Under the existing law the Commission must revoke a license or permit an offending licensee to go unpunished. This provision would permit the Commission to suspend licenses in cases where some punishment was justified but where revocation would be too harsh. The proviso reduces the time within which the licensee may take exception to the Commission's action in revoking or suspending its license to 15 days. This is sufficient for the licensee to take exception and to request a hearing.

Section 313 dealing with the application of the antitrust laws to radio. It is copied from section 15 of the Radio Act.

Section 314 preserves competition in international communications. It is copied from section 17 of the Radio Act.

Section 315 on facilities for candidates for public office is a considerable enlargement of section 18 of the Radio Act. It is identical with a provision of H. R. 7716, Seventy-second Congress, which was passed by both Houses.

This section extends the requirement of equality of treatment of political candidates to supporters and opponents of candidates, and public questions before the people for a vote. It also prohibits any increased charge for political speeches. No station owner is required to permit the use of his station for any of these purposes but if a station permits one candidate or the supporters or opponents of a candidate, or of a public question upon which the people are to vote, to use its facilities, then there is the requirement of equality of treatment and that no higher rates than ordinary advertising rates shall be charged.

Section 316 was also in H. R. 7716, which both Houses passed. It provides that no person shall broadcast by means of any radio station, for which a license is required by any law of the United States, any information concerning any lottery, gift enterprise, or similar scheme offering prizes dependent in whole or in part upon lot or chance.

Sections 317, 318, 319, 320, 321, 322, 323, and 324 are copied, respectively from the Radio Act, sections 19, 20, 21, 22, 23, 24, 25, and 26. They deal with the following subjects: Announcement that matter is paid for, operation of transmitting apparatus, construction permits, distress signals and communications, intercommunication in mobile service, interference between Government and commercial stations, and the use of minimum power.

Section 325 (a) is copied from section 28 of the Radio Act and prohibits false distress signals. Paragraphs (b) and (c) are designed to give the Commission control of all studios or apparatus in the United States used in connection with a broadcasting station in a foreign country for the purpose of furnishing programs to be transmitted back into the United States. The Radio Commission has recommended such legislation. The Senate passed S. 2660 at the present session of Congress containing this provision.

Section 326 prohibits censorship. It is copied from section 29 of the Radio Act.

Sections 327, 328, and 329 are copied, respectively, from the Radio Act, sections 30, 35, and 36, and deal with the use of naval stations, the Philippine Islands, and Canal Zone, and the administration of the act in the Territories and possessions.

All of the sections of the Radio Act, which have been omitted in title III what was either temporary legislation, or administrative, penal, and judicial review sections which are considered in titles I, IV, V, and VI.

Title IV. Procedural and Administrative Provisions

This title contains the applicable procedural and administrative provisions of the Interstate Commerce Act and the Radio Act of 1927.

Section 401 (a-c) is based on sections 20 (9), 16 (12), and 12 (1) of the Interstate Commerce Act. It provides generally for enforcement of the act and of orders of the Commission in the district courts of the United States.

Section 401 (d) extends the Expediting Act (38 Stat. 219), to the orders of the Communications Commission.

Section 402 provides for court review of decisions of the Commission. Under the Interstate Commerce Act all appeals from decisions regarding wire communications can be taken to the district courts under the three-judge court law of October 22, 1913, but appeals from decisions under the radio law can only be taken to the courts of the District of Columbia as provided in the Radio Act.

This system of appeals in radio cases is extremely burdensome to owners of radio stations who live long distances from the District of Columbia. Any station owner finding it necessary to appeal from a decision of the Radio Commission must come to Washington, however great the expense for both himself and his attorney, to file and prosecute the appeal. The expenses incident to repeated trips, added to the regular legal expenses for such appeals, should not be necessary.

Under section 402 (a), the court review now applicable to orders of the Interstate Commerce Commission will apply to suits to enforce, enjoin, set aside, annul, or suspend orders of the Communications Commission, with certain exceptions, so that the special three-judge courts can review them and the appellant can then take his appeal direct to the Supreme Court of the United States.

Under a number of decisions of the Supreme Court, suits to enjoin or set aside orders of the Interstate Commerce Commission as to findings of fact can be disturbed by judicial decree only in cases where the Commission's action has been arbitrary or has transcended the legitimate bounds of the Commission's authority. (See *Seaboard Air Line Ry. Co.* v. *United States*, 254 U.S. 57, and *I.C.C.* v. *Louisville & Nashville R. Co.*, 227 U.S. 88.)

By enacting this provision into this bill, the Communications Commission can rely on well-established principles of law already interpreted by the Supreme Court. This method of appeal will apply in the great majority of cases under this act.

Subsection (a) excludes certain orders of the Commission with respect to radio-station licenses from this method of appeal. It provides that orders relating to the granting or refusal of an application for a new radio-station license or for the renewal or modification of a license shall be appealed only to the Court of Appeals of the District of Columbia. The bill then sets out the method of appeal by following section 16 of the Radio Act of 1927, providing for appeals of radio cases in the courts of the District of Columbia.

Stated briefly, the court appeal provisions of this bill transfer the provisions of the present law with respect to injunctive relief and appeal as now found in the Interstate Commerce Act and the Radio Act to this act, with the exception of the three kinds of radio cases referred to above.

Where a licensee desires to appeal from orders of the Commission affecting his interest, but which he did not originate, he may file his appeal in the three-judge district court in the jurisdiction where he lives. In those cases where he has applied to the Commission for an order and desires to appeal from the Commission's action, he must come to Washington, D.C., to prosecute his appeal, just as he came to Washington to ask for the order.

In fact, appeals from refusals of applications by the Commission could not be prosecuted in the Federal district courts anyhow, and must be prosecuted in the courts of the District of Columbia.

Your committee believes that this appeal section is eminently fair. In nearly all cases in which the Commission makes an order affecting a licensee which the licensee did not seek, the Commission must go to the district court having jurisdiction of such licensee. Where an applicant or a licensee comes to the District of Columbia and applies for an order, he must take his appeal in the courts of the District of Columbia.

Section 403 is adapted from section 13 (2) of the Interstate Commerce Act. It authorizes the Commission to make an investigation upon its own motion of matters concerning which complaint may be made to the Commission.

Section 404 requires the Commission to make written decisions and orders. It is taken from section 14 (1) of the Interstate Commerce Act.

Section 405 is adapted from section 16 (a) of the Interstate Commerce Act with respect to the rehearing of cases.

Section 406 makes section 23 of the Interstate Commerce Act relating to the furnishing of facilities applicable to communications. This remedy is limited to the performance of duties which are so plain and so independent of administrative action by the Commission as not to require a finding by that body (*Baltimore & Ohio R.R.* v. *United States*, 215 U.S. 481). The Commission alone has jurisdiction to determine whether an existing regulation affecting rates, or any other practice is unreasonable, or unjustly discriminatory, and the courts cannot by mandamus control its exercise of these administrative functions (*Morrisdale Coal Co.* v. *Penn. R. Co.*, 183 Fed. 929).

Sections 407 and 408 follow sections 16 (2) and 15 (2), respectively, of the Interstate Commerce Act with respect to enforcement of Commission orders.

Section 409 relates to proceedings before the Commission. The section is largely based upon sections 12, 17(1), 18, 19, and 20 (10) of the Interstate Commerce Act. Examiners and directors, as well as members of the Commission, are authorized to conduct hearings, administer oaths, and issue subpenas, but the provisions of H. R. 7716, referred to above, are adopted in part, restricting an examiner from hearing certain cases involving policy, the revocation of a station license, or new developments in radio.

Section 410, proposed by the State public utility commissions, authorizes the Commission to refer any matter to a joint board to be composed of members of the State commissions affected. The Commission may confer, as to rates, charges, practices, classifications, and regulations, with any State commission having jurisdiction. It is based in part on section 13 (2) of the Interstate Commerce Act.

Section 411 carries forward provisions of the Elkins Act and of section 16 (4) of the Interstate Commerce Act relating to joinder of parties and payment of money.

Section 412 is based upon section 16 (13) of the Interstate Commerce Act relating to the preservation of schedules of charges, classifications, contracts, and statistics contained in annual reports as public record.

Section 413 requires every common carrier subject to the act to maintain an agent in the District of Columbia for the purpose of service of process and orders of the Commission. It is based on United States Code, title 49, section 50, which applies to the Interstate Commerce Commission.

Section 414 provides that remedies under this act are in addition to remedies afforded by other statutes or by common law. It is copied verbatim from section 22 (1) of the Interstate Commerce Act.

Section 415 limits the time for recovery of unlawful charges or of undercharges. This section shortens the periods of limitation in section 16 (3) of the Interstate Commerce Act.

Section 416 relating to service of orders is adapted from section 16 (5-7) of the Interstate Commerce Act.

Title V. Penal Provisions—Forfeitures

Section 501 combines section 10 (1) of the Interstate Commerce Act and section 33 of the Radio Act. It is the general penalty section for violations of the act.

Section 502 provides penalties for violation of rules and regulations of the Commission. It is copied from section 32 of the Radio Act.

Section 503 provides for forfeitures in cases of rebates and offsets, and follows the provisions of the Elkins Act.

Section 504 provides that forfeitures are payable into the Treasury and recoverable by civil suit. It is based on section 16 (9-10) of the Interstate Commerce Act.

Section 504 relating to venue is taken from section 34 of the Radio Act and the Elkins Act.

Title VI. Miscellaneous Provisions

Section 601 transfers to the Commission duties, powers, and functions of the Interstate Commerce Commission and the Postmaster General under certain provisions of law (other than the Interstate Commerce Act) not repealed by the bill; while section 602 repeals the Radio Act of 1927, and the provisions of the Interstate Commerce Act relating to communications. The latter section also makes certain changes in other law, including the Clayton Act, made necessary by the setting up of the new commission and conferring upon it jurisdiction over communications.

Section 603 makes necessary transfers of employees, records, property, and appropriations.

Section 604 defines the effect of transfers, repeals, and amendments made by the bill. Generally speaking, it is provided that all orders, regulations, etc., in effect shall continue until changed by the commission, while pending suits and proceedings are not affected.

Section 605, prohibiting unauthorized publication of communications, is based upon section 27 of the Radio Act and extends it to wire communications.

Section 606 gives the President power over wire and radio communications in time of war, and provides for the payment of just compensation for facilities taken over by him. The section also makes it unlawful in time of war to obstruct or retard interstate or foreign radio communication. It is adapted from the section 6 and 7 of the Radio Act, and the war powers granted by act of Congress of August 10, 1917 (40 Stat. 272).

Sections 607, 608, and 609, respectively, contain the effective date, separability clause, and the short title.

REPORT OF THE HOUSE INTERSTATE AND FOREIGN COMMERCE COMMITTEE
June 1, 1934

Mr. Rayburn, from the Committee on Interstate and Foreign Commerce, submitted the following

REPORT
[To accompany S. 3285]

The Committee on Interstate and Foreign Commerce, to whom was referred the bill (S. 3285) to provide for the regulation of interstate and foreign communications by wire or radio, and for other purposes, having considered the same, report favorably thereon with an amendment, which is a substitute for the Senate bill, and recommend that the bill as so amended do pass.

I. INTRODUCTORY STATEMENT

In the summer of 1933 the Secretary of Commerce appointed an Interdepartmental Committee on Communications to consider a national communications policy. In its report that committee, among other things, recommended the establishment of a Federal Communications Commission to which should be transferred the jurisdiction of the Interstate Commerce Commission over common carriers by wire or wireless, of the Federal Radio Commission, and of the Postmaster General over telegraph companies and telegraph lines.

On February 26, 1934, the President sent the following message to Congress:

To the Congress:

I have long felt that for the sake of clarity and effectiveness the relationship of the Federal Government to certain services known as "utilities" should be divided into three fields: Transportation, power, and communications. The problems of transportation are vested in the Interstate Commerce Commission, and the problems of power, its development, transmission, and distribution, in the Federal Power Commission.

In the field of communications, however, there is today no single Government agency charged with broad authority.

The Congress has vested certain authority over certain forms of communications in the Interstate Commerce Commission, and there is in addition the agency known as the "Federal Radio Commission."

I recommend that the Congress create a new agency to be known as the "Federal Communications Commission," such agency to be vested with the authority now lying in the Federal Radio Commission and with such authority over communications as now lies with the Interstate Commerce Commission—the services affected to be all of those which rely on wires, cables, or radio as a medium of transmission.

It is my thought that a new commission such as I suggest might well be organized this year by transferring the present authority for the control of communications of the Radio Commission and the Interstate Commerce Commission. The new body should, in addition, be given full power to investigate and study the business of existing companies and make recommendations to the Congress for additional legislation at the next session.

Franklin D. Roosevelt

The White House, February 26, 1934.

On February 27, 1934, bills to carry out the recommendations in the President's message were introduced in the House and in the Senate. Extensive hearings were held on the Senate bill which, as amended, was reintroduced as S. 3285, passed the Senate on May 15, 1934, and was referred to this committee.

This committee held hearings for several days on H. R. 8301, which was the companion bill to that originally introduced in the Senate, and has in executive session worked out a substitute bill which is herewith reported as a substitute for the Senate bill S. 3285.

While the Senate bill and the amendment here reported are alike in most respects, there are three principal differences which may be noted as follows:

(1) As passed by the Senate the bill repeals the Radio Act of 1927, as amended, and includes in title III provisions which are substantially the same as the provisions of that act. Certain temporary provisions of that act are not carried over into the Senate bill, and that bill contains certain new provisions not in that act. The amendment of this committee eliminated this title from the bill and substitutes a provision (title III, sec. 301) which transfers to the new commission all the functions of the Federal Radio Commission but leaves the provisions of the Radio Act of 1927, as amended, unchanged and adds no provisions to supplement that act. Both the Senate bill and the amendment provide for abolishing the Federal Radio Commission.

(2) The Senate bill includes an amendment adopted on the floor of the Senate exempting carriers engaged in interstate or foreign communication solely through physical connection with the facilities of a nonaffiliated carrier. The amendment retains this provision except that it makes such carriers subject to sections 201 and

205, providing for regulation of charges and prohibiting discriminations. Such carriers will not, however, be required to file schedules of charges.

(3) The Senate bill provides for the creation of two divisions within the Commission, to be known as the "Radio Division" and the "Telegraph and Telephone Division," and prescribes the jurisdiction of each division. The Senate bill is so written that these divisions would function practically as separate Commissions without their action being subject to review by the full Commission. The amendment here reported rejects this provision and substitutes therefor a provision patterned upon section 17 of the Interstate Commerce Act, authorizing the Commission to create within itself not more than three divisions and to provide for the performance of any of its work, provisions, or functions through such divisions or through individual commissioners or boards of employees. The action of such divisions, individual commissioners, or boards is to be subject to rehearing in the discretion of the Commission.

In considering the bill, the committee had before it the comprehensive report made by Dr. W. M. W. Splawn, special counsel, on the subject of holding companies in the communications field. The bill as reported contains provisions designated to eliminate abuses, the existence of which this report reveals.

General Purposes of the Bill

The communications industry has been subject to disjointed regulation by several different agencies of the Government. The Interstate Commerce Commission has had jurisdiction over common carriers engaged in communication by wire or wireless since 1910, but has never set up any bureau within its organization designed to concentrate on this field. The Radio Commission has had jurisdiction since 1927 over the licensing of radio stations. Certain minor jurisdiction has been vested by a series of acts in the Postmaster General and the Chief Executive.

The report of the interdepartmental committee on communications and the hear ings before both the House and Senate committees have shown the great need for the creation of one central body vested with comprehensive jurisdiction over the industry. In line with the President's message, it is the primary purpose of this bill to create such a commission armed with adequate statutory powers to regulate all forms of communication and to consider needed additional legislation. The bill is largely based upon existing legislation and except for the change of administrative authority does not very greatly change or add to existing law; most controversial questions are held in abeyance for a report by the new commission recommending legislation for their solution. Thus, it is provided that the commission shall make a report to Congress by February 1, 1935, recommending such amendments to the act as are in the public interest. In addition to this general mandate, section 215 expressly directs the commission to study and report upon the following subjects:

(1) Certain transactions of common carriers which may affect the charges made for services rendered to the public. These transactions include those relating to the furnishing of equipment, supplies, research, services, finance, or credit, whether by a

single company or group of companies controlled by the same interests. The Commission is also directed to report on the desirability of requiring competitive bidding in cases where the same company or group of companies are both buyers and sellers.

(2) The methods by which, and the extent to which, telephone companies are furnishing telegraph services and telegraph companies are furnishing telephone services.

(3) The effect of exclusive contracts entered into by common carriers which prevent other competing carriers from locating offices in railroad depots, hotels, and other public places.

It is important to review the legislative history of the regulation of communications by the Interstate Commerce Commission. That body functions under an act of 1887 which has been many times amended. It was originally created to regulate railroads and still is primarily concerned with the transportation field, but in 1910 an amendment to the Interstate Commerce Act made common carriers engaged in the transmission of intelligence by wire or wireless subject to its jurisdiction. While a series of minor amendments have followed this 1910 legislation, the act never has been perfected to encompass adequate regulation of communications, but has really been an adaptation of railroad regulation to the communications field. As a consequence, there are many inconsistencies in the terms of the act and also many important gaps which hinder effective regulation. In this bill the attempt has been made to preserve the value of court and commission interpretation of that act, but at the same time modifying the provisions so as to provide adequately for the regulation of communications common carriers.

II. GENERAL ANALYSIS OF THE BILL

Title I. General Provisions

Section 1 contains a declaration of the purposes of and necessity for the legislation, and establishes the Federal Communications Commission.

Section 2 makes the bill applicable to all interstate and foreign communication by wire or radio, except that independent telephone companies engaged in interstate or foreign communication only through physical connections with another nonaffiliated carrier are subjected only to certain sections of the act designed to insure reasonableness of rates and no discrimination in service. The bill also exempts the intrastate business of any carrier.

Section 3 contains the definitions, which are for the most part taken from the Interstate Commerce Act, the Radio Act, and the international conventions.

Paragraph (h) of this section contains a definition of the terms "common carrier" and "carrier." Since a person must be a common carrier for hire to come within this definition, it does not include press associations or other organizations engaged in the business of collecting and distributing news services, which may refuse to furnish to any person service which they are capable of furnishing, and may furnish service under varying arrangements, establishing the service to be rendered, the terms under which rendered, and the charges therefor.

The bill upon which this committee held hearings (H. R. 8301) contained a definition of the terms "parent," "subsidiary," and "affiliated" for the purposes of those provisions of the bill which applied to parents and subsidiaries of common carriers subject to the act and persons affiliated with such carriers. The Senate bill and the amendment reported herewith both leave out these definitions since the persons intended to be covered are referred to in the Senate bill and the amendment as persons "directly or indirectly controlling or controlled by, or under direct or indirect common control with" any carrier subject to the act. It is believed that this method of referring to such persons is preferable to attempting to cover them through the use of the terms "parent," "subsidiary," and "affiliated." Many difficulties are involved in attempting to define such terms. It is believed that a more satisfactory result will be reached by referring to such persons as in the Senate bill and the amendment. No attempt is made to define "control," since it is difficult to do this without limiting the meaning of the term in an unfortunate manner. Where reference is made to control the intention is to include actual control as well as what has been called legally enforceable control. It would be difficult, if not impossible, to enumerate or to anticipate the many ways in which actual control may be exerted. A few examples of the methods used are stock ownership, leasing, contract, and agency. It is well known that actual control may be exerted through ownership of a small percentage of the voting stock of a corporation, either by the ownership of such stock alone or through such ownership in combination with other factors.

Section 4 provides for a bi-partisan commission of 7 members, holding office for 7-year terms at a salary of $10,000. It also provides for the appointment of personnel and contains other provisions usual in the case of the creation of a new administrative body.

Section 5 authorizes the commission to create not more than three divisions within its membership which have authority to hear and determine cases in the same manner as the Interstate Commerce Commission. It is believed that the commission may find it desirable to set up separate divisions having jurisdiction, respectively, over radio, telegraph, and telephone. The section also follows the Interstate Commerce Act in authorizing action through individual commissioners and boards of employees.

Title II. Common Carriers

This title sets forth the duties and obligations of common carriers engaged in communication service and the powers of the Commission relating thereto. For the most part it follows provisions of the Interstate Commerce Act now applicable to communications or adapts some provisions of that act now applicable only to transportation.

Section 201 (a) requires carriers to furnish service upon reasonable request and to establish with other carriers physical connections, through routes, through rates, and divisions of through rates. It is adapted from section 1 (4) of the Interstate Commerce Act.

Section 201 (b) requires reasonable charges, and limits the contracts for exchange of services between carriers to such contracts as the Commission deems "not contrary to the public interest." It is adapted from section 1 (5), (6) of the Interstate Commerce Act.

Section 202 combines and condenses sections 2 and 3 (1) of the Interstate Commerce Act, making unjust discrimination and undue preference unlawful.

Section 203 (a) adapts section 6 (1), (6) of the Interstate Commerce Act to communications. It requires publication and filing of schedules of charges, classifications, regulations, and practices. Subsections (b), (c), (d), and (e) are all copied from section 6, paragraphs (3), (7), (9), and (10), respectively, of the Interstate Commerce Act.

Section 204 authorizes suspension and investigation of proposed changes in such schedules. It is adapted from section 15 (7) of the Interstate Commerce Act so as to apply to communications.

Section 205 follows sections 15 (1) and 16 (8) of the Interstate Commerce Act, authorizing the Commission to prescribe just and reasonable charges, including maximum and minimum charges.

Sections 206, 207, 208, and 209 are the present law in sections 8, 9, 13 (1), and (2), and 16 (1) of the Interstate Commerce Act, and deal, respectively, with liability for damages, complaints, reparation, and orders for payment of money.

Section 210 permits railroads and communication companies to continue to exchange franks and passes under rules prescribed by the Commission. It adapts the language of section 1 (7) of the Interstate Commerce Act.

Section 211 (a) requires filing of all contracts between carriers engaged in the communication business and between communication companies and other common carriers not covered by this bill. It is similar to section 6 (5) of the Interstate Commerce Act. Subsection (b) authorizes the Commission to require the filing of additional contracts, but permits it to waive the filing of minor contracts.

Section 212 follows the text of section 20 (a) (12) of the Interstate Commerce Act and extends the prohibition against interlocking directorates to communication carriers. It also prohibits any officer or director of a carrier from profiting out of the funds of the capital account. It will not prohibit a corporate official from selling securities which he owns personally and not in an official capacity.

Section 213 differs in some respects from the valuation provisions of section 19 (a) of the Interstate Commerce Act. Except with respect to annual reports of improvements and retirements, the bill is permissive whereas the Interstate Commerce Act is mandatory. The bill omits the detailed requirements of that act for ascertainment and report of various elements of value and does not repeat the elaborate procedural provisions of the act relating to determination of tentative and final valuation. The Interstate Commerce Commission is directed, upon request of the Communications Commission, to complete the valuations now in progress of the property of communication carriers.

Section 214 requires certificates of public convenience and necessity for the construction of new interstate lines or extensions of lines, and for the acquisition of lines. It is similar to section 1(18-22) of the Interstate Commerce Act relating to construction. No certificates are required for the construction of local lines or for wires or cables added to existing pole lines or conduits. The Commission is also permitted to authorize temporary or emergency service without such certificates.

Section 215, authorizing the Commission to make certain investigations and reports, has been referred to above.

Section 216 makes the bill applicable to receivers and trustees of carriers. A similar provision is in the Interstate Commerce Act.

Section 217 provides that the carriers shall be liable for the acts and omissions of its agents and is adapted from the Elkins Act.

Section 218 is based on section 12 (1) of the Interstate Commerce Act and makes it the duty of the Commission to keep itself informed of the conduct of the carriers' business and also of new developments in the art of communication.

Section 219 is based on section 20 (1) and (2) of the Interstate Commerce Act, but also requires annual reports of affiliates of carriers as well as of carriers and requires that all reports shall include statement of the privileges of each class of stock, the names of the 30 largest holders of any class of stock and the amount of stock held by each, and the names of all officers and directors and the amount of salary, bonus, and all other compensation paid to each.

Section 220 (a-g) is taken from section 20 (5-8) of the Interstate Commerce Act dealing with accounts, records, and memoranda. It also adds the new provisions found in subsections (h), (i), and (j). Subsections (h), (i), and (j) are responsive to the requests of the State commissions that the present law be changed so as to permit those bodies to exercise, for State purposes, certain jurisdiction over accounting systems and methods of depreciation accounting.

Section 221 (a) permits mergers of telephone companies and is copied verbatim from section 5 (18) of the Interstate Commerce Act. Paragraphs (b), (c), and (d) conform to recommendations of the State commissions, and will enable those commissions, where authorized to do so, to regulate exchange services in metropolitan areas overlapping State lines.

Title III. Provisions Relating to Radio

Title III consists of a single section which abolishes the Radio Commission and transfers its functions under the Radio Act of 1927 to the Communications Commission.

Title IV. Procedural and Administrative Provisions

This title contains procedural and administrative provisions substantially the same as those of the Interstate Commerce Act.

Section 401 (a-e) is based on sections 20 (9), 16 (12), and 12 (1) of the Interstate Commerce Act. It provides generally for enforcement of the act and of orders of the Commission in the district courts of the United States.

Section 401 (d) extends the Expediting Act (38 Stat. 219), to the orders of the Communications Commission.

Section 402 provides for court review of decisions of the Commission. The review now applicable to orders of the Interstate Commerce Commission will apply to suits to enforce, enjoin, set aside, annul, or suspend orders of the Communications Commission under this act, but this section will not, of course, apply in the case of matters arising in connection with the exercise of the function transferred by title III.

Section 403 is adapted from section 13 (2) of the Interstate Commerce Act. It authorizes the Commission to make an investigation upon its own motion of matters concerning which complaint may be made to the Commission.

Section 404 requires the Commission to make written decisions and orders. It is similar to section 14 (1) of the Interstate Commerce Act.

Section 405 is adapted from section 16 (a) of the Interstate Commerce Act with respect to the rehearing of cases.

Section 406, in effect, makes section 23 of the Interstate Commerce Act relating to the furnishing of facilities applicable to communications.

Sections 407 and 408 follow sections 16 (2) and 15 (2), respectively, of the Interstate Commerce Act with respect to enforcement of Commission orders.

Section 409 relates to proceedings before the Commission. The section is largely based upon sections 12, 17 (1), 18, 19, and 20 (10) of the Interstate Commerce Act. Examiners and directors, as well as members of the Commission, are authorized to conduct hearings, administer oaths, and issue subpenas, but examiners are restricted from hearing certain cases involving policy, the revocation of a station license, or new developments in radio.

Section 410 provides that the Commission may confer, as to rates, charges, practices, classifications, and regulations, with any State commission having jurisdiction. It is based on section 13 (2) of the Interstate Commerce Act.

Section 411 carries forward provisions of the Elkins Act and of section 16 (4) of the Interstate Commerce Act relating to joinder of parties and payment of money.

Section 412 is based upon section 16 (13) of the Interstate Commerce Act relating to the preservation of schedules of charges, classifications, contracts, and statistics contained in annual reports as public record.

Section 413 requires every common carrier subject to the act to maintain an agent in the District of Columbia for the purpose of service of process and orders of the Commission. It is based on present law applicable to carriers subject to the Interstate Commerce Act.

Section 414 provides that remedies under this act are in addition to remedies afforded by other statutes or by common law. It follows section 22 (1) of the Interstate Commerce Act.

Section 415 limits the time for recovery of unlawful charges or of undercharges. This section provides for shorter periods of limitation than are provided in section 16 (3) of the Interstate Commerce Act.

Section 416, relating to service of orders, is adopted from section 16 (5-7) of the Interstate Commerce Act.

Title V. Penal Provisions—Forfeitures

Section 501 is similar to section 10 (1) of the Interstate Commerce Act and section 33 of the Radio Act. It is the general penalty section for violations of the act.

Section 502 provides penalties for violation of rules and regulations of the Commission. It is adapted from section 32 of the Radio Act.

Section 503 provides for forfeitures in cases of rebates and offsets, and follows the provisions of the Elkins Act.

Section 504 provides that forfeitures are payable into the Treasury and recoverable by civil suit. It is based on section 16 (9-10) of the Interstate Commerce Act.

Section 505 relating to venue is taken from section 34 of the Radio Act and the Elkins Act.

Title VI. Miscellaneous Provisions

Section 601 transfers to the Commission duties, powers, and functions of the Interstate Commerce Commission and the Postmaster General under certain provisions of law (other than the Interstate Commerce Act) not repealed by the bill; while section 602 repeals the provisions of the Interstate Commerce Act insofar as they relate to communications. The latter section also makes certain changes in other law, including the Clayton Act, made necessary by the setting up of the new Commission and conferring upon it jurisdiction over communications.

Section 603 makes necessary transfers of employees, records, property, and appropriations.

Section 604 defines the effect of transfers, repeals, and amendments made by the bill.

Section 605, prohibiting unauthorized publication of communications, is based upon section 27 of the Radio Act, but is also made to apply to wire communications.

Section 606 gives the President power over wire and radio communications in time of war. The section also makes it unlawful in time of war to obstruct or retard interstate or foreign radio communication. It is adapted from the war powers granted by act of Congress of August 10, 1917 (40 Stat. 272).

Sections 607, 608, and 609, respectively, contain the effective date, separability clause, and the short title.

THE DEBATE

Senate – 73rd Congress, 2d Session
May 15, 1934

MR. DILL. Mr. President, the communications bill is a bill of 104 printed pages. That, of course, is rather a large legislative document. I call attention, however, in the beginning to the fact that probably 70 to 75 pages of it comprise a rewriting of existing radio law and its amendments and of the Interstate Commerce Act and its amendments, and that the other parts of the bill which are new are the parts which create the new commission and provide for certain additional powers which the committee thought were necessary for the newly created commission to have for effective regulation.

There are a few sections in the bill which adapt certain provisions of the Interstate Commerce Act heretofore applying only to railroads, making them applicable to telephone and telegraph regulation. There are some sections in regard to radio regulation which were in H. R. 7716, a bill passed by both Houses of Congress in 1933, which did not receive the signature of the President and died with the end of the session.

Briefly, the bill creates a new commission to be known as the "Communications Commission." It abolishes the Radio Commission and transfers all radio regulation to one division of the Communications Commission. It also repeals the radio laws which now exist and substitutes the provisions of this bill. It also transfers all powers over telephone and telegraph communications from the Interstate Commerce Commission and the Postmaster General to the Communications Commission.

I invite attention as to why it seemed important to us that we should enact new legislation rather than merely transfer the existing powers in present law. The Interstate Commerce Act has been evolved over a period of about 50 years. I have in my hand a book of 242 pages and a supplement of 59 pages comprising the Interstate Commerce Act and amendments to it written primarily for the control of transportation. In 1910 an amendment was adopted which applied certain provisions of the then Interstate Commerce Act to telephone and telegraph companies and added certain new provisions. Since that time the Interstate Commerce Commission has given what might be called cursory attention to the regulation of telephone and telegraph matters, but in practical operation the regulation of the telephone and telegraph companies has been really nothing effective. It has amounted to very little. The Interstate Commerce Commission has been so busy with railroad questions that it has never given much attention to telephone and telegraph companies, and the latter business has grown only recently to such proportions that there have been sufficient complaints on the part of the public to seem to justify a separate organization to regulate and control them.

The Radio Act had in it certain provisions which have become obsolete. When written it referred to the Commerce Department certain powers for certain purposes.

It also had a number of amendments made to it, and it seemed desirable to collect all those provisions in the new bill.

Then, too, there should be a regulation of the rates of radio telephone and radio telegraph if we are to have regulation of the rates of wire telephone and wire telegraph. I shall not today take the time of the Senate to enlarge at any length upon the size of the industry or all that it involves. I do want to call attention, however, to just a few facts.

The telephone monopoly and associated corporations have a capitalization and a tentative valuation of more than $5,000,000,000. There are more than 20,000,000 individual telephones in the United States. Last year it was reported there were 27,000,000,000 individual telephone calls made by the people of the United States and more than 200,000,000 written messages over telegraph and cable. That is the largest use of communications service of any part of the world; in fact, I think it is as large as all the rest of the world combined.

Before I attempt to analyze the bill in detail, permit me to say that the bill has been prepared with great care. After rather lengthy hearings, a subcommittee of five members was appointed. I then secured the assistance of a representative of the Interstate Commerce Commission, Mr. Stough, who is an examiner; a representative of the Radio Commission; the acting chief counsel, Mr. Porter; and a representative from the State Department, Mr. Stewart, who handles communications. We had also Mr. Boots, of the legislative counsel of the Senate. In addition I had assisting me in connection with the legislation Mr. Stephan, who is an examiner of the Interstate Commerce Commission, and who was loaned to the committee for this work. These gentlemen went over the bill, not once but again and again, line by line, to see that it covered so far as possible all the existing law that is in the statutes which we are proposing to repeal, and also to see that it did not seriously conflict. I am safe in saying, therefore, it is one of the most carefully prepared bills that have been reported for some time, at least by this committee.

After the subcommittee had gone over it with great care and revised it repeatedly, it was reported to the full committee and given some consideration there. Like any other piece of legislation, it may have its mistakes and weaknesses; but from a drafting standpoint, I maintain it is a very carefully prepared bill. . . .

MR. COUZENS. May I ask if my understanding is correct that there is no authority in the bill to permit any consolidation of radio, telegraph, and telephone companies?

MR. DILL. There is not. The bill reenacts section 17 of the present radio law of 1927, which specifically prohibits any merging of radio, telegraph, and cable services. It reenacts, however, that provision of the Interstate Commerce Act which permits the continuation of the merging of telephone companies which has been going on for many years.

MR. COUZENS. But it would not permit the consolidation of the Postal and the Western Union?

MR. DILL. No; it would not permit that, primarily because of the fact that the Postal and the Western Union are tied up with radio and cables in such a manner that a union of their subsidiary corporations would bring about a union which is forbidden by section 17 of the existing radio law. . . .

Now, taking up the bill, title I, containing the general provisions of the bill, creates a commission for the regulation of all radio and telephone and telegraph communications. We have attempted in title I to reserve to the State commissions the control of intrastate telephone traffic. We have kept in mind the fact that the Interstate Commerce Commission, through the Shreveport decision and the decisions in other similar cases, has gone so far in the regulation of railroads that the so-called "State regulation" amounts to very little.

We have attempted, in this proposed legislation, to safeguard State regulation by certain provisions to the effect that where existing intrastate telephone business is being regulated by a State commission, the provisions of the bill shall not apply. We have in mind, for instance, cases where a city has telephone service connecting into a number of States, such as we have right here in Washington, running out into Maryland and out into Virginia, and in New York the service runs into New Jersey, and I think perhaps into Connecticut, though I am not sure about that. There are many cases in the country where, without some saving clause of that kind, the State commissions might be deprived of their power to regulate; and the State commission representatives were jealous, in the preparation of this bill, that those rights should be protected; and we have attempted to do that.

Most of the definitions—and there are a considerable number of definitions—are taken from the present Radio Act, from the Interstate Commerce Act, and from the International Convention on Radio that is in force throughout the world.

This bill creates a commission of five members. They are appointed for terms of 2, 3, 4, 5, and 6 years, and then are to be appointed for terms of 6 years, the salary being $10,000 per year. I think the usual provisions relating to commissions are pretty well followed in the bill, with one exception. The bill sets up in the commission two divisions—one the radio division, the other the telephone and telegraph division—and attempts to prescribe the jurisdiction of these divisions, and provides that the action of a division shall be the action of the commission; each division to have two members, with the chairman acting as the chairman of each division when it is necessary for him to serve in that capacity.

That is a variation from the method that has been previously used, and I desire to say frankly that some members of the committee were doubtful about the wisdom of the provision; but it was kept in the bill, I think, because of this fact: When the commission is created, if the action of a division is allowed to be appealed to the full commission, as is the case in the Interstate Commerce Act, so many applications for changes of power and frequency and allotments of time by radio stations are likely to come to the commission, and whatever may be the decision of a division those decisions will be appealed to the full commission, that the danger is that the full commission will become a body giving all its time or the major part of its time to radio only, and that the regulation, study, and investigation of telephones and telegraphs will not receive the full time and attention that is believed necessary if there is to be any effective regulation.

It may be that the jurisdictional provision which attempts to say what each division shall handle will prove unworkable, or prove somewhat inflexible in operation; but, if that be the case, the commission is specifically directed to report back to the Congress next February any recommendations it may desire to make for new legislation, and the Congress can easily remove the provision that sets up the divisions as I have stated.

I desire to say that the subcommittee and the full committee gave considerable consideration to this provision, recognizing that it is a departure from the ordinary method. It was adhered to in the report of the bill primarily in the hope that a certain number of members of the commission would give their entire time to a study of the telephone and telegraph question, which never has been studied, and because of which there never has been any effective regulation. . . .

Title II—

MR. COUZENS. Mr. President, before the Senator reaches that title, I should like to ask him a question. I was not able to follow the bill all through the committee. May I ask why the committee bill left out all reference to civil service as it appears on page 9?

MR. DILL. I think the bill provides for civil service with the exception of certain employees.

MR. COUZENS. That is what I wanted to draw to the Senator's attention. There is a very long list of exceptions, much longer than usually appears where exceptions are made to civil-service regulations.

MR. DILL. I think not, with the exception that we have provided for a director of each division, and for a clerk to each commissioner. I think one of the weaknesses of the commission system in the civil service is that a commissioner is not able to pick his own clerk; and it seemed to the committee that a commissioner ought to have the right to select one confidential clerk outside the civil service.

MR. COUZENS. I am not out of harmony with the committee's view in that respect, but I wish to draw the Senator's attention to the particular language at the top of page 9, which says:

Without regard to the civil-service laws or the Classification Act of 1923, as amended, (1) the commission may appoint and prescribe the duties and fix the salaries of a secretary, a chief engineer and one or more assistant chief engineers, a general counsel and one or more assistants, experts, and special counsel—

It seems to me the word "experts" includes the whole category.

MR. DILL. No; those are the provisions, I think, that are now in the Radio Act and, I think, to a limited extent in the Interstate Commerce Act. The second provision, providing for a clerk, is new, and also the provision for a director of the division. The director of the division was provided for the reason that it was believed that a great many purely administrative acts requiring no particular discretion can be performed by a director if he is authorized by the commission to perform them, his acts, of course, always being subject to revision, modification, reversal, or appeal to the commission. That is especially true in the radio division, where there are so many thousand amateur applications presented and licenses to be issued; and I think there will be a great deal of work in the telegraph and telephone division that can be done in that way.

Title II is the common-carrier section, and provides for the regulation of telephones and telegraphs, both wire and wireless. Under this title most of the sections are taken from the Interstate Commerce Act; but section 201 is an adaptation of a provision of the Interstate Commerce Act now applying to railroads. It provides that the commission may set up through routes by physical connections if it finds it necessary to do so, just as may be done now with railroads. The committee believed that was a power the commission should have if it was to be effective in its regulation.

Section 202, paragraph (b), is new, and covers the regulation of the charges for chain broadcasting. That section was thought to be desirable because the charges for the use of wires for chain broadcasting have been without any control whatsoever.

Section 203 is a requirement for the publication and filing of schedules and is taken from the Interstate Commerce Act, which at the present time applies only to railroads. It was the thought that that provision should be applied to telephone and telegraph schedules.

Section 204 gives power to suspend new rates, just as is done by section 15 of the Interstate Commerce Act, relating to railroads.

Section 211 expands the interstate commerce provisions so that the communications commission may require copies of all contracts by communication companies instead of only contracts with other carriers, as the law now requires. This was recommended by the Radio Commission.

Section 212 extends the prohibition against interlocking directorates to the communication companies—that is, extends it to the point that the directorates must be approved by the Commission. . . .

MR. BLACK. The Senator has passed over section 207.

MR. DILL. That section is copied from the Interstate Commerce Act. The sections I am not mentioning have been copied from the Interstate Commerce Act practically verbatim.

MR. BLACK. Section 207 provides that a suit can be filed either before the commission or before any district court of the United States of competent jurisdiction. That is not intended to deprive the State court of jurisdiction?

MR. DILL. I do not know that it deprives it of jurisdiction, but it provides specifically that the suit may be brought in that way. The section is copied from the Interstate Commerce Act now applying to telephones and telegraphs. It is the existing law.

Section 213 makes the valuation of communication company properties permissive instead of mandatory, as section 19 (a) of the Interstate Commerce Act does as to railroads.

Section 214 provides for certificates of necessity for communication companies, such as are required for railroads, although there are inserted provisions giving the commission power to be quite liberal in its interpretation of the section.

Section 215 is the investigation section; and I desire to say something about that.

When the bill was originally introduced, we provided that the commission should have control over what are known as "interservice contracts" between the parent and the subsidiary company. The language was quite broad. Mr. Gifford, of the telephone company, was insistent that it would wreck the telephone company's business and make it impossible for the company to do business, and painted a very black picture.

In light of the fact that it was an entirely new power, the committee struck out that provision and substituted, instead, a direction to the commission to make a study of these interservice contracts, and report to Congress regarding them, and to recommend to Congress whether there should be legislation controlling the contracts between the parent and its subsidiaries and affiliates.

I think it is generally well known by those who know anything about the set-up of the telephone monopoly, that under the present arrangement the parent telephone company, the American Telephone & Telegraph, not only owns the operating companies in the principal cities in the United States—I understand there are some 71 companies—but it owns the manufacturing company, the Western Electric, which supplies the operating companies with the equipment of the telephone business, and there is no competitive bidding on the part of those who would sell equipment to the operating companies.

Charges have been made—and they have been quite free and quite broad—that there is a tremendous spread of profit between the cost to the Western Electric of manufacturing the equipment and the prices paid by the operating companies which buy the equipment from Western Electric, the result being not only that there is an enormous profit on the operating equipment but the investment of the operating companies in equipment becomes part of the rate base in the various States, upon which the subscribers must pay a sufficient amount to give a return of a reasonable percentage.

How much of these charges are true I cannot say, but it seemed to the committee that it was highly desirable that the commission should investigate that whole situation and report back to Congress as to whether or not the commission should be given authority to control such contracts and to control competitive bidding.

It is a policy which has developed not only in the telephone business, but we are all familiar with the way it has worked with all corporations which own subsidiaries and affiliates. Particularly is that true in the power business, where they build bridges, dams, and plants through the means of subsidiaries, and pad the costs of the projects.

On page 32 the committee added an amendment providing that the commission should investigate the methods by which the wire-telephone companies are furnishing wire-telegraph service and wire-telephone companies are furnishing wire-telephone service. In the code hearings recently many charges have been made back and forth as to the practices of these companies. The committee, not knowing the facts, felt that this was something the commission should investigate, and that it should make a report to Congress with its recommendations. . . .

MR. BLACK. Looking at section 215, which the Senator was just discussing, does the Senator construe that section as giving authority to the commission to investigate the profits, for instance, of the company which supplies the equipment?

MR. DILL. That is the intent. It may be that it is not broad enough. If the Senator thinks the language needs broadening, I should be very glad to have him suggest an amendment. The intent is to give the commission power to find all the facts and report back to the Congress as to whether the commission should be given power to control the contracts.

MR. BLACK. I assumed that was the intent, and I doubt whether the language is broad enough.

MR. DILL. I shall be very glad to have the Senator offer an amendment, if he thinks it is not sufficiently broad, and I will be glad to consider it.

The sections I am not reading are sections which are copied practically verbatim from the Interstate Commerce Act, and are existing law. Section 219 provides for the reports of subsidiaries and affiliates and requires the naming of stockholders who own more than 5 percent of the stock. Whether that will be particularly effective or not is doubtful. I understand that there is nobody who owns 5 percent of the stock in the telephone business. The telephone company has put on a campaign to have its subscribers buy a share of stock, and in that way make them interested, of course, in the perpetuation of the financial system of the telephone company. But certainly it is not a burdensome requirement, to say the least. We also require reports on the salaries and bonuses of the officers and directors, and that is new as compared with the existing law, as it is provided in the Interstate Commerce Act.

Title III refers to the radio division, and is largely a rewriting of the provisions of the radio law of 1927, which are, in effect, of amendments which have been adopted, and of provisions of H. R. 9716, which passed both Houses, but was not signed by the President, and did not become a law because of the expiration of the Congress on March 4, 1933.

There are one or two new sections in that title which I desire to mention. Section 307 provides for a study of the question of the allocation of facilities for educational and religious broadcasting. I think perhaps every Senator here has had one or more telegrams or letters urging support for an amendment which is pending, offered by the Senator from West Virginia [Mr. Hatfield] and the Senator from New York [Mr. Wagner], seeking to allocate by statute 25 percent of the radio facilities to those engaged in broadcasting on a nonprofit basis.

I may say that the committee considered that amendment, voted on it, and rejected it, but felt that this question was of such importance, and that there was so much public sentiment in this country for a larger use of radio facilities for educational and religious and other nonprofit purposes, for broadcasting on a nonprofit basis, that it would be well to have the commission make a study of the subject and report to Congress as to whether or not Congress should actually legislate on it, or whether the Commission should handle it, and what its plans might be. I shall not discuss that further at this time but will probably have something to say about it when the amendment is presented to the Senate. . . .

MR. BONE. I have in my hand a copy of the so-called "Wagner-Hatfield amendment," and I gather from a hasty reading of it that it provides for the allocation of a certain percentage of licenses to be issued to broadcasting stations. Is that to be confined to new stations, or is it to apply to old stations to be set over to that type of work, or is it to apply to part of the time on present stations?

MR. DILL. The Senator will have to judge that language, and I would rather not discuss the amendment now, because it will be offered at a later time.

MR. BONE. I have not had time to read it carefully.

MR. DILL. We will have time to discuss it later.

I call attention also to section 310, which considerably changes the present law relating to foreign ownership of communication companies and makes these requirements apply to the holding companies.

The holding-company system has made such legislation necessary. A private corporation comes to the Radio Commission and secures a license to do business, and then we find that private corporation is merely a subsidiary of some big company that is interested in a great many other organizations, perhaps communication companies and organizations of another nature, and is in reality the power that determines what use shall be made of those radio facilities.

The committee gave very careful consideration to this provision. It is a controversy which is not new. It has been before the committee and has been brought upon the floor of the Senate, repeatedly. No doubt Senators who have given any study to the subject are familiar with the fact that the officials of the Navy Department insist that we should have 100-percent-owned foreign communications, and that there should be 100-percent American directorates. At first thought, that appeals to many who study the question, but in practical operation, it is found that it is too rigid a requirement, and that it would not be necessary to have such a provision in order to protect our communications system in case of trouble with a foreign country. So, after much consideration and study, the committee has written into the bill a provision that none of the officers of the company shall be foreigners, that not more than one fifth of the capital stock shall be owned and voted by foreigners, and that not more than one fourth of the directors shall be foreigners, and have extended the time for these requirements to go into operation until June 1, 1935.

We did that for the reason that one of the companies thinks it is necessary to go to the legislature of the State in which it was incorporated and secure some change of law in order that it may change its charter. I personally do not think that is necessary, but not desiring to be unjust in any manner to any of these companies, we agreed to this provision.

I think we have amply safeguarded the protection of the American communications service, because, after all, if an emergency shall arise and the country shall go to war, the President will have power under the law to seize all communication companies, and have absolute control of all communication companies with facilities in the United States. So that really I think the law fully protects American rights, and, at the same time, will permit our international communication companies to compete with companies in foreign countries with whom they must compete to establish facilities in those countries.

Title IV is the procedural and administrative section. Most of this title is taken from the existing law, but I wish to speak particularly of section 402, which is the section relating to appeals.

Before I do that, however, I think I ought to say something about sections 313 and 314, which relate to the prohibition against monopoly and to conviction by courts.

We change the law slightly there, so that if the court which has the power to take away the license of a licensee because it has violated the antitrust law, finds the licensee guilty but does not take away that license, then the commission will not be compelled to revoke the license, but, of course, if the court takes away the license, the commission will be prohibited from granting another license. The change was one which was insisted upon by certain organizations, and it seemed fair to the committee to do that.

Section 402, concerning which I started to speak, is what is known as the appeals section relating to the courts. There was considerable difference of opinion in the committee, and especially in the subcommittee, regarding this appeals section. We were confronted with a difficult problem. The Interstate Commerce Act provides for appeals from its orders and appeals from its actions in what are known as the "three-judge" district courts of the country. The Radio Act provides for all appeals under that act in the courts of the District of Columbia.

If we shall have one commission handling the entire wire and wireless system, it would seem rather incongruous to have two systems of appeal. In any case it would hardly be proper that the appeals from the decisions of the commission relating to the common carriers engaged in wire communications should go to one set of courts and those relating to common carriers engaged in wireless communications should go to another set of courts. So we wrote this provision providing that certain of the decisions of the commission should be appealed in the three-judge district courts and that certain exceptions should be made relating to decisions of the commission affecting radio. It provides that the three-judge court appeal provision may apply to orders of the commission "applicable to suits to enforce, enjoin, set aside, annul, or suspend any order of the commission under this act (except any order of the commission granting or refusing an application for a construction permit for a radio station, or for a radio station license, or for renewal of an existing radio station license, or for modification of an existing radio station license."

Those exceptions are to be prosecuted in the district courts as under the existing Radio Act, and we have followed the language of the appeal section of existing radio law as to those particular appeals.

I desire to call attention to what I think is an important fact to consider in this appeal provision. Those owners of radio broadcasting stations living long distances from the District of Columbia should not be required to come to Washington to prosecute an appeal from a decision for which they were not responsible. When I say "were not responsible" I mean a decision which was granted against them or affecting them when they did not bring the case into court. A station owner who lives in the Rocky Mountain area, or who lives in the far West, and who is compelled to come to the District of Columbia to prosecute his appeal, finds himself faced with an expense of from $400 to $500 for the mere trip of coming here, an equal amount for his attorney, if he brings one, and then the attorney fees in addition. I say of personal knowledge that some of the station owners have found it almost impossible to finance appeals in that way. So we provide that where the decisions of the commission are made in cases wherein the stations took no part in beginning the suits, appeal may be taken in the three-judge district courts in the jurisdictions where the stations are located. But in the case where the applicant for the license or the permit, or whatever it may be, comes to the commission and asks for a change in his license or asks for a new license, or asks for something to be done by the commission, then if the commission makes a decision from which he desires to appeal he must make his appeal in the courts of the District of Columbia.

In other words, if the station owner has money enough to come here in the beginning to prosecute his case before the commission, it is fair to assume that he has money enough to continue the appeal here. Not only that, but the refusal of the commission to grant an application is a decision from which no appeal can be taken in the Federal district courts. It must be taken in the courts of the District of Columbia. So we have worked out this amendment, which is not satisfactory to all members of the committee, but which I think is fair, and which I believe will be found to be practicable and to work in a satisfactory manner.

Title V is the penal section, and combines the provisions of the Interstate Commerce Act and of the Radio Act as to penalties and forfeitures, although we have reduced the amounts of the penalties and the forfeitures considerably from what they are in the Interstate Commerce Act, for the reason that we felt that not so much money being involved and not so large interest being involved it was not fair to make the penalties so severe.

In title VI will be found the miscellaneous provisions which are to provide for the transfer of employees and the records and the property of the Radio Commission, and the unexpired appropriations, and the provisions that the new commission may change, of course, the compensation and classification of the employees.

I have made this general statement. I have omitted discussing many parts of the bill for the reason that they are copied directly from existing law or acts which have been previously passed by both Houses. If any Senator desires to ask any question I shall be glad to answer them. If not I shall ask to take up the committee amendments first.

Mr. President, I ask unanimous consent that the bill may be read and that the amendments of the committee may first be considered.

THE PRESIDING OFFICER. (MR. MURPHY in the chair). Is there objection? The Chair hears none, and it is so ordered.

The first amendment was, in section 3, paragraph (r), page 6, line 15, after the word "exchange," to insert a comma and the words "and which is covered by the exchange service charge," so as to make the paragraph read:

(r) "Telephone-exchange service" means service within a telephone exchange, or within a connected system of telephone exchanges within the same exchange area operated to furnish to subscribers intercommunicating service of the character ordinarily furnished by a single exchange, and which is covered by the exchange service charge.

The amendment was agreed to.

The next amendment was, in section 5, paragraph (c), on page 14, line 4, after the word "exceed," to strike out "$8,000" and to insert in lieu thereof "$7,500," so as to make the paragraph read:

(c) Each division may (1) appoint a director, without regard to the civil service laws or the Classification Act of 1923, as amended, at an annual salary which shall not exceed $7,500 per annum; and (2) hear and determine, order, certify, report, or otherwise act as to any matter under its jurisdiction, and in respect thereof the division shall have all the jurisdiction and powers conferred by law upon the commission, and be subject to the same duties and obligations. Any action so taken by a division and any order, decision, or report made or other action taken by either of said divisions in respect of any matters assigned to it shall have the same force and effect, and may be made, evidenced, and enforced in the same manner as if made or taken by the commission. The secretary and seal of the commission shall be the secretary and seal of each division thereof.

The amendment was agreed to.

The next amendment was, in section 5, paragraph (d), on page 14, line 16, after the word "prescribe," to insert a comma and—

And may be affirmed, modified, or reversed: *Provided, however*, That the authority of a director to make orders shall not extend to investigations instituted upon the commission's own motion nor, without the consent of the parties thereto, to contested proceedings involving the taking of testimony at public hearings.

So as to make the paragraph read:

(d) The director for each division shall exercise such of the functions thereof as may be vested in him by the division, but any order of the director shall be subject to review by the division under such rules and regulations as the commission shall prescribe, and may be affirmed, modified, or reversed: *Provided, however*, That the authority of a director to make orders shall not extend to investigations instituted upon the commission's own motion nor, without the consent of the parties thereto, to contested proceedings involving the taking of testimony at public hearings.

The amendment was agreed to.

The next amendment was, in section 202, paragraph (a), page 16, line 8, after the word "discriminate," to insert the word "unjustly"; and on line 10, after the word "with," to strike out the word "such" and to insert in lieu thereof the word "like," so as to make the paragraph read:

SEC. 202. (a) It shall be unlawful for any common carrier to discriminate unjustly in charges, practices, classifications, regulations, facilities, or services for or in connection with like communication service, directly or indirectly, by any means or device, or to make or give any undue or unreasonable preference or advantage to any particular person, class of persons, or locality, or to subject any particular person, class of persons, or locality to any undue or unreasonable prejudice or disadvantage.

MR. COUZENS. May I ask just why the word "unjustly" is inserted? Will the Senator from Washington please interpret that?

MR. DILL. There was some thought on the part of some members of the committee that possibly the word "unjustly" was necessary so that there could not be any doubt as to discrimination. I do not think it is particularly important. Has the Senator any objection to it?

MR. COUZENS. It seems to me that it would put a restriction on the commission which is hardly necessary in the act.

MR. DILL. There might be minor variations which it was felt ought to be overlooked and that it would make the provision a little stronger.

MR. COUZENS. I have always assumed that a discrimination was unjust per se.

MR. DILL. I presume that is true.

THE PRESIDING OFFICER. The question is on agreeing to the amendment reported by the committee.

The amendment was agreed to.

The next amendment was, in section 214, paragraph (a), on page 29, line 7, after the word "service," to insert "or the supplementing of existing facilities," so as to make the paragraph read:

SEC. 214. (a) No carrier shall undertake the extension of any line, or the construction of a new line, or shall acquire or operate any line, or extension thereof, or shall engage in transmission over or by means of such additional or extended line, unless and until there shall first have been obtained from the commission a certificate that the present or future public convenience and necessity require or will require the construction, or operation, or construction and operation, of such additional or extended line: *Provided*, That the authority conferred upon the commission by this section shall not extend to the construction, operation, or extension of (1) a line within a single State, unless said line constitutes part of an interstate line, or (2) local, branch, or terminal lines not exceeding 10 miles in length: *Provided further*, That the commission may, upon appropriate request being made, authorize temporary or emergency service, or the supplementing of existing facilities, without regard to the provisions of this section.

The amendment was agreed to.

The next amendment was, in section 215, on page 32, line 9, to insert a new subsection, as follows:

(b) The Commission shall investigate the methods by which and the extent to which wire telephone companies are furnishing wire telegraph service and wire telegraph companies are furnishing wire telephone service, and shall report its findings to Congress, together with its recommendations as to whether additional legislation on this subject is desirable.

The amendment was agreed to.

The next amendment was, in section 307, paragraph (b), on page 50, line 11, after the word "located," to strike out "*Provided further*, That no frequency used for broadcasting shall be reserved for the use of one station for a distance of more than 2,200 miles, airline, if any person, capable of rendering radio service in the public interest, make application to operate broadcasting apparatus on any frequency so reserved, at a point beyond the distance of 2,200 miles, airline, from the station or stations already licensed and operating on said frequency, and all applications and licenses considered and granted under this provision shall not be counted as a part of the quota of the zone in which said additional stations are located"; on line 23, after the word "may," to strike out "without regard to quota restrictions"; and on line 25, after the word "exceeding," to strike out "250" and to insert in lieu thereof "100," so as to make the paragraph read:

(b) It is hereby declared that the people of all the zones established by this title are entitled to equality of radio broadcasting service, both of transmission and of reception, and in order to provide said equality the Commission shall as nearly as possible make and maintain an equal allocation of broadcasting licenses, of bands of frequency, of periods of time for operation, and of station power, to each of said zones when and insofar as there are applications therefor; and shall make a fair and equitable allocation of licenses, frequencies, time for operation, and station power to each of the States and the District of Columbia, within each zone, according to population. The Commission shall carry into effect the equality of broadcasting service hereinbefore directed, whenever necessary or proper, by granting or refusing licenses or renewals of licenses, by changing periods of time for operation, and by increasing or decreasing station power, when applications are made for licenses or renewals of licenses; *Provided*, That if and when there is a lack of applications from any zone for the proportionate share of licenses, frequencies, time of operation, or station power to which such zone is entitled, the Commission may issue licenses for the balance of the proportion not applied for from any zone, to applicants from other zones for a temporary period of 90 days each, and shall specifically designate that said apportionment is only for said temporary period. Allocations shall be charged to the State or District wherein the studio of the station is located and not where the transmitter is located; *Provided further*, That the Commission may also grant applications for additional licenses for stations not exceeding 100 watts of power if the Commission finds that such stations will serve the public convenience, interest, or necessity, and that their operation will not interfere with the fair and efficient radio service of stations licensed under the provisions of this section.

The amendment was agreed to.

MR. WHITE. Mr. President, I think I appreciate the strength of the sentiment in favor of an amendment of this sort. Certainly that sentiment was indicated in the last Congress. Yet I think we are making a serious mistake when we undertake in this respect to depart from the practice which has heretofore been followed and from the spirit of the present law.

The so-called "Davis allocation amendment" provided for an equal distribution of these facilities among the zones which were set up in the 1927 act, and provided for their distribution among the States within the zones according to the population thereof. This proposal lifts out from under that equalization amendment stations of 100 watts.

I myself have felt very strongly that the wise thing for us to do was either to adhere to the Davis amendment, so-called, adopted in 1930, which provides for equality among the zones and for equality of service among the States, based on population, or that we should repeal the Davis amendment in its entirety and lodge in the licensing authority the jurisdiction and power to make allocations wherever it might seem possible to do it technically without undue interference with other services.

I simply want these views of mine to be a matter of record at this point. I think we are doing an unwise thing.

MR. DILL. Mr. President, I want to say in justification of the amendment, especially for the benefit of some Senators who were not here at the time the Radio Act was passed, that the provision is designed to make it possible to have small stations, not exceeding a hundred watts in power, located in small communities far removed in many cases from existing stations. It is especially needed in those zones of large area, particularly in the western section of the country. We have found that a station of a hundred watts is heard only a short distance, and the Commission has established the policy of requiring most of the hundred-watt stations to be of the same frequency, because they cannot interfere with one another at very far distances.

Yet when applicants from different small communities have come to Washington and made application for a hundred-watt station to supply service to their particular communities, while the evidence might show that such a station could not possibly interfere with the service of any other station, yet because of the quota restriction, that State or that zone having exhausted its quota facilities so that a new station would exceed what is called the "quota" of the zone or State, the application must be denied.

So it seemed to the committee in the bill that was passed a year ago, and it seemed to the committee, I think, again that no serious harm could result in the equality of service by permitting the Commission, in its discretion, when it would not interfere with existing facilities, to violate that equality provision to the extent of a hundred watts, and allow many of the lonely communities of the country to have a radio station which could never have it otherwise. That is why the provision was put in the amendment.

MR. O'MAHONEY. Mr. President, may I ask the Senator why the language in lines 23 and 24 on page 50, "without regard to quota restrictions," is stricken out?

MR. DILL. Primarily because the law has never mentioned quotas. That is a device of the Radio Commission. The law says "equality of service and facilities," and we did not think it wise to give legal sanction to the word "quota." Many of us believe that the method of the present Radio Commission in arriving at this equality is not a sound method, and we did not want to give legal sanction to that method.

MR. O'MAHONEY. Is not the word "quota" used to denominate the restrictions imposed by the Davis amendment?

MR. DILL. No; it is not. It says "equality of radio service and radio facilities." The Commission invented the quota system and arbitrarily set up a certain value. I shall not go into that, for it would take too long; but it set up certain values for certain stations with certain power, and proceeded to charge, according to their own arbitrary figures, districts or zones and States and communities with what they called a "quota." We do not want by this legislation to bind the new commission to that kind of an interpretation of "equality of service and facilities" provided by law.

MR. O'MAHONEY. Did the Senator explain why, in the judgment of the committee, it was wiser to make a limitation of a hundred watts instead of 250 watts?

MR. DILL. I think it was because the bill that passed in 1933 had that provision, and then I think that a 250-watt station might be so large as seriously to interfere with service.

MR. O'MAHONEY. Would we not be safe in giving the commission complete discretion?

MR. DILL. That was what the Senator from Maine [Mr. White] suggested. We debated in committee the wisdom of abolishing the Davis amendment and as to whether or not the whole matter should not be left to the commission. I think I speak for the Senator from Maine as well as for myself when I say that neither of us felt strongly enough about it to propose a change or to make much of a fight. So we just concluded that this legislation should be enacted, and then later if the new commission thinks it ought to be changed or Congress thinks it ought to be changed, we can consider that question.

MR. O'MAHONEY. It is a fact, is it not, that under the Davis amendment there are certain Western States which are in areas not overquotaed, so to speak, and which cannot receive any new licenses although they themselves have very few licenses.

MR. DILL. The Senator's statement is correct. I think it may be said in justification of those of us who wrote the original radio law that when we created the zones we did not create them with any thought of the division of facilities, but we created them for the purpose of representation on the then radio commission. Later we found there was such a tremendous concentration of radio stations in a few centers of population that the wisest way to meet that situation was to use the zones and provide for equality of service.

The Senator from Wyoming was not in the Senate at that time, but there was a very strong feeling about it, and the fight was rather heated. So the creation of the zones was made not on the basis of radio facilities but on the basis of having a representation largely by the population of the country.

I think there is much to be said for the abolition of zones, and yet our experience with the concentration of great stations in a few communities was so unsatisfactory and aroused such bitter feelings that I have hesitated to move at this time to strike it out. It was my thought, and the thought of the committee, I think, that we might experiment to the extent of 100 watts and see whether or not it would cause any serious interference, and that possibly that would result in a sentiment to abolish the entire Davis provision.

MR. O'MAHONEY. As I understand the Senator, the language which is now proposed is such that it will clothe the Commission with the power to establish new stations of 100 watts regardless of zones?

MR. DILL. Yes; if the Commission finds that they will not interfere with other services.

MR. NORRIS. Mr. President, I should like to ask the Senator how close in miles two stations of 100 watts may be located without interference?

MR. DILL. I think generally they try to separate them by a hundred miles, and certainly not much more than that is required, although they might interfere with one another but the service range of a 100-watt station is quite small; it is only a few miles.

MR. NORRIS. How many miles?

MR. DILL. Five, ten, or fifteen miles, at most, and it is not reliable at all beyond that distance. Probably 5 miles is all that it can actually be counted upon, although, in many cases, such a station can be heard for longer distances, and may oftentimes be heard for 15 or 20 miles.

MR. WHITE. Mr. President, the interfering effect of these 100-watt stations, however, may be very great. It is the carrier wave which interferes and this may extend over a very appreciable distance, whereas the receptive quality of the transmission may be very much limited.

MR. DILL. The Commission, however, tried to remedy that by placing these 100-watt stations with a view to wave lengths, letting them interfere with one another if they interfere at all.

THE PRESIDING OFFICER. The clerk will state the next amendment reported by the committee.

The next amendment was, in section 307, paragraph (c), page 51, line 8, after the word "of," to insert the word "nonprofit"; in line 10, after the word "of," to insert "nonprofit"; and at the beginning of line 11 to insert "not later than February 1, 1935," so as to make the paragraph read:

(c) The Commission shall study the proposal that Congress by statute allocate fixed percentages of radio broadcasting facilities to particular types or kinds of nonprofit radio programs or to persons identified with particular types or kinds of nonprofit activities, and shall report to Congress, not later than February 1, 1935, its recommendations, together with the reasons for the same.

The amendment was agreed to.

The next amendment was, in section 310, page 55, line 22, after the word "foreign," to strike out "country: *Provided, however,* That nothing herein," and insert the word "country"; and at the beginning of line 24, to insert "nothing in this subsection", so as to make the section read:

LIMITATION ON HOLDING AND TRANSFER OF LICENSES

SEC. 310 (a) The station license required hereby shall not be granted to or held by—

(1) Any alien or the representative of any alien;

(2) Any foreign government or the representative thereof;

(3) Any corporation organized under the laws of any foreign government;

(4) Any corporation of which any officer or director is an alien or of which more than one fifth of the capital stock is owned of record or voted by aliens or their representatives or by a foreign government or representative thereof, or by any corporation organized under the laws of a foreign country;

(5) Any corporation directly or indirectly controlled by any other corporation of which any officer or more than one fourth of the directors are aliens, or of which more than one fourth of the capital stock is owned of record or voted, after June 1, 1935, by aliens, their representatives, or by a foreign government or representative thereof, or by any corporation organized under the laws of a foreign country.

Nothing in this subsection shall prevent the licensing of radio apparatus on board any vessel, aircraft, or other mobile station of the United States when the installation and use of such apparatus is required by act of Congress or any treaty to which the United States is a party.

(b) The station license required hereby, the frequencies authorized to be used by the licensee, and the rights therein granted shall not be transferred, assigned, or in any manner either voluntarily or involuntarily disposed of, or indirectly by transfer of control of any corporation holding such license, to any person, unless the Commission shall, after securing full information, decide that said transfer is in the public interest, and shall give its consent in writing.

The amendment was agreed to. . . .

THE LEGISLATIVE CLERK. In section 311, page 56, line 15, after the word "station," it is proposed to strike out "to any person, or to any person directly or indirectly controlled by such person" and to insert "to any person (or any person directly or indirectly controlled by such person) whose license has been revoked by a court under section 313, and is hereby authorized to refuse such station license and/or permit to any other person (or to any person directly or indirectly controlled by such person)," so as to make the section read:

SEC. 311. The Commission is hereby directed to refuse a station license and/or the permit hereinafter required for the construction of a station to any person (or to any person directly or indirectly controlled by such person) whose license has been revoked by a court under section 313, and is hereby authorized to refuse such station license and/or permit to any other person (or to any person directly or indirectly controlled by such person) which has been finally adjudged guilty by a Federal court of unlawfulfully monopolizing or attempting unlawfully to monopolize, after this act takes effect, radio communication, directly or indirectly, through the control of the manufacture or sale of radio apparatus, through exclusive traffic arrangements, or by any other means, or to have been using unfair methods of competition. The granting of a license shall not stop the United States or any person aggrieved from proceeding against such person for violating the law against unfair methods of competition or for a violation of the law against unlawful restraints and monopolies and/or combinations, contracts, or agreements in restraint of trade, or from instituting proceedings for the dissolution of such corporation.

The amendment was agreed to.

THE PRESIDING OFFICER. That completes the committee amendments.

MR. WAGNER. Mr. President, I offer an amendment which I ask the clerk to read.

THE PRESIDING OFFICER. The amendment will be stated.

THE LEGISLATIVE CLERK. It is proposed, on page 51, to strike out lines 6 to 12, inclusive; on page 51, line 13, to strike out "(d)" and insert in lieu thereof "(c)"; on page 52, line 1, to strike out "(e)" and insert in lieu thereof "(d)"; and on page 52, after line 3, to insert the following:

(e) To eliminate monopoly and to insure equality of opportunity and consideration for educational, religious, agricultural, labor, cooperative, and similar non-profit-making associations, seeking the opportunity of adding to the cultural and scientific knowledge of those who listen in on radio broadcasts, all existing radio broadcasting licenses issued by the Federal Radio Commission, and any and all rights of any nature contained therein, are declare null and void 90 days following the effective date of this act, anything contained in this act to the contrary notwithstanding.

(f) The Commission shall, prior to 90 days following the effective date of this act, reallocate all frequencies, power, and time assignments within its jurisdiction among the five zones herein referred to.

(g) The Commission shall reserve and allocate only to educational, religious, agricultural, labor, cooperative, and similar non-profit-making associations one fourth of all the radio broadcasting facilities within its jurisdiction. The facilities reserved for, or allocated to, educational, religious, agricultural, labor, cooperative, and similar non-profit-making associations shall be equally as desirable as those assigned to profit-making persons, firms, or corporations. In the distribution of radio facilities to the associations referred to in this section, the Commission shall reserve for and allocate to such associations such radio broadcasting facilities as will reasonably make possible the operation of such stations on a self-sustaining basis, and to that end the licensee may sell such part of the allotted time as will make the station self-supporting.

MR. WAGNER. Mr. President, the amendment is a very simple one. I believe that it is in accord with the sentiment of Congress and I am sure that it is in accord with the sentiment of the country. It simply provides that when the new communications commission reallocates time, power, and frequencies among the different stations 25 percent shall be allotted to cultural, educational, religious, agricultural, labor, co-operative, and similar non-profit-making organizations. . . .

. . . We must consider that the privilege to use the air is allotted to radio stations without any compensation being paid the Federal Government. Commercial stations enjoying the free use of the air have captured 98 percent of the broadcasting today, while non-profit-making stations, devoted to educational, religious, cultural, agricultural, and labor purposes have secured only 2 percent.

This amendment does not in any way interfere with the larger stations. They may continue to use all their time for purely profit-making purposes. But when they have these great privileges certainly we ought to insure that a part of radio time shall be used for the public purposes I have indicated. To me the proposition that at least 25 percent should be allocated to nonprofit ventures seems so fair that I cannot understand the opposition to it. I desire to emphasize that at present they get only 2 percent of the time while 98 percent is allotted by our Government, without charge or tax or regulation, to the large stations which have secured a practical monopoly of the air.

I do not need to go into the question of the power of radio stations to disseminate information and to influence opinion, because that is something which we all understand. . . .

MR. BORAH. I am very much in sympathy with the objective which the Senator's amendment contemplates; but the amendment provides:

All existing radio broadcasting licenses issued by the Federal Radio Commission, and any and all rights of any nature contained therein, are declared null and void 90 days following the effective date of this act, anything contained in this act to the contrary notwithstanding.

Is there nothing in these radio licenses in the way of a right that must be respected when we come to terminate them?

MR. WAGNER. Not so far as I know, Mr. President. Let me indicate to the Senator the conditions upon which frequencies are now allotted. They are allotted for a period of 6 months, at the end of which time the Government can say to them, "Your license is at an end, and we are going to give the use of the air on this frequency to some other station."

MR. BORAH. Yes; I understand that, and I think that is a wise thing to do; but prior to that time have the stations holding licenses no rights which the Government is bound to respect in any way when it comes to terminate them?

MR. WAGNER. None, except that I suppose termination must be in accordance with public convenience and necessity. I know of no other rights which the stations acquire. Let me read to the Senator the condition of the application:

Applicant waives any claim to the use of any particular frequency, or of the ether, as against the regulatory power of the United States because of the previous use of the same, whether by license or otherwise, and requests a station license in accordance with this application.

MR. BORAH. It is true that the stations get no vested right; but during the time the license is in existence do they not enter into obligations with people for the use of the stations?

MR. WAGNER. Yes; but they cannot make their obligations for longer than a period of 6 months, because that is the limit of their grant from the Government.

MR. BORAH. If this provision were to the effect that upon the termination of the several contracts, and so forth, the time should be allotted differently, it would be perfectly clear to me that it was a proper thing to do. It seems rather extraordinary that Congress shall declare null and void contracts which have been let under authority of Congress.

MR. WAGNER. The Senator does not mean the contracts between these commercial stations and individuals whom they serve. He has in mind, rather, the length of the license granted to the stations by the Government.

MR. BORAH. Certainly.

MR. WAGNER. As a matter of fact, no license extends beyond a period of 6 months; so, if the time prescribed in this amendment were lengthened to 6 months, perhaps that would take care of the situation.

MR. BORAH. I think it would. . . .

MR. DILL. There is not any doubt at all in my mind that Congress does not have the power to cut off these licenses. The decision of the Supreme Court, written by Chief Justice Hughes last year, while it is broad and sweeping in its declarations that there were no rights beyond the date of the expiration of the license, was equally decisive, I think, that the Commission could not take away the license unless it could be shown that the station had violated the terms of the license, or had violated the law, and a hearing had been held and the license revoked. I think there is no question at all about that.

MR. WAGNER. Does the Senator mean that the Government which gives a license to a station for a period of 6 months, cannot revoke it at the end of the 6 months?

MR. DILL. Oh, no; but the Senator is saying "3 months."

MR. WAGNER. Very well. I will consult the co-author of the amendment upon that proposition. If there is any fear that 90 days is too short a time, I am quite willing to make it extend to the expiration of the particular license in existence when the act takes affect. May I ask the co-author of the amendment his view in that respect?

MR. HATFIELD. Mr. President, I think that adjustment should be made. I agree with the Senator.

MR. WAGNER. Yes; I am quite willing to have that done, and I thank the Senator for the suggestion.

MR. FESS. Mr. President, I do not like the kind of legislation that the amendment carries, and yet at the same time it seems to me that it is quite essential that something of this sort should be done.

Ever since the radio has been an agency of communication there has been complaint about the slight attention given to matters of an educational character, cultural, as well as religious. I very much dislike to write into the law any compulsion. It is rather antagonistic to my way of thinking of things; and yet I believe everyone must be impressed with the pollution of the air for commercial purposes until it is actually nauseating. The practice is to turn off the radio about as quickly as one gets to it, because so much of the matter broadcast is offensive. Whether or not the extent to which we are going here is justifiable is still a question in my mind.

The Senator from New York probably will recall that some time ago I offered an amendment to the Radio Act allocating not less than 15 percent of the time for educational purposes. I never could get any reaction in favor of it. As soon as it was offered, the stations began a propaganda against it; just why I do not know; and the same thing would be true here.

Whether or not this is the way to place a greater emphasis on the things that are really worth while than merely matters of trade and barter is still a matter of doubt in my mind. I like the suggestion that the Commission shall be authorized to make a study of the subject, but I rather feel inclined to vote for this amendment. . . .

MR. DILL. Mr. President, I call the attention of the Senator to the fact that this amendment does not propose at all what the Senator proposed in the amendment to which he refers. He proposed that the time allotted should be used by educational stations, presumably for educational purposes; but subsection (g) of this amendment provides that the so-called "religious, educational, or agricultural nonprofit stations" are to sell time in the commercial field sufficient to pay for the maintenance of the stations.

I am informed by those who ought to know about the radio business that probably two thirds of the existing radio stations are not able to do more than pay for their own maintenance now. Thus, it is proposed by this amendment to grant 25 percent of the radio facilities to those who call themselves educational, religious, nonprofit stations, but who in reality are planning to enter the commercial field and sell a tremendous amount of their time for commercial purposes. That is not what the people of this country are asking for.

MR. FESS. That is not quite what I had in mind.

MR. DILL. That is not what the Senator from Ohio proposed; but this amendment is in effect a proposal to transfer the control of 25 percent of the radio facilities to organizations or individuals who say that they desire to broadcast for nonprofit purposes, but who are allowed to sell time to commercial purchasers; and if time is sold to a commercial purchaser, he is going to advertise. He is not going to pay for time unless he does advertise.

In my judgment, therefore, this amendment falls of its own weight. . . .

MR. COUZENS. Mr. President, may I point out that section (g) of this amendment does not require any one of these stations to broadcast any religious or educational programs at all. After having once gotten a license under the provisions of this amendment, the whole time allotted to the station can be used for commercial purposes. That is permissible under the provisions of the last few lines on page 2 of the amendment.

MR. FESS. I could hardly support a proposition of that kind.

MR. WAGNER. Mr. President, of course I deny that statement. There certainly is a difference. I think we must be candid about that—between being able to use for commercial purposes a sufficient time to have the station self-sustaining and making a profit out of it. There is a tremendous difference between the two things.

I am willing that the matter should be safeguarded in any other way, except that I think it is fair that the station should be permitted to do sufficient business to make it self-sustaining. We might put in the amendment, if desired, a stipulation that shall not include wages and salaries paid to anybody, because the people who are interested in this proposal represent the type of station which was in existence earlier in this whole adventure, people who used the air for educational and religious purposes, and who time after time since then—because I myself know something about one instance— made application to the Radio Commission for a little more time to use for such purposes. Instead of that, however, they were set aside, and the large commercial stations, as we know, practically secured a monopoly of the air, because apparently they were more persuasive than the small stations conducted by churches and religious institutions.

It is those institutions which I say we should help. If the Senator wants to safeguard the amendment in any other way, I am quite willing to accept an amendment; but I have had some experience in this matter, and I know exactly what I am talking about.

Let us not be too solicitous for the large stations, commercial stations, which, through the favor of the Government, without giving to it a dollar in return, have secured practically a monopoly of the air. This is just an entering wedge to have the Congress declare that at least part of the time shall be used for other purposes. If there is any safeguard the Senator wants to provide, I am sure that my colleague, who is offering this amendment with me, and I will be glad to accept it. . . .

MR. CLARK. I am familiar with the instance to which the Senator from New York has referred, and in which I think an injustice was done by the Federal Radio Commission to a very worthy radio station operated by a religious order. But the Senator from New York has drawn an amendment, having in mind that one particular case, which would open the door and allow many stations, under the guise of religious and educational enterprises, to come in to compete with commercial companies. I happen to know something about that matter myself, as the Senator from New York says he knows about the case of the Paulist Fathers.

In Missouri there were several stations ostensibly organized for religious purposes or for educational purposes, but which, as a matter of fact, were profit-making institutions. As the Senator from Washington said a moment ago, they were simply organized under the guise of religious or educational institutions for the purpose of competing with ordinary radio stations. . . .

MR. WAGNER. The Radio Commission would have power to inquire whether a station represented a profit-making or a non-profit-making institution, and the former would be denied the privileges granted by the amendment. I am quite willing to accept any language which any Senator might offer to insure that only non-profit-making organizations would be encompassed. I hold no brief against the commercial stations, but I do not believe they are entitled to 98 percent of the time. Under the amendment, they will still have 75 percent of it. . . .

MR. COPELAND. I take it that this matter never would have reached the floor of the Senate if there had been some elasticity and yielding on the part of the Radio Commission. I tried, and I have no doubt my colleague has tried, from what he said here today, to get the Commission to make certain concessions which, it seems to me, might have been done; but those concessions were not made. So this particular station has no other means of relief except to come here. . . .

MR. WAGNER. I hope my colleague will not create the impression that this amendment is offered to help one particular station. I believe thoroughly in the principle underlying the amendment. I am one of those public officials who is tired of a few radio stations having a complete monopoly of the air, and using it purely for commercial purposes. . . .

MR. COPELAND. Mr. President, I venture to say that this matter would not have reached the floor of the Senate except for the need of the particular station at the moment, but, nevertheless, the need of that station has emphasized the need of other stations.

I can see no reason why we should not pass a general law which would make it possible for these educational and religious radio stations to broadcast the material they have to broadcast. Why should they not be given the opportunity to sell a part of their time in order to pay the costs of the station? Of course, the commercial stations are making tremendous sums out of the sale of radio time, and, personally, I am glad of that; nevertheless, there is no reason why church bodies and educational institutions should not have the opportunity of taking some of the channels and making use of them for educational and religious purposes primarily, and, incidentally, selling some of the time in order that they may recoup the great expenses involved, because the cost of radio broadcasting is very high. Certainly, as I view it, the amendment offered by my colleague is a perfectly proper one, and should be adopted. . . .

MR. HATFIELD. I may say to the Senator from New York that the amendment is here, in my judgment, because of the support given it by the National Education Association of America.

MR. FESS. Mr. President, I must confess that no particular institution, outside of the educational movement, actuated me in introducing the amendment 4 years ago, and in pressing it, though not unduly, because I had the hope that the reform would ultimately be made without any legislation. Nothing that has been said in reference to any particular interest has had any effect upon my mind. My only concern is that the air should not be polluted, as is permitted to be done, and when we know that it is the profit element that is back of that pollution and makes it possible, it occurs to me that we ought to correct the situation, if that is injurious to the public thinking of the country.

I should hesitate to have Congress do anything that would lead to prescribing what could go over the radio and what could not go over the radio. I would not vote for anything of that sort; I would not want to censor the air; but I do think that there ought to be some assurance that there should be some reform of the present situation, with which everybody is now acquainted. For that reason I have been more or less inclined to vote for some measure that will insure to the country some relief along the line that has been urged so long by the National Education Association. The amendment which I offered was to carry out the wishes of a great body of our people. As I said, I have not pressed it, because I had hoped that under pressure of public opinion the correction would be made without any legislation. . . .

MR. DILL. I wish to call the attention of the Senator in that connection to a resolution adopted by the Committee on the Use of Radio as a Cultural Agency in a Democracy, which met here in Washington on May 7 and 8 under the auspices of the National Committee on Education by Radio at the Interior Building. Among the various paragraphs they adopted in their resolution I call attention to one. I may say that this amendment was called to the attention of that body. I read:

IMPARTIAL STUDIES

Thorough, adequate, and impartial studies should be made of the cultural implications of the broadcasting structure to the end that specific recommendations can be made for the control of that medium to conserve the greatest social-welfare values. These studies should also include an appraisal of the actual and potential cultural values of broadcasting; the effective means for the protection of the rights of children, of minority groups, of amateur radio activities, and of the sovereignty of individual States; the public services rendered by broadcasting systems of other nations; international relationships in broadcasting.

In other words, they do not recommend the adoption of this amendment. They recommend, rather, a study. While they set out some things which are not in the provision of the bill as to studies, it is clear that they are not ready to recommend that 25 percent of the facilities be set aside for educational and religious institutions.

Let me call to the attention of the Senator why what they say is so. It costs a tremendous amount of money to build large radio stations. The religious and educational and cultural organizations do not have the money necessary, and they are trying to work out some system whereby existing stations may be used, probably in addition to the 63 stations which already are in operation, of an educational and nonprofit nature, and still not be burdened with the great expense of building stations. . . .

MR. WAGNER. May I suggest that the Radio Commission has been studying this question since its formation. And while all this study has been going on, application after application for educational purposes has been denied, while the commercial radio stations have kept growing, growing, growing, growing until they have obtained 98 percent of the total facilities. What is the good of this kind of study, and how much more of it do we need? It seems to me it is now time for a congressional declaration of policy.

MR. FESS. Mr. President, the Senator from New York makes rather a strong statement, and it is very impressive. He states that during all the period when there was opportunity for study, we end up with a slight 2 percent of the use of the time for culture. That is a very strong statement, and it is persuasive on the minds of us all.

Since we are creating a specific commission which has to deal with this problem, along with others, and this one, it seems to me, is commanding, I still am concerned about whether it would not be better for the Congress to definitely instruct the proposed commission to report, on this particular subject, rather than for us to write the provision into statute law at this time. In fact, Mr. President, it was my thought that in reporting the bill we ought to confine the bill to the recommendations of the President. It was thought in the committee that we would have to go further than that. My thought was that if we confined the bill to the recommendations of the President, then the commission could go into all these subjects and make their recommendations as a commission to Congress for any needed legislation, in the same way as we look to the Interstate Commerce Commission for recommendations for such amendments to the transportation act as they deem wise.

I should have much preferred to have limited the legislation in such manner. I could have voted for it with much more freedom than I will vote for this provision, because it goes considerably further than I wanted to go.

My only purpose in rising is to state that I am disgusted, as I know a great portion of our people are disgusted, with the pollution of the air for mere commercial purposes. How to correct the situation is a problem. I should prefer to leave it to the study of a select group, which ought to be able to tell us the possibilities of correcting the situation, rather than to write it into the law at the present time, and yet I have an open mind on this subject.

MR. HATFIELD. Mr. President, as a member of the Interstate Commerce Committee, I join with Senator Wagner in the presentation of the amendment which directs the communication commission created by this bill to allocate and assign to educational, religious, labor, farm, fraternal, cooperative, and other institutions dedicated to human welfare and higher education, 25 percent of the radio facilities under control of the Government.

Mr. President, this amendment is offered with the hope that Members of the Senate interested in retaining private initiative in business, with a greater knowledge of the past than is indicated by those in control of commercial radio stations of today, will benefit by past experiences.

Education has been carried to a greater degree in our country than any country in the world. The aim and the object of almost every family is to secure a better education for the children than the parents themselves were permitted to secure. Untold sacrifices have been made by millions of parents of our country to provide a higher education for their offspring.

My State, as many others, provides a State university, at the expense of the taxpayer, for higher education of those who will give the time to secure it.

Despite, Mr. President, the $636,000,000 which the citizens of our country give toward education privately, despite the $2,822,000,000 spent by the National, State, and other political subdivisions of government, at the expense of the taxpayer, for education, we find that radio is today so commercialized that less than 2 1/5 percent of radio time is controlled by educational institutions.

The annual report of the Federal Commissioner of Education indicates that there are some 30,000,000 of our people attending day schools and colleges. These schools employ more than 1,300,000 teachers.

Yearly we spend some $3,000,000,000 on education, 83 percent of which is raised by taxation and the balance is contributed for the support of private schools and colleges in the form of tuition and donations.

Education is, or was, a State function, but is supported chiefly by local taxation. Education was a State function until our schools developed extension courses and radio became an interstate rather than a State or a local matter.

Education is defined in Webster's International Dictionary as—

The process of developing mentally or morally; to cultivate, develop, or expand the mind; the impartation of or acquisition of knowledge, skill, or discipline of character.

The Federal Commissioner of Education states:

Human education is a process of individual growth and development beginning with birth and ending only with death, requiring at the outset much effort on the part of others in discovering, nourishing, and directing inherent potentialities, but, at every stage, demanding increasing, self-reliance and self-control.

The interest of the American people in education may be judged from the fact that the value of public-school properties in 1920 were less than $3,000,000,000, while in 1930 our schools carried a value of more than $6,000,000,000, or an increase in 10 years of more than 100 percent. These figures do not include colleges or schools for higher education.

The question has been raised as to who is interested in promoting the adoption of the amendment offered by Senator Wagner and myself. The answer could well be that every parent, every one of our 1,300,000 teachers, every one of the 30,000,000 attending our schools and colleges seeking an education is interested. And, we might well add, every thoughtful American who realizes that an educated people is an asset of more value than either wealth or physical power.

Indeed, Mr. President, the boys and girls of today are the greatest assets that the American people possess for America.

Naturally, were it possible for all of these many millions to make their demands heard, there would be but little, if any, hesitancy in the speedy adoption of the amendment which has been presented.

The educational, religious, labor, and other groups, however, realizing how this wonderful instrument for education—radio—has been monopolized for private profit, have organized, and they have unanimously demanded that legislation whereby the Radio Commission will be directed to assign a fair portion of the radio facilities to educational and other non-profit-making bodies be enacted by Congress.

The National Education Association, the National Association of State Universities, the National University Extension Association, the National Association of Parents and Teachers, the National Association of Land Grant Colleges and Universities, among others, have petitioned for this legislation through which the radio can be made available for the purpose of spreading education and culture among our millions of radio listeners.

The Reverend John B. Harney, superior general of the Paulist Fathers, appeared before the Interstate Commerce Committee and made a valiant plea for radio facilities to be assigned to educational institutions and other human-welfare, non-profit-making groups.

The National Committee on Education by Radio, sets forth the following:

That colleges and universities, with radio broadcasting stations, have in their possession one of the most powerful and effective tools for popular education which exists at the present time.

That the broadcasting activities of educational institutions should be looked upon as major educational enterprises within these institutions, comparable in service and importance with other major departments.

That the officers of these institutions, their boards of control, and legislative bodies to which they look for appropriations should regard their services to individual students and the general public rendered by means of radio as an important and appropriate extension and supplement to similar services rendered within the classrooms of the institution.

That such services have a valid claim to public support and justify expenditure for equipment and personnel.

That the use of radio broadcasting as a constructive educational procedure is in its infancy, and, Mr. President, education by radio will remain in its infancy unless the Congress of the United States takes a hand and apportions a part of the vast radio opportunity, supposedly controlled by the Government, which can be sent broadcast throughout the country. . . .

Mr. President, if this amendment should be rejected, it would simply mean that the educational institutions of our country, and those who seek programs of a cultural type, will be forced to support government ownership and control of all radio facilities, which will be their only means of providing the people of this country with the type of programs which the average man or woman will welcome into his or her home.

I think, Mr. President, that those who control the radio industry, if we may call it such, are short-sighted. I think they ought to be willing to concede to the educational institutions of America an opportunity to go upon the air and at seasonable hours, which will give those who wish to listen in an opportunity to hear what some of our great educators have to say.

Mr. President, we are the only important country in the world that places control of radio facilities in the hands of those who seek private profit. Canada and England, as well as most other countries, own and control their radio facilities, and, unless this amendment, or some legislation of similar type shall soon be enacted into law, the Congress of the United States will find it essential and necessary to possess and to operate all radio facilities for the benefit of the people as a whole. The retort of those who now operate commercial radio stations to this suggestion may be that we would be placing a tremendous power politically in the administration which happens to be in power. I admit that such may be true, but I do not know of any administration which might be in power which would have a greater control over the radio facilities of this country than is possessed at the present time by an administration which is not held responsible for its own acts. . . .

What I stand for is the placing of responsibility in the administration of radio facilities and fixing that responsibility so that those who represent our educational system may know where to go in order to get what they are entitled to in the way of recognition on the air.

Mr. President, I have no criticism to make of the personnel of the Radio Commission, except that their refusal literally to carry out the law of the land warrants the Congress of the United States writing into legislation the desire of Congress that educational institutions be given a specified portion of the radio facilities of our country.

As was pointed out so ably by my colleague from New York [Mr. Wagner], the Radio Act and the amendments thereto specifically provide that the holder of a broadcasting franchise shall obtain no property or vested right in the air. Yet the rules of the Radio Commission are such that those who possess clear-channel stations under the rules of the Radio Commission are vested with the right to prevent the Radio Commission itself from placing any other broadcasting station, no matter how many hundreds or thousands of miles apart any of these clear-channel stations may be, on the same wave length. This is a clear violation of the letter and the intent of the Radio Act and the amendments thereto. . . .

This amendment, presented jointly by Senator Wagner and myself, is not at all cumbersome, as it simply directs the new Communications Commission to allocate 25 percent of the radio facilities to stations devoted to education and human welfare. As my colleague, in offering this amendment, pointed out a while ago, if there is any thought upon the part of anyone in this body that these groups may undertake to overcommercialize their stations, we will agree to an amendment which will safeguard for all time what this amendment proposes, which is that this 25-percent allocation shall be made for the sole purpose of providing educational facilities and permitting the radio stations to be self-sustaining only.

This is not class legislation, as no one class of our people will secure any gain by this legislation. The gain will be that of all our people, as I believe all our people are interested in education and human welfare. . . .

Radio broadcasting reaches many millions of our people daily. The educators and others in our country who are seeking to build a higher standard for all Americans are denied opportunities which they should have. To my mind, these worthy organizations should be accorded the facility which they can so effectively use for the common good, and, I sincerely trust that the Senate will insist on the adoption of the pending amendment which is beneficial to so many and which is harmful to but few. And I might add that unless legislation of this type is soon enacted the few who might be injured by the amendment may find themselves bereft of the business they are now engaged in as the Congress will find it essential and necessary to take over all radio facilities and operate them for the common good. . . .

MR. COPELAND. . . . I cannot see why the amendment offered by my colleague the junior Senator from New York [Mr. Wagner] and the Senator from West Virginia [Mr. Hatfield] may not be appropriate for adoption by the Senate. I think it would be wise for us to adopt it. If there had been greater readiness on the part of the Radio Commission to deal with the problem it would not have reached us.

The Radio Commission have done a fine job. They have done a splendid work. My sympathies are with them. But there are certain activities which somehow or other have not been taken care of by that body, and this is one of them. If there is no other or better way to deal with it than by the adoption of the amendment, I think the matter should be given this consideration. This appears necessary in order that there may be such use of the radio as to impress upon the American public those ideas in education and religion which are so important to the building of character and to the development of good behavior. . . .

MR. DILL. I wish to call the Senator's attention to the fact that from the organization of the Radio Commission down to January 1, 1932, only 81 applications were presented to the Commission for educational stations. Of this number 32 were granted in full, 27 in part, 10 were denied, and 10 dismissed at the request of the applicants. Thus there were only 71 who would have taken a license if they could have gotten it. Has the Senator stopped to consider the fact that it is financially impossible for these institutions actually to build and operate these stations without becoming commercial and advertising stations?

MR. COPELAND. Yes; I may say I realize that to be a fact. To operate a radio station costs a lot of money. But if we find a religious or educational body willing to take the chance of disposing of certain commercial time in order that the main objective may be reached, which is the dissemination of religion or education, I think certainly we should give consideration to their willingness to do so.

MR. DILL. Does not the Senator think a much more practical result might be obtained by working out some system of requiring stations to permit a certain part of their time to be used for these purposes and requiring that in the licenses of existing stations?

MR. COPELAND. No; I do not think so.

MR. DILL. That is the only way the religious and educational broadcasts can ever be gotten out to the people generally, because they are the only stations which can get those broadcasts out in that way.

MR. COPELAND. There is no question that the existing stations have done a great work along the line suggested by the Senator from Washington. For example, in disseminating the sermons which are broadcast every Sunday, there is no doubt that very great good has been done and much happiness brought to the American people. But there are institutions which have definite programs of character building and definite programs in educational development or progress where it is not possible for the casual use of a station now and again to accomplish what the originators of the various programs have in mind. Therefore I believe that where there are educational and religious bodies willing to assume the responsibility of carrying on the work we might well give consideration to permitting them to have the radio channels in order that they may do the work in question. . . .

MR. DILL. Mr. President, I shall not detain the Senate at any great length, but in light of the statements which have been made by the proponents of the amendment I feel that I should make some explanation of the reason why this amendment was rejected.

The amendment was presented by Father Harney, of the Paulist Fathers, representing station WLWL in New York. Full hearings were had, and the committee considered it carefully and rejected the amendment by an overwhelming vote, but adopted instead a provision in the bill requiring the Commission to make a study of the question of educational broadcasting, and to submit recommendations to Congress.

It might be concluded from the arguments made here by those who propose this amendment that the committee and I are not anxious for educational and religious broadcasts. I think the record of my activities in radio will show that I have always been one of the most insistent among those who wanted to see a larger use of radio for educational, religious, and fraternal purposes and for nonprofit purposes generally. I am extremely anxious now that some plan may be worked out for a larger use of radio for educational and religious purposes; but the amendment presented by the Senators from New York and West Virginia does not suggest the proper method, in my judgment, to bring about such a result.

In the first place, the amendment proposes to wipe out all existing allocations. It did propose to allow 3 months, which now has been changed, I understand, to 6 months, because it would be impossible under the law to wipe out the licenses before they had expired except for violation of the law.

In the second place, it compels a reallocation by the new commission of all the stations in the United States within a period, as the amendment has been changed, of 6 months. I think that is impracticable. I do not believe the new commission will be able to reallocate all the stations in that short period of time.

The third and strongest objection which I have is that these stations are not to be what we understand as educational and religious stations merely, but they are to be stations that are to sell time on the air to advertisers who will make use of the stations for advertising purposes. Thus we are simply changing the ownership of these stations from the present commercial owners to owners who call themselves nonprofit organizations.

The records show that a large percentage of stations are not making any money as it is. It is safe to say that even if these nonprofit organizations could borrow money—and I do not know where they could borrow it, but if they could borrow money with which to build these stations and maintain them, it would require the sale of between 60 and 75 percent of their valuable time to maintain the stations and pay back the money which it would cost to build the new stations.

I remind the Senate that it costs a large sum of money to build a high-power radio station and to employ the engineers that may be necessary, and so to handle the station that its broadcasts may be heard throughout the country. . . .

MR. LOGAN. The Senator says it requires a large sum of money to build and operate a radio station. For my own satisfaction, I should like to know approximately what one of these large radio stations costs?

MR. DILL. Anywhere from one hundred to two hundred thousand dollars.

MR. LOGAN. So an educational or religious or nonprofit association would have to provide some such sum as that in order to establish a station?

MR. DILL. They would have to, if they established a high-powered station. I am told that it costs practically as much each year to operate and maintain a station as it does to build it in the first place.

This is not a new subject. I myself, with the Senator from Michigan, in 1931, induced the Senate to pass a resolution to investigate the question, particularly of educational stations. A series of questions was propounded to the Radio Commission. I have here the answers to some of those questions, and I particularly call attention to the reply to the question—

What applications by public educational institutions for increased power and more effective frequencies have been granted since the Commission's organization? What refused?

Answer. In the period—

Since the organization of the Commission—

from February 23, 1927, to January 1, 1932, the Commission considered 81 applications from
educational institutions for additional and more effective radio facilities, 52 of which were from
public educational institutions and 29 from private educational institutions.
    . . . Thirty-two of these applications were granted in full; 27 were granted in part; 10 were
denied; . . . 10 were dismissed at the request of the applicant.

So, out of 71, all but 10 were granted either in full or in part.

There are today some 63 stations operated in the United States by educational,
agricultural, religious, or nonprofit organizations, but none of them exceeds 5,000
watts. There is one 5,000-watt station, and I think there are one or two 1,500-watt
stations and one or two 1,000-watt stations, but the large percentage of them are small
stations. They are used only for a few hours a day and some of them for only a few
hours a week.

It is the conviction on the part of those who have made a study of this subject that
this question must be solved in some other way. I am not prepared to say what is the
best method. I may say, however, that the owners of large radio stations now
operating have suggested to me that it might be well to provide in the license grant
that a certain percentage of the time of a radio station shall be allotted to religious,
educational, or nonprofit users by their paying the actual cost of operation for the
hours which they actually use such station. . . .

MR. WAGNER. I should like to ask the Senator whether the Commission, in
granting licenses to any of the larger purely commercial stations, ever made it a
condition for granting the license that any part of the time be used for religious,
cultural, or educational purposes?

MR. DILL. I think not; and I suggest that that is one of the possibilities that might
be worked out.

MR. WAGNER. They have had a long time in which to think about it.

MR. DILL. I am not defending the Radio Commission; Heaven knows, I do not
hold any brief for the present Radio Commission; I am glad it is going to be abolished
and that new policies will be established by the Radio Commission. . . .

MR. BONE. As I read the proposed amendment, it would require the Radio
Commission arbitrarily to destroy, or what would amount to destroying, 25 percent of
the radio facilities now existing in any community where anyone else sought to take
advantage of the facilities. They simply would be permitted to use the wave length or
the power in watts of existing stations. Is that correct?

MR. DILL. At the end of the license period they would have a right to allocate to
new stations, but they have that right under existing law.

MR. BONE. I understand; but it is a right which, I assume, has not been exercised.

MR. DILL. Yes; it has been exercised.

MR. BONE. I am trying to get some light on the matter. Suppose in the State of
Washington the Radio Commission should decree that out of 100,000 watts of power
now employed by radio stations there should be a reduction to 75,000 watts. That

would mean, if I understand the amendment aright, that stations now operating with 25,000 watts of power would be summarily cut off and, of course, that value would be destroyed.

MR. DILL. The commission would decide whether it would reduce all stations or certain stations, or would delete and take out of operation certain stations. There is no limit as to the method. Under the law, of course, the public interests would have to be considered in that connection.

Mr. President, I do not want to take the time of the Senate any further. I hope the amendment will be defeated. I believe it would be an extremely bad policy for Congress to begin the allocation of wave lengths. I believe we will do more for educational and religious progress by having the new commission study the matter and let it come back to Congress with some practical plan that will make use of existing facilities, rather than attempt to grant an arbitrary 25 percent and then allow those stations to be turned into commercial stations.

MR. WAGNER. Mr. President, I should like to perfect my amendment in this manner: On page 2, line 5, strike out the words "90 days" and substitute therefor "6 months," and in line 8, strike out "90 days" and insert in lieu thereof "6 months."

THE PRESIDING OFFICER. The Senator has the right to modify his amendment.

MR. WHITE. Mr. President, the pendency of the amendment and the discussion to which we have listened confirm me in the view I have always had as to the unwisdom of offering this legislation in its entirety at this time. I have felt strongly that the wise thing for us to have done would have been to follow the recommendation of the President, as I understood it to be, to enact legislation creating a new commission, to transfer to that commission the present authorities of law, and to enjoin upon the commission the obligation to study the problem of communications during the summer and fall, and to report to the Congress of the United States, when we convene in January next, its recommendations as to comprehensive communications legislation.

I believed when the legislation was first suggested, and I believe now that that is the sound course for Congress to pursue. A majority of the committee were decidedly of the contrary opinion, and I bowed to the judgment of the majority.

One of the particular things to which it seems to me the commission might have given its attention during the summer is the study of the precise problem presented by the pending amendment. The amendment in its substance basically is not new, for even back in 1927, when the present radio law was written, there was pending before the committees of Congress and before the Congress itself and before the conferees the question of giving legislative preference or legislative priority to some particular user of radio communication.

I recall very well when the bill passed the Senate in 1927 there was embodied in it a provision that land-grant colleges should have a preference or priority in the use of frequencies. That provision was dropped in conference. It was dropped because depending upon that provision was a string of applications for special recognition in the law. At that time, when it was being urged that special recognition should be given to land-grant colleges, there were religious organizations or institutions asking that they be given the same legislative preference which was proposed to be given to the land-grant colleges. There were all sorts of groups and organizations throughout the United States asking that if we gave statutory preference to land-grant colleges, we should accord similar recognition to them.

At that time it was the judgment of the Congress that we had to adopt one of two courses. We either had to strike from the legislation special consideration for land-grant colleges and grant to the regulatory body full power and authority with respect to the granting of licenses, or the Congress faced the obligation of making a complete allocation to services.

I object to the pending amendment for the considerations suggested by the Senator from Washington [Mr. Dill] . I object also more strongly because it seems to me it flies in the face of a sound principle. We must, as I said, do one of two things. We must here in the Congress make a complete allocation of the radio spectrum to services, or we must leave it entirely alone. I have long been a believer, and I believe now, that commercial activities occupy too much of the time and use too many of the radio facilities of the country.

I recall very definitely I urged, in legislation which I introduced in the House a number of years ago, that we should give to the regulatory body the power, and we should lay upon them the express duty of establishing priorities in the character of service. That is precisely what the pending proposal is, but it only takes one step in that direction. It proposes that we shall take only 25 percent of the radio facilities, and that we shall give them to a somewhat indefinite group, religious, educational, non-profit-making organizations. They are indefinite almost in number. How many of them there are I do not know. As a practical result, we have all of these non-profit-making organizations contending among themselves not for a place in the entire radio spectrum but for a part of only 25 percent of the radio spectrum. If that shall be granted the controversy will be intensified, and the situation will not be cured at all.

Manifestly, we should either go ahead as a Congress and divide up the entire spectrum among persons and organizations for uses here in the United States or we should leave it alone in its entirety and place the responsibility of allocation where it already is—upon the Federal Radio Commission.

It seems to me that if this amendment should be adopted it would go through the entire radio structure of the United States like a tornado, leaving destruction and chaos in its wake.

I join with the Senator from Washington [Mr. Dill] in expressing the earnest hope that the amendment may not have the approval of this body.

THE PRESIDING OFFICER. The question is on the amendment offered by the Senator from New York [Mr. Wagner] and the Senator from West Virginia [Mr. Hatfield] .

MR. WAGNER. I ask for the yeas and nays on the amendment.

The yeas and nays were ordered. . . .

The result was announced—yeas 23, nays 42. . . .

So the amendment of Mr. Wagner and Mr. Hatfield was rejected.

MR. CLARK. Mr. President, I offer an amendment, which I send to the desk.

THE PRESIDING OFFICER. The clerk will state the amendment.

THE LEGISLATIVE CLERK. It is proposed, on page 2, to strike out lines 20 to 25, inclusive, and to insert in lieu thereof the following:

(b) Nothing in this act shall be construed to apply or to give the commission jurisdiction with respect to charges, classifications, practices, or regulations for or in connection with intrastate communication service of any carrier, or to any carrier engaged in interstate or foreign communication solely through physical connection with the facilities of another carrier not directly or indirectly controlling or controlled by such carrier, or under direct or indirect control with such other carrier.

MR. CLARK. Mr. President, the only purpose of this amendment is to clarify the language contained in the original bill with regard to small independent telephone companies. These independent telephone companies are located in small communities. They are entirely local affairs. I know there are nearly 700 in Missouri, and in a great many instances they are family enterprises; that is, a man will own the local independent telphone company, have the central office located in his own home, and the plant will be operated by the man and his family.

There are 700 independent telephone companies in Missouri. I think that without exception they are located in towns of less than 1,500 inhabitants. Nevertheless, under the terms of the bill, they probably would be subjected to the jurisdiction of the Interstate Commerce Commission, because nearly invariably they have a physical connection with a toll line, for long-distance calls, which would make them engage in interstate commerce.

Every one of these independent telephone lines throughout the United States is already subjected to local regulation by the State public-service commission, and to subject them to further regulation, with a duplication of a system of accounting, would simply mean an intolerable burden on these little companies, who have had a hard time existing anyway.

MR. DILL. Mr. President, I am familiar with the Senator's proposed amendment. I do not believe the amendment is necessary, but I do not think it would do any harm, because its purpose is to accomplish that which we have tried to do throughout the bill; that is, to protect the independent companies. I have no objection to the amendment.

THE PRESIDING OFFICER. The question is on agreeing to the amendment.

The amendment was agreed to.

MR. WHEELER. Mr. President, on page 56, section 311, I notice this language is used:

SEC. 311. The commission is hereby directed to refuse a station license and/or the permit hereinafter required for the construction of a station to any person (or to any person directly or indirectly controlled by such person) whose license has been revoked by a court under section 313, and is hereby authorized to refuse such station license and/or permit to any other person (or to any person directly or indirectly controlled by such person) which has been finally adjudged guilty by a Federal court of unlawfully monopolizing, or attempting unlawfully to monopolize, after this act takes effect.

I move to strike out the words "after this act takes effect." Otherwise it would bring it down, in my judgment, to the present date, and if they have been monopolizing up to the present time, the commission would not be able to act.

MR. DILL. Mr. President, this wording, "after this act takes effect," was copied from existing law, and I think there may be some merit in the Senator's contention. At first I did not think there was, but on further consideration I believe there may be. I do not see that it would do any good to keep the language in, and I have no objection to it being stricken out, because there might be some question, it seems to me, of relieving somebody violating the law at this time. . . .

MR. WHITE. I was in the far reaches of the Chamber and I could not hear the amendment as the Senator stated it.

MR. WHEELER. I am moving to strike out, on line 24, page 56, section 311, the words "after this act takes effect."

MR. WHITE. Will not the Senator explain just what the effect of the amendment would be?

MR. WHEELER. Assuming that someone has been violating the provisions set forth up to the present time, the commission may want to go ahead and act, and it seems to me that they could not act if that language remained in the measure. The purpose of this section is simply to reenact the present law.

MR. DILL. In other words, as I understand, the Senator's contention is that this might exempt those who had been convicted between 1927 and this time. I cannot see that it would do any harm, and I have no objection to the amendment.

THE PRESIDING OFFICER. The question is on agreeing to the amendment.

The amendment was agreed to.

MR. WALSH. Mr. President, I request the Senator to turn to page 9, line 1, where the bill reads, "Without regard to the civil-service laws or the Classification Act of 1923, as amended, (1) the commission may appoint," and so forth; and again on page 14, where it reads, "Each division may (1) appoint a director, without regard to the civil-service laws or the Classification Act of 1923."

I should like to ask the Senator the reason for exempting the operations of the Classification Act in the payment of salaries of these officials, other than the commissioners.

MR. DILL. Mr. President, it is because practically all of the commissions now do that.

MR. WALSH. It is true that all of the emergency commissions which were created do that, but the fact is that the Federal Trade Commission and the Interstate Commerce Commission and other permanent departments comply with the provisions of the Classification Act. I, for one, protest against these new permanent commissions being allowed to fix salaries outside of the stipulations of the Classification Act, and exempt themselves from the general policy fixed.

MR. DILL. We have fixed a maximum above which they may not go.

MR. WALSH. That does not meet the situation. The same question is before the Committee on Education and Labor, of which I am chairman, in connection with the Wagner labor bill. A very similar provision was drafted, leaving employees out of the Classification Act and the civil service. It is one thing leaving them out of the civil service, where experts are needed, but it is an entirely different thing to put lawyers and other various employees outside of the Classification Act. It means that they may get any salary the commission may see fit to fix. Let us have a uniform policy. Let us have all these positions under the Classification Act.

MR. DILL. The Radio Commission has been operating under this kind of a provision, and I think they have found it reasonably satisfactory.

MR. WALSH. It is time to stop it if they have been operating under it. One of the criticisms we hear generally as to the N.R.A. and some of the temporary commissions is that the salaries are out of all proportion to salaries in other fixed bureaus.

MR. DILL. That would not apply in this case.

MR. WALSH. Lawyers and experts doing exactly the same work which is being performed by lawyers and other employees in the permanent commissions are underpaid in comparison with the salaries being paid by the new commissions.

MR. DILL. I remind the Senator that there is a limit fixed for salaries to be paid by this commission; they cannot go above a certain amount.

MR. WALSH. Why should they be taken from under the Classification Act, anyway?

MR. DILL. Because I think there ought to be a specific amount in the case of the chief counsel of a great commission like this. I think he ought to have a substantial salary.

MR. WALSH. That may be so of the chief counsel; but how about these other lawyers?

MR. DILL. I think the same should apply to the chief engineer. It applies only to the chief counsel and the chief engineer. The special counsel are not included.

MR. WALSH. It provides for one or more assistants, experts, and special counsel. It means that the assistant counsel may receive $7,500 per annum. I think that is an excessive salary for attorneys today, in view of conditions in this country.

I am not one who favors low salaries. I have the same question coming up in connection with a bill that will be before us in a few weeks, and if such a policy is to be adopted in regard to the commission to be created under this bill, I want it to apply to the one to be created in the bill to come up later. I am against designating salaries in these bills, because I think these employees and officials should be under the Classification Act. I cannot see any reason for exempting in this case.

MR. DILL. I think one of the worst things about the civil service today in regard to these commissions is the fact that a commissioner cannot choose his own confidential clerk, that he must take someone who is on the civil-service list. If I were the member of a commission I would want my own confidential clerk, and I think the Senator from Massachusetts would want his, and I have purposely inserted in this bill a provision that each Commissioner might have one clerk. I think that is a provision that is highly desirable. I think every man has a right to have one clerk in an organization of this kind. . . .

MR. COUZENS. Let me ask the Senator whether this would be satisfactory to him. I intend to offer an amendment on page 9, beginning with line 4, to cut out the words "and one or more assistant chief engineers and one or more assistants, experts, and special counsel." That would leave free the secretary, the general counsel and the chief engineer.

MR. DILL. I would have no objection to that amendment.

MR. WALSH. As I understand the Senator's amendment it would strike out of this bill the provision "Without regard to the Classification Act of 1923."

MR. COUZENS. Only as applied to the chief engineer and secretary and the general counsel. All the rest would be under civil service.

MR. WALSH. If that is the purpose which the Senator from Michigan has in mind, I would agree to it.

MR. COUZENS. I move, Mr. President, that that amendment be agreed to.

MR. DILL. I have no objection to it.

MR. WALSH. Let us see if we understand it. I understand that with the exception of the few positions named in the amendment, every other employee of this commission shall be subjected to the Classification Act. Am I correct?

MR. DILL. That still leaves this one clerk, about whom I have made explanation, and I appeal to the Senator not to strike him.

MR. WALSH. Who?

MR. DILL. I provided that each commissioner should have one clerk.

MR. COUZENS. On what page?

MR. DILL. Page 9, lines 6 to 8.

MR. WALSH. At a salary of $7,500 per annum?

MR. KING. No, Mr. President; a salary of $4,000 per annum.

MR. DILL. That "each commissioner may appoint and prescribe the duties of an assistant at an annual salary not to exceed $4,000 per annum."

MR. KING. I think that ought to go out.

MR. DILL. I think the Senator from Utah, if he were a commissioner, would desire to have his own clerk.

MR. WALSH. It is quite easy to get one's own clerk from the civil-service list. All that is necessary is to write to the Civil Service Commission asking for a clerk of the type that one designates, who would answer the qualifications, and one can be assigned.

Mr. President, I object to this promiscuous fixing of salaries outside the Classification Act. I gather that the Senator from Michigan is in accord with my views. In connection with these new commissions we are running wild in the matter of salaries, and it is not fair to the old, steady employees in commissions like the Federal Trade Commission, the Post Office Department, or the Interstate Commerce Commission, or other departments. If lawyers and experts are entitled to these substantial salaries in the new commission, those in the old departments and commissions are entitled to the same salaries, and we will have a move here to boost their salaries to a level with the new high salaries. . . .

MR. O'MAHONEY. It has been my experience that the remarks of the Senator from Massachusetts are fully borne out by conditions in the various departments. Even the assistants in the Post Office Department and the Assistant Secretaries in the Department of Commerce and the Department of Labor are governed by the Classification Act. I know of no reason why, for example, an Assistant Secretary of the Treasury or an Assistant Secretary of Labor should be under the Classification Act while an assistant in any new commission should be exempt from it. It would mean, just as the Senator from Massachusetts has said, that these commissions could fix the salaries as they pleased for their particular assistants, with no more responsibility, nor no greater amount of work to be performed than those in the old departments and commissions. I believe the objection is very well founded.

MR. DILL. The salary can be limited.

MR. WALSH. I am pleased the Senator from Wyoming agrees with me.

MR. O'MAHONEY. I am in perfect accord in limiting the salary.

MR. WALSH. May I ask the Senator if the Assistant Secretary of Labor and the assistant secretaries of the major departments are under the Classification Act?

MR. O'MAHONEY. Yes, certainly.

MR. WALSH. Then if the assistant secretary to a Cabinet officer is under the Classification Act, why put experts and attorneys and lawyers and other people outside the Classification Act? . . .

MR. BARKLEY. I think it must be inaccurate to say that all the Assistant Secretaries of Labor and so forth are under the Classification Act.

MR. O'MAHONEY. That is another matter.

MR. BARKLEY. I recall at least one Assistant Secretary of Labor whom I happen to have known for many years, whose name was sent here and who was confirmed by the Senate. I do not know of any Assistant Secretary of Commerce or State or Labor who is in the classified service.

MR. O'MAHONEY. Mr. President, I think the Senator is laboring under a misapprehension. This had no reference whatever to the classified service. This refers only to the Classification Act, which as I understand, fixes the salaries. This is not a question of exempting persons from the civil service.

MR. WALSH. It is not exempting them from high salaries. It is putting their salaries above the salaries of those doing comparable work in other departments.

MR. BARKLEY. I am entirely in sympathy with that, but I understand we are talking here about a provision which allows each one of these new commissioners to appoint a private secretary at a salary not to exceed $4,000 a year. I think the real test in a matter of this sort is whether we would be willing to go to the civil-service list and pick our private secretary from that list. I am frank to say that I would not.

MR. WALSH. I am not requiring that this be under the civil service, but I am asking that the classified salary be the salary which is received by those performing the same class of work in other departments, whether it be $3,500 or $4,000. I am not asking that the commissioner go to the civil service, but I am asking that the salary be under the classified act, in order that the secretaries to these commissioners will be paid the same salary as paid to the secretary to the Postmaster General and the Secretary of Labor.

MR. O'MAHONEY. I might call the attention of the Senator from Kentucky to the language of this section, page 9, line 1:

Without regard to the civil-service laws, or the Classification Act of 1923, as amended.

Those are two different laws. The Senator from Massachusetts is objecting to eliminating the provisions of the Classification Act from this special commission, and I think he is correct.

MR. WALSH. It is an attempt to deceive us for those who are drafting these new acts to come here and sneak in exemptions of this type. I would not have discovered it except for the Secretary of Labor's Department calling our attention to what that classification elimination would mean. We did not realize that by using that exception to the Classification Act they were leaving employees in this new commission out of the regular classified act, and I want to protest and ask the Senators, when these proposals are brought before us, to watch for such things as I have indicated.

MR. BARKLEY. To what extent does the Classification Act conflict with the provision here limiting the salary of secretaries of two commissioners to $4,000?

MR. WALSH. The Classification Act, I understand, fixes the salary of every Government employee, except those salaries which are fixed by law, and it is fixed on the basis of duties performed in the various departments, so that there shall be relationship in the salary of an employee of one department to the salary received by an employee in another department performing the same duty.

MR. BARKLEY. So, if the same language is retained in the bill, then the commissioner could pick his own private secretary, and could fix the salary the same as the salary of an employee engaged in similar work in any other department.

MR. WALSH. The point I am making is, why should the status of the secretary of a member of this new commission be different from that of the secretary to the Postmaster General, for example, so far as his relationship to the Classification Act is concerned?

MR. BARKLEY. I am making no contention about that, but I am asking whether the retention of this language in the bill, while giving the commissioner a right to appoint his own secretary, would mean that the secretary would get the same salary as other employees engaged in the same line of duty would get? . . .

MR. LOGAN. It is not often that I disagree so emphatically with the Senator from Massachusetts, but I draw his attention to the fact that, in view of the difference in the situation between the civil-service employee under the classification service and the secretary who is brought in from the outside, who is not on the Civil Service, there ought to be recognition by a difference in salary. The civil-service employee, subject to the Classification Act, has a lifetime job, or cannot be removed except upon charges. He is safe in the position which he has. When an official goes out to employ someone as his secretary, who is not under Civil Service, that employee gives up his work back home and comes to Washington. He has no fixed tenure of office. He can be told to take his hat and coat and leave at any time. When the official goes out, he goes out. And if we undertake to classify him as a civil-service employee and require him to accept the same salary, we are not treating him fairly.

MR. WALSH. I agree with what the Senator says, but I understand that the Classification Act fixes the salary of other than civil-service employees.

MR. LOGAN. That is very true.

MR. WALSH. I think it fixes the salary of the secretary, for example, to the Secretary of Labor, the secretary to the Secretary of Commerce, and the secretary to the Postmaster General. Such secretary is subject to all the conditions we fix, and his salary is fixed by the Classification Act. Why should the secretaries to these new commissioners have a different status as far as their relationship to the Classification Act is concerned? . . .

MR. O'MAHONEY. Perhaps I may add a word of explanation. The system which is now in vogue permits most of the heads of departments, and most of the assistants, and, I believe, most of the commissioners, to appoint their own personal secretaries free from the civil-service laws, and the salaries paid to those secretaries, occupying what are known as exempt positions, are somewhat greater than the salaries paid similar persons in the civil service, under the circumstances which the Senator has referred to.

MR. WALSH. Are they fixed under the Classification Act?

MR. O'MAHONEY. They are.

MR. WALSH. Why should these secretaries be treated any differently than the other secretaries of whom the Senator spoke?

MR. O'MAHONEY. It is one thing to exempt certain positions from the Civil Service Act. That may and should properly be done in many cases. But to exempt them also from the Classification Act would result in great discrimination between the departments.

MR. WALSH. Even the important officials and experts in the Interstate Commerce Commission, one of the most important independent organizations in the Federal Government, are subject to the Classification Act, every one of them. And yet here we are proposing to exempt certain employees in this new department.

I call attention to what is proposed on page 14.

Each division may (1) appoint a director, without regard to the Civil Service laws or the Classification Act of 1923, as amended, at an annual salary that shall not exceed $7,500 per annum.

Why should not that director be subject to the classification act the same as a director in the Interstate Commerce Commission?

MR. DILL. For the reason that this is the creation of a new kind of position. We do not know exactly what he is going to do, and we have made the limit of salary $7,500.

I think the Senator from Massachusetts is unduly exercised about these limitations of salary for the reason . . . that we are providing for the creation of a new kind of position and we do not know exactly what the officer is going to have to do, but we have provided a limit of $7,500. I think the Senator is unduly exercised about these limitations of salaries. They are not fixed; they are limitations.

MR. WALSH. I am exercised simply because a bill handed to my committee contains exactly the same provisions in the same language, and that all these bills are now being drafted with the idea of lifting these employees out of the civil service in some cases and in all cases out of the Classification Act. There may be some justification for it in the N.R.A. and the Public Works Administration, but in the case of a permanent board such as the one now proposed or the labor board such as is proposed in the bill pending before my committee, I propose that the salaries shall be uniform, that they shall be subject to the terms of the general Classification Act, and that the same salaries shall be paid for the same kind of work performed as are paid in other departments, no more and no less. If that is not a fair proposition, then, I do not know what is fair. . . .

MR. WHEELER. It seems to me also that the language that is used on page 9 places no limitation on the amount the commission might pay its secretary, for it is there provided:

(f) Without regard to the civil-service laws or the Classification Act of 1923, as amended, (1) the commission may appoint and prescribe the duties and fix the salaries of a secretary, a chief engineer and one or more assistant chief engineers, a general counsel and one or more assistants, experts, and special counsel.

MR. WALSH. What do the words "and one or more assistants" mean? They may mean a hundred, to be appointed without regard to the Classification Act.

MR. WHEELER. In addition to that, there is no limitation on the salary of the secretary. The commission may fix the salary of the secretary at $10,000 or $5,000, or any other sum that it sees fit, without any limitation of any kind or character.

MR. WALSH. I suggest to the Senator from Washington, who, I know, is desirous of conforming to the usual practice, and who, undoubtedly, has not had this matter called to his attention, because it was called to the attention of my committee only by mere chance, that this is an attempt to lift a large number of employees out of the salary groups of the Classification Act. The salaries under the Classification Act run up to eight or nine thousand dollars in some cases. I will ask the Senator from Wyoming [Mr. O'Mahoney] if that is not a correct statement?

MR. LOGAN. Mr. President, some salaries may reach that figure in the course of time, but what salaries are paid when the employees enter the service? If the Senator were to be appointed a member of this commission, which, of course, he will not be, because he is not eligible under the Constitution, and he wanted to take his secretary with him and his secretary had to come under the Classification Act, what would he get on going into the service in the beginning? He would probably get $1,600 a year, with a reduction on account of the Economy Act.

MR. WALSH. The Senator is mistaken. He would get the same salary that is paid to the secretary of the Secretary of Labor; he would get the same salary as paid to the secretary to the Attorney General.

MR. LOGAN. Unless he had been in the service for a number of years he could not get the same salary. I had this experience with the Classification Act in Kentucky, as my colleague will bear me witness: Deputy collectors had been receiving $2,200, $2,400, $2,600 up to $3,000, because they had been in the service a good while under a previous administration. New ones were appointed recently; every one of them, under the ruling of the Department, had to go in at $1,800, less 15-percent reduction under the Economy Act; and that is what the Senator's secretary would receive if the

Senator were appointed a member of the commission and he selected his present secretary to be his secretary in the new office. Unless he were placed in grade 8 or grade 9, or something of that kind, he would go in at grade 4, and would not be able to get the salary which should be paid. I do not know much about the civil-service laws now, and do not expect to know much about them, but that is my idea of what would happen.

MR. WALSH. I am sure the Senator from Kentucky does not want this bill to provide for salaries for employees of this commission that are different from the salaries paid by other commissions. The only difference between the Senator and me is that he is willing to have all the subordinate employees, all the clerks and stenographers and filing clerks, and all the lesser employees come under the Classification Act, but he is not willing to let the attorneys, the experts, the directors, and those who are under the Classification Act in other bureaus of the Government come in under the Classification Act under the new commissions. That is the only difference between us.

MR. LOGAN. I should have no objection to their going under the Classification Act if there were not a rule in the classification law which requires that a new employee shall be appointed in a certain grade and which provides a salary that will not enable the commission to get the best men to do the work. I think it would be a mistake to make the salaries so low that the commission would have to take incompetent persons. . . .

MR. O'MAHONEY. I may say to the Senator from Kentucky that that is not the way the law operates. To cite my own case, on the 6th of March 1933 I became First Assistant Postmaster General and I appointed my own secretary. She assumed her office at the same salary as that which was paid to the secretary of my predecessor, except that she suffered the reduction that was required of all employees under the Economy Act, which, of course, has nothing whatever to do with the question now being considered.

MR. LOGAN. I will say to the Senator that perhaps many of us have not been so fortunate as he has been. I have not been able to secure anything of that kind. I do know that in Kentucky when new employees are appointed they have to go in at a certain grade, and they do not get very much salary. That may be just a discrimination against my State.

MR. DILL. Mr. President, I want to say to the Senator from Massachusetts that this provision is not drawn by accident; it is not here without consideration. The only point raised in this connection here today which I overlooked is that the bill fails to limit the salary of the secretary. I think that ought to be limited, and I am also entirely willing to strike out the provision relating to the assistants; but I submit that when a commission of this kind is being created the majority party, having 3 of the 5 members, should have the right, without regard to the civil-service law, to change its chief counsel.

MR. WALSH. I am not objecting to that.

MR. DILL. Or to change its chief engineer.

MR. WALSH. I am not objecting to that, either.

MR. DILL. And to appoint their individual assistants and have them paid a proper salary. If $4,000 is too much, make it $3,600. I do not see anything to be gained by taking advantage of civil-service methods by which one clerk is dismissed and another clerk is appointed who, it is thought, may be a little better. I think that is just a matter of juggling. We ought to be frank about this matter and say that the members of the commission should appoint their own clerks; I think they are entitled to do so; I think we will thereby get better results from the commission.

MR. WALSH. Does the Senator suggest that the only office created in this bill that leaves the salary unsettled is that of the secretary of the commission?

MR. DILL. I say the one which I had overlooked was the salary of the secretary.

MR. WALSH. I call attention to what the Senator from Montana stated, quoting from page 9 of the bill, which provides that—

The commission may appoint and prescribe the duties and fix the salaries of a secretary, a chief engineer, and one or more assistant chief engineers, a general counsel, and one or more assistants, experts, and special counsel.

MR. DILL. And the general counsel and the chief engineer are limited with regard to salaries to $9,000; their assistants and experts to $7,500.

MR. WALSH. Yes; but why limit them to that? I want to have them all come under the Classification Act as to employees doing comparable work in other departments.

MR. DILL. For the simple reason that I do not believe it possible always to get the kind of men required under the salaries provided by the Classification Act.

MR. WALSH. Then let us agree that in the case of all future bills we will put the same language in and leave to the commissioners all questions of salary, and take that power away from Congress which has fixed the policy in adopting the Classification Act.

MR. DILL. The Senator from Michigan has suggested an amendment which I think meets reasonably the objections of the Senator from Massachusetts, and which I think will not seriously interfere with the purpose of the commission.

MR. WALSH. Mr. President, I should like to have the amendment of the Senator from Michigan stated.

MR. COUZENS. Mr. President, I have not written it out, but I should like, with the consent of the chairman of the committee, to amend what I think ought to be amended in paragraph (f). What I suggested, I think, does not go far enough, and I have since talked to the assistant to the chairman of the committee, pointing out to him the part that I thought ought to be amended; and, without having written it out, if he will follow me, I will read what I offer as an amendment. It will read thus:

(f) With regard to the civil-service laws or the Classification Act of 1923, as amended, (1) the commission may appoint and prescribe the duties and fix the salaries of a secretary, a chief engineer, and a general counsel, and (2) each commissioner may appoint and prescribe the duties of an assistant and pay him in accordance with the Classification Act of 1923, as amended.

Then on line 9:

The general counsel, the secretary, and the chief engineer shall receive an annual salary of not exceeding $7,500.

Then I eliminate the following language:

And no assistant or expert shall receive an annual salary in excess of $7,500.

That is eliminated because those officers will come under the Classification Act of 1923, as amended.

MR. DILL. Does the Senator think that $7,500 is a sufficient salary for the chief counsel of a great commission such as this?

MR. COUZENS. I put that provision in largely at the suggestion of the Senator from Utah, but I did not intend to amend that; and if there is any objection to that particular suggestion, I will leave it at $9,000. Then, we may discuss that later. But I should like to have the other provisions of my amendment agreed to.

MR. DILL. It seems to me that $7,500 is a pretty low salary for a general counsel.

MR. WALSH. Is not that the salary of the Assistant Attorneys General? Is not that the salary the chief counsels get for every bureau and department of the Government?

MR. DILL. A good many of them get $10,000.

MR. COUZENS. I think that is true. I will withdraw that provision; and then, if the Senate wants to amend my amendment, and adopt it, we can discuss the other matter separately.

MR. WALSH. The amendment of the Senator from Michigan is infinitely better than the bill as drafted. Yet he adheres to the belief that certain officers should be taken out of the Classification Act. If the Classification Act did not allow substantial salaries, I would agree with what he says, but under that act salaries may be paid up to eight or nine thousand dollars. It does not provide merely for salaries of $2,000, $3,000, $4,000, or $5,000, but provides for the very salaries that are proposed to be paid by this bill. Why make a distinction? Why let the bars down in this case? If we do it in this case, why not do it in other cases and let the various departments and bureaus fix the salaries of those they employ?

MR. O'MAHONEY. Mr. President, I might add that the President within a few months past delegated to the Director of the Budget the duty of examining all the new bureaus and attempting to classify all the salaries there in accordance with the Classification Act for the purpose of maintaining a uniform system throughout the Government service.

MR. WALSH. Yes; and we are proposing, by passing this bill, to undo what the President is trying to do, namely, to create a uniform system. Why not, I will ask the Senator from Michigan, merely strike out the exempting words "the Classification Act of 1923, as amended"? . . .

MR. WHITE. I offer another amendment, on page 58, at the end of line 8, to insert the following—and probably I had better read the amendment, because it is in my own handwriting:

(b) Any station license hereafter granted under the provisions of this act, or the construction permit required hereby and hereafter issued, may be modified by the commission either for a limited time or for the duration of the term thereof, if in the judgment of the commission such action will promote the public interest, convenience, and necessity, or the provisions of this act or of any treaty ratified by the United States will be more fully complied with: *Provided, however,* That no such order of modification shall become final until the holder of such outstanding license or permit shall have been notified in writing of the proposed action and the grounds or reasons therefor, and shall have been given reasonable opportunity to show cause why such an order of modification should not issue.

I may say to the Senator from Washington that the only purpose of the amendment is to put affirmatively into the bill the express authority for modification. We have referred in various places to modification of licenses, but I fail to find any definite and express and affirmative authority to make a modification. I suggest that if this amendment be adopted and is found not to be in proper form, it may be worked out in conference.

MR. DILL. Mr. President, I may say that the Senator from Maine previously called my attention to the amendment. It simply is a method of harmonizing differences that may arise and, as I understand, it provides for hearing before action. I have no objection.

THE PRESIDING OFFICER. The question is on agreeing to the amendment offered by the Senator from Maine.

The amendment was agreed to.

MR. DILL. Mr. President, the Senator from Alabama [Mr. Black] asked me to offer in his behalf an amendment, to which I have no objection. I now offer the amendment.

THE PRESIDING OFFICER. The amendment will be stated.

THE CHIEF CLERK. It is proposed on page 31, line 14, before the period to insert the following:

And in order to fully examine into such transactions the commission shall have access to and the right of inspection of all accounts, records, and memoranda, including all documents, papers, and correspondence now or hereafter existing, of persons furnishing such equipment, supplies, research, services, finances, credit, or personnel.

THE PRESIDING OFFICER. The question is on agreeing to the amendment offered by the Senator from Washington in behalf of the Senator from Alabama [Mr. Black].

The amendment was agreed to.

MR. DILL. I have another amendment of my own which I should like to offer and which I think is desirable.

THE PRESIDING OFFICER. The amendment will be stated.

THE CHIEF CLERK. It is proposed, on page 52, after line 3, to insert the following new paragraph:

(f) In granting applications for licenses or renewal of licenses for frequencies to be used for broadcasting, the commission shall so distribute such licenses that no one licensee nor organization of licensees, whether effected by purchase, lease, chain broadcasting, or other method, shall be able to monopolize or exercise dominant control over the broadcasting facilities of any community, city, or State, or over the country as a whole; and the commission shall, so far as possible, by its distribution of licenses, provide for broad diversification and free competition in broadcast programs to be presented to radio listeners.

MR. DILL. The purpose of the amendment is to make it impossible for any one man or organization to have control of the broadcasting facilities of a community, State, or the country if there are other applications from responsible applicants. At the present time there is growing up in many cities the practice of the owner of an important station leasing the facilities of another important station and then organizing a corporation to control a third station, and as a result the one station gets complete control of the broadcasting of the community. The purpose of the amendment is to give the commission a reason, if there be a suitable applicant, for granting a license to another applicant and to break up that kind of practice if the commission shall find it necessary. It is a permissive amendment.

MR. FESS. Mr. President, may I ask the Senator a question?

MR. DILL. Certainly.

MR. FESS. This would not interfere with WLW?

MR. DILL. Only if WLW reached out and undertook to get control of all the other stations in Cincinnati.

MR. FESS. After that station has been given the frequency it would not be interfered with if operating within the law?

MR. DILL. No; but if it went out and secured all the other stations in Cincinnati, then someone else might get a license.

THE PRESIDING OFFICER. The question is on agreeing to the amendment offered by the Senator from Washington.

The amendment was agreed to. . . .

MR. WALSH. Mr. President, carrying out the views expressed by the Senator from Michigan [Mr. Couzens] , myself, and other Senators upon the floor, we have agreed to the amendment which I send to the desk and ask to have stated.

THE PRESIDING OFFICER. The amendment will be stated.

THE CHIEF CLERK. It is proposed to strike out from line 1 page 9 to the words "per annum" on line 12, and in lieu thereof to insert the following:

(f) Without regard to the civil-service laws or the Classification Act of 1923, as amended, the commission may appoint and prescribe the duties and fix the salaries of a secretary, a chief engineer, and a general counsel; and each commissioner may, without regard to the civil-service laws, appoint and prescribe the duties of an assistant whose compensation shall be fixed in accordance with the Classification Act of 1923, as amended. The general counsel and the chief engineer shall each receive an annual salary of not to exceed $9,000. The secretary shall receive an annual salary not to exceed $7,500.

THE PRESIDING OFFICER. The question is on the amendment offered by the Senator from Massachusetts.

MR. WALSH. Mr. President, in explanation of the amendment, I desire to state that I have obtained the published pamphlet of the civil service retirement and salary classification laws. I find on page 19 of that pamphlet, among the various employees who are classified for the purpose of fixing salaries, a group known as "professional and scientific service." The classification board has classified this group into seven grades; and it is provided that the annual rate of compensation for positions in grade 7 "shall be $7,500, unless a higher rate is specially authorized by law."

I find that all through this compilation of laws an attempt is made by the classification board to establish various classifications of salaries, in some instances salaries which reach as high as $9,000, providing for every official in the Government other than these designated by law.

I understand that this amendment is acceptable to the Senator from Washington.

MR. DILL. I have no objection to the amendment.

MR. KING. Mr. President, I should like to inquire as to the meaning of the word "assistant." That may mean much, and it may mean little. It may mean that an assistant is to have a grade slightly below the principal, at a very large salary.

If the assistant is to fall within the category of secretary, that is one thing. . . .

MR. COUZENS. In drafting this amendment in cooperation with the Senator from Massachusetts, it was understood that the assistant in this case means a commissioner's secretary, and the assistant falls within the salary fixed by the Classification Act.

MR. KING. If it is understood that the word "assistant" does not mean an assistant commissioner, or an "under secretary," such as it is now so common to call officials, or some other high position in the Government, that is one thing. However, I shall accept the explanation made by the able Senator from Michigan and give to the word "assistant" the meaning ascribed to it; but I am afraid that when the commission attempt to interpret the word "assistant" they will attribute to it quite a different meaning and insist that it calls for one who has large experience and has ability to deal with practical questions in connection with radio, and so forth, and claim for the "assistant" compensation greatly in excess of that indicated or which would be required for a secretary.

If the Senator understands that it is really a secretary who is meant, that is a different matter.

MR. DILL. It is really a secretary.

MR. KING. I ask the clerk to read again the compensation provided for the attorney and the engineer. Meanwhile I may say, Mr. President, that I think we have been unwise in fixing the salaries and compensation for many of these new organizations. I think we have gone wild, to use the language of the street, and I know that we are bringing upon ourselves considerable criticism by reason of the fact that some of these new agencies, new bureaus, and new organizations are permitted to pay compensation in excess of that given to many employees in regular organizations and departments of the Government. That common policy results in discontent. When persons working in the Treasury Department or in some other department who have been there for many years, receiving four, five, or six thousand dollars per annum, find that individuals, perhaps with less ability and less qualifications, in some of these new organizations are getting two or three or four thousand dollars more per annum than they get, obviously there will be resentment and a feeling of discrimination.

Mr. President, I think we have gone too far in providing the large salaries in new organizations which have been set up. Notwithstanding the speech made by the Senator from Kentucky, these new organizations ought to come within the Classification Act. We ought to treat all alike. There is no trouble in getting individuals to come here and accept jobs. They come here in myriads seeking them. I have from 25 to 50 callers every day from various parts of the United States who are here seeking positions—lawyers, engineers, accountants, men who have received large salaries and have been employed in responsible positions, and who would be glad now to get $150 or $200 a month; yet when we come to fix the compensation of officials in some of these new organizations we do not take into account the condition of the country, the burdens imposed upon the Government, and the demands made upon the Treasury of the United States. . . .

MR. WALSH. Mr. President, as I understand the amendment that has been offered, when we get through setting up this commission we shall have 5 commissioners, 5 assistant commissioners, and 5 private secretaries.

MR. KING. Yes.

MR. DILL. Oh, no!

MR. WALSH. We shall have a private secretary to each commissioner.

MR. DILL. But not five assistants.

MR. WALSH. Each commissioner is to have an assistant.

MR. DILL. That is his clerk or secretary.

MR. COUZENS. That is what it is intended for.

MR. WALSH. There is quite a difference between an assistant to the commissioner and a secretary to the commissioner.

MR. ROBINSON OF ARKANSAS. Mr. President, this employee has been dignified with the title of assistant commissioner, but he is expected to serve as secretary.

MR. DILL. There will be no assistant commissioners.

MR. KING. May I ask the chairman of the committee what is meant by the provision on page 14—

Each division may . . . appoint a director, without regard to the Civil Service laws or the Classification Act . . . at an annual salary—

It was $8,000 and it has been reduced to $7,500. What is a director?

MR. DILL. A director is a man to be appointed to try to carry out the administrative work of these divisions, to save the commissioners from doing the detail work they now have to do. It is believed that they can avoid employing a great deal of additional help which otherwise would have to be chosen if these directors can be provided. I do not know how the plan will work; it is an experiment; but there are 17,000 amateur licenses in this country, and they are renewed every 6 months. There ought to be somebody handling that work besides the chairman of the Commission.

MR. KING. Mr. President, we find the engineer and the other assistants—

MR. DILL. The Senator was talking about the salary of the engineer and the attorney.

MR. KING. Yes.

MR. DILL. The present chief counsel of the Radio Commission gets $10,000.

MR. KING. That is too much.

MR. DILL. The chief engineer gets $10,000.

MR. KING. That is too much.

MR. DILL. We are cutting it to $9,000, and I think that when we are putting both the great telephone monopoly and the radio, with all the ramifications, under one commission, $9,000 is not an exorbitant salary. Certainly as to the engineer, with the responsibility on him that is coming with the development of radio, $9,000 is not an exorbitant salary.

MR. KING. I will ask that the clerk read the salary to be paid the engineer and the salary to be paid the counsel.

THE PRESIDING OFFICER. The clerk will read.

THE LEGISLATIVE CLERK (reading):

The chief engineer shall receive an annual salary not to exceed $9,000, and the secretary shall receive an annual salary not to exceed $7,500.

MR. KING. Mr. President, I move to strike out "$7,500" and to insert in lieu thereof "$6,000." I think that is sufficient for the secretary of the commission.

THE PRESIDING OFFICER. The question is on agreeing to the amendment offered by the Senator from Utah to the amendment offered by the Senator from Massachusetts.

The amendment to the amendment was rejected.

MR. FESS. Mr. President, I am in favor of the movement that is being made to require, so far as possible, that the civil-service law shall be followed, although I do agree, and have agreed all along, that in the case of experts we really ought to keep the way open, so that special talent may be selected without the requirement of an examination, which would not be the best method for getting the highest talent.

On the question of salaries, I do not see how we can very well classify this commission with other commissions. It will have a duty to perform probably as complicated as that of most of the other commissions. As to the counsel, we ought to realize that where the counsel of this commission will be called in to prosecute a case he will be up against the best talent money can buy, and while I believe legal talent could be found which would lend itself to the service of the Government at a smaller salary, I doubt very much whether it would be wise to cut the salary below what the bill has suggested, for the legal counsel at least. I do not care so much about the engineer or the examiners, but as to the legal counsel, I think that is quite essential.

THE PRESIDING OFFICER. The question is on agreeing to the amendment of the Senator from Massachusetts as modified.

The amendment as modified was agreed to.

MR. WHEELER. Mr. President, there is a provision on page 14 with reference to directors. I am frank to say that I feel it is absolutely wrong to appoint two directors. I think it would result in dividing up the responsibility of the commission. The commissioners are to be appointed, and they are to be paid good salaries, and there are to be lawyers and engineers and assistants and secretaries, and then they are to appoint directors. When those directors are appointed the responsibility which ought to be placed upon the commissioners will be divided.

MR. DILL. Mr. President, I call attention to the fact that in the Interstate Commerce Commission there are nine directors, their salaries ranging from $7,500 to $10,000 a year. The Interstate Commerce Commission has found that they are so important and so valuable that they have nine of them. I do not think it is unreasonable, in a commission of the kind to be appointed under this measure, that there should be two directors, and that their salaries should be $10,500.

MR. WHEELER. My own view about the matter is, as I said a moment ago, that we are loading these commissions up with many high-salaried employees who are not necessary. We talk about getting experts in these commissions, and every Senator knows that, as a matter of fact, they are not experts at all; that we are filling some of the commissions with politicians.

MR. WALSH. May I inquire of the Senator, or, through him, of the Senator from Washington, whether the bill contains a provision taking over the present Radio Commission?

MR. DILL. Yes.

MR. WALSH. So that, in addition to the present personnel of the Radio Commission, we are creating all these new jobs. Has the Senator any conception of what the pay roll will be?

MR. DILL. There is no requirement to keep the employees of the Radio Commission. The new commission are simply empowered to take it over.

MR. WALSH. Those who are now employed in the Radio Commission are under the civil service?

MR. DILL. Not all of them. Quite a number of them are. The assistants who are to be stricken out are not under the civil service today.

MR. WALSH. Does the Senator know what the salaries of the present employees are?

MR. DILL. In the Radio Commission the chief engineer gets $10,000, the chief counsel gets $10,000, and the salaries range below that. I do not know the salaries of the assistants.

MR. WALSH. What are the salaries of the directors?

MR. DILL. There are no directors in the Radio Commission.

MR. WALSH. The Senator is proposing to provide for directors?

MR. DILL. Two are provided for. The Interstate Commerce Commission has 9, and has found it necessary to have that number of directors; so I do not think it is unreasonable to ask for 2 in this bill. . . .

MR. WALSH. Mr. President, I do not mean anything personal toward the Senator from Washington [Mr. Dill] in what I am about to say, but, in view of what I myself have observed before the Committee on Education and Labor, of which I have the honor to be chairman, as to the agitation for new commissions, or in view of the discussion here today, I wish to say that in the future I intend to inquire, when a bill is reported creating a new commission, whether or not the salary list and the number of employees and the amounts to be paid have been referred to the Budget for report. Let the administration take the responsibility of piling up these big salary lists.

MR. KING. Mr. President, will the Senator yield?

MR. WALSH. I yield.

MR. KING. I hope the Senator is not prophesying that there are to be new commissions created. I hope the day has come when we will not create any more.

MR. WALSH. There are four or five in sight, developed here during the last few days.

THE PRESIDING OFFICER. The question is on the engrossment and third reading of the bill.

The bill was ordered to be engrossed for a third reading and read the third time.

THE PRESIDING OFFICER. The question now is, Shall the bill pass? . . .

The bill was passed.

House of Representatives—73rd Congress, 2d Session
June 2, 1934

MR. BANKHEAD. . . . Mr. Speaker, I shall make a very brief statement on the rule, because I think only a brief statement is necessary. I am informed that this bill comes from the Committee on Interstate and Foreign Commerce with a practically unanimous report.

This is a measure that has been under investigation by the Committee on Interstate and Foreign Commerce for some time. It was inaugurated originally with the recommendation of the Secretary of Commerce. It has the approval of the administration, and the provisions of the bill will be fully explained by the chairman and other members of the committee. . . .

I will say that the rule provides for 2 hours' general debate, and to consider the House amendment to the Senate bill as an original bill. . . .

MR. McFADDEN. Mr. Speaker, this is an important bill dealing with the supervision of radio broadcasting and the necessary organization that has control of this important function.

It not only deals with radio but it consolidates under one bureau all lines of communication and takes from the Interstate Commerce Commission its jurisdiction over telephone and telegraph lines of the country, and apparently takes jurisdiction of legislation affecting communications from the Merchant Marine, Radio, and Fisheries Committee and places it all in the Interstate and Foreign Commerce Committee.

The development of radio in the United States and its importance, which is equal to that of the press, was provided for in the Constitution when our forefathers drew that important document. The people of the country were given free and open expression at all times through the press. Of course, in those days nothing like the radio and the important part it was to take in the dissemination of information was thought of. This development of radio is to my mind more important than is the control of the press of the United States. I direct the attention of the membership of the House to the growing control over all lines of communication. I mean by that the attempt at censorship which is being made and to an extent attained, not only over the press but over the radio. Radio is probably the most effective method of reaching every class of people and is more important than any other medium. Many people who do not read the newspapers listen in on radio, and form their opinions from this source. Under this tremendous development of radio during the past few years we have seen built up the use of this particular function to an extent that is almost unbelievable. We see it being used for propaganda purposes, we see it being used effectively for advertising, we see it being used in culture. Those who are in control of the agencies of publicity are particularly alive to the importance of the control of this function of radio. We have seen it used effectively by political parties, by candidates, and I do not hesitate to say that which you all know, that policies of a political party disseminated with the free use over radio can control public sentiment to an extent of political decisions. It is possible to assert personality into radio talks, oftentimes more effectively than by personal contact. Any administration in power which sees fit to use this instrument can control the sentiment of the citizenry, as the same cannot be controlled through any other medium of propaganda, not even by the press. . . .

. . . When the change of administration took place and the Democrats came into office, they found that the control of radio was very much in the hands of and very much to the advantage of the outgoing administration; that it had been used to a great extent by the previous administration and dominated to a great extent by it. . . .

. . . The question of the political control of the use of radio is an important thing to the American people, and I call attention to the fact that the incoming administration felt they had to deal with this subject, else it might be controlled to their detriment. So there was immediate action as to a change in personnel of the Commission. Key men were arranged for. Hanley and Pretty and others were put in, and there was immediately appointed this special committee, of which the Secretary of Commerce was the head, who made this study that has been the basis of this particular legislation which is before you, and this is particularly an administration measure. It is the President's bill. He has seen to it that no changes are made. It was drawn in the administrative departments and was presented to the committees of the Senate and the House and has had very little consideration by either one of those committees. It is true there were hearings held and a lot of protests were entered, but no attention was given to amendments. The bill was kept just as the President wanted it.

This bill we find here today strikes out everything after the enacting clause of the Senate bill and substitutes the House bill. It is proposed here that this bill shall go through this House without any amendment or any proper consideration of it by the House. It is a long bill. The Senate bill is 175 pages long. There is not going to be an opportunity for the Members of the House to do any more, practically, than to listen to the reading of this bill, and I point out that this is another one of those administration measures dealing with an important function which affects all of the people of the United States, and which is being put through in the same manner that all of this other legislation has been proposed and passed by this House. Just as the President wishes, this House is again signing on the dotted line without crossing a "t" or dotting an "i." . . .

MR. CULKIN. Under the present law these licenses for broadcasting continue from year to year if they are extended. Is that not true?

MR. McFADDEN. Yes.

MR. CULKIN. That is, they may be revoked at the end of a year?

MR. McFADDEN. Yes.

MR. CULKIN. What is the advantage of this law over the present statute? What is the necessity for it?

MR. McFADDEN. I suppose it is in order to keep a more complete control over broadcasting. I might say in that connection that the board having jurisdiction over this is exercising a control over the small stations, which are the independent stations, which is a subject which this committee, if it is appointed to make the study, must give very careful consideration to, because I find that the action of the Commission in dealing with the small stations is to drive them out of business, which seems to be the plan of the two big chains. Broadcasting in the United States is rapidly becoming a monopoly in the hands of those two systems. They have now under contract 80 percent of all the available stations and their time. The Columbia Broadcasting System is very responsive to suggestions from the other important system, the National Broadcasting Co. These two outfits dominate the chain systems. It is a situation that looks to me—and anyone who will study it must believe likewise, for he cannot come to any other conclusion—that the purpose is to have a centralized system completely under the control of one dominating influence—and that the National Broadcasting Co., which is owned, operated, and controlled by the Radio Corporation of America. It would seem from the method and manner in which the Commission has been operating, as though it were encouraging doing away with the small stations, just in accordance with the aim of the National Broadcasting Co.

I might say in that connection as an illustration that a station located in western Pennsylvania has recently been going through a critical period with the Commission, in which they are finding all kinds of fault with the operations, which is similar to that which is taking place with all of the small stations throughout the country, making it utterly impossible for those stations to comply with the regulations of the Commission. The Commission in their dealings with the small independent stations, particularly those stations who are not now under contract with N.B.C. or Columbia, are carrying on a policy of absolute intimidation. They do not dare say that their souls are their own, lest the license be taken away from them. If you do not believe this statement, read the hearings on my bill held before the Merchant Marine and Radio Committee just recently.

These facilities are then transferred to other companies. It is a situation which confronts the independent broadcaster in the United States today. . . .

In this connection it would be interesting for the Membership to know that which has occurred with regard to this station at Washington, Pa., operated by Mr. Spriggs, an American citizen, who has invested a large amount of money in the running of a small 100-watt station. They have practically made it impossible for him to continue to operate; and when you go through all of the detail in connection with this one situation, as I have, you cannot fail but to see that the strong hand of influence is drying up the independent broadcasting stations in the United States and the whole thing is tending toward centralization of control in these two big companies, if not one company. . . .

MR. BLAND. Does the gentleman feel that it is fair to try the merits of any particular station on the floor without knowing all the facts? The gentleman has brought a very grave charge against the Federal Radio Commission, one in which I absolutely cannot concur. . . .

MR. RAYBURN. Mr. Speaker, I move that the House resolve itself into the Committee of the Whole House on the state of the Union for the consideration of the bill (S. 3285) to provide for the regulation of interstate and foreign communications by wire or radio, and for other purposes.

The motion was agreed to.

Accordingly the House resolved itself into the Committee of the Whole House on the state of the Union for the consideration of the bill S. 3285, with Mr. Disney in the chair. . . .

MR. RAYBURN. Mr. Chairman, the rule provides an hour to each side for general debate. I shall certainly take a very small part of that time because I do not deem it necessary to take up very much time on this matter.

With reference specifically to the remarks of the gentleman from Pennsylvania [Mr. McFadden], I may say that they do not apply in anywise to this bill, for the reason that in the House draft of the bill we do not in anywise amend or change the Radio Act. I think it is also a fair statement to make that the bill as a whole does not change existing law, not only with reference to radio but with reference to telegraph, telephone, and cable, except in the transfer of the jurisdiction and such minor amendments as to make that transfer effective.

I think I am also justified in saying that this is a unanimous report from the Committee on Interstate and Foreign Commerce. . . .

MR. CULKIN. The gentleman says the existing law is substantially reenacted. Will the gentleman tell the House specifically whether section 29 is reenacted? Section 29 relates to the right of free speech by means of radio and communication and provides that no obscene language may be used. . . .

MR. BLAND. I think a reading of title III in the bill as reported shows that this is not affected in any way, because the gentleman's committee simply transferred the powers of the Federal Radio Commission to this new Communications Commission and does not undertake in any respect to change or to modify the existing radio law.

MR. RAYBURN. That is the statement that I made, and I felt sure I was correct. I am certainly glad to have the assurance of the gentleman from Virginia [Mr. Bland], who knows more about radio legislation than any member of our committee.

MR. CULKIN. May I say briefly that section 29 is of first importance and should be continued in any subsequent legislation.

MR. RAYBURN. That is what we intended to do. . . .

I may say to the gentleman from Virginia that we have brought all of the elements of communication under one head. We did not set out to amend the law with reference to radio especially, a matter about which our committee knows little, because it has not handled that legislation, and we thought we were doing about as much as we might be expected to do at this time. . . .

Section 1 states the purpose of the act and provides for the creation of the Federal Communications Commission.

Section 2 (a) states the application of the act to interstate and foreign communication by wire or radio and transmission of energy by radio. The Canal Zone is excepted, because all radio activities in that area are under military and naval authorities. The Philippine Islands are excepted because their distance from the United States makes it inadvisable for a commission in the United States to try to regulate interference in the Philippines. The present laws governing communications do not apply to either the Canal Zone or the Philippines.

Section 2 (b) exempts from most of the provisions of the act small independent telephone companies whose only interstate business is through physical connection with a nonaffiliated company. The sections to which such independent companies are subjected are those providing for the regulation of rates and prohibiting unjust discrimination in interstate and foreign service.

Section 3 contains definitions taken largely from existing law and international conventions.

Section 4 provides for a bipartisan seven-man commission serving 7-year terms. In paragraph (f) the commission is authorized to appoint certain general officers without regard to the civil-service laws or the Classification Act of 1923. By paragraph (k) the commission is directed to make a special report not later than February 1, 1935, recommending such amendments to the act as it deems desirable in the public interest.

Section 5, authorizing the commission to organize itself into not more than three divisions, follows section 17 of the Interstate Commerce Act. The full commission has the right to review decisions of a division, but such review lies within the discretion of the commission and is not mandatory.

Title II. Common Carriers

Section 201 (a) is based upon section 1 (4) of the Interstate Commerce Act which relates only to transportation. It establishes the duty of common carriers to furnish communication service upon reasonable request; and requires them where ordered by the commission after a hearing to establish physical connections with other carriers and to establish through routes and charges.

Section 201 (b) provides that charges, practices, classifications, and regulations in connection with such interstate and foreign communication service shall be just and reasonable. It is based upon the Interstate Commerce Act, section 1 (5) and (6), which mentions only charges in connection with communications. The types of messages listed in the classification are taken from the Interstate Commerce Act. The proviso permits carriers subject to the act to enter into or operate under contracts with other common carriers for the exchange of services if the Commission is of the opinion that such contract is not contrary to the public interest. The proviso differs from the present law in that it applies to existing contracts and makes such contracts subject to the jurisdiction of the commission, whereas under present law the commission has no jurisdiction of the contracts. The usual type of contract contemplated is that by which the telegraph companies furnish message service to railroads in return for transportation of men and materials and perhaps for rights-of-way.

Section 202 (a), based upon sections 2 and 3 (1) of the Interstate Commerce Act, forbids unjust and unreasonable discriminations. The present law is followed, and there can be no doubt that reasonable classifications are permitted. This is the section against which some newspapers and stock-exchange firms are protesting because of a possible restriction of leased wires. Their protests are really based upon amendments which Postal Telegraph suggested to the section, which amendments were not adopted by the committee. There is no ground for fear that the law will not recognize existing classes of service.

Section 202 (b) is a new provision designed to make doubly sure that charges for wires in connection with chain broadcasting are within the jurisdiction of the commission.

Section 202 (c) is a penal provision which will apply to those small independent companies made subject to sections 201-205, inclusive, but exempted from the other provisions of the act under section 2 (b).

Section 203, regarding the filing of schedules of charges, is based upon section 6 of the Interstate Commerce Act, which relates only to transportation. It is clear that the commission must have information as to the charges made by the carriers if it is to regulate rates.

Section 204 providing for hearing as to the lawfulness of new charges and for the suspension of such new charges for 3 months in proper case is based upon section 15 (7) of the Interstate Commerce Act, which relates to transportation only. It is an essential power if rates are to be regulated. It did not apply to communications in the Interstate Commerce Act because that act did not require the filing of schedules of charges and therefore the Commission had no information as to the new rates upon which to call for a hearing or to base a suspension.

Section 205, authorizing the commission to prescribe just and reasonable charges and to fix maximum and minimum charges, is taken over from section 15 (1) of the Interstate Commerce Act without important change.

Section 206, covering liability of carriers for damages, is based on section 8 of the Interstate Commerce Act.

Section 207, dealing with recovery of damages, is based upon section 9 of the Interstate Commerce Act.

Section 208, relating to complaints to the commission, is based upon section 13 (1) and (2) of the Interstate Commerce Act.

Section 209, relating to orders for payment of money, is based upon section 16 (1) of the Interstate Commerce Act.

Section 210, relating to franks and passes, is based upon section 1 (7) of the Interstate Commerce Act. It carries over existing law permitting communication companies to exchange franks for messages and to exchange such franks with railroads for passes.

Section 211 (a), requiring common carriers to file with the commission copies of their contracts with other common carriers, is taken from section 16 (5) of the Interstate Commerce Act. Section 211 (b) authorizes the commission to require the filing of other contracts of any carrier, but permits it to waive the filing of minor contracts. This new provision is desirable to enable the commission to determine whether any such contracts are designed to enable carriers to escape the effects of the law.

Section 212, relating to interlocking directorates and to the dealing by officials in securities of their companies, is based upon section 20 (a) (12) of the Interstate Commerce Act, relating only to transportation.

Section 213, relating to the valuation of carrier property, differs from section 19 (a) of the Interstate Commerce Act in that valuation is made permissive instead of mandatory and the·commission is left wider discretion as to the method of valuation to be employed.

Paragraph (e) is taken from the Emergency Railroad Transportation Act of 1933 and requires the commission to keep itself informed of new construction and improvements. The Interstate Commerce Commission has made considerable progress in the valuation of telegraph companies. Paragraph (g) permits it to complete such valuations if requested to do so by the communications commission.

Section 214, relating to extension of lines, is based upon section 1 (18) to (24) of the Interstate Commerce Act, which relates only to transportation. It requires a certificate of public convenience and necessity from the Commission for the construction of a new interstate line but permits the construction of local lines and the supplementing of existing lines without such certificate. The section is designed to prevent useless duplication of facilities, with consequent higher charges upon the users of the service.

Section 215 directs the commission to make three separate studies and to report its findings to Congress, with recommendations for any additional legislation which may be found to be needed.

First. Paragraph (a) directs an examination into transactions relating to the furnishing of equipment, supplies, research, services, finances, credit, or personnel which may affect charges or services. It is designed particularly to develop the facts with respect to intercompany transactions and to the relation of holding companies to operating companies. State regulation of communication companies has been greatly handicapped because the State commissions have been unable to get information of the type which the commission is here directed to obtain.

Second. Paragraph (b) directs the commission to investigate the methods by which and the extent to which the telephone companies are furnishing telegraph service and vice versa. The telegraph companies have complained bitterly that they are being subjected to unfair competition through the entry of the telephone company into the telegraph field using its byproduct facilities. It is contended that the telephone company is taking the cream of the telegraph business without assuming common-carrier telegraph obligations, and that its tactics have seriously handicapped the telegraph companies. The commission is directed to find the facts in the matter.

Third. By paragraph (c) the commission is directed to examine into the so-called "exclusive contracts" by which one telegraph company keeps another from competing for public business in public places such as railroad stations and hotels. Such contracts have been objected to on the ground that they operate as a restraint of competition in the face of the congressional mandate that the telegraph business be competitive.

Section 216, relating to the application of the act to receivers and trustees, follows the Interstate Commerce Act.

Section 217, relating to the liability of carriers for acts and omissions of agents, follows the Interstate Commerce Act.

Section 218 follows section 12 (1) of the Interstate Commerce Act in authorizing the commission to make inquiry into the management of business of carriers subject to the act. It contains a new provision directing the Commission to keep itself informed of technical developments and improvements in order that the commission may be able effectively to regulate communications. Another new provision authorizes the commission to obtain from holding and affiliated companies information necessary to enable the commission to carry out its duties.

Section 219 providing for annual and other reports is based upon section 20 (1) of the Interstate Commerce Act. It adds new provisions authorizing the commission to require such reports from holding and associated companies and providing that reports shall show the amount and privileges of each class of stock and the names of the 30 largest holders of each class of stock and the amount held by each.

Section 20, paragraphs (a) to (g), relating to accounts records, memoranda, and depreciation, is based upon section 20 (5) to (8) of the Interstate Commerce Act with changes necessary to permit State commissions to prescribe the systems of accounts for the intrastate operation of carriers. Paragraphs (h) to (j) are new. Paragraph (h) authorizes the commission to classify carriers and to except the carriers of particular classes in any State from the requirements of the section where the State commission regulates accounts or depreciation for the particular class of carriers. Paragraph (i) requires the commission to consult the State commission before prescribing new systems of accounts and paragraph (j) removes any limitation upon the power of a State commission to prescribe, for the purposes of the exercise of its jurisdiction, rates of depreciation. The last three paragraphs named were placed in the bill at the request of the State commissions which feel that their task of regulating intrastate communications will be greatly facilitated by the adoption of these paragraphs.

Section 221 (a), providing the procedure for the consolidation of telephone companies, closely follows section 5 (18) of the Interstate Commerce Act. Paragraph (b) leaves local exchange service to local regulation even where a portion of such local exchange service constitutes interstate communications. It is designed to cover cases of cities located within two States, as Texarkana.

Paragraphs (c) and (d) authorize the commission, in making valuations of telephone property, to value only that part of the property used in interstate or foreign telephone toll service.

Title III. Provisions Relating to Radio

Section 301 abolishes the Federal Radio Commission and transfers its functions and powers to the new Commission.

Title IV. Procedural and Administrative Provisions

Section 401, relating to jurisdiction to enforce the act and orders of the commission, follows sections 20 (9) and 16 (12) of the Interstate Commerce Act.

Section 402, relating to the application of the district court jurisdiction acts, adapts the procedure now applicable to orders of the Interstate Commerce Commission. Inasmuch as the Radio Act of 1927 is not amended by the present bill, the procedure applicable to appeals in matters now coming under that act will continue to be as provided in the Radio Act of 1927. Thus, the review of orders affecting the common-carrier aspects of the commission's jurisdiction will be by the district courts, while that of the radio orders will be by the Court of Appeals of the District of Columbia.

The remaining provisions of the bill are believed to be sufficiently explained in the committee report. . . .

It may be of interest to the House if for just a moment I take the time to explain something about the size and scope of communications in the country.

In the telephone field there are 88,303,231 miles of wire; in telegraph and cable there are 2,336,976 miles of telegraph and cable wire; and power lines are estimated at 200,000 miles.

The capitalization of the telephone is $6,025,678,634; telegraph and cable, $349,542,130; and power—and this is an estimate—$15,000,000,000.

In plant and equipment, the telephone has $4,660,662,997; telegraph and cable, $465,639,421; and in comparison with the railroads, the investments of railroads in plant and equipment is estimated at $26,086,990,995. The capitalization of the railroads is $29,129,250,000.

In the telephone field the average per capita revenue amounts to $8.41 to each person—man, woman, and child—in the United States. In the telegraph and cable field, 88 cents; electric service, $15.82; and in railroad freight, $19.91.

The dividends in these industries for 1932 were about as follows:

In the telephone field $340,000,000; in the telegraph field, $2,500,000; and in the radio communication about one-third of $1,000,000. The estimated number of radio sets in the United States is 16,500,000.

The number of employees is about as follows:

In the telephone field there are 300,000 employees, or 80 percent of all the employees in the communications field; and in the telegraph 65,000, or 15 percent; and in radio about 22,000, or 5 percent.

The telephone companies have sixteen and two-thirds million telephones and 11,000 central offices; the telegraph, 26,000 central offices; and the radio broadcasting is estimated to have 50,000,000 listeners.

The extent of the use of these facilities is about as follows:

In the telephone field it is estimated that per year there are 28,000,000,000 conversations, or 222 per capita. In the telegraph field there are 127,000,000 messages sent per annum, and in radio 2,500,000 messages.

The age of these industries is about as follows:

Telephone, 58 years; telegraph, about 82 years; and the radio had its inception about 38 years ago.

The competition in the industry will run about as follows:

Telephone: American Telephone & Telegraph Co., 95 percent of the business; 100 independent companies, 5 percent of the business.

In the telegraph field: The Western Union, 75 percent; the Postal, 24 percent; and the independents, 1 percent.

In telephone service the American Telephone & Telegraph is practically a monopoly. At present and for several years past American Telephone & Telegraph has paid dividends at the rate of $9 per year.

The things we expect this commission to consider, among others, are these:

There has been great complaint about excessive depreciation charges in these fields. There has been great complaint about so-called "watered stock." There has been no complete regulation of security issues in these fields as there has been since 1920 in the railroad field. They should study this question and make some recommendation to Congress as to further need for regulation along these lines.

These public utilities have been practically a monopoly for quite a long time. There has been no national planning in this field.

Some of the few reasons for the bill are as follows: We think that we ought to bring the regulation of all these communications under one authority.

Today we have the telegraph and telephone and cable, with control and regulation by the Interstate Commerce Commission, but the Interstate Commerce Commission in all these years has had the great question of transportation of the railroads to handle, and they have devoted very little time to any sort of regulation of the telegraph and telephone and cable. There is no hope in the future that they will have more time to devote to it than they have had in the past.

Also, the Post Office has some telegraph jurisdiction and, of course, the Radio Commission has the radio.

The State Department has jurisdiction over cable landings, and the Army and Navy have some radio and telegraph facilities. It is not our intention to take away from the Army or the Navy their small control which they have over radio and telegraph, because we think it would be unwise.

As to the Interior Department, the only control they have is in the public parks of the country, and we think that should remain there. And by and large we think, as the President stated in his message, and by common consent, all these instrumentalities should be brought into this one body.

We are forming a new commission and we are abolishing the existing Commission. The Radio Commission at the present time has a membership of five. We provide that the new commission shall have a membership of seven, and for a very good reason. We anticipate a division of two members for the radio, with the chairman of the commission as a third; we anticipate a division for the telephone of two members, with the chairman of the commission as a third; and we anticipate a division of two for the telegraph, with the chairman as a third. The Senate provided a commission of five and made a division for the telephone and telegraph and one for radio. We believe—and the membership of the House committee believes—that into the telephone and telegraph field at the present time in their breadth and in principle and set-up we should bring some kind of real control, and that there ought to be a division of the telephone and a division of the telegraph. . . .

MR. SNELL. Is there anything in the bill that in any way interferes with the telephone companies in favor of the telegraph companies?

MR. RAYBURN. Not unless it is in the present law. We did not change it.

MR. SNELL. No change in the present law?

MR. RAYBURN. We transfer the jurisdiction to the new commission, and the only amendment as to the telegraph and telephone companies is to make effective their transfer. . . .

MR. MEAD. The Senate provided for a certain fixed percentage of radio-broadcasting. Is there any provision in the House bill of that kind?

MR. RAYBURN. No.

MR. MEAD. What is the gentleman's idea?

MR. RAYBURN. We had up what is known as the "Father Harney amendment," that came to us in the House as it did in the Senate. That provided for the allocation of 25 percent of all the time to religious, educational, and, though I do not believe they used the word "uplift," yet they used a word that corresponds to it. If we begin to take away from the Radio Commission its authority to allocate, we would be in the same position that the Congress would be in if, after giving to the Interstate Commerce Commission its function of regulating railroads and fixing the rates, we would then start out to introduce and pass measures to revise the rate structure. In that way we would probably get into a lot of trouble. Our thought—at least, my thought—was this: If 25 percent should be allocated, or the allocation of it taken away from the Radio Commission, why not take away 30 percent or 40 percent or 100 percent? Also, if you allocate 25 percent to education and religion, then what difficulty is the Radio Commission going to have in dividing that 25 percent between Catholic, Jew, Protestant, and other sects, and also between what colleges, where located, and what else might be supposed to be taken into consideration for morals, education, and uplift? Our committee took that position, and we believe it is a wise one. . . .

MR. BLAND. Would not an attempt by the committee or by anyone to make this change so involve the broadcasting structure all over the United States that it would have to be studied carefully by some other commission in order to arrive at some equitable solution of the problem?

MR. RAYBURN. Yes; and if we do this, then it will practically amount to a revocation of every broadcasting license in the United States, because they must all be revised. . . .

MR. BLAND. I notice there is a section here that deals with procedural and administrative matters. Do the provisions of this bill materially alter the procedural provisions of the existing radio legislation?

MR. RAYBURN. I do not think so. I know they do not as far as the administration under the Interstate Commerce Act is concerned. We did not intend to do that. . . .

MR. DIRKSEN. I understand that some of the stations are now over their quota in their assignment of radio units. Is it the implication of the bill that if the Commission should so find and seek a more equitable distribution to put arbitrarily some of the private radio stations out of business? It would be almost necessary to do that.

MR. RAYBURN. That is a matter in the hands of the Commission, because whatever power the Commission has now this new commission will have in the administration of the law.

MR. DIRKSEN. Was that question raised in the course of the deliberations of the committee?

MR. RAYBURN. All those questions were raised, and we decided to leave them out by leaving the Radio Act as it is at the present time. . . .

MR. MILLIGAN. Under the present Radio Act they can reallocate them. They grant a license for only 6 months.

MR. RAYBURN. Yes.

MR. BLAND. The only possibility which I can see is in the procedural provisions.

MR. RAYBURN. We did not intend to do that.

MR. MILLIGAN. As I understand it, the same procedure is retained for the Radio Commission in this new commission.

MR. RAYBURN. That is my impression also. I thank the Members of the House for their attention. [Applause.] . . .

MR. MERRITT. Mr. Chairman, I have nothing of great importance to add to what the chairman has said. I agree substantially with what he has said.

I approached this question with considerable prejudice against the formation of any new commissions, but I found that the control of the telegraph and telephone, which is now under the Interstate Commerce Act, had not received very much attention, because, as the chairman has said, the Interstate Commerce Commission was entirely occupied with railway communication. Several things of interest have developed in the course of the examination of this question. In the first place, with regard to the very important matter of telephone communication, it developed that some 97½ or 98 percent of all telephone communication is intrastate, which this bill does not affect.

At one of our first hearings we had before us the State commissioners, to see what their attitude was. Their attitude in general was that they needed this bill to help them to do their own intrastate duties well. In the course of that examination I asked the men who represented the State commissioners whether, as far as they knew, there was any nation in the world that had as efficient telephone service as the United States. They all said, "No." Then I said, "Is there any particular criticism as to the rates for the 2½ percent of communication which is interstate?" They said, "No." Then it occurred to me that if that is so, if we have the best service and the interstate rates are not to be criticized, what is the use of doing anything about it? It developed as the hearings went on that by reason of improvements and inventions and the mechanical part of the service, telephone and telegraph and radio are becoming more and more interconnected, so that it is hardly possible to regulate one without regulating the other. I think, however, that the House should feel as I do, that it is very much to the credit of the men who founded and who have developed the great telephone system in this country, that they have done it on such absolutely sound, honest, and conservative lines.

It may interest the Members of this House to know that not only is there no "water" in the capitalization of the telephone companies but that the company has received $114 for every $100 share of stock, so there is no "water" in the company. As the State Commissioners have said, in general there has been no complaint of the rates and no complaint of the service.

I do not know so much about the telegraph companies, but I believe the capitalization of those companies is sound. I know still less as to radio. Of course, there has been great talk as to "water" and supersalesmanship of radio stock. I should have been glad if this legislation had confined itself to setting up a committee to investigate and report; but as to radio, that is exactly what this act does. All legislation about radio is found in section 301, which provides that the Federal Radio Commission is hereby abolished, and all the duties, powers, and functions of the Federal Radio Commission under the Radio Act of 1927, as amended, or under any other provision of law, are hereby imposed upon and vested in the new commission. That is the only thing that is in this bill about the power over radio.

As to the other parts of the bill, with regard to the remarks of the gentleman from Pennsylvania, you will find in section 215 and in section 202 very specific provisions against any discrimination in service or in charges. Of course, it is not possible, with human imperfections, to form any commission which may not do unfair things, but in a Government of this sort, covering such a great extent and such enormous range of matters, I do not see any other solution if any services are to be regulated except to form a commission of this sort and gradually make rules and regulations from experience. As the chairman has said, it is much safer to give this commission the power to do that than to attempt, with what little knowledge we have, to lay down a code which will cover all sorts of conditions and all sorts of individual practices. We found that out in the N.I.R.A. All that any regulatory body can safely do is to lay down a set of general principles and allow the parties who are doing the work to formulate the details as to carrying out those principles. . . .

MR. FULMER. Does this bill give the new commission any more power over the regulation of radio than the present Radio Commission has?

MR. MERRITT. It does not.

MR. FULMER. Is it not a fact that about all this bill hopes to accomplish is to transfer the activities of the Radio Commission and certain jurisdiction on the part of the Post Office Department and the Interstate Commerce Commission to this new commission?

MR. MERRITT. That is right. . . .

MR. FISH. Mr. Chairman, I assume from the fact this bill was reported out unanimously by the Committee on Interstate and Foreign Commerce that the bill must be meritorious and that it merely transfers powers that are already authorized to one separate commission. I, therefore, do not propose to take much time in discussing the merits of the proposals before us; and I do not assume to know very much about it except the general purpose of the legislation.

I admit that I am somewhat worried over the fact that the Democratic administration finds it necessary to employ hundreds of publicity agents to support the socialistic policies of the administration and the policies of the President and of the Democratic Party.

Four or five years ago some of us on the minority side thought that President Hoover knew something about publicity. He probably was the best publicity manager that we had ever had as President of the United States up to that time, but President Hoover was a mere piker compared to this administration, which has completely outclassed him. There are literally hundreds of paid publicity agents throughout the United States receiving substantial salaries. I venture to say that there are over a hundred who receive salaries in excess of $3,000, a very large proportion of them former members of the press—intelligent, likeable, and competent. Go to any department of the Government, small or large, or to any bureau of the Government, and you will find a publicity agent. They are frank and open about it; you will find the title right on the door. It may not always be "publicity agent," for they have various terms; it may be "director of publicity," "agent of publicity," "director of bureau of information," "public-relations division," and so on. Then there are hundreds of people employed at Government expense who clip newspaper articles and who mimeograph publicity articles. The result is that we are in the midst of a government of propaganda, by propaganda and ballyhoo, largely for the Democratic Party at the expense of the taxpayers of America. I think that fair-minded Democrats must sympathize with the Republicans who have not even got a look in. We have not got a chance at all. The only rights we have are once in a while to take the floor of the House of Representatives when there are about a score of Members present and express our views. Until recently it has been very difficult to get on the radio. A year ago Republicans could not get on the radio anywhere, but I imagine they feel they can be generous with the Republicans now because they keep adding to their publicity agents every time a Republican talks on the radio. So they can afford to let one or two of us speak now and then and develop an excuse for some more jobs for deserving Democrats to handle publicity.

I think it is unfortunate that the radio is controlled by the administration or terrorized by the administration to the extent that the policies of the administration literally burn up the radio time day and night. . . .

MR. MALONEY OF CONNECTICUT. Mr. Chairman, I have no special desire to speak at length on this bill today. My natural inclination is to bow to the superior wisdom and experience of our very able and courageous chairman; but I had been hopeful that those who were chiefly responsible for amendments which were offered to this bill on the other side of the Capitol would be afforded an opportunity to make some reference to them in the debate here today. Because they are unavoidably absent, I feel obliged to make some particular reference to one suggested amendment already very briefly discussed.

Those of you who have read the Senate bill know that provision is made therein for a study of the allocation of radio time, which would properly take care of education, religion, agriculture, and labor.

I have not yet heard any serious reason why the Radio Commission, or the new organization which will administer this bill, should not make such a study or should not have authority to reallocate time to those all-important groups and institutions. Of course, every Member of the Congress knows that these particular groups represent the very cornerstone of our Government, and that education, religion, labor, and agriculture should be afforded a proper time to tell their story, and to spread their advantages over the radio broadcasting systems of this country.

During committee consideration of this bill I offered a more modified amendment than had been proposed. I was particularly prompted to do that by the very able presentation of Father Harney, and partially prompted by the interest of many Members of the Congress in some such addition to this bill.

I am not going to offer an amendment now. I choose to go along with the majority of my committee, which has perhaps wisely decided that this is not the time nor the place to offer this amendment. I continue to be hopeful, however, that if the bill is passed in its present form, without amendment by the House, that the conferees will give further careful consideration to that part of the Senate bill. I would like to take these few minutes more of your time to express the hope on my part, and I am sure on the part of many others, that those who will administer this law will be particularly careful of radio, and not permit it to fall into the careless ways of the motion-picture industry. Most of us are hopeful that there will not be built up the tyranny that exists in the motion-picture field, which allows certain producers to ride roughshod over the interests of independent theater owners and a great majority of the careful and clean-thinking people. I have no such fear, but I think I would be a little bit remiss if I did not express my feeling and give what I think is the principal reason why the people concerned with this amendment want this subject further considered.

I know that the great majority of radio-broadcasting companies—and I am certain more than a majority of those representing the great networks—are determined to give these groups a fair allotment of time and proper representation; but there has been evidence of real selfishness on the part of one group, and that particular selfishness is what prompted these proposed amendments; that selfishness is what prompted this particular portion of the Senate bill. These people have now within their own hands a means of correction. [Applause.] . . .

MR. MAPES. Mr. Chairman, I yield myself 5 minutes. I am not going to attempt to discuss the bill in detail. Frankly, I do not know enough about it to do so, but I do want to take the opportunity to express my approval of the general purpose of the bill. For several years there has been an agitation to put all communications by wire and wireless under the jurisdiction of one commission. I think that is desirable, and that is what this bill primarily does. Speaking broadly, it does not attempt to do anything further than that. Under existing law the Postmaster General has certain powers over telegraph companies, the Interstate Commerce Commission has a great deal of power by statute over telegraph and telephone companies, which, for the most part, it has never exercised, and, of course, the Radio Commission has complete control under existing law over the radio. This bill proposes to put all of the powers now exercised by these different agencies under the new communications commission and it abolishes the authority which these other agencies now have in that respect. It abolishes the present Radio Commission. Primarily that is all this bill attempts to do. There are some amendments to the laws relating to telegraph and telephone and cable, but no amendments have been proposed to the radio law. The Interstate and Foreign Commerce Committee has felt it is not sufficiently informed and that there is not enough time remaining during this session of Congress to enable it to go into the various phases of existing law to justify it in recommending any substantial amendments to the law as it now stands. The bill provides that the new commission shall report back to Congress its findings on different matters and make such recommendations for amendments to the law as it thinks should be made. These can be taken up and considered more deliberately some other time than they can be at the close of a session of Congress such as we are in at the present time.

To repeat, I am in sympathy with the general purposes of this bill and shall vote for it. . . .

MR. BACON. . . . Does section 218 prevent a man who has made an invention from patenting that invention?

MR. RAYBURN. Oh, no.

MR. BACON. It does not deprive him of any right that he may have as an inventor?

MR. RAYBURN. None whatever.

MR. BACON. In other words, the company can use any inventions that they might make?

MR. RAYBURN. For the time the patent runs; yes.

MR. BACON. No patent rights are taken away?

MR. RAYBURN. None whatever.

MR. BACON. From either the individual or the company?

MR. RAYBURN. None whatever. . . .

MR. TRUAX. Mr. Chairman, I offer an amendment which I send to the desk.

The Clerk read as follows:

Amendment offered by Mr. Truax: On page 128, line 26, after the word "created," add "the Commission shall investigate the exclusion of addresses of Father Charles E. Coughlin and other crusaders against the international bankers and money kings by the National Broadcasting Co. and Columbia Broadcasting System."

MR. RAYBURN. Mr. Chairman, I make the point of order that that is not germane.

THE CHAIRMAN. The point of order is sustained.

MR. TRUAX. Mr. Chairman, I desire to be heard on the point of order.

THE CHAIRMAN. The Chair is ready to rule on the point of order. The Chair sustains the point of order.

MR. TRUAX. Mr. Chairman, I move to strike out the last word.

Mr. Chairman, it is a well-known fact that the addresses of one of the greatest crusaders for the common people in this country, the Reverend Father Charles E. Coughlin, have been barred by the National Broadcasting Co. and the Columbia Broadcasting System. Why? Simply because he reflects and makes certain charges against the very interests who have the monopoly of the broadcasting systems of this country.

Moreover, they will refuse to sell time to anyone who wishes to address the millions of listeners on old-age pensions. Why? Merely because that is a measure for the benefit of the common people of this country, the poor, the needy, the aged and distressed, against whom their master, J. P. Morgan, is eternally and unalterably opposed.

I want to call the attention of this House and the people of this Nation to the fact that these two major broadcasting companies are thus throttling such magnificent voices raised in behalf of the people in distress as, for instance, Father Coughlin, who has crusaded for months past to abandon the gold standard, for nationalization of the currency, and for such measures as the Frazier-Lemke bill to refinance the farmers of this country, and for the bank pay-off bill. I maintain that the throttling and strangling of this information from the millions of people of this country who are in distress and need aid, and need it now, is something that this Congress should not overlook.

You may strangle the daily press, you may strangle the weekly and the semiweekly publications; but when it comes to that point where we, the people, permit the millionaires of Wall Street to own and control the great systems of broadcasting that come to the ears of the poor man, the farmer, the wage earner, and all of these distressed, toiling millions so that they can hear only what their masters say they shall hear, it is time that this Congress took decisive action to make the air what it used to be and what it should be today, free for all the people. [Applause.] . . .

MR. McGUGIN. Mr. Chairman, the real depository of the liberties of the people is to be found in freedom of speech and freedom of the press. No lesser person than Thomas Jefferson, upon reading the Constitution, made the remark, in substance, that it did not make so much difference the form of government a people had so long as they had a free press; that with a free press a good government could not go far wrong, and with a free press a bad government could not long survive.

With the coming of radio it is not enough to have freedom of speech, which includes the right to stand upon a street corner and speak one's views. With radio there must be reasonable freedom of speech over the air, otherwise the benefits of freedom of speech have been taken away from the people.

I know of no way that radio can be operated except on the basis of a license from the Government, for the simple reason that there are not enough air channels to take care of all the radio stations that might want to operate. Therefore, there must be a limitation upon them.

When the Government has the power to issue licenses to operate radios it inherently follows that this Government agency has too great a control over freedom of speech. Whether the Radio Commission or any other Government agency turns it hand, the fact remains that throughout the years the broadcasting systems which are looking to the Radio Commission for courtesies are going to be found upon the side of the administration in power. So, after all, the real protection of the people yet rests in the freedom of the press rather than in freedom of speech since the coming of radio.

We have had a fair example of this since this administration came into power. I have no concrete evidence that this administration has laid down upon any radio station and said, "You must carry new-deal propaganda, and you must not carry anything to the contrary," yet the fact remains that radio broadcasters currying the favor of a

Government agency, have given unlimited facilities to new-deal propaganda and have unwarrantedly denied the right of the air to those who would rise to criticize any part of the new-deal program.

I have no personal complaint. No Republican Member of Congress can have any personal complaint, so far as I know. It is my understanding that a Republican Member of Congress can get on the air whenever he wants to with either of the chains on any reasonable time or occasion, but there it stops. The ordinary private citizen who is a Republican cannot get on the air to discuss the other side of some of this so-called "new-deal" legislation. . . .

So in conclusion I wish to say that with all the greatness of radio, the liberty of the people of this country yet rests in the press and not in the radio. I hope that at some time a plan may be devised whereby the use of the air will be free without censorship or discrimination. . . .

MR. WEARIN. Mr. Chairman, I rise . . . to ask a few questions of the chairman of the committee, if he will be so kind as to answer them. On page 142 is a provision that "the Commission shall at all times have access to and the right of inspection and examination of all accounts, records, and memoranda," and so forth. That reminds me, and if I am wrong I trust the chairman will correct me, that it is the general procedure to incorporate such a provision in all legislation that creates or, for that matter, reorganizes the existing Commission from the standpoint of investigating books, records of that corporation.

MR. RAYBURN. That is true. That is in the Interstate Commerce Act. Section 20 gives that authority over common carriers.

MR. WEARIN. That is my understanding. But they did not have that provision in the Stockyards Act of 1921. That does not give that authority. Now, there is one other question in reference to the bill from the standpoint of supervision that extends over radio stations: I presume that goes to all stations regardless of their size?

MR. RAYBURN. If that is the law, it now remains in the bill, because we do not amend the Radio Act.

MR. WEARIN. Now, with reference to the operation, does it affect the small mutual companies that operate within the States?

MR. RAYBURN. They are not affected. . . .

The Clerk read as follows:

ORDERS NOT FOR PAYMENT OF MONEY—WHEN EFFECTIVE

SEC. 408. Except as otherwise provided in this act, all orders of the Commission, other than orders for the payment of money, shall take effect within such reasonable time, not less than 30 days after service of the order, and shall continue in force until its further order, or for a specified period of time, according as shall be prescribed in the order, unless the same shall be suspended or modified or set aside by the Commission, or be suspended or set aside by a court of competent jurisdiction.

MR. CULKIN. Mr. Chairman, I move to strike out the last word, and I do so briefly to call to the attention of the Committee and those on both sides of the House who may be conferees on this bill, the importance of the reenactment of section 29, which is found on page 30 of the Radio Laws of the United States, a pamphlet, without number, that covers all radio enactments since the beginning. Section 29 is really the Magna Carta of the whole procedure and covers generally the complaints that have been made here today with regard to the freedom of the air. Section 29 provides:

That nothing in this act shall be understood or construed to give the licensing authority the power of censorship over radio communications or signals transmitted by any radio station, and no regulation or condition shall be promulgated or fixed by the licensing authority which shall interfere with the right of free speech by means of radio communication.

Of course, that section is in the law. It is complicated by the fact that under the law now a broadcasting station is liable for an action in slander and so it must necessarily have power, as a newspaper has to edit what appears in the newspaper, but this section, I am informed, is not in the Senate bill, but it is reenacted in the House bill; and I expressly commend it to the tender care of the House conferees on both sides of the aisle when the bill goes to conference. It is of the highest importance that this section should be retained in the law. . . .

THE CHAIRMAN. The motion occurs on the committee substitute for the Senate bill.

The committee substitute was agreed to.

THE CHAIRMAN. Under the rule the Committee will rise.

Accordingly the Committee rose; and the Speaker having resumed the chair, Mr. Disney, Chairman of the Committee of the Whole House on the state of the Union, reported that that Committee had had under consideration the bill (S. 3285) to provide for the regulation of interstate and foreign communications by wire or radio, and for other purposes; and pursuant to House Resolution 411, he reported the bill back to the House with an amendment adopted in the Committee of the Whole.

THE SPEAKER. Under the rule, the previous question is ordered.

The question is on the adoption of the amendment.

The substitute amendment was agreed to.

THE SPEAKER. The question is on the third reading of the Senate bill.

The bill was ordered to be read a third time, and was read the third time.

THE SPEAKER. The question is on the passage of the bill.

The question was taken, and the bill was passed. . . .

Senate—73rd Congress, 2d Session
June 9, 1934

MR. DILL. Mr. President, I ask unanimous consent for the immediate consideration of the conference report on the bill (S. 3285) to provide for the regulation of interstate and foreign communications by wire or radio, and for other purposes.

There being no objection, the Senate proceeded to consider the report of the committee of conference on the disagreeing votes of the two Houses on the amendment of the House to the bill (S. 3285) to provide for the regulation of interstate and foreign communications by wire or radio, and for other purposes. . . .

I move that the report be agreed to.

MR. KING. Mr. President, I should like to ask the chairman of the committee, the Senator from Washington, whether in the agreement which has been reached there is any provision which will restrict the authority and power of the District of Columbia in handling and exercising jurisdiction over public utilities.

MR. DILL. Mr. President, I think nothing in this bill would seriously restrict in any way, unless it might be in connection with the exchanges of the city which run out into the States. We have attempted in the bill to avoid even that restriction. I think the occasion for the suggestion being made to the Senator is that in the House amendment there was a provision, in the form of a definition, which would have given the commission control of the telephone and telegraph rates in the District of Columbia, but the House receded on that provision; so that, so far as we can know, we believe the power of the District of Columbia will not be interfered with.

MR. KING. Mr. President, I want to be assured of that fact, because I could not support the conference report if I believed that within the pages of the bill and within the report there were provisions which would restrict the District of Columbia, through its government, through Congress, in exercising full and proper authority over the public utilities within the District. That is a matter belonging exclusively to the District of Columbia, and I would not be willing to impinge upon that authority, and if the bill should do so, I should oppose the report.

MR. DILL. I think I can assure the Senator that it does not.

THE VICE PRESIDENT. The question is on agreeing to the conference report.

The report was agreed to.

House of Representatives—73rd Congress, 2d Session
June 9, 1934

CONFERENCE REPORT

The committee of conference on the disagreeing votes of the two Houses on the amendment of the House to the bill (S. 3285) to provide for the regulation of interstate and foreign communications by wire or radio, and for other purposes, having met, after full and free conference have agreed to recommend and do recommend to their respective Houses as follows:

That the Senate recede from its disagreement to the amendment of the House and agree to the same with an amendment as follows:

In lieu of the matter proposed to be inserted by the House amendment insert the following: [The text of the Act as passed follows]

And the House agree to the same.

That the title of the bill be amended to read as follows: "An act to provide for the regulation of interstate and foreign communication by wire or radio, and for other purposes."

Sam Rayburn
Clarence Lea
Carl E. Mapes
Chas. A. Wolverton
Managers on the part of the House

C. C. Dill
E. D. Smith
Carl A. Hatch
James Couzens
Wallace H. White, Jr.
Managers on the part of the Senate

STATEMENT

The managers on the part of the House at the conference on the disagreeing votes of the two Houses on the amendment of the House to the bill (S. 3285) to provide for the regulation of interstate and foreign communications by wire or radio, and for other purposes, submit the following statement in explanation of the effect of the action agreed upon by the conferees and recommended in the accompanying conference report:

The House amendment strikes out all of the Senate bill after the enacting clause. The Senate recedes from its disagreement to the House amendment with an amendment which is a substitute for both the Senate bill and the House amendment. The differences between the House amendment and the substitute agreed upon by the conferees are noted in the following outline, except for incidental changes made necessary by reason of the action of the conferees and minor and clarifying changes.

The Senate bill provides in section 2 for the application of the act to the licensing and regulating of all radio stations as provided in the act. The House amendment omits this provision. In view of the action taken by the conferees in respect of title III of the bill, the substitute retains the provision of the Senate bill.

Section 3 (e) of the Senate bill defines "interstate communication" and "interstate transmission." The House amendment contains a corresponding definition but differs from the Senate bill in certain respects. The Senate bill includes communication or transmission from or to the United States to or from the Philippine Islands or the Canal Zone only insofar as it takes place within the United States. The House amendment includes such communication or transmission in its entirety. The Senate bill excludes wire communication between points within the same State which passes through another State or a foreign country, when such communication is regulated by a State commission. The House amendment includes communication or transmission between points within the same State which passes through another State, but does not include such communication or transmission which passes through a foreign country, irrespective of regulation by a State commission. The Senate bill does not include communication or transmission wholly within the same Territory or possession or the District of Columbia. The House amendment includes such communication and transmission, except in the case of the Philippine Islands and the Canal Zone. The substitute adopts the provisions of the Senate definition.

The Senate amendment defines "common carrier" or "carrier" to mean any person engaged as a common carrier for hire in interstate or foreign communication by wire or radio or in interstate or foreign radio transmission of energy. In the House amendment the terms are defined to mean any person engaged in communication by wire or radio as a common carrier for hire. The substitute (sec. 3 (h)) adopts the Senate provision. It is to be noted that the definition does not include any person if not a common carrier in the ordinary sense of the term, and therefore does not include press associations or other organizations engaged in the business of collecting and distributing news services which may refuse to furnish to any person service which they are capable of furnishing, and may furnish service under varying arrangements, establishing the service to be rendered, the terms under which rendered, and the charges therefor.

The Senate bill provides for a Federal Communications Commission of five commissions with terms of 6 years. The House amendment provides for 7 commissioners with terms of 7 years. The substitute adopts the House provision.

Section 4 (f) of the Senate bill provides for appointment and salaries of officers and employees of the Commission. The House amendment contains a somewhat similar provision, which is retained in the substitute, except that it reduces the maxima of the salaries of the chief counsel and chief engineer from $10,000 to $9,000 per annum and of the directors of divisions from $8,000 to $7,500 per annum, following the Senate bill in both cases. It also fixes the salary of the secretary of the Commission at a maximum of $7,500, as provided in the Senate bill.

Both the Senate bill and the House amendment provide for publication of the Commission's records and proceedings, but the Senate bill authorizes the Commission to withhold publication of such records or proceedings as contain secret information affecting the national defense. The House amendment omits this authorization. The substitute adopts the Senate provision.

The Senate bill provides for two designated divisions of the Commission and fixes the jurisdiction of these divisions and of the Commission over the various subjects of the bill. The House amendment follows the provisions of section 17 of the Interstate Commerce Act, as amended, and provides that the Commission may fix its own divisions (not in excess of three) and make its own assignment of work thereto, and may assign certain of its work to individual commissioners or boards of employees. The substitute adopts the House provision.

Title II of the Senate bill and of the House amendment relate to the regulation of common carriers. The only substantial differences between the House amendment and the substitute are found in sections 214 and 220.

Section 214 of the Senate bill (requiring a certificate of public convenience and necessity for construction, operation, or extension of lines) exempts from the requirements of the section lines within a single State unless such lines constitute part of an interstate line. The House amendment qualifies the words "interstate line" by the word "additional." The substitute adopts the Senate provision. The Senate bill also exempts local, branch, or terminal lines not exceeding 10 miles in length. The House amendment omits the 10-mile limitation. The substitute restores the limitation. The House amendment adds an exemption of wires or cables added to existing pole lines or conduits or other structures constituting established routes. In view of the provision in both the Senate bill and the House amendment, under which the Commission, upon request, may authorize the supplementing of existing facilities without regard to the provisions of section 214, the substitute omits the House provision. The House amendment also excepts lines acquired under section 221 (relating to consolidation of telephone companies). The substitute retains this provision.

Section 220 (j) of the Senate bill (relating to accounts and depreciation charges) authorizes the Commission to investigate and report to Congress upon the desirability of legislation authorizing the Commission to except the carriers of any particular class or classes in any State from the requirements of the section and permitting State commissions to prescribe their own percentage rates of depreciation and systems of accounts for carriers. The House amendment (sec. 220 (h)) specifically authorizes the Commission to except carriers of any particular class or classes in any State and provides (in sec. 220 (j)) that the section shall not limit the power of the State commissions to prescribe percentage rates of depreciation or to require the keeping of accounts. The substitute adopts the House provision as to exception of particular classes of carriers and a modified provision for investigation and report to Congress as to the need for defining or harmonizing Federal and State authority in respect of other matters to which the section relates.

The Senate bill abolishes the Federal Radio Commission and repeals the Radio Act of 1927, but in effect reenacts it in title III, eliminating certain matter no longer effective, and adding certain provisions, most of which are taken from H. R. 7716, Seventy-second Congress, which passed both Houses but was pocket vetoed. Title III of the House bill abolishes the Federal Radio Commission but transfers its functions under the Radio Act of 1927 to the new Commission. Title III of the substitute adopts the provisions of the Senate bill, except that most of the changes from existing law which were not contained in H. R. 7716 have been omitted.

The provisions of the Radio Act of 1927 relating to judicial review have been included in title IV, with certain changes, and those for taking over stations in time of war are in title VI, and so far as they change existing law will be explained below. The other differences between the substitute and the Radio Act of 1927, except where the changes are insubstantial or are for purposes of clarification or of elimination of temporary provisions which no longer serve any purpose, are listed below.

Sections 301, 302 (a), 304, 306, 309, 313, 314, 315, 317, 318, 319, 320, 321, 322, 323, 324, 325 (a), 326, 327, 328, and 329 are, respectively, substantially identical with the following sections of the Radio Act of 1927: 1, 2, 5, 8, 11, 15, 17, 18, 19, 20, 21, 22, 23, 24, 25, 26, 29, 30, 35, and 36.

Section 302 (a) follows closely section 2 of the Radio Act, Section 302 (b) follows H.R. 7716 in removing the Territories and possessions from the zones for which equality of broadcasting facilities is prescribed.

Section 303 combines sections 4 and 5 of the Radio Act with the additions hereafter noted. Section 303 (f) adds the requirement of a public hearing in cases involving changes in the frequency, authorized power, or times of operation of any station. This was contained in H.R. 7716. Section 303 (g) directs the Commission to study new uses for radio and to encourage the more effective use of radio in the public interest. Section 303 (q) requires the painting or illumination of radio towers which constitute a menace to air navigation. This was contained in H.R. 7716.

Section 305 is copied from section 6 of the Radio Act, except that the provision for taking over a station in time of war is transferred to section 606 (c).

Section 307 (a) and (b) through the first proviso are taken from section 9 of the Radio Act, as amended. The second proviso authorizing additional licenses for stations not exceeding 100 watts of power when they will not interfere with the efficient service of other licensed stations, was taken from H.R. 7716. This proviso is substituted for that in the Senate bill which would permit additional noninterfering stations regardless of power.

Section 307 (c) directs the Commission to study the proposal that Congress by statute allocate fixed percentages of broadcasting facilities to particular types of nonprofit programs or to persons identified with particular kinds of nonprofit activities.

Section 307 (d) follows part of section 9 of the Radio Act with the addition taken from H.R. 7716, that the Commission in granting an application for the renewal of a license shall be governed by the same considerations which affect the granting of original applications. The provision of the Senate bill which reduces the maximum terms of broadcasting licenses from 3 years to 1 year, and the maximum for other licenses from 5 years to 3 years, is not included.

The substitute bill agreed to in conference omits the paragraph of the Senate bill no. 307 (f), which carried a new provision requiring the Commission to distribute broadcasting licenses so that no one licensee or organization of licensees should exercise dominant control over the broadcasting facilities of any locality.

Section 308 follows section 10 of the Radio Act as proposed to be modified by H.R. 7716, which added the requirement that modifications and renewals of licenses may be granted only upon written application. This is the present practice of the Radio Commission. The two provisos in subsection (a) permit the Commission to issue temporary licenses for stations on vessels or aircraft in cases of emergency.

Section 310 (a), dealing with limitation on foreign holdings and transfer of licenses, is adapted from section 12 of the Radio Act as proposed to be modified by H.R. 7716, with additional limitations as to foreign ownership.

Section 12 of the Radio Act provides that radio station licenses may not be granted or transferred to any corporation of which any officer or director is an alien or of which more than one-fifth of the capital stock may be voted by aliens, their representatives, a foreign government, or a company organized under the laws of a foreign country. The Senate bill changes this provision by making the restriction apply also where one-fifth of the capital stock is owned of record by the designated persons and altering the words "may be voted" to "is voted." The substitute (sec. 310 (a) (4)) adopts the language of the Senate bill.

Section 12 of the Radio Act, restricting alien control of radio station licenses does not apply to holding companies. The Senate bill, adapted from H.R. 7716, provides that such licenses might not be granted to or held by any corporation controlled by another corporation of which any officer or more than one-fourth of the directors are aliens or of which more than one-fourth of the capital stock is owned of record or voted, after June 1, 1935, by aliens, their representatives, a foreign government, or a corporation organized under the laws of a foreign country. The substitute (sec. 310 (a) (5)) adopts the Senate provision with an addition stating that the license may not be granted to or held by such a corporation if the Commission finds that the public interest will be served by the refusal or the revocation of such license.

Section 310 (b) is substantially section 12 of the Radio Act modified as proposed by H.R. 7716. The section relates to transfer of radio licenses. As in H.R. 7716 the authority to approve or disapprove such transfers is extended to cover transfer of stock control in a licensee corporation. The present law is also modified to require the Commission to secure full information before reaching decision on such transfers.

Section 311 is based upon section 13 of the Radio Act, modified to leave the Commission discretion in refusing licenses where the applicant has been adjudged by a court to be guilty of a violation of the antitrust laws but where the judgment has not extended to the revocation of existing licenses.

Section 312 (a) is based on section 14 of the Radio Act modified as proposed by H.R. 7716 to reduce from 30 to 15 days the period within which a licensee may take exception to the Commission's action in revoking his license. The Senate provision authorizing the Commission to suspend licenses is omitted from the substitute.

Section 312 (b) amplifies the Radio Act along the lines proposed by H.R. 7716 by providing for the modification of station licenses and construction permits in cases where the Commission finds such action in the public interest.

Section 315 on facilities for candidates for public office is the same as section 18 of the Radio Act. The Senate provisions, which would have modified and extended the present law is not included in the substitute.

Section 316 provides that no person shall broadcast by means of any radio station any information concerning any lottery, gift enterprise, or similar scheme offering prizes dependent in whole or in part upon lot or chance. This is not in the present law, but was included in H.R. 7716.

Section 325 (b) and (c) are designed to give the Commission control of all studios or apparatus in the United States used in connection with a broadcasting station in a foreign country for the purpose of furnishing programs to be transmitted back into the United States. The House Committee on Merchant Marine, Radio, and Fisheries has, during the present session, favorably reported a bill, S. 2660, containing provisions similar to these two paragraphs.

Section 326 prohibits censorship, and is the same as section 29 of the Radio Act.

The Senate bill—section 402—for the purposes of cases involving carriers, carries forward the existing method of review of orders of the Interstate Commerce Commission, and, in the main, for "radio" cases carries forward the existing method of review of orders of the Federal Radio Commission; but in "radio" cases involving affirmative orders of the Commission entered in proceedings initiated upon the Commission's own motion in revocation, modification, and suspension matters, review is to be by the method applicable in the case of orders of the Interstate Commerce Commission. The House provision contains a similar provision as to cases involving carriers, but leaves the present section 16 of the Radio Act of 1927, as amended, applicable in all radio cases. The substitute adopts the Senate provision.

Section 405 of the Senate bill, relating to rehearings by the Commission, contained a proviso limiting to 20 days the time within which applications for rehearing of radio cases under title III may be made and providing that such application may be made by any party or any person aggrieved or whose interests are adversely affected. The House amendment omitted the proviso. The substitute adopts the provision of the Senate bill.

Section 410 (a) of the Senate bill provides for joint boards of members of commissions of States affected by or involved in a particular proceeding, to which the Commission may refer such proceedings. The House amendment omits this provision. It is retained in the substitute.

The House amendment contains a provision, similar to one contained in the Senate bill, transferring all appropriations and unexpended balances of appropriations available for expenditure by the Federal Radio Commission to the Federal Communications Commission. The substitute retains the House provision modified to insure that such appropriations and unexpended balances of appropriations will be available for expenditure by the Federal Communications Commission for any and all objects of expenditure authorized by the bill, in the discretion of the Commission and without regard to the requirement of apportionment of the Anti-Deficiency Act of February 27, 1906.

Section 606 (c) and (d) of the Senate bill authorizes the President in time of war or public peril to take over wire and radio offices and stations and to give just compensation therefor to persons entitled thereto. The House amendment omits these provisions. The substitute conforms to the House bill by adopting the present provisions of sections 6 and 7 of the Radio Act of 1927, as amended, which do not apply to wire communications.

The committee of conference recommends that the title of the bill read as follows: "An act to provide for the regulation of interstate and foreign communication by wire or radio, and for other purposes."

> *Sam Rayburn*
> *Clarence Lea*
> *Carl E. Mapes*
> *Chas. A. Wolverton*
> *Managers on the part of the House*

MR. BLAND. Mr. Speaker, it is not customary for me to ask for the rejection of a conference report, I do so very reluctantly on this occasion, particularly, as this report comes from a committee presided over by such a distinguished friend of mine as the gentleman from Texas; but I believe the situation that presents itself on this conference report is one that deserves serious consideration.

The Senate has undertaken to repeal the Radio Act of 1927, which was framed with the greatest care, most meticulous attention being given to every word and every expression that is contained in that act. They do the useless or futile thing, so far as radio is concerned, of repealing the law and then reenacting the same law.

Now, the question might arise, What difference does it make? It may make a most material difference in a new set-up.

Under the Radio Act of 1927 there have been handed down judicial decisions, there have been interpretations, and there has been a coordinating of radio. If we repeal this act, with a new set-up, without a study by the Communications Commission, there is no man on this floor who can tell what the effect of this repeal is.

In order to secure the continuance of this act you have to vote down this conference report.

Has the matter been considered by a committee of this House? I mean no reflection on the distinguished gentlemen of the Interstate and Foreign Commerce Committee, but they conceded themselves upon this floor 1 week ago that they knew nothing about radio, and they said that they believed the wise thing to do—and it was a wise judgment on their part—was to set up a communications commission which could study the law and find out just what ought to be done. They thought it wise then to continue the law as it is at the present time, simply transferring the powers and functions of the Radio Commission to the communications commission; but under the dulcet persuasion of the Senate committee, which is the only committee that has considered this particular legislation, and surrendering to the charm which has been exercised by the distinguished Members of the Senate who are on that committee, our friends, who are usually so very persistent, found themselves writing into the law provisions that they, themselves, had conceded they knew nothing about.

I submit that in as delicate an art as the radio art, and with its effect upon the public and the public interests involved, the conference report ought to be rejected. The result would simply be that the committee would go back, these new provisions would be struck out, and the bill would be returned as it was written by the House. The bill then would set up the communications commission and permit the communications commission to study this most delicate art. That commission would report to what extent the Radio Act of 1927 should be amended.

I mean no reflection upon my friends on the Interstate and Foreign Commerce Committee.

They did not have the time to go to the bottom of this matter; they had most important matters to consider. Radio has always been in the Committee on Merchant Marine, Radio, and Fisheries, and, as I said some time ago, why should this one ewe lamb be taken away? Leave it where it can be studied by that committee; and, gentlemen, do not repeal an act that may materially affect your interests. . . .

MR. LEHLBACH. Mr. Speaker, we have a situation where we are passing most important legislation on the say-so of the Senate which has never been considered by the House of Representatives. We have been called rubber stamps of the Government, but we have never passed 20 pages of a radio act, repealing the existing radio law on the recommendation of the Senate without a single Member of the House who knows anything about radio giving the slightest consideration to it. Why should we be errand boys for the Senate Committee on Commerce to wipe out the old Radio Act and enact a brand-new radio act, a very important measure, without the slightest consideration by any committee or any individual in the House of Representatives.

When this bill was introduced here there was not a change made in the radio law. It merely created a commission and vested the control and administration of the radio law in a communications commission instead of the Radio Commission.

At that time the question was raised whether the jurisdiction over that bill, the communications bill, belonged to the Radio Committee or the Interstate Commerce Committee. It was asserted and emphasized by the Chairman of the Committee on Interstate and Foreign Commerce that there was no change in the bill with respect to the substantive radio law, and that seemed to be the compelling reason why the bill was referred to the Committee on Interstate and Foreign Commerce rather than to the Committee on Merchant Marine, Radio, and Fisheries.

Now, the conferees have written into the bill at the behest of the Senate a radio law consisting of 20 pages—page 20 to page 38 in the conference report.

Why is the House asked to accept the Senate say-so in this radio legislation? Why should not the House in the preservation of its dignity send back the conference report and eliminate the substantive radio act; as my chairman from Virginia says, let the Communications Committee study the law and recommend changes in the law that are desirable to be made, and let the House committee having jurisdiction consider that question and report with respect thereto and, after debate on the floor, enact the law as the House in its dignity ought to do? [Applause.] . . .

MR. McFADDEN. Mr. Speaker, this legislation comes as the result of a message by the President to the Congress. Simultaneously with the delivery of that message there was delivered to the Committee on Interstate and Foreign Commerce, of the House, and a similar committee of the Senate, a draft of the particular legislation which was recommended in the message. The Interstate and Foreign Commerce Committee of the House had never had jurisdiction over the question of radio. The Merchant Marine, Radio, and Fisheries Committee had, and has grown up with the growth of radio in the United States. Under this direction in the message of the President, jurisdiction for the consideration of this message was transferred to the Interstate and Foreign Commerce Committee, who were engaged to the full limit in the consideration of other measures that were being forced through the House under great pressure—the securities bill, railroad legislation, and stock-exchange control legislation. It is only fair to say that which we all know, and the members of that committee know, that they did not have time to fairly consider this bill. Apparently it was not thought necessary that we should carefully consider it, because it was generally understood that this bill was going to be written and perfected in conference, which has been done; and notwithstanding the assurance of the chairman, Mr. Rayburn, that was given to this House, that there was nothing in the House bill that affected the present radio law—and by that statement he was giving the House assurances that nothing in this bill was to change existing law—

MR. RAYBURN. O Mr. Speaker, the gentleman does not undertake to say that I said there would not be anything in the conference report.

MR. McFADDEN. No; I did not say that, but the gentleman was in close enough touch with this general situation to know in advance practically what was to be done in conference. So here we find ourselves in the predicament of considering one of the most important bills that could possibly come before this House, without any consideration on the part of the House, putting it through here in a few minutes. It is a fair example of what we may expect under the administration of this communications law, where we have consolidated all matters of communication in one commission. That applies to telephone and telegraph, radio, national and international, one of the most important parts of government. I say to the House that which I believe: That this bill was written, or at least the controlling and important part of it, in conformity with the wishes of the people who control this industry, and propose to control it as a monopoly, to control public sentiment in the United States, to control it now immediately for political purposes as part of the administration in control, and eventually use it as an international control for the dissemination of information leading toward the destruction of constitutional government in the United States. The passage of this bill is quite in harmony with the regulation that is taking place in Canada, with the regulations of communications that is taking place in Great Britain. It is all tied in together. We have as much of an international finger in this as we have in our financial affairs. I point out to the Membership of the House that this bill is being jammed through under the authority of the administration for these very purposes.

MR. RAYBURN. Mr. Speaker, I did not intend to detain the House at all, but the gentleman from Pennsylvania [Mr. McFadden] as usual has his alarmer at work. In answer to his statement about this bill being put through under the spur of the administration, I remind him that the minority members of the Committee on Interstate and Foreign Commerce, who I think are as wise and patriotic as he or any other Member of the House, signed this report, and that the report is a unanimous report from that conference committee. Also, practically every change in the Radio Act made by this bill was passed in a bill through both the House and the Senate, which went to President Hoover and there met with a pocket veto. As far as jamming legislation through the House is concerned, I introduced a bill to create this commission in the early part of 1933, and the question has been up before the committee and the country ever since. This bill has been in the committee for several weeks. We took it up and had thorough hearings, we had thorough consideration of the bill that passed the House. The Senate and the House in a former Congress considered title III of this bill, and we were assured by the Senate conferees that these amendments were practically every one contained in that bill. . . .

MR. LEHLBACH. The communications bill introduced by the gentleman or drafted by the gentleman in 1933, and the bill that was reported from the committee unanimously in this session of Congress, did not contain substantive radio legislation.

MR. RAYBURN. No.

MR. LEHLBACH. That is what we are complaining about. We are enacting a law dictated by the chairman which we have never considered.

MR. RAYBURN. And we claim that this legislation has already been passed by both the House and the Senate. . . .

MR. RAMSPECK. Mr. Speaker, I join with my colleague from Virginia [Mr. Bland] and my colleague from New Jersey [Mr. Lehlbach] in opposition to this conference report. Every Member of this House, perhaps, has in his district a radio station or several of them. Millions of dollars have been invested in those plants, and we are proposing here in this conference report to wipe out the law under which those stations have been established, or to wipe out everything that has gone heretofore and reenact it under an act which we are asked to pass here in a few minutes and which we have had no opportunity to examine. No committee of the House which has given study or thought to radio legislation has had an opportunity to consider this matter.

It seems to me it is unwise, it is unjust to our people back home, to enact legislation of such far-reaching effect in this manner. Radio stations, under the best conditions, lead a very uncertain life. The Commission has authority to take them off of the air on very short notice. I do not think we ought to place in jeopardy the investments of our people back home by enacting legislation in this manner. I think if we are going to reenact the radio law, which I think is unnecessary, it ought to be considered by the committee of this House which has jurisdiction of it, upon which committee there are Members who have given years of study to that subject.

For that reason I expect to vote against the adoption of the conference report, and I hope it will be rejected. [Applause.] . . .

MR. MAPES. Mr. Speaker, I see nothing unusual in this situation. Of course there are always differences between the Senate and the House to be ironed out in every conference. Otherwise, there would be no occasion for the appointment of a conference committee. The Senate bill referred to the Committee on Interstate and Foreign Commerce, repealed, in effect, the existing radio law, and at the same time it reenacted all of the material provisions of that act. . . .

MR. BLAND. Has the House had an opportunity to consider what are the material provisions of that act that are repealed?

MR. MAPES. Yes; it did when the bill was in the House. Instead of following the action of the Senate in that respect, the House did this: It left the existing law intact but established a new communications commission. It does not seem to me there was any great difference in principle in the action of the two bodies in that respect. The Senate specifically repealed the Radio Act, but reenacted it, or the pertinent part of it, in express terms. The House, instead of reenacting it, left it as it was and created this new commission. . . .

As I was saying there was not such a material difference between the action of the House and the Senate as some would be led to believe from the discussion this afternoon. In conference the Senate conferees accepted the House provision for a new commission, and the House conferees accepted the work of the Senate on this radio provision or made it the basis upon which an agreement was reached. There is nothing in this bill under the radio title of importance which has not been considered by the Committee on Merchant Marine, Radio, and Fisheries of the House of Representatives, and which has not passed both the House and Senate at different times. . . .

The whole matter is set up in the report of the conference on page 47, in the paragraph at about the middle of the page:

> The Senate bill abolishes the Federal Radio Commission and repeals the Radio Act of 1927, but in effect reenacts it in title III, eliminating certain matter no longer effective and adding certain provisions, most of which are taken from H.R. 7716, Seventy-second Congress, which passed both Houses but was pocket vetoed. Title III of the House bill abolishes the Federal Radio Commission, but transfers its functions under the Radio Act of 1927 to the new commission. Title III of the substitute adopts the provisions of the Senate bill, except that most of the changes from existing law which were not contained in H.R. 7716 have been omitted. . . .

MR. LEHLBACH. The statement which has just been read says it reenacts, in effect, leaving out certain matters that are no longer necessary and putting in some other general provisions. Has any Member of the House conference committee examined the old law and the new law that is proposed in order to ascertain just what differences there may be, and if they have not, has any other Member of the House who knows anything about it had that opportunity?

MR. MAPES. Of course, the conferees went over every provision of this new matter and passed upon it, exercising their best judgment in regard to it. Our judgment may not have been as good as the judgment of the members of the Radio Committee would have been, but we were confronted with this legislation and had to exercise such judgment as we had.

MR. LEHLBACH. How could reading a new bill give you any idea how it changed the old law that you did not know and had not read? . . .

MR. WILLFORD. Mr. Speaker, as a member of the Committee on Merchant Marine, Radio, and Fisheries, I have listened while this bill has been both cussed and discussed over quite a period of time. We have listened attentively to the explanation of this bill by the chairman of this great committee, the gentleman from Virginia, Mr. Bland; we have taken the consensus of opinion of the members of this committee and have arrived at the conclusion expressed in the House bill. I believe, however, that more time should be given to a thorough study and consideration of this subject. We had before the committee men who had spent their entire time since its discovery in the study of radio.

I recognize the fact of controversial theory of freedom of speech. However, I believe that a more general version should be given this meaning; and a right to give our views in speech on radio or in the press should be more liberal, as I believe is the right that we are all entitled to and a liberty guaranteed by our Constitution in amendment no. 1, passed during the first session of Congress, September 25, 1789. My attempt is not to make a judicial basis on which to judge freedom of speech, but I wish to apply it to our modern life, in which views, regardless of their nature, should have the right to be brought before our people for their judgment and opinion. As a member of the House Radio Committee, this freedom of speech is a serious consideration. In a news periodical in which the Radio Commission intimated it was not unlawful to allow liquor advertisements to be put on the air but that if any of the stations did advertise liquor they would have difficulty in renewing their licenses, as radio stations must make application for a new one every 6 months—this, in my opinion, is unfair. The Commission, in my judgment, should either state it is unlawful for such advertising or it is lawful. I believe the individual station owners and their respective communities are much concerned over the morals of their people, and, as a matter of fact, it is the listeners and the public themselves that will primarily make the rule by which radio stations and press will follow. This happens to be just one example that has clearly struck me as not being fair. All of us, as individuals, are much concerned with the welfare of our own country and our own communities, but a small percent would attempt to bring before its listeners or readers anything with the intention of degrading our morals. I believe, however, there are subjects, regardless of nature, which should be reviewed by the people and their opinion expressed, as knowledge prevents disaster.

It is unfortunately true that the lack of knowledge on subjects leads into despair and discouragement. We can guide ourselves only by facts and our collective opinions. The people of this country and of the world are privileged to listen to all problems by the wonderful systems of communications, radios, periodicals, and newspapers. The United States, especially, can proudly say that nearly every home in this country has either radio, newspapers, or magazines for their enjoyment and education. By this means of communication, problems of a nation can be quickly presented to them for their opinion and consideration. The press fortunately has enjoyed a broad freedom in which they can advocate or bring to the people their views in editorials and in columns, by various writers. I believe this same privilege should be extended to the radio stations of these United States without any political hatchet ready to sacrifice them if their principles are not pleasing. I do believe that regulation is necessary in all things. However, mere words written or spoken must be judged from several angles and especially from a point of view as to who makes these statements and for what purpose. The right of free speech and printed words can hardly exist without mechanical facilities, whether it is writing a letter, newspapers, publications, or radio. Therefore, I deem it necessary to liberalize the scope in which newspapers, magazines, and radio deal without political curtailment or foreign pressure brought to bear to print or broadcast the opinions expressed by individuals. It might be well to bear in mind the Virginia declaration made in 1786, which was several years before the first amendment to the Federal Constitution. The declaration was—

The State of Virginia had no right or authority over the opinion of any source and should not be involved in any manner or interfere until actual injury had resulted.

This significant amendment has a great bearing in favor of liberalized freedom of speech and press. And if you will recall when the Federalist Party was defeated and Thomas Jefferson became President of the United States he pardoned every man convicted under the alien and sedition law, as he believed that any person had a right to his own opinion and expression. It is my opinion that the radio and newspapers are two of the greatest mediums that the human race has ever had an opportunity of availing themselves of for an interchange of opinion and expression of thought. Therefore, the radio and press should be protected from any interference for our own welfare and education. Fortunately, the value of press and radio are as informatives of the Nation, as has been demonstrated by our President, Franklin D. Roosevelt, who has taken his problems, his plans for the present and future, before the people by personally talking over the radio and interviewing the press reporters who give the American people the information as to the progress of our Government.

I do not personally believe there should be any rivalry between radio broadcasting and the newspapers of this country. They are both serving the people in their respective ways, and I truly believe that they themselves realize they can work hand in hand with a profit to themselves and a direct benefit to this Nation. As a member of the Radio Committee, I am vitally interested in the future of our radio broadcasts, and with this I have in mind the relationship of the newspapers of this country. These two cannot ever be replaced by any substitute. I do not for one moment uphold any unscrupulous broadcaster or newspaperman who deliberately, by direct intent, incites trouble or maliciously attacks a principle or person without foundation of facts; but the truth should never be suppressed, as by that we can best see our mistakes. With what little knowledge and experience I have had in the world I shall always be the defender of free speech of the radio and newspaper. I do not believe that the system of the Radio Commission of a 6-month license is adequate protection or encouraging to the present-day broadcaster. I believe these licenses should be issued for 3 to 5 years and should be inviolable except where charges of malicious intent or violation of such rules that are equitable in fairness of radio broadcasters is violated. I believe radio broadcasters should have the privilege of expressing their views editorially, as newspapers do, and they should not be suppressed by quiet threats or the impossibility of renewal of licenses or any other way that is used against an unfriendly or disliked broadcaster. I am positive in my statement when I say I do not believe that our Radio Commission is responsible for even intent upon this procedure. However, I believe their rules and regulations could be changed for better protection in the interest of radio. In my opinion, the suppression of radio broadcasters as has been used in the past is not fair and equitable. About 4 years ago the Radio Commission issued licenses for 90 days only, and then, on January 1, 1931, Congress allowed the Commission to issue licenses for a 3-year limit. However, the Radio Commission only raised their license limit from 90 days to 6 months, and then every broadcaster had to make application for a renewal. The sad part of this, in my estimation, is that there has been some unscrupulous dealings in the matter of applications, as it is the privilege of any station to make application for a frequency held by another station every 6 months, which would cause an expensive hearing and would cost the broadcaster whose license had been asked for from $500 to $2,000, and if someone with malicious intent and sufficient money should make application every 6 months to someone in the industry that he did not like, it would finally wear him out. This has been done, and I shall do everything I can do to correct this evil.

The radio broadcaster today must be extremely careful in his statements, he must be generous and diplomatic, because if he should say something that was distasteful to authority, he would be censured. He also must be careful not to express any pointed opinion of his own, as the public would quickly take it up, and radio, like no other field, is either praised or condemned instantly. The speaker must present his problem in a generous and even temper. He must present the problem and let the audience be the judge. The listening public will not tolerate continuous propaganda, and even sponsors of programs have found it advisable to be very brief and make simple statements regarding their products—yet they have found that the greatest results have been in these simple statements. There is no doubt, in my mind, that discrimination has taken place when opposite views were presented. This evil should be corrected and freedom of the air should be available to anyone. We must have, if you please, rules and regulations governing our methods and procedure. Let us not, however, put strict censorship on the press or radio. Let us be generous and restrict censorship so that freedom of opinion can be expressed without punishment. It is my purpose as a member of the Radio Committee to acquaint myself with as many facts as possible and at all times work in the interest of our system of education by radio and newspaper. . . .

MR. BLANTON. Mr. Speaker, we have not been able to do it in this session, but I am hopeful that the next Congress will fairly and justly reallocate wave lengths, channels, and power so that broadcasting stations may be granted to and equitably distributed throughout the various districts of the United States. Due consideration must be given to each congressional district. Under the present system the big cities have gobbled up all of the important stations, wave lengths, channels, and power. . . .

MR. LEHLBACH. Does not the gentleman realize that a revision of existing radio laws in the next Congress, desirable as it may be, will be precluded if we enact a new radio law by accepting this conference report?

MR. BLANTON. Nothing will be precluded, and everything will be possible, if a majority of the Members of this House in the next Congress set their heads and concertedly work together, with a determined purpose to fairly and justly distribute and reallocate stations, wave lengths, channels, and power. All obstacles can be overcome, and anything they want done can be done by a determined majority. . . .

MR. RAYBURN. Mr. Speaker, I move the previous question on the adoption of the conference report.

The previous question was ordered.

THE SPEAKER. The question is on the adoption of the conference report.

The question was taken; and on a division (demanded by Mr. Ramspeck and Mr. Lehlbach) there were—ayes 58, noes 40. . . .

So the conference report was agreed to. . . .

THE DECISION

Commentary

In many ways, the most important decision on the powers of the Federal Communications Commission was that rendered in *National Broadcasting Co.* v. *United States*. It upholds the Chain Broadcasting Regulations as within the FCC's regulatory power, and thus endows the commission with authority to deal with what quickly became one of the major problems in broadcasting—the rise and dominance of the networks. But the *NBC* opinion is even broader in its implications. Justice Felix Frankfurter goes out of his way to uphold the standard of "public interest, convenience or necessity" contained in the Communications Act. In *Federal Radio Commission* v. *Nelson Bros. Bond & Mfg. Co.*, 289 U.S. 266 (1933), the Court had upheld the similar standard in the Radio Act of 1927, but had touched upon the matter only very briefly. The *NBC* opinion goes more fully into the matter. It recognizes that, under the Communications Act, the FCC is given very wide authority to regulate broadcasting. According to the Court, "The Commission was, however, not left at large in performing this duty. The touch-stone provided by Congress was the 'public interest, convenience or necessity,' a criterion which 'is as concrete as the complicated factors for judgment in such a field of delegated authority permit.' " In a field where the subject-matter of regulation is as fluid and dynamic as radio, a detailed prescription of standards could have made effective administration impossible. Congress, says the Court, would have frustrated "the purposes for which the Communications Act of 1934 was brought into being by attempting an itemized catalogue of the specific manifestations of the general problems, for the solution of which it was establishing a regulatory agency. That would have stereotyped the powers of the commission to specific details, in regulating a field of enterprise the dominant characteristic of which was the rapid pace of its unfolding."

But where does this leave the requirement of an ascertainable standard in legislation delegating powers to an administrative agency? Plainly, a standard such as that contained in the Communications Act is not mechanical or self-defining; it implies wide areas of judgment and, therefore, of discretion. If such a broad standard is considered adequate, then has not the requirement of a defined standard become a purely formal one and, if that is the case, has not the American law, in practice if not in theory, become similar to that in Britain, where there are no constitutional limitations to restrain Parliament from delegating authority how it will?

The Supreme Court would answer this by asserting that the generality of the phrasing in a statute, such as the Communications Act of 1934, does not mean that the applicable standards are too vague to canalize administrative discretion effectively. The statutory language is not to be read in a vacuum; a general standard may be given specific form and content when looked at in the light of the statutory scheme and its background. Thus the standard of "public interest" in the Communications Act is not so vague and indefinite as to be unconstitutional. As the *NBC* opinion puts it, "It is a mistaken assumption that this is a mere general reference to public welfare without any standard to guide determination. The purpose of the Act, the requirements it imposes, and the context of the provision in question, show the contrary."

One wonders, however, whether a standard such as that contained in the Communications Act really furnishes an effective legislative guide. Certainly a legislative direction to act in the "public interest" appears to add little to an enabling Act. Would the Federal Communications Commission be likely to act any differently in specific cases if the Communications Act did not specifically instruct it to be guided by "public interest, convenience or necessity"?

NATIONAL BROADCASTING CO. v. UNITED STATES
319 U.S. 190 (1943)

MR. JUSTICE FRANKFURTER delivered the opinion of the Court.

In view of our dependence upon regulated private enterprise in discharging the far-reaching role which radio plays in our society, a somewhat detailed exposition of the history of the present controversy and the issues which it raises is appropriate.

These suits were brought on October 30, 1941, to enjoin the enforcement of the Chain Broadcasting Regulations promulgated by the Federal Communications Commission on May 2, 1941, and amended on October 11, 1941. We held last Term in Columbia Broadcasting System v. United States, 316 U.S. 407, 62 S.Ct. 1194, 86 L. Ed. 1563, and Nat. Broadcasting Co. v. United States, 316 U.S. 447, 62 S.Ct. 1214, 86 L.Ed. 1586, that the suits could be maintained under § 402(a) of the Communications Act of 1934, 48 Stat. 1093, 47 U.S.C. § 402(a), 47 U.S.C.A. § 402(a) (incorporating by reference the Urgent Deficiencies Act of October 22, 1913, 38 Stat. 219, 28 U.S.C. § 47, 28 U.S.C.A. § 47), and that the decrees of the District Court dismissing the suits for want of jurisdiction should therefore be reversed. On remand the District Court granted the Government's motions for summary judgment and dismissed the suits on the merits. 47 F.Supp. 940. The cases are now here on appeal. 28 U.S.C. § 47, 28 U.S.C.A. § 47. Since they raise substantially the same issues and were argued together, we shall deal with both cases in a single opinion.

On March 18, 1938, the Commission undertook a comprehensive investigation to determine whether special regulations applicable to radio stations engaged in chain broadcasting[1] were required in the "public interest, convenience, or necessity." The Commission's order directed that inquiry be made, inter alia, in the following specific matters: the number of stations licensed to or affiliated with networks, and the

---

[1]Chain broadcasting is defined in § 3(p) of the Communications Act of 1934, 47 U.S.C.A. § 153(p), as the "simultaneous broadcasting of an identical program by two or more connected stations." In actual practice, programs are transmitted by wire, usually leased telephone lines, from their point of origination to each station in the network for simultaneous broadcast over the air.

amount of station time used or controlled by networks; the contractual rights and obligations of stations under their agreements with networks; the scope of network agreements containing exclusive affiliation provisions and restricting the network from affiliating with other stations in the same area; the rights and obligations of stations with respect to network advertisers; the nature of the program service rendered by stations licensed to networks; the policies of networks with respect to character of programs, diversification, and accommodation to the particular requirements of the areas served by the affiliated stations; the extent to which affiliated stations exercise control over programs, advertising contracts, and related matters; the nature and extent of network program duplication by stations serving the same area; the extent to which particular networks have exclusive coverage in some areas; the competitive practices of stations engaged in chain broadcasting; the effect of chain broadcasting upon stations not licensed to or affiliated with networks; practices or agreements in restraint of trade, or in furtherance of monopoly, in connection with chain broadcasting; and the scope of concentration of control over stations, locally, regionally, or nationally, through contracts, common ownership, or other means.

On April 6, 1938, a committee of three Commissioners was designated to hold hearings and make recommendations to the full Commission. This committee held public hearings for 73 days over a period of six months, from November 14, 1938, to May 19, 1939. Order No. 37, announcing the investigation and specifying the particular matters which would be explored at the hearings, was published in the Federal Register, 3 Fed.Reg. 637, and copies were sent to every station licensee and network organization. Notices of the hearings were also sent to these parties. Station licensees, national and regional networks, and transcription and recording companies were invited to appear and give evidence. Other persons who sought to appear were afforded an opportunity to testify. 96 witnesses were heard by the committee, 45 of whom were called by the national networks. The evidence covers 27 volumes, including over 8,000 pages of transcript and more than 700 exhibits. The testimony of the witnesses called by the national networks fills more than 6,000 pages, the equivalent of 46 hearing days.

The committee submitted a report to the Commission on June 12, 1940, stating its findings and recommendations. Thereafter, briefs on behalf of the networks and other interested parties were filed before the full Commission, and on November 28, 1940, the Commission issued proposed regulations which the parties were requested to consider in the oral arguments held on December 2 and 3, 1940. These proposed regulations dealt with the same matters as those covered by the regulations eventually adopted by the Commission. On January 2, 1941, each of the national networks filed a supplementary brief discussing at length the questions raised by the committee report and the proposed regulations.

On May 2, 1941, the Commission issued its Report on Chain Broadcasting, setting forth its findings and conclusions upon the matters explored in the investigation, together with an order adopting the Regulations here assailed. Two of the seven members of the Commission dissented from this action. The effective date of the Regulations was deferred for 90 days with respect to existing contracts and arrangements of network-operated stations, and subsequently the effective date was thrice again postponed. On August 14, 1941, the Mutual Broadcasting Company petitioned the Commission to amend two of the Regulations. In considering this petition the Commission invited interested parties to submit their views. Briefs were filed on behalf of all of the national networks, and oral argument was had before the Commission on September 12, 1941. And on October 11, 1941, the Commission (again with two members dissenting) issued a Supplemental Report, together with an order amending three Regulations. Simultaneously, the effective date of the Regulations was postponed until November 15, 1941, and provision was made for further postponements from time to time if necessary to permit the orderly adjustment of existing arrangements. Since October 30, 1941, when the present suits were filed, the enforcement of the Regulations has been stayed either voluntarily by the Commission or by order of court.

Such is the history of the Chain Broadcasting Regulations. We turn now to the Regulations themselves, illumined by the practices in the radio industry disclosed by the Commission's investigation. The Regulations, which the Commission characterized in its Report as "the expression of the general policy we will follow in exercising our licensing power," are addressed in terms to station licensees and applicants for station licenses. They provide, in general, that no licenses shall be granted to stations or applicants having specified relationships with networks. Each Regulation is directed at a particular practice found by the Commission to be detrimental to the "public interest," and we shall consider them seriatim. In doing so, however, we do not overlook the admonition of the Commission that the Regulations as well as the network practices at which they are aimed are interrelated: "In considering above the network practices which necessitate the regulations we are adopting, we have taken each practice singly, and have shown that even in isolation each warrants the regulation addressed to it. But the various practices we have considered do not operate in isolation; they form a compact bundle or pattern, and the effect of their joint impact upon licensees necessitates the regulations even more urgently than the effect of each taken singly." (Report, p 75.)

The Commission found that at the end of 1938 there were 660 commercial stations in the United States, and that 341 of these were affiliated with national networks. 135 stations were affiliated exclusively with the National Broadcasting Company, Inc., known in the industry as NBC, which operated two national networks, the "Red" and the "Blue." NBC was also the licensee of 10 stations, including 7 which operated on so-called clear channels with the maximum power available, 50 kilowatts; in addition, NBC operated 5 other stations, 4 of which had power of 50 kilowatts, under management contracts with their licensees. 102 stations were affiliated exclusively with the Columbia Broadcasting System, Inc., which was also the licensee of 8 stations, 7 of which were clear-channel stations operating with power of 50 kilowatts. 74 stations were under exclusive affiliation with the Mutual Broadcasting System, Inc. In addition, 25 stations were affiliated with both NBC and Mutual, and 5 with both CBS and Mutual. These figures, the Commission noted, did not accurately reflect the relative prominence of the three companies, since the stations affiliated with Mutual were, generally speaking, less desirable in frequency, power, and coverage. It pointed out that the stations affiliated with the national networks utilized more than 97% of the total night-time broadcasting power of all the stations in the country. NBC and CBS together controlled more than 85% of the total night-time wattage, and the broadcast business of the three national network companies amounted to almost half of the total business of all stations in the United States.

The Commission recognized that network broadcasting had played and was continuing to play an important part in the development of radio. "The growth and development of chain broadcasting," it stated, "found its impetus in the desire to give widespread coverage to programs which otherwise would not be heard beyond the reception area of a single station. Chain broadcasting makes possible a wider reception for expensive entertainment and cultural programs and also for programs of national or regional significance which would otherwise have coverage only in the locality of origin. Furthermore, the access to greatly enlarged audiences made possible by chain broadcasting has been a strong incentive to advertisers to finance the production of expensive programs. . . . But the fact that the chain broadcasting method brings benefits and advantages to both the listening public and to broadcast station licensees does not mean that the prevailing practices and policies of the networks and their outlets are sound in all respects, or that they should not be altered. The Commission's duty under the Communications Act of 1934, 47 U.S.C.A. § 151 et seq., is not only to see that the public receives the advantages and benefits of chain broadcasting, but also, so far as its powers enable it, to see that practices which adversely affect the ability of licensees to operate in the public interest are eliminated." (Report, p. 4.)

The Commission found that eight network abuses were amenable to correction within the powers granted it by Congress:

Regulation 3.101–Exclusive affiliation of station. The Commission found that the network affiliation agreements of NBC and CBS customarily contained a provision which prevented the station from broadcasting the programs of any other network. The effect of this provision was to hinder the growth of new networks, to deprive the listening public in many areas of service to which they were entitled, and to prevent station licensees from exercising their statutory duty of determining which programs would best serve the needs of their community. The Commission observed that in areas where all the stations were under exclusive contract to either NBC or CBS, the public was deprived of the opportunity to hear programs presented by Mutual. To take a case cited in the Report: In the fall of 1939 Mutual obtained the exclusive right to broadcast the World Series baseball games. It offered this program of outstanding national interest to stations throughout the country, including NBC and CBS affiliates in communities having no other stations. CBS and NBC immediately invoked the "exclusive affiliation" clauses of their agreements with these stations, and as a result thousands of persons in many sections of the country were unable to hear the broadcasts of the games.

"Restraints having this effect," the Commission observed, "are to be condemned as contrary to the public interest irrespective of whether it be assumed that Mutual programs are of equal, superior, or inferior quality. The important consideration is that station licensees are denied freedom to choose the programs which they believe best suited to their needs; in this manner the duty of a station licensee to operate in the public interest is defeated.... Our conclusion is that the disadvantages resulting from these exclusive arrangements far outweigh any advantages. A licensee station does not operate in the public interest when it enters into exclusive arrangements which prevent it from giving the public the best service of which it is capable, and which, by closing the door of opportunity in the network field, adversely affect the program structure of the entire industry." (Report, pp. 52, 57.) Accordingly, the Commission adopted Regulation 3.101, providing as follows: "No license shall be granted to a standard broadcast station having any contract, arrangement, or understanding, express or implied, with a network organization under which the station is prevented or hindered from, or penalized for, broadcasting the programs of any other network organization."

Regulation 3.102–Territorial exclusivity. The Commission found another type of "exclusivity" provision in network affiliation agreements whereby the network bound itself not to sell programs to any other station in the same area. The effect of this provision, designed to protect the affiliate from the competition of other stations serving the same territory, was to deprive the listening public of many programs that might otherwise be available. If an affiliated station rejected a network program, the "territorial exclusivity" clause of its affiliation agreement prevented the network from offering the program to other stations in the area. For example, Mutual presented a popular program, known as "The American Forum of the Air," in which prominent persons discussed topics of general interest. None of the Mutual stations in the Buffalo area decided to carry the program, and a Buffalo station not affiliated with Mutual attempted to obtain the program for its listeners. These efforts failed, however, on account of the "territorial exclusivity" provision in Mutual's agreements with its outlets. The result was that this program was not available to the people of Buffalo.

The Commission concluded that "It is not in the public interest for the listening audience in an area to be deprived of network programs not carried by one station where other stations in that area are ready and willing to broadcast the programs. It is as much against the public interest for a network affiliate to enter into a contractual arrangement which prevents another station from carrying a network program as it would be for it to drown out that program by electrical interference." (Report, p. 59.)

Recognizing that the "territorial exclusivity" clause was unobjectionable in so far as it sought to prevent duplication of programs in the same area, the Commission limited itself to the situations in which the clause impaired the ability of the licensee to broadcast available programs. Regulation 3.102, promulgated to remedy this particular evil, provides as follows: "No license shall be granted to a standard broadcast station having any contract, arrangement, or understanding, express or implied, with a network organization which prevents or hinders another station serving substantially the same area from broadcasting the network's programs not taken by the former station, or which prevents or hinders another station serving a substantially different area from broadcasting any program of the network organization. This regulation shall not be construed to prohibit any contract, arrangement, or understanding between a station and a network organization pursuant to which the station is granted the first call in its primary service area upon the programs of the network organization."

Regulation 3.103—Term of affiliation. The standard NBC and CBS affiliation contracts bound the station for a period of five years, with the network having the exclusive right to terminate the contracts upon one year's notice. The Commission, relying upon § 307(d) of the Communications Act of 1934, under which no license to operate a broadcast station can be granted for a longer term than three years, found the five-year affiliation term to be contrary to the policy of the Act: "Regardless of any changes that may occur in the economic, political, or social life of the Nation or of the community in which the station is located, CBS and NBC affiliates are bound by contract to continue broadcasting the network programs of only one network for 5 years. The licensee is so bound even though the policy and caliber of programs of the network may deteriorate greatly. The future necessities of the station and of the community are not considered. The station licensee is unable to follow his conception of the public interest until the end of the 5-year contract." (Report, p. 61.) The Commission concluded that under contracts binding the affiliates for five years, "stations become parties to arrangements which deprive the public of the improved service it might otherwise derive from competition in the network field; and that a station is not operating in the public interest when it so limits its freedom of action." (Report, p. 62.) Accordingly, the Commission adopted Regulation 3.103: "No license shall be granted to a standard broadcast station having any contract, arrangement, or understanding, express or implied, with a network organization which provides, by original term, provisions for renewal, or otherwise for the affiliation of the station with the network organization for a period longer than two years:[2] Provided, That a contract, arrangement, or understanding for a period up to two years, may be entered into within 120 days prior to the commencement of such period."

Regulation 3.104—Option time. The Commission found that network affiliation contracts usually contained so-called network optional time clauses. Under these provisions the network could upon 28 days' notice call upon its affiliates to carry a commercial program during any of the hours specified in the agreement as "network optional time." For CBS affiliates "network optional time" meant the entire broadcast day. For 29 outlets of NBC on the Pacific Coast, it also covered the entire broadcast day: for substantially all of the other NBC affiliates, it included 8½ hours on weekdays and 8 hours on Sundays. Mutual's contracts with about half of its affiliates contained such a provision, giving the network optional time for 3 or 4 hours on weekdays and 6 hours on Sundays.

In the Commission's judgment these optional time provisions, in addition to imposing serious obstacles in the path of new networks, hindered stations in developing a local program service. The exercise by the networks of their options over the station's time tended to prevent regular scheduling of local programs at desirable hours. The Commission found that "shifting a local commercial program may seriously

---

[2] Station licenses issued by the Commission normally last two years. Section 3.34 of the Commission's Rules and Regulations governing Standard and High-Frequency Broadcast Stations, as amended October 14, 1941.

interfere with the efforts of a [local] sponsor to build up a regular listening audience at a definite hour, and the long-term advertising contract becomes a highly dubious project. This hampers the efforts of the station to develop local commercial programs and affects adversely its ability to give the public good program service. . . . A station licensee must retain sufficient freedom of action to supply the program and advertising needs of the local community. Local program service is a vital part of community life. A station should be ready, able, and willing to serve the needs of the local community by broadcasting such outstanding local events as community concerts, civic meetings, local sports events, and other programs of local consumer and social interest. We conclude that national network time options have restricted the freedom of station licensees and hampered their efforts to broadcast local commercial programs, the programs of other national networks, and national spot transcriptions. We believe that these considerations far outweigh any supposed advantages from 'stability' of network operations under time options. We find that the optioning of time by licensee stations has operated against the public interest." (Report, pp. 63, 65.)

The Commission undertook to preserve the advantages of option time, as a device for "stabilizing" the industry without unduly impairing the ability of local stations to develop local program service. Regulation 3.104 called for the modification of the option-time provision in three respects: the minimum notice period for exercise of the option could not be less than 56 days; the number of hours which could be optioned was limited; and specific restrictions were placed upon exercise of the option to the disadvantage of other networks. The text of the Regulation follows: "No license shall be granted to a standard broadcast station which options for network programs any time subject to call on less than 56 days' notice, or more time than a total of three hours within each of four segments of the broadcast day, as herein described. The broadcast day is divided into 4 segments, as follows: 8:00 a.m. to 1:00 p.m.; 1:00 p.m. to 6:00 p.m.; 6:00 p.m. to 11:00 p.m.; 11:00 p.m. to 8:00 a.m. Such options may not be exclusive as against other network organizations and may not prevent or hinder the station from optioning or selling any or all of the time covered by the option, or other time, to other network organizations."

Regulation 3.105—Right to reject programs. The Commission found that most network affiliation contracts contained a clause defining the right of the station to reject network commercial programs. The NBC contracts provided simply that the station "may reject a network program the broadcasting of which would not be in the public interest, convenience, and necessity." NBC required a licensee who rejected a program to "be able to support his contention that what he has done has been more in the public interest than had he carried on the network program." Similarly, the CBS contracts provided that if the station had "reasonable objection to any sponsored program or the product advertised thereon as not being in the public interest, the station may, on 3 weeks' prior notice thereof to Columbia, refuse to broadcast such program, unless during such notice period such reasonable objection of the station shall be satisfied."

While seeming in the abstract to be fair, these provisions, according to the Commission's finding, did not sufficiently protect the "public interest." As a practical matter, the licensee could not determine in advance whether the broadcasting of any particular network program would or would not be in the public interest. "It is obvious that from such skeletal information [as the networks submitted to the stations prior to the broadcast] the station cannot determine in advance whether the program is in the public interest, nor can it ascertain whether or not parts of the program are in one way or another offensive. In practice, if not in theory, stations affiliated with networks have delegated to the networks a large part of their programming functions. In many instances, moreover, the network further delegates the actual production of programs to advertising agencies. These agencies are far more than mere brokers or intermediaries between the network and the advertiser. To an ever-increasing extent, these agencies actually exercise the function of program production. Thus it is frequently neither the station nor the network, but rather the advertising agency, which determines what broadcast programs shall contain. Under such circumstances, it is especially important that individual stations, if they are to operate in the public interest, should have the practical opportunity as well as the contractual right to reject network programs. . . .

"It is the station, not the network, which is licensed to serve the public interest. The licensee has the duty of determining what programs shall be broadcast over his station's facilities, and cannot lawfully delegate this duty or transfer the control of his station directly to the network or indirectly to an advertising agency. He cannot lawfully bind himself to accept programs in every case where he cannot sustain the burden of proof that he has a better program. The licensee is obliged to reserve to himself the final decision as to what programs will best serve the public interest. We conclude that a licensee is not fulfilling his obligations to operate in the public interest, and is not operating in accordance with the express requirements of the Communications Act, if he agrees to accept programs on any basis other than his own reasonable decision that the programs are satisfactory." (Report, pp. 39, 66.)

The Commission undertook in Regulation 3.105 to formulate the obligations of licensees with respect to supervision over programs: "No license shall be granted to a standard broadcast station having any contract, arrangement, or understanding, express or implied, with a network organization which (a), with respect to programs offered pursuant to an affiliation contract, prevents or hinders the station from rejecting or refusing network programs which the station reasonably believes to be unsatisfactory or unsuitable; or which (b), with respect to network programs so offered or already contracted for, prevents the station from rejecting or refusing any program which, in its opinion, is contrary to the public interest, or from substituting a program of outstanding local or national importance."

Regulation 3. 106—Network ownership of stations. The Commission found that NBC, in addition to its network operations, was the licensee of 10 stations, 2 each in New York, Chicago, Washington, and San Francisco, 1 in Denver, and 1 in Cleveland. CBS was the licensee of 8 stations, 1 in each of these cities: New York, Chicago, Washington, Boston, Minneapolis, St. Louis, Charlotte, and Los Angeles. These 18 stations owned by NBC and CBS, the Commission observed, were among the most powerful and desirable in the country, and were permanently inaccessible to competing networks. "Competition among networks for these facilities is nonexistent, as they are completely removed from the network-station market. It gives the network complete control over its policies. This 'bottling-up' of the best facilities has undoubtedly had a discouraging effect upon the creation and growth of new networks. Furthermore, common ownership of network and station places the network in a position where its interest as the owner of certain stations may conflict with its interest as a network organization serving affiliated stations. In dealings with advertisers, the network represents its own stations in a proprietary capacity and the affiliated stations in something akin to an agency capacity. The danger is present that the network organization will give preference to its own stations at the expense of its affiliates." (Report, p. 67.)

The Commission stated that if the question had arisen as an original matter, it might well have concluded that the public interest required severance of the business of station ownership from that of network operation. But since substantial business interests have been formed on the basis of the Commission's continued tolerance of the situation, it was found inadvisable to take such a drastic step. The Commission concluded, however, that "the licensing of two stations in the same area to a single network organization is basically unsound and contrary to the public interest," and that it was also against the "public interest" for network organizations to own stations in areas where the available facilities were so few or of such unequal coverage that competition would thereby be substantially restricted. Recognizing that these considerations called for flexibility in their application to particular situations, the Commission provided that "networks will be given full opportunity, on proper application for new facilities or renewal of existing licenses, to call to our attention any reasons why the principle should be modified or held inapplicable." (Report, p. 68.) Regulation 3.106 reads as follows: "No license shall be granted to a network organization, or to any person directly or indirectly controlled by or under common control with a network organization, for more than one standard broadcast station where one of the stations covers substantially the service area of the other station, or for any standard broadcast station in any locality where the existing standard broadcast stations are so few or of such unequal desirability (in terms of coverage, power, frequency, or other related matters) that competition would be substantially restrained by such licensing."

Regulation 3.107—Dual network operation. This regulation provides that: "No license shall be issued to a standard broadcast station affiliated with a network organization which maintains more than one network: Provided, That this regulation shall not be applicable if such networks are not operated sumultaneously, or if there is no substantial overlap in the territory served by the group of stations comprising each such network." In its Supplemental Report of October 11, 1941, the Commission announced the indefinite suspension of this regulation. There is no occasion here to consider the validity of Regulation 3.107, since there is no immediate threat of its enforcement by the Commission.

Regulation 3.108—Control by networks of station rates. The Commission found that NBC's affiliation contracts contained a provision empowering the network to reduce the station's network rate, and thereby to reduce the compensation received by the station, if the station set a lower rate for non-network national advertising than the rate established by the contract for the network programs. Under this provision the station could not sell time to a national advertiser for less than it would cost the advertiser if he bought the time from NBC. In the words of NBC's vice-president, "This means simply that a national advertiser should pay the same price for the station whether he buys it through one source or another source. It means that we do not believe that our stations should go into competition with ourselves." (Report, p. 73.)

The Commission concluded that "It is against the public interest for a station licensee to enter into a contract with a network which has the effect of decreasing its ability to compete for national business. We believe that the public interest will best be served and listeners supplied with the best programs if stations bargain freely with national advertisers." (Report, p. 75.) Accordingly, the Commission adopted Regulation 3.108, which provides as follows: "No license shall be granted to a standard broadcast station having any contract, arrangement, or understanding, express or implied, with a network organization under which the station is prevented or hindered from, or penalized for, fixing or altering its rates for the sale of broadcast time for other than the network's programs."

The appellants attack the validity of these Regulations along many fronts. They contend that the Commission went beyond the regulatory powers conferred upon it by the Communications Act of 1934; that even if the Commission were authorized by the Act to deal with the matters comprehended by the Regulations, its action is nevertheless invalid because the Commission misconceived the scope of the Act, particularly § 313 which deals with the application of the anti-trust laws to the radio industry; that the Regulations are arbitrary and capricious; that if the Communications Act of 1934 were construed to authorize the promulgation of the Regulations, it would be an unconstitutional delegation of legislative power; and that, in any event, the Regulations abridge the appellants' right of free speech in violation of the First Amendment. We are thus called upon to determine whether Congress has authorized the Commission to exercise the power asserted by the Chain Broadcasting Regulations, and if it has, whether the Constitution forbids the exercise of such authority.

Federal regulation of radio[3] begins with the Wireless Ship Act of June 24, 1910, 36 Stat. 629, 46 U.S.C.A. § 484 et seq., which forbade any steamer carrying or licensed to carry fifty or more persons to leave any American port unless equipped with efficient apparatus for radio communication, in charge of a skilled operator. The enforcement of this legislation was entrusted to the Secretary of Commerce and Labor, who was in charge of the administration of the marine navigation laws. But it was not until 1912, when the United States ratified the first international radio treaty,

[3] The history of federal regulation of radio communication is summarized in Herring and Gross, Telecommunications (1936) 239-86; Administrative Procedure in Government Agencies, Monograph of the Attorney General's Committee on Administrative Procedure, Sen. Doc. No. 186, 76th Cong., 3d Sess., Part 3, dealing with the Federal Communications Commission, pp. 82-84; 1 Socolow, Law of Radio Broadcasting (1939) 38-61; Donovan, Origin and Development of Radio Law (1930).

37 Stat. 1565, that the need for general regulation of radio communication became urgent. In order to fulfill our obligations under the treaty, Congress enacted the Radio-Communications Act of August 13, 1912, 37 Stat. 302, 47 U.S.C.A. § 51 et seq. This statute forbade the operation of radio apparatus without a license from the Secretary of Commerce and Labor; it also allocated certain frequencies for the use of the Government, and imposed restrictions upon the character of wave emissions, the transmission of distress signals, and the like.

The enforcement of the Radio Act of 1912 presented no serious problems prior to the World War. Questions of interference arose only rarely because there were more than enough frequencies for all the stations then in existence. The war accelerated the development of the art, however, and in 1921 the first standard broadcast stations were established. They grew rapidly in number, and by 1923 there were several hundred such stations throughout the country. The Act of 1912 had not set aside any particular frequencies for the use of private broadcast stations; consequently, the Secretary of Commerce selected two frequencies, 750 and 833 kilocycles, and licensed all stations to operate upon one or the other of these channels. The number of stations increased so rapidly, however, and the situation became so chaotic, that the Secretary, upon the recommendation of the National Radio Conferences which met in Washington in 1923 and 1924, established a policy of assigning specified frequencies to particular stations. The entire radio spectrum was divided into numerous bands, each allocated to a particular kind of service. The frequencies ranging from 550 to 1500 kilocycles (96 channels in all, since the channels were separated from each other by 10 kilocycles) were assigned to the standard broadcast stations. But the problems created by the enormously rapid development of radio were far from solved. The increase in the number of channels was not enough to take care of the constantly growing number of stations. Since there were more stations than available frequencies, the Secretary of Commerce attempted to find room for everybody by limiting the power and hours of operation of stations in order that several stations might use the same channel. The number of stations multiplied so rapidly, however, that by November, 1925, there were almost 600 stations in the country, and there were 175 applications for new stations. Every channel in the standard broadcast band was, by that time, already occupied by at least one station, and many by several. The new stations could be accommodated only by extending the standard broadcast band, at the expense of the other types of services, or by imposing still greater limitations upon time and power. The National Radio Conference which met in November, 1925, opposed both of these methods and called upon Congress to remedy the situation through legislation.

The Secretary of Commerce was powerless to deal with the situation. It had been held that he could not deny a license to an otherwise legally qualified applicant on the ground that the proposed station would interfere with existing private or Government stations. Hoover v. Intercity Radio Co., 52 App.D.C. 339, 286 F. 1003. And on April 16, 1926, an Illinois district court held that the Secretary had no power to impose restrictions as to frequency, power, and hours of operation, and that a station's use of a frequency not assigned to it was not a violation of the Radio Act of 1912. United States v. Zenith Radio Corp., D.C., 12 F.2d 614. This was followed on July 8, 1926, by an opinion of Acting Attorney General Donovan that the Secretary of Commerce had no power, under the Radio Act of 1912, to regulate the power, frequency or hours of operation of stations. 35 Op.Atty.Gen. 126. The next day the Secretary of Commerce issued a statement abandoning all his efforts to regulate radio and urging that the stations undertake self-regulation.

But the plea of the Secretary went unheeded. From July, 1926, to February 23, 1927, when Congress enacted the Radio Act of 1927, 44 Stat. 1162, almost 200 new stations went on the air. These new stations used any frequencies they desired, regardless of the interference thereby caused to others. Existing stations changed to other frequencies and increased their power and hours of operation at will. The result was confusion and chaos. With everybody on the air, nobody could be heard. The situation became so intolerable that the President in his message of December 7, 1926, appealed to Congress to enact a comprehensive radio law:

"Due to the decisions of the courts, the authority of the department [of Commerce] under the law of 1912 has broken down; many more stations have been operating than can be accommodated within the limited number of wave lengths available; further stations are in course of construction; many stations have departed from the scheme of allocations set down by the department, and the whole service of this most important public function has drifted into such chaos as seems likely, if not remedied, to destroy its great value. I most urgently recommend that this legislation should be speedily enacted." (H.Doc. 483, 69th Cong., 2d Sess., p. 10.)

The plight into which radio fell prior to 1927 was attributable to certain basic facts about radio as a means of communication—its facilities are limited; they are not available to all who may wish to use them; the radio spectrum simply is not large enough to accommodate everybody. There is a fixed natural limitation upon the number of stations that can operate without interfering with one another.[4] Regulation of radio was therefore as vital to its development as traffic control was to the development of the automobile. In enacting the Radio Act of 1927, the first comprehensive scheme of control over radio communication, Congress acted upon the knowledge that if the potentialities of radio were not to be wasted, regulation was essential.

The Radio Act of 1927 created the Federal Radio Commission, composed of five members, and endowed the Commission with wide licensing and regulatory powers. We do not pause here to enumerate the scope of the Radio Act of 1927 and of the authority entrusted to the Radio Commission, for the basic provisions of that Act are incorporated in the Communications Act of 1934, 48 Stat. 1064, 47 U.S.C. § 151 et seq., 47 U.S.C.A. § 151 et seq., the legislation immediately before us. As we noted in Federal Communications Comm. v. Pottsville Broadcasting Co., 309 U.S. 134, 137, 60 S.Ct. 437, 438, 84 L.Ed. 656, "In its essentials the Communications Act of 1934 [so far as its provisions relating to radio are concerned] derives from the Federal Radio Act of 1927 ... By this Act Congress, in order to protect the national interest

[4] See Morecroft, Principles of Radio Communication (3d ed. 1933) 355-402; Terman, Radio Engineering (2d ed. 1937) 593-645.

involved in the new and far-reaching science of broadcasting, formulated a unified and comprehensive regulatory system for the industry. The common factors in the administration of the various statutes by which Congress had supervised the different modes of communication led to the creation, in the Act of 1934, of the Communications Commission. But the objectives of the legislation have remained substantially unaltered since 1927."

Section 1 of the Communications Act states its "purpose of regulating interstate and foreign commerce in communication by wire and radio so as to make available, so far as possible, to all the people of the United States a rapid, efficient, Nation-wide, and world-wide wire and radio communication service with adequate facilities at reasonable charges." Section 301 particularizes this general purpose with respect to radio: "It is the purpose of this Act, among other things, to maintain the control of the United States over all the channels of interstate and foreign radio transmission; and to provide for the use of such channels, but not the ownership thereof, by persons for limited periods of time, under licenses granted by Federal authority, and no such license shall be construed to create any right, beyond the terms, conditions, and periods of the license." To that end a Commission composed of seven members was created, with broad licensing and regulatory powers.

Section 303 provides:

"Except as otherwise provided in this Act, the Commission from time to time, as public convenience, interest, or necessity requires, shall—

"(a) Classify radio stations;

"(b) Prescribe the nature of the service to be rendered by each class of licensed stations and each station within any class;

"(f) Make such regulations not inconsistent with law as it may deem necessary to prevent interference between stations and to carry out the provisions of this Act . . .

"(g) Study new uses for radio, provide for experimental uses of frequencies, and generally encourage the larger and more effective use of radio in the public interest;

"(i) Have authority to make special regulations applicable to radio stations engaged in chain broadcasting;

"(r) Make such rules and regulations and prescribe such restrictions and conditions, not inconsistent with law, as may be necessary to carry out the provisions of this Act . . ."

The criterion governing the exercise of the Commission's licensing power is the "public interest, convenience, or necessity." §§ 307(a) (d), 309 (a), 310, 312. In addition, § 307 (b) directs the Commission that "In considering applications for licenses, and modifications and renewals thereof, when and insofar as there is demand for the same, the Commission shall make such distribution of licences, frequencies, hours of operation, and of power among the several States and communities as to provide a fair, efficient, and equitable distribution of radio service to each of the same."

The Act itself establishes that the Commission's powers are not limited to the engineering and technical aspects of regulation of radio communication. Yet we are asked to regard the Commission as a kind of traffic officer, policing the wave lengths to prevent stations from interfering with each other. But the Act does not restrict the Commission merely to supervision of the traffic. It puts upon the Commission the burden of determining the composition of that traffic. The facilities of radio are not large enough to accommodate all who wish to use them. Methods must be devised for choosing from among the many who apply. And since Congress itself could not do this, it committed thé task to the Commission.

The Commission was, however, not left at large in performing this duty. The touchstone provided by Congress was the "public interest, convenience, or necessity," a criterion which "is as concrete as the complicated factors for judgment in such a field of delegated authority permit." Federal Communications Comm. v. Pottsville Broadcasting Co., 309 U.S. 134, 138, 60 S.Ct. 437, 439, 84 L.Ed. 656. "This criterion is not to be interpreted as setting up a standard so indefinite as to confer an unlimited power. Compare N.Y. Cent. Securities Corp. v. United States, 287 U.S. 12, 24, 53 S.Ct. 45 [48], 77 L.Ed. 138. The requirement is to be interpreted by its context, by the nature of radio transmission and reception, by the scope, character, and quality of services. . . ." Federal Radio Comm. v. Nelson Bros. Bond & Mortgage Co., 289 U.S. 266, 285, 53 S.Ct. 627, 636, 77 L.Ed. 1166, 89 A.L.R. 406.

The "public interest" to be served under the Communications Act is thus the interest of the listening public in "the larger and more effective use of radio." § 303 (g). The facilities of radio are limited and therefore precious; they cannot be left to wasteful use without detriment to the public interest. "An important element of public interest and convenience affecting the issue of a license is the ability of the licensee to render the best practicable service to the community reached by his broadcasts." Federal Communications Comm. v. Sanders Bros. Radio Station, 309 U.S. 470, 475, 642, 60 S.Ct. 693, 697, 84 L.Ed. 869, 1037. The Commission's licensing function cannot be discharged, therefore, merely by finding that there are no technological objections to the granting of a license. If the criterion of "public interest" were limited to such matters, how could the Commission choose between two applicants for the same facilities, each of whom is financially and technically qualified to operate a station? Since the very inception of federal regulation by radio, comparative considerations as to the services to be rendered have governed the application of the standard of "public interest, convenience, or necessity." See Federal Communications Comm. v. Pottsville Broadcasting Co., 309 U.S. 134, 138 n. 2, 60 S. Ct. 437, 439, 84 L.Ed. 656.

The avowed aim of the Communications Act of 1934 was to secure the maximum benefits of radio to all the people of the United States. To that end Congress endowed the Communications Commission with comprehensive powers to promote and realize the vast potentialities of radio. Section 303(g) provides that the Commission shall "generally encourage the larger and more effective use of radio in the public interest"; subsection (i) gives the Commission specific "authority to make special regulations applicable to radio stations engaged in chain broadcasting"; and subsection (r) empowers it to adopt "such rules and regulations and prescribe such restrictions and conditions, not inconsistent with law, as may be necessary to carry out the provisions of this Act."

These provisions, individually and in the aggregate, preclude the notion that the Commission is empowered to deal only with technical and engineering impediments to the "larger and more effective use of radio in the public interest." We cannot find in the Act any such restriction of the Commission's authority. Suppose, for example, that a community can, because of physical limitations, be assigned only two stations. That community might be deprived of effective service in any one of several ways. More powerful stations in nearby cities might blanket out the signals of the local stations so that they could not be heard at all. The stations might interfere with each other so that neither could be clearly heard. One station might dominate the other with the power of its signal. But the community could be deprived of good radio service in ways less crude. One man, financially and technically qualified, might apply for and obtain the licenses of both stations and present a single service over the two stations, thus wasting a frequency otherwise available to the area. The language of the Act does not withdraw such a situation from the licensing and regulatory powers of the Commission, and there is no evidence that Congress did not mean its broad language to carry the authority it expresses.

In essence, the Chain Broadcasting Regulations represent a particularization of the Commission's conception of the "public interest" sought to be safeguarded by Congress in enacting the Communications Act of 1934. The basic consideration of policy underlying the Regulations is succinctly stated in its Report: "With the number of radio channels limited by natural factors, the public interest demands that those who are entrusted with the available channels shall make the fullest and most effective use of them. If a licensee enters into a contract with a network organization which limits his ability to make the best use of the radio facility assigned him, he is not serving the public interest. . . . The net effect [of the practices disclosed by the investigation] has been that broadcasting service has been maintained at a level below that possible under a system of free competition. Having so found, we would be remiss in our statutory duty of encouraging 'the larger and more effective use of radio in the public interest' if we were to grant licenses to persons who persist in these practices." (Report, pp. 81, 82.)

We would be asserting our personal views regarding the effective utilization of radio were we to deny that the Commission was entitled to find that the large public aims of the Communications Act of 1934 comprehend the considerations which moved the Commission in promulgating the Chain Broadcasting Regulations. True enough, the Act does not explicity say that the Commission shall have power to deal with network practices found inimical to the public interest. But Congress was acting in a field of regulation which was both new and dynamic. "Congress moved under the spur of a widespread fear that in the absence of governmental control the public interest might be subordinated to monopolistic domination in the broadcasting field." Federal Communications Comm. v. Pottsville Broadcasting Co., 309 U.S. 134, 137, 60 S.Ct. 437. 439, 84 L.Ed. 656. In the context of the developing problems to which it was directed, the Act gave the Commission not niggardly but expansive powers. It was given a comprehensive mandate to "encourage the larger and more effective use of radio in the public interest," if need be, by making "special regulations applicable to radio stations engaged in chain broadcasting." §303(g) (i).

Generalities unrelated to the living problems of radio communication of course cannot justify exercises of power by the Commission. Equally so, generalities empty of all concrete considerations of the actual bearing of regulations promulgated by the Commission to the subject-matter entrusted to it, cannot strike down exercises of power by the Commission. While Congress did not give the Commission unfettered discretion to regulate all phases of the radio industry, it did not frustrate the purposes for which the Communications Act of 1934 was brought into being by attempting an itemized catalogue of the specific manifestations of the general problems for the solution of which it was establishing a regulatory agency. That would have stereotyped the powers of the Commission to specific details in regulating a field of enterprise the dominant characteristic of which was the rapid pace of its unfolding. And so Congress did what experience had taught it in similar attempts at regulation, even in fields where the subject-matter of regulation was far less fluid and dynamic than radio. The essence of that experience was to define broad areas for regulation and to establish standards for judgment adequately related in their application to the problems to be solved.

For the cramping construction of the Act pressed upon us, support cannot be found in its legislative history. The principal argument is that § 303 (i), empowering the Commission "to make special regulations applicable to radio stations engaged in chain broadcasting," intended to restrict the scope of the Commission's powers to the technical and engineering aspects of chain broadcasting. This provision comes from § 4(h) of the Radio Act of 1927. It was introduced into the legislation as a Senate committee amendment to the House bill (H.R. 9971, 69th Cong., 1st Sess.). This amendment originally read as follows:

"(C) The commission, from time to time, as public convenience, interest, or necessity requires, shall— . . .

"(j) When stations are connected by wire for chain broadcasting, determine the power each station shall use and the wave lengths to be used during the time stations are so connected and so operated, and make all other regulations necessary in the interest of equitable radio service to the listeners in the communities or areas affected by chain broadcasting."

The report of the Senate Committee on Interstate Commerce, which submitted this amendment, stated that under the bill the Commission was given "complete authority . . . to control chain broadcasting." Sen.Rep.No.772, 69th Cong., 1st Sess., p. 3. The bill as thus amended was passed by the Senate, and then sent to conference. The bill that emerged from the conference committee, and which became the Radio Act of 1927, phrased the amendment in the general terms now contained in § 303(i) of the 1934 Act: the Commission was authorized "to make special regulations applicable to radio stations engaged in chain broadcasting." The conference reports do not give any explanation of this particular change in phrasing, but they do state that the jurisdiction conferred upon the Commission by the conference bill was substantially identical with that conferred by the bill passed by the Senate. See Sen.Doc.No.200, 69th Cong.,

2d Sess., p. 17; H.Rep.1886, 69th Cong., 2d Sess., p. 17. We agree with the District Court that in view of this legislative history, § 303(i) cannot be construed as no broader than the first clause of the Senate amendment, which limited the Commission's authority to the technical and engineering phases of chain broadcasting. There is no basis for assuming that the conference intended to preserve the first clause, which was of limited scope, and abandon the second clause, which was of general scope, by agreeing upon a provision which was broader and more comprehensive than those it supplanted.[5]

A totally different source of attack upon the Regulations is found in § 311 of the Act, which authorizes the Commission to withhold licenses from persons convicted of having violated the anti-trust laws. Two contentions are made—first, that this provision puts considerations relating to competition outside the Commission's concern before an applicant has been convicted of monopoly or other restraints of trade, and second, that in any event, the Commission misconceived the scope of its powers under § 311 in issuing the Regulations. Both of these contentions are unfounded. Section 311 derives from § 13 of the Radio Act of 1927, which expressly commanded, rather than merely authorized, the Commission to refuse a license to any person judicially found guilty of having violated the anti-trust laws. The change in the 1934 Act was made, in the words of Senator Dill, the manager of the legislation in the Senate, because "it seemed fair to the committee to do that." 78 Cong.Rec. 8825. The Commission was thus permitted to exercise its judgment as to whether violation of the anti-trust laws disqualified an applicant from operating a station in the "public interest." We agree with the District Court that "The necessary implication from this [amendment in 1934] was that the Commission might infer from the fact that the applicant had in the past tried to monopolize radio, or had engaged in unfair methods of competition, that the disposition so manifested would continue and that if it did it would make him an unfit licensee." 47 F.Supp. 940, 944.

That the Commission may refuse to grant a license to persons adjudged guilty in a court of law of conduct in violation of the anti-trust laws certainly does not render

[5] In the course of the Senate debates on the conference report upon the bill that became the Radio Act of 1927, Senator Dill, who was in charge of the bill, said: "While the commission would have the power under the general terms of the bill, the bill specifically sets out as one of the special powers of the commission the right to make specific regulations for governing chain broadcasting. As to creating a monopoly of radio in this country, let me say that this bill absolutely protects the public, so far as it can protect them, by giving the commission full power to refuse a license to anyone who it believes will not serve the public interest, convenience, or necessity. It specifically provides that any corporation guilty of monopoly shall not only not receive a license but that its license may be revoked; and if after a corporation has received its license for a period of three years it is then discovered and found to be guilty of monopoly, its license will be revoked. . . . In addition to that, the bill contains a provision that no license may be transferred from one owner to another without the written consent of the commission, and the commission, of course, having the power to protect against a monopoly, must give such protection. I wish to state further that the only way by which monopolies in the radio business can secure control of radio here, even for a limited period of time, will be by the commission beconing servile to them. Power must be lodged somewhere, and I myself am unwilling to assume in advance that the commission proposed to be created will be servile to the desires and demands of great corporations of the country." 68 Cong. Rec. 2881.

irrelevant consideration by the Commission of the effect of such conduct upon the "public interest, convenience, or necessity." A licensee charged with practices in contravention of this standard cannot continue to hold his license merely because his conduct is also in violation of the anti-trust laws and he has not yet been proceeded against and convicted. By clarifying in § 311 the scope of the Commission's authority in dealing with persons convicted of violating the anti-trust laws, Congress can hardly be deemed to have limited the concept of "public interest" so as to exclude all considerations relating to monopoly and unreasonable restraints upon commerce. Nothing in the provisions or history of the Act lends support to the inference that the Commission was denied the power to refuse a license to a station not operating in the "public interest," merely because its misconduct happened to be an unconvicted violation of the anti-trust laws.

Alternatively, it is urged that the Regulations constitute an ultra vires attempt by the Commission to enforce the anti-trust laws, and that the enforcement of the anti-trust laws is the province not of the Commission but of the Attorney General and the courts. This contention misconceives the basis of the Commission's action. The Commission's Report indicates plainly enough that the Commission was not attempting to administer the anti-trust laws:

"The prohibitions of the Sherman Act [15 U.S.C.A. §§ 1-7, 15 note], apply to broadcasting. This Commission, although not charged with the duty of enforcing that law, should administer its regulatory powers with respect to broadcasting in the light of the purposes which the Sherman Act was designed to achieve. . . . While many of the network practices raise serious questions under the antitrust laws, our jurisdiction does not depend on a showing that they do in fact constitute a violation of the antitrust laws. It is not our function to apply the antitrust laws as such. It is our duty, however, to refuse licenses or renewals to any person who engages or proposes to engage in practices which will prevent either himself or other licensees or both from making the fullest use of radio facilities. This is the standard of public interest, convenience or necessity which we must apply to all applications for licenses and renewals. . . . We do not predicate our jurisdiction to issue the regulations on the ground that the network practices violate the antitrust laws. We are issuing these regulations because we have found that the network practices prevent the maximum utilization of radio facilities in the public interest." (Report, pp. 46, 83, 83n. 3.)

We conclude, therefore, that the Communications Act of 1934 authorized the Commission to promulgate regulations designed to correct the abuses disclosed by its investigation of chain broadcasting. There remains for consideration the claim that the Commission's exercise of such authority was unlawful. . . .

SECURITIES AND EXCHANGE COMMISSION

SECURITIES ACT
1933

SECURITIES ACT
1933

Commentary

The regulatory commissions were created by the Congress to resolve problems arising in particular areas of the economy. As individual industries presented problems of abusive tactics with which traditional economic and legal devices had failed to cope, the new governmental organ made its appearance. Transportation, power, communications—industries with sicknesses stemming from failure to meet public needs adequately—all came under the fostering guardianship of the regulatory commission.

The great depression of 1929 stimulated the growth of federal commissions. The legislative measures of the New Deal were in the main carried out through the medium of the administrative agency, and a whole host of such bodies was created. In the words of James M. Landis, himself a participant in formulating the New Deal program, "As rapidly as—indeed, sometimes more rapidly than—causes could be isolated and problems defined, administrative agencies were created to wrestle with them."

When Franklin D. Roosevelt was first inaugurated, the securities business was patently in need of governmental regulation. Soon after he took office, the President presented to Congress a message urging it to provide for "Federal supervision of traffic in investment securities in interstate commerce." It was essential that full publicity and information be available regarding security issues. In this way, investors would be protected against fraudulent prospectuses and claims by sellers of securities. In the President's phrase, the old adage "Let the buyer beware" had to be supplemented by the principle "Let the seller also beware."

The Securities Act of 1933 was the response to Roosevelt's request. It was more or less a federal "blue sky" law, designed to give the public full information about new offers of securities. It provided for a scheme of registration of security issues, administered by the Federal Trade Commission. Only new security issues were covered, not securities already outstanding. The essential requirement was the registration of all securities offered to the public with the FTC. This requirement was enforced by denying the use of the mails and the facilities of interstate commerce for failure to register, as well as civil and criminal penalties for untrue statements or omission of required information.

The report of the House Commerce Committee contains the President's message as well as the legislative background of the Securities Act (*infra* p. 2573). The report both points out the pressing need for the legislation and summarizes the bill's provisions.

Like most of the New Deal legislation setting up new schemes of economic regulation, the Securities Act of 1933 received brief—if not perfunctory—legislative debate. Only five hours were allowed for debate in the House on May 5, 1933, and the bill passed without a roll call the same day. The House debate began with the bitter objection of Congressman Carl E. Mapes [Rep., Mich.], ranking minority committee member, to the limitation of debate (an objection which was repeated in debates on other regulatory laws during the next five years). As he characterized it, this was "another one of those closed or gag rules which have become so common during this session of Congress."

Congressman Sam Rayburn [Dem., Tex.], chairman of the House Commerce Committee, made the key speech. He discussed the background of the bill and summarized its provisions. The goal, he said, is to give the prospective purchaser of securities "all information that is pertinent that would put him on notice and on guard, and then let him beware." The colloquy with Congressman Edward Cox [Dem., Ga.] shows how the commerce power was being expanded by legislation such as this. The bill itself was basically supported by both parties. One of the principal speeches in support was by Congressman Charles A. Wolverton [Rep., N.J.]. He noted that the bill did not go as far as some of the state "blue sky" laws, since they embodied the concept of a state duty to protect citizens from fraudulent practices which included the evaluation of securities offered for sale.

A leading opponent of the New Deal expansions of federal power, Congressman James M. Beck [Rep., Penn.], made the principal speech against the bill. He relied on a narrow conception of commerce—one that was being left behind by the growing need for federal regulation. His concept of constitutional law was shortly rejected by the Supreme Court itself. Beck also objected to vesting the new power in the FTC, "easily one of the most futile of the bureaucratic agencies in Washington."

The Senate debate was just as brief, taking place in a perfunctory manner on May 8. Senator Duncan U. Fletcher [Dem., Fla.] introduced the bill with a brief statement. There was practically no discussion. The Senate voted, without a roll call, to substitute its committee's bill for the House bill. Though the two bills were very similar, this necessitated a conference. The conference committee report contains only the text of the Act as finally passed; it is explained in the statement of the House managers (*infra* p. 2671). Both houses passed the conference report without discussion or a roll call—the House on May 22 and the Senate the following day. On May 27, 1933, the bill was signed by the President.

SECURITIES ACT
May 27, 1933

Be it enacted by the Senate and House of Representatives of the United States of America in Congress assembled,

TITLE I

Short Title

SECTION 1. This title may be cited as the "Securities Act of 1933."

Definitions

SEC. 2. When used in this title, unless the context otherwise requires—

(1) The term "security" means any note, stock, treasury stock, bond, debenture, evidence of indebtedness, certificate of interest or participation in any profit-sharing agreement, collateral-trust certificate, preorganization certificate or subscription, transferable share, investment contract, voting-trust certificate, certificate of interest in property, tangible or intangible, or, in general, any instrument commonly known as a security, or any certificate of interest or participation in, temporary or interim certificate for, receipt for, or warrant or right to subscribe to or purchase, any of the foregoing.

(2) The term "person" means an individual, a corporation, a partnership, an association, a joint-stock company, a trust, any unincorporated organization, or a government or political subdivision thereof. As used in this paragraph the term "trust" shall include only a trust where the interest or interests of the beneficiary or beneficiaries are evidenced by a security.

(3) The term "sale," "sell," "offer to sell," or "offer for sale" shall include every contract of sale or disposition of, attempt or offer to dispose of, or solicitation of an offer to buy, a security or interest in a security, for value; except that such terms shall not include preliminary negotiations or agreements between an issuer and any underwriter. Any security given or delivered with, or as a bonus on account of, any purchase of securities or any other thing, shall be conclusively presumed to constitute a part of the subject of such purchase and to have been sold for value. The issue or transfer of a right or privilege, when originally issued or transferred with a security, giving the holder of such security the right to convert such security into another security of the same issuer or of another person, or giving a right to subscribe to another security of the same issuer or of another person, which right cannot be exercised until some future date, shall not be deemed to be a sale of such other security; but the issue or transfer of such other security upon the exercise of such right of conversion or subscription shall be deemed a sale of such other security.

(4) The term "issuer" means every person who issues or proposes to issue any security or who guarantees a security either as to principal or income; except that with respect to certificates of deposit, voting-trust certificates, or collateral-trust certificates, or with respect to certificates of interest or shares in an unincorporated investment trust not having a board of directors (or persons performing similar functions) or of the fixed, restricted management, or unit type, the term "issuer" means the person or persons performing the acts and assuming the duties of depositor or manager pursuant to the provisions of the trust or other agreement or instrument under which such securities are issued; and except that with respect to equipment-trust certificates or like securities, the term "issuer" means the person by whom the equipment or property is or is to be used.

(5) The term "Commission" means the Federal Trade Commission.

(6) The term "Territory" means Alaska, Hawaii, Puerto Rico, the Philippine Islands, Canal Zone, the Virgin Islands, and the insular possessions of the United States.

(7) The term "interstate commerce" means trade or commerce in securities or any transportation or communication relating thereto among the several States or between the District of Columbia or any Territory of the United States and any State or other Territory, or between any foreign country and any State, Territory, or the District of Columbia, or within the District of Columbia.

(8) The term "registration statement" means the statement provided for in section 6, and includes any amendment thereto and any report, document, or memorandum accompanying such statement or incorporated therein by reference.

(9) The term "write" or "written" shall include printed, lithographed, or any means of graphic communication.

(10) The term "prospectus" means any prospectus, notice, circular, advertisement, letter, or communication, written or by radio, which offers any security for sale; except that (a) a communication shall not be deemed a prospectus if it is proved that prior to such communication a written prospectus meeting the requirements of section 10 was received, by the person to whom the communication was made, from the person making such communication or his principal, and (b) a notice, circular, advertisement, letter or communication in respect of a security shall not be deemed to be a prospectus if it states from whom a written prospectus meeting the requirements of section 10 may be obtained and, in addition, does no more than identify the security, state the price thereof, and state by whom orders will be executed.

(11) The term "underwriter" means any person who has purchased from an issuer with a view to, or sells for an issuer in connection with, the distribution of any security, or participates or has a direct or indirect participation in any such under-taking, or participates or has a participation in the direct or indirect underwriting of any such undertaking; but such term shall not include a person whose interest is limited to a commission from an underwriter or dealer not in excess of the usual and customary distributors' or sellers' commission. As used in this paragraph the term "issuer" shall include, in addition to an issuer, any person directly or indirectly controlling or controlled by the issuer, or any person under direct or indirect common control with the issuer.

(12) The term "dealer" means any person who engages either for all or part of his time, directly or indirectly, as agent, broker, or principal, in the business of offering, buying, selling, or otherwise dealing or trading in securities issued by another person.

Exempted Securities

SEC. 3. (a) Except as hereinafter expressly provided, the provisions of this title shall not apply to any of the following classes of securities:

(1) Any security which, prior to or within sixty days after the enactment of this title, has been sold or disposed of by the issuer or bona fide offered to the public, but this exemption shall not apply to any new offering of any such security by an issuer or underwriter subsequent to such sixty days;

(2) Any security issued or guaranteed by the United States or any Territory thereof, or by the District of Columbia, or by any State of the United States, or by any political subdivision of a State or Territory, or by any public instrumentality of one or more States or Territories exercising an essential governmental function, or by any corporation created and controlled or supervised by and acting as an instrumentality of the Government of the United States pursuant to authority granted by the Congress of the United States, or by any national bank, or by any banking institution organized under the laws of any State or Territory, the business of which is substantially confined to banking and is supervised by the State or territorial banking commission or similar official; or any security issued by or representing an interest in or a direct obligation of a Federal reserve bank;

(3) Any note, draft, bill of exchange, or banker's acceptance which arises out of a current transaction or the proceeds of which have been or are to be used for current transactions, and which has a maturity at the time of issuance of not exceeding nine months, exclusive of days of grace, or any renewal thereof the maturity of which is likewise limited;

(4) Any security issued by a corporation organized and operated exclusively for religious, educational, benevolent, fraternal, charitable, or reformatory purposes and not for pecuniary profit, and no part of the net earnings of which inures to the benefit of any person, private stockholder, or individual;

(5) Any security issued by a building and loan association, homestead association, savings and loan association, or similar institution, substantially all the business of which is confined to the making of loans to members (but the foregoing exemption shall not apply with respect to any such security where the issuer takes from the total amount paid or deposited by the purchaser, by way of any fee, cash value or other device whatsoever, either upon termination of the investment at maturity or before maturity, an aggregate amount in excess of 3 per centum of the face value of such security), or any security issued by a farmers' cooperative association as defined in paragraphs (12), (13), and (14) of section 103 of the Revenue Act of 1932;

(6) Any security issued by a common carrier which is subject to the provisions of section 20a of the Interstate Commerce Act, as amended;

(7) Certificates issued by a receiver or by a trustee in bankruptcy, with the approval of the court;

(8) Any insurance or endowment policy or annuity contract or optional annuity contract, issued by a corporation subject to the supervision of the insurance commissioner, bank commissioner, or any agency or officer performing like functions, of any State or Territory of the United States or the District of Columbia.

(b) The Commission may from time to time by its rules and regulations, and subject to such terms and conditions as may be prescribed therein, add any class of securities to the securities exempted as provided in this section, if it finds that the enforcement of this title with respect to such securities is not necessary in the public interest and for the protection of investors by reason of the small amount involved or the limited character of the public offering; but no issue of securities shall be exempted under this subsection where the aggregate amount at which such issue is offered to the public exceeds $100,000.

Exempted Transactions

SEC. 4. The provisions of section 5 shall not apply to any of the following transactions:

(1) Transactions by any person other than an issuer, underwriter, or dealer; transactions by an issuer not with or through an underwriter and not involving any public offering; or transactions by a dealer (including an underwriter no longer acting as an underwriter in respect of the security involved in such transaction), except transactions within one year after the last date upon which the security was bona fide offered to the public by the issuer or by or through an underwriter (excluding in the computation of such year any time during which a stop order issued under section 8 is in effect as to the security), and except transactions as to securities constituting the whole or a part of an unsold allotment to or subscription by such dealer as a participant in the distribution of such securities by the issuer or by or through an underwriter.

(2) Brokers' transactions, executed upon customers' orders on any exchange or in the open or counter market, but not the solicitation of such orders.

(3) The issuance of a security of a person exchanged by it with its existing security holders exclusively, where no commission or other remuneration is paid or given directly or indirectly in connection with such exchange; or the issuance of securities to the existing security holders or other existing creditors of a corporation in the process of a bona fide reorganization of such corporation under the supervision of any court, either in exchange for the securities of such security holders or claims of such creditors or partly for cash and partly in exchange for the securities or claims of such security holders or creditors.

Prohibitions Relating to Interstate Commerce and the Mails

SEC. 5. (a) Unless a registration statement is in effect as to a security, it shall be unlawful for any person, directly or indirectly—

(1) to make use of any means or instruments of transportation or communication in interstate commerce or of the mails to sell or offer to buy such security through the use or medium of any prospectus or otherwise; or

(2) to carry or cause to be carried through the mails or in interstate commerce, by any means or instruments of transportation, any such security for the purpose of sale or for delivery after sale.

(b) It shall be unlawful for any person, directly or indirectly—

(1) to make use of any means or instruments of transportation or communication in interstate commerce or of the mails to carry or transmit any

prospectus relating to any security registered under this title, unless such prospectus meets the requirements of section 10; or

(2) to carry or to cause to be carried through the mails or in interstate commerce any such security for the purpose of sale or for delivery after sale, unless accompanied or preceded by a prospectus that meets the requirements of section 10.

(c) The provisions of this section relating to the use of the mails shall not apply to the sale of any security where the issue of which it is a part is sold only to persons resident within a single State or Territory, where the issuer of such securities is a person resident and doing business within, or, if a corporation, incorporated by and doing business within, such State or Territory.

Registration of Securities and Signing of Registration Statement

SEC. 6. (a) Any security may be registered with the Commission under the terms and conditions hereinafter provided, by filing a registration statement in triplicate, at least one of which shall be signed by each issuer, its principal executive officer or officers, its principal financial officer, its comptroller or principal accounting officer, and the majority of its board of directors or persons performing similar functions (or, if there is no board of directors or persons performing similar functions, by the majority of the persons or board having the power of management of the issuer), and in case the issuer is a foreign or Territorial person by its duly authorized representative in the United States; except that when such registration statement relates to a security issued by a foreign government, or political subdivision thereof, it need be signed only by the underwriter of such security. Signatures of all such persons when written on the said registration statements shall be presumed to have been so written by authority of the person whose signature is so affixed and the burden of proof, in the event such authority shall be denied, shall be upon the party denying the same. The affixing of any signature without the authority of the purported signer shall constitute a violation of this title. A registration statement shall be deemed effective only as to the securities specified therein as proposed to be offered.

(b) At the time of filing a registration statement the applicant shall pay to the Commission a fee of one one-hundredth of 1 per centum of the maximum aggregate price at which such securities are proposed to be offered, but in no case shall such fee be less than $25.

(c) The filing with the Commission of a registration statement, or of an amendment to a registration statement, shall be deemed to have taken place upon the receipt thereof, but the filing of a registration statement shall not be deemed to have taken place unless it is accompanied by a United States postal money order or a certified bank check or cash for the amount of the fee required under subsection (b).

(d) The information contained in or filed with any registration statement shall be made available to the public under such regulations as the Commission may prescribe, and copies thereof, photostatic or otherwise, shall be furnished to every applicant at such reasonable charge as the Commission may prescribe.

(e) No registration statement may be filed within the first forty days following the enactment of this Act.

Information Required in Registration Statement

SEC. 7. The registration statement, when relating to a security other than a security issued by a foreign government, or political subdivision thereof, shall contain the information, and be accompanied by the documents, specified in Schedule A, and when relating to a security issued by a foreign government, or political subdivision thereof, shall contain the information, and be accompanied by the documents, specified in Schedule B; except that the Commission may by rules or regulations provide that any such information or document need not be included in respect of any class of issuers or securities if it finds that the requirement of such information or document is inapplicable to such class and that disclosure fully adequate for the protection of investors is otherwise required to be included within the registration statement. If any accountant, engineer, or appraiser, or any person whose profession gives authority to a statement made by him, is named as having prepared or certified any part of the registration statement, or is named as having prepared or certified a report or valuation for use in connection with the registration statement, the written consent of such person shall be filed with the registration statement. If any such person is named as having prepared or certified a report or valuation (other than a public official document or statement) which is used in connection with the registra-tion statement, but is not named as having prepared or certified such report or valuation for use in connection with the registration statement, the written consent of such person shall be filed with the registration statement unless the Commission dispenses with such filing as impracticable or as involving undue hardship on the person filing the registration statement. Any such registration statement shall contain such other information, and be accompanied by such other documents, as the Commission may by rules or regulations require as being necessary or appropriate in the public interest or for the protection of investors.

Taking Effect of Registration Statements
and Amendments Thereto

SEC. 8. (a) The effective date of a registration statement shall be the twentieth day after the filing thereof, except as hereinafter provided, and except that in case of securities of any foreign public authority, which has continued the full service of its obligations in the United States, the proceeds of which are to be devoted to the refunding of obligations payable in the United States, the registration statement shall become effective seven days after the filing thereof. If any amendment to any such statement is filed prior to the effective date of such statement, the registration statement shall be deemed to have been filed when such amendment was filed; except that an amendment filed with the consent of the Commission, prior to the effective date of the registration statement, or filed pursuant to an order of the Commission, shall be treated as a part of the registration statement.

(b) If it appears to the Commission that a registration statement is on its face incomplete or inaccurate in any material respect, the Commission may, after notice by personal service or the sending of confirmed telegraphic notice not later than ten days after the filing of the registration statement, and opportunity for hearing (at a time fixed by the Commission) within ten days after such notice by personal service or the sending of such telegraphic notice, issue an order prior to the effective date of registration refusing to permit such statement to become effective until it has been amended in accordance with such order. When such statement has been amended in accordance with such order the Commission shall so declare and the registration shall become effective at the time provided in subsection (a) or upon the date of such declaration, whichever date is the later.

(c) An amendment filed after the effective date of the registration statement, if such amendment, upon its face, appears to the Commission not to be incomplete or inaccurate in any material respect, shall become effective on such date as the Commission may determine, having due regard to the public interest and the protection of investors.

(d) If it appears to the Commission at any time that the registration statement includes any untrue statement of a material fact or omits to state any material fact required to be stated therein or necessary to make the statements therein not misleading, the Commission may, after notice by personal service or the sending of confirmed telegraphic notice, and after opportunity for hearing (at a time fixed by the Commission) within fifteen days after such notice by personal service or the sending of such telegraphic notice, issue a stop order suspending the effectiveness of the registration statement. When such statement has been amended in accordance with such stop order the Commission shall so declare and thereupon the stop order shall cease to be effective.

(e) The Commission is hereby empowered to make an examination in any case in order to determine whether a stop order should issue under subsection (d). In making such examination the Commission or any officer or officers designated by it shall have access to and may demand the production of any books and papers of, and may administer oaths and affirmations to and examine, the issuer, underwriter, or any other person, in respect of any matter relevant to the examination, and may, in its discretion, require the production of a balance sheet exhibiting the assets and liabilities of the issuer, or its income statement, or both, to be certified to by a public or certified accountant approved by the Commission. If the issuer or underwriter shall fail to cooperate, or shall obstruct or refuse to permit the making of an examination, such conduct shall be proper ground for the issuance of a stop order.

(f) Any notice required under this section shall be sent to or served on the issuer, or, in case of a foreign government or political subdivision thereof, to or on the underwriter, or, in the case of a foreign or Territorial person, to or on its duly authorized representative in the United States named in the registration statement, properly directed in each case of telegraphic notice to the address given in such statement.

Court Review of Orders

SEC. 9. (a) Any person aggrieved by an order of the Commission may obtain a review of such order in the Circuit Court of Appeals of the United States, within any circuit wherein such person resides or has his principal place of business, or in the Court of Appeals of the District of Columbia, by filing in such court, within sixty days after the entry of such order, a written petition praying that the order of the Commission be modified or be set aside in whole or in part. A copy of such petition shall be forthwith served upon the Commission, and thereupon the Commission shall certify and file in the court a transcript of the record upon which the order complained of was entered. No objection to the order of the Commission shall be considered by the court unless such objection shall have been urged before the Commission. The finding of the Commission as to the facts, if supported by evidence, shall be conclusive. If either party shall apply to the court for leave to adduce additional evidence, and shall show to the satisfaction of the court that such additional evidence is material and that there were reasonable grounds for failure to adduce such evidence in the hearing before the Commission, the court may order such additional evidence to be taken before the Commission and to be adduced upon the hearing in such manner and upon such terms and conditions as to the court may seem proper. The Commission may modify its findings as to the facts, by reason of the additional evidence so taken, and it shall file such modified or new findings, which, if supported by evidence, shall be conclusive, and its recommendation, if any, for the modification or setting aside of the original order. The jurisdiction of the court shall be exclusive and its judgment and decree, affirming, modifying, or setting aside, in whole or in part, any order of the Commission, shall be final, subject to review by the Supreme Court of the United States upon certiorari or certification as provided in sections 239 and 240 of the Judicial Code, as amended (U.S.C., title 28, secs. 346 and 347).

(b) The commencement of proceedings under subsection (a) shall not, unless specifically ordered by the court, operate as a stay of the Commission's order.

Information Required in Prospectus

SEC. 10. (a) A prospectus—

(1) when relating to a security other than a security issued by a foreign government or political subdivision thereof, shall contain the same statements made in the registration statement, but it need not include the documents referred to in paragraphs (28) to (32), inclusive, of Schedule A;

(2) when relating to a security issued by a foreign government or political subdivision thereof shall contain the same statements made in the registration statement, but it need not include the documents referred to in paragraphs (13) and (14) of Schedule B.

(b) Notwithstanding the provisions of subsection (a)—

(1) when a prospectus is used more than thirteen months after the effective date of the registration statement, the information in the statements contained therein shall be as of a date not more than twelve months prior to such use.

(2) there may be omitted from any prospectus any of the statements required under such subsection (a) which the Commission may by rules or regulations designate as not being necessary or appropriate in the public interest or for the protection of investors.

(3) any prospectus shall contain such other information as the Commission may by rules or regulations require as being necessary or appropriate in the public interest or for the protection of investors.

(4) in the exercise of its powers under paragraphs (2) and (3) of this subsection, the Commission shall have authority to classify prospectuses according to the nature and circumstances of their use, and, by rules and regulations and subject to such terms and conditions as it shall specify therein, to prescribe as to each class the form and contents which it may find appropriate to such use and consistent with the public interest and the protection of investors.

(c) The statements or information required to be included in a prospectus by or under authority of subsection (a) or (b), when written, shall be placed in a conspicuous part of the prospectus in type as large as that used generally in the body of the prospectus.

(d) In any case where a prospectus consists of a radio broadcast, copies thereof shall be filed with the Commission under such rules and regulations as it shall prescribe. The Commission may by rules and regulations require the filing with it of forms of prospectuses used in connection with the sale of securities registered under this title.

Civil Liabilities on Account of False Registration Statement

SEC. 11. (a) In case any part of the registration statement, when such part became effective, contained an untrue statement of a material fact or omitted to state a material fact required to be stated therein or necessary to make the statements therein not misleading, any person acquiring such security (unless it is proved that at the time of such acquisition he knew of such untruth or omission) may, either at law or in equity, in any court or competent jurisdiction, sue—

(1) every person who signed the registration statement;

(2) every person who was a director of (or person performing similar functions) or partner in, the issuer at the time of the filing of the part of the registration statement with respect to which his liability is asserted;

(3) every person who, with his consent, is named in the registration statement as being or about to become a director, person performing similar functions, or partner;

(4) every accountant, engineer, or appraiser, or any person whose profession gives authority to a statement made by him, who has with his consent been named as having prepared or certified any part of the registration statement, or as having prepared or certified any report or valuation which is used in connection with the registration statement, with respect to the statement in such registration statement, report, or valuation, which purports to have been prepared or certified by him;

(5) every underwriter with respect to such security.

(b) Notwithstanding the provisions of subsection (a) no person, other than the issuer, shall be liable as provided therein who shall sustain the burden of proof—

(1) that before the effective date of the part of the registration statement with respect to which his liability is asserted (A) he had resigned from or had taken such steps as are permitted by law to resign from, or ceased or refused to act in, every office, capacity, or relationship in which he was described in the registration statement as acting or agreeing to act, and (B) he had advised the Commission and the issuer in writing that he had taken such action and that he would not be responsible for such part of the registration statement; or

(2) that if such part of the registration statement became effective without his knowledge, upon becoming aware of such fact he forthwith acted and advised the Commission, in accordance with paragraph (1), and, in addition, gave reasonable public notice that such part of the registration statement had become effective without his knowledge; or

(3) that (A) as regards any part of the registration statement not purporting to be made on the authority of an expert, and not purporting to be a copy of or extract from a report or valuation of an expert, and not purporting to be made on the authority of a public official document or statement, he had, after reasonable investigation, reasonable ground to believe and did believe, at the time such part of the registration statement became effective, that the statements therein were true and that there was no omission to state a material fact required to be stated therein or necessary to make the statements therein not misleading; and (B) as regards any part of the registration statement purporting to be made upon his authority as an expert or purporting to be a copy of or extract from a report or valuation of himself as an expert, (i) he had, after reasonable investigation, reasonable ground to believe and did believe, at the time such part of the registration statement became effective, that the statements therein were true and that there was no omission to state a material fact required to be stated therein or necessary to make the statements therein not misleading, or (ii) such part of the registration statement did not fairly represent his statement as an expert or was not a fair copy of or extract from his report or valuation as an expert; and (C) as regards any part of the registration statement purporting to be made on the authority of an expert (other than himself) or

purporting to be a copy of or extract from a report or valuation of an expert (other than himself), he had reasonable ground to believe and did believe, at the time such part of the registration statement fairly represented the statement of the expert or was fair copy of or extract from the report or valuation of the expert; and (D) as regards any part of the registration statement purporting to be a statement made by an official person or purporting to be a copy of or extract from a public official document, he had reasonable ground to believe and did believe, at the time such part of the registration statement became effective, that the statements therein were true, and that there was no omission to state a material fact required to be stated therein or necessary to make the statements therein not misleading, and that such part of the registration statement fairly represented the statement made by the official person or was a fair copy of or extract from the public official document.

(c) In determining, for the purpose of paragraph (3) of subsection (b) of this section, what constitutes reasonable investigation and reasonable ground for belief, the standard of reasonableness shall be that required of a person occupying a fiduciary relationship.

(d) If any person becomes an underwriter with respect to the security after the part of the registration statement with respect to which his liability is asserted has become effective, then for the purposes of paragraph (3) of subsection (b) of this section such part of the registration statement shall be considered as having become effective with respect to such person as of the time when he became an underwriter.

(e) The suit authorized under subsection (a) may be either (1) to recover the consideration paid for such security with interest thereon, less the amount of any income received thereon, upon the tender of such security, or (2) for damages if the person suing no longer owns the security.

(f) All or any one or more of the persons specified in subsection (a) shall be jointly and severally liable, and every person who becomes liable to make any payment under this section may recover contributions as in cases of contract from any person who, if sued separately, would have been liable to make the same payment, unless the person who has become liable was, and the other was not, guilty of fraudulent misrepresentation.

(g) In no case shall the amount recoverable under this section exceed the price at which the security was offered to the public.

Civil Liabilities Arising in Connection with Prospectuses and Communications

SEC. 12. Any person who——

(1) sells a security in violation of section 5, or

(2) sells a security (whether or not exempted by the provisions of section 3, other than paragrpah (2) of subsection (a) thereof), by the use of any means or instruments of transportation or communication in interstate commerce or of

the mails, by means of a prospectus or oral communication, which includes an untrue statement of a material fact or omits to state a material fact necessary in order to make the statements, in the light of the circumstances under which they were made, not misleading (the purchaser not knowing of such untruth or omission), and who shall not sustain the burden of proof that he did not know, and in the exercise of reasonable care could not have known, of such untruth or omission,

shall be liable to the person purchasing such security from him, who may sue either at law or in equity in any court of competent jurisdiction, to recover the consideration paid for such security with interest thereon, less the amount of any income received thereon, upon the tender of such security, or for damages if he no longer owns the security.

Limitation of Actions

SEC. 13. No action shall be maintained to enforce any liability created under section 11 or section 12 (2) unless brought within two years after the discovery of the untrue statement or the omission, or after such discovery should have been made by the exercise of reasonable diligence, or, if the action is to enforce a liability created under section 12 (1), unless brought within two years after the violation upon which it is based. In no event shall any such action be brought to enforce a liability created under section 11 or section 12 (1) more than ten years after the security was bona fide offered to the public.

Contrary Stipulations Void

Sec. 14. Any condition, stipulation, or provision binding any person acquiring any security to waive compliance with any provision of this title or of the rules and regulations of the Commission shall be void.

Liability of Controlling Persons

SEC. 15. Every person who, by or through stock ownership, agency, or otherwise, or who, pursuant to or in connection with an agreement or understanding with one or more other persons by or through stock ownership, agency, or otherwise, controls any person liable under section 11 or 12, shall also be liable jointly and severally with and to the same extent as such controlled person to any person to whom such controlled person is liable.

Additional Remedies

SEC. 16. The rights and remedies provided by this title shall be in addition to any and all other rights and remedies that may exist at law or in equity.

Fraudulent Interstate Transactions

SEC. 17. (a) It shall be unlawful for any person in the sale of any securities by the use of any means or instruments of transportation or communication in interstate commerce or by the use of the mails, directly or indirectly——

(1) to employ any device, scheme, or artifice to defraud, or

(2) to obtain money or property by means of any untrue statement of a material fact or any omission to state a material fact necessary in order to make the statements made, in the light of the circumstances under which they were made, not misleading, or

(3) to engage in any transaction, practice, or course of business which operates or would operate as a fraud or deceit upon the purchaser.

(b) It shall be unlawful for any person, by the use of any means or instruments of transportation or communication in interstate commerce or by the use of the mails, to publish, give publicity to, or circulate any notice, circular, advertisement, newspaper, article, letter, investment service, or communication which, though not purporting to offer a security for sale, describes such security for a consideration received or to be received, directly or indirectly, from an issuer, underwriter, or dealer, without fully disclosing the receipt, whether past or prospective, of such consideration and the amount thereof.

(c) The exemptions provided in section 3 shall not apply to the provisions of this section.

State Control of Securities

SEC. 18. Nothing in this title shall affect the jurisdiction of the securities commission (or any agency or office performing like functions) of any State or Territory of the United States, or the District of Columbia, over any security or any person.

Special Powers of Commission

SEC. 19. (a) The Commission shall have authority from time to time to make, amend, and rescind such rules and regulations as may be necessary to carry out the provisions of this title, including rules and regulations governing registration statements and prospectuses for various classes of securities and issuers, and defining accounting and trade terms used in this title. Among other things, the Commission shall have authority, for the purposes of this title, to prescribe the form or forms in which required information shall be set forth, the items or details to be shown in the balance sheet and earning statement, and the methods to be followed in the preparation of accounts, in the appraisal or valuation of assets and liabilities, in the determination of depreciation and depletion, in the differentation of recurring and nonrecurring income, in the differentiation of investment and operating income, and in the preparation, where the Commission deems it necessary or desirable, of consolidated balance sheets or income accounts of any person directly or indirectly controlling or controlled by the issuer, or any person under direct or indirect common control with the issuer; but insofar as they relate to any common carrier subject to the provisions of section 20 of the Interstate Commerce Act, as amended, the rules and regulations of the Commission with respect to accounts shall not be inconsistent with the requirements imposed by the Interstate Commerce Commission under authority of such section 20. The rules and regulations of the Commission shall be effective upon publication in the manner which the Commission shall prescribe.

(b) For the purpose of all investigations which, in the opinion of the Commission, are necessary and proper for the enforcement of this title, any member of the Commission or any officer or officers designated by it are empowered to administer oaths and affirmations, subpena witnesses, take evidence, and require the production of any books, papers, or other documents which the Commission deems relevant or material to the inquiry. Such attendance of witnesses and the production of such documentary evidence may be required from any place in the United States or any Territory at any designated place of hearing.

Injunctions and Prosecution of Offenses

SEC. 20. (a) Whenever it shall appear to the Commission, either upon complaint or otherwise, that the provisions of this title, or of any rule or regulation prescribed under authority thereof, have been or are about to be violated, it may, in its discretion, either require or permit such person to file with it a statement in writing, under oath, or otherwise, as to all the facts and circumstances concerning the subject matter which it believes to be in the public interest to investigate, and may investigate such facts.

(b) Whenever it shall appear to the Commission that any person is engaged or about to engage in any acts or practices which constitute or will constitute a violation of the provisions of this title, or of any rule or regulation prescribed under authority thereof, it may in its discretion, bring an action in any district court of the United States, United States court of any Territory, or the Supreme Court of the District of Columbia to enjoin such acts or practices, and upon a proper showing a permanent or temporary injunction or restraining order shall be granted without bond. The Commission may transmit such evidence as may be available concerning such acts or practices to the Attorney General who may, in his discretion, institute the necessary criminal proceedings under this title. Any such criminal proceeding may be brought either in the district wherein the transmittal of the prospectus or security complained of begins, or in the district wherein such prospectus or security is received.

(c) Upon application of the Commission the district courts of the United States, the United States courts of any Territory, and the Supreme Court of the District of Columbia, shall also have jurisdiction to issue writs of mandamus commanding any person to comply with the provisions of this title or any order of the Commission made in pursuance thereof.

Hearings by Commission

SEC. 21. All hearings shall be public and may be held before the Commission or an officer or officers of the Commission designated by it, and appropriate records thereof shall be kept.

Jurisdiction of Offenses and Suits

SEC. 22. (a) The district courts of the United States, the United States courts of any Territory, and the Supreme Court of the District of Columbia shall have jurisdiction of offenses and violations under this title and under the rules and regulations promulgated by the Commission in respect thereto, and, concurrent with State and Territorial courts, of all suits in equity and actions at law brought to enforce any liability or duty created by this title. Any such suit or action may be brought in the district wherein the defendant is found or is an inhabitant or transacts business, or in the district where the sale took place, if the defendant participated therein, and process in such cases may be served in any other district of which the defendant is an inhabitant or wherever the defendant may be found. Judgments and decrees so rendered shall be subject to review as provided in sections 128 and 240 of the Judicial Code, as amended (U.S.C., title 28, secs. 225 and 347). No case arising under this title and brought in any State court of competent jurisdiction shall be removed to any court of the United States. No costs shall be assessed for or against the Commission in any proceeding under this title brought by or against it in the Supreme Court or such other courts.

(b) In case of contumacy or refusal to obey a subpena issued to any person, any of the said United States courts, within the jurisdiction of which said person guilty of contumacy or refusal to obey is found or resides, upon application by the Commission may issue to such person an order requiring such person to appear before the Commission, or one of its examiners designated by it, there to produce documentary evidence if so ordered, or there to give evidence touching the matter in question; and any failure to obey such order of the court may be punished by said court as a contempt thereof.

(c) No person shall be excused from attending and testifying or from producing books, papers, contracts, agreements, and other documents before the Commission, or in obedience to the subpena of the Commission or any member thereof or any officer designated by it, or in any cause or proceeding instituted by the Commission, on the ground that the testimony or evidence, documentary or otherwise, required of him, may tend to incriminate him or subject him to a penalty or forfeiture; but no individual shall be prosecuted or subjected to any penalty or forfeiture for or on account of any transaction, matter, or thing concerning which he is compelled, after having claimed his privilege against self-incrimination, to testify or produce evidence, documentary or otherwise, except that such individual so testifying shall not be exempt from prosecution and punishment for perjury committed in so testifying.

Unlawful Representations

SEC. 23. Neither the fact that the registration statement for a security has been filed or is in effect nor the fact that a stop order is not in effect with respect thereto shall be deemed a finding by the Commission that the registration statement is true and accurate on its face or that it does not contain an untrue statement of fact or omit to state a material fact, or be held to mean that the Commission has in any way passed upon the merits of, or given approval to such security. It shall be unlawful to make, or cause to be made, to any prospective purchaser any representation contrary to the foregoing provisions of this section.

Penalties

SEC. 24. Any person who willfully violates any of the provisions of this title, or the rules and regulations promulgated by the Commission under authority thereof, or any person who willfully, in a registration statement filed under this title, makes any untrue statement of a material fact or omits to state any material fact required to be stated therein or necessary to make the statements therein not misleading, shall upon conviction be fined not more than $5,000 or imprisoned not more than five years, or both.

Jurisdiction of Other Government Agencies over Securities

SEC. 25. Nothing in this title shall relieve any person from submitting to the respective supervisory units of the Government of the United States information, reports, or other documents that are now or may hereafter be required by any provision of law.

Separability of Provisions

SEC. 26. If any provision of this Act, or the application of such provision to any person or circumstance, shall be held invalid, the remainder of this Act, or the application of such provision to persons or circumstances other than those as to which it is held invalid, shall not be affected thereby.

Schedule A

(1) The name under which the issuer is doing or intends to do business;

(2) the name of the State or other sovereign power under which the issuer is organized;

(3) the location of the issuer's principal business office, and if the issuer is a foreign or territorial person, the name and address of its agent in the United States authorized to receive notice;

(4) the names and addresses of the directors or persons performing similar functions, and the chief executive, financial and accounting officers, chosen or to be chosen if the issuer be a corporation, association, trust, or other entity; of all partners, if the issuer be a partnership; and of the issuer, if the issuer be an individual; and of the promoters in the case of a business to be formed, or formed within two years prior to the filing of the registration statement;

(5) the names and addresses of the underwriters;

(6) the names and addresses of all persons, if any, owning of record or beneficially, if known, more than 10 per centum of any class of stock of the issuer, or more than 10 per centum in the aggregate of the outstanding stock of the issuer as of a date within twenty days prior to the filing of the registration statement;

(7) the amount of securities of the issuer held by any person specified in paragraphs (4), (5), and (6) of this schedule, as of a date within twenty days prior to the filing of the registration statement, and, if possible, as of one year prior thereto, and the amount of the securities, for which the registration statement is filed, to which such persons have indicated their intention to subscribe;

(8) the general character of the business actually transacted or to be transacted by the issuer;

(9) a statement of the capitalization of the issuer, including the authorized and outstanding amounts of its capital stock and the proportion thereof paid up, the number and classes of shares in which such capital stock is divided, par value thereof, or if it has no par value, the stated or assigned value thereof, a description of the respective voting rights, preferences, conversion and exchange rights, rights to dividends, profits, or capital of each class, with respect to each other class, including the retirement and liquidation rights or values thereof;

(10) a statement of the securities, if any, covered by options outstanding or to be created in connection with the security to be offered, together with the names and addresses of all persons, if any, to be allotted more than 10 per centum in the aggregate of such options;

(11) the amount of capital stock of each class issued or included in the shares of stock to be offered;

(12) the amount of the funded debt outstanding and to be created by the security to be offered, with a brief description of the date, maturity, and character of such

debt, rate of interest, character of amortization provisions, and the security, if any, therefor. If substitution of any security is permissible, a summarized statement of the conditions under which such substitution is permitted. If substitution is permissible without notice, a specific statement to that effect;

(13) the specific purposes in detail and the approximate amounts to be devoted to such purposes, so far as determinable, for which the security to be offered is to supply funds, and if the funds are to be raised in part from other sources, the amounts thereof and the sources thereof, shall be stated;

(14) the remuneration, paid or estimated to be paid, by the issuer or its predecessor, directly or indirectly, during the past year and ensuing year to (a) the directors or persons performing similar functions, and (b) its officers and other persons, naming them wherever such remuneration exceeded $25,000 during any such year;

(15) the estimated net proceeds to be derived from the security to be offered;

(16) the price at which it is proposed that the security shall be offered to the public or the method by which such price is computed and any variation therefrom at which any portion of such security is proposed to be offered to any persons or classes of persons, other than the underwriters, naming them or specifying the class. A variation in price may be proposed prior to the date of the public offering of the security, but the Commission shall immediately be notified of such variation;

(17) all commission or discounts paid or to be paid, directly or indirectly, by the issuer to the underwriters in respect of the sale of the security to be offered. Commissions shall include all cash, securities, contracts, or anything else of value, paid, to be set aside, disposed of, or understandings with or for the benefit of any other persons in which any underwriter is interested, made, in connection with the sale of such security. A commission paid or to be paid in connection with the sale of such security by a person in which the issuer has an interest or which is controlled or directed by, or under common control with, the issuer shall be deemed to have been paid by the issuer. Where any such commission is paid the amount of such commission paid to each underwriter shall be stated;

(18) the amount or estimated amounts, itemized in reasonable detail, of expenses, other than commissions specified in paragraph (17) of this schedule, incurred or borne by or for the account of the issuer in connection with the sale of the security to be offered or properly chargeable thereto, including legal, engineering, certification, authentication, and other charges;

(19) the net proceeds derived from any security sold by the issuer during the two years preceding the filing of the registration statement, the price at which such security was offered to the public, and the names of the principal underwriters of such security;

(20) any amount paid within two years preceding the filing of the registration statement or intended to be paid to any promoter and the consideration for any such payment;

(21) the names and addresses of the vendors and the purchase price of any property, or good will, acquired or to be acquired, not in the ordinary course of business, which is to be defrayed in whole or in part from the proceeds of the security

to be offered, the amount of any commission payable to any person in connection with such acquisition, and the name or names of such person or persons, together with any expense incurred or to be incurred in connection with such acquisition, including the cost of borrowing money to finance such acquisition;

(22) full particulars of the nature and extent of the interest, if any, of every director, principal executive officer, and of every stockholder holding more than 10 per centum of any class of stock or more than 10 per centum in the aggregate of the stock of the issuer, in any property acquired, not in the ordinary course of business of the issuer, within two years preceding the filing of the registration statement or proposed to be acquired at such date;

(23) the names and addresses of counsel who have passed on the legality of the issue;

(24) dates of and parties to, and the general effect concisely stated of every material contract made, not in the ordinary course of business, which contract is to be executed in whole or in part at or after the filing of the registration statement or which contract has been made not more than two years before such filing. Any management contract or contract providing for special bonuses or profit-sharing arrangements, and every material patent or contract for a material patent right, and every contract by or with a public utility company or an affiliate thereof, providing for the giving or receiving of technical or financial advice or service (if such contract may involve a charge to any party thereto at a rate in excess of $2,500 per year in cash or securities or anything else of value), shall be deemed a material contract;

(25) a balance sheet as of a date not more than ninety days prior to the date of the filing of the registration statement showing all of the assets of the issuer, the nature and cost thereof, whenever determinable, in such detail and in such form as the Commission shall prescribe (with intangible items segregated), including any loan in excess of $20,000 to any officer, director, stockholder or person directly or indirectly controlling or controlled by the issuer, or person under direct or indirect common control with the issuer. All the liabilities of the issuer in such detail and such form as the Commission shall prescribe, including surplus of the issuer showing how and from what sources such surplus was created, all as of a date not more than ninety days prior to the filing of the registration statement. If such statement be not certified by an independent public or certified accountant, in addition to the balance sheet required to be submitted under this schedule, a similar detailed balance sheet of the assets and liabilities of the issuer, certified by an independent public or certified accountant, of a date not more than one year prior to the filing of the registration statement, shall be submitted;

(26) a profit and loss statement of the issuer showing earnings and income, the nature and source thereof, and the expenses and fixed charges in such detail and such form as the Commission shall prescribe for the latest fiscal year for which such statement is available and for the two preceding fiscal years, year by year, or, if such issuer has been in actual business for less than three years, then for such time as the issuer has been in actual business, year by year. If the date of the filing of the registration statement is more than six months after the close of the last fiscal year, a

statement from such closing date to the latest practicable date. Such statement shall show what the practice of the issuer has been during the three years or lesser period as to the character of the charges, dividends or other distributions made against its various surplus accounts, and as to depreciation, depletion, and maintenance charges, in such detail and form as the Commission shall prescribe, and if stock dividends or avails from the sale of rights have been credited to income, they shall be shown separately with a statement of the basis upon which the credit is computed. Such statement shall also differentiate between any recurring and nonrecurring income and between any investment and operating income. Such statement shall be certified by an independent public or certified accountant;

(27) if the proceeds, or any part of the proceeds, of the security to be issued is to be applied directly or indirectly to the purchase of any business, a profit and loss statement of such business certified by an independent public or certified accountant, meeting the requirements of paragraph (26) of this schedule, for the three preceding fiscal years, together with a balance sheet, similarly certified, of such business, meeting the requirements of paragraph (25) of this schedule of a date not more than ninety days prior to the filing of the registration statement or at the date such business was acquired by the issuer if the business was acquired by the issuer more than ninety days prior to the filing of the registration statement;

(28) a copy of any agreement or agreements (or, if identic agreements are used, the forms thereof) made with any underwriter, including all contracts and agreements referred to in paragraph (17) of this schedule;

(29) a copy of the opinion or opinions of counsel in respect to the legality of the issue, with a translation of such opinion, when necessary, into the English language;

(30) a copy of all material contracts referred to in paragraph (24) of this schedule, but no disclosure shall be required of any portion of any such contract if the Commission determines that disclosure of such portion would impair the value of the contract and would not be necessary for the protection of the investors;

(31) unless previously filed and registered under the provisions of this title, and brought up to date, (a) a copy of its articles of incorporation, with all amendments thereof and of its exisitng bylaws or instruments corresponding thereto, whatever the name, if the issuer be a corporation; (b) copy of all instruments by which the trust is created or declared, if the issuer is a trust; (c) a copy of its articles of partnership or association and all other papers pertaining to its organization, if the issuer is a partnership, unincorporated association, joint-stock company, or any other form of organization; and

(32) a copy of the underlying agreements or indentures affecting any stock, bonds, or debentures offered or to be offered.

In case of certificates of deposit, voting trust certificates, collateral trust certificates, certificates of interest or shares in unincorporated investment trusts, equipment trust certificates, interim or other receipts for certificates, and like securities, the Commission shall establish rules and regulations requiring the submission of information of a like character applicable to such cases, together with such other information as it may deem appropriate and necessary regarding the character, financial or otherwise, of the actual issuer of the securities and/or the person performing the acts and assuming the duties of depositor or manager.

Schedule B

(1) Name of borrowing government or subdivision thereof;

(2) specific purposes in detail and the approximate amounts to be devoted to such purposes, so far as determinable, for which the security to be offered is to supply funds, and if the funds are to be raised in part from other sources, the amounts thereof and the sources thereof, shall be stated;

(3) the amount of the funded debt and the estimated amount of the floating debt outstanding and to be created by the security to be offered, excluding intergovernmental debt, and a brief description of the date, maturity, character of such debt, rate of interest, character of amortization provisions, and the security, if any, therefor. If substitution of any security is permissible, a statement of the conditions under which such substitution is permitted. If substitution is permissible without notice, a specific statement to that effect;

(4) whether or not the issuer or its predecessor has, within a period of twenty years prior to the filing of the registration statement, defaulted on the principal or interest of any external security, excluding intergovernmental debt, and, if so, the date, amount, and circumstances of such default, and the terms of the succeeding arrangement, if any;

(5) the receipts, classified by source, and the expenditures, classified by purpose, in such detail and form as the Commission shall prescribe for the latest fiscal year for which such information is available and the two preceding fiscal years, year by year;

(6) the names and addresses of the underwriters;

(7) the name and address of its authorized agent, if any, in the United States;

(8) the estimated net proceeds to be derived from the sale in the United States of the security to be offered;

(9) the price at which it is proposed that the security shall be offered in the United States to the public or the method by which such price is computed. A variation in price may be proposed prior to the date of the public offering of the security, but the Commission shall immediately be notified of such variation;

(10) all commissions paid or to be paid, directly or indirectly, by the issuer to the underwriters in respect of the sale of the security to be offered. Commissions shall include all cash, securities, contracts, or anything else of value, paid, to be set aside, disposed of, or understandings with or for the benefit of any other persons in which the underwriter is interested, made, in connection with the sale of such security. Where any such commission is paid, the amount of such commission paid to each underwriter shall be stated;

(11) the amount or estimated amounts, itemized in reasonable detail, of expenses, other than the commissions specified in paragraph (10) of this schedule, incurred or borne by or for the account of the issuer in connection with the sale of the security to

be offered or properly chargeable thereto, including legal, engineering, certification, and other charges;

(12) the names and addresses of counsel who have passed upon the legality of the issue;

(13) a copy of any agreement or agreements made with any underwriter governing the sale of the security within the United States; and

(14) an agreement of the issuer to furnish a copy of the opinion or opinions of counsel in respect to the legality of the issue, with a translation, where necessary, into the English language. Such opinion shall set out in full all laws, decrees, ordinances, or other acts of Government under which the issue of such security has been authorized. . . .

THE ORIGINS

REPORT OF THE HOUSE COMMITTEE ON INTERSTATE AND FOREIGN COMMERCE (WITH MINORITY VIEWS)
May 4, 1933

MR. RAYBURN, from the Committee on Interstate and Foreign Commerce, submitted the following

REPORT
[To accompany H.R. 5480]

The Committee on Interstate and Foreign Commerce, to whom was referred the bill (H.R. 5480) to provide full and fair disclosure of the character of securities sold in interstate and foreign commerce and through the mails, and to prevent frauds in the sale thereof, and for other purposes, report favorably thereon and recommend that the bill do pass with the following amendments:

Page 6, line 18, strike out "or any political."

Page 6, line 19, strike out "subdivision thereof" and insert "or by any political subdivision of a State or Territory, or by any public instrumentality of one or more States or Territories exercising an essential governmental function."

Page 6, line 23, after the words "national bank," insert "or by any banking institution organized under the laws of any State or Territory, the business of which is substantially confined to banking and is supervised by the State or territorial banking commission or similar official;".

Page 8, line 19, after the word "underwriter" insert "and not involving any public offering."

I. INTRODUCTORY STATEMENT

1. The President's Message

On March 29, 1933, the President sent the following message to Congress:

To the Congress:
I recommend to the Congress legislation for Federal supervision of traffic in investment securities in interstate commerce.

In spite of many State statutes the public in the past has sustained severe losses through practices neither ethical nor honest on the part of many persons and corporations selling securities.

Of course, the Federal Government cannot and should not take any action which might be construed as approving or guaranteeing that newly issued securities are sound in the sense that their value will be maintained or that the properties which they represent will earn profit.

There is, however, an obligation upon us to insist that every issue of new securities to be sold in interstate commerce shall be accompanied by full publicity and information, and that no essentially important element attending the issue shall be concealed from the buying public.

This proposal adds to the ancient rule of caveat emptor, the further doctrine "let the seller also beware." It puts the burden of telling the whole truth on the seller. It should give impetus to honest dealing in securities and thereby bring back public confidence.

The purpose of the legislation I suggest is to protect the public with the least possible interference to honest business.

This is but one step in our broad purpose of protecting investors and depositors. It should be followed by legislation relating to the better supervision of the purchase and sale of all property dealt in on exchanges, and by legislation to correct unethical and unsafe practices on the part of officers and directors of banks and other corporations.

What we seek is a return to a clear understanding of the ancient truth that those who manage banks, corporations, and other agencies handling or using other people's money are trustees acting for others.

Franklin D. Roosevelt

2. The Situation that Demands Action

The background of the President's message is only too familiar to everyone. During the post-war decade some 50 billions of new securities were floated in the United States. Fully half or $25,000,000,000 worth of securities floated during this period have been proved to be worthless. These cold figures spell tragedy in the lives of thousands of individuals who invested their life savings, accumulated after years of effort, in these worthless securities. The flotation of such a mass of essentially fraudulent securities was made possible because of the complete abandonment by many underwriters and dealers in securities of those standards of fair, honest, and prudent dealing that should be basic to the encouragement of investment in any enterprise. Alluring promises of easy wealth were freely made with little or no attempt to bring to the investor's attention those facts essential to estimating the worth of any security. High-pressure salesmanship rather than careful counsel was the rule in this most dangerous of enterprises.

Equally significant with these countless individual tragedies is the wastage that this irresponsible selling of securities has caused to industry. Because of the deliberate overstimulation of the appetites of security buyers, underwriters had to manufacture securities to meet the demand that they themselves had created. The result has been that investment bankers with no regard for the efficient functioning of industry forced corporations to accept new capital for expansion purposes in order that new securites might be issued for public consumption. Similarly, real-estate developments would be undertaken, not on the basis of caring for calculated needs but merely as an excuse for the issuance of more securities to satisfy an artificially created market. Such conduct has resulted both in the imposition of unnecessary fixed charges upon industry and in the creation of false and unbalanced values for properties whose earnings cannot conceivably support them. Whatever may be the full catalogue of the forces that brought to pass the present depression, not least among these has been this wanton misdirection of the capital resources of the Nation.

The irresponsibility which fostered this tragic distribution of securities derived in the main from the abnormal profits possible from the business of selling securities. Despite the fact that that business demands the assumption of responsibilities of a character fully equivalent to those of trusteeship, compelling full and fair disclosure not only of the character of the security but of the charges made in connection with its distribution, the literature on the faith of which the public was urged to invest its savings was too often deliberately misleading and illusive. Even dealers through the exertion of high-pressure tactics by underwriters were forced to take allotments of securities of an essentially unsound character and without opportunity to scrutinize their nature. These then would be worked off upon the unsuspecting public. One would have to turn the pages of history back to the days of the South Sea bubble to find an equivalent fantasy of security selling. It is these facts that have led the President, speaking for the Nation, rightly to demand that such a situation can no longer be tolerated.

3. Principles of the President's Message

Because only the dishonest man could object to the principles of the legislation outlined in the President's message, these principles have met with wide approval from the public, investment bankers, dealers, and industry alike. In brief, the aims set forth by the President are:

(1) An insistence that there should be full disclosure of every essentially important element attending the issue of a new security.

(2) A requirement that whatever action taken by the Federal Government for such disclosure should be limited to that purpose and should be so devised as not to be capable of being construed as an approval or guarantee of a security issue.

(3) A demand that the persons, whether they be directors, experts, or underwriters, who sponsor the investment of other people's money should be held up to the high standards of trusteeship.

The achievement of these ends is the principal purpose of this bill.

4. Disclosures Required

Resting upon the power of Congress under the Constitution over interstate and foreign commerce the bill closes the channels of such commerce to security issues unless and until a full disclosure of the character of such securities has been made. The items required to be disclosed, set forth in detailed form, are items indispensable to any accurate judgment upon the value of the security. But to require a disclosure of these items by the filing of a registration statement with the Federal Trade Commission would be insufficient, if by the mere act of such filing a privilege immediately to sell these securities was granted. High-pressure salesmanship with all its demonstrated evil effects would not even be scotched. Instead, heightened pressure would be exerted to effect the distribution of an issue before the investing public could digest the information demanded. For this reason and because some check should be exercised as to whether or not the disclosures demanded have been made, a period of 30 days intervenes between the act of disclosure by the filing of the registration statement and the date upon which that statement becomes effective so as to permit the sales of the securities registered under it. The type of information required to be disclosed is of a character comparable to that demanded by competent bankers from their borowers, and has been worked out in the light of these and other requirements. They are, in the judgement of your committee, adequate to bring into the full glare of publicity those elements of real and unreal values which may lie behind a security. To require anything else would permit evasions; but to require these disclosures fulfills the President's demand that "there is an obligation upon us to insist . . . that no essentially important element attending the issue shall be concealed from the buying public."

5. The Nonassumption by the Federal Government of any Guarantee

The mechanism devised by your committee for compelling disclosures and for insisting that disclosures shall be both adequate and true has been carefully framed, so that neither action nor nonaction by the Federal Trade Commission can be interpreted as a guarantee or approval of any particular security issued. The right to sell a security follows automatically upon the termination of the stipulated period after the filing of the registration statement. Nonaction by the Commission has no effect to disturb the acquisition of this right to sell the security in interstate commerce. Such functions as are given the Commission, with reference to the initial filing of the registration statement, are limited merely to determining whether the information so filed is complete and accurate on its face. The Commission may inquire to see whether the questions that should have been answered have been answered. But with the truth or falsity of the answers the Commission has no initial concern. If the statement is incomplete and inaccurate on its face. the Commission may require that these gaps shall be filled in before the statement is to become effective.

If, in an unusual case, the Commission is of the opinion that the statements made are materially untrue or materially inadequate, the Commission may institute an investigation and after giving an opportunity for a hearing, if convinced that the statements are untrue or inadequate, issue a stop order that will prevent further distribution of the security. The power so to suspend the right of underwriters and dealers to continue selling the security to the public, after proof that the statements upon the fact of which the security is sold are false, is essential for the protection of the investing public.

Thus the grant of control to the Federal Trade Commission conveys with it no right to pass upon the merits of any security, but simply to insist that whatever its merits, facts essential to its character are to be disclosed. An additional safeguard against the construction that the Government in any way approves a security registered with the Commission, is the provision of the bill expressly prohibiting any statement that registration of a security with the Commission is evidence either that the requirements of the act have been met or that the Commission has in any way approved the security.

6. The Imposition of Standards of Trusteeship

The character of civil liabilities imposed by this bill are described in detail elsewhere. Their essential characteristic consists of a requirement that all those responsible for statements upon the face of which the public is solicited to invest its money shall be held to standards like those imposed by law upon a fiduciary. Honesty, care, and competence are the demands of trusteeship. These demands are made by the bill on the directors of the issues, its experts, and the underwriters who sponsor the issue. If it be said that the imposition of such responsibilities upon these persons will be to alter corporate organization and corporate practice in this country, such a result is only what your committee expects. The picture of persons, assumed to be responsible for the direction of industrial enterprises, occupying 50 or more directorships of corporations is the best proof that some change is demanded. Directors should assume the responsibility of directing and if their manifold activities make real directing impossible, they should be held responsible to the unsuspecting public for their neglect. But to require them to guarantee the absolute accuracy of every statement that they are called upon to make, would be to gain nothing in the way of an effective remedy and to fall afoul of the President's injunction that the protection of the public should be achieved with the least possible interference to honest business. Whereas to insist upon the assumption of duties of trusteeship is to return to the ancient truths of fair dealing. The demands of this bill call for the assumption of no impossible burden, nor do they involve any leap into the dark. Similar requirements have for years attended the business of issuing securities in other industrialized nations. They have already been readily assumed in this country by honest and conservative issuers and investment bankers. Instead of impeding honest business, the imposition of liabilities of this character carries over into the general field of security selling, ethical standards of honesty and fair dealing common to every fiduciary undertaking.

II. GENERAL ANALYSIS OF THE BILL

1. Its Scope

The bill affects only new offerings of securities sold through the use of the mails or of instrumentalities of interstate or foreign transportation or communication. It does not affect the ordinary redistribution of securities unless such redistribution takes on the characteristics of a new offering by reason of the control of the issuer possessed by those responsible for the offering. It carefully exempts from its application certain types of securities and securities transactions where there is no practical need for its application or where the public benefits are too remote.

In respect of unexempted security offerings it provides in substance that:

(1) Any such offering is unlawful until—

(*a*) A registration statement setting forth prescribed information has been filed with the Federal Trade Commission; and

(*b*) Such "registration statement" has remained on file for not less than 30 days, subject to public inspection, thereby giving adequate opportunity for appropriate scrutiny by State securities commissions and independent securities services and advisers.

(2) After such waiting period, such securities may be sold through the mails, or through the use of any instrumentalities of interstate or foreign communication or transportation only if the buyer is given a substantial replica of the information included in the "registration statement"; and if sales are made without giving the buyer such information, or if even after the waiting period the Commission discovers that the "registration statement" is or has become false, inadequate, or misleading, because it includes an untrue statement of a material fact or omits to state a material fact, the Commission may by stop order, subject to court review, temporarily or permanently stop the further sale of such securities.

(3) Newspaper articles, "tipster's sheets," and other descriptions of or comments upon securities not purporting to offer such securities for sale must disclose any financial interest of the writer or publisher in their sale.

(4) The directors and officers of the issuers, the accountants, appraisers, and other experts authorizing and furnishing the information included in the "registration statement," and the underwriters of the offering, are jointly and severally liable to any buyer for rescission of any sale or for damages, if the registration statement or the information given to the buyer in the course of a sale is false and misleading and the defendant cannot prove both that he did not know and by the exercise of due care could not have known of such false or misleading character.

(5) The Commission may apply to the courts to enjoin any device, scheme, or artifice to defraud, employed in connection with the sale in interstate or foreign commerce of any securities, whether new or already outstanding.

2. Exempted Securities and Transactions

The exemption sections, 3 and 4, exempt, among other transactions in securities, transactions by individuals; the execution by brokers of customer's orders in open market; transactions by a dealer in securities not connected by time or circumstance with distribution of a new offering; securities issued in a reorganization subject to the approval of a court; certificates issued by a receiver or by a trustee in bankruptcy, with the approval of a court; short-term commercial paper; general obligations of the Federal Government and its corporate instrumentalities, of national banks, of the Federal Reserve banks, of State banks (as suggested by a committee amendment), and the States and their political subdivisions; railroad securities subject to the jurisdiction of the Interstate Commerce Commission; insurance policies subject to the supervision of a State insurance commissioner; and the securities of a nonprofit corporation and of certain building and loan associations. The Commission is given a further discretionary power carefully limited to exempt additional transactions and securities where the aggregate amount of the offering does not exceed $100,000. This power is deemed necessary for the effective administration of the bill, but is expected to be used only in a sparing manner, which keeps in mind the prima facie requirement that every security and transaction not specifically exempted by the terms of the bill should be kept within its scope. Section 5 (c) also exempts sales within a State of entire issues of local issuers. In view of these exemptions and the restriction of the bill's application to new offerings, the bill does not affect transactions beyond the need of public protection in order to prevent recurrences of demonstrated abuses.

3. The Character of Registration and the Conditions to Its Effectiveness

Sections 5, 6, 7, 8, and 9 include the provisions for the filing of the "registration statement" with the Commission, the required lapse of an inspection period between the first availability of such information to the public through the "registration statement" and the time when selling of securities therein described may lawfully commence, and the power in the Commission to stop the further improper distribution of securities. It should be noted that the Commission is not empowered to affect at any time the validity, as such, of sales already lawfully made.

The information required to be filed in and with the "registration statement" is set forth in the schedules annexed to the bill. Because of the basic importance of this "registration statement," both as a source of information to the prospective buyer and as a foundation for civil liability if the information therein given is false or misleading, the requirements of this "registration statement" have, of course, been designed to reach items of distribution profits, watered values, and hidden interests that usually have not been revealed to the buyer despite their indispensable importance in appraising the soundness of a security. A balance sheet that gives an intelligent idea of the assets and liabilities of the issuer and a profit and loss statement that gives a fair picture of its operations for the preceding 3 years, must be certified by an independent public accountant. The requirements in respect of securities of foreign governments have been worked out with particular care. To assure the necessary knowledge for judgment, the bill requires enumerated definite statements. Mere general power to require such information as the Commission might deem advisable would lead to evasions, laxities, and powerful demands for administrative discriminations. No honestly conceived and intelligently worked out offering, floated at a fair but not exorbitant profit, will be injured by the revelation of the whole truth which these requirements seek to elicit. The requirement of comparable information, at the time of the offering, of many of the most fraudulent issues, in which the public has suffered the greatest losses in late years, would have presented their flotation. A compulsory revelation of the whole truth will give impetus to honest dealing in securities and help to bring back public confidence.

4. The Waiting Period

The compulsory 30-day inspection period before securities can be sold is deliberately intended to interfere with the reckless traditions of the last few years of the securities business. It contemplates a change from methods of distribution lately in vogue which attempted complete sale of an issue sometimes within 1 day or at most a few days. Such methods practically compelled minor distributors, dealers, and even salesmen, as the price of participation in future issues of the underwriting house involved, to make commitments blindly. This has resulted in the demoralization of ethical standards as between these ultimate sales outlets and the securities-buying public to whom they had to look to take such commitments off their hands. This high-pressure technique has assumed an undue importance in the eyes of the present generation of securities distributors, with its reliance upon delicate calculations of day-to-day fluctuations in market opportunities and its implicit temptations to market manipulation, and must be discarded because the resulting injury to an underinformed public demonstrably hurts the Nation. It is furthermore the considered judgment of this committee that any issue which cannot stand the test of a waiting inspection over a month's average of economic conditions, but must be floated within a few days upon the crest of a possibly manipulated market fluctuation, is not a security which deserves protection at the cost of the public as compared with other issues which can meet this test. There is no more appropriate function of government than that it should encourage reasonable saving by protecting the fruits of that saving.

5. Prospectuses

Section 10 of the bill requires that any "prospectus" used in connection with the sale of any securities, if it is more than a mere announcement of the name and price of the issue offered and an offer of full details upon request, must include a substantial portion of the information required in the "registration statement." The Commission is given power to classify prospectuses according to the nature and circumstance of their use and to prescribe the form and contents appropriate to each class. While a leeway is given to the Commission to meet the varying exigencies of business transactions, fundamental safeguards necessary to insure a fair disclosure are to be preserved.

"Prospectus" is defined in section 2 (1) to include "any prospectus, notice, circular, advertisement, letter, or other communication offering any security for sale."

The purpose of these sections is to secure for potential buyers the means of understanding the intricacies of the transaction into which they are invited. The full revelations required in the filed "registration statement" should not be lost in the actual selling process. This requirement will undoubtedly limit the selling arguments hitherto employed. That is its purpose. But even in respect of certain types of listed issues, reputable stock exchanges have already, on their own initiative, recognized the danger of abbreviated selling literature and insisted upon supervising the selling of literature distributed in connection with such issues, to make certain that such literature includes the same information concerning the issue required in a formal circular filed with and approved by such exchanges. Any objection that the compulsory incorporation in selling literature and sales argument of substantially all information concerning the issue, will frighten the buyer with the intricacy of the transaction, states one of the best arguments for the provision. The rank and file of securities buyers who have hitherto bought blindly should be made aware that securities are intricate merchandise.

6. Civil Liabilities

Sections 11 and 12 create and define the civil liabilities imposed by the act and the machinery for their enforcement which renders them practically valuable. Fundamentally, these sections entitle the buyer of securities sold upon a registration statement including an untrue statement or omission of material fact, to sue for recovery of his purchase price, or for damages not exceeding such price, those who have participated in such distribution either knowing of such untrue statement or omission or having failed to take due care in discovering it. The duty of care to discover varies in its demands upon participants in security distribution with the importance of their place in the scheme of distribution and with the degree of protection that the public has a right to expect. The committee is fortified in these sections by similar safeguards in the English Companies Act of 1929. What is deemed necessary for sound financing in conservative England ought not be unnecessary for the more feverish pace which American finance has developed.

The committee emphasizes that these liabilities attach only when there has been an untrue statement of material fact or an omission to state a material fact in the registration statement or the prospectus—the basic information by which the public is solicited. All who sell securities with such a flaw, who cannot prove that they did not know—or who in the exercise of due care could not have known—of such misstatement or omission, are liable under sections 11 and 12. For those whose moral responsibility to the public is particularly heavy, there is a correspondingly heavier legal liability—the persons signing the registration statement, the underwriters, the directors of the issuer, the accountants, engineers, appraisers, and other professionals preparing and giving authority to the prospectus—all these are liable to the buyer not only if they cannot prove they did not know of the flaw in the information offered the public but also if they cannot prove that they could not have found that flaw "after reasonable investigation" and that they "had reasonable ground to believe and did believe . . . that such statement was true or that there was no such omission." This throws upon originators of securities a duty of competence as well as innocence which the history of recent spectacular failures overwhelmingly justifies. As a proper safeguard, anyone who has been given an apparent responsibility by the terms of the registration statement can avoid subsequent liability only by disclaiming such responsibility in a public way prior to the effective date of the registration statement or at the first opportunity.

The provisions throwing upon the defendant in suits under sections 11 and 12 the burden of proof to exempt himself are indispensable to make the buyer's remedies under these sections practically effective. Every lawyer knows that with all the facts in the control of the defendant it is practically impossible for a buyer to prove a state of knowledge or a failure to exercise due care on the part of defendant. Unless responsibility is to involve merely paper liability it is necessary to throw the burden of disproving responsibility for reprehensible acts of omission or commission on those who purport to issue statements for the public's reliance. The responsibility imposed is no more nor less than that of a trust. It is a responsibility that no honest banker and no honest business man should seek to avoid or fear. To impose a lesser responsibility would nullify the purposes of this legislation. To impose a greater responsibility, apart from constitutional doubts, would unnecessarily restrain the conscientious administration of honest business with no compensating advantage to the public.

The constitutionality of the imposition of liabilities of the character provided by the bill raises no serious question. Even though the activities of the particular persons concerned may be actually intrastate in character, they are, nevertheless, an integral part of a process calling for the interstate distribution of securities. Liability is imposed upon them as a condition of the acquisition of the privilege to do business through the channels of interstate or foreign commerce. The statements for which they are responsible, although they may never actually have been seen by the prospective purchaser, because of their wide dissemination, determine the market price of the security, which in the last analysis reflects those manifold causes that are the impelling motive of the particular purchase. The connection between the statements made and the purchase of the security is clear, and, for this reason, it is the essence of fairness to insist upon the assumption of responsibility for the making of these statements.

7. State Security Laws

The bill carefully preserves the jurisdiction of State security commissions to regulate transactions within their own borders. It goes further and makes that control more effective by preventing evasion of State security legislation by the device of selling in interstate or foreign commerce from outside the State. The fact that security dealers who wish to evade State laws have so frequently resorted to methods of selling securities without entering the State and thus never subjecting themselves to State control makes the elimination of this evil imperative.

The bill thus withdraws securities sold in violation of State laws from the protection that the method of selling them in interstate commerce would otherwise give them. It also makes it unlawful to use the instruments of interstate or foreign commerce in an effort to evade protective State legislation. In this aspect the bill builds itself upon existing precedents. Congress, by the Reed amendment of 1917, forbade sellers of intoxicating liquor from shielding their distribution of liquor in violation of State law behind the cloak of interstate commerce. The same principle was approved by this House, with reference to the sale of securities, by the passage of the Denison bill which sought in this respect to effectuate the same end. In the light of these precedents, together with the upholding of the Webb-Kenyon Act by the Supreme Court of the United States in *Clark Distilling Company* v. *Western Maryland Railway Company* (242 U.S. 311) there can be slight doubt as to the existence of a power in the Nation to prevent the use of means, such as interstate commerce, over which it has control, being employed to evade the settled policies of the States, whether these policies concern securities or intoxicating liquor. The right to withdraw protection of the interstate commerce clause from a commodity, because otherwise it would be sold in violation of State law (upheld by the Supreme Court in the Clark Distilling case), implies of necessity a power in the Nation to punish an attempt to use interstate commerce in defiance of the very purpose for which the protection of the interstate commerce clause was withdrawn. The wisdom of such an exertion of congressional power bases itself upon the uncontested fact that dealers in securities have cleverly organized their means of distributing securities so as to evade State blue-sky legislation by never entering the State. Such a policy does not interfere with legitimate business, but only by a resort to such a policy can interstate commerce be closed to illegitimate business.

III. SUMMARY OF THE BILL BY SECTIONS

Section 1. Title

This section provides a short title for the bill.

Section 2. Definitions

Paragraph (1) defines the term "security" in sufficiently broad and general terms so as to include within that definition the many types of instruments that in our commercial world fall within the ordinary concept of a security. The definition is broad enough to include as securities, for example, certificates of interest in oil, gas, or mining leases or royalties. The definition is again comprehensive enough to bring within its terms certificates of deposit issued by protective committees. It also includes warrants or rights to subscribe to a security, so that the control exerted by this bill commences with the initiation of any scheme to sell securities to the public.

Paragraph (2) defines "person" in terms sufficiently broad to include within that conception not only an individual but also every form of commercial organization that may issue securities. It includes within the concept of "person" a government or a political subdivision thereof, although later sections of the bill exempt from its provisions securities issued by the United States, a State, or a Territory, or a political subdivision of any of these governmental units. The term "trust" is defined to exclude the ordinary noncommercial trust but to include that type of organization, commonly known as a "business trust" or a "Massachusetts trust," which, without resort to the device of incorporation, is used to achieve many of the purposes of the ordinary business corporation.

Paragraph (3) defines the term "sale" or "sell" broadly to include every attempt or offer to dispose of a security for value. It includes within the definition of "sale" an offer to buy, thereby preventing dealers from making offers to buy between the period of the filing of the registration statement and the date upon which such a statement becomes effective. Otherwise, the underwriter, although only entitled to accept such offers to buy, after the effective date of the registration statement, could accept them in the order of their priority and thus bring pressure upon dealers, who wish to avail themselves of a particular security offering, to rush their orders to buy without adequate consideration of the nature of the security being offered. From the definition of sale, however, is excluded the exchange of an instrument for another instrument which merely evidences exactly the same right embodied in the original instrument, thus exchanges of a stock certificate for another stock certificate of the same character or of an interim receipt for the permanent security are excluded from the operation of the act. Special care is taken to except from the definition of "sale" preliminary negotiations and agreements between an issuer and an underwriter. Underwriting agreements can thus be entered into prior to the time of the filing of the registration statement between the issuer and underwriters, so as to delay the actual organization of the selling group and the disposition of the security to the dealers until the registration statement shall have become effective.

This paragraph also exempts from the concept of "sale" the giving to a holder of a security, at the time of the sale of such security to the holder, a right either to conversion or a warrant to subscribe, where neither of these rights are immediately exercisable. This makes it unnecessary to register such a security prior to the time that it is to be offered to the public, although the conversion right or the right to subscribe must be registered. When the actual securities to which these rights appertain are offered the public, the bill requires registration as of that time. This permits the holder of any such right of conversion or warrant to subscribe to judge whether upon all the facts it is advisable for him to exercise his rights.

Paragraph (4) defines the term "issuer" not only to include the actual issuer of the security but also the guarantor, if there be such a guarantor, in order that adequate disclosure may be made to the investor as to the worth of any such guaranty. Special provisions govern the definition of "issuer" in connection with security issues of an unusual character, such as fixed investment trusts and certificates of deposit. In instances of this nature basic securities are acquired by a depositing committee or corporation, which then deposits these securities with a trustee. The trustee actually issues the new securities, which represent an interest in the securities deposited with the trustee. These are then delivered to the depositor and are then distributed by the depositor to the public. Under such an arrangement, although the actual issuer is the trustee, the depositor is the person responsible for the flotation of the issue. Consequently, information relative to the depositor and to the basic securities is what chiefly concerns the investor—information respecting the assets and liabilities of the trust rather than of the trustee. For these reasons the duty of furnishing this information is placed upon the actual manager of the trust and not the passive trustee, and this purpose is accomplished by defining "issuer" as in such instances referring to the depositor or manager.

Paragraphs (5) and (6) are self-explanatory.

Paragraph (7) defines interstate commerce to include foreign commerce.

Paragraphs (8) and (9) need no detailed explanation.

Paragraph (10) defines "prospectus" broadly as including any written or radio communication offering a security for sale. Thus communications of this character, by virtue of this definition, must comply with the requirements of section 10. The bill, apart from section 16 (b), is not concerned with communications which merely describe a security. It is, therefore, possible for underwriters who wish to inform a selling group or dealers generally of the nature of a security that will be offered for sale after the effective date of the registration statement, to circulate among them full information respecting such a security. This could easily and effectively be done by circulating the offering circular itself, if clearly marked in such a manner as to indicate that no offers to buy should be sent or would be accepted until the effective date of the registration statement. From the definition of "prospectus" two exceptions are made: The first allows dealers, after they have opened negotiations with a prospective purchaser by giving him the requires prospectus, to give him such additional information as they may deem desirable. This additional information, of course, by virtue of the provisions contained in sections 12 (2) and 16 (a) (2) must not contain fraudulent statements or statements that are themselves untrue, either because of the misstatements that they contain or the facts of a relevant character that are omitted. The second exception to the inclusive definition of "prospectus" permits the ordinary type of broker and dealer advertising. Brokers and dealers are allowed to advertise a security by name and to state the price at which they will procure it for purchasers, provided that they also inform prospective purchasers where a detailed prospectus can be obtained. To avoid the inclusion in such advertisements of misleading and insufficient statements, dealers and brokers are not permitted to go farther in their advertising, unless they are willing to set forth the detailed statements required by the prospectus. It should be noted in this connection that section 10 (b) (4) permits the Commission to prescribe forms for prospectuses to be used in newspaper, periodical, and other general advertising.

Paragraph (11) sets forth the important definition of "underwriter." The term is defined broadly enough to include not only the ordinary underwriter, who for a commission promises to see that an issue is disposed of at a certain price, but also includes as an underwriter the person who purchases an issue outright with the idea of then selling that issue to the public. The definition of underwriter is also broad enough to include two other groups of persons who perform functions, similar in character, in the distribution of a large issue. The first of these groups may be designated as the underwriters of the underwriter, a group who, for a commission, agree to take over pro rata the underwriting risk assumed by the first underwriter. The second group may be termed participants in the underwriting or outright purchase, who may or may not be formal parties to the underwriting contract, but who are given a certain share or interest therein.

The term "underwriter," however, is interpreted to exclude the dealer who receives only the usual distributor's or seller's commission. This limitation, however, has been so phrased as to prevent any genuine underwriter passing under the mark of a distributor or dealer. The last sentence of this definition, defining "issuer" to include not only the issuer but also affiliates or subsidiaries of the issuer and persons controlling the issuer, has two functions. The first function is to require the disclosure of any underwriting commission which, instead of being paid directly to the underwriter by the issuer, may be paid in an indirect fashion by a subsidiary or affiliate of the issuer to the underwriter. Its second function is to bring within the provisions of the bill redistribution whether of outstanding issues or issues sold subsequently to the enactment of the bill. All the outstanding stock of a particular corporation may be owned by one individual or a select group of individuals. At some future date they may wish to dispose of their holdings and to make an offer of this stock to the public. Such a public offering may possess all the dangers attendant upon a new offering of securities. Wherever such a redistribution reaches significant proportions, the distributor would be in the position of controlling the issuer and thus able to furnish the information demanded by the bill. This being so, the distributor is treated as equivalent to the original issuer and, if he seeks to dispose of the issue through a public offering, he becomes subject to the act. The concept of control herein involved is not a narrow one, depending upon a mathematical formula of 51 percent of voting power, but is broadly defined to permit the provisions of the act to become effective wherever the fact of control actually exists.

Paragraph (12) defines the term "dealer" to include not merely the ordinary dealer in securities but also the broker. Transactions by a broker, however, provided that they are true brokerage transactions, are not brought within the scope of the bill by the specific exemptions granted in paragraph (2) of section 4. The sole object of this definition is thus to subject brokers to the same advertising restrictions that are imposed upon dealers, so as to prevent the broker from being used as a cloak for the sale of securities.

Section 3. Exempted Securities

This section lists securities that are exempt from the act. Paragraph (1) of subsection (a) exempts securities which prior to 60 days after the enactment of the act have either been sold or disposed of by the issuer or have been bona fide offered to the public. Adequate care is taken to prevent the exemption of securities whose issuance has been authorized prior to this time but which have never been offered to the public. Also the exemption does not apply to any redistribution of outstanding issues which would otherwise come within the act.

Paragraph (2) exempts United States, Territorial, and State obligations, or obligations of any political subdivision of these governmental units. The term "political subdivision" carries with it the exemption of such securities as county, town, or municipal obligations, as well as school district, drainage district, and levee district, and other similar bonds. The line drawn by the expression "political subdivision" corresponds generally with the line drawn by the courts as to what obligations of States, their units and instrumentalities created by them, are exempted from Federal taxation. By such a delineation, any constitutional difficulties that might arise with reference to the inclusion of State and municipal obligations are avoided. Securities of instrumentalities of the Government of the United States are also exempted, as well as securities issued by a national bank or by a Federal Reserve Bank. Securities issued by Governmental instrumentalities are not generally sold in the market while adequate supervision over the issuance of securities of a national bank is exercised by the Comptroller of the Currency. A committee amendment makes it clear that there are also exempt securities issued by a public instrumentality of one or more State or Territories exercising an essential governmental function.

Paragraph (3) exempts short-term paper of the type available for discount at a Federal Reserve bank and of a type which rarely is bought by private investors.

Paragraph (4) exempts securities of a noncommercial character issued by eleemosynary institutions.

Paragraph (5) exempts the securities of building and loan associations and similar institutions, but insists that such institutions as a condition to being exempt from the act must do a true building and loan business by confining their business to the making of loans to their members.

Paragraph (6) exempts all securities issued by common carriers, the issuance of whose securities is already by virtue of section 20a of the Interstate Commerce Act subject to the control and approval of the Interstate Commerce Commission.

Paragraph (7) exempts receiver's certificates and trustee certificates when such certificates have already been approved by the court under whose control the receiver or trustee acts.

Paragraph (8) makes clear what is already implied in the act, namely, that insurance policies are not to be regarded as securities subject to the provisions of the act. The insurance policy and like contracts are not regarded in the commercial world as securities offered to the public for investment purposes. The entire tenor of the act would lead, even without this specific exemption, to the exclusion of insurance policies from the provisions of the act, but the specific exemption is included to make misinterpretation impossible.

Subsection (b) gives a general authority to the Commission to add to the class of express exemptions any security which because of the small amount involved or the limited character of the public offering should properly be excluded from the provisions of the act. To confer such a power upon the Commission permits the Commission by adequate rules and regulations to provide against needless registration of issues of such an insignificant character as not to call for regulation. This general power of the Commission, however, is closely limited by the requirement that it shall not extend to any issue whose aggregate amount exceeds $100,000. The Commission is thus safeguarded against any untoward pressure to exempt issues whose distribution may carry all the unfortunate consequences that the act is designed to prevent.

Section 4. Exempted Transactions

The provisions of this section exempt certain transactions from the provisions of section 5, which section requires both the registration of securities as a condition precedent to offering them for sale in interstate or foreign commerce or for transporting them in such commerce, and which section also requires that after the effective date of registration prospectuses relating to such securities shall conform to the requirements of the act.

Paragraph (1) broadly draws the line between distribution of securities and trading in securities, indicating that the act is, in the main, concerned with the problem of distribution as distinguished from trading. It, therefore, exempts all transactions except by an issuer, underwriter, or dealer. Again, it exempts transactions by an issuer unless made by or through an underwriter so as to permit an issuer to make a specific or an isolated sale of its securities to a particular person, but insisting that if a sale of the issuer's securities should be made generally to the public that that transaction shall come within the purview of the act. Recognizing that a dealer is often concerned not only with the distribution of securities but also with trading in securities, the dealer is exempted as to trading when such trading occurs a year after the public offering of the securities. Since before that year the dealer might easily evade the provisions of the act by a claim that the securities he was offering for sale were not acquired by him in the process of distribution but were acquired after such process had ended, transactions during that year are not exempted. The period of a year is arbitrarily taken because, generally speaking, the average public offering has been distributed within a year, and the imposition of requirements upon the dealer so far as that year is concerned is not burdensome. Transactions by an underwriter are not exempted. It is true, however, that there is a point of time when a person who has become an underwriter ceases to exercise any underwriting function and, therefore, ceases to be an underwriter. When that point is reached such a person would be subject only to whatever restrictions would be imposed upon him as a dealer.

Paragraph (2) exempts the ordinary brokerage transaction. Individuals may thus dispose of their securities according to the method which is now customary without any restrictions imposed upon the individual or the broker. This exemption also assures an open market for securities at all times, even though a stop order against further distribution of such securities may have been entered. Purchasers, provided they are not dealers, may thus in the event that a stop order has been entered, cut their losses immediately, if there are losses, by disposing of the securities. On the other hand, the entry of a stop order prevents any further distribution of the security.

Paragraph (3) exempts stock dividends or additional capital stock distributed among the stockholders of a corporation when such distribution is by way of dividend and not by sale. Any crediting of stock dividends to income is to be disclosed by the issuer in whatever income statement may precede the issuance of a security, together with the basis upon which such credit is computed, by the express provisions of paragraph (26) of Schedule A. This paragraph also exempts the distribution of additional capital stock of a corporation when distributed among its own stockholders provided that no commission is paid in connection with such distribution. This paragraph also exempts the distribution of securities during a boda fide reorganization of a corporation when such reorganization is carried on under the supervision of a court.

Reorganizations carried out without such judicial supervision possess all the dangers implicit in the issuance of new securities and are, therefore, not exempt from the act. For the same reason the provision is not broad enough to include mergers or consolidations of corporations entered into without judicial supervision.

Paragraph (4) exempts subscriptions to the capital stock of a corporation where no expense is incurred or commission paid in connection with the subscriptions. No sales pressure being present in connection with subscriptions of this character and no promotion for pecuniary profit being involved, the reason for their exemption is clear.

Section 5. Prohibitions Relating to Interstate or Foreign Commerce and the Mails

Subject to the exemptions allowed by sections 3 and 4, it is made unlawful for any person to make use of the mails or any means or instruments of interstate or foreign commerce (a) before the effective date of registration, or while the registration is suspended, to sell any security or to carry or cause to be carried any security for the purpose of sale or delivery after sale, and (b) after the effective date of registration to transmit any prospectus relating to the sale of any such security that does not meet the requirements set in section 10, or to carry or cause to be carried any such security for the purpose of sale or delivery after sale, unless accompanied or preceded by a prospectus meeting such requirements.

The provisions of this section as to the use of the mails, however, do not apply to the sale of a security where the issue of which it is a part is sold only to persons resident within a single State, where the issuer is a resident and doing business within such State.

Section 6. Registration of Securities and Signing of Registration Statement

(a) A security may be registered so as to permit its sale by use of the mails or instruments of interstate and foreign commerce by filing a registration statement in triplicate with the Federal Trade Commission. The registration statement must be signed by the issuer, its principal executive, financial and accounting officers, and by a majority of its board of directors. When the issuer is a foreign or territorial person, the statement must be signed by its duly authorized representative in the United States, except that in case of a foreign government or political subdivision thereof, it need only be signed by the underwriter.

(b) At the time of filing, the applicant must pay a fee of one hundredth of 1 per centum of the maximum aggregate price at which the securities are propsed to be offered, but in no case less than $50.

(c) The filing of a registration statement or of an amendment takes place upon the receipt thereof or if forwarded in the United States by registered mail, upon the mailing thereof.

(d) The information contained or filed with any registration statement shall be available to the public under appropriate regulations of the Commission, and copies, printed, photostatic, or otherwise, shall be furnished to anyone who applies therefor at a reasonable charge.

(e) No registration statement may be filed within 30 days after the enactment of the act.

Section 7. Information Required in Registration Statement

The registration statement when relating to a security other than a security issued by a foreign government, or political subdivision thereof, shall contain the information and be accompanied by the documents specified in schedule A and when relating to the security of a foreign government or political subdivision thereof the information and documents specified in schedule B. The Commission, however, may by its rules and regulations provide that any such information or documents need not be included in respect to a class of issuers or securities if it finds that such information or documents are inapplicable to such class and that disclosure fully adequate for the protection of investors is otherwise required. The Commission may further provide by its rules and regulations for the inclusion of such additional information and documents as it may deem necessary or appropriate to effectuate the purposes of the act.

The requirements of schedule A, relating principally to corporate securities, may be briefly summarized as follows:

(1) The investor must be given these essential facts concerning the property in which he is invited to acquire an interest:

(a) The name, locality, and character of the business.

(b) A detailed statement of the capitalization of the issuer with a description of the rights of the holders of the various classes of securities.

(c) The specific purposes for which the security to be offered is to supply the funds.

(d) A list, and the general effect concisely stated, of all material contracts, not made in the ordinary course of the business, including all management contracts, profit-sharing arrangements, and contracts for the giving or receiving of technical or financial advice or service.

(*e*) A balance sheet that will give an intelligent idea of the assets and liabilities of the issuer, in such form and such detail as the Commission may prescribe.

(*f*) A profit and loss statement that will give an intelligent idea of the earnings and operations of the issuers for at least 3 years, year by year, in such form and in such detail as the Commission may prescribe.

(2) The investor must be given these essential facts concerning the identity and the interests of the persons with whom he is dealing or to whom the management of his investment is entrusted:

(*a*) The names of the promoters, directors, and principal executive, financial and accounting officers of the issuer, and the names of the underwriters and of all persons owning more than 10 percent of any class of stock or more than 10 percent in the aggregate of all stock, together with a statement of the amount of the securities of issuer held by all such persons as of the date of the filing of the registration statement and as of 1 year prior thereto.

(*b*) A statement of the securities of the issuer covered by options and the names of any persons holding more than 10 percent of such options.

(*c*) The remuneration paid the directors during the past year, and to be paid during the ensuing year and the remuneration to officers or other persons, exceeding $25,000 per year during any such year.

(*d*) All commissions paid or to be paid to the underwriters.

(*e*) Any amounts paid within 2 years to any promoter and the consideration therefor.

(*f*) Particulars concerning the acquisition of any property acquired or to be acquired, not in the ordinary course of the business, to be paid in whole or in part out of the proceeds of the security to be offered, the names of the vendors and the interest of any director, officer, or principal stockholders of the issuer in any such property.

(*g*) Names of counsel approving legality of the issue.

(3) The investor must be given these essential facts in regard to the price and cost of the security he is buying and its relation to the price and cost of earlier offerings:

(*a*) Estimated net proceeds to be derived from the security offered.

(*b*) Proposed price of security to be offered to the public.

(*c*) Estimated amount of expenses in connection with the sale of the security.

(*d*) Net proceeds from any security of the issuer sold during the preceding 2 years, price at which such security was offered to the public, and the names of the underwriters.

The requirements of schedule B relating to securities of a foreign government or political subdivision thereof may be briefly summarized as follows:

(1) That investor must be given these essential facts concerning the borrowing government or subdivision thereof:

(*a*) The name of the borrower and authorized agent, if any, in the United States.

(*b*) A description of the funded and floating debt of the borrower and a statement of the terms of the loan to be floated and of the security therefor.

(*c*) Any default in the principal or interest of any external obligation during the preceding 20 years and the terms of any succeeding arrangement.

(*d*) The specific purposes of the loan.

(*e*) The receipts, reasonably classified by source, and the expenditures, reasonably classified by purpose, in such detail and form as the Commission may prescribe, for the preceding 3 years, year by year.

(2) The investor must be given these essential facts with regard to the underwriters and counsel:

(*a*) The names of the underwriters, and all commission paid or to be paid to such underwriters.

(*b*) The names of counsel approving the legality of the issue.

(3) The investor must be given these essential facts in regard to the price and cost of the security he is buying:

(*a*) The estimated proceeds to be derived from the sale in the United States of the security to be offered.

(*b*) The price at which the security is to be offered to the public in the United States.

(*c*) The estimated amount of the expenses to be incurred in connection with the sale of the security to be offered.

Schedules A and B are to be accompanied by important documents such as the underwriting agreements, opinions of counsel, and the underlying indentures and agreements in regard to the securities of the issuer.

Section 8. Taking Effect of Registration Statements and Amendments Thereto

(*a*) The registration statement becomes effective 30 days after filing. If any amendment is filed prior to the effective date of the registration statement, the registration statement is deemed to have been filed when the amendment was filed; except that an amendment filed with the consent of the Commission prior to the effective date of the registration statement, is treated as if filed with the original statement. This subdivision, as has been expalined above, is to afford a waiting or cooling period of 30 days so as to eliminate many of the abuses connected with high-pressure salesmanship and the sale of securities to the public under circumstances permitting an inadequate examination by informed critics of the essential facts.

(*b*) If it appears to the Commission that a registration statement is on its face incomplete or inaccurate in any material respect, the Commission may, after con-firmed telegraphic notice not later than 20 days after the filing of the registration statement and opportunity for hearing within 10 days after such notice, issue an order prior to the effective date of registration refusing to permit such statement to become effective until it has been amended in accordance with such order. When the statement has been amended in accordance with such order the Commission shall so declare and the registration shall become effective at the time provided in subsection (*a*) or upon the date of such declaration, whichever date is the later. This subsection is intended to enable the Commission to make a preliminary check-up of any obvious departures from the standards set by the law without imposing upon the Commission any responsibility as to the truth of the registration statement or as to the soundness of the securities to be offered thereunder.

(*c*) If any amendment filed after the effective date of the registration statement appears to the Commission to be not incomplete or inaccurate on its face, it becomes effective on such date as the Commission may determine, having regard to the public interest and the protection of investors.

(*d*) If it appears to the Commission at any time that the registration statement includes any untrue statement of a material fact or omits to state any material fact, the Commission may, after the sending of confirmed telegraphic notice after opportunity for hearing within 15 days after such notice, issue a stop order suspending the effectiveness of the registration statement. When such statement has been amended to meet the objections of the Commission, the Commission shall so declare, and thereupon the stop order shall cease to be effective. In determining whether a stop order should issue, the Commission will naturally have regard to the facts as they then exist and will stop the further sale of securities even though the registration statement was true when made, it has become untrue or misleading by reason of subsequent developments. This subdivision is intended to enable the Commission to prevent any imposition upon its authority by the filing of any untrue, inadequate, or misleading statement. At the same time, it limits the scope of the issues to be considered by the Commission on any stop order and thereby avoids any undue interference with private rights.

(*e*) The Commission is given adequate power to make a complete examination in order to determine whether a stop order should issue. If any issuer, representative, or underwriter fails to cooperate, or obstructs or refuses to permit the making of an examination, such conduct is proper ground for the issuance of a stop order.

(*f*) Any notice under this section shall be sent to the issuer, or in case of a foreign government, to the underwriter, or in case of a foreign or territorial person to its authorized representative in the United States.

Section 9. Court Review of Orders

Any person aggrieved by an order of the Commission may obtain a review of such order on questions of law in the Court of Appeals of the District of Columbia. The jurisdiction of such court is exclusive, and its judgment and decree final, subject to review by the Supreme Court of the United States. Proceedings before the court, unless specifically ordered by the court, do not operate as a stay of any order of the Commission.

Section 10. Information Required in Prospectus

(*a*) A prospectus must contain the same statements made in the registration statement, except that the documents accompanying the registration statement need not be included.

(*b*) Notwithstanding the provisions of subsection (*a*), (1) when a prospectus is used more than 12 months after the effective date of the registration statement, the information contained therein must be of a date not more than 12 months prior to its use, (2) there may be omitted from the prospectus any of the statements that would otherwise be required under subsection (*a*), which the Commission may by rules and regulations designate as not being necessary or appropriate in the public interest or for the protection of investors, and (3) the prospectus must contain such other information as the Commission may by rules or regulations require as being necessary or appropriate in the public interest or for the protection of investors. The Commission is given power to classify prospectuses according to the nature and circumstances of their use and to prescribe as to each class the form and contents which it may find appropriate to such use and consistent with the public interest and protection of investors. Copies of all radio broadcasts must be filed with the Commission, and the Commission may by rules and regulations require the filing with it of forms of prospectuses used or to be used in connection with the sale of any securities registered under the act.

Section 11. Civil Liabilities on Account of False Registration Statement

(*a*) In case any part of the registration statement contained, at the time it became effective, an untrue statement of a material fact or omitted to state a material fact, any person who shall have acquired such security (unless it be proved that at the time of the acquisition he knew of such untruth or omission) is given the right to sue either at law or in equity in any court of competent jurisdiction—(1) every person who signed the registration statement; (2) every person who was a director of (or person performing similar functions) or partner in, the issuer at the time of the filing of the registration statement; (3) every person who with his consent is named in the registration statement as being or about to become a director, a person performing similar functions, or a partner; (4) every accountant, engineer, or appraiser, or any person whose profession gives authority to a statement made by him, who has prepared or certified any part of the registration statement, with respect to the part prepared or certified by him; (5) every underwriter.

Inasmuch as the value of a security may be affected by the information given in the registration statement, irrespective of whether a particular sale takes place in interstate or intrastate commerce, the civil remedies accorded by this subsection against those responsible for a false or misleading statement filed with the Federal Trade Commission are given to all purchasers regardless of whether they bought their securities in an interstate or intrastate transaction and regardless of whether they bought their securities at the time of the original offer or at some later date, provided, of course, that the remedy is prosecuted within the period of limitations provided by section 13. In this connection, it must be borne in mind that no one is obliged to register a security under this act unless he desires to make use of the mails or of the channels of interstate or foreign commerce in the distribution of the security. But if a person does avail himself of the privilege of registration accorded by this act, it is obviously within the constitutional power of Congress to accord a remedy to all purchasers who may reasonably be affected by any statements in the registration statement. The separability clause in section 25 of the bill makes certain that congressional power in this instance has been vested as far and to whatever circumstances the Constitution allows.

(b) The provisions of subsection (a), however, do not impose an absolute liability. Any person liable under such subsection, other than an issuer, may exempt himself if he sustains the burden of proof——

(1) That before the effective date of the registration statement with respect to which his liability is asserted (A) he had resigned from or had taken steps permitted by law to resign from or ceased or refused to act in, every official capacity or relationship in which he was described in the registration statement as acting or agreeing to act; (B) he had advised the Commission and the issuer in writing that he had taken such action and that he would not be responsible for such registration statement (of course, the Commission upon being so advised would not permit a registration statement to become effective until the name of the person disavowing responsibility was removed from the registration statement and the Commission would be put on its guard, unless such disavowal was clearly explained, to investigate the truth and adequacy of the statement); or

(2) That if the registration statement became effective without his knowledge, upon becoming aware of such fact, he forthwith acted and advised the Commission, in accordance with paragraph (1), and in addition gave reasonable public notice that the registration statement had become effective without his knowledge; or

(3) That as regards any part of the registration statement not purporting to be made on the authority of an expert, and not purporting to be a copy of or extract from a report or valuation of an expert, and not purporting to be made on the authority of a public official document or statement, he had, after reasonable investigation, reasonable ground to believe and did believe, at the time such registration statement became effective, that the statements therein were true and that there was no omission to state a material fact; and as regards any part of the registration statement purporting to be made on the authority of an expert, or purporting to be a copy of or extract from a report or valuation of an expert, or purporting to be made on the authority of a public official document or statement, he had reasonable ground to believe and did believe, at the time the registration statement became effective, that the statements therein were true and that there was no omission to state a material fact, and that the registration statement fairly represented the statement of the expert or of the official person, or was a fair copy of or extract from the report or valuation of the expert, or was a fair copy of or extract from the public official document.

(c) In determining for the purpose of paragraph (3) of subsection (b) of this section what constitutes reasonable investigation and reasonable ground for belief, the standard of reasonableness shall be that required of a person occupying a fiduciary relationship. While subsections (b) and (c) permit a person who has conscientiously and with competence met the responsibilities of his trusteeship to be relieved of liability, they prevent any person who has not fulfilled his trust from escaping liability by any trick of procedure or unjustified delegation of his duties.

(d) If any person becomes an underwriter after the part of the registration statement with respect to which his liability is asserted, has become effective, then for the purposes of paragraph (3) of subsection (b) such part of the registration statement is considered as having become effective with respect to him as of the time when he became an underwriter.

(e) Suits authorized under subsection (a) may be either (1) to recover the consideration paid for such securities with interest thereon, less the amount of any income received thereon, upon the tender of such security, or (2) for damages if the person suing no longer owns the security.

(f) All or any one or more of the persons specified in subsection (a) are jointly and severally liable, but contribution is allowed among them as in cases of contract, unless the person who has become liable was, and the other was not, guilty of fraudulent misrepresentation.

(g) In no case is the amount recoverable under this section to exceed the price at which the security was offered to the public.

Section 12. Civil Liabilities Arising in Connection With Prospectuses and Communications

If any person (1) sells a security in violation of section 5, or (2) sells a security, whether or not exempted by section 3, by the use of the instruments of interstate or foreign commerce or of the mails by means of a prospectus or oral communication which includes an untrue statement of a material fact or omits to state a material fact (the purchaser not knowing of such untruth or omission) and does not sustain the burden of proof that he did not know, and in the exercise of reasonable care could not have known, of such untruth or omission, he is made liable to the person purchasing such security from him, and the purchaser may sue either at law or in equity in any court of competent jurisdiction to recover the consideration paid for such security with interest thereon, less the amount of any income received thereon, upon the tender of such security, or for damages if he no longer owns the security. The committee has deemed this shift in the burden of proof as both just and necessary, inasmuch as the knowledge of the seller as to any flaw in his selling statements or the failure of the seller to exercise reasonable care are matters in regard to which the seller may readily testify, but in regard to which the buyer is seldom in a position to give convincing proof.

Section 13. Limitation of Actions

No action may be maintained to enforce any liability created under section 11 or 12 of this act unless brought within 2 years after the discovery of the untrue statement or of the omission, or after the discovery should have been made by the exercise of reasonable diligence, or, if the action is based upon a violation of section, unless brought within 2 years after such violation. In no event may any action be brought after 10 years after the security was offered to the public.

Section 14. Contrary Stipulations Void

Any condition, stipulation, or provision binding any person acquiring any security to waive compliance with any provision of the act or of the rules and regulations of the Commission is made void.

Section 15. Additional Remedies

The rights and remedies provided by the act are in addition to any and all other rights and remedies that may exist at law or in equity.

Section 16. Fraudulent Interstate Transactions

(*a*) It is made unlawful for any person in the sale of any securities by the use of any means or instruments of interstate or foreign commerce or by use of the mails (1) to employ any device, scheme, or artifice to defraud, (2) to obtain money or property by means of any untrue statement of, or omission to state, a material fact, or (3) to engage in any transaction, practice, or course of business which operates or would operate as a fraud upon the purchaser.

(*b*) It is made unlawful for any person, by use of any means or instruments of interstate or foreign commerce or by use of the mails, to publish, give publicity to, or circulate, any advertisement, newspaper, article, letter, investment service, or communication which, though not purporting to offer a security for sale, describes such security, for a consideration received or to be received, directly or indirectly, from an issuer, underwriter, or dealer, without fully disclosing the receipt, whether past or prospective, of such consideration and the amount thereof. This subsection is particularly designed to meet the evils of the "tipster sheet," as well as articles in newspapers or periodicals that purport to give an unbiased opinion but which opinions in reality are bought and paid for.

(*c*) The exemptions provided in section 3 of the act do not apply to this section.

Section 17. State Control of Securities

Nothing in this act is intended to affect the jurisdiction of the security commission (or any agency or office performing like functions) of any State over any security or any person.

Section 18. Unlawful Sending into States

(*a*) It is made unlawful for any person to make use of the mails or any means or instruments of interstate commerce to sell or deliver any security to any person in any State, where such sale or delivery, if it had taken place wholly within such State, would be in violation of the laws thereof relating to the sale of securities.

(*b*) The exemptions provided in section 3 of this act do not apply to this section.

Section 19. Special Powers of Commission

(*a*) The Commission is given full power and authority to make, amend, and rescind such rules and regulations as may be necessary to carry out the provisions of the act, including rules and regulations governing registration statements and prospectuses for various classes of securities and issuers and defining accounting and trade terms used in the act. The Commission further is given authority to prescribe the forms in which required information shall be set forth and the methods to be followed in the preparation of accounts.

(*b*) For the purpose of investigations under the act, the Commission or officers designated by it are empowered to subpena witnesses, examine them under oath, and require the production of books, papers, and documents.

Section 20. Injunction and Prosecution of Offenses

The Commission is given power, upon complaint or otherwise, to make investigations if it appears to the Commission that the provisions of this act or any rule or regulation prescribed under authority thereof have been or are about to be violated. Whenever it appears to the Commission that the transactions investigated constitute or will constitute a violation of the act or any rule or regulation prescribed thereunder, it may bring an action in the district court of the United States, the United States court of any Territory, or the Supreme Court of the District of Columbia to enjoin the continuance of such transactions, and it may transmit such evidence as may be available to the Attorney General who may institute the necessary criminal proceedings under this act. Any such civil or criminal proceeding may be brought either in the district where the transmitter of the prospectus or security begins or in the district where such prospectus or security is received.

Section 21. Jurisdiction of Offenses and Suits

(*a*) The district courts of the United States, the United States courts of any Territory, and the Supreme Court of the District of Columbia are given jurisdiction of offenses and violations under this act and, concurrent with State and Territorial courts, of all suits in equity and actions at law brought to enforce any liability or duty created by this act. Any such suit or action may be brought in the district wherein the defendant is an inhabitant or has its principal place of business or in the district where the sale took place if the defendant participated therein and process therein may be served in the district of which the defendant is an inhabitant or wherever the defendant may be found. Judgments and decrees so rendered are subject to review as provided in section 128 to 240 of the Judicial Code. No case arising under this act and brought in any State court of competent jurisdiction is removable to any court of the United States.

(*b*) In case of contumacy or refusal to obey a subpena issued to any person, any of the said United States courts within the jurisdiction of which said person resides, upon application by the Commission, may issue to such person an order requiring such person to appear before the Commission or one of its commissioners, there to testify or produce evidence; and any failure to obey such order of the court may be punished as a contempt.

(*c*) No person shall be excused from testifying or producing evidence before the Commission on the ground that the testimony or evidence may tend to incriminate him or subject him to a penalty or forfeiture; but no person shall be prosecuted or subject to a penalty or forfeiture for or on account of any transaction concerning which he is compelled to testify or produce evidence, except that such person so testifying shall not be exempt from prosecution or punishment for perjury.

Section 22. Unlawful Representations

Neither the fact that the registration statement for a security has been filed or is in effect, nor the fact that a stop order is not in effect in respect thereof shall be deemed a finding by the Commission that the registration statement is true and accurate on its face or that it does not contain an untrue statement of fact or omit to state a material fact, or be held to mean that the Commission has in any way passed on the merits of, or given approval to, such security. It is unlawful to make to any prospective purchaser any representation contrary to the provisions of this section.

Section 23. Penalties

Any person who willfully violates any of the provisions of this act or the rules and regulations promulgated under authority thereof, or who willfully, in a registration statement filed under this act, makes any untrue statement of a material fact or omits to state a material fact shall, upon conviction, be fined not more than $5,000 or imprisoned for not more than 5 years, or both.

Section 24. Jurisdiction of Other Government Agencies over Securities

Nothing in this act is to be construed to relieve any person from submitting to the respective supervisory units of the Government of the United States information, reports, or other documents that are now or may hereafter be required by any law of the United States.

Section 25. Separability of Provisions

If any provision of this act or the application of such provision to any person or circumstance shall be held invalid, the remainder of this act or the application of such provision to persons or circumstances other than those as to which it is held invalid, shall not be affected thereby.

MINORITY VIEWS

This bill follows a commendable and constructive purpose to provide a uniform and protective plan of national control for the marketing of interstate securities.

Section 18, however, injects a destructive principle which detracts from the value of the general scheme of constructive control. It destroys the uniformity of the plan of regulation by giving each State arbitrary control of the sale of interstate securities within its boundaries.

This section also denies the Federal Government its proper function of acting as arbiter between the States in the regulation of interstate commerce.

This section also makes the Federal Government responsible for the enforcement of various laws of the States affecting the sale of interstate securities. It will result in burdensome and vexatious handicaps in the administration of the law and in the transaction of the business it regulates.

Scope of Section 18

In substance this section makes it unlawful to sell any interstate security in any State where such sale would be unlawful if it had taken place wholly within that State.

A newspaper or radio advertisement of such a security in interstate commerce, published within such State, is made a criminal offense.

Under section 23 any person who willfully violates any of the provisions of the act commits a Federal offense. Thus a violation of any State law under section 18 is made a severe Federal offense, punishable by the Federal Government at its expense.

Under a State law the maximum penalty for a specific violation of its blue-sky law might be $50. Under this bill the Federal maximum penalty for the same act would be $5,000 or imprisonment for 5 years.

Section 18 makes the Federal Government the enforcing agency for legislation of the State without any discretion as to the wisdom of the State laws. It is proposed that Congress shall give a blindfolded approval thereof.

The State laws that may be violated are largely created by the rules and regulations of State commissions which are subject to constant change without any reference to the uniformity of interstate regulations.

Under section 20 it is the duty of the Commission to apply for injunctions to enforce the provisions of the act which would include the blue-sky laws of every State.

Under the same section it is the duty of the Attorney General to institute criminal prosecutions of violation of the act which includes State laws.

The Federal Government is made to assume the burden of prosecuting criminal offenses created without the knowledge or consent of Congress. This section attempts to prospectively approve laws hereafter passed by the State legislatures and rules and regulations hereafter adopted by State commissions.

It invites the States to recklessly make laws and place the burden of their enforcement on the Federal Government. It withdraws the Federal Government from its impartial control of the conflicting interests of States.

It leaves the commerce of States defenseless against the unfriendly legislation of their sister States except as they too may resort to retaliation as a method of defense.

Burden on Business

This section would impose unwarranted burdens on the sale of securities. The dealer, in addition to establishing his right to engage in interstate commerce by complying with the Federal act, would be forced to register and meet the individual requirements of each of the 48 States in which he transacts business. That means registration fees, lawyer's fees, and traveling expenses for each filing. That may be accomplished only by vexatious delays and burdensome expense which, in the case of many legitimate stocks, would probably bar their sale in many States.

This Committee properly refused to approve a provision authorizing the commission to pass on the soundness of a security offered for registration. Many of the State laws require the exercise of that power by their commissions. Thus section 18 compels the Federal Government to be responsible for a policy of State control of interstate commerce that it refuses to adopt on its own account. It subjects the dealer in interstate securities to that burden in every State which sees fit to impose it.

Sacrifices Sound Principles of Federal Regulation

The policy, or the lack of policy, of section 18 is not without plausible reasons for its support. It appeals to the disposition of a State to consider an immediate specific local advantage of more worth than the maintenance of sane and just principles of government, which though less personal in their benefits, are deeper and farther reaching in the penalties their violations impose.

The section purports to give the State uniform control of State and interstate securities within its own boundaries. For that meed of contentment it surrenders the wholesome advantages of uniform regulations for its own commerce in each of the other 47 States. It tears down one barrier to the exercise of its power but it builds up 47 other barriers that may rise to harass the commerce of its own people and their sister States. It would surrender that protection of interstate commerce on which the commercial success of the Nation has so largely been builded—free trade, untrammeled commerce between the States.

Burden on Enforcement

This section would impose an undue burden on the Federal Trade Commission. That Commission would have to serve as a clearing house for information for each of the 48 States. It assumes responsibility for initiating the enforcement of the laws of each State through its own proceedings and through references to the Attorney General.

The diversified laws of 48 States constantly changed by legislative action, judicial interpretations, and rules and regulations of their commissions would provide harassing handicaps not only to the commission but to every person attempting to legitimately sell stock in interstate commerce.

Violates Interstate Principle of Regulation

The interstate clause of the Constitution is well founded on reason and historical facts.

Under the Articles of Confederation each State regulated interstate commerce. There was no uniform protection or regulation for interstate traffic. The States penalized the commerce of their neighbors and passed retaliatory acts of favoritism to their local commerce and discrimination against that of their sister States. Out of this grew a contention in some States that they would rather be allied with foreign countries than with their sister States in America. Out of this situation grew "this wretchedness of the commercial relations, between the States at home." Out of this situation arose the beginning of the great demand of Madison for a Federal Government with "uniform commercial regulations."

The Constitution supplanted State control by Federal control of interstate commerce.

The interstate commerce clause of the Constitution is the remedy prescribed by the Constitution for preventing the evils of State control of interstate commerce.

The first conception of that clause is the necessity of uniform regulation.

The second conception is that of the Federal Government as the impartial promoter of interstate commerce and the impartial umpire to protect commerce against the conflicting and selfish policies of the States.

In other words, the interstate commerce clause is founded on a conception of "my country" instead of "my State."

Section 18 violates every principle of the interstate commerce clause. Instead of affording the country the encouragement and aid of a uniform system of regulation, it proposes that Congress shall abdicate that function and surrender to each of the 48 States carte blanche authority to deny protection to this interstate commerce coming into their borders. It subordinates interstate commerce to the whims and diversities of State regulation.

Harmony of State and Federal Regulations

The Constitution has attempted to establish livable relations between the State and Federal Governments. That means State control of State affairs, Federal control of interstate affairs.

The State has police power which it may exercise and incidentally and indirectly impose burdens on interstate commerce where necessary for the protection of the health, morals, and safety of its people.

The Federal Government, within the scope of its authority, exercises a police power which may incidentally and indirectly impose burdens on State commerce. The exercise of this police power by each government is a measure of tolerance to fit into our dual form of government. Beyond that, each government is supreme within its own sphere.

Thus the sane plan of the Constitution for harmonizing State and Federal jurisdiction is not joint or independent control of each subject by both governments, but separate control by each government within the sphere of its own jurisdiction.

The Senate committee has wisely omitted this section from its bill. Judge Healy, the attorney for the Federal Trade Commission, has advised the committee of the burden and impracticability of this section, which should be eliminated from the bill.

Clarence F. Lea
Schuyler Merritt

THE DEBATE

MR. POU. Mr. Speaker, I call up House Resolution 130 and ask for its immediate consideration. . . .

Mr. Speaker, this resolution brings before the House the securities bill reported by the Committee on Interstate and Foreign Commerce. It provides for 5 hours of general debate. It provides that amendments may be offered by authority of the committee only.

I am informed that the securities bill had practically a unanimous report from the Committee on Interstate and Foreign Commerce. There may have been differences of opinion, but the committee was practically unanimous as to the bill as a whole.

I cannot see that any extended discussion of the rule can avail anything. It may be called another gag rule, but almost every rule that is brought in here fixing an order of business is more or less restrictive in its nature. It limits the procedure in this House that would take place if measures were considered under the general rules of the House. So the Committee on Rules felt that we were pursuing the wiser course in allowing 5 hours of debate and in confining amendments to the committee that has been working on this bill over a long period.

I am informed by members on both sides of the Committee on Interstate and Foreign Commerce that every line in the bill from beginning to end has been carefully considered by that committee, and, inasmuch as it comes here with the unanimous support of that great and powerful committee, after having given it such prolonged and careful consideration, the Committee on Rules felt that the House would not want the measure thrown open to indiscriminate amendments, and in this belief we have reported this rule, and we hope it will be unanimously adopted. [Applause.] . . .

MR. MAPES. Mr. Speaker, this is another one of those closed or gag rules which have become so common during this session of Congress; in fact, they have become the regular thing instead of the exception. Under it the bill will not be read under the 5-minute rule, and the individual Member will have no opportunity to offer any amendment to any part of the bill. The only amendments that will be in order are those that may be offered by the committee, and the committee does not intend to offer any very important ones, as I understand it.

The Republican members of the Committee on Rules voted against this rule, the same as they have voted against other gag rules which have been reported at this session. They are opposed to this rule. It is subject to the same objections that have been made to the other rules, but it is apparent that the large majority of the House is going to pass gag rules, and it would probably be futile to reiterate at this time the statements and objections which have been made to the other rules of the same character as this one, except I should like to point out that the viciousness of this sort of rule is demonstrated in the pending rule perhaps as well or better than any other rule which has been considered during this session of Congress. This securities bill contains something like 38 pages and 25 different sections. It deals with a very complex and controversial subject, and there are two outstanding provisions involving fundamental principles of public policy upon which the House of Representatives ought to be allowed to express itself sometime during the consideration of the bill. Under this rule there will be no such opportunity for it to do so.

One of the questions that the House ought to express itself upon is the one referred to in the minority views filed by the gentleman from California [Mr. Lea] and the gentleman from Connecticut [Mr. Merritt], relating to the question of putting into effect in this Federal statute the blue sky laws of the different States, and another is the matter of making responsible for false statements or for omitting to state material facts the members of the boards of directors of corporations filing statements with the Federal Trade Commission giving information relating to such securities. I shall have more to say about this provision later, but the House as a whole ought to have the right to vote upon these two propositions especially.

But under this rule the House of Representatives will not be allowed to express itself on these two important questions. The Constitution guarantees freedom of speech to the ordinary citizen, but the House of Representatives during this session of Congress has not had freedom to express itself on important policies of legislation submitted to it. So much for that. I do not want to take any more time in the discussion of the rule, because I want to use a part of my time to discuss the merits of the legislation which the rule seeks to make in order. . . .

MR. BYRNS. The gentleman was a member of the subcommittee that considered this bill.

MR. MAPES. I was.

MR. BYRNS. I do not suppose any bill was ever brought before the gentleman's committee which received closer and more undivided attention than this particular bill.

MR. MAPES. I think in a general way the gentleman's statement is correct.

MR. BYRNS. I understand the gentleman himself approved of the bill in committee.

MR. MAPES. That is correct, although there is one important provision in the bill about which I differed from the rest of the subcommittee. I shall explain that later; but the general purpose of the bill I am in hearty accord with, and I can support the legislation with a great deal of enthusiasm.

MR. BYRNS. The gentleman is a very able Member of the House and is in the habit of giving legislation his careful attention, particularly that which comes before the Committee on Interstate and Foreign Commerce. I want to ask the gentleman this question: After giving this matter 2 weeks of close, undivided attention, having rewritten, as I understand, the bill in many particulars, does the gentleman think any particular advantage could occur in the consideration of amendments offered from the floor to this bill, having in mind that the rule gives the right of free expression from Members of the House in general discussion?

MR. MAPES. As I have said, for the most part I approve of the bill; but, regardless of my position on the bill, I do not believe it is good policy to bring in a rule which does not give the Membership of the House of Representatives generally an opportunity to express itself upon the different provisions of a bill of this importance. I believe that every Member should have an opportunity to express himself if he so desires. Debate is often very helpful and brings out points which may not have been thought of by the committee, but whatever may be the fact in that respect I do not believe that the committee, no matter how able or powerful it may be, ought to be allowed to say to a membership of 435, all of them equals, "You have got to swallow this particular piece of legislation as it is or reject it altogether." . . .

. . . As I have said in answer to the questions of the distinguished gentleman from Tennessee [Mr. Byrns], the majority leader, I am very much in favor of the object sought to be accomplished by this legislation. It has been very carefully considered by a subcommittee, and by the full committee, of the Committee on Interstate and Foreign Commerce, with the help of the drafting service and others who were called in for consultation. Practically every word of the 38 pages of the bill has been weighed and considered, first by the subcommittee and then by the full committee, and I think, from the standpoint of drafting, the bill is in very excellent condition, and few indeed will question the general purposes sought to be accomplished by the legislation. . . .

I wish the gentleman would permit me to proceed for just a few minutes, if he will pardon me. The administration of the legislation, if the bill is enacted into law, will come under the supervision of the Federal Trade Commission. The object of the legislation, in brief, is to require those who issue securities to be sold to the public through the mails or by the use of the instruments of interstate commerce to furnish material information to the public about the securities which they are asking the public to buy. That, in my judgment, will be the chief and primary accomplishment of the legislation. It will make available to the public the information upon which the public is asked to invest its money. The information must be given in a statement to be filed with the Federal Trade Commission before the mails or the instruments of interstate commerce can be made use of to sell securities. Certain securities are expected, but I shall not attempt to name the exceptions at this time.

The bill is not foolproof. It will not prevent anybody from putting his money into rat holes or into highly speculative ventures if he sees fit to do so, but in the exercise of reasonable care he can go to the Federal Trade Commission or to the underwriter or the dealer in the securities and find out the facts relating to the business of the corporation issuing the securities, the profits which the dealers are to receive in selling them, and the amount of money that is to go back into the treasury of the corporation after the sale is made—how much of the $100 per share, or whatever amount he pays for his stock, is really going back to the corporation, going into the treasury for the promotion of the business of the corporation.

It is not necessary here to dwell upon the need for this kind of legislation. Mr. Huston Thompson in testifying before the committee made the statement that the United States is farther behind than any other civilized nation that he knew of with respect to preserving the rights of the purchasers of securities. The American public in the last few years has become particularly "investment minded," and there probably is no other country where securities are so widely distributed among the people. It is said that during the 13 years immediately after the war something like $50,000,000,000 of securities—bonds and stocks together—were bought by the investing public in the United States. A large part of those were, as a matter of general information, of little value, and some of them had no value at all. Anything that this Congress can do to supplement the blue-sky laws of the States to protect the public in investing its money ought to be done. Of the 48 States in the Union, all but 1 have some sort of blue-sky legislation. This law does not interfere with, but supplements, those laws and makes it impossible for dealers and underwriters to evade the State laws by the shipment of their securities and prospectuses and other material in interstate commerce or through the mails.

The enactment of this law will prevent that sort of thing. I have always wanted to believe in the copy-book statements that those who occupy high positions in the business and financial world were not only men of ability but men of character as well; that the fact that they occupied such positions was an evidence that they were men worthy of confidence. The revelations of the last few years have had a tendency to shake my faith in that respect. For example, I have in my hand a report of a Senate committee which quotes from another report of a Senate committee, namely, "Report No. 1655, Seventy-first Congress, third session," relating to what took place in the District of Columbia relating to the sale of bonds of the Wardman Realty Co. I am not going to take the time to read it, but under the leave which has been granted me, I will put in an excerpt from it in the Record.

The excerpt is as follows:

Four members of the Investment Bankers' Association of America, namely, Halsey, Stuart & Co., Inc., Hambleton & Co., A. B. Leach & Co., Inc., and Rogers Caldwell & Co., Inc., together with William R. Compton Co., sponsored and participated in the public offering throughout the country of what they designated on their circular to be "$11,000,000 first and refunding mortgage 6½-percent serial gold bonds" of the Wardman Real Estate Properties, Inc. Even the printed description of this issue was deceptive, for, in reality, the authorized issue of bonds was $16,000,000 and the security back of the bond issue was not a first mortgage on all of the property of the issuing corporation but a second, and possibly third, mortgage as to some of the properties involved.

The same properties were made the basis of a $2,500,000 so-called "general mortgage," which was, in reality, a third or fourth mortgage as to some of the hotels and apartments listed as security for the issues. In addition the very questionable and doubtful "equities" in the properties, encumbered by the various mortgages mentioned, were made the basis for two issues of so-called "gold debentures" in the amount of $4,900,000. The companies issuing these various securities also issued common stocks to the amount of 200,000 shares.

As this excerpt shows, four investment banking houses supposed to be reputable—at least, they had a reputation for being reputable before they were put to the test by this depression—namely, Halsey, Stuart & Co., Hambleton & Co., A. B. Leach & Co., Rogers Caldwell & Co., and William R. Compton Co., put out statements which were totally misleading and in some respects false, in order to secure the sale of these bonds. With this legislation in effect that sort of thing will not be possible. If it is done, those responsible for it will be held responsible, both in the civil and criminal courts. . . .

I have not the time to go into the details of this bill and to make a close analysis of the different provisions of it, but I do want to call attention to one feature of it about which there were some differences of opinion in the subcommittee. I will say at the outset that I was the only member of the subcommittee which took the view which I am going to dwell upon. . . .

The particular point of the bill to which I was about to call attention is the difference between the House bill and the bill reported by the committee of the Senate, and the original draft of the legislation which accompanied the President's message and which was introduced in the House of Representatives, as to the liability of the directors of issuing corporations, for false statements which are made in the registration statement filed with the Federal Trade Commission, and upon which the innocent investing public has relied in putting its money into securities.

I have taken so much time with the interruptions that I will not have time to go into this matter in detail, but the Senate committee in its report states the question at issue this way:

> The question is whether ignorance of an untruth should excuse the director and leave the loss upon the buyer. To do so, in our opinion, would fail to give the buyer the needed relief and fail to restore confidence. If one of two presumably innocent persons must bear a loss, it is familiar legal principle that he should bear it who has the opportunity to learn the truth and has allowed untruths to be published and relied upon. Moreover, he should suffer the loss who occupies a position of trust in the issuing corporation toward the stockholders, rather than the buyer of stock who must rely upon what he is told. . . .
>
> If a director can excuse himself by saying that he has in good faith relied upon an accountant's statement, or the statement of some other person, then the investor will continue in the same position from which the Nation is struggling to extricate him. It has been stated in prospectuses repeatedly that the information given is believed by the company to be true, but not guaranteed.

Let me say that the original draft as introduced in the House contained a provision which made directors responsible and liable to the investing public for the return of its money if misstatements of material facts were made or if there were any omissions of material facts in this statement which is required to be filed with the Federal Trade Commission. That has been changed in the bill as reported by the committee so that a director, if he shows that he exercised reasonably good faith and believed that the statements were true, or that no omission to give material facts had been made, then he is not liable. I may say that the issuer himself in all such cases is responsible for the return of the money to an innocent investor if he desires to rescind his contract. That is a good provision and has a tendency to some extent to take care of the situation which I have in mind. The directors, however, are not responsible if they can show the exercise of good faith and reasonable diligence. It seems to some of us that, as between directors and the innocent investing public, that the directors should be held civilly liable as well. . . .

Stripped of legal phraseology the original bill proposes that if the directors of a company misstate a material fact they shall give the purchaser's money back to him, even though the directors, in the exercise of due diligence, did not know the statement of that fact to be untrue. Give the purchaser's money back—not the vendors' money—for it was never rightfully theirs.

The new draft proposes that, even if the directors make a mistake about a material fact, they shall retain the purchaser's money with all their incidental profits, if upon the exercise of reasonable care they believed the statements to be true. We are discussing ascertainable facts—not opinions or expectancies concerning which both drafts are silent. . . .

It should be kept in mind that no one is asked to guarantee the success of any enterprise. He is only asked to tell the truth about existing facts. If he makes the statement that he is organizing a company to drill oil wells and so states, that is a perfectly fair statement, and everybody who puts money into the proposition takes his chances and has no redress even though nothing but dry wells are found; but if a misstatement relative to a material fact is made, then it seemed to some of us that the members of the board of directors ought to be held responsible as against the rights of the innocent investors who made their investments relying upon such statements even though the directors acted in good faith. . . .

In closing I should like to say this one thing more. The investing public should keep clearly in mind that this legislation does not contemplate that the Federal Trade Commission will attempt to pass upon the soundness or unsoundness of any security. The investor must do that for himself. It will make the material facts relating to any security available to him if he cares to investigate them, but he must exercise his own judgment as to the merits of the investment. The bill expressly provides that it shall be unlawful for anyone to represent to a prospective purchaser that the Federal Trade Commission has in any way passed upon the merits or given approval to any security coming within the purview of the act. [Applause.] . . .

MR. GREENWOOD. Mr. Speaker, my study of this bill convinces me that there is no politics involved in the bill. I think all of us are agreed that a situation exists in the sale of securities in our country that calls for some reform and regulation.

I never have read a bill that appeared to be more carefully drawn, with reference to all of its features and technicalities, than this bill. I am informed that the Committee on Interstate and Foreign Commerce itself and through its subcommittee, has spent a great deal of time and careful thought and has called before it many experts as draftsmen students of economy, commerce, and banking and that they used more care upon particular features of this bill than any bill that has come before the House in many a day.

The bill uses the commerce clause of the Constitution conferring power upon Congress to regulate through interstate agencies of communication the sale of securities. All lines of publicity, whether by use of the mails, the telegraph, the telephone, radio, prospectuses, or any other form of publicity that will lead an investor to purchase securities have been covered by this bill.

This bill should not be mutilated or garbled by amendments that have not been thought out; and I take it that we legislate in this House largely through our committees. The majority party is simply expressing its confidence in this committee and the subcommittee that have drawn this particularly technical bill by giving them the special authority of amending the bill, allowing abundance of time for debate—5 hours in addition to the rule—in which all phases of the bill will be explained.

The House retains its privilege of adopting or rejecting the rule or of accepting or rejecting the bill as written. The bill is directed to transactions that reach out into every nook and corner of our land. Wherever there are savings accounts, wherever people invest their funds in postal savings, building and loan companies, or in banks they have suffered because of lack of information concerning investment that have been recommended to them—very often by their bankers who thought they were recommending with full faith and understanding securities both foreign and domestic—this measure will afford protection. These investments have drained funds from local saving accounts through the channels of banking and have taken them into the metropolitan centers, there to be invested in securities many times that were worth scarcely more than the paper they were written upon.

Commercial banking has been confused with investment banking. International bankers and investment bankers in the cities have sent out their lines of contact with every bank in America. By that contact, by their high-powered salesmen, and by their publicity they have induced these corresponding banks to take allotments of investments, and oftentimes the local bankers in good faith have taken them solely on the word of the investment banker and the international banker as to the worth and value of the securities. So instead of confining their efforts to commercial banking, they have gone into this field of investment banking or sent their money to the financial centers to be invested in securities. They have failed to use their funds locally for the needs of the community and its industries; they have failed to put it into the channels of trade and deprived the local community of the money because an opportunity to make profits has been offered to peddle questionable securities.

The time has come when the full light of publicity must be thrown upon these transactions of promoting sales of these securities and the manner in which they are sold, so that the investor may know more about the value of the security he is buying.

It has been said that we have drifted into a gambler's civilization, in which men are no longer inclined to invest their money in proven and honest business; but, believing they can make more money in the negotiation and sale of securities, sometimes upon a margin and upon a basis of gambling, our whole financial system has taken on the psychology of gambling instead of honest methods of banking and industry.

So publicity concerning investments will have a wholesome psychological effect in every community and many of these banks will cease their high-powered promotion in connection with big city banks, which procedure in the past has induced their depositors to send their funds out of the communities where funds should remain to assist local enterprise.

If there is any one thing that has destroyed confidence in the banking system of America it is this system of gambling in securities. The channels of publicity I have outlined, the forms of contact, and the use of high-powered salesmen have resulted in the people losing their savings in large part and even their confidence in their local bankers.

So the necessity for this legislation to help restore confidence in our local banking institutions is great. These practices must stop. The President of the United States called attention to this in a special message. We are attempting here to reform these crooked methods.

There is a peculiar fact with respect to such investments in that the corporation that issues the securities knows more about them than anyone else, and the old rule of caveat emptor, or the buyer beware, certainly should not apply to this character of investments. The man who sells them ought to give all the facts, and the Government ought to require the issuer of securities to give all the facts, and be honest with the public.

This is the purpose of the legislation, so that every investor may know more about the assets behind the securities, the practices of the corporation issuing the securities, the motives that are behind the negotiating bank, whether it is a promoter who wants to make a commission rather than to serve the public in an honest way or not. These are the facts that the American people are entitled to know not only to save the investment funds of the small investor but to restore confidence in the banking system of America.

I think this panic has demonstrated one fact, that we have one of the worst banking systems in the world, because many of the leading bankers of the country no longer have the old-time sense of ethics that the bankers of a former generation had. The banker has become so impersonal in dealing with the public that he no longer has a strict sense of ethics or pays attention to the strict detail of honest business like the bankers of a former day. The investment bankers send their men out and they are none too particular in telling the small banks or the investors all the facts concerning the investments they are peddling over the country. The sale of such securities has reached the point where it is a scandal and a gigantic racket in America, and the Federal Government is the agency to stop it.

No State has power to control publicity of securities. Some issues come from abroad, some of them are national in character, and no State has such authority or power. It is the duty of the Federal Government, using the commerce clause of the Constitution and the mails, to compel these investment bankers to lay their cards on the table and to show all the facts concerning the securities they are asking the American people to buy. . . .

MR. MOTT. Did I understand the gentleman to say that no blue-sky law would prohibit the advertising of a foreign security within the State where these advertisements are printed?

MR. GREENWOOD. No; that was not my statement. I say this system of sale is Nation-wide, and, perhaps, there is a different blue-sky law in every State, and some States have none, and, therefore, there ought to be uniform security for every investor in America, and the Federal Government is the power that can provide this uniform system of protection. The States can assist and support the Federal Government. . . .

MR. SAMUEL B. HILL. You cannot have such uniformity if you incorporate in this bill in section 18 the blue-sky law of the various States, because each State has its own particular blue-sky law. I agree with most of what the gentleman has said here, but if you pass this rule in its present form, there will be no opportunity to eliminate from the bill section 18, which, in my judgment, is absolutely vicious. . . .

MR. SHANNON. Mr. Speaker, there is not a Member of this House on either side whose heart is not in sympathy with remedial legislation along the lines proposed in this measure.

However, we are now confronted with a rule, an unnecessary one, a gag rule, which permits amendments to be offered only by the committee which has had the bill under consideration. We cannot even offer an amendment to the amendments offered by the committee on the floor.

If I am a reader of the hearts of men, the heart of the Chairman of the Rules Committee is not for these rules that he brings in here day after day.

We are absolutely in the position of the striker in an old-fashioned blacksmith shop. In the blacksmith shop of old, the master smith took his light hammer in one hand and his tongs in the other, and by gentle movements of the hammer he directed the striker, who struck the powerful blows that finally welded into form the work of the shop.

This House is made the striker. We drive these measures through by our votes, as shown in the Record. The master smith is the committee, which directs the work, aided, too frequently, by the soft, velvety, and unseen hand of those backing the measure.

The strikers in this congressional shop are given another duty of the striker in the blacksmith shop. By 5 hours debate we do the work of furnishing the hot air for the bellows; the more we pump the greater the heat to pass a measure we are not permitted to amend, even to the extent of dotting an "i" or crossing a "t," and yet this is called "deliberative legislation."

The gentleman who just left the floor said we had 5 hours to debate this measure. There you have it; we can blow hot and cold on this measure for 5 hours after adopting this infamous rule. [Laughter and applause.] . . .

MR. SABATH. Mr. Speaker, ladies and gentlemen of the House, I regret that it was necessary for the Rules Committee to bring in this rule depriving the Members of an opportunity to offer amendments. But I have been for many years vitally interested in legislation of this kind. Three years ago, and again 2 years ago, I pleaded with the committee to give favorable consideration to my bill to regulate the stock exchanges and the issuance and sale of stock.

I realize that there is no perfection in anything and that this proposed legislation is, after all, a compromise. This bill does not go as far as I had hoped it would go. I should like to see included in this bill a provision that would apply not only to the stocks that will be listed but to all stocks that have been listed on the many stock exchanges in the United States. . . .

. . . We have today millions upon millions of shares of stock outstanding that were at the time of listing of questionable value and are now of no value at all, but that are still being manipulated in. The gentlemen who control and manipulate the stock exchanges, hungry as they are for profit and more profit, have listed stocks that should never have been listed, and they will continue for many years to unload worthless stocks upon the American people until we pass a law that will prevent them from perpetrating the frauds that have been practiced upon the people of this Nation for many years. [Applause.]

During the years 1928 and 1929 they listed over 300 different stocks, the majority of which should not have been listed. Yet not only did they do that but they issued false statements to induce people to invest their entire savings in these securities, knowing full well that the securities were worthless and that they were committing fraud upon the Nation.

We are today a nation suffering from the misdeeds of these investment bankers and crooked manipulators on the stock exchanges. I had hoped that we would enact a bill at this time that would forever prevent dishonest listings and transactions. But unfortunately the committee came to the conclusion that at this time they could not do it all in one bill. Consequently I am in favor of this proposed legislation, although I deplore the lack of the provision I mentioned. I believe this measure will remedy to some extent the evils that have been practiced by these dishonest bankers and unprincipled manipulators on the stock exchange.

But I renew the notice that I served on the House three and a half years ago that I will not desist until these invidious and thoroughly reprehensible practices of short selling, "selling against the box," and floor trading are abolished.

Mr. Speaker, ladies, and gentlemen, I am satisfied that if my advice had been heeded and my bill and resolution adopted in 1929 the liquidation of securities then, though necessarily severe, due to the criminal inflation, would never have reached the catastrophic proportions of that in the last 3 years that has brought about a terrific loss in all property value, that has closed thousands of banks, that has forced tens of thousands of small merchants into bankruptcy, and that has thrown 15,000,000 people out of employment. [Applause.]

MR. POU. Mr. Speaker, I feel constrained to say a word in conclusion. We have here a measure which will be passed by this House with probably very few dissenting votes. And yet we have had the usual complaint about gag rules. I believe the country is more concerned about what we do than about the way we do it, and I believe that the country is more concerned about the results of our deliberations here than about the way that measures are considered. During this session already quite a number of great measures have been passed. So far as I can judge, the country almost unanimously approves these measures. And yet we have heard someone complain about gag rules whenever these measures were presented to the House. I believe the country is practically unanimous behind this measure, and I believe that when it becomes law there will be very little thought given to whether or not Mr. A from this State or Mr. B from some other State had opportunity to offer amendment. With the Nation facing imminent complete economic breakdown our people demanded action, prompt action. This House has responded. It will hardly be denied that the Nation approves what we have done.

I demand the previous question.

The previous question was ordered.

THE SPEAKER. The question is on the adoption of the resolution.

The resolution was agreed to.

MR. RAYBURN. Mr. Speaker, I move that the House resolve itself into the Committee of the Whole House on the state of the Union for the consideration of the bill (H. R. 5480) to provide full and fair disclosure of the character of securities sold in interstate and foreign commerce and through the mails, and to prevent frauds in the sale thereof, and for other purposes.

The motion was agreed to. . . .

MR. RAYBURN. . . . I am compelled to do something today that I do not usually do, and that is ask the indulgence of the House while I read at least a part of my remarks. I have been with this matter for 3 weeks, day and night, and, frankly, I am just a little tired. If gentlemen will bear with me until I can give them the background and some of the conditions that have grown up in this country which call for this legislation without interruption, then I shall be very glad to answer any questions I can about this very technical measure. In the 20 years that I have been a Member of Congress I have dealt with matters touching interstate commerce. When you deal with matters affecting interstate commerce in transportation you do so with a law that has been upon the statute books for more than 40 years. You have the decisions of the courts as your chart, and you have the decisions of the Interstate Commerce Commission and of the various State commissions. With this bill we are embarking upon a practically new and untried sea; and, as I say, since I have been a Member of Congress, this is the most technical matter with which I have ever been called upon to deal.

The first permanent settlement of English-speaking people in Virginia was accomplished through a joint-stock company. The successors of these early Colonies, through a series of amazing adventures, have wrested a continent from the aborigines, have explored and utilized its natural resources until more than a hundred million people comprise the citizenship of this Republic. The initiative, self-reliance, inventive genius, organizing ability, and industry of the people who have occupied this continent have created a national wealth of some $300,000,000,000.

The production and distribution of goods by the Americans have given rise to new institutions and to many refinements and new uses of old methods. The corporation has reached a development and has been put to uses never dreamed of by the adventurers who united their slender capital in a joint-stock company to found a colony in the wilderness of Virginia.

The conquest of this continent was made by individual human beings, each pursuing his own happiness in his own way. There was impatience with restraint. Rugged individualism characterized the pioneer. Thomas Jefferson and Andrew Jackson, the idols of frontiersmen, were trusted and followed as they taught that the best government is the least government. Those were the days of a self-reliant agricultural people. During the past 75 years this country has experienced an industrial revolution. Through corporations, great aggregations of capital have been assembled to build railroads, develop mines, fell forests, fabricate goods, and finally to carry on the ordinary processes of merchandising.

The early corporations were in each case composed of a few stockholders who contributed to a joint fund. These stockholders never traded in their own stock. The corporations usually were closed. If the ventures were successful, the profits were divided between those who contributed the capital; if unsuccessful, the contributors of the capital lost what they had risked—that is, the amount they had paid into the capital stock. As corporations became older, as their founders died, as their operations became more extensive, as they came to demand increasing and frequent additions of capital, their stockholders ceased to be a few fellow adventurers known to each other and became a multitude. The relations between the stockholder and the corporation ceased to be personal and became impersonal.

The thousands of stockholders of a great corporation have come to trust implicitly the board of directors. The directorates have come to be composed of men who sit on many such boards. In our investigation of the stock ownership and control of railroads, we found that the chairman of the board of one railroad was a director in some 70 other corporations. In such a situation—and this is rather typical—the board of directors have to rely on the officials of the corporation. Where the stock is widely distributed, as is the case of so many American corporations, the officials of a company, through the use of proxies and of the advantage they have in obtaining proxies, are able to continue in office without much regard to their efficiency. The proof is that when a corporation goes into receivership some official of the corporation is usually appointed receiver. Two hundred companies own 25 percent of the total wealth of the United States. We have in this country more than 300,000 corporations. The total assets of all nonbanking corporations in 1930 have been estimated at $165,000,000,000. (American Economic Review, March 1931, pp. 15 and 16.) The combined assets of the 200 largest of these corporations amounted in 1930 to $81,000,000,000. That is, 200 big corporations control half of the wealth of all the nonbanking companies. Two hundred companies have as much assets as the more than 300,000 smaller companies. When we look to the New York Stock Exchange, we find that 130 of the largest companies control more than four fifths of all the assets of all the companies represented by securities listed by the exchange.

To indicate the importance to the American people of stocks and bonds, we merely have to call to mind that 75 percent, probably 80 percent, of American business wealth is owned and controlled by corporations and that 200 of the biggest corporations control 40 percent or more of all business wealth. In 1928 the National Industrial Conference Board estimated that the total national wealth was $360,000,000,000. In this wealth is included agricultural land and improvements, residential real estate, personal property including automobiles, and a large volume of Government property. In agriculture the corporation is still relatively unimportant. Yet when we consider the total national wealth, we find that 200 corporations control roughly one fourth of the total wealth of this country. To recapitulate, 200 of our biggest companies out of more than 300,000 corporations control one fourth of the total national wealth, two fifths of the business wealth other than banking, one half of the corporate wealth, and more than four fifths of the wealth represented by the securities traded in on the stock exchange. The influence of these 200 big companies is not limited to themselves. They dominate or in some measure determine the policies of many of the smaller corporations. About 2,000 individuals making up the dominant directors and officials of our largest corporations really control or dominate more than one half of the industry of this country.

During the past 10 years the big corporations have grown in size much more rapidly than the smaller companies. Further, to illustrate the rapidity of the growth of our big corporations, the National Industrial Conference Board—in its bulletin no. 30, published February 25, 1930—estimated an increase between 1922 and 1928 in the national wealth of 12½ percent as compared with an increase in the assets of 200 of the largest corporations of 45 percent. That is, while the national wealth was increasing at an annual rate of 2 percent, the assets of 200 big companies was increasing at an annual rate of 6 percent. A list of these 200 non-banking corporations may be found in a book by Berle and Means entitled "The Modern Corporation and Private Property," page 19.

In 1800 the corporation was used in this country mainly for undertakings of public interest, such as the construction of turnpikes, bridges, and canals, and the operation of banks and insurance companies. Up to 1800, 355 profit-seeking corporations had been formed in the United States. Today we have a thousand corporations for one that existed in 1800. The operation of half of our industry is now in the hands of 200 companies. This concentration has brought a change in this character of competition, and production is carried on under the ultimate control of a very few individuals. What is of great concern is that the value of tangible goods is becoming increasingly dependent upon these corporate organizations.

With the concentration of the ownership of our national wealth in corporations there has also developed a dispersion of stock ownership. Of 144 companies out of the 200 largest corporations in this country, 20 each had less than 5,000 stockholders, 71 companies each had over 20,000 stockholders, and more than one half of the assets belonging to the 200 largest corporations were held by companies each with 50,000 stockholders or more. These 144 largest companies whose stock lists have been examined reported 5,800,000 stockholders of record. According to an investigation made by your Committee on Interstate and Foreign Commerce, under authority given by this House, it was found that the largest stockholding of the Santa Fe Railroad was only three fourths of 1 percent of the total and there were over 59,000 stockholders. The largest holding of the Southern Pacific Co. was 1.65 percent of the total and there were over 65,000 stockholders. The largest holding of the Southern Railway Co. was 1.9 percent of the total and there were over 20,000 stockholders. The largest holding of the Baltimore & Ohio was 2½ percent of the total and there were nearly 40,000 stockholders. In 1931 the Pennsylvania Railroad reported more than 240,000 shareholders of record; the United States Steel Corporation, 174,500; the American Telephone & Telegraph, 642,000.

The managements of these big corporations, as a rule, own an insignificant percentage of the outstanding voting stock. For example, the management of 44 steam railroads owns only 1.2 percent of the common stock, the management of 22 gas companies owns only 1.4 percent of the common stock, the management of 36 mining corporations owns only 1.8 percent of the common stock, the management of 378 transportation and public utility companies owns only 1.2 percent of the common stock, the management of 46 electric light and power companies owns only about 4 percent of the common stock, the management of 102 telephone companies owns only about 5 percent of the common stock, the management of 53 petroleum mining companies owns only about 5 percent of the common stock, the management of 43 coal mining companies owns only 8 percent of the common stock, the management of 1,363 manufacturing companies owns only about 15 percent of the common stock, the management of 4,367 corporations engaged in all sorts of industries owns less than 11 percent of the common stock.

It is estimated that in 1928 there were 18,000,000 stockholders of corporations in the United States. This is an increase of about 50 percent over 1920. Much of this increase in numbers has been due, in a very large measure, to the sale of securities to customers and to employees of corporations.

Merely to bring home to the Members of this House the great importance of supervising trading in the securities of corporations, in the interest of honesty and fair dealing, I will give you some figures compiled in 1922. The total par value of outstanding stock in mining and quarrying in 1922 was $8,775,000,000, and the estimated number of stockholders of record was 2,000,000. Of manufacturing corporations, the par value of outstanding stock in 1922 was estimated at $3,400,000,000, with over 3,000,000 stockholders of record. In transportation, the total par value of outstanding stock was $17,532,000,000, with 3,293,000 stockholders, of which the steam railroads had $8,600,000,000 par value of stock, with 965,000 stockholders. As a further illustration of the importance of corporation securities to American investors, it has been estimated that in 1922, 54 percent of the reported income from investment was received from corporate securities, and in 1927, 63 percent.

When we consider the welfare of our people the enacting of this bill into law seems imperative. Any casual consideration of the development of this country impresses on one that the size of our industrial unit is increasing, and with its growth there has come a dispersion in the ownership of the unit. Today an important part of the wealth of individual citizens consists of interest in great enterprises of which no single person owns a major portion. Today the owner does not possess actual physical properties but he holds a piece of paper which represents certain rights and expectations. But the owners of these pieces of paper have little control over the physical property; the owners of these pieces of paper carry no actual responsibility with respect to the enterprise or its physical property.

As Professor Berle so well says:

The spiritual values that formerly went with ownership have been separated from it. . . . Physical property capable of being shaped by its owner could bring to him direct satisfaction apart from the gain it yielded. . . . It represented an extension of his own personality. . . . This quality has been lost to the property owner.

Again the value of the wealth of a particular person is coming more and more to depend on forces beyond his own reach and control. The wealth of the individual is represented by securities subject to the great swings in the appraisal by society of its own immediate future. Wealth in this form can be directly enjoyed by its owner in a less and less degree. Only through sale in the market can the owner obtain direct use of his wealth. In other words, the owner of securities is chained to the market. The purpose of this bill is to place the owners of securities on a parity, so far as is possible, with the management of the corporations, and to place the buyer on the same plane so far as available information is concerned, with the seller. Many of us in this House come from small communities where most of the wealth consists of real estate and improvements. In such a situation, the corporation is of importance only as our constituents purchase and consume the products and services of corporate endeavor. Those in this House who come from industrial centers, from the so-called "metropolitan areas" in which we have permitted an amazing concentration of activity, are familiar with the fact that today the owner of shares in a corporation possesses a mere symbol of ownership, while the power, the responsibility, and the substance which have characterized ownership in the past have been transferred to a separate group which holds control. It is for the protection of these 18 million owners of symbols that this bill has been drawn.

We have, on the one hand, 18,000,000 passive citizens having no actual contact with their companies; on the other hand, a few hundred powerful managers directing and controlling the destinies of the companies and the physical properties which they own. The owners of these symbols are entitled to know what the symbols represent. Those who are interested in purchasing these pieces of paper have the right to demand information as to the actual condition of the issuing company. Up to this time such information has depended on the grace of an intrenched management. These managers are truly trustees. One of their duties as trustees is to furnish security owners, in being and in prospect, with reliable information. This bill has been drawn to enforce that responsibility.

MR. BRITTEN. Mr. Chairman, will the gentleman yield there for the purpose of giving us his definition of the word "management"?

MR. RAYBURN. The ones in active control—the president, the vice president, and the board of directors.

A few individuals really control the destinies of these companies. Millions of people own the stocks and bonds of the corporations; that is to say, the actual wealth, the physical property, the mines, the railroads, the ships, the factories, the warehouses, the office buildings, the gold in the vaults of the central banks, the raw materials awaiting the processing of the manufacturer, the finished products in the warehouse or in transit are owned in most cases by corporations. The rank and file of the people possess stocks and bonds; that is, evidences of a share in equities or of a claim in the event of corporate failure.

The conditions under which these stocks and bonds are issued have been those of the greatest freedom. P. T. Barnum once remarked that the American people pay to be gulled. Millions of citizens have been swindled into exchanging their savings for worthless stocks. The fraudulent promoter has taken an incredible toll from confiding people. So-called "blue sky laws" have been passed by the States in an effort to arrest the predatory promoter and outright swindler.

May I say right in this connection that the bill as proposed by the committee preserves the jurisdiction of the States' securities commissions to regulate transactions within the States. We think it is proper to uphold the laws of the States and by this measure we prohibit the sale through the instrumentality of interstate commerce or by the mails of a security, the sale of which is unlawful in that State. Upon this section of the bill two members of the committee filed a minority report. The other members of the committee cannot agree with their reasoning. We not only believe that Congress has the power to enact such a provision but we believe that it is only just that we should do so.

This bill is not so much a response to the frauds of criminals as it is to the reticence of financiers. Today we are forced to recognize that the hired managers of great corporations are not as wise, not as conservative, and sometimes are not as trustworthy as millions of American investors have been persuaded to believe. During the last 12 years, an era that is falsely designated as one of prosperity, American people lost perhaps a hundred billion dollars through the purchase of stocks and bonds. This catastrophe so colossal as to stagger the imagination did not come upon our people through the machinations of the common fraud. This loss of an amount equal to perhaps a third of the total national wealth did not follow from the kind of confidence game against which parents warn their sons. It came through the leadership that the average investor had a right to believe that he could trust. These securities were peddled among the people by firms like Halsey, Stuart & Co. and by great financial houses like the National City Bank.

Through the deliberate action of the hired officials of our greatest corporations, we have had during the past 15 years an amazing inflation of credit. The printing press has been used to turn out bright new stock certificates to distribute among the stockholders. These new stocks have been distributed as dividends, have been impounded to support issues of bonds. These bonds have been offered over the counter of every bank in exchange for the savings and surplus funds of depositors. The printing presses were not slowed down until the market for securities was paralyzed through the literal impoverishment of millions of people. More than $200,000,000,000 in bonds were issued and sold and are now outstanding. Hundreds of billions of stock were sold, not as offerings in highly speculative enterprises, but they were represented to be evidences of valuable equities in established and going concerns. As the result of this bald inflation directed by the hired managers of our big corporations, we have bonds outstanding almost to the amount of the actual wealth of this country. This orgy of inflation has imposed upon the physical properties of this country fixed charges far beyond the present productive capacity of the country to meet. This unbridled expansion has rendered the stocks almost worthless. A friend of mine, the other day, showed me a list of holdings which within the past few years had been purchased for $165,000 in cash. Last week when we were going over the list, the value according to the quotations of the day was less than $25,000.

These hired officials of our great corporations who permitted, who promoted, who achieved the extravagant expansion of the financial structure of their respective companies today present a pitiable spectacle. Five years ago they arrogated to themselves the greatest privileges. They scorned the interference of the Government. They dealt with their stockholders in the most arbitrary fashion. They called upon the people to bow down to them as the real rulers of the country. Safe from the pitiless publicity of Government supervision, unrestrained by Federal statute, free from any formal control, these few men, proud, arrogant, and blind, drove the country to financial ruin. Some of them are fugitives from justice in foreign lands; some of them have committed suicide; some of them are under indictment; some of them are in prison; all of them are in terror of the consequences of their own deeds.

This bill is drawn to enable a would-be purchaser of a bond or of a stock to require some information from the officials of the issuing company. The financial statements of the most conservative and the most reputable of our corporations are more mystifying than enlightening. The average stockholder cannot tell much about the condition of his company from the statements he receives. The inquiring investor has been able to get little except blurbs. This bill undertakes to define the duty of officers of corporations issuing securities, of syndicates underwriting issues, the duties of these corporate officials to the investing public. It undertakes to fix responsibility for information.

As set forth fully in the report, this bill prohibits the sale of securities in interstate commerce which are not registered with the Federal Trade Commission. The registration statement must contain complete information and all facts asked for under schedule A to be found in the last pages of the bill. If the Commission finds that any of the questions asked or information demanded, are not full and complete, they have the authority to refuse registration. If after registration it is discovered that the registration statement omits to state any material fact or makes a false statement, the Commission may issue a stop order, and the security can only be sold after issuance of the stop order in violation of the laws and subjects the seller to both civil and criminal liability.

The prospectus or advertisement of the security, if it is more than a mere announcement of the name and price of the issue offered, must include any part of the matter contained in the registration statement which the Commission, in its discretion, may require. The purpose of this section is to insure that prospective buyers of securities may have a complete understanding of the transaction in which they are invited to participate.

Let me repeat that what we seek to attain by this enactment is to make available to the prospective purchaser, if he is wise enough to use it, all information that is pertinent that would put him on notice and on guard, and then let him beware. On the other hand, we demand of the seller that he give full and complete information with reference to the security offered, under penalty of both civil and criminal liability if he evades or conceals material facts. If the seller is a wise man he will also beware. The people expect the Government of the United States to be clean. They expect the men who run it to be clean. This must be so if the people are to have confidence in, and respect for, their Government and fight in peace and in war to preserve it. Their Representatives have the right to demand that the men who run the business of the country shall conduct a clean business, to be fair and honorable with the other people of the country. In this bill we demand not only a new deal, we also demand a square deal. Less than this no honest man expects nor a dishonest man should have. When a people's faith is shaken in a business the business becomes halting and lame; when a people lose faith and confidence in the men who administer government it follows as the night the day they lose faith in government. Only one thing can follow in the wake in this destroyed confidence, that is, lack of support; and in its wake must follow the evils that attend socialism, bolshevism, and communism. We have reached the time in this country when we need the best brains and the greatest patriotism of large business, small business, the little man, big man, and all Americans who love the flag, to protect and defend their institutions if they are in these awful times to be preserved. [Applause.] ...

MR. KELLER. Mr. Chairman, does the requirement of registration apply to stocks already listed on the stock exchange or only to new stock?

MR. RAYBURN. New stocks.

MR. KELLER. Does the gentleman mean to say that all stocks now listed on all of the stock exchanges are entirely free from the operation of this law?

MR. RAYBURN. They are to this extent: If a company has put its stock upon the market but goes out and buys that up and makes a new issue, then that new issue will come under the provisions of this bill. If a corporation had authorized an issue and had sold none of it and holds it in its treasury, that all comes under this bill. If it has sold 10 percent or 20 percent or 50 percent, what it still holds in its treasury is subject to the provisions of this bill.

MR. KELLER. Why should it not apply to all stocks already issued?

MR. RAYBURN. Frankly, the committee discussed that very thoroughly, and we doubt very seriously whether or not we can do that, and we doubt very seriously whether or not it would be very helpful in trying to gather up those stocks that are scattered throughout the country. In other words, there must be a provision in this bill somewhere that has to do with an isolated transaction. Otherwise we will follow those stocks through. This bill makes absolutely responsible the issuer, the underwriter, and the dealer. It makes him responsible civilly if he sells stocks upon a misrepresentation; it makes him guilty of fraud and criminally liable if he sells it with misrepresentation and fraudulent intent. We believed if we went as far as this bill goes, as far as we probably can go, we would have been challenged by lawyers throughout the country and the act would have been held up in the courts at a very early date. If we can from now on with the stocks that are issued, if we can from now on with the stocks that have been issued and not sold, if we can, when these great corporations go out and buy up their own stocks that they have distributed to the public and then reissue, if we can cover those things, our committee thought we were going a long way for one enactment, and that we had better try that out for a while before we entered the broader and more uncertain field.

MR. KELLER. I can only say that I am sorry there is not some application made as to all stocks. ...

MR. COX. I, of course, agree with the gentleman on the desirability of the things sought to be accomplished, but I wonder if the gentleman is prepared to discuss the question of the competency of Congress to do the things which are proposed in the resolution that is before us. For instance, I presume it is conceded that it is in the exercise of the commerce powers of the Constitution that this resolution comes to this House. As I understand from a hurried reading of the bill, it is proposed to extend that power beyond the point of where the courts have heretofore said an article becomes a part of commerce. In other words, the courts have held, without dissent, that no article is a part of commerce until it has entered the channel of commerce. Here it is proposed, as I take it from a reading of the bill, to reach back to the point of the preparation or production or manufacture of the article which is intended to be put into commerce. . . .

Is it the position of the gentleman that Congress has a right to supervise and control, or exercise any influence whatsoever, upon the formation of a corporation, which is a thing done entirely within the domain of the State?

MR. RAYBURN. Not at all, and if a man does not intend to sell these securities in interstate commerce he is not compelled to register them.

MR. COX. But does the gentleman contend that the mere intention to put his products in interstate commerce empowers the Congress to impose a condition that attaches then, and prior to the time the article does actually enter commerce?

MR. RAYBURN. No; and that is not what this bill does.

MR. COX. Then what does the language of section 20 mean?

MR. RAYBURN. This bill says to the man who issues a security, "You may register that security; you are not compelled to register that security, but if you do not register it and you send it through interstate commerce we will penalize you."

MR. COX. That, I understand, is probably within the power of Congress; but what is the meaning of the language in section 20?—

> Whenever it shall appear to the Commission, either upon complaint or otherwise, that the provisions of this act, or of any rule or regulation prescribed under authority thereof, have been or are about to be violated, it may, in its discretion, either require or permit such person to file with it a statement in writing, under oath——

And so forth. In other words, what is the meaning of the language "about to be violated" if it is not proposed in this resolution to extend the power of Congress to the point of the mere intention to do a certain thing which cannot, under the rulings of the court as heretofore held, be a part of commerce until it actually enters the channel of commerce?

MR. RAYBURN. Well, if a man has any property in interstate commerce or the Commission decides he has made a false statement in his registration, and that the seller is making false representations in circulars that he is circulating——

MR. COX. But is a mere circular, is a mere representation, commerce, within the meaning of the law?

MR. RAYBURN. It is not commerce unless something you are selling in commerce attends it.

MR. COX. But a mere representation, a mere prospectus, or a mere advertisement, is that property, in the sense that the advertisement represents something of value?

MR. RAYBURN. If it travels in interstate commerce or through the mails I do not see any reason why Congress has not the power to deal with it.

MR. COX. Does not the gentleman see in this measure the projection of the Federal power, under Congress exercising its authority under the commerce clause to the point of uprooting and destroying all police power of States, insofar as the regulation of purely intrastate matters is concerned?

MR. RAYBURN. No; because this bill specifically provides that nothing in this act shall be construed to in anywise interfere with any State law on this subject, but it goes farther than that and says that the States shall be protected, and that it shall be unlawful to ship into a State through the instrumentalities of interstate commerce or the mails, a security, the sale of which is prohibited in that State.

MR. COX. But is it the contention of the gentleman that it is in the competency of Congress to confer any commerce powers upon a State?

MR. RAYBURN. That is a moot question.

MR. COX. It is not a moot question in law, but it may be moot here, as far as the attitude of the gentleman is concerned. . . .

MR. SUMNERS OF TEXAS. I understood from the statement of my colleague that what is attempted to be done is the establishment of conditions precedent to engaging in interstate commerce.

MR. RAYBURN. That is right.

MR. COX. Of course it is within the power of Congress to fix a condition.

MR. SUMNERS OF TEXAS. A condition precedent.

MR. COX. Yes; a condition precedent.

MR. SUMNERS OF TEXAS. As I understood my colleague, the intention was to undertake to establish regulatory conditions for engaging in the interstate commerce of securities.

MR. RAYBURN. That is true.

MR. COX. And merely gives the use of the instrumentalities of commerce upon the condition that these conditions have been complied with. It is not within the power of Congress to confer——

MR. RAYBURN. That is exactly what this bill seeks to do. In effect it says to a man, "You do not have to register this security, but if you are going to sell it in interstate commerce, or through the mails, you will violate the law unless you do register.

MR. PARKER OF NEW YORK. . . .Mr. Chairman, no one could possibly object to the principles set forth in this bill. There are certain clauses in the bill that I personally do not like.

This is the worst time in the history of the country to write a bill of this kind. As the gentleman from Texas so well said, this is the most intricate bill we have ever seen, and he and I have been members of the Committee on Interstate Commerce for the same length of time, 20 years.

This bill is written, and we cannot help it. It is written in the spirit of prejudice, because we have had before us in the past 3 or 4 years perfectly colossal, rotten failures in several large corporations and in several of the large banks of the country, which does not leave us in the proper mental attitude to write a bill of this magnitude and have it as clear as it should be. We are very apt to bend over backwards.

Two things must be considered in connection with this bill. We want to protect the gullible investor, the investor who has been imposed upon. This is tremendously important. But more important is the protection of the honest business man upon the success of whose business depends the success of the country. Under present conditions we are apt to think only of the man who has lost his money and not think of protecting the men who are trying to do business and do business honestly.

The gentleman from Michigan spoke about the directors being guarantors. The gentleman from Texas very emphatically brought out the small percentage of interest that the directors have in the large corporations.

For illustration, let us say you are a director of the United States Steel Corporation. It is nothing unusual for this corporation to bring out an issue of $10,000,000 of stock or debentures. If the directors of this company have got to be guarantors of every single statement that is made, nobody would sign the statement, because the directors cannot know. They must depend upon their accountants, their engineers, and their appraisers for statement.

Now, if they willfully make a misstatement, I am willing to go as far as anybody possibly could go. Send them to jail if the misstatement is willful. But if it is a statement founded on a mistake made by somebody else after the use of due diligence, I do not believe they should be held personally responsible.

MR. COX. Is the gentleman conceding that the commerce clause of the Constitution confers upon Congress authority to carry the Federal power to the point of holding liable one who merely participates in the formation of a corporation within a State?

MR. PARKER OF NEW YORK. I am not. I am not discussing the constitutionality of it; I am discussing the wisdom of it.

MR. COX. Does not the gentleman appreciate the fact that the extension of the principle announced in this bill simply means the swallowing up of the police power of the States by the Federal Government?

MR. PARKER OF NEW YORK. In answer I will simply say that the Senate bill does carry that absolute guaranty to the investor.

MR. COX. Could not Congress accomplish what it seeks—that is, the full play of State laws—by making possible their application to all these matters, as it did when it made subject to State laws liquor transported within a State where traffic was prohibited?

MR. PARKER OF NEW YORK. That is an entirely different question.

MR. COX. Certainly. This is the proposition: It is within the power of Congress to withdraw immunity from any article entering commerce which it may see fit to do, subjecting the article to the operation of State law.

MR. PARKER OF NEW YORK. Yes.

MR. BRITTEN. Mr. Chairman, that is not quite correct, I am sure. The gentleman has confined his question to intrastate business and not interstate business.

MR. PARKER OF NEW YORK. This law does not affect intrastate business in the least.

MR. BRITTEN. Of course it does not, but the gentleman answered in the affirmative.

MR. COX. Let me make this observation: It is within the power of Congress to declare that an article loses its interstate character upon entering a State where the article is under the condemnation of State law.

MR. PARKER OF NEW YORK. I will answer the gentleman in this way: If, in the gentleman's State, it is illegal to sell a certain article, this law makes it illegal to ship it in from another State. Is that clear?

MR. COX. I did not catch the gentleman's statement.

MR. PARKER OF NEW YORK. If it is illegal to sell any particular article or any bond in the gentleman's State———

MR. COX. The sale of which is claimed to be legal because of its interstate character?

MR. PARKER OF NEW YORK. No; because your State makes it illegal by your own law.

MR. COX. Here is the position I take——

MR. PARKER OF NEW YORK. Let me answer the gentleman's question first. If the laws of your State make it illegal——

MR. COX. That is, have outlawed traffic in a certain article——

MR. PARKER OF NEW YORK. All right, then, it is illegal to ship it in interstate commerce into your State under this bill.

MR. COX. That is correct, sir, but could not Congress do that same thing as applied to all the States without involving the question of encroachment upon the sovereign rights of States——

MR. PARKER OF NEW YORK. I do not think they have.

MR. COX. By simply making a declaration to the effect that any article in commerce entering any State, traffic in which is prohibited by that State, loses its interstate character?

MR. PARKER OF NEW YORK. I will say to the gentleman that it was the intention of the committee to do exactly what the gentleman is advocating, as I understand it.

To get back to the liability of directors, if you should follow out the policy of making the directors civilly liable—I would make them criminally liable for any misstatements if they were made intentionally, but that is a different proposition—when you make a man liable for a misstatement when he has employed the very best accountants he can get, the very best engineers he can get, the very best appraisers he can get, and then he sits in his office with the board of directors and they go over these figures and use the utmost diligence in setting forth what is correct, I believe they should have the opportunity to go before the Commission and prove that they did not know and therefore should not be held. The burden of proof under this bill is not on the buyer; the burden of proof is on the director, and he must go before the Commission and prove that he did not make a false statement knowingly. . . .

MR. STUDLEY. Does this bill reach the dealer in securities as well as the directors?

MR. PARKER OF NEW YORK. Yes; just the same.

MR. STUDLEY. And the brokerage and bond houses that sell the securities?

MR. PARKER OF NEW YORK. Yes; just the same.

There was some discussion about stocks that are already listed. If the theory of the gentleman from Missouri and the gentleman from Illinois were carried out and the stocks that are now listed on the market were required to be registered, you would close every market for months at least, or until they could get the registration papers ready; and allow me to say that in the New York Stock Exchange, the Curb Exchange, and I presume in the Chicago Exchange, they require more data to be filed with them before a stock is registered than we require under this bill.

MR. MOTT. Will the gentleman yield?

MR. PARKER OF NEW YORK. Yes.

MR. MOTT. I am pleased to hear the gentleman state that. Does the gentleman know that the Insull stock and the stock of the Central Public Service Corporation of Illinois, two of the biggest rackets in the country, were listed on the New York and Chicago Stock Exchanges?

MR. PARKER OF NEW YORK. That is perfectly true, but you can go right down the list and take any stock that you have in mind, and you will find that taking any railroad stock, for instance, they have gone down, and gone down to practically nothing.

MR. MOTT. The gentleman knows why they listed that stock on the New York Stock Exchange.

MR. PARKER OF NEW YORK. I am not defending the stock exchange or going into that question at all. . . .

MR. BRITTEN. I am interested in the statement the gentleman just made. He indicated to his former questioner that the New York Stock Exchange and the Chicago Stock Exchange require greater detail in statements upon the listing of new securities than may be required by this bill.

MR. PARKER OF NEW YORK. As great, anyway; yes.

MR. BRITTEN. How are we going to protect the prospective investors in the future if they have not been protected in the past by the filing of statements of a more detailed character than the ones we are now requiring?

MR. PARKER OF NEW YORK. I will answer the gentleman in this way: When they file a misstatement with the New York Stock Exchange or any of the other large exchanges their stock is immediately taken off the board, and it is a greater penalty to the stockholders to have that stock taken off the board than any fine you could possibly put on.

MR. BRITTEN. If I may ask the gentleman one more question, if that is true—and I am satisfied it is—what protection are we giving to the poor lamb in the street who may buy more stock, when we are not improving existing conditions?

MR. PARKER OF NEW YORK. We have gone as far as human ingenuity can go. If you will take the bill and read schedule A and schedule B, if there is anything you can think of that we have not asked them to file, I wish the gentleman would tell me what it is.

They have to file what compensation the company is going to get from the sale, and as the gentleman from Texas says, they have to register and wait 30 days before they sell. . . .

MR. BRITTEN. Will not the effect of the bill be this because of the deflation in value? Will not the bill have this effect: That the big corporations from now on will issue no more stock, but continue to do business for years with the present stock issue, whereas if the legislation was not in force they might reduce the outstanding stock 3 to 1 or even 10 to 1? This bill prevents that, and I think it is a bad thing.

MR. PARKER OF NEW YORK. If they can go on and do business with the present stock issue, I do not think it is a hardship. We are trying to protect the man who buys stock. There have been millions and millions of fraudulent stocks sold in this country in the last 10 years, and that is what we are trying to stop. I do not want to stop the honest man from doing business. . . .

MR. HASTINGS. I am much interested in this discussion. I was wondering if the committee had considered having the stock that is now issued and previously issued registered.

MR. PARKER OF NEW YORK. Yes; but did not approve.

MR. HASTINGS. I can see a difficulty with reference to the outstanding issues of stock; there is so much of the stock that in order to protect the public the committee should have taken into consideration the outstanding stock issued before this time.

MR. PARKER OF NEW YORK. The gentleman from Oklahoma does not understand the question. That stock is already on the market now; it is being peddled and distributed by individuals who are selling their holdings. That is not covered. If you paid $100 for stock, and it is now down to $10, all right, you get your $10. That is not covered in this bill. You will have to accept your loss. . . .

MR. MOTT. The gentleman is very familiar with the provisions of the bill, and I would like to name three outstanding financial wreckages. One is the Insull Co., the second is the Central Co., and the other is the Foshay Co. How, if this bill had been in force at the time that stock was sold, would it protect the public from the investment?

MR. PARKER OF NEW YORK. In this way: They have up to 10 years to go through the registration and certificate, and if the registration certificate were not correct on it you could sue them civilly and criminally.

MR. MOTT. What good would it do to sue them criminally 7 or 8 years afterward?

MR. PARKER OF NEW YORK. There is an old saying that you cannot protect a fool from his folly. . . .

MR. SAMUEL B. HILL. After this bill goes into effect I understand that stocks listed on the stock exchange will have to be registered just the same as other stocks?

MR. PARKER OF NEW YORK. Stocks that are listed now?

MR. SAMUEL B. HILL. That will be listed.

MR. PARKER OF NEW YORK. Yes.

MR. SAMUEL B. HILL. Do the securities that are listed on the stock exchanges and which become the subject of open-market operations through those exchanges enjoy exemptions which are not equally applicable to other stock issues?

MR. PARKER OF NEW YORK. Not at all.

MR. SAMUEL B. HILL. So there is nothing here that really places the stock listed on the stock exchanges in a preference class as against other stocks?

MR. PARKER OF NEW YORK. Not at all. The only preference they get is the confidence of the people that they are sound, because as a matter of fact more people will look at the stock market than will ever look at the prospectuses that are gotten out by the Federal Trade Commission; they know that if a stock is listed that at least the prospectus has been filed with the Federal Trade Commission.

MR. SAMUEL B. HILL. Section 18 prohibits the sale through the channels of interstate commerce in the States having so-called "blue sky laws," and the language is:

To sell or deliver, directly or indirectly.

To what extent does that section prohibit sending advertising matter, circulars, newspapers, through the mails or by radio, which does not result in a sale or delivery, directly or indirectly, of the securities? In other words, does it prohibit the advertising through the channels of interstate commerce within those States, without first having complied with the securities acts of the various States?

MR. PARKER OF NEW YORK. Yes. I am not clear upon that, but my impression is that it does.

MR. SAMUEL B. HILL. The language is "to sell or to deliver directly or indirectly," and I am wondering if when it does not result in a sale or delivery whether there will be any violation of the act.

MR. PARKER OF NEW YORK. There will be no harm done in that case. . . .

MR. BRITTEN. What is the penalty for a dealer, a so-called "corporation," dealing in its own stocks?

MR. PARKER OF NEW YORK. It is just the same as though they were putting out new stock. To use an illustration, if Cities Service should put up its own stock and advertise it and sell it to the gentleman at 50 under a fraudulent statement, a fraudulent registration, then the gentleman can recover from them in a civil suit.

MR. BRITTEN. But they would not be registered at all.

MR. PARKER OF NEW YORK. They have got to register when they operate as a dealer.

MR. BRITTEN. Suppose they sell through a dealer?

MR. PARKER OF NEW YORK. Then the dealer has to register.

MR. BRITTEN. He will not register that stock.

MR. PARKER OF NEW YORK. He cannot help it, unless it is an isolated transaction.

MR. BRITTEN. I am talking about stocks now on the board.

MR. PARKER OF NEW YORK. He cannot get rid of it, if he is going to sell it to the public, unless he registers it.

MR. BRITTEN. The gentleman means because it comes from a corporation?

MR. PARKER OF NEW YORK. It does not make any difference where it comes from.

MR. BRITTEN. Evidently I have not made myself clear to the gentleman. I am talking about stocks now outstanding. The corporation buys it in, paying a small amount of money for it.

MR. PARKER OF NEW YORK. Yes.

MR. BRITTEN. It inflates that stock in value as they have done in the past, illegally or otherwise.

MR. PARKER OF NEW YORK. Yes.

MR. BRITTEN. It then has its broker offer that stock for sale.

MR. PARKER OF NEW YORK. Yes.

MR. BRITTEN. Surely that stock is not going to be listed.

MR. PARKER OF NEW YORK. That stock would have to be listed. It is practically new stock. The only thing that is exempted would be an isolated transaction. If the gentleman had some stock and sold it through a broker to me, that would not have to be registered. If the gentleman advertised it for sale, it would have to be registered, be it old or new stock.

MR. BRITTEN. Suppose the corporation, being the owner of the stock, does not advertise it, but merely through ordinary channels turns it over to its broker.

MR. PARKER OF NEW YORK. The broker could not sell until he had it registered. He would have to have it registered through the corporation, and be subject to the Federal Trade Commission.

MR. BRITTEN. That stock will never have been listed, I am sure, even under the provisions of this bill.

MR. PARKER OF NEW YORK. I am certain they would not sell it, unless they violate the law.

MR. REILLY. What becomes of the banker in another State that sells the stock, stock issued under this law, which has the approval of the Federal Trade Commission? Suppose it comes to my State and a local banker sells the stock, and it turns out to be fraudulent. Is he liable under the bill?

MR. PARKER OF NEW YORK. No; it would be the original sellers. . . .

MR. KELLER. The gentleman was chairman of this same committee for some years.

MR. PARKER OF NEW YORK. Yes.

MR. KELLER. Does the gentleman think this bill will help matters?

MR. PARKER OF NEW YORK. I think it will very decidedly.

MR. KELLER. The gentleman knows of the investigation of the Pujo Committee?

MR. PARKER OF NEW YORK. Oh, yes; I was in Congress at that time.

MR. KELLER. Why was not a bill of this kind written some years ago?

MR. PARKER OF NEW YORK. Your powers of prophecy are just as good as mine. I could not tell.

MR. KELLER. Not to embarrass the gentleman, but what I am trying to ask is, Could this not have been prevented if a proper law had been passed years ago?

MR. PARKER OF NEW YORK. It could have been prevented, but still this speculation of the last 4 or 5 years is what brought this to the public attention. As the gentleman from Texas [Mr. Rayburn], so well pointed out, corporate interests did not amount to much 20 years ago. They have grown by leaps and bounds until practically everything in this country is run by corporations, and we are all stockholders. There are very few of us who have any property except pieces of paper which represent an interest in a certain corporation.

MR. KELLER. As a matter of fact, has not every one of the panics in recent years, since the Civil War, been precipitated by a stock crash on the New York Stock Exchange?

MR. PARKER OF NEW YORK. Well, to a certain extent, the gentleman is probably correct. . . .

MR. ADAMS. As I understand it, certain information must be given to the commission prior to the registration?

MR. PARKER OF NEW YORK. Yes.

MR. ADAMS. Does this bill, in the gentleman's opinion, make adequate provision for the availability of that information to the public?

MR. PARKER OF NEW YORK. Why, it is a public record.

MR. ADAMS. I am asking for information.

MR. PARKER OF NEW YORK. Yes; it is a public record; and after the application, if you are going to form a corporation and you file your prospectus, answer all these questions, and I am going to underwrite or handle it for you, I cannot sell it for 30 days after you have filed your prospectus, so that everybody will have a chance at least to be put on notice as to what is behind that stock.

MR. ADAMS. In other words, there are no rules and regulations by which the public may be prevented from getting the information?

MR. PARKER OF NEW YORK. Not at all. . . .

MR. BRITTEN. The hearings before the gentleman's committee bear out my contention quite conclusively.

MR. PARKER OF NEW YORK. I think the gentleman has the Senate hearings.

MR. BRITTEN. Well, they were just handed me.

MR. PARKER OF NEW YORK. That is the Senate hearing.

MR. BRITTEN. Mr. Huston Thompson says this:

As I said before, my interpretation is that any security that has been put on the market and is being sold is exempt.

Exempt from this act. I was talking about securities that are on the market and are being resold. They will never be listed, and this same inflation, this same method of extraction from the public, will occur again unless by some means that stock can be listed.

MR. PARKER OF NEW YORK. It is specifically stated in this bill that if a company buys and trades in its own stock, advertises and puts it back on the market, it must be registered.

MR. BRITTEN. On a reissue?

MR. PARKER OF NEW YORK. Yes; and on an old issue, too. The minute they become dealers, dealing in their own stock, they must register the stock. . . .

MR. McFADDEN. That does not prevent the organization of pools entirely outside the company from accumulating that stock and reselling it?

MR. PARKER OF NEW YORK. It absolutely does, because they are dealers under the definition of "dealers," if the gentleman will read that definition.

MR. McFADDEN. I am referring to stock that is not under this rule and is not a new issue, but is an established issue, like United States Steel or General Electric.

MR. PARKER OF NEW YORK. Yes.

MR. McFADDEN. Pools can be organized and accumulate that stock when it is low and then unload it on the public when it is high. Does the gentleman mean to tell me they must register that stock?

MR. PARKER OF NEW YORK. If they are dealers, they certainly must. If they advertise through interstate commerce, they certainly must register that stock.

MR. McFADDEN. Suppose there is a confidential pool that is buying just through three or four brokers and accumulating it; does the gentleman mean to say that those brokers must register that stock with this board?

MR. PARKER OF NEW YORK. I think a confidential pool would come under the heading of fraud, because they must register it, and if they do not register it, it would be pure and simple fraud. . . .

MR. BULWINKLE. Mr. Chairman—

We advocate protection of the investing public by requiring to be filed with the Government and carried in advertisements of all offerings of foreign and domestic stocks and bonds true information as to bonuses, commissions, principal invested, and interests of the sellers.

These are the words of a plank in the Democratic national platform of 1932.

In compliance with that platform pledge, the President of the United States on March 29, 1933, in a message transmitted to the first session of the Seventy-third Congress, among other things said:

Of course, the Federal Government cannot and should not take any action which might be construed as approving or guaranteeing that newly issued securities are sound in the sense that their value will be maintained or that the properties which they represent will earn profit.

There is, however, an obligation upon us to insist that every issue of new securities to be sold in interstate commerce shall be accompanied by full publicity and information, and that no essentially important element attending the issue shall be concealed from the buying public.

This proposal adds to the ancient rule of caveat emptor, the further doctrine "let the seller also beware." It puts the burden of telling the whole truth on the seller. It should give impetus to honest dealing in securities and thereby bring back public confidence.

The purpose of the legislation I suggest is to protect the public with the least possible interference to honest business.

The necessity for this declaration in the party platform and the necessity of the message of the President of the United States arose from the fact that for the past 10 years the United States has been flooded with not only worthless stock but fraudulent stock as well. The amount in value that the people of the United States paid for these securities is purely a conjecture, but it is safe to say that it runs well into the billions.

Many of these securities that were worthless were in a sense handled by American dealers, who made vast profits upon the same, and the American public who bought them have held the bag ever since. Every Member here present is familiar with the testimony of the various investment bankers before the Senate committee, and nearly everyone has read those lurid advertisements issued by American concerns advising the American public to purchase these securities.

During the past 10 years, therefore, the American dealers, the American underwriters, the American investment bankers, and the officers of American corporations in many instances were responsible for the sale of these worthless and fraudulent securities. But they alone were not to blame. The administration aided in no small degree the sale to the American public of these securities.

The necessity for this legislation is apparent to all, and the objective to be sought by the legislation is the publicity of all necessary and material facts connected with the sale of securities in interstate commerce. In other words, the title of the bill is—

To provide full and fair disclosure of the character of securities sold in interstate and foreign commerce and through the mails, and to prevent frauds in the sale thereof, and for other purposes.

The committee, after extended hearings, referred the matter to a subcommittee, consisting of the chairman and four other members of the committee, who diligently and carefully, with the assistance of the capable legislative drafting service, brought before the full committee the bill now under consideration, H. R. 5480.

The necessity for legislation of this character having been admitted by practically all, including many of the investment houses and dealers in securities in the United States, and the objective being, as I have stated before, to give full publicity to the sale of all securities in interstate commerce, the question will then be asked, "How do you propose to attain this objective?" And it is not amiss for me, in the brief time that I have at my disposal, to state how the end will be accomplished under the bill if it is enacted into law.

Every issuer, every dealer, every underwriter, who would sell securities in interstate commerce, either by newspaper advertisement or by radio or any means of transportation or communication, must obtain a registration statement from the Federal Trade Commission. This statement must show all the information required in schedule A or schedule B, under such rules and regulations as the Federal Trade Commission should hereafter prescribe. And the careful study by you of schedule A and schedule B will show the extent of the information which will be required by every issuer, dealer, or underwriter who attempts the sale of securities in interstate commerce. The registration statement should be—

Signed by the issuer or issuers, its principal executive officers, its principal financial officers, its comptroller or principal accounting officers, and the majority of its board of directors or persons performing similar functions (or, if there is no board of directors or persons performing similar functions, by the majority of the persons or board having the power of management of the issuer), and, in the event that the issuer is a foreign or Territorial person, by its duly authorized representative in the United States—

And so forth.

The requirements here are that the board of directors of a corporation and its managing officers must know what they are signing. They are not only liable civilly for an untrue statement of a material fact and for the omission to state a material fact, but they are also criminally liable when they fail to do that which was required of them and which was done with the purpose to defraud the purchaser of the security.

There are many classes of exempted securities from the provisions of this bill, as well as exempted transactions. Any security issued prior to within 60 days after the passage of this act is exempt, and also any security issued by the United States or any Territory, or by the District of Columbia, or by any State of the United States, or any political subdivision thereof, or by any corporation created and controlled or supervised by and acting as an instrumentality of the United States, Federal bank, State bank, notes, drafts, bills of exchange, or bankers' acceptance; securities issued by religious, educational, benevolent, fraternal, and charitable bodies for reformatory purposes and not for pecuniary profits; securities issued by building and loan associations, savings and loan associations; securities issued by a common carrier; certificates issued by a receiver or by trustee in bankruptcy; any insurance policy issued by a corporation subject to the supervision of the insurance commissioner; and also the Commission may from time to time, by its rules and regulations, add any class to these exempted securities if it is found by the Commission that the enforcement of the act is not necessary for the public interests.

And then we have the exempted transactions, transactions by an issuer and by a broker, and the distribution by a corporation of its stock dividends, and so forth. Subscribers of shares of the organization of the corporation are under certain restrictions. So you can find that with the exempted transactions and the exempted securities under the act and under the rules and regulations of the Commission, that the public and business will in no wise be affected. . . .

MR. SAMUEL B. HILL. Directing the gentleman's attention to page 9 of the bill, line 5, can he tell us if open market transactions on the stock exchange are exempted; are they permitted?

MR. BULWINKLE. Yes.

MR. SAMUEL B. HILL. This portion of the bill does not refer to transactions in securities that are registered, or, to ask the question in another way, need the securities be registered in order to be exempt under this provision?

MR. BULWINKLE. No. . . .

MR. ARENS. Was it the intention of the committee to exclude from the exemptions enumerated on page 7, lines 4 and 5, cooperative organizations? Was it the intention of the committee that the provisions of this act should apply also to farm cooperative organizations?

MR. BULWINKLE. May I ask the gentleman if the cooperatives he has in mind lend money except for the business of the members of the organization?

MR. ARENS. I do not know of any that do, but they do sell stocks and securities.

MR. BULWINKLE. If they sell stocks as an issuer or a dealer or underwriter, then of course they will come under the provisions of this act.

MR. ARENS. Cooperatives should be exempted from the operation of this act, for they are not organized for profit.

MR. BULWINKLE. That is correct.

MR. ARENS. Was it the intention of the committee to include cooperatives that are not organized for profit?

MR. BULWINKLE. To be frank about it, the consideration of cooperatives did not come up before the committee, but I do not see how the ordinary stock of the cooperatives will come under the provisions of this act.

MR. ARENS. Would the committee accept an amendment specifically naming them in the exemptions?

MR. BULWINKLE. I would suggest that the gentleman take it up with the chairman of the committee. Personally, I would have no objection to it at all. . . .

MR. BRITTEN. Of course, if the stock of the cooperative enters into interstate commerce and is sold, and it is a new issue, that stock will have to be listed under the provisions of this bill.

MR. BULWINKLE. Certainly; but I understood that the gentleman from Minnesota wanted to exempt the original issue, although I think it is covered under the exemptions. It may not be. So far as I am concerned personally I will be perfectly willing that they be included.

MR. ARENS. I think the intent of the bill is to exempt cooperatives, but the language is not plain. Several of the cooperatives have asked me to offer an amendment of the nature I have indicated.

MR. RAYBURN. I may say to the gentleman that no such provision was ever suggested either to the full committee or to the subcommittee. As far as I am concerned individually, if an amendment of the nature indicated by the gentleman is adopted in the Senate, speaking for myself alone, as a conferee I would certainly agree to it. . . .

MR. DOBBINS. As I understand the bill, it does not exempt the securities of public-utilities companies?

MR. BULWINKLE. No.

MR. DOBBINS. The only public-utilities securities which are excepted are common carriers.

MR. BULWINKLE. Common carriers come under the jurisdiction of the Interstate Commerce Commission.

MR. DOBBINS. Was any consideration given in the committee to exempting them since they have already been passed upon by existing commissions?

MR. BULWINKLE. They are not exempted.

MR. DOBBINS. I am glad they are not, but some State laws do exempt them. . . .

MR. STUDLEY. Is this bill intended to reach municipal bonds?

MR. BULWINKLE. No; they are exempt.

MR. STUDLEY. Is the bill intended to reach bonds of irrigation districts or levee-improvement districts?

MR. BULWINKLE. Those are all exempted.

MR. STUDLEY. There is nothing in the bill which could prevent the issuance of these bonds and their sale in interstate commerce?

MR. BULWINKLE. The act does not apply to any subdivision of a State government or any instrumentality of any State government.

Furthermore, under the provisions of the act, an applicant shall have 30 days after the filing with the Commission, except as otherwise provided, and if the Commission should find that the statement is incomplete in any material respect, the Commission may cause amendments thereto to be filed. And, also, if it appears to the Commission, if the registration statement contains any untrue statement of facts or omits to state any true condition of facts, a hearing can be had, and the Commission can issue a stop order.

The power is given to the Commission not to guarantee the securities to the purchasers thereof but merely to require that there be filed with the Commission a true and accurate statement of all material facts, which the purchaser of a security should have knowledge of.

Then, the advertisement, which covers all notices, circulars, communications by radio, and so forth, must contain certain facts which the investing public have a right to know before purchasing the securities. Then, in addition to that, the registration statement is a public record, which under the proper rules and regulations, any person can examine, or cause to be examined, before purchasing the securities. Under the provisions, then, of this act there can be no more "old counselors," who, by means of radio, cause the widows and others to invest in securities which are worthless. For the information of the new counselors it will be so that any person of ordinary intelligence, by due care and due diligence, can protect himself against purchasing securities which are either fraudulent or worthless. . . .

MR. BRITTEN. Is there anything in this bill which will preclude an issuing house from carrying in its advertisements the fact that an issue has been listed with the Federal Trade Commission, or approved by the United States Government, and by so doing convey a false representation of its character?

MR. BULWINKLE. Yes. Under the original bill which was introduced an express provision was put in the bill that they could not advertise that they had listed. In my opinion, and I think I am correct, under this bill that subject is covered.

MR. HUDDLESTON. If the gentleman will permit, that subject is covered by section 22 of the bill and is fully covered to the satisfaction of everyone.

MR. BULWINKLE. Yes; it is fully covered.

The machinery of the bill is not complicated or it is not hard to understand. It will not prove unjust to any issuer of securities, dealer, or underwriter, but it will prove an aid to every purchaser of securities. It fully complies with the Democratic platform. If fully complies with the message of the President of the United States, and it should be enacted into law for the benefit of the public as well as the benefit of all legitimate sellers of securities. [Applause.] . . .

MR. PETTENGILL. . . . A burned child fears the fire, and the public has taken such a terrific burning with worthless securities in recent years that I doubt if investment can be tempted back into industry unless the public feels more sure in the future than it has been warranted in feeling in the past, that when they again buy securities they are going to buy not only with open eyes but with honest information, so that they can see what they are buying—that the cards will not be stacked against them. This is a part of a new deal; and if there is any bill in the President's program that fits into the description of a new deal with respect to the shuffling of a pack of cards, it is this particular bill, because the cards have not been shuffled honestly in recent years, as we all know. They have been shuffled very dishonestly—so much so that the testimony before our committee is that the American public has been swindled out of $25,000,000,000 in the last dozen years, almost as much as the World War cost us.

The particulars of the bill have been well covered by previous speakers, and I think I would be trespassing on your time if I were to attempt to again go over the bill itself; but in view of the long years that this bill has been maturing in the minds of liberal and progressive thinkers of America, and as a tribute to a great man in the rich evening of his life, I want to go back just a little in the historic background of the bill. The President in his message urging Congress to enact this legislation said:

What we seek is a return to a clearer understanding of the ancient truth, that those who manage banks, corporations, and other agencies, handling or using other people's money, are trustees acting for others.

In his inaugural address the President said:

There must be a strict supervision of all banking and credits and investments. There must be an end to speculation with other people's money.

These words of the President, "other people's money," were first used to attract the attention of the Nation 20 years ago by a man who for the past 40 years has taken a preeminent part in progressive and liberal thinking, and in behalf of honest relationships between human beings, a man whom I consider of all the men who have participated in public life in the last 40 years, who are still active, as the outstanding one of them all, the economic prophet, and the greatest liberal of our time, Mr. Justice Louis D. Brandeis, now of the United States Supreme Court. . . .

Twenty years ago Mr. Justice Brandeis saw the necessity of this very legislation, and I am quoting from his book in which he speaks of the fraudulent practices prevailing then. This bill, this part of the new deal, is a child of the new freedom of the Wilson administration, because I am convinced from my reading of Wilson's speeches that if we had not entered the World War, if the attention of the American people had not been distracted by the World War, as early as 1914, legislation along this line would have been enacted in Wilson's first term. Justice Brandeis says:

We must break the money trust or the money trust will break us. . . .

MR. McFADDEN. I am wondering whether, under this bill, there are provisions that will secure the innocent investing public from further losses when those securities are dealt out to the public by concerns of the type of J. P. Morgan & Co.

MR. PETTENGILL. Does the gentleman have any specific question in mind?

MR. McFADDEN. I have this in mind: That the public is being exploited by banking houses of that reputation, whose very names lend confidence to the public. Their very names lend confidence to the public, when upon minute examination in 1929 and previously, as the gentleman has referred to, those securities are not worth the paper they are written on.

MR. PETTENGILL. That is correct; yes.

MR. McFADDEN. That is what I want to deal with, and I want to know whether this bill will cover situations like that.

MR. PETTENGILL. I can only express my judgment on it. I think this bill does cover the situation. . . .

MR. MOTT. Will the gentleman state how this bill covers that situation—how, if this law had been in effect at the time of the New York, New Haven & Hartford swindle which the gentleman just mentioned, it would have saved any investors in that company?

MR. PETTENGILL. Well, with respect to railroad securities, they have been previously placed under the control of the Interstate Commerce Commission and therefore do not come under this bill, because their sale is already regulated; but speaking of securities generally, if the gentleman will read the bill carefully and will read the schedules that are attached at the back of the bill and will see the information that must be filed with the Federal Trade Commission showing the amount of commissions that the bankers are receiving from the sale, showing the prior liens of all kinds and their character, showing how much properties actually cost to the exclusion of "water" and "balloon juice," showing the conversion rights of other classes of securities that may be ahead of the one that is to be sold, and a multitude of other particulars, then I think that, with the information which is to be furnished under schedule A to the Federal Trade Commission, all of which becomes a matter of public record, to which any investor may refer, he will have as clear a picture of the value and worth and prospects of that security as it is possible to furnish. I might say as a member of the committee which reported the bill, if the gentleman can suggest any additional safeguards in the way of honest information to the investing public, I personally should be glad to have the gentleman's recommendations. . . .

MR. MOTT. Does the gentleman mean suggestions by others that have been given to the committee or suggestions for amendments that may be made here now?

MR. PETTENGILL. Well, under the rule the bill is still capable of amendment by agreement on the part of the committee. As I say, I am speaking for myself; but if the gentleman can suggest any way of strengthening this bill, personally I should be glad to receive his suggestions.

MR. MOTT. I can suggest a half a dozen ways to improve the bill, and all securities commissioners in the United States, who are the only people who have any practical experience in the administration of any securities laws, can do so, too. The State blue sky laws constitute the entire corpus juris of security regulation. I cannot amend that bill in committee. Your committee did not call the governor of any State or any securities commissioner or any authority on the subject. . . .

MR. RAYBURN. . . . I will say the committee did not call anybody. People volunteered, and if we started out to call commissioners of States and governors we would never have gotten through the hearings.

MR. MOTT. I will state for the information of the chairman of the committee that on the second day on which the committee had this bill under consideration I appeared before the committee for the purpose of offering some suggestions and was advised that the testimony had been closed and that no further testimony would be taken.

MR. RAYBURN. Of course, if the gentleman did not appear until after the testimony had been closed, that could not be helped; but if the gentleman had come to me and told me he wanted time before the testimony was closed, he certainly would have had it.

MR. MOTT. Of course, I supposed this bill would receive more than 1 or 2 days' hearings, given by people who are familiar with security regulations. . . .

MR. HUDDLESTON. If the gentleman from Oregon [Mr. Mott] will be kind enough to read the bill, he will see very clearly that this is not that kind of bill at all.

MR. MOTT. Not what kind of bill?

MR. HUDDLESTON. This is not a blue sky bill. The gentleman totally mis-comprehends the purpose of the legislation. It is merely to give information to those who want to buy securities. In no sense is it a blue sky bill.

MR. MOTT. It depends on what the gentleman means by a blue sky bill.

MR. HUDDLESTON. It is in no sense what the gentleman means by a blue sky bill, as he has indicated by what he has said.

MR. MOTT. I beg the gentleman's pardon, but it is exactly what the gentleman has in mind.

MR. HUDDLESTON. I am reading the gentleman's thought and not undertaking myself to describe what a blue sky law is.

MR. MOTT. I might remind the gentleman there are some 45 so-called "blue sky" laws. They are regulatory statutes.

MR. HUDDLESTON. The gentleman is giving information which others have to an equal degree with himself. . . .

MR. WOLVERTON. Mr. Chairman, the purpose of the bill under consideration is to protect the investing public from fraud in transactions involving the sale of stock, bonds, and other securities.

When it is realized that more than one half of the entire wealth of the United States is represented by securities in one form or another, that corporate securities alone amount to more than $160,000,000,000, and that by conservative estimates at least $1,700,000,000 is lost each year by the purchase of spurious or worthless securities, then the need for effective legislation on the subject can be readily understood.

Legislation seeking to give protection to the purchaser of securities has been enacted in a variety of forms by nearly every State. However, notwithstanding the general existence of statutes to prevent such frauds, the fact, nevertheless, remains that the fabulous amount already mentioned is lost each year by innocent purchasers of securities having little or no value, who have been misled by fraudulent misrepresentations and deception as to the real character and value of such securities.

The failure to prevent such losses is not due to any lack of stringency in the statutes already enacted by the several States, but, in a large measure, because of the inability of State laws to reach interstate transactions in such securities. Fraudulent securities are largely sold and distributed by agencies of communication which extend beyond State lines. The jurisdiction of State regulatory measures is necessarily confined or limited to transactions within the State. The channels of interstate commerce are open and free from such State regulation and control. Thus securities that may be precluded from sale in an intrastate transaction are immune when the transaction extends beyond the boundaries of that particular State.

Because of the ineffectiveness of State statutes to give adequate protection, there is a demand for the Federal Government to enact regulatory legislation to supplement and make more effective the State regulation designed to protect the investing public. This bill now before us for consideration, representing the thought of the Committee on Interstate and Foreign Commerce, is the answer to such demand.

The theory upon which this bill has been drawn is to give the public complete information as to the security offered for sale, rather than a governmental approval of the security. Until the detailed information required by the act has been filed with the Federal Trade Commission, such security cannot become a subject of interstate and foreign commerce. However, when there has been a compliance with the provisions of the bill, the information so filed is made available to prospective purchasers, and thereupon the duty and responsibility of passing upon the desirability of the security as an investment is placed upon the individual who contemplates purchase thereof and not upon the Government.

To have adopted the alternative theory, to wit, the assumption of a governmental responsibility as to the worthiness of such securities, it would have been necessary to set up a vast and extensive bureau of investigation, charged with the appraisal of property, estimating the probable usefulness of patent rights, or likelihood of productivity of every kind of enterprise. Furthermore, the effort to protect, by the adoption of such a principle, might easily lead to injustices through hampering developments based upon patent or other rights that at the time the security was offered would have little if any other than a problematical or possible future value. A very apt illustration, and one with which I am thoroughly familiar, is the development of the talking machine by the Victor Co., of Camden, N.J., my home city. In the beginning, the recording of the human voice was only an idea in the brain of the originator. Those who were willing to invest their money in order that the idea might be developed had no security that would have gained the approval of any governmental agency charged with a responsibility to pass upon the desirability of such an investment. Yet, in subsequent years, by wise and judicious development, it has brought financial reward in large measure to those early investors. Thus it would seem that a more proper sphere for governmental activity would be for it to require full and complete information to be placed at the disposal of the prospective investor, that he might intelligently decide for himself whether or not the investment is desirable, rather than the Government itself decide the question of what is or is not desirable.

There are other reasons that might be urged if time permitted as further justification of the policy adopted by the committee in this matter. Permit me to point out the care with which provision has been made to preclude any unwarranted use being made of the fact of registration of any security, and to preclude the possibility of any prospective purchaser from being misled thereby into believing that the Government has approved such security as an investment. The bill in section 22 specifically provides that the fact that the registration statement for a security has been filed or is in effect shall not be "held to mean that the Commission has in any way passed upon the merits of or given approval of such security." Furthermore, "it shall be unlawful to make, or cause to be made, to any prospective purchaser any representation contrary to the foregoing provisions."

Thus the theory that underlies this proposed legislation is different in its scope from that which forms the basis of many of the so-called "blue sky" laws enacted by the States. The latter quite frequently embody the thought that there is a duty upon the State in the fulfillment of its obligation to protect its citizens from fraudulent practices, to determine the quality of the security to be offered before granting a permit for the sale thereof. This is well illustrated in the act of one of the States which contain this provision:

> If the commissioner of corporations finds that the proposed plan of business of the investment company is unfair, unjust, or inequitable, or that it does not intend to do a fair and honest business, he shall refuse to issue the certificate—

And so forth.

And in another act of the same State it is further provided:

> If he (commissioner) finds ... that the securities that it proposes to issue and the methods to be used by it in issuing or disposing of them are not such as, in his opinion, will work a fraud upon the purchaser thereof, the commissioner shall issue to the applicant a permit authorizing it to issue and dispose of securities, as herein provided, in this State, in such amounts and for such considerations and upon such terms and conditions as the commissioner may in said permit provide. Otherwise he shall deny the application and refuse such permit—

And so forth.

Though there is a wide difference between the principle of merely requiring the filing of full and true information concerning the proposed security as provided for in the bill and the principle of assuming an obligation to pass upon the "honest" intent of the issuer and determine whether it "will work a fraud upon the purchaser" and actually fix the "terms and conditions" including the "amounts" and "considerations," yet it cannot be denied that the information required to be filed by schedules A and B of this bill will give all the information that is necessary for any prudent person to have in passing upon the desirability of the investment security. By requiring the purchaser to be judge of his own investment, based upon facts made available to him, the Government is thereby relieved of a responsibility that some would not be willing to acknowledge as a proper function of government.

Every possible precaution to obtain the full truth has been provided by the terms of the bill. Power is given to the commission to withhold the right to deal in any proposed security until every requirement has been complied with. And, to insure care and remove possibility of untrue or extravagant statements of fact, civil as well as criminal responsibility is fixed upon the issuer, every officer, director, or agent who permits his name to be used in connection therewith.

While it denies to no one the right to offer any security to the public, after the facts required by the statute have been disclosed, yet it attaches personal responsibility respecting the truthfulness of the facts submitted, and provides a right of recovery in money damages for anyone aggrieved by any misstatement of material fact. The bill makes no attempt to change the rule "Let the buyer beware," but extends it to include "Let the seller also beware." The bill denies the seller the immunity so long provided by the duty of the buyer alone to beware, and brings the seller into a position of fixed and determined responsibility as well.

The merit of this bill lies in the fact that it provides a means of protection to the investing public without the Government's assuming the stupendous task of passing upon the value, quality, or desirability of the multitude of various types and kinds of securities that are subjects of interstate and foreign commerce.

The plan or policy of the bill is sound. It will prove highly beneficial to any investor who is intelligent and prudent enough to utilize the information made available by its provisions. [Applause.] . . .

MR. McFADDEN. Is there not the implied obligation that in order to give out the information which the Government under this bill is going to give out, they have got to analyze these companies to see that the statements are correct? Otherwise the Government possibly will be giving false information.

MR. WOLVERTON. No. If the gentleman will read section 22 of this bill, he will find that the Government, through the agency of the Federal Trade Commission under this bill, does not in any way whatsoever assume to pass upon the desirability, the value, or the quality of the security offered or the truthfulness of the statements.

MR. McFADDEN. The point I am making is, if the gentleman will yield, that any information which the Government gives to a prospective investor is going to be considered as absolutely correct and will determine the individual's judgment as to whether he will purchase a particular security.

MR. WOLVERTON. If the gentleman will read section 22 of the bill, he will find that so far as legislative enactment is concerned it has been made just as plain and definite as words could possibly make it that it is not to be assumed that the Commission, by the acceptance of the information, accepts it as true and accurate, or that it does not contain untrue statements of fact or omit to state a material fact or to be held to mean that the Commission has in any way passed upon the merits or given approval to such security. The bill further provides that it shall be unlawful to make or cause to be made to any prospective purchaser any representation contrary to the foregoing provisions of this section. . . .

MR. REILLY. Does not the merit of this bill lie in the fact that it will prevent the sending in interstate commerce of securities that should not be so sent? And is it not a fact that the judgment of the ordinary citizen will to a large extent be influenced by the fact that the Government has permitted the security to be sold?

MR. WOLVERTON. The gentleman may be correct. . . .

MR. PETTENGILL. I wish to direct the gentleman's attention to 2 or 3 lines from a book written by Mr. Justice Brandeis. I quote from page 103 of his book entitled "Other People's Money and How the Bankers Use It."

And it should not seek to prevent investors from making bad bargains. But it is now recognized in the simplest merchandising that there should be full disclosures. The archaic doctrine of caveat emptor is vanishing. The law has begun to require publicity in aid of fair dealing. The Federal pure food law does not guarantee quality or prices; but it helps the buyer to judge of quality by requiring disclosure of ingredients.

MR. WOLVERTON. I agree with the statement of Mr. Justice Brandeis. A careful reading of the bill will show that the basic theory on which it has been drawn is in accord with the view expressed by Mr. Justice Brandeis in the quotation which you have just read. . . .

MR. BECK. Mr. Chairman, that this bill has been drawn with great care and that its aims are very praiseworthy is a matter about which I imagine no Member of this House will disagree. There are features of it, however, that seem to me to justify the careful consideration of the House. My chief concern is that the bill is a perversion of the commerce power to accomplish ends that, if the Constitution any longer means anything, were reserved to the police powers of the States. The act is based, as far as constitutional power is concerned, upon two grounds: One, the power of the United States over post roads, and therefore the mails; and the other, the commerce clause.

The power over the mails is a much broader power than the power over interstate commerce. The United States mails are the instrumentality of the Government, and therefore, while its power with respect to those mails is not absolute or arbitrary, yet it is much broader than that over that indefinable field called "interstate commerce," as to which the citizen has the primary and fundamental right to engage in interstate commerce. This right was not created by the Constitution.

The Constitution was called into existence to insure the freedom of commerce between the States. Before it was adopted every State burdened the free flow of commerce with conflicting and hostile regulations. To emancipate commerce, the power to put it into shackles was taken from the States by the simple grant that Congress should have power to regulate such commerce. It was never intended that Congress should then proceed to put upon commerce the very shackles that it had been created to destroy, and this is shown by the fact that in the first century of our existence under the Constitution Congress never exercised any power to regulate interstate commerce, unless we except the subsidies of land to the transcontinental railroads.

In the absence of any Federal regulation it was held by the Supreme Court that the failure of Congress to exercise its power of regulation was its mandate that commerce should be free, and for 100 years this policy of freedom remained, and, under it, a great continent was conquered, the Atlantic and Pacific linked by steel rails, and the Republic became one of the greatest nations in the world.

Exactly one century after the Constitution was adopted Congress abandoned that policy and began to forge the chains for commerce by bureaucratic regulation. That year it created the Interstate Commerce Commission, and this was followed in 1890 by the Sherman antitrust law, which vainly attempted to limit the inevitable tendency of business to combine into larger units. Ever since, there has been an ever-increasing regulation of American business by Federal bureaus, until today our Government may differ in degree but not in kind from that of Moscow and Berlin in seeking to regulate all forms of industry by an elaborate and oppressive bureaucracy.

In the first century of the Republic it was generally recognized that Federal powers could only be exercised to accomplish Federal purposes, but the destruction of the Constitution began when Congress entered upon the revolutionary policy of utilizing Federal powers to usurp the powers reserved to the States. It was soon seen that if Congress could appropriate moneys for non-Federal purposes without challenge, it could supervise the use of such moneys, and thus usurp fields of power, which were the exclusive province of the States.

About a generation ago it was first asserted that Congress could deny the privilege of engaging in interstate commerce to anyone who did not conform to the views of Congress as to the methods of production. This heresy has now been carried to the extreme of holding that no one can engage in interstate commerce as of right, and that the Government may license or refuse to license a citizen to engage in interstate commerce. Such a right was not created by the Constitution. Indeed, it is one of the natural rights which are included in the solemn guaranty of the right to "life, liberty, and the pursuit of happiness," but the present theory is that unless the manufacturer conforms to the wishes of the Federal Government in regard to the hours of labor, his maximum output, a minimum-wage law, and other restrictions, he can be proscribed by his own Government and denied the privilege of selling his products in interstate trade.

This is economic slavery. It destroys not merely the rights of the States but the basic freedom of the individual to engage in lawful occupations. It concerns both employer and employee, and, to quote Jefferson's words in his first inaugural, it "takes from the mouth of labor the bread it has earned."

The two basic industries of America are concerned with the production of agricultural products and the manufacture of goods. The Constitution did not attempt to give any power over the production of either class of commodities. If they required regulation, such power belonged to the States, and, as stated, the Federal Government acted upon this theory for more than a century. The Government could tax products and it could regulate their interstate transportation or their exportation to foreign countries. Nothing would have more amazed the generation which created the Constitution than the idea that the Federal Government, which they were creating, could regulate the conditions of the farm or the factory. Notwithstanding this, the Federal Government for many years past has, through its many bureaus and commissions, and notably through its Departments of Agriculture and Labor, attempted to control both the factory and the farm, and if the legislative proposals which are now before Congress, with the powerful imprimatur of the President and the "brain trust," become law, the Government's control will be complete. . . .

I was about to say that the power over the mails might have been invoked, I think, to justify this legislation. If the Congress has power to prevent fraudulent matter from being sent through the mails, it has the equal power, by preventive methods, to determine whether a matter is fraudulent that is about to be sent through the mails. Even there, please note the contrast between the solicitude that once prevailed in this Chamber in respect to the rights of the States and the apathetic indifference that now prevails on both sides of the aisle as to whether another reserved right of the States shall be torn from them and vested in an already excessively centralized Government. Ninety-eight years ago in this Chamber, at a time when it was of the utmost importance to the Union that antislavery literature should be excluded from the mails, an attempt was made to pass a law authorizing any postmaster to exclude from the mails any literature of an antislavery character. It passed the Senate. It reached the House. John Quincy Adams then rendered one of his great public services. He was not an abolitionist, because he believed that slavery had been recognized by the Constitution and was as much a part of it as any other guaranty of the Constitution. Nevertheless John Quincy Adams rose in the House of Representatives and protested against any power to use the mails in order to achieve the ulterior purpose of suppressing an agitation that even then was menacing the existence of the Union; and this House, in its very deep solicitude for the rights of the States, and above all, its jealousy of any attempt to pervert Federal power to accomplish ulterior ends, refused to pass the bill.

However, we have long passed that period of extreme solicitude for the rights of the States.

We have now reached possibly the necessary conclusion that a Federal instrumentality, like the United States mails, may not be used in the frustration of Federal authority.

If this act sought as its constitutional basis the power to exclude from the mails even in a preventive or anticipatory way the distribution of securities, it might well be within the powers of Congress.

This bill deals with the issuance of securities and their purchase and sale as though it were interstate commerce. It defines it as interstate commerce. Our Supreme Court from the time of Paul against Virginia, decided 70 years ago, and in a long line of cases have said again and again that choses in action of the same character as a share of capital stock, a bill of exchange, or any similar matter, is not a commodity of commerce, which can be regulated by the Federal Government but is purely intrastate in character. Yet this bill says in effect that if I telegraph tomorrow to New York to buy 500 shares of Pennsylvania that in purchasing this stock on the floor of the New York Stock Exchange I have engaged in interstate commerce. This, to my mind, is a false idea; and if carried to its extreme there is no power of the States that cannot be taken from them by the Federal Government in this highly complicated civilization by simply misusing the commerce powers to achieve that end.

This is a striking vindication of a prophecy I heard uttered 25 years ago at a public dinner of the Pennsylvania Society of New York. The chief speaker was a man whose rank as a lawyer and a statesman is such that no one would question it, Elihu Root. Mr. Root said then, in substance—and his speech attracted adverse comment, especially in the South—that if the States were not wise enough to suppress fraud and bring about good government within their borders, the Federal Government would do for the American people what the States thus neglected. As I said before, this was very widely criticized at the time as an extreme assertion of Hamiltonian federalism.

His prediction has come true to the uttermost letter, for anyone who for 25 years has studied the legislation of Congress and the decisions of the Supreme Court, which slowly and reluctantly yields to one usurpation of Federal power after another, must realize that the commerce power, with its infinite ramifications, has now been used to take from the States reserved police powers given to them by the Constitution. This is strikingly illustrated by proposed legislation about to come before this body, where an attempt will be made to regulate, through the commerce power, the hours of labor in manufactories, and the Labor Department will be given the power to prescribe the maximum of output and minimum wages.

The whole system of our dual government can be torn down, as it has been very largely torn down, if you allow some of these tremendous powers of the Federal Government to be used for purposes, for which they were not given by the Constitution. . . .

I recognize that the term "commerce" not only includes navigation but the transportation, by whatever agencies, of commodities or of passengers, even on foot, or the transmission of ideas, and it is immaterial whether such transportation is connected with a sale. I argued as much in the famous *Lottery case* (188 U.S.). Included in the term "transportation" are all the services in connection with the receipt and delivery of the property transported. A contract may or may not be a transaction of interstate commerce. If it is in the form of a bill of lading, it is; but if in the form of a bill of exchange, or of a contract to perform labor outside the State, or of a contract for future delivery to be executed in another State, or of the contract of a private banker with his depositors, it is not.

Let us consider this question realistically. A group of business men project a corporate enterprise.

Is that interstate commerce? No.

Their lawyers prepare the papers for a charter and the form of the securities.

Is that interstate commerce? No.

They then list the securities and sell them on the New York Stock Exchange.

Is that interstate commerce? No; even when the buyer, represented by a New York broker, lives in another State.

Securities, negotiable or otherwise, may then be shipped from New York to another State.

Is that interstate commerce? Possibly, but it is a very slender thread to hang Federal supervision of corporate securities upon it. No one has hitherto dreamed that such a construction could be put upon the commerce power until the "brain trust" evolved the idea. A bill of lading is an instrumentality of commerce because it represents the property, but a bill of exchange, which is a matter of banking, is not a part of interstate commerce even when sent from one State to another. There is no limit to the Federal power over all business transactions if the commerce power can be perverted to regulate instrastate business transactions. This is "nullification by indirection," a term I first used about 25 years ago, when I addressed the Rhode Island bar. I then predicted that this pernicious doctrine, by which the reserved rights of the

States could be destroyed by the indirect effect of the commerce power, would one day destroy our dual form of government. That prediction is in process of verification, if it be not already verified. I was a Cassandra then, as it is probable that in my present warning I am a Cassandra now.

This bill, on its face, shows that it seeks a power to reach police regulations which the States ought to have passed.

No one need question the abhorrence I have for corporate abuses. I practiced for 17 years in the city of New York and had a good many influential clients. Some of them, I am very glad to say, were honest men.

MR. PETTENGILL. How many?

MR. BECK. I would not attempt to take a census, but if Diogenes, with his lamp, in his eternal quest for an honest man, had gone into Wall Street in those days, his search would not have been short or easy. [Laughter.] Let me give you my opinion of one great cause of the financial immorality of some Wall Street adventurers.

Philosophically, it is the device known as the "corporation." The corporation, of all artificial institutions of man, is at once the most beneficent and the most maleficent. It is the most beneficent in combining capital so that large and important undertakings can be carried on, for which the capital even of a Rockefeller might not be adequate. Our stupendous growth as a nation has resulted from the corporate form of transacting business. It is, unfortunately, also infinitely maleficient, because the corporation dissipates moral responsibility. I have seen it, and any practicing lawyer I suppose has seen it, that a man who, in his private life will be scrupulously honest, yet as president of a corporation he will at times do things of an immoral character on the theory that he is only the trustee for the stockholders and is acting in their interests.

The financial irresponsibility that has resulted from the corporation is immeasurable.

This has been greatly increased by the fact, and this is a strange fact—I am dealing with moral psychology now—that of all the peoples of the world the freeman of America is the last to resent being robbed. You let a corporation fail in England, even honestly, and all the stockholders want to know the reason why and ask the managers to give an accounting of their stewardship; but a corporation here can fail to the extent of hundreds of millions of dollars, in which thousands of investors have lost their all, and not a stockholder will ever appear at a meeting, ask a question, or commence a civil suit, or institute a criminal proceeding.

Why, in England they have a minimum of regulations by law of corporations, but they have prosecuting officers who prosecute. . . .

From what I have seen of corporate business in this country, I believe that if we had prosecuting attorneys and judges who would speed the trial of criminal cases, and as a result, if there were more of this class of predatory millionaires in jail and less of them in palatial homes on Fifth Avenue, we would not have any necessity for this legislation. [Applause.]

I mention all this because it is a kind of psychological background to the question. The American will not fight for his rights, I do not know why.

In the second place, the corporate skullduggery of this country has been also due to the greed of States in their mad rush to get a few little fees for chartering corporations, under which they have issued piratical letters of marque and reprisal to prey upon the people of the country.

With this disposition of the States to make corporation laws so simple that a man can put a coin in a slot and draw out a charter and do anything he pleases, and with all the artificial divisions into holding companies and affiliated securities, and God knows what other skullduggery, the corporate life in this country is rotten to the core [applause], and if a pragmatic sanction is necessary for this legislation, it has it in this fact. This may justify the usurpation of power that now seeks to use the commerce power to deal with a situation that is essentially not one of interstate commerce, as the Supreme Court has held, but wholly of the police powers of the States. The losses have been in billions, and it is not unnatural that an outraged citizenry, Constitution or no Constitution, want to enact this legislation—but what are you going to accomplish when you do it?

You have put the power not in the Secretary of Commerce but in the Federal Trade Commission, easily one of the most futile of the bureaucratic agencies in Washington. The Commission will undoubtedly employ more men and subdivide itself into new bureaus and will receive these papers, which nobody will read, and when this is done the high-pressure salesman will go out to the people and tell everybody to whom they want to sell a rotten bond, "Oh, you know this has been supervised by the Federal Trade Commission." The United States Government has given its imprimatur, and the poor woman who has a little money to invest— . . .

MR. HUDDLESTON. I just want to call the gentleman's attention to the fact that there is a section of the bill that puts such a man in jail.

MR. BECK. Yes; but it is very hard to catch him, may I say to my friend.

MR. HUDDLESTON. Of course, you have to catch a rabbit before you can have hash.

MR. BECK. I know this is a very carefully drawn bill, and has sought to safeguard against this result; but I know my friend from Alabama will agree with me that in the actual detection of these fugitive and peripatetic salesmen they will have a hard time in ever proving he ever said anything of the kind, but he will have said it nevertheless, and I am inclined to think the bill may thus increase the sale of rotten securities, and not decrease them. . . .

MR. PETTENGILL. I want to applaud what the gentleman has said about rottenness of corporation regulation, but I would like to get clear in my mind whether the gentleman thinks this is outside of interstate commerce under Paul against Virginia, which was an insurance-policy case.

MR. BECK. Yes. . . .

Creating a Sacred Circle Around the House of Thieves

MR. KELLER. Mr. Chairman, first I want to congratulate the House for having heard from the chairman of the committee a statement of the facts justifying this bill, the like of which I have never heard before in one short address. I hope the gentleman will publish it in pamphlet form, so that it may be for general use over the country, because of the immense amount of information contained in it.

Next, we seem to get the idea here that we are discussing a new subject. There never was a greater mistake than that. This is an old subject. It was already an old crime in 1909. Chief Justice Hughes, then Governor of New York, had an investigation of this very important subject made by a powerful committee, the report of which ought to be read by every man who wants to be informed about the subject.

The Pujo Committee

Then the Congress of the United States in 1912 had an investigation made by what is known as the "Pujo Committee" of this House. I hold in my hand a copy of the report of that committee, that was printed in 1913. It sets out all the difficulties that have been set out before us here today. It proposes the proper remedy. It presents a legal brief that will instruct any man who wants information. It suggests and furnishes the legal authority to prevent the things which we have had to endure on a terrible scale during the last three and a half years.

The panic of 1907 was inexcusable, as also were the panics of 1921 and 1929, and also they were all as inexcusable as the panics of 1893 and 1873, because there was absolutely no excuse, and never has been, for permitting any of the procession of panics that have so often devastated this young, vigorous Nation, growing up in the country of the greatest possible natural resources. Every one of these panics have been followed by business depressions, destructive of industry to a terrible degree.

Mr. Melvin A. Traylor, president of the First National Bank of Chicago, in his address before the International Chamber of Commerce here in Washington City 2 years ago said:

I am not an economist, but I must admit that at least the last three panics were all precipitated by crashes on the New York Stock Exchange.

It took courage for a banker to say this. His whole address on this occasion is a notable contribution to progressive thought. It ought to be read by every Member of the Congress.

I happened to know Mr. Traylor, and at that time I was at work on a book on this subject, one chapter of which I have here in my hand. I wrote to him, saying that not only was that statement true with relation to the last three panics, but that it was also true in relation to the panics of ninety-three and seventy-three.

Now, all the conditions we have before us we had also in all those panics since the Civil War, except insofar as the extent of them is concerned. At that time we began to use labor-saving machinery on a very large scale. As our chairman pointed out, the increase of corporations ensued to a tremendous extent. And I point out that gambling in stocks increased just as the number of shares increased. The principle underlying the previous panics was not different from the last one, except that they were on a smaller scale and a smaller number of victims involved.

The Rule for Panics

I repeat a rule for you, if I may, and that is that every panic in this country, with its inevitably ensuing depression, has been precipitated by a stock crash on the New York Stock Exchange. To that rule there is no exception, and the extent and intensity of the depressions were foreshadowed exactly by the intensity and scope of the stock crashes themselves.

Should Include Present Stocks and Bonds

I am sorry that we have not the opportunity of including present stock issues under the provisions of this bill. They ought to be included for the reason that if we go on without prohibiting the fraud on people on stocks and bonds already listed, we are leaving the same gang in control that has been in control with exactly the same opportunity of robbing the people of this country just as they have been doing heretofore.

The effect of not including those stocks at present listed on the stock exchanges is to place the stamp of approval of the Congress upon them. In other words, we are placed in a position of saying to the American people: "We will protect you against any future fraud in the sale of securities, but you must take your own chance against those now listed on the exchanges. We believe that these stocks and bonds are all O.K."

We are supposed to act upon measures before us with intelligence, yet no intelligent man would set his stamp of approval upon any security without a thorough analysis of the value behind it, and we refuse him that opportunity on one security and afford it on another.

Schedule A of this bill enumerates 32 qualifications which must be met to the satisfaction of the Federal Trade Commission before authority will be granted for the sale of any new security. If these qualifications are important, and they are, why should they not be met by securities now on the market, regardless of their date of issue?

Are There More Kreugers and Insulls?

Who is there among us able to say that we shall not tomorrow be faced with another Kreuger or Insull? Undoubtedly there are others; the nefarious influence of these two erstwhile gentlemen is too widespread for comfort on the part of investors.

Why do we not take this opportunity to guarantee to the American investing public that there shall be no further fraud perpetrated upon them? Why are we so eager to protect a few and unwilling to protect the many? What honest man will object?

Do you think that the same outfit that engineered the stock panic of 1929 cannot and will not do it again unless the law prevents it?

Unless we include the issues of stocks and bonds presently on the market we shall create a sacred ring around the "house of thieves."

MR. REILLY. What would the gentleman write into the bill to do that?

MR. KELLER. I am very glad the gentleman has asked me that question. There are eight things I set out in my book on that subject.

First. I would compel responsible incorporation under the law of all stock exchanges.

Second. I would prevent the payment of a higher rate of interest on call loans, either directly or indirectly by commissions or otherwise, than the statutory rate of interest in the State where the stock-exchange is located.

Third. I would compel brokers, operators, banks, and their promotional affiliates to assume financial responsibility for their statements in newspapers, advertisements, prospectus, or for other propaganda for the selling of stock.

Fourth. I would compel promotional institutions to assume responsibility for the statements of all their agents.

Fifth. The right to have the shares of any corporation dealt in on the stock exchange is a privilege at present arbitrarily held by the very brokers who buy and sell these same shares. The power to list or refuse to list a stock is capable of such abuse, and has so often been shamelessly abused that it cannot longer be left in the hands of the stock exchange. It is necessary therefore that those companies desiring to have their stocks listed on the stock exchange, and who are thereby given the privilege of having them dealt in on a Nation-wide scale shall have the right to come into a proper court of national jurisdiction and, by making proper showing have their stocks listed on the stock exchange by order of the court.

Sixth. I would prevent banks from owning or having any interest in affiliates or promotional organizations, either through interlocking directorates or otherwise.

Seventh. I would compel brokers to keep actual records of all transactions in the names of the actual parties at interest. I would make it a crime to use an assumed name in stock transactions.

Eighth. I would make the infraction of any of these laws a crime involving compulsory imprisonment.

H.R. 4365 Offers Greater Protection

I have had before the Committee on Interstate and Foreign Commerce a bill, H.R. 4365, that would accomplish the things I have just set forth.

The Panic of 1873

The conditions which precede and follow any panic are the same that precede and follow all panics. The procedure is simple. Let us set out the conditions which preceded and followed the panic of 1873: General prosperity prevailed; there were very few business or bank failures; money in actual use was plentiful, and credit was easily obtained; profits in business were good; labor was well employed; everybody was at work and spending money; not a cloud was on the business sky; every justifiable reason why prosperity should continue indefinitely; speculation on the stock market had put stocks up; new issues of stock were listed on the stock exchanges; many of the "big ones" sold out toward the top of the market. Then short selling precipitated a full-fledged panic on the New York Stock Exchange; stock prices collapsed; credit was destroyed; bank failures started; panic spread to all business; unemployment, poverty, misery, and crime followed; industrial paralysis set in; the inevitable Nation-wide depression ensued; Government officials and leading financiers assured the country that the condition was purely temporary; that business would pick up in the spring; that the business of the country was sound; that the depression could not last; and the newspapers repeated this "hopeful stuff that dreams are made out of." But with all this reassurance, business failure, uncertainty, fear, lost confidence, and lack of enterprise, characterized the long years of recovery—"starving through" by the people who had no part in precipitating the panic. After some years of toil, shamelessly imposed upon them by the greed of others, the people paid the terrible costs of the panic of 1873. Nobody did anything about it. Nobody tried to find out what brought the panic. Nobody tried to prevent the coming of other panics. So, of course, other panics came.

The Panics of 1893, 1907, 1921

The panic of 1893 came about under the same conditions and brought the same results as the panic of 1873. The panic of 1907 fits the description precisely, both in its approach and outcome. The panic of 1921 was distinguished from the other three solely by having had governmental aid and cooperation through the stupid or criminal use of the Federal Reserve System in "deflating" the currency and credits of the country.

The Panic of 1929

The same conditions preceded the panic of 1929, and the same financial chaos, unemployment, poverty, and starvation followed it, with the Federal Reserve System again helping the stock gamblers, both before and after the panic. It will be noted that the stock panic on the New York Stock Exchange always brings a panic in industry, and through industry injures every man, woman, and child in America. Every panic inevitably brings in its train the condition known as business depression—the periods in which all the wrongs and abuses which produce panics are expiated. Here were five Nation-wide panics within a period of 57 years, literally destructive of the rights of men, and, calculated at present price levels, they have cost us more than our total national wealth, yet the United States Government has taken little interest in what caused these panics and has not at all investigated the means of preventing their recurrence. We appear to have concluded that nothing can be done about it.

The reason for bringing about the panic of 1907, the methods of conducting it on the New York Stock Exchange, and the disastrous results of it to the whole country constituted such a flagrant crime against society that the United States Senate in 1908 started an investigation of "wash sales"; that is, of bogus sales made for the purpose of misleading and defrauding the people. Abuses along this line were so palpable, and the evidence so indisputable, that the representatives of the New York Stock Exchange appeared before the Senate committee and agreed to prevent the continuance of that abuse. The investigation was therefore stopped and no record kept of the matter. But after 24 years the same practice in a different form, true enough, was, in the evidence produced before the Senate committee of the Seventy-second Congress (1932) under the chairmanship of Senator Norbeck, shown still to exist on a very large scale.

When the downright dishonesty, chicanery, thievery, and conspiracy to cheat and defraud which for so long a time has controlled and now does control the stock exchanges of the country are for a certainty done away with, we shall find the very conditions which business security demands and which all honest men want. The American people under conditions of reasonable national income save out of their earnings as much as $7,000,000,000 a year.

Legitimate Capital Required

The permanent improvements which the expansion of business requires for the continued development of the country must necessarily get legitimate capital from the savings from industry, not from the continual extending of credit. The people who save have a right to invest their money in the best securities—actual securities—which America has. They will do this gladly when they know they are putting their money into actual things worth as an honest investment what they are asked to pay. The buying and selling of this class of securities would soon bring into the market all the capital necessary to carry on the Nation's business. The honest handling of this immense amount of stored-up energy for the benefit of America, in the interest of the individual producer, at a fair profit to the legitimate broker would be the inspiring business of the stock exchanges of the near future, which must grow directly out of the present stock exchanges, or which will succeed their necessary destruction, if they further refuse to be reformed.

Honest Business Does Not Require Secrecy

Open the books. Honest business does not require secrecy. Crooked business should not be permitted to profit by secrecy. Business must come with clean hands into court of humanity before it can claim the protection of that court. This is a very moderate program, in full keeping with our past experiences, with our system of government; its adoption will eliminate the causes of our present misfortunes. It will be attacked by those interests which are fighting to keep control. But it will be well for those interests to consider that 13,000,000 idle men are not going to remain idle. They have been wonderfully patient under the shameless conditions of the past three and a half years. Patience sometimes ceases to be a virtue. To this day and generation has come the ability to see and understand the causes which have underlain and moved men in government throughout all history—and the opportunity to reinterpret those principles in the interest of humanity. . . .

MR. MOTT. Mr. Chairman, the discussion thus far has demonstrated again the utter futility and the farce of debating a bill of this kind under the gag rule. I agree with the gentleman from Missouri that the discussion of the bill has been interesting and enlightening, but nevertheless it has been entirely futile because we are not permitted under the rule to try to improve it; we cannot amend it, we can only take it or leave it just as it is written. I think if the debate upon this bill shows anything, it shows that a gag rule, whatever may be the claims for its justification in partisan matters, is entirely improper in connection with a bill of this kind. I desired very much to offer an amendment to this bill. Other gentlemen did also. And as I listened to the discussion for the last several hours, I came to the conclusion that almost every suggestion that has been offered here in the course of the debate would, if incorporated in the bill in the shape of an amendment, have improved the bill.

I am going to vote for this bill, of course, I doubt if there will be one dissenting vote in the House. But I am going to vote for it, not because I think it is a good securities bill, for I do not, but because I know that it is the only securities bill we shall be permitted to vote on this session. I doubt very much if there is a State securities commissioner in the United States who would undertake from his knowledge of securities regulation to endorse this bill as an adequate remedy for the evils arising out of the sale of securities in interstate commerce. The reason is that this bill omits the very feature which is necessary to make any securities bill effective and workable, and that is the requirement that before an issuer or dealer may offer his security for sale he must qualify that security with the governmental agency which is intrusted with the administration of the act, and must secure from that governmental agency a permit to offer that security in interstate commerce. This bill omits that feature entirely, and it omits it purposely, as the gentleman from New Jersey [Mr. Wolverton] has stated. It is my opinion that because it does omit it, it will fail of its purpose, just as every State securities act which does not contain the permit feature has been a failure.

On the other hand, every State securities law which does make the issuance of a permit a condition precedent to the sale of securities has been a success. It has been effectively administered, and it has actually protected the investing public.

Now, what is the purpose of any securities regulatory law? Obviously it is to protect the investor. The gentleman from New Jersey [Mr. Wolverton] was entirely correct when he said there were two theories of protection of the investor by a regulatory securities statute.

My objection to this bill is that it is based upon the wrong theory. The first theory of the protection of investors in the sale of securities is based upon the proposition that worthless and illegitimate and fundamentally unsound securities should not be permitted to be sold at all, and that the investing public should be protected against them in the first instance by prohibiting their sale. The securities laws based upon this theory take into consideration several important facts. In the first place, it recognizes the fact that the average investor knows nothing about securities or securities transactions. He knows nothing about the financial structure of the corporations which issue securities. The average investor does not know how to read or interpret a balance sheet, even when he has all the facts before him which went into the make-up of the balance sheet.

It also takes into consideration another important factor, and that is that unless the average investor is protected against the worthless and fraudulent security by prohibition of its sale in the first instance, he has no remedy at all in 9 cases out of 10, because by the time he discovers he has been defrauded, the corporation from which he purchased the security will have become insolvent.

Under this theory of securities regulation, protection to the investor is afforded by investing the securities commissioner with authority to make an investigation of every security proposed to be sold. The scope of the investigation is unlimited and is made by a staff of experts trained in that particular field. Based upon his investigation, the law then imposes upon the commissioner the duty of determining whether the security examined is legitimate and offered in good faith. If it is, the commissioner may issue a permit authorizing its sale. If it is not, then it is his duty under the law to deny the permit. Thus is the investor protected from fraud in the first instance—the only instance, as experience has shown, where he can be given any real protection at all. By issuing a permit the State, of course, does not guarantee that the investor will not lose money, because even legitimate enterprises may, and often do, fail. Neither does the State in issuing a permit undertake to approve the security sold under it. It does undertake to say, however, that the security sold under the permit is at least a legitimate security, and that it is issued honestly and in good faith, and that the investor who buys it is not patronizing a financial racket operated for the very purpose of robbing the investor. This much the State should undertake to guarantee; and if it cannot do this much, then no securities law is of any practical value whatever.

The other theory of securities regulation—and the one upon which this bill is based—is that the sale of worthless, illegitimate, and fraudulent securities should not be prohibited in the first instance. That all that is necessary to properly protect the public and all the protection the public is properly entitled to is that the facts regarding the security offered shall be made known to the public through the filing of a certain statement and information regarding it with the governmental agency charged with the administration of the act. When that is done, then the law, under this theory, applies the old rule of caveat emptor and the seller is liable under the law only for actual legal fraud.

This theory ignores entirely the fact that the average investor cannot read and interpret a balance sheet. It ignores the fact that he is entirely unfamiliar with securities transactions and with the financial structures of the corporations issuing the paper. It ignores the fact that a balance sheet can be technically accurate and still convey to the untutored investor the idea that an unsound company is sound, and this without the risk of either civil or criminal liability on the part of the seller. And, finally, it completely ignores the most important factor of all: that in most cases the issuers of fraudulent securities cannot respond in a judgment, and that when the defrauded investor finally discovers the fraud his only remedy under this theory is a civil judgment which cannot be collected.

It has been estimated by securities commissioners in many States that fully 50 percent of the losses to investors have been through the purchase of securities in corporations which were insolvent at the time the securities were sold. The pending bill, when enacted, will do practically nothing toward protecting this class of investors because this bill does not undertake to prohibit the sale of any securities in the first instance, no matter how fraudulent they may be. All that is necessary is that the issuer file his statement, wait 30 days, and then go ahead and sell the stock.

You will recall that 2 or 3 times this afternoon I have asked gentlemen who were discussing this bill to explain how under it the bill would protect any person buying stock in companies like Insull, the Central Public Service Corporation, or the Foshay Co. None of them could explain how the bill would give any protection whatever to persons buying securities of this kind. The reason is that companies of this kind are financial rackets which a bill based upon this theory of regulation does not even undertake either to control or regulate. The companies I have mentioned could disclose to the commission every fact regarding their financial set-up which is required under this bill, and under the bill the Federal Trade Commission could not stop the sale of a single dollar's worth of their securities offered in interstate commerce. Every State securities commissioner whose State blue sky law does not contain the permit feature knows this to his sorrow. Every commissioner whose State securities law does contain the permit feature knows that with the permit club he can keep these racketeers out of his State, and that if by any chance they do succeed in robbing his people he can compel them to disgorge if he acts before such companies go bankrupt.

I have had a good deal to say about State securities laws and securities commissioners. The reason is that any Federal securities law is inseparably bound up with every State securities law. A Federal securities law is nothing more or less than an adaptation of a State securities law, or a class of State securities laws, to the regulation of the sale of securities in interstate commerce. Any proposal for a Federal securities law must of necessity be an adaptation of the regulatory features of some existing State law to traffic in securities between the States, because the existing State securities statutes in the aggregate constitute the entire corpus juris of securities regulation in this country. And that is what this bill is. My objection to it is that it has adapted the wrong class of blue sky laws to that purpose. It is an adaptation of the second theory of securities regulation, instead of the first. In its national scope, therefore, it must fail of much of its purpose, just as the class of State securities laws from which it is taken have already failed.

As I have stated, I intend to vote for this bill, because we need a Federal securities law, and this one is better than no law at all. But it is at least a start. As several gentlemen have said, "It is a step in the right direction." I do not think it is a very long step, but it is a step, nevertheless, and it may have a tendency to make some issuers and dealers who want to engage in interstate commerce a little more careful than they have been. It will, indeed, help to some extent the shrewd investor by making easily available to himself certain information which he would otherwise have to secure for himself through the various investment manuals and other sources of information at his command. It will not help the poor or the untutored investors, who are the ones who have suffered most from the operations of financial racketeers.

In time I hope this law may be amended so as to become a real Federal blue sky law, and I think eventually that will be done. I should like to have a law sometime that will protect in the first instance the average person who has saved his money and wants to invest it and who is now the legitimate prey of every interstate financial racketeer in the country. I want to do away with the rule of caveat emptor altogether where the sale of a fraudulent security is concerned. I want to make it impossible by law for any financial crook to operate in the United States. . . .

MR. SAMUEL B. HILL. The statement has been made that this is not a blue sky law; and insofar as its main purpose goes, it is not a blue sky law. To this extent I am in entire agreement with the purposes of the proposed legislation.

I doubt the advisability in any instance of a so-called "blue sky" law that implies the approval of the State or of the Government of securities listed under registration provisions. If we must have a blue sky law, it would be better if it were a national law so that but one registration and one approval of a security issued would be required.

In addition to the main purpose of requiring registration of security issues, the bill under consideration contains a provision that ties it up with every blue sky law of the various States. In this sense it is a blue sky law, or a bill that would result in a blue sky law. In my opinion, this feature of the bill is entirely vicious; and if the rule under which the bill is being considered permitted, I would move to amend by striking out section 18 dealing with this particular subject. In the original draft of the bill this was section 14. I appeared before the committee at the hearings in the effort to have it eliminated, and had hoped that the committee would cut out that particular provision.

It declined to do so, but did modify it in the bill as rewritten. This provision appears in the present bill as section 18. I understand that the provision in question has been omitted from the companion bill in the Senate, and I urge that it be eliminated in the conference between the two Houses. . . .

MR. BEEDY. Mr. Chairman, casual reference by one of the Members of the House was just made to a provision in what he termed "the original securities bill." This reference to the original bill suggests the propriety of comparing a provision or two of that bill with the pending measure. And this pending bill is quite properly being considered regardless of party lines. However, the various stages through which the pending proposal has passed, and in the time allotted I can make but brief reference to one or two of them, serve to illustrate the compromises and departures from original intentions which are very generally made in formulating legislative proposals, by whatever party is in power.

Many times during the last 12 years of my membership in this House I have listened passively to accusations from the Democratic side that the Republican Party legislates for the protection of property; that the Republican Party stands for property rights as opposed to human rights. This accusation is generally followed by the proud claim that "the Democratic Party puts human rights above property rights." Of course, the truth of the matter is that without a government of laws, obedience to which is duly observed, there would be neither human rights nor property rights. It is indeed difficult to conceive of any respectable Government under which both human and property rights are not zealously guarded and righteously valued, irrespective of party platforms.

The pending bill, we have been told, is a part of the administration program. Some Member on the Democratic side this afternoon made inquiry, doubtless to leave the implication that the Republican Party had failed to enact similar legislation at an earlier date, "Why such a law had not been passed years ago." The gentleman from New York [Mr. Parker] made a very proper reply. The fact is, that the rapid succession of events brings changed conditions; abuses of one period suggest one remedy, while abuses of another period suggest yet other remedies, and the culmination of abuses in the sale of securities during the last few years has made this particular legislation advisable, if not imperative.

Unquestionably, legislation seeking to curb abuses in the marketing of securities would be a most natural, if not an inevitable, part of the program of whatever party found itself entrusted with power. It is, therefore, conceded without question that the purpose for which this bill is written is highly laudable.

In the first place, the bill aims to bring the fullest light of publicity upon the proposed issue and sale of securities in general. All this is as it should be, but unquestionably the real meat of this proposed legislation is to be found in the sections which provide a remedy for the purchasing public against those who should properly be made responsible for unconscionable practices in the marketing of securities. The real test of the efficacy of this legislative proposal is to be determined by the relentless vigor with which it proposes that the defrauded purchaser may puruse properly responsible parties.

Let us now proceed to compare briefly what may be nominated the liability features of the original bill, which was introduced by the Chairman of the Committee on Interstate and Foreign Commerce [Mr. Rayburn] on the 29th day of last March, with the liability features of the bill which he introduced on May 4 and which is now before us for passage on this 5th day of May. The changes made in the last bill as against the former serve to illustrate that however bold a start may be made by any political party newly entrusted with power there is sure to be a yielding to the demands of those who are primarily concerned with the protection of property rights.

If you will turn to page 6, section 4, of the original bill of March 29, you will find that its provisions called for the filing of—

A registration statement signed by the issuer or issuers, its or their principal executive officer or officers, the principal financial officer or advisors, *and the directors,* trustees, or managers.

Note that this original bill required the registration statement to be signed by *all the directors* and not by a part of them. This is conceded to be the correct interpretation of the phrase "and the directors."

The March 29 bill further provided on page 19, section 9, that—

In case any such statement shall be false in any material respect, any persons acquiring any securities to which such statement relates, either from the original issuer or from any other person, shall have the right to rescind the transaction and to obtain the return, either at law or in equity, of any and all consideration given or paid for any such securities upon the surrender thereof either from any vendor knowing of such falsity or *from the persons signing such statement jointly or severally* .

You will note that this first proposal of the administration for the regulation of the sale of securities and the protection of the public against unconscionable practices in the marketing of the same afforded a plain and unconditional remedy. The purchaser aggrieved could go into a court of law or equity and seek recovery from any one of the persons signing the registration statement. And you will remember that every director, as a matter of law (had the administration pressed the bill of March 29 for enactment into law) would have been compelled to sign the registration statement. No director could escape the signing of the registration statement, and therefore no director could have escaped liability for any representation contained in the registration statement which proved to be "false in any material respect."

Now, what has happened since this bold declaration of rights and proposed remedies was made in the original securities bill sponsored by the present administration? The party in power has been duly impressed with its responsibility for the protection of property rights. Representatives of big business with large property holdings undoubtedly have contacted the leaders in the present administration. They have represented most forcefully that to attempt to hold boards of directors to any such strict rule of accountability would work a hardship upon legitimate industry; that to boast of placing human rights above property rights sounds well in a political campaign, but that as a matter of fact unless property rights are duly protected, human rights themselves will be unduly prejudiced. Apparently the administration has listened to the representatives of big business. Accordingly we find a marked change from the original bill in those sections of the pending bill, introduced on May 4, which provide just who shall sign the registration statement and just what degree of liability may be imposed upon these signers by the aggrieved purchasers of securities.

The pending bill, on page 11, section 6, provides that the registration statement—

Shall be signed by the issuer or issuers, its principal executive officers, its principal financial officers, its controller, or principal accounting officers, and the majority of its board of directors or persons performing similar functions.

Bear in mind that this provision is important because when the pending bill later outlines the remedy for any person acquiring securities, it is expressly stated that such persons may sue "every person who signed the registration statement." Observe that in the original bill all the directors must sign the statement, while in the pending bill only a majority of the directors shall sign or—please observe this also—the directors may be relieved from signing if a majority of "persons performing similar functions" sign. . . .

The remedy sections in the pending bill are to be found on page 20. Here is the provision in lines 21 and 22 that suit may be brought against "every person who signed the registration statement." In the original bill this would have guaranteed a right of action against every member of the board of directors. In the pending bill a right of action is given against the majority of the board of directors or against a majority of such persons as perform duties similar to the duties of a board of directors.

Under the provision of the new bill other persons also may be sued, but if you will study the provisions of the bill, beginning on page 21, line 14, and continuing to page 24, line 5, you will see that all persons who may be sued under the provisions of the bill can escape liability if they prove, although there was an "untrue statement of a material fact" or omission "to state a material fact," that they "after reasonable investigation" had "reasonable ground to believe and did believe" and irrespective of whether the statements in the registration statement were made by experts or others, they in fact "did believe at the time such registration statement became effective that the statements therein were true and that there was no omission to state a material fact," and so forth.

I call your attention to these radical departures in the pending bill from those provisions in the original bill which provided a remedy for the investing public in securities to emphasize the fact that the public itself because of the provisions in this bill may not look for any easy recovery of funds from persons of whom they have purchased securities. As for myself, I believe that in practice the investing public has fully as adequate a remedy under existing law as is given by any of the provisions of the pending bill. It is fair to say in concluding our discussion of this feature of the bill that the party in power has herein seen fit to afford ample protection to those extensive moneyed interests having to do with the issuance and sale of securities.

There is just one other provision of the pending bill to which I would call your attention. It is to be found at the top of page 20 and reads as follows:

The statements or information required to be included in a prospectus by or under authority of subsection (a) or (b) when written shall be placed in a conspicuous part of the prospectus in type as large as that used generally in the body of the prospectus.

This is a very wise provision. It would compel those who as initial to the sale of securities are publishing their prospectuses to print essential information contained in such prospectuses in sizable type, and not print in some inconspicuous space and in small type statements equally material. Clearly, the provision aims to make concealment of material facts difficult. It aims to make prospectuses honest and in no sense misleading or calculated to deceive. It sets up a standard of business morality in this country for men engaged in the private business of issuing and selling securities. I commend it. I endorse it. . . .

MR. BLACK. Mr. Chairman, every State in the Union has one or more laws against larceny. The Federal Government has a law against larceny through the mails. Here is another law on a grand scale against larceny. I hope it does more good than the laws of the 48 States and the present laws of the Union.

Why do we need this law? We need this law because of the nonenforcement of all the present statutes all over this country against larceny. Why are they not enforced? What has brought this situation to the attention of the people? Those laws have not been enforced because of the imposing names and impressive titles of the present-day big crooks.

Our President was Governor of the State of New York for 4 years while a great number of these crimes which are talked about on this floor were committed. He probably now realizes that the States do not have adequate force to meet the situation, so he suggests this bill, and he is behind it.

There is a Federal law that has been on the books that could have taken care of anybody who has been charged before the Senate committee or generally in the public press, with having swindled the public, but that law has not been enforced. Why? Again, because of the imposing names of the men who violated those laws. . . .

I think we are doing the usual thing when we do not want to enforce laws. We pass another one. I say it will do the country more good and restore the confidence of the people quicker than any statute if this Congress would appropriate a large sum of money to organize a flying squad for the prosecution of every case under the mail-fraud section where the amounts involved are large. Let the Attorney General get a special crew of lawyers; let the Post Office Department assign to them a special crew of post-office-inspectors and take the information they get from the Senate committee and go out and indict and convict them. We will not need this law to restore confidence. There have been plenty of violations of the mail-fraud section already evidenced before the Senate committee. The men who have done those things are men of high-sounding names.

They are men responsible for the crash. I said from the beginning you would not restore confidence in the banks, you would not restore prosperity in this country, until the men who have been leading the financial situation of the country, who have been involved in violations of law, are convicted of crimes. You will not convict them by passing new laws. Let the Attorney General be directed to enforce all the present laws and not take up the time of Congress in passing a new law as is usually done when they do not want to enforce the laws on the statute books. Take some of the big bankers from behind the bank cages and put them in others.

I have little patience with the men from the West and the South who are always finding fault with New York in connection with stock operations. The New York Stock Exchange has served a very important function in the development of this country, because it has been the channel through which the West and the South and the undeveloped portions of the country got the money for their development. They sold their securities in the East through the medium of the stock exchange.

The stock exchange has provided a market for those who had securities on hand that were listed to sell them, but the banks with affiliated securities companies did not provide any market for those who held their securities. You took them and kept them when they were no good. If in the course of the operation of the stock exchange there has been fraud in the prospectuses of corporations or in their financial statements, that fraud was not committed by members of the stock exchange or by the brokers. That fraud was committed by the business man, by the banker, by the industrialist, by the utilities man who went to the stock exchange and made the misstatement. And he does not come from New York. The wildcat oil operator, the wildcat mine operator who took a New York address in order to swindle the men in the East, are among the men who gave false statements. . . .

MR. RAYBURN. Mr. Chairman, I ask that the committee amendments be read.

THE CHAIRMAN. (Mr. Arnold). If there is no further debate, the Clerk will report the first committee amendment.

The Clerk read as follows:

Committee amendment: Page 6, line 15, after the word "States", strike out the words "or any political subdivision thereof" and insert "or by any political subdivision of a State or Territory, or by any public instrumentality of one or more States or Territories exercising an essential governmental function."

MR. RAYBURN. I will state for the information of the committee that that is simply a clarifying amendment.

THE CHAIRMAN. The question is on the adoption of the committee amendment.

The committee amendment was agreed to.

THE CHAIRMAN. The Clerk will report the next committee amendment.

The Clerk read as follows:

Second committee amendment: On page 6, line 23, after the word "bank", insert the words "or by any banking institution organized under the laws of any State or Territory, the business of which is substantially confined to banking and is supervised by the State or Territorial banking commission or similar official."

MR. RAYBURN. This amendment, Mr. Chairman, simply places State banks and their issues on the same ground as Federal banks or national banks.

THE CHAIRMAN. The question is on the committee amendment.

The committee amendment was agreed to.

THE CHAIRMAN. The Clerk will report the next committee amendment.

The Clerk read as follows:

Page 8, line 19, after the word "underwriter," insert the words "and not involving any public offering."

MR. RAYBURN. This simply clarifies the language, I may say, Mr. Chairman.

The committee amendment was agreed to. . . .

THE CHAIRMAN. Under the rule, the Committee rises.

Accordingly the Committee rose; and the Speaker having resumed the chair, Mr. Arnold, Chairman of the Committee of the Whole House on the state of the Union, reported that the committee having had under consideration the bill (H.R.5480) to provide full and fair disclosure of the character of securities sold in interstate and foreign commerce and through the mails, and to prevent frauds in the sale thereof, and for other purposes, pursuant to House Resolution 130, he reported the bill back to the House with sundry amendments adopted by the committee. . . .

THE SPEAKER. Is a separate vote demanded on any amendment? If not, the Chair will put them en gros.

The amendments were agreed to.

The bill was ordered to be engrossed and read a third time, was read the third time, and passed. . . .

Senate – 73rd Congress, 1st Session
May 8, 1933

MR. FLETCHER. I move that the Senate proceed to the consideration of Senate bill 875.

THE PRESIDING OFFICER. The question is on the motion of the Senator from Florida, that the Senate proceed to the consideration of a bill, the title of which will be stated.

THE LEGISLATIVE CLERK. A bill (S. 875) to provide for the furnishing of information and the supervision of traffic in investment securities in interstate commerce.

MR. McNARY. Mr. President, I inquire if the motion is to proceed to the consideration of the Senate bill or the House bill?

MR. FLETCHER. I have moved that the Senate proceed to the consideration of the Senate bill.

MR. McNARY. I will say to the Senator from Michigan [Mr. Couzens] that the Senator from Florida has moved that the Senate proceed to the consideration of the Senate bill. The Senator from Michigan expressed to me and others this morning a desire to have the House bill referred to the committee. Has an agreement been reached with regard to that matter?

MR. COUZENS. Mr. President, the Senator from Florida and I discussed the matter, and it seemed to be the consensus of opinion that we ought to go on and discuss the Senate bill, so as to ascertain, if possible, what the differences are between the House bill and the Senate bill. So far as I am concerned, I am in agreement with the plan of going ahead with the securities bill.

MR. FLETCHER. In any case, I may say to the Senator that the bill will have to go to conference, and my view is that we can proceed with the Senate bill and pass it, if we may, and then substitute it for the House bill. That will throw the whole subject into conference. It will have to be thrashed out by the conferees, anyway, and I think that is the best method of procedure. The conferees will then be able to adjust the differences between the House and the Senate. If we should now refer the House bill to the Senate Committee on Banking and Currency, that would lead to considerable delay, and I do not know that we could get any closer together by that method than we can in conference, anyway. So, as a matter of practical procedure and in order to make progress, I think we should take up the Senate bill, which I believe we can pass without taking a great deal of time on it. Then the Senate bill can be substituted for the House bill and the measure then go to conference in all its details. I believe we can proceed without any loss of time in that way.

We would not save any time by referring the House bill to the Senate committee, which has already considered the whole subject, held hearings on it extending over weeks, and reported this bill. I think there are not a great many differences between the two bills. I may say that in principle and in purpose the bills are the same. There is a different use of language in one as compared to the other, but I do not think there is any very serious difference. So I think we had better proceed with the Senate bill and dispose of it, if we may. . . .

MR. FLETCHER. In a general way, Mr. President, I need not say, for Senators are familiar with the conditions, that for some years past there have been offered to the public various securities, foreign and domestic, by various concerns, corporations, organizations, and what not. Such securities have been disposed of to the public in a loose and haphazard sort of way. Bankers, brokers, syndicates, and financial institutions have been handling them, and super-powered agents have been selling them. People have been persuaded to invest their money in securities without any information respecting them, except the advertisements put forth by the agents or representatives of those issuing the securities, and such advertisements have not given full information to the public. The result was that we had a saturnalia of speculation throughout the country, almost as far back as 1920, and certainly during 1927, 1928, 1929, and 1930. People were persuaded to put their money into these investments sometimes because they were attracted by the high rates of interest and often because they were told that the price of the securities would go up and they would make money easily and rapidly by investing in them.

Some persons, under some circumstances, have been persuaded to dispose of perfectly good securities and invest in worthless securities which were offered to them by agents all over the country. There are instances which were brought out by the testimony before the committee where widows who owned Liberty bonds, having invested the accumulations of a lifetime in such bonds, were persuaded by some of these agents to sell their bonds and invest their all in valueless securities by all sorts of misrepresentations, such as that they were bound to increase in value, that returns would be considerable, and all that sort of thing. There are instances where persons who had savings deposits were inveigled into withdrawing those deposits and investing in worthless securities. It is estimated that something like $90,000,000,000 in the hands of people have during recent years been invested in such securities, most of which have become practically worthless.

The idea is that, in the first place, these securities move in interstate commerce. It is therefore, on the commerce clause of the Constitution that we base our jurisdiction with respect to this proposed legislation. The securities also move in the mails, and it is under the postal law of the country that Congress has further jurisdiction to legislate in this connection. Acting under those two provisions of the Constitution, we have undertaken to impose certain restrictions and to provide certain regulations in reference to securities that are being offered to the public throughout the country from time to time.

We have no Federal legislation covering this situation, and so in order to protect the public and in order to protect investors, this bill has been devised. We gave lengthy hearings on it, hearings extending over weeks, and finally reached the conclusion to amend, in many respects, the original bill that had been introduced; in fact, in so many respects that we reported a new bill as a substitute for the original bill.

The purpose of the bill is to protect the investing public and honest business. The basic policy is that of informing the investor of the facts concerning securities to be offered for sale in interstate and foreign commerce and providing protection against fraud and misrepresentation. That is the general purpose of the bill. The aim is to prevent further exploitation of the public by the sale of unsound, fraudulent, and worthless securities through misrepresentation; to place adequate and true information before the investors; to protect honest enterprise, seeking capital by honest presentation, against the competition afforded by questionable securities offered to the public through crooked promotion; to restore the confidence of the prospective investor in sound securities; to bring into productive channels of industry and development capital which has grown timid to the point of hoarding; and to aid in providing employment and in restoring buying and consuming power. Those are the general purposes of the bill, and we have endeavored to write a piece of proposed legislation which will bring about that result.

There is need for such legislation. The President in his special message called attention to such need and pointed out the demand for this kind of legislation. The President said:

> I recommend to the Congress legislation for Federal supervision of traffic in investment securities in interstate commerce.
> In spite of many State statutes the public in the past has sustained severe losses through practices neither ethical nor honest on the part of many persons and corporations selling securities.
> Of course, the Federal Government cannot and should not take any action which might be construed as approving or guaranteeing that newly issued securities are sound in the sense that their value will be maintained or that the properties which they represent will earn profit.

We have endeavored to accomplish all those purposes. It is expressly provided in the bill that the Government shall not be responsible as to guaranteeing the value of the securities offered. We provide, in the first place, for registration. Any concern, corporation or what not, desiring to issue securities must register with the Federal Trade Commission and furnish facts with reference to the securities offered. An inquiry is made by the Federal Trade Commission, and then, after the registration takes place, they are authorized to issue the securities, without the Government guaranteeing their value at all, but with the requirement that information shall be furnished to the public generally as to the character of what is offered and what is back of it.

That is the prime purpose of the first portion of the bill. There are other provisions with reference to punishment for fraud and with reference to the civil liability of those who issue securities. One of the chief differences, I think, between the House bill and the Senate bill is that the House bill rather limits this liability and makes a corporation and its directors, or what not, applying for the registration of securities, seeking the authorization of the Commission, liable civilly for any damage or loss that may arise by reason of misrepresentation or lack or omission as to representation with respect to the securities and the facts. The House bill, as I recall, limits the liability to those who have not acted in good faith; in other words, it provides that people signing the application for registration and obtaining the registration document shall not be liable if they act in good faith upon reasonable judgment and information. . . .

Mr. President, I wish to propose an amendment to come on page 37, lines 1 and 2, to strike out the words "with respect to each other class." . . .

THE PRESIDING OFFICER. The Clerk will state the amendment.

THE LEGISLATIVE CLERK. On page 37, line 1, after the word "class" and the comma, the Senator from Florida proposes to strike out the words "with respect to each other class," so as to read:

(4) A statement of the capitalization of the issuer, including the authorized and paid up amounts of its capital stock, the number and classes of shares into which such capital stock is divided, the par value thereof, or if it has no par value, the stated or assigned value thereof; a description of the respective voting rights, preferences, conversion and exchange of rights, rights to dividends, profits, or capital of each class, including the retirement and liquidation rights or values thereof.

The amendment to the amendment was agreed to.

MR. FLETCHER. Mr. President, on page 38, line 21, after the word "investment," I move to insert the words "and the net amount received or to be received thereafter by the issuer," so as to read:

A detailed statement of the plan upon which the issuer proposes to dispose of the securities offered for registration, the price at which they are offered to the public, the net amount returnable to capital investment, and the net amount received or to be received thereafter by the issuer.

The amendment to the amendment was agreed to.

MR. FLETCHER. On page 47, line 22, after the word "investment," I move to insert the same words "and the net amount received or to be received thereafter by the issuer," so as to read:

The price at which it is offered to the public, the net amount to be returned to capital investment, and the net amount received or to be received thereafter by the issuer.

The amendment to the amendment was agreed to.

MR. FLETCHER. On page 47, line 23, after the words "amount of," to insert the words "discount, rebate," so as to read:

The price at which it is offered to the public, the net amount to be returned to capital investment, and the net amount received or to be received thereafter by the issuer, as well as the maximum amount of discount, rebate, commission, or other form or remuneration to be paid in cash or otherwise, directly or indirectly, for or in connection with the sale or offering for sale of such securities.

The amendment to the amendment was agreed to.

MR. FLETCHER. On page 52, lines 18 and 19, I move to strike out the words "or other public utility," so as to read:

(b) Any security issued by and representing an interest in or a direct obligation of any common carrier subject to regulation or supervision as to the issue of its securities or its accounts by a commission, board, or officers of the Government of the United States; or any such security issued by any national bank; or by any corporation created and controlled by and acting as an instrumentality of the Government of the United States pursuant to authority granted by the Congress of the United States.

The amendment to the amendment was agreed to.

MR. ADAMS. Mr. President, I want to offer an amendment. . . .

On page 29, lines 23 and 24, I move to strike out the words "when such paper is not offered or intended to be offered for sale to the public."

The matter has been discussed with the Senator from Florida [Mr. Fletcher], and it is intended to protect from the operation of the act certain paper which should not be included along with commercial paper, since it merely circulates among banks, instead of the general public.

MR. FLETCHER. I think it is a very good amendment.

THE PRESIDING OFFICER. The question is on agreeing to the amendment to the amendment.

The amendment to the amendment was agreed to. . . .

MR. FESS. Mr. President, I should like to have the attention of the Chairman of the Committee on Banking and Currency. I have had much correspondence from certain business groups in Ohio regarding the pending bill, making specific recommendations as to changes. I had not an opportunity of studying the bill until today. I think the changes have already been made, and I want to make sure of it.

I have a letter from the Chamber of Commerce of Cleveland urging that the bill be limited to issues in the future rather than to those already outstanding.

MR. FLETCHER. The bill provides for that. It refers only to future issues, except in the case of fraud.

MR. FESS. That is cared for, then. Another item to which attention has been called I think has also been cared for. The chamber of commerce suggests that not more than three fourths of the directors or trustees be required to sign the registration statement.

MR. FLETCHER. The bill provides for that.

MR. FESS. They ask also, in respect of section 6, that the party who would be a defendant be given a chance for hearing. I think section 6 has already provided for a public hearing.

MR. FLETCHER. Section 7, on page 45, provides for hearings and appeals.

MR. FESS. Yes; beginning with line 6. I think that is all taken care of.

MR. FLETCHER. That is cared for.

MR. FESS. Another suggestion that has been made is as to the requirement in section 9. The chamber of commerce says:

We feel that it should be limited only to situations in which the signer has personal knowledge of the falsity of the statement.

I cannot find that that is taken care of, that if the statement is proven to be erroneous, in order that action may be sustained it must be shown that the falsity of the statement was known to the person who made it; in other words, that he willfully made a false statement. I have read the bill pretty carefully, and I do not think that matter is taken care of.

MR. FLETCHER. He would not be liable criminally without willfully and knowingly making a false statement.

MR. KEAN. But financially, under the bill, he would be liable for everything he had.

MR. FLETCHER. Liable civilly.

MR. FESS. Mr. President, before taking my seat I should like to state that I have assumed from the beginning that there would have to be some legislation of this character. When blue sky law legislation was proposed in the several States I was not very favorably impressed with the general proposition. One of the first States to enact such legislation was my own. During the Ohio Constitutional Convention in 1912 the question of blue sky legislation was considered in extenso. It being an innovation, there was tremendous opposition to it on the ground that the formula of business was caveat emptor—"let the buyer beware." We had not then reached the point "let the seller beware," and there was much opposition to the proposal. I, myself, voted for it with considerable trepidation, thinking that it probably was not of importance, and we might be unnecessarily cluttering up the statute books by giving constitutional sanction to that kind of legislation. However, in the 20 years' duration of that legislation in Ohio there have been many prosecutions, which indicates that advantage has often been taken of investors. So the protection of the public from transactions in fraudulent securities seems to have come to be recognized as a proper legislative function.

The present Presiding Officer [Mr. Barkley in the chair] knows that while he was a Member of the other House there was much effort on the part of that body to bring about the enactment of a Federal blue sky law. Our friends from Illinois made great efforts for years to have that kind of legislation enacted. I do not think, however, it ever came over to the Senate. I do not now recall that heretofore any effort has been made in the Senate to secure Federal blue sky legislation, but I think that conditions we have observed in the States justify legislation of this character. It should avoid unneccesary obstructions to business; and I think probably this bill does remove the objections of those who, while not opposed to the legislation itself, thought it might provide obstacles that ought not to be thrown in the way of business. As those objections have been removed, I do not see any particular reason why the bill should not be passed, since the field it embraces was entered upon years ago and such legislation has become general in the States.

I recognize the danger that the Senator from Utah [Mr. King] has suggested; but what is the use of attempting to withstand the enactment of these proposals? We are in this movement; we are legislating for everything; and I do not know what the limit is to be. At any rate, it is true that there has been advantage taken of the public in security-sale transactions; and I shall go along with the committee in supporting the pending bill.

MR. KING. Mr. President, I might suggest to the Senator from Ohio if we are dealing with blue sky laws that "the sky is the limit." [Laughter.]

MR. FESS. That is true. . . .

MR. FLETCHER. Mr. President, I presume the words "title I" ought to be inserted after line 1, on page 29; and then that preceding the amendment offered by the Senator from California the words "title II" ought to be inserted after line 4, on page 61.

THE PRESIDING OFFICER. Without objection, the corrections and amendments will be made. . . .

The Chair lays before the Senate House bill 5480.

The Senate, by unanimous consent, proceeded to consider the bill (H.R. 5480) to provide full and fair disclosure of the character of securities sold in interstate and foreign commerce and through the mails, and to prevent frauds in the sale thereof, and for other purposes, which was read twice by its title.

MR. FLETCHER. I move to strike out all after the enacting clause of the House bill and to insert in lieu thereof the Senate bill as it has been amended. . . .

MR. KEAN. Mr. President, the only question that I should like to call to the attention of the Senate is this: On page 34 of the bill there is a requirement that three fourths of all the directors of a corporation shall sign the registration statement.

This provision is taken from the English Companies Act. Directors under the English Companies Act are really responsible and do the detail work of the corporation. They receive as salary from a thousand to two thousand or three thousand pounds a year. Here, however, we are trying to bind people who receive but $5 or $10 a month in the same way that it is proposed to bind men who receive $10,000 a year. It seems to me that the responsiblity of the directors is different in the two cases. Nobody is going to be a director of a corporation if he is compelled to assume a liability, amounting perhaps to $10,000,000, for something about which he does not know, when he receives perhaps only $10 a month. I should like to limit the responsibility of the directors so that the bill would apply to them only when they knowingly commit fraud. If they knowingly commit fraud, the greatest penalty the Senate can impose upon them is not too great for me; but to provide when they sign the statement and not knowingly commit fraud that they shall be liable for ten or fifteen million dollars, although they receive fees of but $10 a month, it seems to be perfectly absurd.

Insistence upon the officers of a corporation signing the statement is perfectly proper. They are in charge of the business; they are responsible for the statement; and, if they make a false statement, they ought to be liable for it; but, in my opinion, that is not true of the directors. . . .

MR. FLETCHER. Mr. President, let me say that the committee considered the suggestion of the Senator from New Jersey very carefully, and, after considerable discussion about it, agreed, if the public is to be protected, that we had better leave the language as it is. The liability provision reads, in part:

In case any such registration statement shall be false or deceptive in any material respect, any persons acquiring any securities to which such statement relates, either from the original issuer or from any other person, shall have the right to rescind the transaction and to obtain the return, either at law or in equity, of any and all consideration given or paid for any such securities upon the surrender thereof.

That is the liability which everybody signing the registration statement assumes, and I think it ought to remain that way. I think that is the only basis on which we can make the proposed act effective. . . .

MR. KEAN. Mr. President, in order to bring the question directly before the Senate I move, on page 34, line 3, to strike out the words "and the directors, trustees, and managers; or, if there is no board of directors, by the persons or board having the power of management of the person."

THE PRESIDING OFFICER. The question is on agreeing to the amendment offered by the Senator from New Jersey to the amendment.

The amendment to the amendment was rejected.

MR. SHIPSTEAD. Mr. President, would it be possible to have an explanation of the essential differences between the House bill and the Senate bill as amended?

MR. FLETCHER. Mr. President, it is a long story, and we have been over it, I will say to the Senator, during his absence. We discussed the differences this morning. It would be quite difficult to point out all the differences. Mainly the purposes and objects of both bills are the same, and they will accomplish very much the same thing. There are some features in the House bill which are not in the Senate bill; for instance, one provision in the House bill is that 30 days must elapse before securities can issue after registration has been made. We think that that ties matters up indefinitely and would operate badly upon all business transactions of this kind.

Then there is another provision about the revocation of the permit. The House bill provides for a stop order instead of a revocation. There is not a great deal of difference in that.

There is another provision in the House bill, section 18, which provides for recognizing all the laws of the different States, which would somewhat complicate matters. We have not that provision in the Senate bill. That was the basis of the minority report of the House. It is not in the Senate bill. In the main the principles and purposes are the same.

THE PRESIDING OFFICER. The question is on the motion of the Senator from Florida to substitute the Senate bill as amended for the language of the House bill.

The motion was agreed to.

THE PRESIDING OFFICER. The question is, Shall the amendment be engrossed and the bill read a third time?

The amendment was ordered to be engrossed and the bill to be read a third time.

MR. SHIPSTEAD. Mr. President, has the bill been explained to the Senate?

MR. COUZENS. Mr. President, it has been explained several times in detail.

THE PRESIDING OFFICER. The question is on the third reading and passage of the bill.

The bill was read the third time and passed. . . .

House of Representatives—73rd Congress, 1st Session
May 22, 1933

MR. BLANTON. Certainly; the gentleman is correct, and I might add that he is usually correct; and I deem it an honor that I find myself voting with him many times, except on partisan party questions.

MR. CLARKE OF NEW YORK. There had not been a name called.

MR. BLANTON. There are precedents which hold that where the yeas and nays have been ordered, but no Member has yet responded to his name on roll call, that it is deemed that the roll call has not yet begun, and a motion to adjourn would be in order. Our distinguished Speaker is so uniformly correct in his rulings that if he ruled against the gentleman's contention he must have been of the opinion that the roll call had begun.

MR. CLARKE OF NEW YORK. The roll call had been ordered, but no names had been called.

THE SPEAKER. The Chair thinks several names were called, but there had been no response.

SECURITIES REGULATION BILL

MR. RAYBURN. Mr. Speaker, I call up the conference report on the bill (H.R. 5480) to provide full and fair disclosure of the character of securities sold in interstate and foreign commerce and through the mails, and to prevent frauds in the sale thereof, and for other purposes, and ask unanimous consent that the statement may be read in lieu of the report. . . .

CONFERENCE REPORT

The committee of conference on the disagreeing votes of the two Houses on the amendment of the Senate to the bill (H.R. 5480) to provide full and fair disclosure of the character of securities sold in interstate and foreign commerce and through the mails, and to prevent frauds in the sale thereof, and for other purposes, having met, after full and free conference, have agreed to recommend and do recommend to their respective Houses as follows:

That the House recede from its disagreement to the amendment of the Senate and agree to the same with an amendment as follows:

In lieu of the matter proposed to be inserted by the Senate amendment insert the following: [The text of the Act follows]

And the Senate agree to the same.

Sam Rayburn
Geo. Huddleston
Clarence Lea
James S. Parker
Carl E. Mapes
Managers on the part of the House
Duncan U. Fletcher
Carter Glass
Robert F. Wagner
Managers on the part of the Senate

STATEMENT

The managers on the part of the House at the conference on the disagreeing votes of the two Houses on the bill (H.R. 5480) to provide full and fair disclosure of the character of securities sold in interstate and foreign commerce and through the mails, and to prevent frauds in the sale thereof, and for other purposes, submit the following statement in explanation of the effect of the action agreed upon by the conferees and recommended in the accompanying conference report:

The Senate amendment struck out all of the House bill after the enacting clause. The House recedes from its disagreement to the amendment of the Senate, with an amendment which is a substitute for both the House bill and the Senate amendment. The differences between the House bill and the substitute agreed upon by the conferees are noted in the following discussion, except for incidental changes made necessary to harmonize various provisions affected by the agreements reached, and minor and clarifying changes to make clear and effective the administrative procedure provided for and to remove uncertainties.

The House bill did not apply to traffic in securities wholly within the District of Columbia, but the Senate amendment did. This feature was omitted from the House bill upon the basis of a misunderstanding, and is incorporated in the substitute.

The House bill (sec. 2 (11)) and the Senate amendment contained differences as to the definition of the term "underwriter" as used in the act. The substitute amends the definition of underwriter contained in the House bill so as to make clear that a person merely furnishing an underwriter money to enable him to enter into an underwriting agreement is not an underwriter. Persons, however, who participate in any underwriting transaction or who have a direct or indirect participation in such a transaction are deemed to be underwriters. The test is one of participation in the underwriting undertaking rather than that of a mere interest in it.

The House bill (sec. 3 (a)(5)) exempted the securities of building and loan associations and other similar institutions when their business was substantially confined to their members. The Senate amendment limited this exemption by further requiring that these associations must not charge withdrawal or other fees in excess of 2 percent of the face value of the security. This provision in the Senate amendment was accepted with the change of extending the exemption only to institutions that did not charge in excess of 3 percent of the face value of the security by way of a withdrawal fee or otherwise.

The Senate amendment also exempted the securities of farmers' cooperatives. This exemption is incorporated in the substitute.

The Senate amendment provided for an exemption in the case of annuity contracts. The House bill contained no such exemption. The substitute, however, only exempts such contracts when issued by a corporation subject to the supervision of the appropriate State or Territorial governmental agency.

The Senate agreed to the House exemption (sec. 4 (3)) of the issuance of securities to the existing security holders or other existing creditors of a corporation in the process of a bona fide reorganization of such corporation under the supervision of any court. It is clear that under section 3 (a)(1) protective committees even though not under the supervision of a court will not be covered by the act if they have in good faith commenced to solicit deposits of claims or securities within 60 days after the enactment of the act although deposits continue to be solicited after such 60 days.

The House provision (sec. 4 (3)) exempting stock dividends and the sale of stock to stockholders is omitted from the substitute, since stock dividends are exempt without express provision, as they do not constitute a sale, not being given for value. Sales of stock to stockholders become subject to the act unless the stockholders are so small in number that the sale to them does not constitute a public offering. The Senate agreed that the mere exchange with its security holders of one form of security for another by an issuer where no commission or other remuneration is paid, shall be exempt. This exemption is considered necessary to permit certain voluntary readjustments of obligations. Inasmuch as any exchange that involves the payment of a commission of any sort is not exempt, there is no danger of the provision being used for purposes of evasion.

The House provision (sec. 4 (4)) exempting subscriptions for shares prior to incorporation where no expense is incurred or commission paid, is omitted from the substitute. This exemption is unnecessary in view of section 4 (1), which exempts transactions by any person other than an issuer, underwriter, or dealer.

The House bill (sec. 6 (b)) provided that the minimum fee for registration should be $50. The Senate amendment made the minimum fee $25. The provisions of the Senate amendment on this point are contained in the substitute.

The House bill (sec. 8) provided that a registration statement had to be on file with the Commission for 30 days before it became effective. Under the Senate amendment the registration statement became effective upon filing, but the grounds for revocation after filing were considerably broader than those for a stop order under the House bill. In the substitute the registration statement becomes effective only 20 days after filing.

This time is sufficient for public scrutiny, while the Commission is expected during this period to make only a preliminary check-up. The stop-order provisions are retained as in the original House measure. Where the security is that of a foreign public authority which has continued the full service of its obligations in the United States and the proceeds of which are to be devoted to the refunding of obligations payable in the United States, the registration statement becomes effective 7 days after the filing of such statement.

The House bill (sec. 9) provided that any review from an order of the Commission should be taken only in the Court of Appeals of the District of Columbia. The Senate amendment permitted these appeals from the Commission's orders to be taken to the appropriate circuit courts of appeal. The substitute embodies this provision. It also, in accordance with phraseology contained in the Senate amendment, makes clear that review over the orders of the Federal Trade Commission shall extend only to questions of law.

A point of difference between the House bill and the Senate amendment concerned the civil liability of persons responsible for the flotation of an issue. The Senate amendment imposed upon the issuer, its directors, its chief executive and financial officers, a liability which might appropriately be denominated as an insurer's liability. They were held liable without regard to whatever care they may have used for the accuracy of the statements made in the registration statement. The House bill, on the other hand, measured liability for these statements in terms of reasonable care, placing upon the defendants the duty, in case they were sued, of proving that they had used reasonable care to assure the accuracy of these statements. The standard by which reasonable care was exemplified was expressed in terms of a fiduciary relationship. A fiduciary under the law is bound to exercise diligence of a type commensurate with the confidence, both as to integrity and competence, that is placed in him. This does not, of course, necessitate that he shall individually perform every duty imposed upon him. Delegation to others of the performance of acts which it is unreasonable to require that the fiduciary shall personally perform is permissible. Especially is this true where the character of the acts involves professional skill or facilities not possessed by the fiduciary himself. In such cases reliance by the fiduciary, if his reliance is reasonable in the light of all the circumstances, is a full discharge of his responsibilities. In choosing between these two standards of liability the Senate accepted the standards imposed by the House bill.

Though the standards of the Senate amendment were more severe than those embodied in the House bill, the classes of persons upon whom liability was imposed were less. The House bill imposed liability upon the underwriters and also upon the experts, such as accountants, appraisers, and engineers, who gave the authority of their names to statements made in the registration statement. The Senate accepted the provisions of the House bill with reference to this matter, but with the modification that, to protect an unauthorized use of the expert's name, written consent to the use of his name, as having prepared or certified part of the registration statement or as having prepared a report to which statements in the registration statement were attributed, should be filed at the time of the filing of the registration statement. The necessary changes to effectuate this end have been made in the substitute.

The Senate amendment imposed liability upon persons making false and deceptive statements in connection with the distribution or sale of a security. The House bill made the liability depend upon the making of untrue statements or omissions to state material facts. This phrase has been clarified in the substitute to make the omission relate to the statements made in order that these statements shall not be misleading, rather than making mere omission—unless the act expressly requires such a fact to be stated—a ground for liability where no circumstances exist to make the omission in itself misleading.

The House bill (sec. 12) imposes civil liability for using the mails or the facilities of interstate commerce to sell securities (including securities exempt, under section 3, from other provisions of the bill) by means of representations which are untrue or are misleading by reason of omissions of material facts. The substantially similar provisions of the Senate amendment did not apply to any of the securities exempted under the Senate amendment. The substitute exempts from the operation of this section sales of securities covered by section 3 (a) (2), which relates, broadly speaking, to securities issued or guaranteed by the United States or any State, Territory, or the District of Columbia, or by a public instrumentality, or by a Federal Reserve bank or national bank, or by a supervised State bank.

The Senate amendment contained provisions referred to as "dummy provisions" which were calculated to place liability upon a person who acted through another, irrespective of whether a direct agency relationship existed but dependent upon the actual control exercised by the one party over the other. The House bill did not contain these provisions. The various provisions of the Senate amendment on this subject have been welded into one and incorporated as a new section in the substitute.

The House bill (sec. 18) contained a provision prohibiting the selling of securities in interstate commerce in any State, Territory, or the District of Columbia where such sale would have been a violation of the laws thereof relating to the sale of securities if it had taken place wholly therein. This provision is not in the Senate amendment and is eliminated from the substitute.

The House bill (sec. 21) limited the venue of actions brought in the district courts to enforce civil liabilities under the act to the district in which the defendant was an inhabitant or had its principal place of business or in the district where the sale took place. The Senate amendment extended this provision to permit suit in the district where the defendant might be found or where he transacts business. The substitute incorporates the provision of the Senate bill in this respect.

The schedules of the House bill required the disclosure of certain material contracts made not in the ordinary course of business. The Senate amendment contained no such provision. The substitute clarifies the meaning of "material contract" as used in the House bill, and also provides against any disclosure of the content of any portion of a material contract when the Commission finds that such disclosure would both impair the value of the contract and would not be necessary for the protection of investors. Ample protection is thereby afforded against the disclosure of secret formulae, trade secrets, or competitive advantages achieved by agreement.

Numerous differences between the House bill and the Senate amendment resolve themselves about the powers of the Federal Trade Commission. In some instances the provisions of the Senate amendment on these matters are contained in the substitute, in others the provisions of the Senate amendment have been adapted to the basic machinery underlying the House bill. Throughout, the aim has been to invest the Federal Trade Commission with full and adequate powers to perform the duties vested upon it under the act. Care has also been taken to avoid any conflict between the exercise of such powers by the Federal Trade Commission and the exercise of similar powers by any other Federal agency. . . .

Sam Rayburn
Geo. Huddleston
Clarence Lea
James S. Parker
Carl E. Mapes
Managers on the part of the House

MR. RAYBURN. Mr. Speaker, there are two typographical errors. In title II, section 202, where "12" is used, it should be "6," and in the same section, near the end of the section, the words "three fourths" should be "two thirds."

I ask unanimous consent that the corrections may be made.

THE SPEAKER. Is there objection to the request of the gentleman from Texas? There was no objection.

MR. RAYBURN. Mr. Speaker, I move the adoption of the conference report.

The conference report was agreed to. . . .

Senate–73rd Congress, 1st Session
May 23, 1933

MR. FLETCHER. Mr. President, may I ask the indulgence of the Senate for just a moment? I am very much occupied now in the Senate Office Building, where the Banking and Currency Committee are conducting hearings, and I should like to have the Senate act on the conference report on the securities bill. The report has been agreed to by the House of Representatives, and I do not know of any opposition to it in the Senate.

THE PRESIDING OFFICER. What is the Senator's request?

MR. FLETCHER. That the Senate now consider the conference report on the so-called "securities bill." . . .

Mr. President, I ask that the conference report may be agreed to. . . .

THE PRESIDING OFFICER. Is there objection to the request of the Senator from Florida for the present consideration of the conference report?

There being no objection, the Senate proceeded to consider the report.
THE PRESIDING OFFICER. The question is on agreeing to the report.
The report was agreed to. . . .

SECURITIES EXCHANGE ACT
1934

Commentary

Even at the time of its enactment, it was apparent that the Securities Act of 1933 was only a partial answer to the problem posed by the condition of the securities business in the early 1930's. The celebrated Pecora investigation of the stock exchanges showed clearly that more was necessary than a law simply requiring the registration of securities sold. Only an independent commission, it was felt, endowed with broad authority over both the exchanges and the security issues, could do the needed regulatory job.

The Securities Exchange Act of 1934 sought to create just such a regulatory agency. It provided for the setting up of the Securities and Exchange Commission. To this new body was transferred the power over the registration of securities which the Act of 1933 had vested in the Federal Trade Commission. Furthermore, the SEC was given wide authority to police the stock exchanges under a comprehensive system of licensing and control.

The regulatory authority of the SEC, like that of the FCC over broadcasting, is based primarily on the licensing power. The Securities Act of 1933 set up what amounts to a nationwide scheme for the licensing of security issues. Registration statements containing prescribed information must be filed with the commission. Although they take effect automatically within twenty days, "if it appears to the commission at any time that the registration statement includes any untrue statement of a material fact or omits to state any material fact required to be stated therein or necessary to make the statements therein not misleading," the commission may issue a so-called "stop order" suspending the effectiveness of such registration statement.

Analogous licensing powers over securities exchanges are given to the SEC under the Securities Exchange Act of 1934. Among the powers conferred are those to permit or deny registration of securities for trading on a securities exchange and to license the exchanges themselves and brokers who deal on them.

Licensing authority of the type conferred on the SEC is a regulatory weapon of tremendous import. It enables the scheme of regulation to be applied at the source, for those who do not conform can be barred from further participation in the business. Its aim is primarily preventive rather than punitive (although it can be used as a punitive device in connection with past misconducts). The agency's power to revoke or suspend is extremely effective in guaranteeing compliance by those to whom licenses have already been granted. The strength of the licensing device is the fact that it makes the right to pursue a given livelihood wholly dependent upon the observance of prescribed standards of conduct.

The commission, as a practical matter, has all but unfettered discretionary authority. It is true that those aggrieved by the commission's acts have a legal right to review by the courts. However, when the commission refused to permit a registration statement in respect to the issue and sale of securities to become effective, the right to judicial review is almost always devoid of practical content.

The reason was pointed out by James M. Landis after he left the chairmanship of the SEC. "The ability to sell a substantial block of securities," he said, "depends upon creation of a belief that that issue is, like Calpurnia, above suspicion. It depends further upon a wise choice as to the time for offering the securities to the public. The very institution of proceedings is frequently sufficient to destroy the former quality, for the commission's allegation that some untruthfulness attends their registration is sufficient to create grave suspicion as to their merit."

Timing is of the essence in security transactions, and the harm done by SEC action in such cases cannot, as a practical matter, be undone by court review. Reversal by a reviewing court may show the commission to have been in error, but, as Landis neatly put it, "the time that elapses before such relief can be procured will have permanently chilled the market for the securities."

The background of the Securities Exchange Act is given in the report of the House Commerce Committee (*infra* p. 2712). The immediate catalyst was the February 9, 1934 message of President Franklin Roosevelt, (*infra* p. 2712). Various plans for stock exchange regulation had been put forward. The Commerce Committees of the two Houses conducted lengthy hearings and reported bills of their own.

The House bill was introduced by Congressman Sam Rayburn [Dem., Tex.], Chairman of the House Committee. The debate on it began April 30, 1934. The rule voted by the House called for seven hours debate and then the right to offer amendments under the five-minute rule. Congressman Adolph Sabath [Dem., Ill.] presented the need for the rule and referred to the pressures against the bill. Congressman John Cooper [Rep., Ky.], for the minority, criticized the bill as going too far. After the rule was adopted, the House went into Committee of the Whole House. Mr. Rayburn then delivered the principal address for the bill. He discussed its history and the pressures against it; no bill, he declared, had been attacked so viciously. He answered the claim that self-regulation would adequately protect the public and then analyzed the key sections of the bill, notably those dealing with margin requirements and the power given the FTC over exchanges.

Opponents of the bill urged that the bill would impair confidence; it went too far and would enable the commission to control every corporation in the country. They also attacked the role of Messrs. Landis, Corcoran, and Cohen—"the youthful legislative wizards from the little red house in Georgetown"—in the bill's drafting. This, they said, was a bill to Russianize everything—"Lenin and Trotsky never envisaged such far-reaching possibilities for strangulation." Congressman Elmer Studley [Dem., N.Y.] (whose district included the New York financial area) plaintively asked, "Why wreak vengeance on Wall Street?"

Congressman Harold McGugin [Rep., Kan.] urged that the bill "is not the Fletcher-Rayburn bill; it is the Corcoran-Cohen bill." Rayburn answered, admitting the help of men like Corcoran and Cohen. The committee, as laymen, needed expert help. He was seconded by Congressman Charles Wolverton [Rep., N.J.], a Republican committee member, who praised the help given by the so-called "brain trust." Wolverton summarized the four principal features of the bill and stressed the overwhelming need for the legislation.

The most interesting aspect of the debate was the difference over the question of who should exercise the regulatory power. The House bill provided for vesting of regulatory authority in the FTC. The Bulwinkle amendment provided for a new regulatory commission. Its supporters urged both the need for a commission of experts in the securities field and the fact that the FTC was overburdened. The strong opposition of the House leadership led to the amendment's defeat and the bill, as passed by the House, provided for the FTC as the regulatory agency.

Also of interest was the debate on the Fish amendment to take away the FTC's rule-making power. This led to a debate on the need for delegation of such power. As Rayburn put it, the real question was whether the administrative body was to have "the power to make the law effective and the power to enforce it." The discussion here gains pertinence from current controversy over the FTC's rule-making power (See National Petroleum Refiners Assn. *v.* FTC, 340F. Supp. 1343(D.C. 1972).

The House debate ended on May 4, with passage of the bill by 282 to 84 (with the Speaker expressly voting in favor).

The Senate debate began on May 7, with consideration of the bill reported by the Senate Commerce Committee. Senator Duncan Fletcher [Dem., Fla.] introduced the bill and made the principal speech in support. He discusses the history of the bill and emphasizes its careful committee consideration (after 21 volumes of hearings). The chief feature of the bill was its provision for a new commission of five members. The reasons for the new commission are given by Senators Alben Barkley [Dem., Ky.] and Carter Glass [Dem., Va.] (Fletcher had favored the FTC as the regulatory agency). The new body was necessary to avoid having securities regulation as "a sort of a lean-to under the [Federal Trade] Commission's original activities." Fletcher succinctly summarizes the bill's provisions and states that a new commission is provided for to meet the demand for specialists. He answers the Corcoran-Cohen argument by asserting that the authorship of the bill is wholly irrelevant.

Opponents of the bill, notably Senators Frederick Steiwer [Rep., Oreg.] and Daniel Hastings [Rep., Del.], contended that the bill went too far. It was compared to prohibition; it would turn over the operation of the exchanges to the government. Senator Hastings objected to the high salaries for the new commission and staff, as well as the power to levy on exchanges for expenses. He actually compared it to the Revolution and the protest against taxation without representation. The bill was characterized as punitive and placing business in a strait-jacket.

Among the most interesting parts of the debate is the interchange between Senator Steiwer and Senator (later Mr. Justice) Black on rule-making power, penalties, and the power to acquire information. Steiwer urged that the bill was "more far-reaching in its effect and more un-American in principle than anything written in the N.R.A." He asserted that the reporting requirement would be devastating in its effect.

As in the House, there was debate on the FTC versus a new agency. The Costigan amendment restoring the FTC as the regulator was supported by Senator

George Norris [Rep., Nebr.] who declared that when the committee substituted a new commission, "they pulled out a good healthy tooth that was already in the bill."

Toward the end of the debate, various amendments introduced by Senator Fletcher were adopted. They are explained in two memoranda, (*infra* pp. 2904, 2910). Then, on May 12, the Senate passed its bill as a substitute for the House bill, by 62 to 13.

The differences between the House and Senate bills were straightened out in conference. The conference report is explained in the statement by the House managers (*infra* p. 2928), as well as the brief explanatory speeches by Senator Fletcher and Representative Rayburn. The conference report retained the Senate provision for a new Securities and Exchange Commission of five members. As Mr. Rayburn explains it, the House yielded on this in order to get a regulatory law. After brief debate, the conference report was agreed to without roll calls on June 1 by both Houses. The bill became law when it was signed by the President on June 6, 1934.

SECURITIES EXCHANGE ACT
June 6, 1934

Be it enacted by the Senate and House of Representatives of the United States of America in Congress assembled,

Title I—Regulation of Securities Exchanges

Short Title

SECTION 1. This Act may be cited as the "Securities Exchange Act of 1934."

Necessity for Regulation as Provided in this Title

SEC. 2. For the reasons hereinafter enumerated, transactions in securities as commonly conducted upon securities exchanges and over-the-counter markets are affected with a national public interest which makes it necessary to provide for regulation and control of such transactions and of practices and matters related thereto, including transactions by officers, directors, and principal security holders, to require appropriate reports, and to impose requirements necessary to make such regulation and control reasonably complete and effective, in order to protect interstate commerce, the national credit, the Federal taxing power, to protect and make more effective the national banking system and Federal Reserve System, and to insure the maintenance of fair and honest markets in such transactions:

(1) Such transactions (a) are carried on in large volume by the public generally and in large part originate outside the States in which the exchanges and over-the-counter

markets are located and/or are effected by means of the mails and instrumentalities of interstate commerce; (b) constitute an important part of the current of interstate commerce; (c) involve in large part the securities of issuers engaged in interstate commerce; (d) involve the use of credit, directly affect the financing of trade, industry, and transportation in interstate commerce, and directly affect and influence the volume of interstate commerce; and affect the national credit.

(2) The prices established and offered in such transactions are generally disseminated and quoted throughout the United States and foreign countries and constitute a basis for determining and establishing the prices at which securities are bought and sold, the amount of certain taxes owing to the United States and to the several States by owners, buyers, and sellers of securities, and the value of collateral for bank loans.

(3) Frequently the prices of securities on such exchanges and markets are susceptible to manipulation and control, and the dissemination of such prices gives rise to excessive speculation, resulting in sudden and unreasonable fluctuations in the prices of securities which (a) cause alternately unreasonable expansion and unreasonable contraction of the volume of credit available for trade, transportation, and industry in interstate commerce, (b) hinder the proper appraisal of the value of securities and thus prevent a fair calculation of taxes owing to the United States and to the several States by owners, buyers, and sellers of securities, and (c) prevent the fair valuation of collateral for bank loans and/or obstruct the effective operation of the national banking system and Federal Reserve System.

(4) National emergencies, which produce widespread unemployment and the dislocation of trade, transportation, and industry, and which burden interstate commerce and adversely affect the general welfare, are precipitated, intensified, and prolonged by manipulation and sudden and unreasonable fluctuations of security prices and by excessive speculation on such exchanges and markets, and to meet such emergencies the Federal Government is put to such great expense as to burden the national credit.

Definitions and Application of Title

SEC. 3. (a) When used in this title, unless the context otherwise requires—

(1) The term "exchange" means any organization, association, or group of persons, whether incorporated or unincorporated, which constitutes, maintains, or provides a market place or facilities for bringing together purchasers and sellers of securities or for otherwise performing with respect to securities the functions commonly performed by a stock exchange as that term is generally understood, and includes the market place and the market facilities maintained by such exchange.

(2) The term "facility" when used with respect to an exchange includes its premises, tangible or intangible property whether on the premises or not, any right to the use of such premises or property or any service thereof for the purpose of effecting or reporting a transaction on an exchange (including, among other things, any system of communication to or from the exchange, by ticker or otherwise, maintained by or with the consent of the exchange), and any right of the exchange to the use of any property or service.

(3) The term "member" when used with respect to an exchange means any person who is permitted either to effect transactions on the exchange without the services of another person acting as broker, or to make use of the facilities of an exchange for transactions thereon without payment of a commission or fee or with the payment of a commission or fee which is less than that charged the general public, and includes any firm transacting a business as broker or dealer of which a member is a partner, and any partner of any such firm.

(4) The term "broker" means any person engaged in the business of effecting transactions in securities for the account of others, but does not include a bank.

(5) The term "dealer" means any person engaged in the business of buying and selling securities for his own account, through a broker or otherwise, but does not include a bank, or any person insofar as he buys or sells securities for his own account, either individually or in some fiduciary capacity, but not as a part of a regular business.

(6) The term "bank" means (A) a banking institution organized under the laws of the United States, (B) a member bank of the Federal Reserve System, (C) any other banking institution, whether incorporated or not, doing business under the laws of any State or of the United States, a substantial portion of the business of which consists of receiving deposits or exercising fiduciary powers similar to those permitted to national banks under section 11(k) of the Federal Reserve Act, as amended, and which is supervised and examined by State or Federal authority having supervision over banks, and which is not operated for the purpose of evading the provisions of this title, and (D) a receiver, conservator, or other liquidating agent of any institution or firm included in clauses (A), (B), or (C) of this paragraph.

(7) The term "director" means any director of a corporation or any person performing similar functions with respect to any organization, whether incorporated or unincorporated.

(8) The term "issuer" means any person who issues or proposes to issue any security; except that with respect to certificates of deposit for securities, voting-trust certificates, or collateral-trust certificates, or with respect to certificates of interest or shares in an unincorporated investment trust not having a board of directors or of the fixed, restricted management, or unit type, the term "issuer" means the person or persons performing the acts and assuming the duties of depositor or manager pursuant to the provisions of the trust or other agreement or instrument under which such securities are issued; and except that with respect to equipment-trust certificates or like securities, the term "issuer" means the person by whom the equipment or property is, or is to be, used.

(9) The term "person" means an individual, a corporation, a partnership, an association, a joint-stock company, a business trust, or an unincorporated organization.

(10) The term "security" means any note, stock, treasury stock, bond, debenture, certificate of interest or participation in any profit-sharing agreement or in any oil, gas, or other mineral royalty or lease, any collateral-trust certificate, preorganization certificate or subscription, transferable share, investment contract, voting-trust

certificate, certificate of deposit, for a security, or in general, any instrument commonly known as a "security"; or any certificate of interest or participation in, temporary or interim certificate for, receipt for, or warrant or right to subscribe to or purchase, any of the foregoing; but shall not include currency or any note, draft, bill of exchange, or banker's acceptance which has a maturity at the time of issuance of not exceeding nine months, exclusive of days of grace, or any renewal thereof the maturity of which is likewise limited.

(11) The term "equity security" means any stock or similar security; or any security convertible, with or without consideration, into such a security, or carrying any warrant or right to subscribe to or purchase such a security; or any such warrant or right; or any other security which the Commission shall deem to be of similar nature and consider necessary or appropriate, by such rules and regulations as it may prescribe in the public interest or for the protection of investors, to treat as an equity security.

(12) The term "exempted security" or "exempted securities" shall include securities which are direct obligations of or obligations guaranteed as to principal or interest by the United States; such securities issued or guaranteed by corporations in which the United States has a direct or indirect interest as shall be designated for exemption by the Secretary of the Treasury as necessary or appropriate in the public interest or for the protection of investors; securities which are direct obligations of or obligations guaranteed as to principal or interest by a State or any political subdivision thereof or any agency or instrumentality of a State or any political subdivision thereof or any municipal corporate instrumentality of one or more States; and such other securities (which may include, among others, unregistered securities, the market in which is predominantly intrastate) as the Commission may, by such rules and regulations as it deems necessary or appropriate in the public interest or for the protection of investors, either unconditionally or upon specified terms and conditions or for stated periods, exempt from the operation of any one or more provisions of this title which by their terms do not apply to an "exempted security" or to "exempted securities."

(13) The terms "buy" and "purchase" each include any contract to buy, purchase, or otherwise acquire.

(14) The terms "sale" and "sell" each include any contract to sell or otherwise dispose of.

(15) The term "Commission" means the Securities and Exchange Commission established by section 4 of this title.

(16) The term "State" means any State of the United States, the District of Columbia, Alaska, Hawaii, Puerto Rico, the Philippine Islands, the Canal Zone, the Virgin Islands, or any other possession of the United States.

(17) The term "interstate commerce" means trade, commerce, transportation, or communication among the several States, or between any foreign country and any State, or between any State and any place or ship outside thereof.

(b) The Commission and the Federal Reserve Board, as to matters within their respective jurisdictions, shall have power by rules and regulations to define technical, trade, and accounting terms used in this title insofar as such definitions are not inconsistent with the provisions of this title.

(c) No provision of this title shall apply to, or be deemed to include, any executive department or independent establishment of the United States, or any lending agency which is wholly owned, directly or indirectly, by the United States, or any officer, agent, or employee of any such department, establishment, or agency, acting in the course of his official duty as such, unless such provision makes specific reference to such department, establishment, or agency.

Securities and Exchange Commission

SEC. 4 (a) There is hereby established a Securities and Exchange Commission (hereinafter referred to as the "Commission") to be composed of five commissioners to be appointed by the President by and with the advice and consent of the Senate. Not more than three of such commissioners shall be members of the same political party, and in making appointments members of different political parties shall be appointed alternately as nearly as may be practicable. No commissioner shall engage in any other business, vocation, or employment than that of serving as commissioner, nor shall any commissioner participate, directly or indirectly, in any stock-market operations or transactions of a character subject to regulation by the Commission pursuant to this title. Each commissioner shall receive a salary at the rate of $10,000 a year and shall hold office for a term of five years, except that (1) any commissioner appointed to fill a vacancy occurring prior to the expiration of the term for which his predecessor was appointed, shall be appointed for the remainder of such term, and (2) the terms of office of the commissioners first taking office after the date of enactment of this title shall expire, as designated by the President at the time of nomination, one at the end of one year, one at the end of two years, one at the end of three years, one at the end of four years, and one at the end of five years, after the date of enactment of this title.

(b) The Commission is authorized to appoint and fix the compensation of such officers, attorneys, examiners, and other experts as may be necessary for carrying out its functions under this Act, without regard to the provisions of other laws applicable to the employment and compensation of officers and employees of the United States, and the Commission may, subject to the civil-service laws, appoint such other officers and employees as are necessary in the execution of its functions and fix their salaries in accordance with the Classification Act of 1923, as amended.

Transactions on Unregistered Exchanges

SEC. 5. It shall be unlawful for any broker, dealer, or exchange, directly or indirectly, to make use of the mails or any means or instrumentality of interstate commerce for the purpose of using any facility of an exchange within or subject to the jurisdiction of the United States to effect any transaction in a security, or to report any such transaction, unless such exchange (1) is registered as a national securities exchange under section 6 of this title, or (2) is exempted from such registration upon application by the exchange because, in the opinion of the Commission, by reason of the limited volume of transactions effected on such exchange, it is not practicable and not necessary or appropriate in the public interest or for the protection of investors to require such registration.

Registration of National Securities Exchanges

SEC. 6. (a) Any exchange may be registered with the Commission as a national securities exchange under the terms and conditions hereinafter provided in this section, by filing a registration statement in such form as the Commission may prescribe, containing the agreements, setting forth the information, and accompanied by the documents, below specified:

(1) An agreement (which shall not be construed as a waiver of any constitutional right or any right to contest the validity of any rule or regulation) to comply, and to enforce so far as is within its powers compliance by its members, with the provisions of this title, and any amendment thereto and any rule or regulation made or to be made thereunder;

(2) Such data as to its organization, rules of procedure, and membership, and such other information as the Commission may by rules and regulations require as being necessary or appropriate in the public interest or for the protection of investors;

(3) Copies of its constitution, articles of incorporation with all amendments thereto, and of its existing bylaws or rules or instruments corresponding thereto, whatever the name, which are hereinafter collectively referred to as the "rules of the exchange"; and

(4) An agreement to furnish to the Commission copies of any amendments to the rules of the exchange forthwith upon their adoption.

(b) No registration shall be granted or remain in force unless the rules of the exchange include provision for the expulsion, suspension, or disciplining of a member for conduct or proceeding inconsistent with just and equitable principles of trade, and declare that the willful violation of any provisions of this title or any rule or regulation thereunder shall be considered conduct or proceeding inconsistent with just and equitable principles of trade.

(c) Nothing in this title shall be construed to prevent any exchange from adopting and enforcing any rule not inconsistent with this title and the rules and regulations thereunder and the applicable laws of the State in which it is located.

(d) If it appears to the Commission that the exchange applying for registration is so organized as to be able to comply with the provisions of this title and the rules and regulations thereunder and that the rules of the exchange are just and adequate to insure fair dealing and to protect investors, the Commission shall cause such exchange to be registered as a national securities exchange.

(e) Within thirty days after the filing of the application, the Commission shall enter an order either granting or, after appropriate notice and opportunity for hearing, denying registration as a national securities exchange, unless the exchange applying for registration shall withdraw its application or consent to the Commission's deferring action on its application for a stated longer period after the date of filing. The filing with the Commission of an application for registration by an exchange shall be deemed to have taken place upon the receipt thereof. Amendments to an application may be made upon such terms as the Commission may prescribe.

(f) An exchange may, upon appropriate application in accordance with the rules and regulations of the Commission, and upon such terms as the Commission may deem necessary for the protection of investors, withdraw its registration.

Margin Requirements

SEC. 7. (a) For the purpose of preventing the excessive use of credit for the purchase or carrying of securities, the Federal Reserve Board shall, prior to the effective date of this section and from time to time thereafter, prescribe rules and regulations with respect to the amount of credit that may be initially extended and subsequently maintained on any security (other than an exempted security) registered on a national securities exchange. For the initial extension of credit, such rules and regulations shall be based upon the following standard: An amount not greater than whichever is the higher of—

(1) 55 per centum of the current market price of the security, or

(2) 100 per centum of the lowest market price of the security during the preceding thirty-six calendar months, but not more than 75 per centum of the current market price.

Such rules and regulations may make appropriate provision with respect to the carrying of undermargined accounts for limited periods and under specified conditions; the withdrawal of funds or securities; the substitution or additional purchases of securities; the transfer of accounts from one lender to another; special or different margin requirements for delayed deliveries, short sales, arbitrage transactions, and securities to which paragraph (2) of this subsection does not apply; the bases and the methods to be used in calculating loans, and margins and market prices; and similar administrative adjustments and details. For the purposes of paragraph (2) of this subsection, until July 1, 1936, the lowest price at which a security has sold on or after July 1, 1933, shall be considered as the lowest price at which such security has sold during the preceding thirty-six calendar months.

(b) Notwithstanding the provisions of subsection (a) of this section, the Federal Reserve Board, may, from time to time, with respect to all or specified securities or transactions, or classes of securities, or classes of transactions, by such rules and regulations (1) prescribe such lower margin requirements for the initial extension or maintenance of credit as it deems necessary or appropriate for the accommodation of commerce and industry, having due regard to the general credit situation of the country, and (2) prescribe such higher margin requirements for the initial extension or maintenance of credit as it may deem necessary or appropriate to prevent the excessive use of credit to finance transactions in securities.

(c) It shall be unlawful for any member of a national securities exchange or any broker or dealer who transacts a business in securities through the medium of any such member, directly or indirectly to extend or maintain credit or arrange for the extension or maintenance of credit to or for any customer—

(1) On any security (other than an exempted security) registered on a national securities exchange, in contravention of the rules and regulations which the Federal Reserve Board shall prescribe under subsections (a) and (b) of this section.

(2) Without collateral or on any collateral other than exempted securities and/or securities registered upon a national securities exchange, except in accordance with such rules and regulations as the Federal Reserve Board may prescribe (A) to permit under specified conditions and for a limited period any such member, broker, or dealer to maintain a credit initially extended in conformity with the rules and regulations of the Federal Reserve Board, and (B) to permit the extension of maintenance of credit in cases where the extension or maintenance of credit is not for the purpose of purchasing or carrying securities or of evading or circumventing the provisions of paragraph (1) of this subsection.

(d) It shall be unlawful for any person not subject to subsection (c) to extend or maintain credit or to arrange for the extension or maintenance of credit for the purpose of purchasing or carrying any security registered on a national securities exchange, in contravention of such rules and regulations as the Federal Reserve Board shall prescribe to prevent the excessive use of credit for the purchasing or carrying of or trading in securities in circumvention of the other provisions of this section. Such rules and regulations may impose upon all loans made for the purpose of purchasing or carrying securities registered on national securities exchanges limitations similar to those imposed upon members, brokers, or dealers by subsection (c) of this section and the rules and regulations thereunder. This subsection and the rules and regulations thereunder shall not apply (A) to a loan made by a person not in the ordinary course of his business, (B) to a loan on an exempted security, (C) to a loan to a dealer to aid in the financing of the distribution of securities to customers not through the medium of a national securities exchange, (D) to a loan by a bank on a security other than an equity security, or (E) to such other loans as the Federal Reserve Board shall, by such rules and regulations as it may deem necessary or appropriate in the public interest or for the protection of investors, exempt, either unconditionally or upon specified terms and conditions or for stated periods, from the operation of this subsection and the rules and regulations thereunder.

(e) The provisions of this section or the rules and regulations thereunder shall not apply on or before July 1, 1937, to any loan or extension of credit made prior to the enactment of this title or to the maintenance, renewal, or extension of any such loan or credit, except to the extent that the Federal Reserve Board may by rules and regulations prescribe as necessary to prevent the circumvention of the provisions of this section or the rules and regulations thereunder by means of withdrawals of funds or securities, substitutions of securities, or additional purchases or by any other device.

Restrictions on Borrowing by Members, Brokers, and Dealers

SEC. 8. It shall be unlawful for any member of a national securities exchange, or any broker or dealer who transacts a business in securities through the medium of any such member, directly or indirectly—

(a) To borrow in the ordinary course of business as a broker or dealer on any security (other than an exempted security) registered on a national securities exchange except (1) from or through a member bank of the Federal Reserve System, (2) from any nonmember bank which shall have filed with the Federal Reserve Board an agreement, which is still in force and which is in the form prescribed by the Board, undertaking to comply with all the provisions of this Act, the Federal Reserve Act, as amended, and the Banking Act of 1933, which are applicable to member banks and which relate to the use of credit to finance transactions in securities, and with such rules and regulations as may be prescribed pursuant to such provisions of law or for the purpose of preventing evasions thereof, or (3) in accordance with such rules and regulations as the Federal Reserve Board may prescribe to permit loans between such members and/or brokers and/or dealers, or to permit loans to meet emergency needs. Any such agreement filed with the Federal Reserve Board shall be subject to termination at any time by order of the Board, after appropriate notice and opportunity for hearing, because of any failure by such bank to comply with the provisions thereof or with such provisions of law or rules or regulations; and, for any willful violation of such agreement, such bank shall be subject to the penalties provided for violations of rules and regulations prescribed under this title. The provisions of sections 21 and 25 of this title shall apply in the case of any such proceeding or order of the Federal Reserve Board in the same manner as such provisions apply in the case of proceedings and orders of the Commission.

(b) To permit in the ordinary course of business as a broker his aggregate indebtedness to all other persons, including customers' credit balances (but excluding indebtedness secured by exempted securities), to exceed such percentage of the net capital (exclusive of fixed assets and value of exchange membership) employed in the business, but not exceeding in any case 2,000 per centum, as the Commission may by rules and regulations prescribe as necessary or appropriate in the public interest or for the protection of investors.

(c) In contravention of such rules and regulations as the Commission shall prescribe for the protection of investors to hypothecate or arrange for the hypothecation of any securities carried for the account of any customer under circumstances (1) that will permit the commingling of his securities without his written consent with the securities of any other customer, (2) that will permit such securities to be commingled with the securities of any person other than a bona fide customer, or (3) that will permit such securities to be hypothecated, or subjected to any lien or claim of the pledgee, for a sum in excess of the aggregate indebtedness of such customers in respect of such securities.

(d) To lend or arrange for the lending of any securities carried for the account of any customer without the written consent of such customer.

Prohibition Against Manipulation of Security Prices

SEC. 9. (a) It shall be unlawful for any person, directly or indirectly, by the use of the mails or any means or instrumentality of interstate commerce, or of any facility of any national securities exchange, or for any member of a national securities exchange—

(1) For the purpose of creating a false or misleading appearance of active trading in any security registered on a national securities exchange, or a false or misleading appearance with respect to the market for any such security, (A) to effect any transaction in such security which involves no change in the beneficial ownership thereof, or (B) to enter an order or orders for the purchase of such security with the knowledge that an order or orders of substantially the same size, at substantially the same time, and at substantially the same price, for the sale of any such security, has been or will be entered by or for the same or different parties, or (C) to enter any order or orders for the sale of any such security with the knowledge that an order or orders of substantially the same size, at substantially the same time, and at substantially the same price, for the purchase of such security, has been or will be entered by or for the same or different parties.

(2) To effect, alone or with one or more other persons, a series of transactions in any security registered on a national securities exchange creating actual or apparent active trading in such security or raising or depressing the price of such security, for the purpose of inducing the purchase or sale of such security by others.

(3) If a dealer or broker, or other person selling or offering for sale or puchasing or offering to purchase the security, to induce the purchase or sale of any security registered on a national securities exchange by the circulation or dissemination in the ordinary course of business of information to the effect that the price of any such security will or is likely to rise or fall because of market operations of any one or more persons conducted for the purpose of raising or depressing the prices of such security.

(4) If a dealer or broker, or other person selling or offering for sale or purchasing or offering to purchase the security, to make, regarding any security registered on a national securities exchange, for the purpose of inducing the purchase or sale of such security, any statement which was at the time and in the light of the circumstances under which it was made, false or misleading with respect to any material fact, and which he knew or had reasonable ground to believe was so false or misleading.

(5) For a consideration, received directly or indirectly from a dealer or broker, or other person selling or offering for sale or purchasing or offering to purchase the security, to induce the purchase or sale of any security registered on a national securities exchange by the circulation or dissemination of information to the effect that the price of any such security will or is likely to rise or fall because of the market operations of any one or more persons conducted for the purpose of raising or depressing the price of such security.

(6) To effect either alone or with one or more other persons any series of transactions for the purchase and/or sale of any security registered on a national securities exchange for the purpose of pegging, fixing, or stabilizing the price of such security in contravention of such rules and regulations as the Commission

may prescribe as necessary or appropriate in the public interest or for the protection of investors.

(b) It shall be unlawful for any person to effect, by use of any facility of a national securities exchange, in contravention of such rules and regulations as the Commission may prescribe as necessary or appropriate in the public interest or for the protection of investors—

(1) any transaction in connection with any security whereby any party to such transaction acquires any put, call, straddle, or other option or privilege of buying the security from or selling the security to another without being bound to do so; or

(2) any transaction in connection with any security with relation to which he has, directly or indirectly, any interest in any such put, call, straddle, option, or privilege; or

(3) any transaction in any security for the account of any person who he has reason to believe has, and who actually has, directly or indirectly, any interest in any such put, call, straddle, option, or privilege with relation to such security.

(c) It shall be unlawful for any member of a national securities exchange directly or indirectly to endorse or guarantee the performance of any put, call, straddle, option, or privilege in relation to any security registered on a national securities exchange, in contravention of such rules and regulations as the Commission may prescribe as necessary or appropriate in the public interest or for the protection of investors.

(d) The terms "put," "call," "straddle," "option," or "Privilege" as used in this section shall not include any registered warrant, right, or convertible security.

(e) Any person who willfully participates in any act or transaction in violation of subsection (a), (b), or (c) of this section, shall be liable to any person who shall purchase or sell any security at a price which was affected by such act or transaction, and the person so injured may sue in law or in equity in any court of competent jurisdiction to recover the damages sustained as a result of any such act or transaction. In any such suit the court may, in its discretion, require an undertaking for the payment of the costs of such suit, and assess reasonable costs, including reasonable attorneys' fees, against either party litigant. Every person who becomes liable to make any payment under this subsection may recover contribution as in cases of contract from any person who, if joined in the original suit, would have been liable to make the same payment. No action shall be maintained to enforce any liability created under this section, unless brought within one year after the discovery of the facts constituting the violation and within three years after such violation.

(f) The provisions of this section shall not apply to an exempted security.

Regulation of the Use of Manipulative and Deceptive Devices

SEC. 10. It shall be unlawful for any person, directly or indirectly, by the use of any means or instrumentality of interstate commerce or of the mails, or of any facility of any national securities exchange—

(a) To effect a short sale, or to use or employ any stop-loss order in connection with the purchase or sale, of any security registered on a national securities exchange, in contravention of such rules and regulations as the Commission may prescribe as necessary or appropriate in the public interest or for the protection of investors.

(b) To use or employ, in connection with the purchase or sale of any security registered on a national securities exchange or any security not so registered, any manipulative or deceptive device or contrivance in contravention of such rules and regulations as the Commission may prescribe as necessary or appropriate in the public interest or for the protection of investors.

Segregation and Limitation of Functions of Members, Brokers, and Dealers

SEC. 11. (a) The Commission shall prescribe such rules and regulations as it deems necessary or appropriate in the public interest or for the protection of investors, (1) to regulate or prevent floor trading by members of national securities exchanges, directly or indirectly for their own account or for discretionary accounts, and (2) to prevent such excessive trading on the exchange but off the floor by members, directly or indirectly for their own account, as the Commission may deem detrimental to the maintenance of a fair and orderly market. It shall be unlawful for a member to effect any transaction in a security in contravention of such rules and regulations, but such rules and regulations may make such exemptions for arbitrage transactions, for transactions in exempted securities, and, within the limitations of subsection (b) of this section, for transactions by odd-lot dealers and specialists, as the Commission may deem necessary or appropriate in the public interest or for the protection of investors.

(b) When not in contravention of such rules and regulations as the Commission may prescribe as necessary or appropriate in the public interest or for the protection of investors, the rules of a national securities exchange may permit (1) a member to be registered as an odd-lot dealer and as such to buy and sell for his own account so far as may be reasonably necessary to carry on such odd-lot transactions, and/or (2) a member to be registered as a specialist. If under the rules and regulations of the Commission a specialist is permitted to act as a dealer, or is limited to acting as a dealer, such rules and regulations shall restrict his dealings so far as practicable to those reasonably necessary to permit him to maintain a fair and orderly market, and/or to those necessary to permit him to act as an odd-lot dealer if the rules of the exchange permit him to act as an odd-lot dealer. It shall be unlawful for a specialist or an official of the exchange to disclose information in regard to orders placed with such specialist which is not available to all members of the exchange, to any person other than an official of the exchange, a representative of the Commission, or a specialist who may be acting for such specialist; but the Commission shall have power to require disclosure to all members of the exchange of all orders placed with specialists, under such rules and regulations as the Commission may prescribe as necessary or appropriate in the public interest or for the protection of investors. It shall also be unlawful for a specialist acting as a broker to effect on the exchange any transaction except upon a market or limited price order.

(c) If because of the limited volume of transactions effected on an exchange, it is in the opinion of the Commission impracticable and not necessary or appropriate in the public interest or for the protection of investors to apply any of the foregoing provisions of this section or the rules and regulations thereunder, the Commission shall have power, upon application of the exchange and on a showing that the rules of such exchange are otherwise adequate for the protection of investors, to exempt such exchange and its members from any such provision or rules and regulations.

(d) It shall be unlawful for a member of a national securities exchange who is both a dealer and a broker, or for any person who both as a broker and a dealer transacts a business in securities through the medium of a member or otherwise, to effect through the use of any facility of a national securities exchange or of the mails or of any means or instrumentality of interstate commerce, or otherwise in the case of a member, (1) any transaction in connection with which, directly or indirectly, he extends or maintains or arranges for the extension or maintenance of credit to or for a customer on any security (other than an exempted security) which was a part of a new issue in the distribution of which he participated as a member of a selling syndicate or group within six months prior to such transaction: *Provided*, That credit shall not be deemed extended by reason of a bona fide delayed delivery of any such security against full payment of the entire purchase price thereof upon such delivery within thirty-five days after such purchase, or (2) any transaction with respect to any security (other than an exempted security) unless, if the transaction is with a customer, he discloses to such customer in writing at or before the completion of the transaction whether he is acting as a dealer for his own account, as a broker for such customer, or as a broker for some other person.

(e) The Commission is directed to make a study of the feasibility and advisability of the complete segregation of the functions of dealer and broker, and to report the results of its study and its recommendations to the Congress on or before January 3, 1936.

Registration Requirements for Securities

SEC. 12. (a) It shall be unlawful for any member, broker, or dealer to effect any transaction in any security (other than an exempted security) on a national securities exchange unless a registration is effective as to such security for such exchange in accordance with the provisions of this title and the rules and regulations thereunder.

(b) A security may be registered on a national securities exchange by the issuer filing an application with the exchange (and filing with the Commission such duplicate originals thereof as the Commission may require), which application shall contain—

(1) Such information, in such detail, as to the issuer and any person directly or indirectly controlling or controlled by, or under direct or indirect common control with, the issuer, and any guarantor of the security as to principal or interest or both, as

the Commission may by rules and regulations require, as necessary or appropriate in the public interest or for the protection of investors, in respect of the following:

(A)   the organization, financial structure and nature of the business;

(B)   the terms, position, rights, and privileges of the different classes of securities outstanding;

(C)   the terms on which their securities are to be, and during the preceding three years have been, offered to the public or otherwise;

(D)   the directors, officers, and underwriters, and each security holder of record holding more than 10 per centum of any class of any equity security of the issuer (other than an exempted security), their remuneration and their interests in the securities of, and their material contracts with, the issuer and any person directly or indirectly controlling or controlled by, or under direct or indirect common control with, the issuer;

(E)   remuneration to others than directors and officers exceeding $20,000 per annum;

(F)   bonus and profit-sharing arrangements;

(G)   management and service contracts;

(H)   options existing or to be created in respect of their securities;

(I)   balance sheets for not more than the three preceding fiscal years, certified if required by the rules and regulations of the Commission by independent public accountants;

(J)   profit and loss statements for not more than the three preceding fiscal years, certified if required by the rules and regulations of the Commission by independent public accountants; and

(K)   any further financial statements which the Commission may deem necessary or appropriate for the protection of investors.

(2) Such copies of articles of incorporation, bylaws, trust indentures, or corresponding documents by whatever name known, underwriting arrangements, and other similar documents of, and voting trust agreements with respect to, the issuer and any person directly or indirectly controlling or controlled by, or under direct or indirect common control with, the issuer as the Commission may require as necessary or appropriate for the proper protection of investors and to insure fair dealing in the security.

(c) If in the judgment of the Commission any information required under subsection (b) is inapplicable to any specified class or classes of issuers, the Commission shall require in lieu thereof the submission of such other information of comparable character as it may deem applicable to such class of issuers.

(d) If the exchange authorities certify to the Commission that the security has been approved by the exchange for listing and registration, the registration shall become effective thirty days after the receipt of such certification by the Commission or within such shorter period of time as the Commission may determine. A security registered with a national securities exchange may be withdrawn or stricken from listing and registration in accordance with the rules of the exchange and, upon such terms as the Commission may deem necessary to impose for the protection of investors, upon application by the issuer or the exchange to the Commission; whereupon the issuer shall be relieved from further compliance with the provisions of this section and section 13 of this title and any rules or regulations under such sections as to the securities so withdrawn or stricken. An unissued security may be registered only in accordance with such rules and regulations as the Commission may prescribe as necessary or appropriate in the public interest or for the protection of investors. Such rules and regulations shall limit the registration of an unissued security to cases where such security is a right or the subject of a right to subscribe or otherwise acquire such security granted to holders of a previously registered security and where the primary purpose of such registration is to distribute such unissued security to such holders.

(e) Notwithstanding the foregoing provisions of this section, the Commission may by such rules and regulations as it deems necessary or appropriate in the public interest or for the protection of investors permit securities listed on any exchange at the time the registration of such exchange as a national securities exchange becomes effective, to be registered for a period ending not later than July 1, 1935, without complying with the provisions of this section.

(f) The Commission is directed to make a study of trading in unlisted securities upon exchanges and to report the results of its study and its recommendations to Congress on or before January 3, 1936. Notwithstanding the foregoing provisions of this section, the Commission may, by such rules and regulations as it deems necessary or appropriate for the protection of investors, prescribe terms and conditions under which, upon the application of any national securities exchange, such exchange (1) may continue until June 1, 1936, unlisted trading privileges to which a security had been admitted on such exchange prior to March 1, 1934, and for such purpose exempt such security and the issuer thereof from the provisions of this section and sections 13 and 16, or (2) may extend until July 1, 1935, unlisted trading privilege to any security registered on any other national securities exchange which security was listed on such other exchange on March 1, 1934. A security for which unlisted trading privileges are so continued shall be considered a "security registered on a national securities exchange" within the meaning of this title. The rules and regulations of the Commission relating to such unlisted trading privileges for securities shall require that quotations of transactions upon any national securities exchange shall clearly indicate the difference between fully listed securities and securities admitted to unlisted trading privileges only.

Periodical and Other Reports

SEC. 13. (a) Every issuer of a security registered on a national securities exchange shall file the information, documents, and reports below specified with the exchange (and shall file with the Commission such duplicate originals thereof as the Commission may require), in accordance with such rules and regulations as the Commission may prescribe as necessary or appropriate for the proper protection of investors and to insure fair dealing in the security—

(1) Such information and documents as the Commission may require to keep reasonably current the information and documents filed pursuant to section 12.

(2) Such annual reports, certified if required by the rules and regulations of the Commission by independent public accountants, and such quarterly reports, as the Commission may prescribe.

(b) The Commission may prescribe, in regard to reports made pursuant to this title, the form or forms in which the required information shall be set forth, the items or details to be shown in the balance sheet and the earning statement, and the methods to be followed in the preparation of reports, in the appraisal or valuation of assets and liabilities, in the determination of depreciation and depletion, in the differentiation of recurring and nonrecurring income, in the differentiation of investment and operating income, and in the preparation, where the Commission deems it necessary or desirable, of separate and/or consolidated balance sheets or income accounts of any person directly or indirectly controlling or controlled by the issuer, or any person under direct or indirect common control with the issuer; but in the case of the reports of any person whose methods of accounting are prescribed under the provisions of any law of the United States, or any rule or regulation thereunder, the rules and regulations of the Commission with respect to reports shall not be inconsistent with the requirements imposed by such law or rule or regulation in respect of the same subject matter, and, in the case of carriers subject to the provisions of section 20 of the Interstate Commerce Act, as amended, or carriers required pursuant to any other Act of Congress to make reports of the same general character as those required under such section 20, shall permit such carriers to file with the Commission and the exchange duplicate copies of the reports and other documents filed with the Interstate Commerce Commission, or with the governmental authority administering such other Act of Congress, in lieu of the reports, information and documents required under this section and section 12 in respect of the same subject matter.

(c) If in the judgment of the Commission any report required under subsection (a) is inapplicable to any specified class or classes of issuers, the Commission shall require in lieu thereof of the submission of such reports of comparable character as it may deem applicable to such class or classes of issuers.

Proxies

SEC. 14. (a) It shall be unlawful for any person, by the use of the mails or by any means or instrumentality of interstate commerce or of any facility of any national securities exchange or otherwise to solicit or to permit the use of his name to solicit any proxy or consent or authorization in respect of any security (other than an exempted security) registered on any national securities exchange in contravention of such rules and regulations as the Commission may prescribe as necessary or appropriate in the public interest or for the protection of investors.

(b) It shall be unlawful for any member of a national securities exchange or any broker or dealer who transacts a business in securities through the medium of any such member to give a proxy, consent, or authorization in respect of any security registered on a national securities exchange and carried for the account of a customer in contravention of such rules and regulations as the Commission may prescribe as necessary or appropriate in the public interest or for the protection of investors.

Over-the-Counter Markets

SEC. 15. It shall be unlawful, in contravention of such rules and regulations as the Commission may prescribe as necessary or appropriate in the public interest and to insure to investors protection comparable to that provided by and under authority of this title in the case of national securities exchanges, (1) for any broker or dealer, singly or with any other person or persons, to make use of the mails or any means or instrumentality of interstate commerce for the purpose of making or creating, or enabling another to make or create, a market, otherwise than on a national securities exchange, for both the purchase and sale of any security (other than an exempted security or commercial paper, bankers' acceptances, or commercial bills, or unregistered securities the market in which is predominantly intrastate and which have not previously been registered or listed), or (2) for any broker or dealer to use any facility of any such market. Such rules and regulations may provide for the regulation of all transactions by brokers and dealers on any such market, for the registration with the Commission of dealers and/or brokers making or creating such a market, and for the registration of the securities for which they make or create a market and may make special provision with respect to securities or specified classes thereof listed, or entitled to unlisted trading privileges, upon any exchange on the date of the enactment of this title, which securities are not registered under the provisions of section 12 of this title.

Directors, Officers, and Principal Stockholders

SEC. 16. (a) Every person who is directly or indirectly the beneficial owner of more than 10 per centum of any class of any equity security (other than an exempted security) which is registered on a national securities exchange, or who is a director of an officer of the issuer of such security, shall file, at the time of the registration of such security or within ten days after he becomes such beneficial owner, director, or officer, a statement with the exchange (and a duplicate original thereof with the Commission) of the amount of all equity securities of such issuer of which he is the beneficial owner, and within ten days after the close of each calendar month thereafter, if there has been any change in such ownership during such month, shall file with the exchange a statement (and a duplicate original thereof with the Commission) indicating his ownership at the close of the calendar month and such changes in his ownership as have occurred during such calendar month.

(b) For the purpose of preventing the unfair use of information which may have been obtained by such beneficial owner, director, or officer by reason of his relationship to the issuer, any profit realized by him from any purchase and sale, or any sale and purchase, of any equity security of such issuer (other than an exempted security) within any period of less than six months, unless such security was acquired in good faith in connection with a debt previously contracted, shall inure to and be recoverable by the issuer, irrespective of any intention on the part of such beneficial owner, director, or officer in entering into such transaction of holding the security purchased or of not repurchasing the security sold for a period exceeding six months. Suit to recover such profit may be instituted at law or in equity in any court of competent jurisdiction by the issuer, or by the owner of any security of the issuer in the name and in behalf of the issuer if the issuer shall fail or refuse to bring such suit within sixty days after request or shall fail diligently to prosecute the same thereafter; but no such suit shall be brought more than two years after the date such profit was realized. This subsection shall not be construed to cover any transaction where such beneficial owner was not such both at the time of the purchase and sale, or the sale and purchase, of the security involved, or any transaction or transactions which the Commission by rules and regulations may exempt as not comprehended within the purpose of this subsection.

(c) It shall be unlawful for any such beneficial owner, director, or officer, directly or indirectly, to sell any equity security of such issuer (other than an exempted security), if the person selling the security or his principal (1) does not own the security sold, or (2) if owning the security, does not deliver it against such sale within twenty days thereafter, or does not within five days after such sale deposit it in the mails or other usual channels of transportation; but no person shall be deemed to have violated this subsection if he proves that notwithstanding the exercise of good faith he was unable to make such delivery or deposit within such time, or that to do so would cause undue inconvenience or expense.

(d) The provisions of this section shall not apply to foreign or domestic arbitrage transactions unless made in contravention of such rules and regulations as the Commission may adopt in order to carry out the purposes of this section.

Accounts and Records, Reports, Examinations of Exchanges, Members, and Others

SEC. 17. (a) Every national securities exchange, every member thereof, every broker or dealer who transacts a business in securities through the medium of any such member, and every broker or dealer making or creating a market for both the purchase and sale of securities through the use of the mails or of any means or instrumentality of interstate commerce, shall make, keep, and preserve for such periods, such accounts, correspondence, memoranda, papers, books, and other records, and make such reports, as the Commission by its rules and regulations may prescribe as necessary or appropriate in the public interest or for the protection of investors. Such accounts, correspondence, memoranda, papers, books, and other records shall be subject at any time or from time to time to such reasonable periodic, special, or other examinations by examiners or other representatives of the Commission as the Commission may deem necessary or appropriate in the public interest or for the protection of investors.

(b) Any broker, dealer, or other person extending credit who is subject to the rules and regulations prescribed by the Federal Reserve Board pursuant to this title shall make such reports to the Board as it may require as necessary or appropriate to enable it to perform the functions conferred upon it by this title. If any such broker, dealer, or other person shall fail to make any such report or fail to furnish full information therein, or, if in the judgment of the Board it is otherwise necessary, such broker, dealer, or other person shall permit such inspections to be made by the Board with respect to the business operations of such broker, dealer, or other person as the Board may deem necessary to enable it to obtain the required information.

Liability for Misleading Statements

SEC. 18. (a) Any person who shall make or cause to be made any statement in any application, report, or document filed pursuant to this title or any rule or regulation thereunder, which statement was at the time and in the light of the circumstances under which it was made false or misleading with respect to any material fact, shall be liable to any person (not knowing that such statement was false or misleading) who, in reliance upon such statement, shall have purchased or sold a security at a price which was affected by such statement, for damages caused by such reliance, unless the person sued shall prove that he acted in good faith and had no knowledge that such statement was false or misleading. A person seeking to enforce such liability may sue at law or in equity in any court of competent jurisdiction. In any such suit the court may, in its discretion, require an undertaking for the payment of the costs of such suit, and assess reasonable costs, including reasonable attorneys' fees, against either party litigant.

(b) Every person who becomes liable to make payment under this section may recover contribution as in cases of contract from any person who, if joined in the original suit, would have been liable to make the same payment.

(c) No action shall be maintained to enforce any liability created under this section unless brought within one year after the discovery of the facts constituting the cause of action and within three years after such cause of action accrued.

Powers with Respect to Exchanges and Securities

SEC. 19. (a) The Commission is authorized, if in its opinion such action is necessary or appropriate for the protection of investors—

(1) After appropriate notice and opportunity for hearing, by order to suspend for a period not exceeding twelve months or to withdraw the registration of a national

securities exchange if the Commission finds that such exchange has violated any provision of this title or of the rules and regulations thereunder or has failed to enforce, so far as is within its power, compliance therewith by a member or by an issuer of a security registered thereon.

(2) After appropriate notice and opportunity for hearing, by order to deny, to suspend the effective date of, to suspend for a period not exceeding twelve months, or to withdraw, the registration of a security if the Commission finds that the issuer of such security has failed to comply with any provision of this title or the rules and regulations thereunder.

(3) After appropriate notice and opportunity for hearing, by order to suspend for a period not exceeding twelve months or to expel from a national securities exchange any member or officer thereof whom the Commission finds has violated any provision of this title or the rules and regulations thereunder, or has effected any transaction for any other person who, he has reason to believe, is violating in respect of such transaction any provision of this title or the rules and regulations thereunder.

(4) And if in its opinion the public interest so requires, summarily to suspend trading in any registered security on any national securities exchange for a period not exceeding ten days, or with the approval of the President, summarily to suspend all trading on any national securities exchange for a period not exceeding ninety days.

(b) The Commission is further authorized, if after making appropriate request in writing to a national securities exchange that such exchange effect on its own behalf specified changes in its rules and practices, and after appropriate notice and opportunity for hearing, the Commission determines that such exchange has not made the changes so requested, and that such changes are necessary or appropriate for the protection of investors or to insure fair dealing in securities traded in upon such exchange or to insure fair administration of such exchange, by rules or regulations or by order to alter or supplement the rules of such exchange (insofar as necessary or appropriate to effect such changes) in respect of such matters as (1) safeguards in respect of the financial responsibility of members and adequate provision against the evasion of financial responsibility through the use of corporate forms or special partnerships; (2) the limitation or prohibition of the registration or trading in any security within a specified period after the issuance or primary distribution thereof; (3) the listing or striking from listing of any security; (4) hours of trading; (5) the manner, method, and place of soliciting business; (6) fictitious or numbered accounts; (7) the time and method of making settlements, payments, and deliveries and of closing accounts; (8) the reporting of transactions on the exchange and upon tickers maintained by or with the consent of the exchange, including the method of reporting short sales, stopped sales, sales of securities of issuers in default, bankruptcy or receivership, and sales involving other special circumstances; (9) the fixing of reasonable rates of commission, interest, listing, and other charges; (10) minimum units of trading; (11) odd-lot purchases and sales; (12) minimum deposits on margin accounts; and (13) similar matters.

(c) The Commission is authorized and directed to make a study and investigation of the rules of national securities exchanges with respect to the classification of members, the methods of election of officers and committees to insure a fair representation of the membership, and the suspension, expulsion, and disciplining of members of such exchanges. The Commission shall report to the Congress on or before January 3, 1935, the results of its investigation, together with its recommendations.

Liabilities of Controlling Persons

SEC. 20. (a) Every person who, directly or indirectly, controls any person liable under any provision of this title or of any rule or regulation thereunder shall also be liable jointly and severally with and to the same extent as such controlled person to any person to whom such controlled person is liable, unless the controlling person acted in good faith and did not directly or indirectly induce the act or acts constituting the violation or cause of action.

(b) It shall be unlawful for any person, directly or indirectly, to do any act or thing which it would be unlawful for such person to do under the provisions of this title or any rule or regulation thereunder through or by means of any other person.

(c) It shall be unlawful for any director or officer of, or any owner of any of the securities issued by, any issuer of any security registered on a national securities exchange, without just cause to hinder, delay, or obstruct the making or filing of any document, report, or information, required to be filed under this title or any rule or regulation thereunder.

Investigations; Injunctions and Prosecution of Offenses

SEC. 21. (a) The Commission may, in its discretion, make such investigations as it deems necessary to determine whether any person has violated or is about to violate any provision of this title or any rule or regulation thereunder, and may require or permit any person to file with it a statement in writing, under oath or otherwise as the Commission shall determine, as to all the facts and circumstances concerning the matter to be investigated. The Commission is authorized, in its discretion, to publish information concerning any such violations, and to investigate any facts, conditions, practices, or matters which it may deem necessary or proper to aid in the enforcement of the provisions of this title, in the prescribing of rules and regulations thereunder, or in securing information to serve as a basis for recommending further legislation concerning the matters to which this title relates.

(b) For the purpose of any such investigation, or any other proceeding under this title, any member of the Commission or any officer designated by it is empowered to administer oaths and affirmations, subpena witnesses, compel their attendance, take evidence, and require the production of any books, papers, correspondence, memoranda, or other records which the Commission deems relevant or material to the inquiry. Such attendance of witnesses and the production of any such records may be required from any place in the United States or any State at any designated place of hearing.

(c) In case of contumacy by, or refusal to obey a subpena issued to, any person, the Commission may invoke the aid of any court of the United States within the jurisdiction of which such investigation or proceeding is carried on, or where such person resides or carries on business, in requiring the attendance and testimony of witnesses and the production of books, papers, correspondence, memoranda, and other records. And such court may issue an order requiring such person to appear before the Commission or member or officer designated by the Commission, there to produce records, if so ordered, or to give testimony touching the matter under investigation or in question; and any failure to obey such order of the court may be punished by such court as a contempt thereof. All process in any such case may be served in the judicial district whereof such person is an inhabitant or wherever he may be found. Any person who shall, without just cause, fail or refuse to attend and testify or to answer any lawful inquiry or to produce books, papers, correspondence, memoranda, and other records, if in his power so to do, in obedience to the subpena of the Commission, shall be guilty of a misdemeanor and, upon conviction, shall be subject to a fine of not more than $1,000 or to imprisonment for a term of not more than one year, or both.

(d) No person shall be excused from attending and testifying or from producing books, papers, contracts, agreements, and other records and documents before the Commission, or in obedience to the subpena of the Commission or any member thereof or any officer designated by it, or in any cause or proceeding instituted by the Commission, on the ground that the testimony or evidence, documentary or otherwise, required of him may tend to incriminate him or subject him to a penalty or forfeiture; but no individual shall be prosecuted or subject to any penalty or forfeiture for or on account of any transaction, matter, or thing concerning which he is compelled, after having claimed his privilege against self-incrimination, to testify or produce evidence, documentary or otherwise, except that such individual so testifying shall not be exempt from prosecution and punishment for perjury committed in so testifying.

(e) Whenever it shall appear to the Commission that any person is engaged or about to engage in any acts or practices which constitute or will constitute a violation of the provisions of this title, or of any rule or regulation thereunder, it may in its discretion bring an action in the proper district court of the United States, the Supreme Court of the District of Columbia, or the United States courts of any Territory or other place subject to the jurisdiction of the United States, to enjoin such acts or practices, and upon a proper showing a permanent or temporary injunction or restraining order shall be granted without bond. The Commission may transmit such evidence as may be available concerning such acts or practices to the Attorney General, who may, in his discretion, institute the necessary criminal proceedings under this title.

(f) Upon application of the Commission the district courts of the United States, the Supreme Court of the District of Columbia, and the United States courts of any Territory or other place subject to the jurisdiction of the United States, shall also have jurisdiction to issue writs of mandamus commanding any person to comply with the provisions of this title or any order of the Commission made in pursuance thereof.

Hearings by Commission

SEC. 22. Hearings may be public and may be held before the Commission, any member or members thereof, or any officer or officers of the Commission designated by it, and appropriate records thereof shall be kept.

Rules and Regulations; Annual Reports

SEC. 23. (a) The Commission and the Federal Reserve Board shall each have power to make such rules and regulations as may be necessary for the execution of the functions vested in them by this title, and may for such purpose classify issuers, securities, exchanges, and other persons or matters within their respective jurisdictions.

(b) The Commission and the Federal Reserve Board, respectively, shall include in their annual reports to Congress such information, data, and recommendation for further legislation as they may deem advisable with regard to matters within their respective jurisdictions under this title.

Information Filed with the Commission

SEC. 24. (a) Nothing in this title shall be construed to require, or to authorize the Commission to require, the revealing of trade secrets or processes in any application, report, or document filed with the Commission under this title.

(b) Any person filing any such application, report, or document may make written objection to the public disclosure of information contained therein, stating the grounds for such objection, and the Commission is authorized to hear objections in any such case where it deems it advisable. The Commission may, in such cases, make available to the public the information contained in any such application, report, or document only when in its judgment a disclosure of such information is in the public interest; and copies of information so made available may be furnished to any person at such reasonable charge and under such reasonable limitations as the Commission may prescribe.

(c) It shall be unlawful for any member, officer, or employee of the Commission to disclose to any person other than a member, officer, or employee of the Commission, or to use for personal benefit, any information contained in any application, report, or document filed with the Commission which is not made available to the public pursuant to subsection (b) of this section: *Provided,* That the Commission may make available to the Federal Reserve Board any information requested by the Board for the purpose of enabling it to perform its duties under this title.

Court Review of Orders

SEC. 25. (a) Any person aggrieved by an order issued by the Commission in a proceeding under this title to which such person is a party may obtain a review of such order in the Circuit Court of Appeals of the United States, within any circuit wherein such person resides or has his principal place of business, or in the Court of Appeals of the District of Columbia, by filing in such court, within sixty days after the entry of such order, a written petition praying that the order of the Commission be modified or set aside in whole or in part. A copy of such petition shall be forthwith served upon any member of the Commission, and thereupon the Commission shall certify and file in the court a transcript of the record upon which the order complained of was entered. Upon the filing of such transcript such court shall have exclusive jurisdiction to affirm, modify, and enforce or set aside such order, in whole or in part. No objection to the order of the Commission shall be considered by the court unless such objection shall have been urged before the Commission. The finding of the Commission as to the facts, if supported by substantial evidence, shall be conclusive. If either party shall apply to the court for leave to adduce additional evidence, and shall show to the satisfaction of the court that such additional evidence is material and that there were reasonable grounds for failure to ad-duce such evidence in the hearing before the Commission, the court may order such additional evidence to be taken before the Commission and to be adduced upon the hearing in such manner and upon such terms and conditions as to the court may seem proper. The Commission may modify its findings as to the facts, by reason of the additional evidence so taken, and it shall file such modified or new findings, which, if supported by substantial evidence, shall be conclusive, and its recommendation, if any, for the modification or setting aside of the original order. The judgment and decree of the court, affirming, modifying, and enforcing or setting aside, in whole or in part, any such order of the Commission, shall be final, subject to review by the Supreme Court of the United States upon certiorari or certification as provided in section 239 and 240 of the Judicial Code, as amended (U.S.C., title 28, secs. 346 and 347).

(b) The commencement of proceedings under subsection (a) shall not, unless specifically ordered by the court, operate as a stay of the Commission's order.

Unlawful Representations

SEC. 26. No action or failure to act by the Commission or the Federal Reserve Board, in the administration of this title shall be construed to mean that the particular authority has in any way passed upon the merits of, or given approval to, any security or any transaction or transactions therein, nor shall such action or failure to act with regard to any statement or report filed with or examined by such authority pursuant to this title or rules and regulations thereunder, be deemed a finding by such authority that such statement or report is true and accurate on its face or that it is not false or misleading. It shall be unlawful to make, or cause to be made, to any prospective purchaser or seller of a security any representation that any such action or failure to act by any such authority is to be so construed or has such effect.

Jurisdiction of Offenses and Suits

SEC. 27. The district courts of the United States, the Supreme Court of the District of Columbia, and the United States courts of any Territory or other place subject to the jurisdiction of the United States shall have exclusive jurisdiction of violations of this title or the rules and regulations thereunder, and of all suits in equity and actions at law brought to enforce any liability or duty created by this title or the rules and regulations thereunder. Any criminal proceeding may be brought in the district wherein any act or transaction constituting the violation occurred. Any suit or action to enforce any liability or duty created by this title or rules and regulations thereunder, or to enjoin any violation of such title or rules and regulations, may be brought in any such district or in the district wherein the defendant is found or is an inhabitant or transacts business, and process in such cases may be served in any other district of which the defendant is an inhabitant or wherever the defendant may be found. Judgments and decrees so rendered shall be subject to review as provided in sections 128 and 240 of the Judicial Code, as amended (U.S.C., title 28, secs. 225 and 347). No costs shall be assessed for or against the Commission in any proceeding under this title brought by or against it in the Supreme Court or such other courts.

Effect on Existing Law

SEC. 28. (a) The rights and remedies provided by this title shall be in addition to any and all other rights and remedies that may exist at law or in equity; but no person permitted to maintain a suit for damages under the provisions of this title shall recover, through satisfaction of judgment in one or more actions, a total amount in excess of his actual damages on account of the act complained of. Nothing in this title shall affect the jurisdiction of the securities commission (or any agency or officer performing like functions) of any State over any security or any person insofar as it does not conflict with the provisions of this title or the rules and regulations thereunder.

(b) Nothing in this title shall be construed to modify existing law (1) with regard to the binding effect on any member of any exchange of any action taken by the authorities of such exchange to settle disputes between its members, or (2) with regard to the binding effect of such action on any person who has agreed to be bound thereby, or (3) with regard to the binding effect on any such member of any disciplinary action taken by the authorities of the exchange as a result of violation of any rule of the exchange, insofar as the action taken is not inconsistent with the provisions of this title or the rules and regulations thereunder.

Validity of Contracts

SEC. 29. (a) Any condition, stipulation, or provision binding any person to waive compliance with any provision of this title or of any rule or regulation thereunder, or of any rule of an exchange required thereby shall be void.

(b) Every contract made in violation of any provision of this title or of any rule or regulation thereunder, and every contract (including any contract for listing a security on an exchange) heretofore or hereafter made the performance of which involves the violation of, or the continuance of any relationship or practice in violation of, any provision of this title or any rule or regulation thereunder, shall be void (1) as regards the rights of any person who, in violation of any such provision, rule, or regulation, shall have made or engaged in the performance of any such contract, and (2) as regards the rights of any person who, not being a party to such contract, shall have acquired any right thereunder with actual knowledge of the facts by reason of which the making or performance of such contract was in violation of any such provision, rule or regulation.

(c) Nothing in this title shall be construed (1) to affect the validity of any loan or extension of credit (or any extension or renewal thereof) made or of any lien created prior or subsequent to the enactment of this title, unless at the time of the making of such loan or extension of credit (or extension or renewal thereof) or the creating of such lien, the person making such loan or extension of credit (or extension or renewal thereof) or acquiring such lien shall have actual knowledge of facts by reason of which the making of such loan or extension of credit (or extension or renewal thereof) or the acquisition of such lien is a violation of the provisions of this title or any rule or regulation thereunder, or (2) to afford a defense to the collection of any debt or obligation or the enforcement of any lien by any person who shall have acquired such debt, obligation, or lien in good faith for value and without actual knowledge of the violation of any provision of this title or any rule or regulation thereunder affecting the legality of such debt, obligation, or lien.

Foreign Securities Exchanges

SEC. 30. (a) It shall be unlawful for any broker or dealer, directly or indirectly, to make use of the mails or of any means or instrumentality of interstate commerce for the purpose of effecting on an exchange not within or subject to the jurisdiction of the United States, any transaction in any security the issuer of which is a resident of, or is organized under the laws of, or has its principal place of business in, a place within or subject to the jurisdiction of the United States, in contravention of such rules and regulations as the Commission may prescribe as necessary or appropriate in the public interest or for the protection of investors or to prevent the evasion of this title.

(b) The provisions of this title or of any rule or regulation thereunder shall not apply to any person insofar as he transacts a business in securities without the jurisdiction of the United States, unless he transacts such business in contravention of such rules and regulations as the Commission may prescribe as necessary or appropriate to prevent the evasion of this title.

Registration Fees

SEC. 31. Every national securities exchange shall pay to the Commission on or before March 15 of each calendar year a registration fee for the privilege of doing business as a national securities exchange during the preceding calendar year or any part thereof. Such fee shall be in an amount equal to one five-hundredths of 1 per centum of the aggregate dollar amount of the sales of securities transacted on such national securities exchange during the preceding calendar year and subsequent to its registration as a national securities exchange.

Penalties

SEC. 32. Any person who willfully violates any provision of this title, or any rule or regulation thereunder the violation of which is made unlawful or the observance of which is required under the terms of this title, or any person who willfully and knowingly makes, or causes to be made, any statement in any application, report, or document required to be filed under this title or any rule or regulation thereunder, which statement was false or misleading with respect to any material fact, shall upon conviction be fined not more than $10,000, or imprisoned not more than two years, or both, except that when such person is an exchange, a fine not exceeding $500,000 may be imposed; but no person shall be subject to imprisonment under this section for the violation of any rule or regulation if he proves that he had no knowledge of such rule or regulation.

Separability of Provisions

SEC. 33. If any provision of this Act, or the application of such provision to any person or circumstances, shall be held invalid, the remainder of the Act, and the application of such provision to persons or circumstances other than those as to which it is held invalid, shall not be affected thereby.

Effective Date

SEC. 34. This Act shall become effective on July 1, 1934, except that sections 6 and 12(b), (c), (d), and (e) shall become effective on September 1, 1934; and sections 5, 7, 8, 9(a), (6), 10, 11, 12(a), 13, 14, 15, 16, 17, 18, 19, and 30 shall become effective on October 1, 1934.

Title II–Amendments to Securities Act of 1933

SECTION 201. (a) Paragraph (1) of section 2 of the Securities Act of 1933 is amended to read as follows:

"(1) The term 'security' means any note, stock, treasury stock, bond, debenture, evidence of indebtedness, certificate of interest or participation in any profit-sharing agreement, collateral-trust certificate, preorganization certificate or subscription, transferable share, investment contract, voting-trust certificate, certificate of deposit for a security, fractional undivided interest in oil, gas, or other mineral rights, or, in general, any interest or instrument commonly known as a 'security,' or any certificate of interest or participation in, temporary or interim certificate for, receipt for, guarantee of, or warrant or right to subscribe to or purchase, any of the foregoing."

(b) Paragraph (4) of such section 2 is amended to read as follows:

"(4) The term 'issuer' means every person who issues or proposes to issue any security; except that with respect to certificates of deposit, voting-trust certificates, or collateral-trust certificates, or with respect to certificates of interest or shares in an unincorporated investment trust not having a board of directors (or persons performing similar functions) or of the fixed, restricted management, or unit type, the term 'issuer' means the person or persons performing the acts and assuming the duties of depositor or manager pursuant to the provisions of the trust or other agreement or instrument under which such securities are issued; except that in the case of an unincorporated association which provides by its articles for limited liability of any or all of its members, or in the case of a trust, committee, or other legal entity, the trustees or members thereof shall not be individually liable as issuers of any security issued by the association, trust, committee, or other legal entity; except that with respect to equipment-trust certificates or like securities, the term 'issuer' means the person by whom the equipment or property is or is to be used; and except that with respect to fractional undivided interests in oil, gas, or other mineral rights, the term 'issuer' means the owner of any such right or of any interest in such right (whether whole or fractional) who creates fractional interests therein for the purpose of public offering."

(c) Paragraph (10) of such section 2 is amended to read as follows:

"(10) The term 'prospectus' means any prospectus, notice, circular, advertisement, letter, or communication, written or by radio, which offers any security for sale; except that (a) a communication shall not be deemed a prospectus if it is proved that prior to or at the same time with such communication a written prospectus meeting the requirements of section 10 was sent or given to the person to whom the communication was made, by the person making such communication or his principal, and (b) a notice, circular, advertisement, letter, or communication in respect of a security shall not be deemed to be a prospectus if it states from whom a written prospectus meeting the requirements of section 10 may be obtained and, in addition, does no more than identify the security, state the price thereof, and state by whom orders will be executed."

SEC. 202. (a) Paragraph (2) of section 3 (a) of such Act is amended to read as follows:

"(2) Any security issued or guaranteed by the United States or any Territory thereof, or by the District of Columbia, or by any State of the United States, or by any political subdivision of a State or Territory, or by any public instrumentality of one or more States or Territories, or by any person controlled or supervised by and acting as an instrumentality of the Government of the United States pursuant to authority granted by the Congress of the United States, or any certificate of deposit for any of the foregoing, or any security issued or guaranteed by any national bank, or by any banking institution organized under the laws of any State or Territory or the District of Columbia, the business of which is substantially confined to banking and is supervised by the State or Territorial banking commission or similar official; or any security issued by or representing an interest in or a direct obligation of a Federal Reserve bank";

(b) Paragraph (4) of such section 3 (a) is amended by striking out "corporation" and inserting in lieu thereof "person."

(c) Such section 3 (a) is further amended by striking out the period at the end of paragraph (8) and inserting in lieu thereof a semicolon, and by inserting immediately after such paragraph (8) the following new paragraphs:

"(9) Any security exchanged by the issuer with its existing security holders exclusively where no commission or other remuneration is paid or given directly or indirectly for soliciting such exchange;

"(10) Any security which is issued in exchange for one or more bona fide outstanding securities, claims or property interests, or partly in such exchange and partly for cash, where the terms and conditions of such issuance and exchange are approved, after a hearing upon the fairness of such terms and conditions at which all persons to whom it is proposed to issue securities in such exchange shall have the right to appear, by any court, or by any official or agency of the United States, or by any State or Territorial banking or insurance commission or other governmental authority expressly authorized by law to grant such approval;

"(11) Any security which is a part of an issue sold only to persons resident within a single State or Territory, where the issuer of such security is a person resident and doing business within or, if a corporation, incorporated by and doing business within, such State or Territory."

SEC. 203. (a) Paragraph (1) of section 4 of such Act is amended (1) by striking out "not with or through an underwriter and"; and (2) by striking out "last" and inserting in lieu thereof "first."

(b) Paragraph (3) of such section 4 is hereby repealed.

SEC. 204. Subsection (c) of section 5 of such Act is hereby repealed.

SEC. 205. Paragraph (1) of section 10(b) of such Act is amended to read as follows:

"(1) When a prospectus is used more than thirteen months after the effective date of the registration statement, the information in the statements contained therein shall be as of a date not more than twelve months prior to such use, so far as such information is known to the user of such prospectus or can be furnished by such user without unreasonable effort or expense."

SEC. 206. (a) Section 11 (a) of such Act is amended by adding after the last line thereof the following new sentence: "If such person acquired the security after the issuer has made generally available to its security holders an earning statement covering a period of at least twelve months beginning after the effective date of the registration statement, then the right of recovery under this subsection shall be conditioned on proof that such person acquired the security relying upon such untrue statement in the registration statement or relying upon the registration statement and not knowing of such omission, but such reliance may be established without proof of the reading of the registration statement of such person."

(b) Clauses (C) and (D) of paragraph (3) of section 11 (b) of such Act are amended to read as follows: "(C) as regards any part of the registration statement purporting to be made on the authority of an expert (other than himself) or purporting to be a copy of or extract from a report or valuation of an expert (other than himself), he had no reasonable ground to believe and did not believe, at the time such part of the registration statement became effective, that the statements therein were untrue or that there was an omission to state a material fact required to be stated therein or necessary to make the statements therein not misleading, or that such part of the registration statement did not fairly represent the statement of the expert or was not a fair copy of or extract from the report or valuation of the expert; and (D) as regards any part of the registration statement purporting to be a statement made by an official person or purporting to be a copy of or extract from a public official document, he had no reasonable ground to believe and did not believe, at the time such part of the registration statement became effective, that the statements therein were untrue, or that there was an omission to state a material fact required to be stated therein or necessary to make the statement therein not misleading, or that such part of the registration statement did not fairly represent the statement made by the official person or was not a fair copy of or extract from the public official document."

(c) Subsection (c) of such section 11 is amended to read as follows:

"(c) In determining, for the purpose of paragraph (3) of subsection (b) of this section, what constitutes reasonable investigation and reasonable ground for belief, the standard of reasonableness shall be that required of a prudent man in the management of his own property."

(d) Subsection (e) of such section 11 is amended to read as follows:

"(e) The suit authorized under subsection (a) may be to recover such damages as shall represent the difference between the amount paid for the security (not exceeding the price at which the security was offered to the public) and (1) the value thereof as of the time such suit was brought, or (2) the price at which such security shall have been disposed of in the market before suit, or (3) the price at which such security shall have been disposed of after suit but before judgment if such damages shall be less than the damages representing the difference between the amount paid for the security (not exceeding the price at which the security was offered to the public) and the value thereof as of the time such suit was brought: *Provided,* That if the defendant proves that any portion or all of such damages represents other than the depreciation in value of such security resulting from such part of the registration statement, with respect to which his liability is asserted, not being true or omitting to state a material fact required to be stated therein or necessary to make the statements therein not misleading, such portion of or all such damages shall not be recoverable. In no event shall any underwriter (unless such underwriter shall have knowingly received from the issuer for acting as an underwriter some benefit, directly or indirectly, in which all other underwriters similarly situated did not share in proportion to their respective interests in the underwriting) be liable in any suit or as a consequence of suits authorized under subsection (a) for damages in excess of the total price at which the securities underwritten by him and distributed to the public were offered to the public. In any suit under this or any other section of this title the court may, in its discretion, require an undertaking for the payment of the costs of such suit, including reasonable attorney's fees, and if judgment shall be rendered against a party litigant, upon the motion of the other party litigant, such costs may be assessed in favor of such party litigant (whether or not such undertaking has been required) if the court believes the suit or the defense to have been without merit, in an amount sufficient to reimburse him for the reasonable expenses incurred by him, in connection with such suit, such costs to be taxed in the manner usually provided for taxing of costs in the court in which the suit was heard."

SEC. 207. Section 13 of such Act is amended (a) by striking out "two years" wherever it appears therein and inserting in lieu thereof "one year"; (b) by striking out "ten years" and inserting in lieu thereof "three years"; and (c) by inserting immediately before the period at the end thereof a comma and the following: "or under section 12(2) more than three years after the sale."

SEC. 208. Section 15 of such Act is amended by inserting immediately before the period at the end thereof a comma and the following: "unless the controlling person had no knowledge of or reasonable ground to believe in the existence of the facts by reason of which the liability of the controlled person is alleged to exist."

SEC. 209. (a) The first sentence of subsection (a) of section 19 of such Act is amended by inserting after the word "accounting" a comma and the word "technical."

(b) Subsection (a) of such section 19 is further amended by adding at the end thereof the following new sentence: "No provision of this title imposing any liability shall apply to any act done or omitted in good faith in conformity with any rule or regulation of the Commission, notwithstanding that such rule or regulation may, after such act or omission, be amended or rescinded or be determined by judicial or other authority to be invalid for any reason."

SEC. 210. Upon the expiration of sixty days after the date upon which a majority of the members of the Securities and Exchange Commission appointed under section 4 of title I of this Act have qualified and taken office, all powers, duties, and functions of the Federal Trade Commission under the Securities Act of 1933 shall be transferred to such Commission, together with all property, books, records, and unexpected balances of appropriations used by or available to the Federal Trade Commission for carrying out its functions under the Securities Act of 1933. All proceedings, hearings, or investigations commenced or pending before the Federal Trade Commission arising under the Securities Act of 1933 shall be continued by the Securities and Exchange Commission. All orders, rules, and regulations which have been issued by the Federal Trade Commission under the Securities Act of 1933 and which are in effect shall continue in effect until modified, superseded, revoked, or repealed. All rights and interests accruing or to accrue under the Securities Act of 1933, or any provision of any regulation relating to, or out of action taken by, the Federal Trade Commission under such Act, shall be followed in all respects and may be exercised and enforced.

SEC. 211. The Commission is authorized and directed to make a study and investigation of the work, activities, personnel, and functions of protective and reorganization committees in connection with the reorganization, readjustment, rehabilitation, liquidation, or consolidation of persons and properties and to report the result of its studies and investigations and its recommendations to the Congress on or before January 3, 1936.

Approved, June 6, 1934, 12:15 p.m.

THE ORIGINS

REPORT ON SECURITIES EXCHANGE BILL
April 27, 1934

Committed to the Committee of the Whole House on the state of the Union and ordered to be printed

Mr. Rayburn, from the Committee on Interstate and Foreign Commerce, submitted the following

REPORT
[To accompany H. R. 9323]

The Committee on Interstate and Foreign Commerce, to whom was referred the bill (H. R. 9323) to provide for the regulation of securities exchanges and of over-the-counter markets operating in interstate and foreign commerce and through the mails, to prevent inequitable and unfair practices on such exchanges and markets, and for other purposes, report favorably thereon without amendment and recommend that the bill do pass.

I. Introductory Statement

The President's Message and Letter

On February 9, 1934, the President sent the following message to Congress:

To the Congress:

In my message to you last March proposing legislation for Federal supervision of national traffic in investment securities I said: "This is but one step in our broad purpose of protecting investors and depositors. It should be followed by legislation relating to the better supervision of the purchase and sale of all property dealt with on exchanges."

This Congress has performed a useful service in regulating the investment business on the part of financial houses and in protecting the investing public in its acquisition of securities.

There remains the fact, however, that outside the field of legitimate investment naked speculation has been made far too alluring and far too easy for those who could and for those who could not afford to gamble.

Such speculation has run the scale from the individual who has risked his pay envelope or his meager savings on a margin transaction involving stocks with whose true value he was wholly unfamiliar, to the poor of individuals or corporations with large resources, often not their own, which sought by manipulation to raise or depress market quotations far out of line with reason, all of this resulting in loss to the average investor, who is of necessity personally uninformed.

The exchanges in many parts of the country which deal in securities and commodities conduct, of course, a national business because their customers live in every part of the country. The managers of these exchanges have, it is true, often taken steps to correct certain obvious abuses. We must be certain that abuses are eliminated and to this end a broad policy of national regulation is required.

It is my belief that exchanges for dealing in securities and commodities are necessary and of definite value to our commercial and agricultural life. Nevertheless, it should be our national policy to restrict, as far as possible, the use of these exchanges for purely speculative operations.

I therefore recommend to the Congress the enactment of legislation providing for the regulation by the Federal Government of the operations of exchanges dealing in securities and commodities for the protection of investors, for the safeguarding of values, and, so far as it may be possible, for the elimination of unnecessary, unwise, and destructive speculation.

Franklin D. Roosevelt

The White House,
February 9, 1934.

On March 26, 1934, the President sent the following letter to the chairman of this committee:

The White House
Washington, March 26, 1934

Hon. Sam Rayburn,
Chairman Interstate and Foreign Commerce,
House of Representatives

My Dear Mr. Chairman: Before I leave Washington for a few days holiday, I want to write you about a matter which gives me some concern.

On February 9, 1934, I sent to the Congress a special message asking for Federal supervision of national traffic in securities.

It has come to my attention that a more definite and more highly organized drive is being made against effective legislation to this end than against any similar recommendation made by me during the past year. Letters and telegrams bearing all the earmarks of origin at some common source are pouring in to the White House and the Congress.

The people of this country are, in overwhelming majority, fully aware of the fact that unregulated speculation in securities and in commodities was one of the most important contributing factors in the artificial and unwarranted "boom" which had so much to do with the terrible conditions of the years following 1929.

I have been definitely committed to definite regulation of exchanges which deal in securities and commodities. In my message I stated, "it should be our national policy to restrict, as far as possible, the use of these exchanges for purely speculative operations."

I am certain that the country as a whole will not be satisfied with legislation unless such legislation has teeth in it. The two principal objectives are, as I see it—

First, the requirement of what is known as margins so high that speculation, even as it exists today, will of necessity be drastically curtailed; and

Second, that the Government be given such definite powers of supervision over exchanges that the Government itself will be able to correct abuses which may arise in the future.

We must, of course, prevent insofar as possible manipulation of prices to the detriment of actual investors, but at the same time we must eliminate unnecessary, unwise, and destructive speculation.

The bill, as shown to me this afternoon by Senator Fletcher, seems to meet the minimum requirements. I do not see how any of us could afford to have it weakened in any shape, manner, or form.

Very sincerely,

Franklin D. Roosevelt

The General Purpose of the Bill

To reach the causes of the "unnecessary, unwise, and destructive speculation" condemned by the President's message, this bill seeks to regulate the stock exchanges and the relationships of the investing public to corporations which invite public investment by listing on such exchanges.

The bill is conceived in a spirit of the truest conservatism. It attempts to change the practices of exchanges and the relationships between listed corporations and the investing public to fit modern conditions, for the very purpose that they may endure as essential elements of our economic system. The lesson of 1921-29 is that without changes they cannot endure.

The bill is not a moral pose or a vengeful striking back at brokers for the losses which nearly the entire Nation has suffered in the last 5 years. Nor is its purpose or effect to regiment business in any way. It is simply an earnest attempt to make belated intelligent adjustments, long required by changing conditions, in a faulty system of distributing shares in corporate enterprise among the public—a system which from the coldly objective viewpoint of the welfare of a conservative public simply has not worked. The out-of-date unsuitability to post-war conditions of a whole series of economic interrelationships of which the stock exchanges are the nerve center has uncontrollably accentuated natural moderate fluctuations of our economic system into mad booms and terrible depressions. And such booms and depressions constitute a more real danger to the stability of a moderate, honest, individualistic state than all the unsound theories in the world. This bill seeks to save, not destroy, stock markets and business, by making necessary changes in time.

The fundamental fact behind the necessity for this bill is that the leaders of private business, whether because of inertia, pressure of vested interests, lack of organization, or otherwise, have not since the war been able to act to protect themselves by compelling a continuous and orderly program of change in methods and standards of doing business to match the degree to which the economic system has itself been constantly changing—changing in the proportion of the wealth of the Nation invested in liquid corporate securities traded in on the stock exchanges, changing in the relationship of the distribution of securities and the trading in securities to the balanced utilization of the Nation's credit resources in the financing of agriculture, commerce, and industry. The repetition in the summer of 1933 of the blindness and abuses of 1929 has convinced a patient public that enlightened self-interest in private leadership is not sufficiently powerful to effect the necessary changes alone—that private leadership seeking to make changes must be given Government help and protection.

Since the war the interest of the public at large in the ownership of corporate enterprise has grown bigger, the size of the corporate unit has increased, the diffusion of corporate ownership has widened, all correlatively. Not only is nearly one half of the entire national wealth of the country represented by corporate stocks and corporate and Government bonds, but nearly one half of that corporate wealth is vested in the 200 largest nonbanking corporations which, piercing the thin veil of the holding company and disregarding a relatively few notable exceptions, are owned in each case by thousands of investors and are controlled by those owning only a very small proportion of the corporate stock. Ownership and control are in most cases largely divorced. It is estimated that more than 10,000,000 individual men and women in the United States are the direct possessors of stocks and bonds; that over one fifth of all the corporate stock outstanding in the country is held by individuals with net incomes of less than $5,000 a year. Over 15,000,000 individuals hold insurance policies, the value of which is dependent upon the security holdings of insurance companies: Over 13,000,000 men and women have savings accounts in mutual savings banks and at least 25,000,000 have deposits in national and State banks and trust companies—which are in turn large holders of corporate stocks and bonds.

With this growth in security ownership by the public, the security markets have grown proportionately in importance. Two hundred and thirty-seven million corporate shares were sold on the New York Stock Exchange in 1923; despite the depression 654,000,000 shares were sold in 1933.

With such concentration of national wealth in the form of liquid corporate securities the economic machinery of the whole country is now affected by, and is organized primarily to serve, security markets which are as sensitive as a hair trigger. A magnificently organized lending machinery which operates by wire, can, with an offer of call-loan safety and 1 percent higher interest, draw funds from local banks which would otherwise seek moderate investment in local business enterprise, to finance the pool of a far-away metropolitan speculator distributing through the stock exchanges the securities of a huge corporate merger designed ultimately to swallow and destroy local enterprise. And there is a demonstrable direct relationship between easy credit for the purchase of new securities in the stock market and the trend toward industrial monopolies so accentuated since the war.

A rise in the security markets stimulates economic activity in all lines of business, a fall in the market precipitates a decline. If the rise in the market is occasioned by an excessive use of credit, a decline in the market loosens a process of deflation which feeds on itself and ruins not only security prices but all business as well. Between 1922 and 1929 brokers' loans increased from 1½ billion dollars to 8½ billion dollars. Five billion dollars of this increase took place in 3 years, 1½ billion dollars in the last 3 months. In the crash of 1929 the same loans declined 3 billion dollars in the first 10 days and 8 billion dollars in the next 3 years. These figures alone will enable the economic historian of the future to describe the unhealthy prosperity of 1929 and the inevitable grief and suffering that followed in the succeeding years—grief and suffering that overwhelmed and carried away not merely the speculative gains of those who participated in the speculative debauch, not merely the savings of the most frugal and most thrifty invested in securities, but eventually the operating profits of every business in the country no matter how unrelated to stock exchanges.

All through these years the machinery of the stock exchanges and of corporate management have only grown bigger without growing different. But this significant growth in size and importance of the exchanges and the business they do with the public has necessitated a real difference in kind in the treatment of that public by the law and by business ethics. Stock exchanges which handle the distribution and trading of a very substantial part of the entire national wealth and which have developed a technique of sucking funds from every corner of the country cannot operate under the same traditions and practices as pre-war stock exchanges which handled substantially only the transactions of professional investors and speculators. And standards of corporate management adequate to inspire investor confidence in the "caveat stockholder" era of closely held stockholder-managed companies cannot be stably perpetuated in an era where one company boasts over 700,000 stockholders, and 200 corporations control one half the corporate wealth of the country.

If investor confidence is to come back to the benefit of exchanges and corporations alike, the law must advance. As a complex society so diffuses and differentiates the financial interests of the ordinary citizen that he has to trust others and cannot personally watch the managers of all his interests as one horse trader watches another, it becomes a condition of the very stability of that society that its rules of law and of business practice recognize and protect that ordinary citizen's dependent position.

Unless constant extension of the legal conception of a fiduciary relationship—a guarantee of "straight shooting"—supports the constant extension of mutual confidence which is the foundation of a maturing and complicated economic system, easy liquidity of the resources in which wealth is invested is a danger rather than a prop to the stability of that system. When everything everyone owns can be sold at once, there must be confidence not to sell. Just in proportion as it becomes more liquid and complicated, an economic system must become more moderate, more honest, and more justifiably self-trusting.

When corporations were small, when their managers were intimately acquainted with their owners and when the interests of management and ownership were substantially identical, conditions did not require the regulation of security markers. Even those who in former days managed great corporations were by reason of their personal contacts with their shareholders constantly aware of their responsibilities. But as management became divorced from ownership and came under the control of banking groups, men forgot that they were dealing with the savings of men and the making of profits became an impersonal thing. When men do not know the victims of their aggression they are not always conscious of their wrongs. President Wilson showed a keen prophetic sense when he stated:

Society cannot afford to have individuals wield the power of thousands without personal responsibility. It cannot afford to let its strongest men be the only men who are inaccessible to the law. Modern democratic society, in particular, cannot afford to constitute its economic undertakings upon the monarchical or aristocratic principle and adopt the fiction that the kings and great men thus set up can do no wrong which will make them personally amenable to the law which restrains smaller men; that their kingdom, not themselves, must suffer for their blindness, their follies, and their transgressions of right.

II. General Analysis of the Bill

Its Scope and Constitutionality

The causes of dangerous speculation in the securities markets go far deeper than defects and abuses in stock-exchange machinery alone. They include inadequate central control of a national credit system that too easily provides for speculation funds which the national welfare much more requires in local commerce, industry, and agriculture. They include inadequate corporate reporting which keeps in ignorance of necessary factors for intelligent judgment of the values of securities a public continually solicited to buy such securities by the sheer advertising value of listing. They include exploitation of that ignorance by self-perpetuating managements in possession of inside information. Speculation, manipulation, faulty credit control, investors' ignorance, and disregard of trust relationships by those whom the law should regard as fiduciaries, are all a single seamless web. No one of these evils can be isolated for cure of itself alone. A stockmarket pool, for instance, is only an effect and not a cause; the manipulator, a shell-game artist who can live only by following the county fair of too easy credit and ignorance.

A bill seeking effectively to control and regulate the securities markets therefore necessarily covers a wide field—necessarily touches more than a few willful speculators of Wall Street, necessarily calls for the cooperation of the widespread economic interests which the securities market affects. Business which was engulfed and nearly destroyed by the speculations of 1929 has its contribution to make in the form of fair and informing reports. Banks whose assets were carried away in loans based upon values inflated by reckless speculation must cooperate in permitting coordinated control of the delicate credit system which has been left to their management despite the fact that the Nation has had to expend billions of dollars to insure their solvency.

The factual situation which makes the legislation necessary is set forth in section 2. These recitals of fact: the use of the security markets as interstate markets in which ownership passes from residents of one State to those of another; the constant use of the postal facilities for the conduct of these markets; the abundant use of the credit facilities of national banks and of member banks of the Federal Reserve System; the effect of security prices upon transactions in interstate commerce, upon bank loans, upon taxes and upon credit available for trade, transportation, and industry—are common knowledge not only among economists but among bankers and business men everywhere. This legislation is not an attempt to reach out and correct the morals of the citizens of any one State; it is an attempt to deal with very vital economic problems going to the root of the functioning of our national credit system.

The constitutional significance of the wide delegation of powers to the Federal Reserve Board and to the Federal Trade Commission, which would administer the act, has been considered with particular care—and the delegation made only with the indication of such maximum standards for discretion as, in the considered judgment of the Committee, the technical character of the problems to be dealt with would permit. The bill legislates specifically just as far as the Committee feels it can. The original bill submitted to the Committee dealt very specifically and definitely with a number of admitted abuses. In many cases, however, the argument was made that while the solutions offered might be correct, their effects were so far-reaching as to make it inadvisable to put these solutions in the form of statutory enactments that could not be changed in case of need without Congressional action. Representatives of the stock exchanges constantly urged a greater degree of flexibility in the statute and insisted that the complicated nature of the problems justified leaving much greater latitude of discretion with the administrative agencies than would otherwise be the case. It is for that reason that the bill in dealing with a number of difficult problems singles out these problems as matters appropriate to be subject to restrictive rules and regulations, but leaves to the administrative agencies the determination of the most appropriate form of rule or regulation to be enforced. In a field where practices constantly vary and where practices legitimate for some purposes may be turned to illegitimate and fraudulent means, broad discretionary powers in the administrative agency have been found practically essential, despite the desire of the Committee to limit the discretion of the administrative agencies so far as compatible with workable legislation. It has been represented that the pleas of the representatives of the stock exchanges for the vesting of broad discretionary powers in the administrative agencies have been made with a view to subjecting the bill to constitutional attack at a later date. The Committee has, however, taken the pleas in good faith believing that the nature of the legislation is such as to justify within constitutional limitations that measure of flexibility required in dealing with so intricate a subject matter.

Organization of Bill

The chief provisions of the bill may be grouped under six headings: (*a*) control of credits; (*b*) control of manipulative practices; (*c*) provision of adequate and honest reports to securities holders by registered corporations; (*d*) control of unfair practices of corporate insiders; (*e*) control of exchanges and over-the-counter markets; (*f*) administration.

Control of Credits

The underlying theory of the bill with respect to control of credit is as follows:

(1) Without adequate control the too strong attraction of a speculative stock market for credit prevents a balanced utilization of the Nation's credit resources in commerce, industry, and agriculture;

(2) To effect such better balance, all speculative credit should be subjected to the central control of the Federal Reserve Board as the most experienced and best equipped credit agency of the Government.

(3) To achieve that control the Federal Reserve Board should be vested with the most effectual and direct power over speculative credit, i.e., the power to control margins on the actual ultimate speculative loans themselves.

(4) Both for the direction and the protection of the Federal Reserve Board in the administration of flexible powers, Congress should offer the Board some definite margin standard to indicate the judgment of Congress that the amount of credit previously routed through the stock markets has been excessive and to indicate the approximate proportion in which such amount should be reduced.

To accomplish these purposes, sections 6 and 7 of the bill gives the Federal Reserve Board power to control speculative credit. The problem of control has been approached from several directions because of the certainty that no purpose of the bill will be more tempting to evasion. Borrowings by brokers to finance their customers are confined to borrowings from or through member banks of the Federal Reserve System or those nonmember banks which apply for a license from the Board. With respect to loans to the ultimate speculating customer, the Board is substantially given power by rules and regulations to fix margins on (*a*) all loans on securities from brokers to customers, and (*b*) loans from banks and others to customers made on equity securities and to carry or purchase securities. For the purposes of guiding and protecting the Board from undue speculative pressure in the exercise of its discretion, the bill includes as a standard for the rules and regulations of the Board a limitation of credit on the initial granting of loans to 55 percent of the current market price of the securities offered as collateral, or 100 percent of the lowest market price of the preceding 3 years, whichever is the greater.

To avoid any conceivable deflationary effects upon presently existing loans on securities, all such loans, and renewals and extensions thereof, are exempt from the application of section 6 until January 1, 1939.

The main purpose of these margin provisions in section 6 is not to increase the safety of security loans for lenders. Banks and brokers normally require sufficient collateral to make themselves safe without the help of law. Nor is the main purpose even protection of the small speculator by making it impossible for him to spread himself too thinly—although such a result will be achieved as a byproduct of the main purpose.

The main purpose is to give a Government credit agency an effective method of reducing the aggregate amount of the nation's credit resources which can be directed by speculation into the stock market and out of other more desirable uses of commerce and industry—to prevent a recurrence of the pre-crash situation where funds which would otherwise have been available at normal interest rates for uses of local commerce, industry, and agriculture, were drained by far higher rates into security loans and the New York call market. Increasing margins—i.e., decreasing the amounts which brokers or banks may lend for the speculative purchase and carrying of stocks—is the most direct and the most effective method of discouraging an abnormal attraction of funds into the stock market.

When margins are discussed with this main purpose in mind differences between the collateral value of gilt-edged bonds and speculative stocks, the credit-worthiness of particular borrowers and similar considerations which have been urged as reasons why each loan should be treated as a particular problem in itself—considerations which affect not a general national credit policy, but only the safety of a particular stock transaction from the standpoint of a particular lender and particular borrower—are unimportant.

Section 6 empowers the Federal Reserve Board to prescribe margins for both brokers and banks on securities registered on exchanges licensed under the bill (hereinafter referred to as registered securities)—both for the initial opening and for the maintenance or carrying of accounts. The Board is given complete legal authority to fix margins at any point. But a standard is included in the bill as an indication by Congress to the Board that from the standpoint of a general policy of utilization of national credit resources, the Board should control the credit available to the stock market to an amount roughly corresponding to such standard.

To protect margin requirements from evasion brokers may lend only on listed securities excepting exempted securities. Banks are subject to margin limitations only on loans on registered equity securities in cases where the loan is sought for the purpose of purchasing or carrying securities. The Board is not required to fix the same margins for banks as for brokers and is given a free hand in fixing margins for maintenance as distinguished from margins for the initial opening of accounts.

It has seemed necessary to empower the Board to fix margins for banks as well as for brokers (*a*) to prevent evasion of restrictions on brokers' margins through loans by banks; (*b*) to increase the powers of the Board over speculative loans by its member banks; and (*c*) to give the Board an effective power (it has no powers at present) over speculative loans by nonmember banks.

The margin standard in Section 6 has been expressed as a percentage of market value which may be lent upon securities rather than of the amount which the customer is required to deposit at the time of his purchase. The basic loan value provided by the standard for the initial opening of an account is 55 percent of market value of the securities lent upon, i.e., from the standpoint of what the customer must "put up," a 45-percent margin. This standard is not indicated for the purposes of maintenance of the account. The 55-percent loan value indicated would govern in the long run of a rising market. But to afford easier margins for the present market and for a possible future declining market a more favorable alternative standard is indicated in Section 6 (*a*) (2), which, by the finding of Standard Statistics Service, would operate to permit, at the present time, an average initial loan value of 65 1/2 percent of market value on the stocks now listed on the New York Stock Exchange, or, from the customer's point of view, a margin of only 34 1/2 percent.

Under this alternative standard, the margin is only 25 percent in the case of a security that is selling at not more than 33-1/3 percent above its 3-year low. As the security increases in price the margin required gradually increases proportionately until, when the security has reached a price that is more than 80 percent above its 3-year low, a margin of 45 percent is required. This flexible margin standard permits a relatively low margin in the case of stable securities such as bonds, while it requires a higher margin in the case of volatile securities after they have risen substantially in market price. Since the margin increases as the price of the security rises, pyramiding on paper profits is made difficult.

Section 6 seems to furnish a very practical program of controlling the volume of stock-market credit, since it embodies a combination of a basic formula, initially setting minimum margins, with a more general discretionary administrative control, which should be based on the total amount of credit outstanding, the level of stock prices, the phase of the business and financial cycle, and so forth. Between the times when changes are made by the Federal Reserve Board, margin requirements would be automatically raised or lowered by the movements of stock prices. Such a self-adjusting mechanism would probably function better, in actual practice, than any system wherein margin requirements are changed only by deliberate action of the Board and remain unadjusted except when the Board takes such action.

The 55-percent standard expressed in the statute is, however, so deliberately over-lenient for the purpose of encouraging the markets at this particular point in the recovery program, that the Board in exercising its discretion would be expected to lower this 55-percent figure considerably after the market reaches more normal levels.

Control of Manipulative Practices

To insure to the multitude of investors the maintenance of fair and honest markets, manipulative practices of all kinds on national exchanges are banned. The bill seeks to give to investors markets where prices may be established by the free and honest balancing of investment demand with investment supply. Investors are free to buy and sell virtually without restraint. But wash sales and matched orders and other devices designed to create a misleading appearance of activity with a view to enticing the unwary into the market on the hope of quick gains are definitely prohibited. False and misleading statements designed to induce investors to buy when they should sell and to sell when they should buy are also outlawed and penalized.

But the most subtle manipulating device employed in the security markets is not simply the crude form of a wash sale or a matched order. It is the conscious marking up of prices to make investors believe that there is a constantly increasing demand for stocks at higher prices, or the conscious marking down of stocks to make investors believe that an increasing number of investors are selling as prices recede. Legitimate investors desire to buy at as low a price as possible and to sell at as high a price as possible, and honest markets are made by the balancing of investment demand and investment supply.

The provisions concerning manipulative practices have been drawn in light of the results of the recent investigation conducted by the Senate Committee on Banking and Currency. Despite all the talk of good pools and bad pools, no evidence has been submitted to this Committee that would justify the recognition of a good stock-market pool. As the Twentieth Century Fund in its recent report on "Stock-Market Control" states—

As a matter of fact, any pool which seeks to bring about a change in the price of a security through manipulation is "illegitimate" according to our definition, inasmuch as it thereby lessens the efficiency of an exchange in the performance of those functions which, as we indicated, are the only justification for its existence.

If the pool to "rig" or "jiggle" the market is wrong, it necessarily follows that the market must be purged of reports about activities for the "rise" or operations for the "decline." If brokers and other interested persons are permitted to spread through brokerage and publicity channels constant reports regarding such activities, it is doubtful whether stimulated activity would not accomplish much the same effect as is accomplished by the direct mark-up or mark-down prices by the pool. For that reason the circulation of reports of market operations conducted for a rise or for a decline is prohibited.

The evidence as to the value of pegging and stabilizing operations, particularly in relation to new issues, is far from conclusive. While abuses are undoubtedly associated with such manipulation, because of the desire of the Committee to proceed cautiously such operations have not been forbidden altogether, but have been subjected to such control as the administrative commission may find necessary in the public interest or for the protection of investors.

The granting of options to pools and syndicates has been found to be at the bottom of most manipulative operations, because the granting of these options permits large-scale manipulations to be conducted with a minimum of financial risk to the manipulators. The bill, therefore, gives the administrative commission power to regulate dealing in options or trading in options. The connection of pool activity with the option has recently been recognized in the rules of the New York Stock Exchange. As it is not always easy to trace and prove manipulative activity, it is necessary to rid the market of devices which commonly accompany or cloak these activities. Short selling and stop-loss orders, which have been the source of much abuse, are brought within the regulatory power of the administrative commission.

There is plenty of room for legitimate speculation in the balancing of investment demand and supply, in the shrewd prognostication of future trends and economic directions; but the accentuation of temporary fluctuations and the deliberate introduction of a mob psychology into the speculative markets by the fanfare of organized manipulation menace the true functioning of the exchanges, upon which the economic well-being of the whole country depends.

To make effective the prohibitions against manipulation civil redress is given to those able to prove actual damages from any of the prohibited practices.

Provision of Adequate and Honest Reports to Securities Holders by Registered Corporations

No investor, no speculator, can safely buy and sell securities upon the exchanges without having an intelligent basis for forming his judgment as to the value of the securities he buys or sells. The idea of a free and open public market is built upon the theory that competing judgments of buyers and sellers as to the fair price of a security brings about a situation where the market price reflects as nearly as possible a just price. Just as artificial manipulation tends to upset the true function of an open market, so the hiding and secreting of important information obstructs the operation of the markets as indices of real value. There cannot be honest markets without honest publicity. Manipulation and dishonest practices of the market place thrive upon mystery and secrecy. The disclosure of information materially important to investors may not instantaneously be reflected in market value, but despite the intricacies of security values truth does find relatively quick acceptance on the market. That is why in many cases it is so carefully guarded. Delayed, inaccurate, and misleading reports are the tools of the unconscionable market operator and the recreant corporate official who speculate on inside information. Despite the tug of conflicting interests and the influence of powerful groups, responsible officials of the leading exchanges have unqualifiedly recognized in theory at least the vital importance of true and accurate corporate reporting as an essential cog in the proper functioning of the public exchanges. Their efforts to bring about more adequate and prompt publicity have been handicapped by the lack of legal power and by the failure of certain banking and business groups to appreciate that a business that gathers its capital from the investing public has not the same right to secrecy as a small privately owned and managed business. It is only a few decades since men believed that the disclosure of a balance sheet was a disclosure of a trade secret. Today few people would admit the right of any company to solicit public funds without the disclosure of a balance sheet.

The need of proper and adequate reporting as an adjunct of the proper functioning of the exchanges has been expressed by the realistic and responsible Executive Assistant of the Committee on Stock List of the New York Stock Exchange:

It has been said a hundred times that accounting is a matter of conventions, and it is questionable whether these conventions have kept pace with the changes in modern business conditions. As the art stands today, it appears to the business man to have evolved with primary emphasis upon two objects:

(a) To give to management that accurate information and aid which is essential to the successful conduct of a business, and (b) to give to actual and prospective creditors that accurate information essential to the determination of the volume of credit which may safely be expended and the conditions under which it may be allowed.

Under conditions of ownership where the number of partners or stockholders was small, where enterprises were largely managed by their owners, or by the personally chosen representatives of a few owners in close contact with the business, and where it was the custom to finance permanently but little beyond minimum needs and to borrow largely to meet peak needs, accounting adequately performing these two functions probably sufficiently served the needs of the then situation. In the meantime the widespread diffusion of corporate ownership, with which we are all familiar, has occurred. There are few large enterprises which have not taken on the corporate form and a large proportion of the total ownership is in the hands of millions of relatively small investors who have no direct contact with management and whose only knowledge of the company is derived from its financial reports. In recent years there has been a marked tendency to finance more or less permanently for peak requirements, becoming lenders of money at the time of minimum requirements, and so tending to lessen the aggregate volume of bank credit needed.

Because of these changes, coupled with a growing tendency toward extreme broadness and flexibility in the corporation laws of many States, the time appears to have arrived for some changes of emphasis as to the objects to be achieved by sound accounting practice. While there have been able efforts devoted toward this end, the result so far generally attained does not seem to me sufficient to meet the needs. The need of accurate information for the aid of management is still paramount; but, under conditions of today, the next object in order of importance has become "to give to stockholders, in understandable form, such information in regard to the business as will avoid misleading them in any respect and as will put them in possession of all information needed, and which can be supplied in financial statements, to determine the true value of their investments."

This is, of course, the object in which the stock exchange is particularly interested. The primary object of the exchange is to afford facilities for trading in securities under the safest and fairest conditions attainable. In order that parties may trade on even terms they should have, as far as is practicable, the same opportunities for knowledge in regard to the subject matter of the trade.

The exchange is interested in the accounts of companies as a source of reliable information for those who deal in stocks. It is not sufficient for the stock exchange that the accounts should be in conformity with the law or even that they should be conservative; the stock exchange desires that they should be fully and fairly informative.

The president of the New York Stock Exchange has effectively answered those who contend that such publicity will give advantage to competitors:

The public, today, insists upon more complete and accurate financial statements from publicly owned companies and I am sure that the officials and directors of these corporations, realizing the reasonableness of this demand, will furnish investors with adequate information. There have not been many instances where the failure to give complete information was due to a desire on the part of directors or officers to secure unfair personal advantage. However, many company officials did not publish complete financial statements because they were afraid that the disclosure of too much information would put their companies at a disadvantage in meeting competition, not only from other American corporations, but frequently from foreign companies engaged in the same line of business. This fear, though genuine, has in large measure proved to be unfounded.

The reporting provisions of the proposed legislation are a very modest beginning to afford that long-denied aid to the exchanges in the way of securing proper information for the investor. Thy provisions carefully guard against the disclosure of trade secrets or processes. But the idea that a fair report of corporate assets and profits give unfair advantage to competitors is no longer seriously entertained by any modern business man. The realistic corporate executive knows that his alert competitors have a pretty good notion of what his business is and if he is unable to compete with them it is because he is hopelessly behind in the keen competitive struggle. The reporting provisions of the legislation have been approved by such conservative investment services as Moody's and Standard Statistics and, despite the wild fears spread throughout the country by powerful lobbyists against this bill, intelligent business men recognize that general knowledge of business facts will only help and cannot hurt them. The possession of these facts has for a number of years been the exclusive perquisite of powerful banking and industrial groups. Making these facts generally available will be of material benefit and guidance to business as a whole.

Control of Unfair Practices by Corporate Insiders

A renewal of investors' confidence in the exchange markets can be effected only by a clearer recognition upon the part of the corporate managers of companies whose securities are publicly held of their responsibilities as trustees for their corporations. Men charged with the administration of other people's money must not use inside information for their own advantage. Because it is difficult to draw a clear line as a matter of law between truly inside information and information generally known by the better-informed investors, the most potent weapon against the abuse of inside information is full and prompt publicity. For that reason, this bill requires the disclosure of the corporate holdings of officers and directors and stockholders owning more than 5 percent of any class of stock, and prompt disclosure of any changes that occur in their corporate holdings. Short selling and selling against the box by insiders are prohibited. These provisions have been called the "anti-Wiggin provisions" of the bill. The Committee is aware that these requirements are not air-tight and that the unscrupulous insider may still, within the law, use inside information for his own advantage. It is hoped, however, that the publicity features of the bill will tend to bring these practices into disrepute and encourage the voluntary maintenance of proper fiduciary standards by those in control of large corporate enterprises whose securities are registered on the public exchanges.

Fair corporate suffrage is an important right that should attach to every equity security bought on a public exchange. Managements of properties owned by the investing public should not be permitted to perpetuate themselves by the misuse of corporate proxies. Insiders having little or no substantial interest in the properties they manage have often retained their control without an adequate disclosure of their interest and without an adequate explanation of the management policies they intend to pursue. Insiders have at times solicited proxies without fairly informing the stockholders of the purposes for which the proxies are to be used and have used such proxies to take from the stockholders for their own selfish advantage valuable property rights. Inasmuch as only the exchanges make it possible for securities to be widely distributed among the investing public, it follows as a corollary that the use of the exchanges should involve a corresponding duty of according to shareholders fair suffrage. For this reason the proposed bill gives the Federal Trade Commission power to control the conditions under which proxies may be solicited with a view to preventing the recurrence of abuses which have frustrated the free exercise of the voting rights of stockholders.

Control of the Exchanges and Over-the-Counter Markets

The importance of the actual workings of the exchanges themselves, although great, should not be exaggerated. The stronger and more subtle economic forces affecting speculation come from without the exchanges. But as this speculation converges upon the exchanges, the control of the exchange mechanism is a necessary part of any effective regulation. It is for that reason that the bill gives the Federal Trade Commission broad powers over the exchanges to insure their efficient and honest functioning. Theoretically floor trading has been assumed to be of value in stabilizing prices and preventing undue fluctuations. The studies conducted by the special counsel for the Senate Committee on Banking and Currency have thrown considerable doubt upon the value of floor trading. The large floor traders seldom stem the tide but run with it. Their activity tends to accentuate the moves of the market and to stimulate undue speculation. The importance of active, constant trading can readily be exaggerated. A relatively stable market over a period is of much greater importance to investors than a fictitiously stable market that involves no more than one eighth of a point spread between sales but results in wide fluctuations over days or weeks. The market's liquidity depends upon its relative stability and not upon the spreads between momentary sales. To prevent the artificial stimulation of the market that comes from excessive speculative trading unrelated to investment, the Commission is given power to regulate and, if need be, prevent floor trading. The Commission is further given power to prevent excessive trading by members off the floor who at times are tempted to stimulate the market by numerous in and out transactions which cost them nothing more than the nominal commissions paid to the $2 brokers.

No issue has been more disputed than that centering about the functions of the specialist. There are many who believe that the exchange mechanism would function better without the specialist, that the work done by the specialist could be done more effectively by a clerk or official of the exchange clearing the orders in a purely mechanical way, much as they are cleared today on the New York Stock Exchange in the "bond crowd." There are others who believe that a specialist should be obliged to act either as a dealer or as a broker and should not be permitted to combine the functions of dealer and broker. The jobber on the London Stock Exchange is essentially a dealer-specialist who deals only with other jobbers and with brokers, and does not act as a broker himself or deal with the public directly. It is generally admitted that there are serious abuses in connection with the work of specialists. The New York Stock Exchange tightened its rules in regard to specialists on the very eve of the hearings held by the Committee. It is true that some of the worst evils associated with the specialist have centered around their participation in pools, but there are inherent difficulties in the situation where under normal circumstances the available orders are known to the specialist only—and perhaps his favored friends—and not to everyone dealing in the security involved. Inasmuch as the stock exchanges objected to the laying down of any statutory rule governing specialists, their suggestion has been adopted of giving the Commission effective power to control the activities of specialists and to experiment with various devices of control.

Another perplexing problem in regard to the working of the exchanges has been that centering about the dealer-broker relationship. There is an inherent inconsistency in a man's acting both as a broker and a dealer. It is difficult to serve two masters. And it is particularly difficult to give impartial advice to a client if the dealer-broker has his own securities to sell, particularly when they are new securities for which there is no ready market. The combination of the functions of dealer and broker has persisted over a long period of time in American investment banking and it was found difficult to break up this relationship at a time when the dealer business was in the doldrums and when it was feared that the bulk of the dealer-brokers would, if compelled to choose, give up their dealer business and leave, temporarily at least, an impaired mechanism for the distribution of new securities. Consequently it was deemed impracticable at this time to do more than require the dealer-broker to disclose to his customer the capacity in which he was acting and to refrain from taking into margin accounts new securities in the distribution of which he had participated during the preceding 6 months.

The bill proceeds on the theory that the exchanges are public institutions which the public is invited to use for the purchase and sale of securities listed thereon, and are not private clubs to be conducted only in accordance with the interests of their members. The great exchanges of this country upon which millions of dollars of securities are sold are affected with a public interest in the same degree as any other great utility. The Commission is empowered, if the rules of the exchange in any important matter are not appropriate for the protection of investors or appropriate to insure fair dealing, to order such changes in the rules after due notice and hearings as it may deem necessary. The exchanges may alter their rules if more effective means are discovered to meet the same or new problems. Although a wide measure of initiative and responsibility is left with the exchanges, reserved control is in the Commission if the exchanges do not meet their responsibility. It is hoped that the effect of the bill will be to give to the well-managed exchanges that power necessary to enable them to effect themselves needed reforms and that the occasion for direct action by the Commission will not arise.

The committee has been convinced that effective regulation of the exchanges requires as a corollary a measure of control over the over-the-counter markets. The problem is clearly put in the recent report of the Twentieth Century Fund on "Stock Market Control":

The benefits that would accrue as the result of raising the standards of security exchanges might be nullified if the over-the-counter markets were left unregulated and uncontrolled. They are of vast proportions and they would serve as a refuge for any business that might seek to escape the discipline of the exchanges; and the more exacting that discipline, the greater the temptation to escape from it. Over-the-counter markets offer facilities that are useful under certain conditions, but they should not be permitted to expand beyond their proper sphere and compete with the exchanges for business that, from the point of view of public interest, should be confined to the organized markets. This constitutes the sanction for Federal regulation of over-the-counter dealers and brokers. To leave the over-the-counter markets out of a regulatory system would be to destroy the effects of regulating the organized exchanges.

Administration

The bill places the administration of the legislation, apart from credit phases, in the Federal Trade Commission. It provides, however, for the enlargement of that commission by two members and the creation within it of a special division which will administer both this bill and the Securities Act of 1933. Unquestionably these two measures are so closely related that they should be administered by the same body, and unquestionably if no new commission were to be appointed that administration should be lodged in the Federal Trade Commission, which has so ably organized the administration of the Securities Act of 1933.

Insofar as the proposals of the stock exchanges suggest a separate stock-exchange authority, it should be kept in mind that the name by which the body administering the act is known is not important. The legislative essentials are the same whether the body is called an authority or a board or a Federal commission. Those essentials are how much power the administrative body shall have and whether it shall be made up entirely of representatives of none but the public interest, or of "expert" representatives, as such, of stock exchanges and of other distinct classes in the community.

Insofar as "experts" are concerned, it is a commonplace of administrative states-manship that boards of men who are experts in details rarely agree among themselves, and in their very expertness with the trees seldom perceive the woods of broad public policy. The well-learned lesson of democratic government with "experts" is that they should be kept on tap but not on top.

Insofar as making up a permanent Government regulatory body from representatives of special vested interests is concerned, it has been long ago learned that no harmony of policy can result from a regulatory body packed with advocates of warring interests, and that the inevitable result of placing on a regulatory authority able advocates who have at heart the definite interest of a particular class which will profit by the least possible regulation is stultification of the regulation.

III. Analysis of the Bill by Sections

Section 1. Short Title

This section provides that the act may be cited as the "National Securities Exchange Act of 1934."

Section 2. The Necessity for Regulation as Provided in This Act

The purpose of this section is to indicate the facts which give rise to the necessity for the legislation and justify the exercise of congressional power. The evidence submitted to the committee, together with that produced before the Senate Banking and Currency Committee during its recent extensive investigation and facts that have become common knowledge during the national economic crisis of the past few years, abundantly justify the findings recited in this section.

Section 3. Definitions and Application of Act

(a) This subsection defines the terms used in the act. Most of these definitions are self-explanatory. Banks are expressly exempted from the definitions of "broker" and "dealer." The definition of "bank" in paragraph (6) includes banks organized under the laws of the United States, members of the Federal Reserve System, and any other bank performing the normal functions of receiving deposits or exercising fiduciary powers and which is subject to supervision and examination by State or Federal authorities. In paragraph (10) the words "oil, gas, or other" have been stricken out of that part of the definition of "security," as it appeared in earlier prints of the bill, which included any "certificate of interest or participation in any profit-sharing agreement or in any oil, gas, or other mineral royalty or lease." From the use of the words "other mineral royalty or lease" in the earlier print it is clear that an oil or gas royalty or lease was considered to be one kind of mineral royalty or lease, and thus no actual change is made by striking out the words indicated above. An "exempted security" is defined in paragraph (12) to include certain specified classes of securities. In addition, the Secretary of the Treasury may designate for exemption the securities of corporations in which the United States has a direct or indirect interest; and the Federal Trade Commission (elsewhere referred to as the "Commission") is given power to place in the category of "exempted securities" any other securities (including unregistered securities the market in which is predominantly intrastate) where it deems such action necessary or appropriate in the public interest or for the protection of investors. A large number of the provisions in the act expressly exclude "exempted securities." Thus the Commission is able to remove from the operation of any one or more of these provisions any securities as to which it deems them inappropriate. It may attach such conditions to such exemption as it deems desirable. The Commission may therefore make appropriate exemptions for the protection of the holders of defaulted securities and foreign securities if the issuers refuse to register.

(b) The Commission and the Federal Reserve Board are given power to define accounting, technical, and trade terms.

(c) The act is not to apply to instrumentalities and agencies of the United States, except where they are specifically included.

Section 4. Transactions on Unregistered Exchanges

This section forbids the use of the mails and interstate commerce to any exchange which is not registered as a "national securities exchange" under section 5, but authorizes the Commission to exempt from this prohibition small exchanges as to which it finds that registration would be impracticable and unnecessary in the public interest or for the protection of investors. Such exemption may be withdrawn under stated circumstances.

Section 5. Registration of National Securities Exchanges

Subsection (a) provides for registration as a "national securities exchange" upon application by any exchange which agrees to comply and to require its members to comply, with the act and the rules and regulations thereunder, and which furnishes the Commission with required information.

An exchange desiring registration is required by subsection (b) to provide for the disciplining of members who are guilty of conduct "inconsistent with just and equitable principle of trade," and must include in this category any willful violation of the act or any rule or regulation thereunder.

It is provided in subsection (c) that exchanges may adopt any rules not inconsistent with the act or the rules and regulations thereunder or the laws of the State in which it is located.

Subsection (d) directs the Commission to grant an application for registration if it appears that the exchange is so organized as to be able to comply with the act and rules and regulations thereunder and to insure fair dealing and the protection of investors.

Subsection (e) provides that the Commission's order granting or denying an application for registration shall be made within 30 days unless the application has been withdrawn.

Subsection (f) permits an exchange to withdraw its registration upon such terms as the Commission may deem necessary for the protection of investors.

Section 6. Margin Requirements

The Federal Reserve Board is directed by subsection (a) to prescribe by rules and regulations the maximum amount of credit which may be extended and maintained on any security (other than an exempted security) which is registered on a national securities exchange. As far as the initial extension of credit is concerned it is indicated by the act that this should be based on a standard of 55 percent of the current market price of the security or 100 percent of its lowest market price during the preceding 36 calendar months, but in no case more than 75 percent of the current market price. Until July 1, 1936, the lowest price on or after July 1, 1933, is to be considered as the lowest price during the preceding 36 calendar months. Matters of detail concerning the maintenance of margins, substitutions, additional purchases, withdrawals, and transfers of accounts are left to be determined by the Board, which is also given power to prescribe regulations with regard to margins in the case of delayed deliveries, short sales, arbitrage transactions, securities which have not been on the market for 36 months, and similar matters of administrative adjustment.

Under subsection (b) the Federal Reserve Board may depart from the standard indicated in subsection (a) for the initial extension of credit by (1) lowering margin requirements insofar as it deems necessary for the accommodation of commerce and industry, having due regard to the general credit situation, and (2) prescribing such higher margin requirements as it may deem necessary or appropriate to prevent the excessive use of credit to finance speculative transactions in securities. Thus the effect is to make the margin provisions of the act completely elastic, giving the Federal Reserve Board discretion, but at the same time indicating a standard to which it is to adhere except under the circumstances indicated.

Subsection (c) makes it unlawful for a member of a national securities exchange or a broker or dealer who does business through such a member to extend or maintain credit in violation of the regulations prescribed under subsections (a) and (b), or without collateral or on collateral other than an exempted security or a security registered upon a national securities exchange, except insofar as this is permitted by rules and regulations of the Federal Reserve Board where such use of credit is not for the purpose of purchasing or carrying securities or of evading the margin requirements for registered securities.

Subsection (d) authorizes the Board to make rules and regulations so far as may be necessary to prevent evasion of this section through loans from persons who are not covered by subsection (c) and permits the imposition, upon loans made for the purchasing or carrying of registered securities, of limitations similar to those which may be imposed upon members, brokers, and dealers. It is expressly provided that such regulations shall not apply to loans not made in the course of business (such as purely personal loans), to loans on exempted securities, to loans to aid dealers in the distribution of securities not through the medium of a national securities exchange, to bank loans on any security other than an "equity security", or to such other loans as the Board may deem it necessary or appropriate to exempt. (An equity security is defined in sec. 3 (a) (11), and is, to speak generally, a stock or a security convertible into a security similar thereto.)

Subsection (e) makes the provisions of this entire section inapplicable to credit outstanding at the effective date of the act until January 31, 1939. This is designed to prevent forced liquidation.

Section 7. Restrictions on Borrowing by Members, Brokers, and Dealers

By subsection (a), borrowing on registered securities (other than exempted securities) by members, brokers, and dealers who do a business through members is confined to loans from member banks of the Federal Reserve System or from nonmember banks which agree to comply with the provisions of this act, the Federal Reserve Act, and the Banking Act of 1933, insofar as they relate to the use of credit to finance transactions in securities. This, however, is subject to certain exceptions in case of transactions between members, brokers, and dealers and in emergency cases.

Subsection (b) prohibits a member, broker, or dealer to permit his indebtedness (except on exempted securities) in the ordinary course of business as a broker to exceed 2,000 percent of his net capital or such lower percentage thereof as the Commission may prescribe.

A broker is forbidden by subsection (c) to commingle the securities of customers without their written consent; and by subsection (d) regardless of such consent to pledge customers' securities with those of persons who are not customers or under circumstances that will subject customers' securities to a lien in excess of the aggregate indebtedness of the customers. This means that a broker cannot risk the securities of his customers to finance his own speculative operations. He is also forbidden by subsection (e) to lend a customer's securities without the latter's written consent.

Section 8. Prohibition Against Manipulation of Security Prices

Subsection (a) makes it unlawful for any person to use the mails, or interstate commerce, or any facility of a national securities exchange, or for any member of a national securities exchange by use of any means, to participate in certain practices in connection with securities registered on a national securities exchange.

Under paragraph (1) of this subsection it is made unlawful for the purpose of creating a misleading appearance as to the real nature of the market or activity of trading in the security, (A) to effect any transaction which involves no change in the beneficial ownership of the security, or (B) to enter orders for the purchase of a security with the knowledge that orders of substantially the same size, at substantially the same time and at substantially the same price, for the sale of such security will be entered by or for the same or different parties, or (C) to enter orders for the sale of a security with the knowledge of orders of substantially the same size, at substantially the same time and at substantially the same price, for the purchase of such security, will be entered for the same by or for the same or different parties. These provisions strike at wash sales and matched orders.

Paragraph (2) makes it unlawful to effect any series of transactions in a security for the purpose of raising or depressing the price of such security. Of course, any extensive purchases or sales are bound to cause changes in the market price of the security. If a person is merely trying to acquire a large block of stock for investment, or desires to dispose of a big holding, his knowledge that in doing so he will affect the market price does not make his action unlawful. His transactions become unlawful only when they are made for the purpose of raising or depressing the market price. This provision catches the rigging and jiggling of the market, and prevents the marking up or down of prices by pools.

Inducing the sale or purchase of securities by the making of a false or misleading statement of a material fact is outlawed by paragraph (4), unless the person making the statement had no reason to believe the statement was false or misleading.

Paragraphs (3) and (5) make it unlawful to induce the purchase or sale of a security by circulating in the ordinary course of business or for a consideration information that a security will change in price as a result of market operations for a rise or fall. These provisions are aimed at the "tipster sheet" and the practice of customer's men in inducing customers to buy or sell by spreading rumors with regard to the operations of pools.

The "pegging" of security prices is regulated by paragraph (6). Many experts are of the opinion that the artificial stabilization of a security at a given price serves no useful economic function. On the other hand the practice has been wide-spread on the part of many investment bankers who regard it legitimate, particularly if the public is aware of the plan. Instead of being prohibited, therefore, this practice is left to such regulation by the Commission as it may deem necessary for the prevention of activities detrimental to the interests of investors.

Subsection (b) is concerned with the use of options in connection with transactions on national securities exchanges. Options and trading against options are the usual concomitants of pool operations. Inasmuch, however, as it has been urged that all options are not affected with the manipulative taint it is made unlawful to trade in or against options only when in violation of such rules and regulations as the Commission may deem necessary in the public interest or for the protection of investors.

Subsection (c) empowers the Commission to make regulations regarding the guaranteeing of options for registered securities by members of national security exchanges.

Subsection (d) makes it clear that the options to be regulated under subsections (b) and (c), which include so-called "puts," "calls," "straddles," and "privileges"—which are commonly used for manipulative and speculative purposes—do not include duly registered warrants or rights to subscribe to a security or the right of the holder of a registered convertible security to have it converted.

Subsection (e) provides that persons who willfully participate in the manipulative or speculative practices which are forbidden by subsections (a), (b), and (c) shall be liable for the damages they cause to innocent investors who have bought or sold the security in question at a price which has been effected by such unlawful practices. A defendant may recover contribution from any other participant in the illegal transactions who would have been liable if sued jointly. Suits for recovery under this subsection must be commenced within 3 years after the violation.

Subsection (f) exempts from the operation of this section all "exempted securities."

Section 9. Regulation of the Use of Manipulative Devices

This section makes it unlawful to use the mails or interstate commerce or any facility of a national securities exchange to effect a short sale of, or to employ any stop-loss order in connection with a transaction in, a registered security in contravention of the regulations of the Commission.

Section 10. Segregation and Limitation of Functions of Members, Brokers, and Dealers

Subsection (a) directs the Commission to regulate or prevent, by rules and regulations, floor trading on the part of members. By this means those who are actually on the scene of speculation may be restricted from taking undue advantage of this privilege. The Commission is also directed by rules and regulations to prevent such excessive speculation on the part of members who operate from off the floor as it may deem detrimental to the maintenance of a fair and orderly market. The Commission may make such exemptions as are necessary or appropriate in the case of "exempted securities," arbitrage transactions, and transactions by odd-lot dealers and specialists.

Subsection (b) authorizes the registration of members as odd-lot dealers or specialists, or both, pursuant to the rules of the exchange, and subject to rules and regulations of the Commission. The odd-lot dealer may be permitted to deal for his own account only so far as necessary in the performance of his particular function. The Commission is directed to limit the specialist in his dealings for his own account to those which are necessary for the maintenance of a fair and orderly market. The specialist is forbidden to reveal the orders on his books to favored persons. This information must be available to all members or else kept confidential. The specialist is likewise prohibited from exercising purely discretionary orders as distinct from market or limited price orders.

Subsection (c) authorizes the Commission to exempt small exchanges from the provisions of this section. This will prevent hardship on those exchanges where the functions of members are not as highly specialized as on the larger markets. Provision is made for withdrawing the exemption in proper cases.

Subsection (d) provides that any member, or any person doing business through a member, who acts both as a broker and dealer shall not use the mails, or interstate commerce, or any national securities exchange to effect any transaction which involves purchasing for a customer on margin, or selling to him on margin, any security which the broker or dealer has been engaged in distributing within 6 months. This strikes at one of the greatest potential evils inherent in the combination of the broker and dealer function in the same person, by assuring that he will not induce his customers to buy on credit securities which he has undertaken to distribute to the public. A broker-dealer must also reveal to his customers whether he acts as principal or as agent in order that the customer may be aware of any factors tending to influence the broker's advice.

Subsection (e) directs the Commission to investigate and report to Congress by January 3, 1936, on the question of completely segregating the activities of brokers and dealers.

Section 11. Registration Requirements for Securities

Subsection (a) prohibits members, brokers, and dealers from effecting any transaction on a national securities exchange in any security which is not exempted or registered under the provisions of this act.

The application to be filed by the issuer of a security with the exchange and with the Commission as a prerequisite to registration is described in subsection (b).

In paragraph (1) is indicated the information which the Commission may require an issuer to file in its application for registration. These provisions are self-explanatory.

Under paragraph (2) various documents such as articles of incorporation, bylaws, and underwriting arrangements may be called for.

Subsection (c) authorizes the Commission if it deems any of the information specified under subsection (b) to be inappropriate in a given case or class of cases to require in lieu thereof the submission of appropriate information of a comparable character. This assures adequate elasticity without giving the Commission unconfined authority to elicit any information whatsoever.

If an exchange approves the registration of a security and so certifies to the Commission, the registration becomes effective within 30 days under subsection (d), subject, however, to the provisions of section 18. An issuer may cancel its registration at any time subject to such conditions as the Commission may prescribe as necessary for the protection of investors. Registration of unissued securities for trading on a "when, as, and if issued" basis is permitted subject to regulations of the Commission in cases where the registration is not primarily designed to distribute the security to investors other than the present security holders of the company. This permits the creation of an adequate market in which the holders of rights to unissued securities may trade them as against the value of the unissued securities. At the same time the Commission will be able to prevent the practice of running up the price of a security prior to its issuance, so that it is finally issued at an excessive price.

In order to preclude congestion during the period when the act first comes into force, subsection (e) would permit the provisional registration of securities already listed on exchanges without compliance with the registration requirements set forth in this section. Such registrations may be effective until July 1, 1935, by which date there should be more than adequate time for formal registration.

Subsection (f) provides that unlisted trading (the practice of admitting securities to trade upon the application of a member of the exchange and without any action on the part of the corporation) shall be permitted by the rules and regulations of the Commission until July 1, 1935, in securities admitted to unlisted trading before March 1, 1934. Such securities are to be regarded as registered securities, except that they are exempt from the requirements of sections 11, 12, and 15, but in quoting transactions exchanges must specify the securities which are admitted merely to unlisted trading.

Section 12. Periodical and Other Reports

Subsection (a) requires the issuers of registered securities to keep the information filed under section 11 reasonably up to date and to make annual reports, certified by independent public accountants if the Commission deems this necessary, and such quarterly reports as may be deemed essential.

Subsection (b) permits the Commission to specify the form in which reports shall be made, the details to be shown in financial statements and the methods to be followed in calculating the items indicated in their preparation. The purpose is to give some assurance that reports will not hide the true condition of the company. In the case of the reports of any person whose accounting is subject to the provisions of any law of the United States or of any State, the rules and regulations of the Commission imposing requirements with respect to reports are not to be inconsistent with the requirements imposed by such law; but if the Commission believes that such requirements are inadequate from the point of view of the investor, it may impose additional requirements. In other words, while the act carefully avoids unnecessary duplication of reports, it permits the Commission to require the reporting of all matters regarded as essential under the act for the protection of investors.

Section 13. Proxies

Subsection (a) prohibits the solicitation of proxies in contravention of such rules and regulations as the Commission may prescribe in the interest of the issuer and its security holders.

By subsection (b) it is made unlawful for a member of a national securities exchange or a broker or dealer who transacts a business in securities through a member to give proxies with respect to securities carried for a customer in contravention of such rules and regulations as the Commission may prescribe for the protection of investors.

Section 14. Over-the-Counter Markets

The use of the mails and interstate commerce for the creation of markets, other than regular exchanges, is made the basis for such regulation of these markets as the Commission may find to be necessary or appropriate to insure to investors protection comparable to that which is accorded in the case of registered exchanges under the act. Such rules and regulations may include provision for the registration of brokers and dealers and of the securities traded. Securities already traded in on exchanges at the time the act becomes effective may be subjected to special regulation if they do not become registered under section 11. This will enable the Commission to distinguish between the securities of the type normally subject to speculative and manipulative abuse and those not customarily bought or sold on exchanges.

Section 15. Directors, Officers, and Principal Stockholders

Under subsection (a) directors and officers of the issuer of a registered equity security (other than an exempted security) and holders of more than 5 percent of any class of a registered equity security (other than an exempted security), are required at the time of registration to file with the Commission a list of their holdings of the issuer's securities and to file monthly reports of their dealings in such securities. This is to give investors an idea of the purchases and sales by insiders which may in turn indicate their private opinion as to prospects of the company.

By subsection (b) directors, officers, and principal security holders are forbidden to sell registered securities (other than exempted securities) short or to sell for delivery after 20 days. The latter provision is for the purpose of preventing "sales against the box" whereby those in possession of inside information sell their holdings but keep the stock registered in their name, so that their change of position does not become known until delivery is made at a later date.

Section 16. Accounts and Records, Reports, Examination
of Exchanges, Members, and Others

By subsection (a) national securities exchanges, their members, and brokers and dealers who do business through them, as well as brokers and dealers who maintain over-the-counter markets, are required to keep such records as the Commission may prescribe in the public interest or for the protection of investors. These records shall be open to reasonable inspection by the Commission.

Subsection (b) gives the Federal Reserve Board necessary powers as to reports and examinations in connection with the exercise of its functions under the act.

Section 17. Liability for Misleading Statements

Subsection (a) provides that any person who makes or causes to be made any statement in an application, report, or document, which is false or misleading as to a material fact, shall be liable to a person who in reliance on the statement and in ignorance of its false or misleading character has purchased the security to which it relates at a price affected by it, unless the person sued proved that he acted in good faith without knowledge of the false and misleading character of the statement.

Subsection (b) provides for contribution between persons who would be liable to be sued jointly, and subsection (c) limits the time for bringing a suit to 3 years after the violation.

Section 18. Powers with Respect to Exchanges and Securities

Subsection (a) authorizes the Commission when it deems such action necessary—(1) to suspend or withdraw registration of an exchange which the Commission finds has violated the act or the rules and regulations thereunder or has failed to take adequate steps to enforce compliance therewith by its members, (2) to deny, postpone, suspend, or withdraw the registration of the security in case of violation by the issuer, (3) to suspend or expel a member or officer of an exchange who is guilty of a violation or of aiding a violation by acting as broker for a person whom he has reason to believe is engaged in a violation, and (4) summarily to suspend trade in any registered security for a period not exceeding 10 days or with the approval of the President of the United States summarily to suspend all trade on a registered exchange for not more than 90 days. Orders issued pursuant to (1), (2), and (3), must be preceded by appropriate notice and opportunity for hearing; action under (4) is of an emergency nature and therefore limited in time.

Subsection (b) authorizes the Commission to amend the rules of an exchange in certain particulars by rules and regulations, after the exchange has failed to comply with the Commission's written request for such amendment of the rules of the exchange as the Commission deems necessary or appropriate for the protection of investors or to insure fair dealing or administration of the exchange.

Section 19. Liabilities of Controlling Persons

By subsection (a) a person who controls a person subject to the act or a rule or regulation thereunder is made liable to the same extent as the person controlled unless the controlling person acted in good faith and did not induce the act in question.

Subsection (b) makes it unlawful for any person to do, through any other person, anything that he is forbidden to do himself.

Subsection (c) makes it unlawful for a director, officer, or security owner, without just cause, to hinder, delay, or obstruct the making of reports required of an issuer under this act.

In this section and in section 11, when reference is made to "control," the term is intended to include actual control as well as what has been called legally enforceable control. (See Handy & Harmon v. Burnet (1931) 284 U.S. 136.) It was thought undesirable to attempt to define the term. It would be difficult if not impossible to enumerate or to anticipate the many ways in which actual control may be exerted. A few examples of the methods used are stock ownership, lease, contract, and agency. It is well known that actual control sometimes may be exerted through ownership of much less than a majority of the stock of a corporation either by the ownership of such stock alone or through such ownership in combination with other factors.

Section 20. Investigations; Injunctions and Prosecution of Offenses

(a) The Commission is authorized to investigate violations of the act. The Commission is further authorized to investigate and to publish information concerning any facts, conditions, practices, or matters which it may deem necessary or appropriate to aid in the enforcement of the act or in prescribing rules and regulations.

(b) The Commission is authorized through its members, or officers designated by it, to administer oaths and affirmations, subpena witnesses, compel their attendance, and require the production of books, papers, correspondence, memoranda, and other records.

(c) This subsection relates to compelling attendance and testimony of witnesses and the production of evidence.

(d) This subsection is similar to one contained in the Federal Trade Commission Act, and provides that no person shall be excused from attending and testifying, but relieves any natural person from prosecution with respect to or on account of any matter concerning which he may testify or produce evidence.

(e) The Commission is authorized to seek the aid of the United States district courts to enjoin acts or practices in violation of the provisions of the act or rules and regulations.

(f) The district courts of the United States are given jurisdiction to issue writs of mandamus commanding any person to comply with the provisions of the act or any order made thereunder.

Section 21. Hearings by Commission

This section provides that hearings of the Commission may be public and may be held before the Commission or any member or members thereof or any designated officer or officers and requires that appropriate records of hearings shall be kept.

Section 22. Rules and Regulations; Annual Reports

(a) The Commission and the Federal Reserve Board, respectively, are authorized to make such rules and regulations as may be necessary for the execution of the functions granted to them under the act and are authorized for such purposes to classify issuers, securities, exchanges, and other persons or matters.

(b) The Commission and the Federal Reserve Board are directed to include in their annual reports to Congress such information and such recommendations for further legislation as they may deem advisable relating to the matters within their respective jurisdictions under the act.

Section 23. Information Filed with the Commission

(a) This subsection makes it clear that no person is to be required to reveal trade secrets or processes in applications, reports, or other documents.

(b) Any person filing information may object in writing to the public disclosure thereof, and the Commission is authorized to hear objections when it deems it advisable. In cases where objections are made the Commission is not to make the information public unless in its judgment disclosure thereof is in the public interest.

(c) It is made unlawful for any member, officer, or employee of the Commission to make disclosure of information which is not made available to the public as authorized in subsection (b).

Section 24. Court Review of Orders

(a) This section relates to review by United States Circuit Courts of Appeal of orders of the Commission, on the petition of any person aggrieved. On such review the court is to have exclusive jurisdiction to affirm, modify, and enforce or set aside the order, in whole or in part. Findings of fact by the Commission are to be conclusive if supported by substantial evidence. The judgment and decree of the court is to be final subject to review by the Supreme Court in accordance with section 239 and 240 of the Judicial Code.

(b) The commencement of proceedings under subsection (a) is not to operate as a stay of the Commission's order unless the court so orders.

Section 25. Unlawful Representations

No action or failure to act by the Commission or Federal Reserve Board is to be construed to indicate approval of any security or transaction or to indicate a finding that any statement or report is true and accurate or not false or misleading. It is declared to be unlawful to make any representation that any such action or failure to act is to be so construed or has such effect.

Section 26. Jurisdiction of Offenses and Suits

The district courts of the United States, the Supreme Court of the District of Columbia, and the United States courts of any Territory or other place subject to the jurisdiction of the United States are given jurisdiction of violations of the act and of rules and regulations thereunder, and of suits in equity and actions at law brought to enforce any liability or duty created by the act or by the rules and regulations thereunder.

Section 27. Effect on Existing Law

(a) This subsection reserves rights and remedies existing outside of those provided in the act, but limits the total amount recoverable to the amount of actual damages. It provides that the jurisdiction of State commissions shall not be affected insofar as it does not conflict with the provisions of the act or the rules and regulations thereunder.

(b) It is provided that nothing in the act shall be construed to modify existing law with regard to certain relationships between exchanges and their members.

Section 28. Validity of Contracts

(a) This subsection declares void any condition or stipulation requiring any person to waive compliance with any provision of the act or any rule or regulation thereunder or any rule of exchange.

(b) This subsection declares void contracts made in violation of the provisions of the act or the rules or regulations thereunder, and contracts made prior to the enactment of the act which involve the continuance of any relationship or practice prohibited by the act or any rule or regulation thereunder.

(c) This subsection includes provisions to negative any construction of the act which would affect the validity of loans and liens in certain cases. Cases are specified in which the act is to be construed to afford a defense to the collection of any debt or obligation or the enforcement of a lien.

Section 29. Foreign Securities Exchanges

(a) This subsection makes it unlawful for brokers or dealers to use the mails or any instrumentality of interstate commerce to effect upon an exchange outside the United States transactions in securities of issuers who reside in or are organized under the laws of, or have their principal place of business in, the United States or any place subject to the jurisdiction thereof, in contravention of the rules and regulations of the Commission.

(b) It is provided that the act shall not apply to any person insofar as he transacts a business in securities outside the jurisdiction of the United States unless he transacts such business in contravention of the rules and regulations of the Commission prescribed to prevent evasion of the act.

Section 30. Registration Fees

An annual registration fee for exchanges is provided for in this section. Such fee is to be an amount equal to one five-hundredth of 1 percent of the aggregate dollar amount of the securities sales transacted on the exchange during the preceding calendar year. Amounts received as fees will be desposited in the Federal Treasury.

Section 31. Members and Employees of Federal Trade Commission

(a) This subsection provides for two additional members of the Federal Trade Commission. It authorizes the Commission to divide the members thereof into divisions (each to consist of not less than three members) and to direct that any of its functions arising under this act or any other provision of law may be assigned or referred to any such division. Provision is made for rehearing before the full Commission of decisions, orders, or other action by a division. A rehearing is not to suspend the operation of that division unless the Commission makes an order to that effect.

(b) For the purposes of this act and of the Securities Act of 1933 the Commission is authorized to employ and fix the compensation of attorneys, examiners, and other special experts without regard to the provisions of other laws applicable to the employment and compensation of officers and employees of the United States.

Section 32. Penalties

Penalties are provided for willful violation of the act or any rule or regulation thereunder the violation of which is expressly made unlawful, or for the making or causing to be made any statement in any application, report, or document filed under the act if such statement is false or misleading with respect to any material fact. The penalty provided is a fine of not more than $10,000 or imprisonment for not more than 2 years, or both, except that when the violation is by an exchange a fine not to exceed $500,000 may be imposed.

Section 33. Separability of Provisions

This section declares the policy of Congress that if any provision of the act or the application of such provision to any person or circumstance is held invalid the remainder of the act or the application of such provision to persons or circumstances other than those to which it is held invalid, shall not be affected thereby.

Section 34. Effective Date

The act is to take effect upon its enactment, except that certain of its provisions are to become effective July 1, 1934, and certain other provisions are to become effective on August 1, 1934.

MINORITY VIEWS
[To accompany H.R. 9323]

There can be no doubt that the securities exchange bill, as reported by the House Committee on Interstate and Foreign Commerce, is greatly improved over the bill as originally produced.

The original bill, drawn under the natural resentment which resulted from the revelation of many abuses in the stock exchanges and in other agencies for distributing stocks, was primarily a punitive and preventive measure. As is often the case, those who drew the bill were so intent upon the relatively few who had committed these offenses that its effect on innocent and honest people was overlooked. The provisions of the bill would practically have stopped business on the stock exchanges and would have frozen the liquid assets of the Nation, and so still further restricted business and caused still further disasters to the banks.

Many of the original provisions of the bill which would have produced these disasters have been modified or elminated. So far as the bill relates to practices of stock exchanges it cannot be severely criticized.

But the original fundamental objection still remains, namely, that it gives the commission which is in charge of administering the bill indeterminate power over all issues of stock, and thus over all corporations in the country. This may seem a broad statement, but from the best statistics which can be obtained, it is estimated that there are 10 million stockholders of record in this country after allowing for duplication, and that, not allowing for duplication, there are about 26 million stockholders of record; that is, 26 million individual stock holdings. It is evident that the value of all these stock holdings may be affected by the action of the commission under this bill.

In addition to this there are, of course, thousands of millions of dollars of bonds and other obligations issued by corporations which are held by insurance companies and savings banks and other trustees for the benefit of millions of owners. It is not contended that this bill is going to ruin all these people, but it is sure that the handling of all this immense amount of liquid capital is going to be more complicated and less free than without the legislation.

As will be seen by reference to the bill, the powers of the commission are varied and important. The commission has power to license an exchange, to exempt an exchange from registration, and to withdraw such exemption. The commission also has power to suspend trading on an exchange for the violation of its regulations. It can control over-the-counter markets, it can make rules and regulations for the segregation and limitation of functions of members, brokers, and dealers on the exchanges.

The bill provides very minute directions as to the registration of a security on a national exchange and requires detailed information as to its organization, as to the directors and officers of a corporation, giving their salaries and any bonus or other profit-sharing arrangements. It requires also a statement of any remuneration, including bonuses, for any employee whose total compensation exceeds $10,000 per annum, and other information going into great detail as to the management of a corporation, which information most corporations, for good reasons, would prefer to consider confidential. Annual and quarterly statements are required, and finally, the commission is given blanket power to require information, and provided any report required under the bill is found inapplicable to any specified class or classes or issuers, to require such reports of comparable character as the commission may deem applicable.

The commission has full power as to the solicitation of proxies for any special or annual meeting. There is a provision that any person who is a large stockholder, and owns or controls more than 5 percent of any class of stock, shall file a statement with the exchange of the amount of his holdings, and at the end of each month shall file a statement indicating any change in his ownership.

Any person who makes a false or misleading statement with regard to any material fact is liable to a suit for damages by anyone who suffers, unless the person making the statement can prove that he acted in good faith and did not believe that the statement was false and misleading.

The commission, whenever it thinks any person has violated any provision of the act, or any rule or regulation thereunder, can investigate, and for that purpose any member of the commission or any officer designated by it can subpena witnesses and compel their attendance and require the production of books, etc., from any place in the United States or any State at any designated place of hearing. And finally, anyone who willfully violates any provision of the act shall, upon conviction, be fined not more than $10,000 and imprisoned not more than 2 years, or both, except that when such person is in an exchange a fine not exceeding $500,000 may be imposed.

The above brief enumeration of some of the provisions of the bill will be enough to show why this bill has created the greatest attention and interest throughout the length and breadth of the Nation. It is safe to say that no bill has produced more correspondence for Members of Congress than this bill.

This interest has been referred to by some members of the administration and by some leading Members of the House and Senate as propaganda, but bearing in mind the 10 million individuals who are holders of stocks, their interest in this bill is perfectly natural and proper and should not be attributed to propaganda. It is simply a legitimate desire on the part of the owners to protect their property from undue and unnecessary depreciation.

There can be no question that there has been very wide-spread fear of such depreciation from the enactment of this bill. It may be argued that there is nothing in the bill to warrant the fear and that such fear is uncalled for. The same arguments were used with reference to the Securities Registration Act, which it is now proposed to modify, and it may be that the arguments have force as to both the acts, but fear is a psychological state which cannot be overcome at once by argument. When a man reads a complicated bill relating to his own industry or his own property, and finds it filled with intricate instructions and directions and which gives broad and undefined powers to a commission to make further rules and regulations and to impose penalties, and when further the bill winds up with a statement of possible heavy fines and imprisonment for a violation of any of these rules and regulations, almost anyone is justified in feeling fearful as to doing business in connection with organizations or securities covered by the bill.

What is essential to any sound recovery of business and to any real extension of employment and the use of credit in enterprise is confidence. The creation of new commissions having power over business and the creation of new regulations and penalties do not tend to quiet and confidence, but to the contrary, and thus retard business.

A minority of the committee suggest that however sound many of the provisions of the bill may be, the immediate consequences of its enactment would not be helpful, but rather the reverse, in the existing economic situation.

It is not probable, and, it may be said, hardly possible, that there should be any dangerous speculation or inflation of credit on the stock exchanges during this year. The stock exchanges have of their own motion made rules and regulations to do away with many of their previous evil practices. It is noticeable in the committee, which has given long and careful study to this bill, that the longer it was studied the more every member of the committee became convinced of the far-reaching effects of the bill, not only as to its extent over the Nation, but as to its ramifications in all branches of business. If there is no immediate crisis which would seem to call for legislation, it would seem to be the part of wisdom, before enacting legislation of such far-reaching consequences, to enable those who are especially expert in the business and those who are especially affected by the bill to study it carefully and submit their recommendations concerning it to the next Congress.

For the above reasons, therefore, it is recommended that the bill should not be passed by this Congress.

Schuyler Merritt

THE DEBATE

House of Representatives—73rd Congress, 2d Session
April 30—May 4, 1934

MR. BANKHEAD. Mr. Speaker, by direction of the Committee on Rules, I call up House Resolution 363, for the consideration of the bill H.R. 9323, and ask that it be reported. . . .

MR. SABATH. Mr. Speaker, I am so very much interested in this rule and the proposed legislation that I shall refrain from answering my colleague from Illinois [Mr. Britten], but I shall do so in the near future and point out to him that no injustice was done him by my extension of remarks and the statistics included in my speech, which do not descend to the regrettable depths of unfairness and viciousness he has displayed toward me.

Mr. Speaker, ladies, and gentlemen, the resolution before us is broad and liberal. It calls for 7 hours of general debate.

After that, notwithstanding the bill is of a very technical nature, the rule provides that the bill shall be read under the 5-minute rule giving each and every Member opportunity to offer amendments and to speak on the amendments.

I am of opinion that this is the most important piece of legislation that has ever been considered by the Congress. For many years efforts have been made to regulate the stock exchanges. After every panic serious efforts have been made to enact legislation that would make impossible the panics that were brought about by the manipulation of the stock exchange. In 1894, after the 1893 panic, an effort was made to secure legislation. In 1903 a commission was appointed to investigate the stock exchange, and in 1912 a bill was introduced to accomplish that purpose. The Pujo Committee reported and demanded action in 1912. The bill was considered, but the same tactics that are pursued against this bill were utilized then to bring about the defeat or delay of the legislation.

During the last 30 days I have received, and each and every Member must have received, hundreds of letters and telegrams from misled business men telling us that this legislation will be detrimental to the best interests of the Nation. I say to these business men that they are misled. This legislation will restore confidence, will not injure legitimate business, and all it will do is restrict the gambling activities of a small group of men who have no interest in the welfare of the Nation, but who, regardless of the effect everybody knew it would have upon conditions of the country, ruthlessly manipulated the markets and brought about the conditions from which the Nation is now suffering. Had it not been for the manipulators of Wall Street, for the criminal inflation for which they were responsible and carried on in 1927, 1928, and 1929, the crash would not have occurred. The people who were responsible for the inflation of 1928 and 1929 are also the very men responsible for the crash in 1929. This legislation is absolutely necessary for the best interests of the Nation, because not until we pass this measure will confidence be restored. All this bill aims to do is to prohibit the reckless gambling and manipulation on the exchange. . . .

The privilege of a seat at the gambling table in New York was worth as much as $650,000 at one time. True, it is not worth that much today, but that was the price in the good old days of 1929. No wonder that every ingenuity and every effort is being made to mislead the House and the Membership about this legislation now pending.

I regret that the propaganda going on is so unfair and unjustifiable. As I stated before, they are trying in every conceivable way to mislead the Members and the country in regard to the legislation. I myself am indeed grateful and overjoyed that I have the opportunity to speak for the rule that will make the legislation in order, because ever since 1929 I have appealed to the stock-exchange officials and I appealed to the then President, Mr. Hoover, urging that we suspend these operations. I have pleaded that they should stop short-selling and the many vicious activities that were detrimental to the Nation, but nothing has been done. They now say, "Give us a chance and we will amend our rules." They have refused to act before, and they will refuse to act in the future.

Regardless of what they promise, regardless of what they say, they are not sincere, they do not want any legislation, they believe that it is their own privilege and their God-given right to control this gambling den that brought about destruction to America, brought about the closing of our banks and manufacturing plants, nearly ruined all of the insurance companies, brought about the unemployment of 16,000,000 men in the United States and that caused untold hardships and suffering and, above all, that was responsible for thousands of suicidal deaths. I doubt very much that any flood, fire, or plague ever caused as much destruction and loss as the inflations of 1928 and 1929 and its resultant crash. In fact, it destroyed the values of not only stocks and bonds, but the value of city and farm properties, as statistics show that the value of listed stocks fell to the extent of 83 percent, causing a loss of more than $100,000,000,000. I say that had we had legislation of this nature on our statute books in 1893, 1907, and 1929 the then panics and losses would not have been possible. Therefore, I am amazed that so many well-meaning business men permit themselves to be used by the most vicious propagandists in the history of America. To the business men of America I want to say they should not be alarmed by this proposed legislation. Instead of stifling business it will encourage business and restore confidence.

I repeat that the passage of the bill will to a still greater extent stimulate business and improve conditions, and, therefore, it is manifestly unfair that this institution, through its activities, should create alarm just for the purpose of stopping the proposed legislation to regulate it.

Mr. Speaker, ladies and gentlemen of the House, the stock exchanges have had plenty of opportunity to eliminate the vicious practices that have been going on, as has been testified to and disclosed by the Senate investigating committee. It is high time that the unscrupulous Wall Street investment bankers, who are part and parcel of the New York Stock Exchange, be stopped in reenacting shortly, as they would, another crash. Before concluding I want to congratulate our courageous President, Franklin D. Roosevelt, upon his determination to effect the passage of this proposed legislation, because I know that he recognizes the tremendous, powerful opposition, and, understanding the good that will be accomplished by the adoption of the bill, he remains praiseworthily steadfast for its adoption.

In conclusion, Mr. Speaker, let me call attention to the fact that the same tactics and the same fight have been waged against the Federal Reserve Act and other beneficial legislation by these overlords of high finance, which gives the lie to the selfish and unworthy lobbyists and propagandists who have tried to put the fear of God in everybody they could reach. . . .

MR. COOPER OF OHIO. Mr. Speaker, I do not rise at this time to oppose the adoption of this rule. I am of the opinion that the measure which will be considered on the adoption of this rule is one of the most important pieces of legislation that this or any other Congress has considered. It has been continually before the Committee on Interstate and Foreign Commerce for the last 8 or 10 weeks. Only the members of the committee themselves know how hard we have worked to try to put this legislation into shape to present it to the House. It has been a tremendously difficult task to undertake to write this legislation in order that Congress might consider it. I want to pay my respects to the Chairman of the Committee on Interstate and Foreign Commerce [Mr. Rayburn], who has worked hard in order to try to get this legislation before the House. It has been my pleasure and privilege to serve with him on the Interstate and Foreign Commerce Committee for 18 years. I do not believe that in all my experience on this committee, any chairman has had such a tremendous task before him as has Mr. Rayburn, chairman of our committee, during the committee consideration of this measure. [Applause.]

I am sure there are many good things in this bill. I do not question the right of the Federal Government to regulate stock exchanges. I think they should have been regulated long ago. We all know something of the manipulations and practices that have been carried on by some of the stock exchanges in the past. People who have invested their money in securities must look some place for protection. Therefore I believe it is absolutely necessary to pass legislation for the regulation of the stock exchanges, which will protect the people of our country who invest their money in securities. So with that part of the bill I am fully in accord.

But I feel confident that this measure goes far and beyond the regulation of the stock exchanges, by giving to the Federal Trade Commission the power to regulate industries, corporations, businesses, banks, and credits. Industry and business today want to be let alone for a little while. They want to try to get on their feet. They are trying to recover. They are doing everything that is humanly possible to try to bring our country back to a sound economic situation again; but they are afraid that the restrictions placed upon them in this bill will retard economic recovery and not assist it.

I have numerous letters and telegrams from industrialists, business men, especially those in the great industrial district in which I live, who are afraid of this bill. I know they are honest and sincere men. They have no desire to evade any law. I do not believe that they attempt to engage in any corrupt practices in placing their securities and stocks on the market. They suffered tremendous loss during the last 3 years of economic depression; but notwithstanding that they have kept their industries operating in order to try to give men work, to try to keep their families alive. They are afraid of this bill. They say it will make it hard for them to go forward and it will tighten up credits. . . .

What industry wants today is a relaxation of credit, especially the heavy industries. If there can be a little relaxation of credit so that they can get credit money and put it into productive activity, we will step along pretty fast toward economic recovery. . . .

MR. RAYBURN. Mr. Speaker, I move that the House resolve itself into the Committee of the Whole House on the state of the Union for the consideration of the bill H.R. 9323, to provide for the regulation of securities exchanges and of over-the-counter markets operating in interstate and foreign commerce and through the mails, to prevent inequitable and unfair practices on such exchanges and markets, and for other purposes.

The motion was agreed to.

Accordingly the House resolved itself in the Committee of the Whole House on the state of the Union for the consideration of the bill H.R. 9323, with Mr. Taylor of Colorado in the chair. . . .

MR. RAYBURN. Mr. Chairman, the Committee on Interstate and Foreign Commerce of the House for the past 9 weeks has been wrestling with the problems raised by this suggested legislation.

A draft of a bill was submitted to Senator Fletcher, of the Senate Banking and Currency Committee and to me as Chairman of the House Committee on Interstate and Foreign Commerce. We took the draft bill as a basis for discussion, began hearings. For 5 weeks, with an intermission of 1 week, we conducted hearings and those who were in so-called "opposition" to the legislation had at least three fourths of this time. To every section of the country and to every interest affected opportunity for hearing was accorded.

The bill that is before you today, it matters not what the propagandists who oppose any sort of legislation may say, is the bill of no one man or group of men, except the 25 members of the Committee on Interstate and Foreign Commerce of the House. Partisanship has been abolished in the committee during the hearings and during the consideration of this bill in executive session, and may I pay to my Republican colleagues on the committee the compliment which I believe they, as well as my Democratic colleagues, deserve for the way in which they went about the solution of this problem. Especially do I want to remark about the two minority members of the subcommittee, Messrs. Cooper and Mapes. They were courteous and cooperative with me throughout. May I pay a special compliment to the gentleman from Michigan [Mr. Mapes] for his help, his wisdom, and his good judgment in working out the definite and concrete provisions of the bill. I congratulate him and thank him for the way in which he has cooperated with me.

Few bills have ever had such thorough consideration as this stock-exchange bill. As a practical matter, the matters with which it deals have been the subject of hearings ever since the investigation of the Senate Banking and Currency Committee started some 2 years ago. And to complete the certainty that the bill in its present form has been given consideration at least so far as hearing opposition is concerned, we have worked out the terms of this bill under the pressure of the most vicious and persistent lobby that any of us have ever known in Washington—a lobby that has relentlessly opposed the bill, not only in the original form, but in the present form as my committee brings it to you, and which would, I am convinced, protest against it in any form so long as there was a tooth left in it.

Before we begin discussing the provisions of the bill in its present form, and consider objections still being made to it, I want to talk about that lobby, because the possibility that that lobby has inspired most of the protests against the bill is something which has to be taken into consideration in valuing those protests fairly. I am not suggesting that persons affected by a proposed regulation have not the right to protest fairly against it to the limit of their powers. I do not object to the effort of the New York Stock Exchange and of other exchanges to rally brokers against the bill on the frank ground that it will cut down on the profits they can take from the public. But I do object to the unfair and insidious campaign of exploitation of ignorance which the stock exchanges have waged to get business, banks, investors, and anyone else they could reach to pull their chestnuts out of the fire with exaggerated interpretations of the bill and terroristic prophesies of general disaster. My experience with those who have personally interviewed me to protest against this bill and thereby given me a chance to cross-examine them on what they really know about it, has convinced me that not one critic in five hundred has even carefully read the bill or the sections he came in to talk about. They have been simply and sincerely following like so many sheep the suggestion carefully planted in their minds by those who want to prevent this or any other kind of effective stock-exchange legislation from being enacted at this session. As I have said, I believe in encouraging frank and honest and intelligent protest by those who know what they are talking about. But I do resent a deliberate campaign to swamp Congress and the press with a false appearance that the thinking criticism of the bill is much wider than it is.

There has not been a bill introduced into the Congress of the United States in all the years that it has been my privilege to serve in this body that has been attacked as viciously and in many instances as senselessly as this legislation has been attacked. Propaganda unequaled by any that I have ever before witnessed has been leveled against this legislation, against the members of the committee, and especially against the chairman of the committee.

I resent, as I think does everyone in this House, the campaign of personal pressure that has been carried on against every Congressman in this House, and I do not need to expand on the tactics of that campaign. There is not one of us who has not recognized how subtly and how cleverly the sources of pressure against us have been chosen, how there have been sent against each of us the most carefully chosen delegations of our personal friends and of our political friends, nor how bluntly there has been drummed into us the fact that this is an election year, when we need friends. These things do not need to be told, except to assure each of us that his own experience has been repeated by every other one of us.

But I do think that there have been certain phases of this campaign of manufacturing public opinion that are probably only best known to those who have actually been working with the bill. For instance, take the flood of letters we have received. It is commonplace talk that it has been an inspired flood. But only an analysis of a representative group of those letters will show how inspired and how untrustworthy they are. As the best illustrative sample I have had an examination made of approximately 5,000 letters and telegrams received by the President. I have those communications here with me and any unbeliever may examine them if he wishes. . . .

The first interesting revelation is that apparently even the authenticity of some of this mail is not above suspicion. . . .

. . . It is significant that the names signed to 50 communications from Pasadena, Calif., alone could not be found by the Postal Service or in the city directory.

But beyond the problem of genuineness, internal evidence makes it clear that the vast majority of the letters are of the chain variety written not of the writer's own free will and consideration but as the result partly of compulsion and partly of ignorance bred of a fear carefully nurtured by a whispering campaign. . . .

I do not doubt that every brokerage house in the country waged a . . . concerted campaign to create protest against this bill. . . .

And let me say to you about this bill, the impression has been created that everybody who operated on an exchange, that everybody who was a member of an exchange, that everybody who was a manufacturer or a business man is opposed to this legislation; and yet men came to my office and filed strong statements advocating a strong stock exchange bill and asking me to put their statements in the Record without filing their names. . . .

Business men throughout the country have come to me and said that they wanted a good strong bill.

But here is a letter that caps the climax. Three writers ask in identical words, "What would Jefferson think of the Fletcher-Rayburn bill? He would, of course, use every influence to defeat it." May I ask you what that great democrat—not speaking in a partisan sense of the word—what would that great democrat, who believed in honesty in Government and honesty in all the affairs of men, have said about 1929 and the conditions and the practices that brought about the loss of untold millions to the people of this country? What would Jackson have said, what would Lincoln have said, what would Cleveland have said, what would Theodore Roosevelt have said? They would have said the same thing, that this President Roosevelt today says; that he "wants a law that will prevent the elements getting so mixed that it will bring about conditions like we had in 1927, 1928, culminating in 1929." [Applause.] . . .

Now, if the Membership of the House expects any man or any group of men to write any sort of a bill or law that will be accepted and endorsed by the people who do not want any sort of regulation, then they are mistaken. It matters not how you revise this bill, not what you take out of it, the people who operate the exchanges do not want it. They want self-regulation; and when temptation comes, self-regulation will mean the kind of regulation you had in 1929.

The New York exchange holds itself up by rules adopted recently establishing self-regulation and say that such rules ought to be sufficient. But it must be remembered that the New York Stock Exchange is not the only exchange in the country, and furthermore, the New York Stock Exchange, if it can pass a rule, can revoke that rule as well.

We want to lodge the authority, power, and direction somewhere in some agency of the Government as representing the people of the country, with the right to approve or disapprove the rules and regulations of the exchanges, and with the power and authority to enforce the rules and regulations if in the public interest it is found necessary.

Another clear source of inspiration for these letters in addition to the pressure brought by brokers' houses on their customers and employees is the propaganda conducted by many of the larger corporations of big business men. For example, the Associated Gas & Electric Co., the utility now under investigation in New York State, relayed to thousands of small, ignorant stockholders, who could not understand the bill even if they had an opportunity to read it, the exaggerated account of it given by the New York Stock Exchange.

Many almost illiterate stockholders and bondholders have been frightened by this campaign into thinking that passage of the bill will destroy what little value remains of the securities previously sold them by high-pressure methods, and have written pathetic letters often enclosing the company's circular or mentioning it by name. . . .

The blunt fact about the reaction of that portion of the public which has been induced by this campaign to protest against the bill—particularly that part of the business public which is excited about the regimentation of industry supposed to lurk in the bill—is that it has either been unable to comprehend the necessarily complicated provisions of this long bill and the many drafts of it which have followed one another in the course of its revision, or that it has simply swallowed the opinions of propagandists whole without reading what they are supposed to be talking about.

I tell you from my own experience at the center of all this agitation that that part of the public which has been used by the New York Stock Exchange in its propaganda to create an appearance of a furore of protest against this bill is not representative of anything but the smallest portion of the public as a whole—and the public as a whole, perfectly conscious of the propaganda, are watching with interest to see whether we succumb to it. For every frightened security holder and every brokerage-house clerk and every nervous corporation executive who has let the stock exchange do this thinking for him, there are thousands whom experience with securities has made hard-headed who are doing some thinking for themselves, and are watching to see whether Congress hesitates to regulate the great financial powers of Wall Street whom tradition says cannot be controlled by the forces of Government.

One of the things that has been most frequently used to frighten people, particularly business men, are the provisions of the bill that have to do with reporting by corporations. When, for example, the business man whom I have referred to as admitting to me that he had been "played as a sucker," came to me with the memorandum mimeographed at the Washington headquarters of the New York Stock Exchange, I told him that I would take the bill and sit down with him and if there was a line in the bill or a sentence that did an injustice to or put an unreasonable burden upon business in this country I would be the first to move to strike it out. I then took the bill up and said to this gentleman, "Your first amendment is to strike out section 2 of the bill entirely. Why do you want to strike that out? It simply declares that this matter has reached the point where it is charged with a public interest, that there is necessity for regulation." He then said that he did not care whether it was stricken out or not, but I said, "You move to strike it out."

At every place in the bill where the term "or appropriate in the public interest" occurs, they have proposed to strike it out. Just why should a statement like that be objectionable? If the Commission that administers this law must find, before it can reach a rule or regulation, that it is in the public interest or for the interest of the investing public, what objection is there to that? It seems to me that that is a loosening of the bill. But that gets back to another thing. This bill now is criticized because it gives too much power to the administrative authorities, but all through the hearings the representatives of the exchanges and the so-called "representatives of business" in this country pounded into the committee the unwisdom of particularizing in the legislation, or going further than simply fixing the outstanding standards for the administrative body to go by. We went through the bill, and everywhere that we could find a place to give authority to the Commission to make rules and regulations to govern these matters we gave it to them, and now you will hear throughout this House those who are not voting against the bill but voting for every amendment which pulls the teeth of it, saying that they fear that we are giving to a commission or board here in Washington unheard-of powers to look into the affairs of business.

Mr. Chairman, there is no use trying to write a bill that will be effective, which will cure these evils, that will protect the public in general and investors in particular, which will please also the great exchanges of this country. These stock exchange amendments were offered in the committee. We were able to vote them down. They will be offered on the floor of this House, and I intend to brand every one of them as they come. Some people in this country may want the New York Stock Exchange and its satellites and hirelings to write this legislation. I do not. [Applause.] I do want to write a bill that will deal justly and fairly with every group and with every individual in this land. I have been held up I know as an enemy to business, but there is nothing in my career in Congress that warrants it. Twenty-four months ago I was called one of the arch reactionaries of the House and of the country, but when I went out with the securities' bill and tried to pro- tect the investing public in this country by giving them information about securities that were offered to them, and stopping a lot of pretty bad practices that were going on, I was then advertised as a radical or a bolshevik. When I came along following the recom- mendation of the President of the United States and the platform upon which he was elected and upon which each and every one of you on my right was elected, trying to carry out this legislation in the protection of the people against the rapacities of the past, I am again branded as one who is willing to go out and destroy business.

Let me tell you something, and I say this to representatives of the exchanges who are doing me the honor to sit in the galleries this afternoon. They have not yet lost hope that they will be able to pull the teeth of this bill so they are still around here, and I am glad to have them here.

They are engaged in a business that ought to go on, that has a very legitimate and important function to perform. We should have a market place for the exchange of securities but it should be a clean and honest market place.

They are in a business that, since 1929, has not stood in such high favor in the United States. In their own selfish interest, if their judgment was used, instead of their fear, they would want a strong bill for the regulation of the exchanges in order to reestablish the faith and confidence of the people so that they will again in the future, if they forget their unhappy experience of the past, use these exchanges as a place of barter and trade for securities.

Then I took up sections 11 and 12 of this bill with this business man, and I said to him, "if you will point out one thing in sections 11 and 12," and that is the registration requirements for securities, "one line that regiments business, that interferes with the operation of your own business, that makes it unduly burdensome, I will take it out." I sat down with him, and I began to read these things to him. What are they supposed to do? When they try to scare you about what the Commission is asking them to do, let me show you what the committee on stock list of the New York Stock Exchange asks them to do and the questions which they ask them to answer. Here I hold in my hand the printed list of requirements; observe all those questions covering several pages, which must be answered. The New York Curb Exchange also has detailed requirements. Now, what do we ask them to report? You know there is a remarkable thing about this bill. It contained a provision that they should report to the stock exchange and to the Commission. They objected to reporting to the Commission. Why I was never able to figure out; but they were perfectly willing that a copy of the report that they made to the stock exchange, when they had an application for a listing of their securities, should be filed with the Commission. What the difference is in that I do not know, but we did put in the bill a provision that they should file the original with the stock exchange and a duplicate with the Commission if the Commission asked them to do it.

Now, what do we ask them to do?

(A) The organization, financial structure, and nature of business.

Is that harmful? Is that irksome?

(B) The terms, position, rights, and privileges of the different classes of securities outstanding.
(C) The terms on which their securities are to be, and during the preceding 3 years have been, offered to the public or otherwise.
(D) The directors and officers, their remuneration (including amounts paid, or which may become payable, as a bonus or under a profit-sharing agreement), and their interests in the securities of, and their material contracts with, the issuer and any person directly or indirectly controlling or controlled by, or under direct or indirect common control with, the issuer.

Is it asking too much that they give us their bonus lists? I think, my friends, that when an officer of a company is paid a salary sufficient unto his labor, then if the company happens to make profits, those profits are the property of the stockholders. I think it is a very bad thing not only from the standpoint of what I think is the right thing to do but also from the standpoint of the very looks of things for a man to receive $150,000 a year as a salary and eight or nine hundred thousand dollars at the end of the year as a bonus.

It appears to me that if a man is paid from $75,000 to $150,000 a year, he is reasonably compensated; and if not he alone but all of the people in the organization and all the people that labor to produce what it sells should make $900,000, it either ought to be distributed to the stockholders or among those who made it possible. We ask merely that the stockholders be informed of the bonuses. If that is regimentation of business, then that is it.

Then we ask for:

Remuneration (including amounts paid, or which may become payable, as a bonus or under a profit-sharing agreement) in excess of $10,000 per annum, to any person other than directors and officers.

(F) Management and service contracts of material importance to investors;

(G) Options existing or to be created with respect to their securities;

(H) Balance sheets for the 3 preceding years certified by independent public accountants or otherwise, as the Commission may prescribe; and

(I) Profit-and-loss statements for the 3 preceding years, certified by independent public accountants or otherwise, as the Commission may prescribe.

Such copies of articles of incorporation, bylaws, trust indentures, or corresponding documents by whatever name known, underwriting arrangements, and other similar documents.

And so forth.

Now, I want to say that before a man can list his stock on the New York Stock Exchange, he may be required to file that much or more (apart from the disclosure of bonuses, which certainly the investing public has a right to know), but there seems to be a fear running around that the Government is going to regiment business. If any gentleman on the floor of this House during the consideration of this bill—and we have had all of these amendments—can demonstrate to the membership of this committee on either side of the House that there is regimentation of business in this bill, we are willing to take it out.

Now, the talk has been that they would have uniform accounting for all corporations of the country. There is nothing like that in this bill. There is no attempt to do it, but if an agency of the Government is going to try to regulate the sale or dealing in securities of any corporation doing business in interstate commerce, there must be intelligent reporting so that somebody can understand it.

I asked some of our railroad brethren years ago, when we were trying to get them to bring about a system of uniform accounting, which we afterward had to pass a law to make them do, why they did not get up figures that somebody could understand. It took a Philadelphia lawyer to understand their figures. Finally, by act of Congress, they were forced to bring about a uniform system of accounting, which they fought very strenuously, and today each railroad will tell you that they themselves would oppose the repeal of that requirement.

I do not say that the average business in the country is on the same footing with the railroads, but the railroads are strictly a regimented industry, being public-service corporations and subject in all of their dealings to the law.

I do challenge these people to show me where there is any interference, but they cannot show it. This fear went out from Washington. Propaganda was spread throughout the land. It went to every manufacturer; it went to every bank; it went to every employee of these houses throughout the country, a campaign of misrepresentation and attempted fright. . . .

"Why then," say opponents of the bill, "is not the problem of reports of corporation left to the exchanges without Government interference?" One answer is that the exchanges are not in a position as a practical matter to require issuing corporations to give them as much information as modern standards consider is indispensably necessary to aid decent appraisal by an investor of the value of a security he proposes to buy or sell. Exchanges can only go so far before selfish managements and interlocking banking control decide that it is more advisable to fight the exchanges' requirements than to tell shareholders the entire truth about the use of their money. Another reason is that when the amount of information which is to be furnished depends upon the power of exchanges to enforce requirements as a matter of private contract in return for the advantages of listing, the trading positions of exchanges vary greatly. Requirements which the great New York Stock Exchange can insist upon, smaller exchanges cannot insist upon and get enough business to live. Writing minimum listing requirements for all listed corporations into sections 11 and 12 assures a decent minimum of listing requirements for securities listed on all exchanges, and having the information filed not only with the exchanges, but with a Federal agency, assures that the information will really be available and readily accessible to investors who might have difficulty approaching the exchanges.

The information asked for by sections 11 and 12 goes no further than the present requirements of the New York Stock Exchange except in respect of the revelation of the remuneration of officers, directors, and high-salaried employees. As a legal matter, the New York Stock Exchange can demand far more than is required by sections 11 and 12 since there is no limit to what, by private contract, the exchange can demand of applicants. It requires as part of its listing agreement that the applicant "furnish the New York Stock Exchange, on demand, such reasonable information concerning the company as may be required." Companies that are subject to such demands upon them on the part of private interest operating a public-securities market, can hardly be heard to object to the minimum listing requirements set forth in sections 11 and 12.

As for the new requirements set out in sections 11 and 12 for the revelation of the compensation and remuneration which officers, directors, and high-salaried employees take out of the business, that is an advance which the public investors of the United States who are paying that compensation and remuneration will demand regardless of the protests of the managements whom they are paying and the charges that such revelation may interfere with essential secrecy in the operation of corporations.

Now, coming back to this campaign of fear, the President of the United States wrote me a letter before he went away on a short vacation, in which he called attention to this propaganda and pointed out that it came from a common source; and, of course, it was paid for from a common source. I, too, can bear witness to this organized propaganda. I have in my hands a batch of more than 200 letters. As you may observe, they came from a common source, from the same neighborhood. Every one is in the same colored envelope, but they are written in different hands.

As I pointed out before, the Associated Gas & Electric System is circularizing everybody who owns any of its stock. While it may not be information to you, it is true nevertheless, that the Associated Gas & Electric System throughout its existence—and it is a concern whose securities run into hundreds of millions of dollars—has been the most noncooperative organization in the United States, both with regard to State commissions and to legislative bodies. This system, of course, is dominated by the personality of Mr. Hobson; and he is pretty hard to get before a committee, as some of you may know. . . .

MR. COOPER OF OHIO. The objections of most of the utilities were met by an amendment accepted by the committee, which amendment inserted the words "or any State." I think this was the principal objection from the utility companies.

MR. RAYBURN. Of course, we put the language in the bill "of any State"; but we also provided that the commission should be allowed to call for other things, because we know some of the States do not have any laws with reference to this question and some have very poor laws with respect to it.

MR. COOPER OF OHIO. If I may make this further observation, the fear expressed by the utilities was that they would have to set up a double-accounting system. They now have to conform to a system set up by each State public utility commission; and the thing about which they complained in the bill in its original form was that it would probably cause them to set up a double-accounting system.

MR. RAYBURN. The requirement that adequate and intelligent reports be made for the benefit of investors does not necessitate the keeping of two sets of books. . . .

In section 3 of the bill we set forth the definitions; and I shall insert in the Record at this point some further definitions of terms which may be used in connection with the discussions of the bill in nontechnical language and are only intended to assist the Members in understanding the bill.

A "put" is an option to sell a security at a given price within a given time.

A "call" is an option to buy a security at a given price within a given time.

A "straddle" is a combination of a "put" and a "call," giving the holder the right either to sell or to buy the security at specified prices within a given time.

The term "pool" is used to describe operations to control the price of a security, usually by means of a syndicate or joint account. Under the bill all efforts to raise or lower the price of a security are outlawed. Pools to peg or stabilize the price are subject to regulation by the Commission.

A "short sale" is a sale by a person who does not own the security sold. He borrows the security to make delivery to the buyer and subsequently buys the security in order to return it to the lender. His profit is the difference between the price at which he sells and that at which he subsequently buys.

"Floor trading" is trading on the premises of an exchange by members for their own account. As used in the bill it also includes trading for a discretionary account.

"Arbitrage" is the simultaneous buying of a security in one market at a price and selling it in another market at another price for the purpose of profiting from the difference in prices in such markets.

"Over-the-counter market," as used in this bill, refers to a market maintained off a regular exchange by one or more dealers or brokers. The market must be maintained both for the purchase and the sale of the securities in question. A dealer or broker who merely undertakes a request to find a purchaser for a person who wants to sell or to find a seller for a person who wants to buy, would not usually be considered to be creating a market. But the dealer who normally is willing to quote "a market," that is, both the price at which he will buy and the price at which he will sell, is creating an over-the-counter market.

Section 6 is the section around which a great controversy has raged. It deals with the all-important problem of credit control or margins. I have from the beginning considered this problem paramount. A reasonably high margin requirement is essential so that a person cannot get in the market on a shoe string one day and be one of the sheared lambs when he wakes up the next morning. I do not believe people ought to be allowed to go into the market on a 10-, 15-, 20-, or 25-percent margin.

Originally we proposed in this bill that the margin should be 60 percent for the initial margin or 40 percent as the initial loan. Then in order to bring about an agreement, I proposed 50 percent for margins and 50 percent for loan values. The subcommittee finally went to an initial margin of 45 percent and a borrowing of 55 percent, which the full committee accepted. And considerable flexibility in the application of the margin rules is afforded by the provision permitting a broker to lend 100 percent of the 3-year low, not exceeding 75 percent of the market. Indeed, according to the calculations of Standard Statistics, the margins required on the basis of the present level of the market would not exceed 35 percent.

Governor Black [member of Federal Reserve Board] has been quoted all around as wanting this bill flexible as far as margins are concerned. A proposal was made from some source that we have a marginal requirement in the bill, but that no standard should be set up and that the margin business should be turned over entirely to the administrative body. May I say one thing about these margins? It matters not whether this bill is administered by a board or a commission and the Federal Reserve Board in conjunction with them, but it is important that the margin requirements for member banks of the Federal Reserve System, the margin requirements for nonmember banks, and the margin requirements for brokers be put under the administration of the same body. If the margins for the member banks are under the Federal Reserve System, then the margins for the nonmember banks and for the brokers should be handled by the same agency. As Governor Black said, whether or not there was a standard fixed in the bill the margin requirements should be administered by the same body for the reason that if the Federal Reserve Board fixed one marginal requirement for member banks and another administrative authority fixed another margin for brokers and nonmember banks, speculative loans would move from the brokers and nonmember banks to member banks, or from member banks to the brokers and nonmember banks, depending upon which margin requirements were the higher.

But believing that we should set up a flag somewhere, and that we should give some congressional expression to what we regarded as a proper margin requirement, we set up 45 percent as the initial margin, and yet we give the Federal Reserve Board, when it finds it in the public interest, and necessary to the free flow of trade and commerce, power to vary even the 45-percent margin for initial opening of accounts. Not only that, but we go farther and say that the maintenance of the account shall be left entirely with the administrative body. It seemed to those of us who believe in some sort of a standard being fixed by Congress, some kind of a bright line drawn or signal set up, that we would have failed in our duty if we did not give some indication to the Reserve Board as to what we regarded as a fair minimum-margin requirement.

I believe that the House, after discussion and when we begin to read this bill under the 5-minute rule, will come to the same conclusion that the subcommittee and the full committee came to, namely, that we should have a marginal requirement in this bill. . . .

MR. CLAIBORNE. Assume a man employed by a company whose stock is dealt with on an exchange. If that man wants to buy further of his company's stock and goes to the banker to make a loan in order to increase his stock holdings, does this bill limit his banker as to the amount of money the banker may lend him to buy his company's stock?

MR. RAYBURN. If it is listed on the exchange, yes.

MR. CLAIBORNE. So that young men who have built themselves up by buying their company's stock, of which they know much, are limited in the future and may not be able to do so?

MR. RAYBURN. They will unless by rules and regulations it is provided otherwise, if the stock is listed on the New York exchange.

If there has been a thing in the world that has been abused throughout this country, and if there is one way in which management perpetuates itself in office, it is by the use of proxies. We treat that situation here and say that the proxies shall be used under such rules and regulations as the administrative body may promulgate. . . .

MR. McFADDEN. I wanted to inquire about the other provision. May I ask the gentleman whether or not his committee considered the question of taking stockbrokers or members of the exchange out of the banking business and forbidding them lending money to their customers, and compelling the customers to either have the cash or go to the banks and get it? Did the committee consider that question?

MR. RAYBURN. The rules and regulations give wide authority to the administrative body over loans. Stock-exchange brokers cannot lend on unlisted securities, but banks may lend any amount they deem proper.

MR. McFADDEN. There is no restriction on the brokers borrowing money from the banks and in turn lending to their customers.

MR. RAYBURN. That is precisely what the margin regulations cover.

We have a liability clause in here covering false and misleading statements. It appeared to us that there ought to be some way of protecting a man against false and misleading statements.

The first provision of the bill as originally written was very much challenged on the ground that reliance should be required. This objection has been met. In other words, if a man bought a security following a prospectus that carried a false or misleading statement, he could not recover from the man who sold to him, nor could the seller be punished criminally, unless the buyer bought the security with knowledge of the statement and relied upon the statement. It seemed to us that this is as little as we could do.

I will proceed to section 18, which deals with powers with respect to exchanges and securities. The Commission is authorized, if in its opinion such action is necessary or appropriate for the protection of investors, after appropriate notice and opportunity for hearing, by order, to suspend not only an exchange for a period but to suspend trading in a security on an exchange. In other words, they may force the delisting of the security if the issuer of such security has failed to comply with any provision or the rules and regulations thereunder.

May I say something about the hearings before the Commission? The hearings may be public. There are some issues which will come before the Commission where the people who are being heard would not want open hearings, because it might give away trade secrets that they would not want given out. We have protected in this bill, as far as language can protect, the trade secrets of corporations.

We come to the penalty clause of the bill, which was very drastic in the beginning. The maximum penalty for violation was 10 years' imprisonment, a $25,000 fine, or both.

Of course, I did not think it made a great deal of difference, since this was the maximum penalty and the court could impose such fine or imprisonment as it deemed appropriate to the particular offense. But to show that the committee wanted to take as much of this so-called "fright" out of the bill as possible, we reduced the maximum penalty to a fine of $10,000 or 2 years in prison, and in the case of an exchange, to a fine of not more than $500,000.

All in all, as we believe we will be able to demonstrate under the 5-minute rule in answer to questions and in the discussion of amendments, we have a reasonable bill, one that will not be irksome to any legitimate industry, but will protect the public from conditions that have existed in the past and in the long run will not only help investors and the public in general, but will be a great boon to the stock exchanges themselves and the traders on the stock exchanges. . . .

MR. MAY. I am very much in favor of regulating the stock exchanges and have a great deal of confidence in the information of the chairman of this committee, but I would like to state a concrete proposition that affects my own particular neighborhood and see if it meets the requirements of this legislation. In my district I have an operating coal company that is a $30,000,000 concern with a $6,000,000 defaulted bond issue in receivership. I have another coal company that has a statement involving $8,000,000 with a $35,000,000 bond issue in default and it is also in receivership. I have a gas company that owns a good many leases of gas wells in production and has a default of $4,500,000 of bonds. Under the provisions of this proposed legislation, could these receivers enter into an agreement with the bondholders by which they could refund these bonds by an issue of preferred or common stock, without having to meet the requirements of this legislation? In other words, would they have to list these stocks on the exchanges?

MR. RAYBURN. If they are not listed stocks, they would not have to do it.

MR. MAY. If they are not already listed stocks?

MR. RAYBURN. Yes; primarily this does not have anything to do with securities except those listed on a national exchange, and the exchange must make application and be granted the right to register them before it comes under the National Securities Act. The commission also has power to regulate the over-the-counter markets, but in so doing they can only regulate the brokers or dealers who create a public market for both the purchase and sale of such securities, and cannot compel corporations not interested in having a public market for their shares to file any statements or submit to any regulation.

MR. MAY. Then it would not affect small corporations at all who have not such registered stocks?

MR. RAYBURN. Not at all.

MR. BROWN OF KENTUCKY. If the gentleman will permit, the company that the gentleman from Kentucky is speaking of would be affected by this legislation and, as a matter of fact, it ought to be affected, because before they offer such a security to the gullible public, such as the securities of a company that has been in receivership, the public ought to be protected by some sort of law.

MR. RAYBURN. I think the Securities Act of 1933 is the one to which the gentleman is referring.

MR. MAY. My question does not have any reference to the gullible public. I am talking about the bondholders of the concern taking stock for it.

MR. BROWN OF KENTUCKY. Is not this company listed on the New York Stock Exchange?

MR. MAY. I do not know whether it is or not, but it is a New York corporation.

MR. RAYBURN. Now, Mr. Chairman, I am going to close, because I am fearfully tired and I would rather answer the questions you are going to ask me under the 5-minute rule, because we are going to have unlimited debate at that time.

I want to wind up what I say here today by repeating what I stated in a radio address when I told the people of the country something about this bill.

The people of this country, I think, are high-minded and honest. I think the vast majority of business in this country is high-minded and honest. I do not think we have to pass restrictive laws for a great deal of business, but I do think that business with a reputation to protect, that over a long period of years has built up a reputation and a good will among the people that is worth a great deal to it, has the right to be protected from the desperadoes who are making it hard on the man who wants to conduct a straightforward and honest business.

I think the people of this country want corruption driven from high places. I think they want and expect their public officials to be clean, and we must not forget, when we are harassed by this propaganda of a few thousands of people, the unnumbered millions throughout this country who have not been articulate in this fight, who have no interests to serve except the common good. They are looking to you and to me as their spokesmen and as their Representatives, not only now but in the future. They want to see this country clean in business and clean in politics, so that the faith and confidence of our people may not be shattered and destroyed, so that under a faith and confidence that are constant and patriotic the institutions of this country, great as they are, may be transmitted to posterity in such a way that those who live at that time can be of the most service to those who live about them. [Applause.] I thank you. . . .

MR. MERRITT. Mr. Chairman and members of the Committee, I repeat what has been already said in appreciation of the work of our committee, which reported this bill, and particularly the immense amount of work our chairman, Mr. Rayburn, has done. I think you will perceive from his remarks that at times he was a little worn by the number of people who wanted to see him, and by letters and telegrams he received. That is not strange. You will also agree, I think, that all the Members of Congress—I know it is true of all the members of the committee—have received an enormous number of telegrams and letters regarding the bill.

The chairman has characterized, and I suppose stigmatized all those communications as propaganda, but I think that if you have in mind the fact that by the best estimates we can get there are some 10,000,000 separate stockholders in the United States, and also that this bill directly and indirectly may affect every one of those 10,000,000 people, you will perceive why the bill has created a tremendous amount of interest throughout the United States and why the people have written in to their Congressmen.

I do not believe that the bulk of these communications have been brought about by anything except a legitimate desire of the people to protect their own property against undue depreciation.

It seems to me that it is not quite fair to the stockholders, these people seeking to protect their interests, to impute their action to unfair motives. I never have heard any objection to the farmers getting together to protect their own interests.

You doubtless appreciate that in the past 50 years the amount of liquid personal property in stocks and bonds in this country has increased tremendously, and very much to the advantage of the people of this country.

You will agree, I think, also, that while the so-called "panic of 1929" was largely connected with this personal property, and that while the blow-up was more evident on the stock exchange than anywhere else, the stock exchange was not primarily to blame.

You know, as any well-informed man knows, that these speculative eras and collapses afterward have been with us ever since civilization began and people have been possessed of personal property.

You will appreciate that stock exchanges have done a tremendous amount of good. If it had not been for the stock exchanges, which make capital liquid, which enable men to realize quickly on their holdings, the distress of the collapse would have been much greater.

You will all agree that more frozen assets of this country have been connected with real estate than they have with stocks.

I personally have not had very much business with the stock exchange, but I have known a great many people who have. I know that the New York Stock Exchange—that is credited with more of the evils than all the rest of them put together—I know that the business ethics are higher on that exchange than in the average business. It is conducted by word of mouth, and on honor, and violations of that honor are very rare.

I am not saying that there have not been abuses that should be corrected. What I am pleading for here is that in considering this legislation it should not be undertaken in any vindictive spirit. It should not be conducted with a notion that anybody who has made or may make a suggestion concerning the bill has been actuated by anything but an honest motive, and not by any propaganda.

In my own case, coming from New England, I have not been so much interested in the great corporations whose stocks are traded in on the New York Stock Exchange, and which become part of these great speculative movements, as I have in the smaller corporations and manufacturers who exist throughout New England and throughout the United States in general. I have not been so concerned with the regulation of stock-exchange practices, and I have not, as I said in my minority views, specially criticized the bill as a stock-exchange regulative bill, but I am concerned that the Commission which is set up under the bill should have such tremendous power over every manufacturing corporation and almost every other form of corporation in the country, and should have such tremendous power to regulate the care and management of these billions of liquid property in the United States. . . .

MR. RICH. I was under the impression from what the chairman of the committee, Mr. Rayburn, said a few moments ago, that the smaller businesses were not affected by this bill if they did not deal on the listed-stock exchanges.

MR. MERRITT. That is partly true, but the fact of the matter is that the Commission under this bill still has the power to force every corporation into some stock exchange. It also has the power to exempt them, and that was put in for the relief of these smaller corporations, and I think it is a very valuable feature of the bill, but, nonetheless, it is true that the Commission could act so that those small businesses would be bound to register on some exchange. . . .

MR. BRITTEN. I rise to accentuate the statement of the gentleman that the Federal Trade Commission really can control and regulate the corporation whose securities are not on any listed exchange. Is not that so?

MR. MERRITT. Rather indirectly, I think. I think it may make regulations which would force the small corporations to register their securities if the Commission so desired.

MR. BRITTEN. Could it not also make regulations which would more or less limit their credit?

MR. MERRITT. Yes.

MR. BRITTEN. And in the limitation of their credit they would have to do what the Commission required?

MR. MERRITT. Yes.

MR. BRITTEN. So that the Commission could indirectly, under the bill, control every industry in the United States if it wanted to.

MR. MERRITT. It could control the business in its securities. . . .

MR. BLOOM. I believe the gentleman stated that the Commission could force these different businesses into the exchange?

MR. MERRITT. Yes.

MR. BLOOM. Could it force the exchange to accept them? If it has the right to force the different businesses into an exchange, can it force the exchange to accept the different business interests?

MR. MERRITT. It can force an exchange to become a national exchange if it wants to. It can exempt from the effects of the bill the smaller exchanges.

MR. BLOOM. The exchange today needs to accept the different business interests it wants to list on the exchange. Is not that right?

MR. MERRITT. Yes.

MR. BLOOM. Suppose the exchange refuses to accept the business interests that the Commission would force into the exchange.

MR. MERRITT. It could not do that, because they have to come in under general rules, and the general rules of all exchanges are subject to the Commission. . . .

MR. MAPES. I dislike to interrupt my friend, but the question which has been propounded to the gentleman from Connecticut is so vital and the country is so much interested in the question and the answer that I feel I should say that I do not interpret the bill as giving the Federal Trade Commission power to compel any corporation to list on any exchange.

MR. MERRITT. Not directly; no.

MR. MAPES. And the only provision in the bill that relates to small or local corporations in that respect, as I understand it, is the one in the over-the-counter market section, which gives the Federal Trade Commission authority in its regulations of the dealers and brokers in the over-the-counter markets to require that such dealers and brokers cease to handle the securities of any corporation unless they are listed with them, but in no case is a corporation required to so list unless it sees fit to do so. I say again I beg the gentleman's pardon for interrupting him, but I think this is a very vital feature of the bill.

MR. MERRITT. I think what I said before is correct, that the Commission could not do it directly; but I think if the bill is carefully read the gentleman will find that if the Commission starts out to do it by indirection it could either do that or else fix it so that the stock of any particular company could not be used as collateral, and would be very much depreciated. . . .

Now, for the purchase of capital goods, and indeed for business in general, the first essential is confidence. It is very generally thought by business men and writers on economics that the Security Registration Act which was passed at the last session of this Congress has been very detrimental. It had a great many severe provisions with regard to underwriters, with regard to directors, and putting on them responsibilities and liabilities which drove a great many of them out of business and prevented new securities being issued. I do not mean to say that the lack of issuing new securities has been altogether due to that act, but I do say it has been a large factor. In this act we should be careful not to overdo it. The difficulty with all acts like this is that those who write them are so intent on punishing a few guilty people that they overlook the fact that they are really punishing still more, a greater percentage of honest people. In all corporations there are a certain number of selfish men who will endeavor to feather their own nests at the expense of the corporation or of their fellow stockholders, but, after all, those men are a very small percentage. The time has not yet come when great corporations or any corporations can get along without character and without brains. The difficulty with the Securities Registration Act and with this act, to my mind, is that it is so filled with directions and regulations which are indefinite and uncertain, and cannot be enforced. That was illustrated, for instance, by the colloquy between the gentleman from Michigan [Mr. Mapes] and myself. We have both been working on this bill for weeks, and the gentleman from Michigan thinks it produces one result and I think it produces another. There can be no doubt that the result from the Securities Registration Act, and the result from this act, will be that responsible people, a great many thousands of directors of corporations, will be forced out of those corporations. These men go on boards of directors not because they want to but because they are known in their communities, and their services are sought after because they are men of judgment and character. Such men are not going on those boards to make money on the stock, and if by going on a board of directors they are going to subject themselves to suits by any blackmailer that comes along, they will not go on. The result is that the corporation will not be formed or you will have boards of directors and managements not as able as you would wish. . . .

MR. BRITTEN. Undoubtedly there is considerable opinion in the House for a change in the bill which grants this authority to the Federal Trade Commission. Many Members of the House, and I am one of them, would like to see a different form of commission set up, by the enactment of legislation. I am wondering if the gentleman contemplates presenting an amendment that, for instance, would provide a commission composed of a member of the Federal Reserve Board, a member of the Federal Trade Commission, and one or two members from the stock exchange, members who would know all about this very complicated machinery which operates the exchanges?

MR. MERRITT. The gentleman perhaps knows that the bill as reported by the Senate committee provides for a separate commission.

MR. BRITTEN. The Senate bill provides for a purely political commission, three Democrats and two Republicans.

MR. MERRITT. I think so.

MR. BRITTEN. My thought is that that would be just as bad as the provisions in this act now before the House. I have been much impressed with the testimony before the gentleman's committee, to the effect that a distinctly nonpartisan, nonpolitical commission of some sort should be established, and there should be upon that commission one or two men who know every angle of the operations of the stock exchanges of this country.

MR. MERRITT. I agree with the gentleman, and if he will allow me, I will give him better authority than perhaps either he or I, for that statement. This whole legislation came from a commission which was appointed by President Roosevelt and headed by Mr. Dickinson, who is Assistant Secretary of Commerce. That commission made a report, and this bill follows that report. I regret to say that Mr. Dickinson was not a member of the committee which drew the bill, but his letter to the President, which finally resulted in the drawing of the bill, has this phrase:

Should it be determined that a separate commission should be set up, such commission should be composed of at least three members without regard to political affiliations, appointed for a term of at least 7 years.

Now, this is the point:

In either case it is suggested that one of the members of the commission or authority should be required by law to be a man thoroughly experienced in stock-exchange practices.

I think the longer the committee considered this bill the more the members were impressed with the feeling of its enormous importance and the enormous interests which will be affected by the bill. . . .

MR. BEEDY. Is the gentleman going to offer an amendment embracing the suggestions made by the gentleman from Illinois and Mr. Dickinson?

MR. MERRITT. I think it will be offered. I do not know that I shall offer it. . . .

MR. BULWINKLE. The gentleman refers to the separate authority or commission?

MR. BRITTEN. Yes.

MR. BULWINKLE. Yes; I am going to offer such an amendment. . . .

In substance it will empower the President to appoint 3 men to serve for 2, 4, and 6 years, 2 of one political party and 1 of another.

MR. BRITTEN. . . . my thought is that instead of the President naming three gentlemen of the political parties—and, of course, any commissioner named by the President would be a high type of man—that at least one member of the commission should be thoroughly qualified and experienced in the manipulations of the stock exchanges.

MR. BULWINKLE. Answering the gentleman from Illinois, I may say that I do not think any President ought to be tied down to the selection of a man from any certain group.

MR. BRITTEN. Does not the gentleman think it would be wise to suggest in the legislation that at least one man should be thoroughly experienced in the manipulation of stock exchanges?

MR. BULWINKLE. No; I do not. . . .

MR. MERRITT. . . . In closing I call the attention of the committee to the letter of the President addressed to the chairman of our committee on March 26, in which the President said in the paragraph summing up his letter:

> We must, of course, prevent insofar as possible manipulation of prices to the detriment of actual investors; but at the same time we must eliminate unnecessary, unwise, and destructive speculation.

This sentence, you see, applies to stock-exchange practices. I cannot criticize the provisions of this bill in that regard especially, but I do think the bill goes beyond the expressed sentiments of the President. I think it will tend to continue the unsettled state of mind of business men and manufacturers so that they will not be willing to make forward contracts; they will not be willing to buy capital goods and contract to furnish capital goods because they cannot tell at what moment the Commission may decide to change its rules, may decide to put some increased burden on their corporation, may decide to make some new regulation of the stock exchanges which will freeze what ought to be their liquid assets.

This bill has been drawn with the greatest care; and I suppose that with the knowledge we have now it may be considered a good bill to cover these subjects, if we want to cover them; but I still doubt if there is a man on our committee who has been studying this subject who would be willing to say with certainty what the bill will do in very many directions. . . .

I think, therefore, the part of wisdom, as I have suggested in the minority report, would be to allow this bill to sleep. Perfect it by debate, yes; give the Members an opportunity to debate, to state their own opinions, and hear the opinions of others, but allow the enactment of the bill to wait until the next Congress. It is only 7 months before another Congress will meet; and, surely, nothing is going to happen in that time; there is not going to be any destructive speculation. I think it will be the part of much greater wisdom to let the bill go over another 6 months instead of rising the enactment of a bad law which will be difficult to remove from the statute books once it is enacted. . . .

MR. WADSWORTH. Mr. Chairman, I do not propose to discuss in detail the provisions of this bill, but rather to touch upon a few matters which have occurred to me during its consideration in the committee as being extraordinarily important.

When the gentleman from Connecticut states that the committee worked hard, he stated the truth, and when he stated that the chairman of the committee had been hard driven he stated the truth. It has been a big task, and for one I take my hat off to the chairman of the committee for the manner in which he has stood up under the pressure exerted upon him from all sides. At the same time I do not think we should belittle the concern that a very, very large number of people scattered all over the country have felt about this measure, and I think we can get a better understanding of this concern if we go back and look for a moment at the bill as it was originally introduced. It was a very different proposition than the one now confronting us.

The bill as originally introduced was not drawn under the auspices of the so-called "Roper committee," but by another group selected for the purpose, and the selection was not made by the members of the Interstate and Foreign Commerce Committee. That first bill was calculated to throw fear not only into the minds of brokers and dealers and those engaged in the marketing of securities, but into the minds of bankers and security owners all over the country, and those who are responsible for the management of great business enterprises. I think we ought to review for just a moment some of the things which that bill proposed to do, in order that we may understand the fear that spread over the country and the actual harm that was done by the destruction of confidence. Of course, not all will agree with me in my criticism of the original proposal. But, for example, in the original bill the margin requirement was to be 60 percent. The best informed people in the United States, as we have encountered them, or at least as I have encountered them, were thoroughly convinced that if that provision were frozen in the law we would embark upon another painful period of deflation.

Various errors were committed, probably unintentionally. For example, the first bill forbade dealing in convertible bonds on the stock exchange. This happily has been corrected. The first bill, as I recollect, would have compelled the separation of the broker-dealer business, and in this event nearly every small broker in the country would have been driven out of business, because he would have been forbidden to do any business as a dealer. It was perfectly apparent that the small house cannot live, cannot command enough income unless it is permitted under proper regulation to do both kinds of business. That very provision is the one that started a great deal of this campaign of opposition to the bill as a whole, for if it had gone into effect literally thousands of employees in broker-dealer houses throughout the country would have lost their places.

Under the original bill it was not definitely clear that a State bond was to be put in the exempt class, as was provided for United States bonds or obligations. This, of course, caused concern at the seat of every State government and was of special concern to those who make a specialty of dealing in municipal and State bonds. Their number, of course, is very large. That needed clarification.

As to the reports to be required from corporations desiring to list their stocks, there were some extraordinary provisions in the first measure introduced, and, as though to cover everything in case anything should be forgotten, the Federal Trade Commission was authorized to require any kind of report that it saw fit to ask for. Furthermore, the Commission was charged with the initial function of granting permission for the listing of the securities on the exchange. In other words, the exchanges, in the first place, would have nothing to say about the matter; the Commission alone would pass judgment on the proposal to list a given security. That very thing, with the extraordinary report required under the first draft of this measure, would have centered here in the Federal Trade Commission a very practical control over all the corporations in the country whose securities might be listed upon any exchange.

The same is true with respect to the first draft concerning the accounts or the method of keeping accounts which these same corporations might be required to adopt under orders from the Commission. As we all know, hundreds and hundreds of utilities must keep their accounts in accordance with the laws of the State in which they operate and under which they are regulated. To authorize a commission here in Washington to prescribe a different form of keeping accounts would, of course, impose a tremendous expense on those companies, and to no public benefit. Naturally, they were nervous. The keeping of accounts now under the various State laws is a highly expensive piece of business. Of course, it must be done, but most of these companies are having a hard enough time to get along, and any unnecessary or additional expense is something to be avoided. We cured that in the final redraft of the bill.

Then, as to the publicity of this information which the Commission was authorized under the previous draft to gather in, there was grave doubt as to the wisdom of the publicity section, because under a certain construction of this section the trade secrets and business practices of all these concerns might be given out to the public or made available to the public—practices and secrets which have nothing whatsoever to do with dealing in securities on stock exchanges. In the first draft the bill went so far beyond the mere regulation of stock exchanges that it is not surprising that it attracted national interest rather than simply so-called "Wall Street" interest.

My experience with those who have protested against certain provisions of this bill as originally introduced has been a very informing one.

I confess I knew nothing about the practices of stock exchanges, never having come in contact with them in a single instance. In the hearings, it is true, three fourths of the time was consumed by critics of the bill, but in nearly every instance those who criticized the bill expressed the hope we would get a good bill regulating the dealing in securities.

I remember very well that the representatives of the Curb Exchange came before the committee and pointed out that under the provisions of the bill as then drafted there was no question whatsoever but that the Curb Exchange in New York must close. Do you blame them for coming to us and protesting? This has been cured in the redraft.

I can also remember the original proxy provisions as contained in the bill first introduced. They provided, for example, that any person soliciting proxies from a shareholder in a company must at the same time furnish such shareholder with a complete list of all the other shareholders in the company. This would be an extraordinary undertaking for the Pennsylvania Railroad, with its over 100,000 shareholders, or the American Telegraph & Telephone Co., with its 680,000 shareholders, living in all 48 States and in 80 foreign countries. Every one of them would have had to receive from the corporation's headquarters three volumes, each as large as the Washington telephone directory, with every name and address of the shareholders printed in the volume. Is it strange that we have had opposition and criticism? This has been cured to a very considerable degree in the redraft of the bill.

My experience has been very pleasant in having these things pointed out and teaching me, and I think they have taught us a great deal more than we ever knew before about the business of the United States. . . .

MR. COOPER OF OHIO. A moment ago the gentleman spoke about section 11, which is the report section, and the gentleman stated he thought we had cured that.

We have modified it, but I call the gentleman's attention to page 34, beginning with the word "except" in line 18, where we find these words:

Except that this provision shall not be construed to prevent the Commission from imposing such additional requirements with respect to such reports, within the scope of this section and section 11.

Now, section 11 is the report section, so that while we have modified the bill, yet it does give the Federal Trade Commission the power to impose any additional requirements on reports that it may see fit to make. . . .

MR. RAYBURN. But it states that the Commission cannot go further than the requirements of section 11.

MR. COOPER OF OHIO. Section 11 is the report section.

MR. RAYBURN. Yes; that is a limitation.

MR. COOPER OF OHIO. Then the bill says that the Commission has power to impose additional requirements with respect to such reports within the scope of this section and section 11.

MR. WADSWORTH. The gentleman from Ohio is correct. While modifications were made in this so-called "report section," and I think rather important modifications, there still does reside in the Federal Trade Commission the power which the gentleman from Ohio has mentioned. . . .

MR. BEEDY. Does not the gentleman still consider that very provision leaves the business interests affected laboring under great fear and doubt as to the possibilities of future regulations that may be imposed?

MR. WADSWORTH. I will answer that question in this way. When I said the provision has been modified, the enumeration of the subjects to be covered in the reports required has been shortened. Some things that the committee believed were utterly unnecessary and put in merely for annoyance purposes have been eliminated. I regret myself that the sentence which the gentleman from Ohio has just read was put in the measure. It was put in after another modification had been made, which we thought was to be the final modification. . . .

I have been asked to find out where the modifications are which make the bill a better measure than the original one.

We will start with the marginal requirements. Under the original bill it was 60 percent. Most people thought that would bring a deflation and place the country in a worse condition than it is today. That has been reduced to 45 percent. Or he can borrow 100 percent of its lowest market price during the preceding 36 calendar months, but in no case more than 75 percent of the current market price. If I had my way, I would make the first alternative 40 percent instead of 45 percent.

Now, we are dealing with a very delicate thing when we deal with margins. We cannot tell here in the House of Representatives what is going to happen in the next 3 months or the next 6 months or the next year with respect to the demand for securities, the demand of the public for securities for investment as well as speculation.

I should have preferred that the whole provision be left absolutely flexible with the Federal Reserve Board to keep its hand on the situation. But the committee finally decided to write their formula into the statute. The Senate bill does not contain the formula, but leaves it to the Federal Reserve Board.

As I am informed—I may not be correct about it—that is substantially the way that it is done in London. Instead of the Federal Reserve Board, the control is by the Bank of England.

It is further modified by the fact that the bill gives the Federal Reserve Board the right to change the formula if it deems it wise so to do for the benefit of trade and commerce and so forth.

I suppose there will always remain in the minds of the Federal Reserve Board the fact that the Congress has written the formula, and it will take quite a situation to persuade the Board to abandon the formula and substitute its own regulation. It would be a matter of courage. Generally those decisions have to be made, if made at all, under very stressful conditions; but if we are to trust government at all, I should think we could trust the Federal Reserve Board to rise to the occasion with respect to changing margin conditions.

Instead of separating broker-dealer concerns and forcing segregation and putting any number of them out of business, this bill permits broker-dealers to continue in business under regulations fixed by the Federal Trade Commission, and implies that a study shall be made of that to see what the developments may be and whether further legislation is necessary.

State bonds and municipal bonds are now definitely placed in the exempt clause by this bill.

As I said, the proxy provision has been toned down, and although I regard the section as absolutely unnecessary, having nothing to do with the regulation of stock exchanges, I suppose it can be said that it is not going to impose much hardship or annoyance on anybody.

I hesitate to bring up a constitutional question. This bill, I assume, is founded upon the interstate-commerce clause of the Constitution. There is a long argument in the first two pages of the bill. In fact section 2 is a speech, and I would advise you all to read it. I have never seen anything quite like it proposed in legislation. It starts by stating that certain things are important and certain things are evil, and then goes on to say that the important things should be handled and the evil things should be prevented, and it ends up with an exhortation that the whole thing is the right thing to do and is well within the provisions of the Constitution, or words to that effect. That, of course, is designed to control the Supreme Court. If I had my way, as a matter of bill drafting, I would strike it out. It has no place in a statute of the United States. You do not put your arguments in statutes; you put your arguments in the reports of the committee or you make them on the floor of the House or the Senate.

May I now call the attention of Members to one matter which has been one of deep concern to me, although, perhaps, not so many others. This bill imposes a marginal requirement not only upon brokers and dealers but also upon all bankers. That establishes in my view a new thought and a new principle in the treatment of bankers and banks under a statute of the United States. Under this bill a banker may not loan to one of his customers more than 55 percent of the market value of the stock which that customer is purchasing and wants to carry with the aid of the loan.

We are speaking now, of course, of listed securities. The same provision, of course, applies to the broker. He may not lend more than 55 percent. I can very well understand how a statute controlling the broker in this regard is defensible, and I make no complaint against it, but I have my doubts as to the soundness of having these margin provisions apply to all the banks. A broker, when he makes a loan to a customer, makes little or no inquiry as to the customer's financial standing, otherwise than connected with the collateral he puts up. Of course, in most instances he does not see the customer, as the orders come in by telegraph very often. He makes no inquiry as to the customer's character or standing in the community, or as to his other assets. He does not inform himself as to the nature of the customer's business. Those things do not interest the broker. All he must do is to comply with the rules of the exchange or the statute of the United States, as the case may be, with respect to the customer's margin; but when the customer of a bank goes to that bank, known to the president of the bank, to the directors of the bank, as a man of substance and standing in the community, and proposes that the bank make him a loan with which he may purchase a listed security and carry it with the aid of the loan, and the banker knows with whom he is talking and knows about the man's other assets and about his character and all about his business, how long he has been living in the town, all about his family, as he will, if he is anything like a wise banker, then the banker may be doing a perfectly sound thing, a perfectly safe thing, a thing which will aid in a small way the business transactions of the town, if he should loan to that man on a smaller margin than 45 percent. Yet this law is to step in between the individual customer and his own banker, whether that banker be in Oshkosh or Wichita, or some place in Montana, or in Texas, or in New York City. . . .

MR. SABATH. In the case the gentleman describes, if the man is a man of such standing as he describes, the banker could make a loan without this collateral security, or he could also make a loan to that extent, 45 percent, and then make a separate loan for an amount that he believes this man is entitled to receive. Is not that true? So that there is no danger of that provision at all.

MRS. KAHN. That would be a direct evasion of the law. . . .

MR. WADSWORTH. Mr. Chairman, of course the question propounded by the gentleman from Illinois [Mr. Sabath], if answered in the affirmative—and I do not know that I am competent to answer it either in the affirmative or in the negative—but if answered in the affirmative, and that answer were taken as true, means that this section is not worth anything. If it is to be evaded that easily, why have it at all with respect to banks?

I may be somewhat old fashioned in my regard for the function of a banker. I do not like to see him put in the same category as the broker. I think the banker is expected to use judgment, and the broker is not expected to use judgment to anything like the same extent in making loans.

I know my suggestion will not be and cannot be carried out; that is, to take the banks entirely out of this margin provision. That was discussed in committee, and it was decided otherwise. I dread it somewhat. I believe it will cramp the style, if I may use that phrase, of prospective investors away back in the hinterland, who want to go to their county banks and make loans, who cannot put up any such amount of collateral, or it would cause great hardship upon them if compelled to do so, as is imposed by this statute. I would rather trust the judgment of the banker who is well acquainted with his customer than I would the law. . . .

MR. FORD. Mr. Chairman, I am not going to discuss the details of the bill, but shall make just a few observations on the broader aspects of it.

No more controversial measure has been before this House than H.R. 9323, known as the "securities exchange bill of 1934."

The bill as first written brought down an avalanche of criticism and objections. It is my conviction that the bill as first drawn was too drastic. Therefore, much of the criticism of that first draft has proved to be justified.

But extended public hearings have been held. Every objection has been given careful consideration. Revision after revision has been made with the purpose of eliminating the provisions that seemed to be too drastic.

Now, I think, we have a bill that will protect the public by preventing inequitable and unfair practices and that will in the end prove beneficial to legitimate operators on our stock exchanges.

This bill does three things. It protects investors, controls market manipulations that are destructive to values, and tends to curb destructive speculation.

This measure strikes directly at what I believe is the most vicious practice of the stock exchanges—that is, the making of what is known as "wash sales" and "matched orders." This kind of manipulation is on a par with the use of loaded dice or other devices utilized by crooked professional gamblers in the conduct of their profession. It is, however, more reprehensible. No sane man enters a gambling house expecting to get a fair break for his money. But hundreds of thousands of good, honest American citizens pay their money to brokers, thinking that they are dealing with conservative, responsible, business men who are affording them the facilities of the market on an even chance with all others who use the market for the purpose of buying and selling securities. These people think they are investing their money in legitimate securities. That should be the case. If this measure is enacted into law, I believe that will be the case henceforth.

I hold no brief for those who would deliberately interfere with or hamper legitimate business. On the other hand, I insist that since the stock market has in the past been guilty of practices that transcend the legitimate, they, as well as all other offenders, should be brought within the law that calls for an honest, fair, and open chance for the citizen who desires to invest his money in legitimate securities. If in so doing he loses through the natural or ordinary hazard in industry and commerce, that is a loss he is willing to take. But if he is sheared like a lamb through a rigged market, through manipulations resulting from wash sales and matched orders, he has a legitimate cause for complaint, and it is his Government's business, through its legislative and executive branches, to throw about this stock-purchasing and stock-selling business such safeguards as will make these tricky devices, so long indulged in, impossible in the future.

This is a measure that President Roosevelt strongly recommends. In the face of the terrific drive against the measure, the President has repeated his recommendations. He is acting in the interest of honest business and honest investors. His motives are the highest. Shall we listen to the uninformed protestors or to the special interests who are objecting to this bill? Or shall we follow the leadership of the best friend the people of the United States ever had? Let us have the courage to pass this bill, knowing that it is an honest bill, framed for the benefit of honest people. [Applause.] . . .

MR. BLACK. . . . We have plenty of laws in New York against wash sales and matched orders; and we have the provisions of the United States mail fraud law against the same thing. We do not need this bill to give that particular protection. I do not think the gentleman will find anyone who has lost money recently on the New York Stock Exchange because of wash sales or matched orders.

MR. FORD. Not recently; but how about the past?

MR. BLACK. That may have been the case years and years ago. . . .

MR. LEA OF CALIFORNIA. Mr. Chairman, this measure is a new venture in Federal regulation. I do not regard it as premature. I regard it as tardily recognizing conditions that make it the duty of the Federal Government to regulate such matters. The reason for this legislation, as I view it, is amply demonstrated by a history of our economic developments in the past 15 years. We have been passing through a new economic period in our country. Stock exchanges have become the market places of the Nation. A large portion of the wealth of the country represented by stock certificates and bonds finds its market in these stock exchanges. The list prices of the stock exchanges are published even in fourth-class newspapaers of the Nation. All over the United States hundreds of thousands of American citizens read those papers. They hurriedly pass over the glaring headlines that may tell of the latest sensations, to read the news of the stock market. They are interested, because they are investors or speculators to an unusual degree. It is claimed that 10,000,000 people, citizens of this Republic, scattered to the remotest sections, are holders of shares, and interested in the market on the exchanges.

This bill, although it is called a bill to regulate national security exchanges, is much broader in its practical operation. In fact, the object of this measure is not merely to regulate the exchanges—that is only incidental to its purpose. The real purpose of this regulatory measure is to protect the investors of the United States against fraud and imprudent investments, and to give integrity to the securities by the sale of which American business must be financed.

The great abuses that have occurred through the use of the stock market in recent years is illustrative of the fact that power always carried with it susceptibility to abuse. The stock exchange is not a reprehensible organization in the business life of our country. It is not an unnecessary burden on the business of the Nation. It performs a very useful service. It is the outgrowth of the development of the economic forces of this country.

Above everything else, this is the corporate age of America. This is the age in which people have resorted to corporate investments as the most practical and in many respects the most desirable manner of carrying on the business of the United States.

It is estimated that about half the wealth of the United States is represented by the securities issued by corporations and by the wealth that is in the banks in the form of deposits. These security exchanges afford a liquid market that has no comparison in the past history of the world. A large percentage of the total wealth of America, as illustrated by the bonds and stocks of corporations, has a definite price on the exchanges today and every business day of the year. It may be a manufacturing plant in New Jersey, a sugar-production plant in Utah, or a gold mine in Alaska, but they are alike financed through a stock exchange in a distant city. Every day in the year, at least, at some cash price the securities of that corporation are salable. Every holder of these stocks and bonds knows that he can convert them into cash today to whatever may be the price on those exchanges.

A system which gives liquidity to a large proportion of the investments of the American people is a marvelous institution. I do not say this in praise; neither do I say it in condemnation of the exchange. I state the fact. We must properly appraise the function of the exchange in order to pass legislation to regulate and control, not for the purpose of destroying but for the purpose of protecting, for the constructive purpose of conserving the business of the United States. If this legislation is successful in carrying out the purpose for which it is designed, it will give greater stability, more credence, and greater integrity to the stocks listed on the exchanges of the country. They will be more valuable.

The stocks and bonds of the corporations and the bank accounts of this country constitute liquid assets and a convenient form of investment. Before the corporate phase of American business developed, the man with a few hundred or a few thousand dollars at his command was frequently at a loss to know what to do with it. The chances were he did not have sufficient money with which to go into business on his own account, or if he had sufficient money, did not have the business experience and perhaps not the time to manage a small business. In recent years, under quantity production, expanding trade and industries, the stock market has invited him to become a purchaser of its securities. The stock market furnished a convenient method of investing with the hope of security and a prospect of a fair or possibly a speculative return.

A problem that will more acutely develop, particularly if this bill functions as intended, will be the tendency of the stock markets to drain credits from local investments. I take it the best investment the citizen can make is a local investment. Where an individual invests his money in a local enterprise, he builds up his local community, adds to local labor employment and community progress, and does more for the country than by contributing to the financing of the great business organizations of the country with remote control. This was one of the great difficulties in 1929. The stock markets drained local credit throughout the United States and caused an unbalanced credit situation which weakened our stability from the financial standpoint. Our people were turning away from safe investments to the more enticing and uncertain rewards of speculation.

It is well to realize that today the vast wealth invested in stocks, bonds, corporate securities, and bank deposits represents nearly one half the wealth of the United States and involves the separation of ownership and control. At no other time in the history of the world has there been such a vast proportion of the wealth of a nation invested in undertakings where ownership and control were separated. We have had this remarkable situation in the United States. It means that those in control of our great corporations, those who issue and control these securities, those who sell these stocks and profit from their transfer, are not the people who primarily suffer from fraud or imprudent investments these stocks may represent. There is the greatest temptation that managements have ever had to be unfaithful to their trusts.

In the main, the men controlling these great corporations are not large owners of the stocks of the corporations they control. Too often they have yielded to the temptation to control these great business institutions to their own interests, and with a zeal out of proportion to the loyalty they have shown their stockholders. Thus in recent years we have seen the directors of corporations, without the knowledge of their stockholders, voting themselves vast bonuses out of all proportion to what legitimate management would justify. We have had revelations of salaries paid to directors and officers of great corporations which showed shameful mismanagement; which showed that the men in charge of some of these corporations were more concerned in managing its affairs for their own benefit than for the benefit of the stockholders. The history of the past few years has revealed that in a number of instances these unconscionable bonuses and unconscionable salaries exacted from the stockholders were continued notwithstanding the fact that dividends were cut, and notwithstanding the fact that in some cases the common-stock holders were deprived of any dividends. We have had the ugly picture of corporate officials juggling with the stocks of their own companies, preying on their own stockholders through inside information they obtained as trustees of the trust they violated.

One of the most serious phases of this indirect or remote control of capital by those who are not the owners is lack of contact. In the old days when the man in charge of a local corporation committed an offense, embezzled the company's money, or conducted the company's business in an unconscionable way, he was branded in the local community. He lost his prestige, and the victims of his mismanagement or fraud were known to the community. Their suffering was present and visible. At the present time, however, under remote stock transactions, the victims of mismanagement of a corporation are remote from those who inflict the injury, the associates of the perpetrator do not ostracize or upbraid him. The victims are unseen by those who inflict their injuries. This bill proposes to hold these wrongdoers to a higher degree of responsibility.

This measure, as I suggested, goes a good deal further than the regulation of stock exchanges. The purpose of the bill is not simply the regulation of stock exchanges. It proposes the protection of the investor against fraud, to give more integrity to securities listed on the exchanges. To accomplish these purposes we must follow the stock from its issuance to the hands of the purchasers. The question of the integrity of the management of the corporation is involved; the question of the prudence of the investment represented by the stock is involved.

We do not mean that the Federal Government will attempt to substitute its judgment for the judgment of the stockholder in the matter of determining the prudence of the investment. That is a problem which must be assumed by the investor and of which the Government does not try to relieve him; but it is the problem of the Federal Government under the theory of this bill to require that when the corporation registers its stock on an exchange it must make a full and complete revelation of all facts that legitimately affect its securities. The information which corporations are required to give by this bill do not materially differ from that required by the New York Stock Exchange at this time. I take it, the first substantial step toward securing effective regulation is to require a complete revelation of all material facts that an investor should know in order to invest his money properly.

When these market exchanges are open for the investors of the Nation the Government has a right to expect that the corporations whose stocks are listed there and offered to the public will give truthful information and make a full revelation of the facts tending to show the merits or the demerits of their stock. Without giving such information their stocks are not entitled to the credence which listing should carry.

When it comes to the exchanges themselves, this bill provides for their regulation. We recognize that an exchange is a private institution. It is run for the profit of its members. Yet it performs a useful function of value to the people of the United States. It aids business by giving a market and by giving liquidity to this vast portion of the wealth of our country. We require that the exchange shall register and give full information as to its set-up to the commission that will administer this law. We require that the exchanges shall agree to enforce compliance by their members of all the regulations and rules of the commission. They agree to submit to regulation themselves. They agree that the exchanges will, if necessary, change their rules with reference to membership or in reference to stocks and other matters, so as to conform to the requirements of the regulatory commission.

These exchanges must not be charged with all the sins that have occurred in connection with the sale of stock in recent years. If I undertook to try to fix the responsiblity for the debacle that came to the stock market since 1929 I would not attempt to place my finger on the exchanges and blame them alone. I recognize the part they played in the matter, but I also recognize another man who is very largely responsible for the misfortunes of the country and the excessive stock speculation and debacle. That is Mr. American Citizen who wants to get something for nothing. He had a large part in the misfortunes of the American people in reference to the stock speculation.

However, that is no answer to the purposes of this bill. This bill cannot do everything. It does not attempt that, but it does attempt to perform a useful service, to insist on reliable information to the investor. . . .

These stock exchanges are the bottle necks through which these certificates flow after they are issued by the corporation and before they reach the ultimate investor. This furnishes an opportunity to control and regulate that may serve a useful purpose to the Nation.

We must first go to the corporation that issues the stock and look into the prudence and integrity of that corporation. Then we must go to the exchange where this stock is sold; then to the broker and the dealer who handle these stocks, and some of whom have been guilty of the manipulative practices of recent years. Then we must look into the question of the credit advanced and on which the stock is floated in the markets of the United States.

The Government in connection with every city assumes responsiblity for its water supply. It assumes the responsiblity to see that the water supply is clean, drinkable, and beneficial to the public. Here we have this great market supply of the Nation. In this bill the Federal Government attempts to assert its regulatory powers to keep as clean and trustworthy as possible this vast flow of stock from the corporations to the investors and business life of the United States.

When we come to the question of the broker and the dealer, a good deal of controversy was involved as to what control should be established; whether or not these positions should be separated; whether or not we would permit a man to act in the capacity of both broker and dealer; whether or not we should permit floor trading or permit specialists to be on the floor; and other problems.

In attempting to deal with these questions I am candid to admit that the committee proposed to confer a large regulatory power on the regulatory commission.

There were two reasons for this: The first was that we recognized we are not experts and tried to act with a caution becoming our inexperience. Where in doubt as to what should be done, we thought better to resolve the doubt in favor of maintaining the present business practices than to establish some fixed rule that might prove unfortunate. In the second place, where we gave the regulatory commission the power, it would be a flexible power. If the commission finds a mistake has been made, it can readily change its rules to more favorable ones and thus accomplish the purposes of Congress.

The manipulative practices that have so stigmatized the stock market in recent years revolve largely around the broker and the dealer. This bill is severe in its denunciation and penalties for manipulative violations of the law. It not only prescribes criminal penalties for those who engage in these manipulative practices, but it also gives a civil suit in behalf of the man who is the victim of such practices. It is going to be dangerous for a man to engage in window dressing, fraudulent and deceptive methods for the purpose of defrauding investors. This bill proposes to punish persons guilty of fraudulent statements in reference to stocks listed on these national exchanges where damage results.

There has been a great deal of controversy about the question of controlling credit as it is embodied in the margin sections of this bill. Restrained credit is not primarily for the benefit of the purchaser of the stock. It is not necessary from the standpoint of the broker. It is necessary for the business welfare of the Nation, for its vital need of credit protection. . . .

MR. WOLVERTON. Mr. Chairman, the subject matter of the bill (H.R. 9323) now under consideration presents more intricate and a greater variety of problems affecting the economic, financial, and individual welfare of our people than any legislation heretofore presented at this session of Congress.

Propaganda

The wide-spread interest manifested throughout the country is not entirely due to propaganda alleged to have been instigated by opponents of this measure; although I can say that the propaganda against this bill has been more highly organized and more extensive than any I have ever previously experienced. However, the fact remains that beneath the deluge of inquiries and protests received by every Member of Congress there has been an apparent and unmistakable fear that in some way or other the proposed legislation would adversely affect the business enterprises of our Nation.

While it is true that the original bill did contain some provisions that might create an honest concern upon the part of thoughtful business men, yet, I am inclined to believe that statements, unwarranted in many instances, originating from prominent business men have had more to do with creating this psychology of fear than the actual provisions of the bill. [Applause.]

Protection of Legitimate Business

I wish to assure the Members of the House that the Committee on Interstate and Foreign Commerce has not been insensible to the necessity of taking every precaution to preclude even the possibility of curing one evil by creating another or greater one. And, for the further assurance of the House permit me to say that in our consideration of the many vital questions or problems that we were called upon to decide there has been no division of thought along strictly party lines. The uppermost thought that has dominated out individual and collective decisions has been a desire to correct existing evils, or conditions that have proved harmful, without destroying, curtailing, or handicapping legitimate business.

And, in this connection, I wish to express my appreciation of the faithful and conscientious endeavor of our chairman [Mr. Rayburn] to present to this House legislation on this important subject that would prove beneficial to the public interest. [Applause.] At all times he was fair, open-minded, and willing to give every opportunity to the members of the committee to present conflicting viewpoints. His attitude of fairness to the members of the committee and interested parties desiring to be heard, is still further emphasized by his request to the Rules Committee for an open rule whereby the membership of the House is likewise given the opportunity to express their viewpoint and offer amendments to the bill. It is a pleasure and a privilege to hold membership on a committee that is willing, under the leadership of its chairman, to submit its work on a matter as important as this to the House for approval in a manner that does not preclude the fullest expression of opinion.

[Applause.] Similar procedure should likewise be adopted for the consideration of all important legislation. Such a course is in accord with the dignity and intelligence of the House.

Prevailing Conditions Require Action

The need for legislation of this character is apparent to everyone who has given thoughtful and unbiased consideration to the underlying causes and conditions that brought about or culminated in the stock market catastrophe of 1929, with its attendant destruction of business and individual distress.

In 1929, at the peak of the security market, the total value of stocks listed on the New York Stock Exchange alone, was nearly $89,000,000,000. In 1932, it had shrunk to less than $16,000,000,000. In those 3 years the average value per share of stock had declined from $89 to $12. Bonds listed on the exchange declined from $49,000,000,000 in September 1930 to $31,000,000,000 in April 1933. In addition to this enormous loss of value there must also be added the depreciation in value of stocks and bonds on other exchanges than the New York Stock Exchange, and the depreciation of all stocks, bonds, mortgages, real estate, and every class of securities throughout the country. It was the collapse of security values in 1929 and subsequent years that has resulted in the closing of nearly 6,000 banks in the United States, paralyzing business and bringing distress to millions of our people.

It may properly be said that the New York Stock Exchange was not the sole cause for these results, yet the fact remains that the practices prevailing on the exchange, prior to 1929, constituted a direct and contributing cause to the collapse of security values.

Wild and unrestrained speculation, made possible by highly organized pools and other manipulative practices, encouraged by false and misleading statements, influenced thousands of individuals to enter the stock market. They not only utilized their own savings, but borrowed large sums to finance their stock-market transactions. They had little, if any, information as to the real value of the stocks they traded in, and no knowledge of the intricacies of market practices. The vast majority were as innocent and gullible as lambs.

Extent of Stock-Market Trading

As an indication of the extent to which stock-market speculation became a fascinating venture, it is only necessary to consider the rapidity and extent of increased trading in the years immediately preceding and including 1929.

In the 10 years before the World War the yearly transactions in stock on the New York Stock Exchange averaged about 155,000,000 shares. During this period the maximum days's trading was less than 3,000,000 shares. In 1925 the number of shares traded in had increased to 450,000,000, or approximately three times greater than the average for the pre-war decade. In 1929 the volume had reached the tremendous total of 1,125,000,000—an increase of 150 percent in 4 years and more than 700 percent over the pre-war period. During the busy days of 1929 the total number of shares bought and sold in 1 day reached as many as 16,000,000. In 1929, 1 day of such trading was equal to one third of the entire volume of trading for the year 1914. Or, expressed differently, 3 days of such trading in 1929 was equal in volume to the entire trading of the full year in 1914. And, astounding as it may seem, notwithstanding, the experiences of the past, in the summer of 1933 there was a repetition of the orgy of speculation that characterized the year 1929, and in 1933, despite the depression 654,000,000 shares were bought and sold on the New York Stock Exchange.

These contrasting figures indicate the constantly increasing public interest in stock-market transactions, and the necessity of controlling and regulating such exchanges to the end that the public interest shall be served and the investing public protected.

Speculative Financing

While unrestrained and unrestricted speculation played a large part in creating conditions that eventually contributed to the stock-market collapse of 1929, yet there is another condition closely identified with it that challenges our thoughtful consideration, namely, the extensive use of credit in financing stock-market transactions.

The report of the Committee on Interstate and Foreign Commerce presents a striking analysis of the situation and the result that inevitably follows. Between 1922 and 1929 brokers' loans increased from one and one half billion to eight and one half billion dollars. Five billion dollars of this increase took place in 3 years, one and one half billion dollars in the last 3 months. In the crash of 1929 the same loans declined $3,000,000,000 in the first 10 days and $8,000,000,000 in the next 3 years. These figures alone will enable the economic historian of the future to describe the unhealthy prosperity of 1929 and the inevitable grief and suffering that followed in the succeeding years—grief and suffering that overwhelmed and carried away not merely the gains of speculative debauch, not merely the savings of those who had invested in securities, but eventually the savings of the frugal and thrifty who had deposited their funds in banking institutions, and finally destroyed the operating profits of every business in the country no matter how unrelated to stock exchanges.

To finance these stock transactions, and to provide funds for new security issues, of every conceivable kind and character, increased interest and other inducements were made that had the effect of drawing into this whirlpool of speculation the funds of local banks from the remotest parts of our country. These funds would otherwise have been utilized in financing local enterprises. When the bubble burst, the harmful effects were consequently felt in every locality throughout the land. The innocent suffered with the guilty. The individual who had deposited his or her life's savings in a bank, a building-and-loan association, or a home, felt the effect and suffered the loss, although he had never purchased a share of stock on any exchange. It is not necessary to pursue this thought any further to illustrate the necessity of preventing, as far as humanly possible, a recurrence of such conditions in the future.

Federal Regulation a Necessity

How, and by what means, can the public interest and the investing public be best served? Certainly, it cannot be by the abolition of exchanges. Their usefulness and necessity as a part of the highly organized economic and financial machinery of present-day business makes their continuation an absolute necessity. This fact is well and forcibly set forth in the summary of the research findings and recommendations of the stock market survey staff of the Twentieth Century Fund, wherein it is said:

> The security markets supply a means by which those who hold securities may exchange them for others or convert them into cash. The more effective the marketing processes become, the easier it is for owners of stocks and bonds to sell them. It is unnecessary to describe in detail the public as well as the private advantages of such a ready market. To clarify the picture, imagine the indescribable difficulties which would follow a condition in which the owner of high-grade stocks or bonds who wants to sell would meet the uncertainty and delay which faces the owner of real estate today if he is in need of ready cash. Such a situation would involve a complete revolution in banking and insurance, not to mention the financial affairs of millions of our people who hold securities.

If the stock market is to perform a useful as well as an essential service to the economic, financial, and business life of the Nation, it must be so conducted, by control or regulation in the public interest, as to insure a ready market for securities, with continuity of prices for securities as near as possible to the actual value.

To effect this purpose, the bill under consideration has four principal objectives, namely, (1) to establish Federal supervision over securities exchanges; (2) to prevent manipulation of security prices and to protect the public against unfair practices; (3) to prevent excessive fluctuations in security prices due to speculative influences; (4) to discourage and prevent the use of credit in the financing of excessive speculation in securities.

The necessity for Federal regulation and control of exchanges is made apparent by the inability of such exchanges, conducted as private institutions, to adequately control or eliminate the harmful practices that have grown up in dealing with securities, both within and outside of recognized exchanges. Furthermore, the business of buying and selling securities is largely interstate in character. Consequently, proper regulation and control must be found through Federal agencies rather than State.

Plan of Regulation

The plan of regulation and control, set up under the provisions of this bill, makes it unlawful for any exchange to function as such or utilize any of the facilities of interstate commerce until it has first made application and received permission from the Federal authority set up for that purpose. And the granting of such right is further conditioned upon an agreement to comply, and to require its members to comply, with the provisions of this act and the rules and regulations set up thereunder by the Federal Commission. The penalties and actions provided are amply sufficient to require and insure strict compliance.

A question as to the right, power, or authority of Congress to legislate on the subject matter of the bill and in the manner proposed by the bill has been raised by eminent counsel. I am convinced, however, that the constitutionality of the method as well as the power of Congress to legislate for the purposes set forth in the bill has well been sustained by a brief submitted to the committee by Thomas C. Corcoran and Benjamin V. Cohen, who have also faithfully and ably assisted the committee in its consideration of the intricate problems directly and indirectly related to the subject matter of the proposed legislation. If it be true, as stated, that these young men are part of the so-called "brain trust," then I can testify that there have been no misnomer in so doing. [Applause.] They have each shown rare ability and fidelity in the performance of their duty and have rendered a most worth-while service in this important matter of legislation.

No Improper Regulation of Business

Aside from the constitutional feature, the next most important question that has been raised against the bill is that with respect to whether or not its provisions place an undue or improper burden upon legitimate business enterprises.

Whatever justification may have existed for this complaint as based upon the provisions of the original bill, there is no legitimate objection in the one now before this House. This bill requires no information to be given by issuers or securities traded in on a stock exchange other than what is essential and necessary to properly and fully inform the investing public as to the merits of the particular investment, and in no way, directly or indirectly, curtails or handicaps legitimate business in the fullest measure of management in the interest of its shareholders. It does preclude, however, the management of business enterprises from utilizing inside information to their own benefit without making such fact known to the shareholder. It, furthermore, seeks to make more difficult the use of official positions to self-perpetuate the controlling management, and thereby enables the individual stockholder in conjunction with others to have a more reasonable opportunity to change the management when occasion seems to justify. There is also a curtailment or restriction on the right to use surplus funds, by loans or otherwise, to finance or supply credit for stock-market speculation, and a requirement that full disclosure must be made of remuneration received by officers of the company, including any bonus.

Certainly there can be no proper complaint made to provisions such as these, the only purpose of which is to protect the investing public. Accurate knowledge of the financial condition of the security issuer and an assurance that full and true information is available to the small investor on the outsider as well as to the insider cannot help but produce a more ready and substantial market for securities.

Margin Trading

Another feature of the bill that has met with considerable opposition is that which seeks to restrict or control margin trading as a speculative influence. It would be impossible to correct the evils incidental to stock-market operations without assuming jurisdiction to regulate or control margin trading. There is nothing more harmful to the maintenance of an orderly market or the continuity of price levels based upon actual investment value of securities than the upsetting influence of unrestrained or unrestricted speculation. Margin requirements have a direct relation to speculation. The amount of margin required can create or curtail speculation. No one denies it can be utilized either as an accelerator or a brake. Everyone, therefore, admits the necessity of providing some authority to regulate its use.

Some have held that this important function should remain in the hands of stock-exchange officials with some power given to the Federal regulatory body to supervise the stock exchange in its control of the matter. Others are of the opinion that the public interest demands that there shall be an entire separation of its control from private hands. I am of the opinion that the importance of the subject, as well as the difficulties to be otherwise encountered, require that a flexible power of control should be lodged in a Federal administrative authority with the fullest opportunity given to such authority, preferably the Federal Reserve bank, to raise or lower the margin requirements according as prevailing business conditions may seem to require and with due respect to different classes of securities and their earning possibilities. This latter method has been adopted by this bill except that it contains definitely fixed margin requirements as a declaration of congressional policy, but, in the final analysis, giving unrestricted discretionary authority to the Federal Reserve bank, because of its general supervision of the subject of bank credits, to raise or lower the margin requirements set forth in the bill. The Twentieth Century research staff had recommended to the committee the advisability of fixing margin requirements upon the basis of earnings of the security issuer. It was agreed that this method presented problems too intricate to be made a part of this bill at this time and required further study. In a former draft of this proposed legislation the Federal Reserve Board and associated agencies were directed to make such study and report the result of the same to the next session of Congress. I regret it was not made a part of this bill. However, the general direction to make reports annually by the agencies of government having to do with the administration of this act may be sufficient without specific direction to do so. I hope it may be so considered.

Control of Stock-Market Credit

In order that the fullest control may be exercised at all times over loans and credits extended to stock-exchange members, brokers, and dealers for stock-market transactions, and thereby preclude undue or improper speculation, borrowing on registered securities—other than exempted securities—is determined by definite restrictions laid down by the provisions of the bill.

Furthermore, a broker is forbidden to commingle the securities of customers without their written consent; and in no event is he permitted to pledge customers' securities with those of persons who are not customers or under circumstances that will subject customers' securities to a lien in excess of the aggregate indebtedness of the customers. These provisions prevent a broker from risking the securities of his customer to finance his own speculative operations. The provisions of this section of the bill, together with the margin-requirement section, will prove a strong deterrent and preventive against unrestrained orgies of speculation in the future.

Manipulative Practices

The need for regulation of stock exchanges and corporate securities having the benefit of the Nation-wide facilities afforded by such exchanges was revealed, if not already known, by the recent investigation conducted by the Senate Committee on Banking and Currency. Manipulative price-control methods were found to be practiced by corporate officers and others who utilized the stock-exchange facilities to advance their nefarious and unconscionable schemes.

The bill now under consideration recognizes and labels distinctly and unmistakably each and every such fraudulent and improper device heretofore used. In specific and plain language it makes unlawful (1) creating a false or misleading appearance of active trading in any security registered on the exchange; (2) to effect any transaction which involves no change in the beneficial ownership of such security; (3) to enter an order for the purchase or sale of a security with the knowledge that an order of substantially the same size, same price, and, at the same time has been or will be entered by or for the same or different parties; (4) to effect singly or jointly any transaction for raising or depressing the price of a security; (5) to induce the purchase or sale of any registered security by circulating the information that the price is likely to rise or fall because of market operations of any person conducted for the purpose of raising or depressing the price of such security; (6) to induce the purchase or sale of a security by knowingly making a false or misleading statement; (7) in contravention of prescribed rules and regulations to effect alone or jointly any transactions for the purposes of "pegging," "fixing," or stabilizing the price of a security, or any transaction to acquire any "put," "call," "straddle," or other option or privilege of buying or selling a security without being bound to do so, or, to endorse or guarantee any such. And, in addition to the declaration of criminal responsibility, there is also provided a civil liability in favor of any person injured by any such transaction. If anyone should desire to observe a real, genuine set of legislative teeth, he can do so by giving consideration to section 8 of this act.

There are many other important features of the bill which, if the time allotted had permitted, I would have discussed. Furthermore, the full and complete report, together with the exhaustive explanation of Mr. Rayburn, chairman of the committee, make further detailed reference to the provisions of the bill unnecessary. While there may be some features with which I do not agree, yet a close study of the bill with an open mind will reveal that every care has been taken to adequately protect the public interest and give protection to the investor. Yet equal care has been taken to do no harm to legitimate business. Furthermore, I would like to assure employees of stock exchanges and those in other activities directly or indirectly incident thereto that whatever justification for fear of dismissal there may have been by reason of the provisions of the original bill, such does not exist in the present bill.

Type of Regulatory Authority

In conclusion, I wish to express my views with respect to the type of authority to be set up for the administration of the act. The bill provides that the authority for such administration shall be the Federal Trade Commission, and that the membership of the Commission shall be increased to 7 commissioners by the addition of 2 new commissioners, and that the Commission shall be divided into divisions of not less than 3 members each. The work of administering the provisions of this act and the Securities Act of 1933 to come under the jurisdiction of one of such divisions. There is much to commend this plan, inasmuch as the Federal Trade Commission already has exercised jurisdiction in industrial and other closely related subjects. However, I am of the opinion that as the administrative work to be pursued in the regulation and control of the exchanges and the jurisdiction to be exercised in the many matters related thereto require a high degree of technical skill and knowledge, that it would be more advantageous if the administration of the act should be placed in a Federal securities exchange commission to be composed of 5 members appointed by the President, by and with the advice and consent of the Senate, not more than 3 members to be of the same political party, such commission to take over also the administration of the Securities Act of 1933. In either case, however, as the Dickinson report to the President set forth, after its study of the general subject matter of stock-exchange control:

The staff of the agency must be specifically fitted for their tasks and the Commissioners charged with the work must be men of unusual qualifications who must hold the respect of the country; and such an agency should give continuous representations to the views both of the investing public and of the exchanges in an endeavor to provide that no hasty or ill-advised regulations would be promulgated by inexperienced men.

Creating New Confidence in Security Markets

It is my hope and expectation that a wise and judicious administration of the provisions of this act will create a new confidence in the integrity of the security markets. The report of the Twentieth Century Survey and study, aptly states:

If there were a justifiable belief that security markets actually were "free and open," that all buyers and sellers met on substantially equal terms, that the outsider was not victimized by the insider, that pool activities did not distort investment values, that brokers could be relied upon to give undivided loyalty toward their customers, that reckless speculation would not occur—if, in short, a new atmosphere of this sort could be created, the response would be a greater investment interest in securities and a consequent improvement in all phases of the security business.

It is needless to say that it has been the constant endeavor of the Committee on Interstate and Foreign Commerce, throughout its long and tedious consideration of this subject, to produce a bill that will recreate confidence by an assurance that past evils cannot and will not occur again in the security market. We believe this bill will accomplish that purpose. [Applause.] . . .

MR. MALONEY OF CONNECTICUT. Mr. Chairman, this bill has been declared the most important piece of legislation to be considered by this Congress. It has excited thousands of columns of newspaper space, made boom business for the Post Office Department and the telegraph companies, has seized the interest of the public as few pieces of legislation have done—and has worked certain interests to the point where it has been said they would spend millions to have it cast aside.

All this has naturally intensified the interest of the members of the Committee on Interstate and Foreign Commerce, which has been considering the bill. That interest and that sense of its importance has driven us to go over it time and again, line by line, paragraph by paragraph, and page by page. We have called on representatives of all interests to help us, defenders of high finance from Wall Street, conservative investment bankers from all parts of the country, industrialists, lawyers, commercial bankers, and Government servants filling high posts in the Federal Reserve Board and other departments. Because of its importance, we have never attempted to hurry and we have never used or felt the partisan whip. Whenever reasonable doubts have existed, we have called a halt to discuss at full length the problem involved. Time and again the bill has been redrafted to meet the directions of the committee for further changes. I think the committee can be proud of the dispassionate and devoted effort it has given to the formulation of the bill which has been reported out. The time all this has required has been justified by the improvement which the existing bill represents over the much more drastic measure originally introduced as a basis for suggestion and hearings.

But on the other hand the very conscientiousness with which the bill has been reworked by the committee has, paradoxically, been largely the cause of the uneasiness about its provisions which have been described as existing in certain parts of the country and, according to my colleague, Mr. Merritt, particularly in my own New England. In the first place, the changes of sections and even the complete redrafts of the bill have been too many and have succeeded each other too quickly for the public to follow and distinguish between them. I am still receiving protests which I am sure are based not on the bill which the committee has reported to the House, but on the bill which was originally introduced nearly 10 weeks ago. In the second place, the intervening 10 weeks have afforded a golden opportunity for propagandists. With their great resources and many contacts the stock exchanges were able to gather their forces and take full advantage of the public confusion over the terms of the bill. We are unfortunate in that our very conscientiousness has made things more difficult.

Two things particularly impressed me in the long hearings. One was the seeming inability of the brokers and big business men to consider the broader point of view of the whole social structure, and to understand the degree to which their own prosperity is completely tied up with a sound stability in the economic system as a whole. They seemed to realize so little the degree to which the prosperity of each of them depends upon the common good, and that if we do not learn somehow to hang together, we shall soon again, as in 1929-32, hang separately. As Chairman Rayburn stated in his speech before the House yesterday, fundamentally it is impossible to have a bill which will completely satisfy those interests. They really want no bill at all.

Another thing about the hearings that impressed me to a considerable extent was the absence of those who suffered most during the period of financial madness. We were endeavoring to perfect a measure that would remove the possibility of future frauds, that would protect the little banks, the small industries, the business men of America, and the hundreds of thousands of individuals who have periodically been caught in the vortex of the waters of juggled finance, and there were none of them at court. Their representatives were a few Government servants and these men were roundly suspected and damned for their efforts.

I came to the conclusion that some of them were beyond the opportunity to testify, that others among them were indifferent because their faith in a Congress to meet the challenge was very slight, and the rest because they had lost their pride, their spirit was crushed, and their courage gone.

Some of these absentees would be the people who would again suffer most if we could not evolve some way of preventing a repetition of that nightmare. Here we are endeavoring to perfect a measure to remove the possibility that soon again, as in the years before 1929, the operations of a comparatively few irresponsible financial monarchs and their camp followers—monarchs who would later abdicate into bankruptcy like Livermore or into oblivion like Kreuger, or to a far-away place like Insull, and leave the common folks to work out of the mess without their help—might ruin the little banks, the small industries, the average business man, and the thousands of investor-speculators who are periodically caught in and pay the price for speculative madnesses which political reactionaries fatalistically regard as regrettable but inevitable fluctuations in the economic cycle. Almost a hundred witnesses and hundreds more of highly paid lawyers and agents appeared and lobbied directly or indirectly for the cause of those who dwell in high financial places. Only five or six Government employees, and a few other people, appeared for the hundreds of thousands of the solid little fellows.

Of course, we were not alone the representatives of those who lost when the masts and funnels of finance were shot away. We had, however, felt the evidence that would have been theirs had they testified, as we lived in the terrible times ourselves, and the finding of this committee, as it is presented for your final judgment this week, was based upon a desire to be fair to those men who labor in the money marts, and just to those who make this great financial business possible. It became very clear to me that there was a particular duty upon us, hearing in substance only one side in this great debate. We were in a sense compelled to represent that great inarticulate mass and in a sense to be their advocate in weighing the testimony so pressed upon us by well-paid lawyers for the other side.

I think that this Congress, so likely to hear only the side of the articulate big man, should be careful that it adopts a bill fair not only to those who operate financial markets with other people's money, but to those millions who self-stinting thrift, and possibly pathetic faith in the integrity of those operators and in the stability of those markets, makes great financial business possible. And I feel that the bill as reported by the committee is fair enough in that way, and is effective, and should be adopted now.

Yesterday I heard my colleague from Connecticut, Mr. Merritt, plead with you not to enact this bill into law at this session, because it might interfere with business, even though only indirectly, and because reviving business confidence might be disturbed by the existence of that possibility magnified into a real fear by clever propaganda. I have for Mr. Merritt a feeling of affection and regard that goes far beyond the warm feeling of good will that men who are friends feel toward one another. I tremendously admire him for the sincerity of his convictions, even as I disagree with him.

I know, and I understand, and I share the concern of my Connecticut colleague as he aims to protect the typical Connecticut business man from actual Government domination or from any reasonable fear of that domination. But I do disagree with him on the existence of any fair basis for fear, and on the wisdom of postponing this legislation because unjustifiable fears have been created.

For myself I want to declare that I am whole-heartedly for this bill in its present form. I am for it because I am firmly convinced that industry will have a haven of safety behind its remparts, because it will no longer allow the small banks scattered over the land to be the unknowing tools and victims of a small financial clique run wild, because it affords once more a better chance to the small business man on Main Street, and because it gives a greater measure of protection to the unschooled small investor in every hamlet in America.

Honest and sincere men will arise on the floor of this House before the close of this debate, as my colleague did yesterday, and plead with you not to permit the enactment of a law that will tie the hands of industry, retard the flow of credit, and slow up the wheels of progress. Many of them will be blessed with a greater gift of words than I possess, and I regard the abilities of some of them so highly that I am sure there will be a plausibility in their argument. I urge you to watch for the concrete case of where the bill does harm.

Among those who will express fear, both in this House and elsewhere, are other men of noble character and high purpose from my own State. For some of them I have a high regard. The difference between us—and it is a wide difference—is our opinion concerning the responsibility of government. Theirs is that philosophy of government so clearly and so pitifully exemplified in the days just before the Seventy-third Congress. Theirs is that governmental view which expresses the thought that it is unwise to try things heretofore untried. They belong to the old order and the old guard. They are the political reactionaries.

I am not in sympathy with the view which attacks these men or attacks the Mellons and the Morgans. From the law they know and the view they have, I am certain that theirs is no less a noble purpose than that of other men. I do, however, join in the attack upon the manipulation of our system of government by men of high finance, and I do join in the attack upon every set-up, whether it be in Wall Street or Pittsburgh, which permits an abuse of power by men who have been given that power by the sweat of another man's brow.

I think I can show in a few minutes that there is no ground for the fear that this bill will interfere with the conduct of business corporations. But right now let me say that I have no faith in a business confidence that is so tender a plant that it cannot stand the sunshine of immediate curative legislation for admitted existing abuses. I do not believe that any business recovery like the one through which we are rapidly passing can be ruined by a sound piece of stabilizing legislation designed to keep that recovery from running away like the boom of last year. A confidence that comes from the real knowledge that crazy stock-exchange speculation cannot again upset the balance of things is the only kind of confidence on which business can really build. A nervous postponement of necessary adjustments until an inevitable "next year" is a basis on which nothing can be built except the hope that political accident may make it impossible to pass any bill next year. This bill does not offer us any simplified choice of reform or recovery. We are in a situation where without reform there can be no sound recovery.

I do not believe that a generation should fatalistically suffer its woes in the sackcloth and ashes of passive acceptance, fearing to do anything but wait for the operation of so-called "economic natural laws" to restore prosperity to the next generation. I do not believe in changing our form of Government. But I do believe that this generation has the intelligence and resource to grapple with our problems as boldly and concretely, and as experimentally if need be, as our constitutional fathers grappled with their problems 150 years ago. That is part of the reason why I have long advocated a governmental regulation of working hours, and an old-age pension system.

I consider that the truly dangerous radical in times like these, when all the plans of a generation are standing at the forks of the road, is the disbeliever in our power to control our own economic destiny. I cannot comprehend the feeling of those who fatalistically shake their heads face to face with our admitted problem, remark on human futility, and have no recommendation but that things be allowed to work themselves out. In a thousand years' view of human history it perhaps makes no difference to the philosopher that this generation in Meriden and in New Haven, Conn., 1934, are trapped in a burning structure, while the philosophers watch the flames burn out and reflect that in another 10 years the workings of the natural laws of economics will create prosperity for another generation. But it means everything to those people in Meriden and in New Haven in 1934 to try to take hold of the situation and do some things for themselves now.

I represent an even more highly industrialized constitutency than does Mr. Merritt. Mine is a constituency of moderate-sized closely owned business firms, managed by those who have had to make profits while paying the highest wage scales in the country, and employing clear-headed, sober, intelligent workingmen who have tried to invest intelligently. It is a constituency of democratic decentralized industrial units which has tried to live by its own self-reliant standards and which has had very little part in the speculation of the rest of the country. But it has learned—and it was a bitter lesson—that the completely national scale on which our business and finance is now organized leaves the native conservatism of any community rather helpless before the speculation of less conservative communities. My New England constituency will not only be unharmed by the passage of this bill but gains from it the protection of its habitual methods of doing business and of investing money to a greater extent than practically any other section of the country. The small New England business man, who always operated on a cautious, stable basis, can only gain by control of the stream of credit which has upset his careful plans, and profits, by alternately flushing his huge poorly managed competitors with stock-market funds to expand in the fever of a boom—and leaving his market glutted with productive facilities when the boom collapsed. And I am convinced that there has been a direct relationship between the flotation of huge mergers on the basis of too easy stock-market credit and the tendency toward monopolization of industry which has gone on in the past 10 years to the destruction of the democratic decentralization and diversification of small industry on which New England stability is based.

I think the New England investor likewise has everything to gain and nothing to lose. The provisions for adequate corporate reporting, the provisions by which credit controls will tend to make securities sell on an investment basis, and the provisions outlawing market manipulations give him the materials for a stable investment policy based on stable investment values which he has always sought. In the House committee the other day I heard general agreement that the New England securities market was the best and perhaps the only true investment market in the country—that securities were bought in New England for investment holding and not for speculative trading to a degree unequaled in any other section of the country. Not a little of that sort of investment demand comes from its carefully conservative banks, and from its magnificently operated insurance companies, which safeguard the humble estates men endeavor to create by real self-sacrifice. A bill that tends to stabilize securities markets for such insurance companies, banks, and other investors, that gives them adequate corporation reports on which to base their judgments to buy and sell—that gives them assurances that the values reflected in these corporate reports will not be unpredictably upset by alternate booms and panics in the stock market—is a bill which will put at a premium the qualities on which New England's financial life is based. New England has less reason to be afraid of this bill than has any other section of the country.

The talk about the effect of this proposed legislation upon business usually starts with the statement that it is only right and proper to regulate the abuses on the stock exchanges, but that this legislation goes far beyond the stock exchanges and that under the guise of stock-exchange regulation it reaches out and affects industry of all kinds, both the large and small. It is interesting to know that this talk first came from the representatives of the great stock exchanges, who took it upon themselves, in the true spirit of benevolent philanthropy, to awaken industry to its great peril. While I have no doubt that this propaganda has caused genuine fear to be entertained by many business men, I am equally certain that when the business men of this country become acquainted with the actual provisions of the law, as distinguished from the stigma placed upon it by Wall Street lawyers and public-relations counsel, theirs will be a greatly changed opinion. Wall Street has done more to regiment and monopolize business than this bill could ever hope to.

It is the small industries of New England that carry on the best traditions of American business. It is these industries that sustain themselves by an economy of low-cost production and in the quality of their service, and not by monopoly based on banking control. If this legislation had any tendency to interfere with the self-reliant small industries I should be the first to oppose it and the last to accept it. The curb that this legislation puts upon the excessive flow of credit into the stock market will, in my judgment, be a great boon to these small industries. It will guarantee them adequate credit facilities when business is fully revived, because it will prevent money flowing from local banks into a vortex of speculation in a few metropolitan centers.

The small New England business man should note that under section 4 of the bill it is contemplated that the very small exchanges on which the securities of small, closely held New England corporations are often traded may, as exchanges, be exempted by the administrative commission from all or any of the provisions of the bill. The small business man should also note how carefully the bill, which is fundamentally only concerned with the trading on the exchanges in the shares of companies which have a sufficiently wide distribution to be traded in on such exchanges and made the subject of abuses incident to such trading, provides that the administrative commission may exempt securities, the markets of which are predominantly intrastate in character. Because of the tremendous difference in circumstances, it was not possible to draw definite lines of classification with which to exclude small corporations. But it should be noted that even a listed security of a small corporation which fits the classification given could probably be exempted by the Commission from all or a large part of the bill, and securities not listed would not be within the scope of the bill at all, except for the purposes of the over-the-counter market section in section 14. The sections of which industry has been told it should be afraid are sections 11, 12, 13, 14, and 15.

The provisions of sections 11 and 12 have been so much discussed on the floor already that I shall not repeat the arguments made by the chairman and Mr. Mapes to show that they are in substance merely a standardization of minimum listing requirements on exchanges, analogous to requirements already made by exchanges and actually less burdensome to issuing corporations than the power now exercised by the New York Stock Exchange.

There have been attempts to make it appear that the control given to the Commission in this section 14 to regulate the over-the-counter markets is really aimed at small industry. Nothing could be further from the truth. The provision for the control of brokers and dealers in the over-the-counter market is not intended as a catch-all by which the Commission can dominate the affairs of unlisted companies. It is simply an absolutely necessary protection for the market on the exchanges which the bill seeks so much to improve. . . .

If one wants to put effective restraints upon excessive speculation on the exchanges, it is obviously necessary to guard against the same sort of excessive speculation on the unregulated markets. But those who tell you that the over-the-counter provisions of the bill will interfere directly or indirectly with the small industrial concern are either willfully misleading you or are ignorant of what the bill really does. The control of the Commission with respect to the over-the-counter markets may be exercised only over dealers or brokers who maintain a public market. The Commission has no power to cause any corporation to file any statement or to subject itself in any way to regulation. Even the dealer or broker is not subject to control if he does no more than to try to find a buyer for a person who wants to sell some shares or to find a seller for a person who wants to buy some shares. A dealer or broker creates or maintains an over-the-counter market as it is defined in the bill only if he stands ready both to buy and sell; that is, if he stands ready to quote you a price at which he will buy your shares as well as a price at which he will sell your shares.

Now, if a corporation is small, and has only a few stockholders, it has no concern to see its shares constantly traded in. If the corporation is of such a size that its stockholders demand a public market, then it should be ready to file the very reasonable information for its stockholders that is required of companies whose shares are registered. But even in the case of a large corporation there is no mandatory requirement in the bill that the corporation register its shares on an exchange or meet any requirement that the Commission may impose as a condition to permitting a broker or dealer to create or maintain a public market for its shares. And it is important to note that the over-the-counter provisions of the bill are so framed that the Commission may, but need not, require the filing of information by a corporation as a condition to permitting a dealer or broker to create or maintain a public market for its securities. The over-the-counter markets present so many variants that the bill wisely gives the Commission the broadest discretion, because it is impossible to foresee at the moment whether considerable regulation may be required if the threatened delisting by large publicly owned corporations should occur—which I for one do not anticipate. Certainly the corporation, large or small, with less than 100 security holders, would remain for all practical purposes unaffected by any over-the-counter regulations.

Under this bill a bank may lend any amount it deems proper upon an unlisted security and is not in this respect subject to any margin requirement. Under these circumstances the holder of an unlisted security need not fear being deprived of any legitimate credit facility.

Small, self-reliant industry, such as New England prides itself upon, has nothing to fear and much to gain from such provisions.

Everyone here knows that when you establish a flexible power in a law you are bound to give men power to do harm, but our intention is to give men power to do good, and what reason is there to believe that the power would be abused? Recent history has taught men that those who have had a part in manipulation of the money marts have less of friendship for the folks and no greater love of their country than those now engaged in management of governmental affairs.

This bill is primarily designed to prevent a manipulation of securities—the kind of manipulation that threatened the lives of the insurance companies of America, and thereby the humble estates men endeavored to create by the sweat of the brow and real self-sacrifice. It would remove a chance at manipulation that not only threatened the banking system of the country but actually left many banks broken wreckage upon the rocks. It would forever forbid a manipulation that boiled a market to the point where it attracted credit away from the proper channels of industry into the uncertain paths of speculation.

While there were other contributing causes, none seems to deny that stock gambling, with its now known abuses, ruined many an industry and crippled or destroyed business establishments and working people.

Many of those who would thwart the aim of this bill, and quite sincerely in most instances, approach the situation with an unconscious selfishness that makes them victims of their own blindness. Among them are the men who are schooled in that class which believes in business monopoly. They would maintain a monarchy of business and sit upon its throne. I believe in a far-reaching democracy of business, and I would make more rigid the antitrust laws when the uncertainties of this depression permits that change. They believe in a cash-and-carry plan, and I am sufficiently old-fashioned to still have a regard for those little storekeepers who carried the burden of the neighbors in other dark days—those men who gave the groceries to the neighbor's youngster when he brought no more evidence of money to the store than a badly worn little brown book with a picture of a meat rack and a butcher on the cover.

Manipulation and misleading statements to be hereafter forbidden by law did not stop after crippling banks, insurance companies, industry, and investors.

It dulled the faith of conservative investors in the investment banking houses long engaged in the business of selling high-grade securities. Though the operators of these establishments kept their hands unsoiled they were smeared by the splashing in the muddy waters, and people in business, as well as those out of work, became afraid.

It cannot be that we have staggered through the wilderness for 4 years without having learned the need for the revision of the system. As we try to revive business by experiment it is our sacred responsibility to provide against a reoccurrence of what has happened in our generation.

Those who are loudest in their condemnation of this bill are those who look with scorn upon such social reforms and economic necessities as regulated working hours and old-age pensions. Their influence has been so effective up to now that they could build an opposition to legislation by people who would benefit from it.

Time will undoubtedly find flaws in this particular bill, as it almost always does, because the men of the committee which wrote the bill possess the customary frailties of human nature and finite minds.

This bill does no more than insist upon the truth, and it denies an opportunity to one class of investors that has heretofore been denied to others—or rather it gives the man on the outside a knowledge up to now reserved to himself by the man on the inside.

President Wilson, in 1919, recommended the enactment of a law to prevent the fraudulent methods of promoters by which our people are annually fleeced of many millions of hard-earned money. Prior to that time, or in 1907, President Roosevelt admonished the Congress that the Federal Government should supervise the issuance of securities of any combination doing an interstate business. We now have a President who observed greater abuses in this field than his illustrious predecessors had known, and he insisted that the law be written. His insistence is not my special reason for supporting this measure, for I have strayed from the administrative path when my convictions were in serious conflict with those of our great national leadership. I feebly helped lead the fight against the so-called "municipal bankruptcy bill" in the last session, and I could not bring myself to the conclusion of those who saw wisdom in the recent decision of this House on the tariff proposal. My mind fails to justify the silver opinion we expressed in this body, and I cannot enter the class of those men who yielded to the inflationary temptation of the much-discussed and widely advertised plan to make good for every bank loss of the panic period.

All of this is to emphasize that I am inspired by no socialistic notion or romantic dream. I regard myself as a liberal conservative. This is a conservative bill.

I urge you to pass it in its present form. [Applause.] . . .

MR. COOPER OF OHIO. . . . I believe the measure now before us for consideration is the most important piece of legislation that has come before this Congress. Especially is this true from the standpoint of the public interest.

Regulation of Stock Exchanges

I am very much in favor of the provisions of the bill relating to the regulation of stock exchanges. People who invest their money in securities are entitled to some protection; and if those who are charged with holding these securities do not protect them, then they have a right to come to this legislative body and ask for protection.

Legislation for the regulation of stock exchanges should have been passed long ago. We all know the unfair practices and the crooked manipulations and excessive speculations that have gone on on some stock exchanges of our country in the past, and especially in the last few years. During the deliberations of the committee who had charge of this legislation I favored all the provisions of the measure which related to the regulation of stock exchanges, and I hope that this Congress will pass some legislation to that effect.

Government Regulation of Industry and Business

However, as most of the members of the committee know, I was more interested in that part of the bill which went far beyond the regulation of the stock exchanges than I was in the regulation of the stock exchanges themselves. I cannot agree with my good friend the chairman of this committee, nor with my colleague the gentleman from

Michigan [Mr. Mapes], when they stand on the floor of the House and try to leave the impression that the opposition to this measure which has been expressed by business and industry was all inspired by the New York Stock Exchange.

I have more confidence in that great organization of business men in the industrial district in which I live than to believe that the New York Stock Exchange has inspired their opposition to this measure. Again, I think they have a perfect right to oppose this measure. It has been intimated here in a way that they are all wrong when they come to Congress and protest against some of the provisions of this legislation. If they cannot protest to Congress, which is considering the measure, to whom will they go? I do not question the right of the industries and business men in my district and those scattered throughout the great State of Ohio to protest to a Member of Congress and tell him there are some provisions of the bill which they believe will be detrimental to their interests. I, like many other Members, have received numerous telegrams and letters from business houses and industrial corporations protesting against the passage of this bill. In not one of these protests that I have received is there any objection to the regulation of the stock exchanges. As a matter of fact, 99 percent of the protests that I have received from business men and corporations say they favor the regulation of the stock exchanges. I call attention now to a few of the hundreds of protests that I have received. This telegram I have in my hand comes from the Goodyear Tire & Rubber Co., the B. F. Goodrich Co., and the Firestone Rubber Co., of Akron, Ohio, the greatest rubber industrial center in the world. These three organizations employ upward of 50,000 men and women in their plant. Can anyone standing here on the floor say that any one of these organizations has ever tried to take advantage of its stockholders?

Can you say that they have brought forward certain practices in order to beat their stockholders out of the earnings of their securities? I believe these men are honest. They are charged with the investment of the people's money. As I said a few days ago, the big, heavy industries in our country today, like the rubber and the steel companies, have sweat blood during the last 3 years. In my own district, which is the second largest steel-producing section of the United States, during the years 1930 to 1933, every one of the companies lost millions of dollars in the operation of their plants, but they kept them open because they had invested money in those institutions, and they wanted to give as many workingmen employment in order that they might provide some sort of livelihood for their families. Do you classify them as crooked manipulators who are trying to rob American people who have invested their money in their securities.

I have here another telegram from several large corporations in Cleveland, protesting against that part of this bill which has no direct relation whatsoever to the regulation of the stock exchanges. They believe certain provisions of the bill will very materially affect their business and make it harder for them to bring about economic recovery. . . .

Now, I will tell you what heavy industry needs today. I have talked to the men who have charge of those industries—those men who, as I said a moment ago, sweat blood during the last few years in trying to keep their plants in operation. What they need today is relaxation of credit. They have told me that if there could only be a little relaxation of credit and they could get the money, it would not be long before we should be well on the road to recovery, as far as heavy industry is concerned. . . .

MR. TRUAX. I agree with the last statement made by the gentleman, but is it not true that that is what everybody, including the farmer and the small business man, needs today, namely, relaxation of credit? [Applause.]

MR. COOPER OF OHIO. I agree with the gentleman; yes, sir. Now, of course, we all want to see recovery from the terrible economic depression we have passed through. I have been informed that the one thing business and industry are afraid of, with regard to the passage of this bill, is that it will make it a great deal harder to get credit in the future. Of course, if they cannot get credit in a lawful way they should not have it.

I received a letter from the general counsel of the largest steel industry in my district, in which he said if it were not for the Securities Act of 1933, there would have been $10,000,000 invested in this district during the last year.

I want to be fair and say that there has been some modification of this bill. When we first received the bill, it was much more objectionable than it is now. I am glad the committee saw fit to make some of the modifications. I personally should like to have the bill framed along the line of the commission report which the President selected. Early last year the President selected a committee known as the "Roper Committee." Secretary Roper, of the Department of Commerce, was at the head of that committee. He wanted them to proceed along the line of writing legislation for the regulation of the stock exchanges. They did. That is a public report, and you can get it. During the hearings on this bill, which we are considering, the Assistant Secretary of Commerce, Mr. Dickinson, appeared before our committee.

I say to you that in all my experience in Congress I have never heard a more brilliant man or a more sound man, a clearer thinker or speaker than Mr. Dickinson. He made some very strong objections to the legislation which we then had before us. We asked him why the President's report was not accepted and written into legislation. I forget what his answer was, but the truth of the matter is that the President's committee report was set to one side. Mr. Landis, of the Federal Trade Commission, Mr. Tom Corcoran and Mr. Ben Cohen wrote the legislation which was presented to our committee in the first instance. There is no question about that, because Mr. Landis made that statement before our committee himself. I say the bill has been modified to a great extent, and it is not as objectionable as it was when it was first presented to our committee. Therefore I do not want it understood here today that I am directly opposing the passage of this legislation for the regulation of the stock exchanges, and we should have had it long ago, but I want to call attention to the fact that sections 11,12, 13, 14, 15, 17, 19, 23, 28, and 32 of this bill have no direct relation to the regulation of stock exchanges. Section 13 deals with proxies.

Proxies

Strong objections have been made by business and industries from all parts of the country against this section. They maintain it has no place in stock-exchange regulation.

If it is desirable that the solicitation of proxies should be governed by rules and regulations of the Federal Trade Commission for listed securities, a similar rule or regulation will be adopted by the Commission with regard to unlisted securities under the authority of section 14, and section 14 gives to the Federal Trade Commission the power to set up rules and regulations in regard to unlisted securities that are not on one of our national stock exchanges.

Again, section 13 means that any person soliciting a proxy—I want the House to pay attention to this, and I am only bringing it up so that you may know what is in the bill—section 13 provides that any person soliciting a proxy, listed or unlisted on the exchange, is subject to the rules and regulations of the Federal Trade Commission, and that to solicit a proxy in violation of any rule or regulation the Commission may prescribe is made a criminal offense, punishable by fine and imprisonment. The Federal Trade Commission, under this bill, has the power to set up any rule or regulation that it desires regarding the solicitation of proxies.

The solicitation of a proxy in violation of any rule or regulation the Commission may prescribe is made, not a misdemeanor but a criminal offense, punishable by fine and imprisonment. This section gives to the Federal Trade Commission the power by rule and regulation to create criminal offenses in connection with the matter of soliciting proxies, and shows the extent to which the bill goes in an endeavor to control the conduct of individuals in the moral and everyday business activities of life.

Over-the-Counter Markets

Section 14 deals with over-the-counter markets. I wonder if we realize the extent of the grant of power given to the Federal Trade Commission in this section. Over-the-counter markets are defined in this section, which relates to the buying and selling of securities of any corporation which securities are not listed on any national stock exchange. This section gives the Commission the broad power to make rules and regulations governing entirely intrastate transactions—not interstate, but intrastate transactions. The violation of such rules and regulations is declared to be unlawful and is made punishable by fine and imprisonment. Such business today is not only governed by provisions of law but there already exists in almost every State "blue sky" laws for the protection of investors, laws designed to eliminate abuses. The Federal Securities Act of 1933 also covers transactions of this sort. Section 14, should it become law, will make every corporation whose securities are bought and sold, even though locally, subject to the rules and regulations of the Federal Trade Commission.

Contracts

Section 28 (b) makes void every contract made in violation of any provision of the act, or any rule or regulation thereunder, and every contract the performance of which involves the continuance of any relationship or practice prohibited by the act.

The far-reaching consequence of this subsection is little comprehended. This provision, coupled with the use throughout the acts of the words "it shall be unlawful," opens the door to a vast amount of litigation which may involve many of the daily commercial and banking transactions of our country. If, perchance, through the error of a clerk, or even of a partner, a miscalculation has been made as to the amount that could be legally loaned or borrowed, it could not be corrected, for if a transaction be void, neither party can seek redress in a court of law. The infinite number of questions which arise from an examination of this section makes it clear that it should be carefully considered by the House.

Section 32. Criminal Penalties

I now come to the penalty section, and with this I close. This section makes no distinction between acts which are intended to be criminal, such as the manipulative practices set out in section 8, and the violation of ever-changing rules and regulations of the Commission. I believe the criminal penalties should be confined to the specific things which are intended to be made criminal.

I wonder if we want to write into this bill, however, a provision which provides a fine and imprisonment for the violation of a rule or regulation having no direct connection with the regulation of the stock exchange. Should we go so far as to subject any person, business man, banker, official of industry, or employee to the hazard of criminal prosecution for the possible violation of a rule or regulation of the Commission? This provision gave very much concern to the committee having the bill in charge and under consideration. It will be said that the criminal provisions are confined to a willful violation of the rules and regulations of the Commission. Ah, my friends, the proof of whether the violation was willful or not will have to be made in court. We should remember, however, that it is the indictment of the individual which is likely to destroy his standing and reputation in the community in which he lives, not whether he may be found guilty; and he could be indicted for violating a rule or regulation. The proof of his innocence by showing that the violation was accidental and not willful is not news. Papers would not have much to say about that; it would not be given the same publicity as his indictment was. The mere indictment of a prominent citizen is a sad thing to him no matter in what community he may live.

Mr. Chairman, in a brief time I have tried to set forth my views on some parts of this legislation. As I said, I believe we ought to have regulation of the stock exchange, but I trust we can modify the bill to some extent, at least so that business and industry which are fighting for their life today would feel more confident that they are going to be able to carry forward in a legitimate and lawful way. If they are permitted to work out their own business without too much governmental regulation, they will succeed and at the same time be of great benefit to the country at large. [Applause.] . . .

MR. MOTT. I wish to ask the gentleman a rather pertinent question. During the course of his remarks the gentleman named several men with whose names I am not acquainted. If I remember correctly, the gentleman stated they were the people who drafted this legislation.

MR. COOPER OF OHIO. They drafted the first bill; yes.

MR. MOTT. I want to ask the gentleman as a member of the committee if he knows whether any of these people who drafted any of this legislation have ever had any personal and practical experience in the regulation of the sale of securities; whether any of them has ever held office as securities commissioner or has otherwise been connected with the regulation of securities?

MR. COOPER OF OHIO. I believe one of the three gentlemen who was responsible for the drafting of this bill did make the statement before our committee that at one time he worked for some broker on the New York Stock Exchange.

MR. MOTT. That is not the regulation of securities. I think I know at least by reputation, if not personally, almost every securities commissioner of the country, although their names may be unfamiliar to me. I used to be securities commissioner in my own State. . . .

MR. STUDLEY. Mr. Chairman, Wall Street is in my district, so is Main Street. I must do justice to both.

Somebody ought to tell the truth about Wall Street.

Why wreak vengeance on Wall Street?

By passing this bill you will not reach the malefactors of great wealth whom you so zealously desire to punish.

Instead of reaching them, your wrath will fall impotently on an army of real-estate owners, of bookkeepers, clerks, stenographers, stockholders, and bondholders, who will be thrown out of employment, or who will fail to collect their incomes, and so you will add to the sum of human misery and unemployment.

When you want to get money to build your roads, pave your streets, lay out a city park, install waterworks, or build a levee, where do you go for it? To Wall Street.

Obligingly and courteously Wall Street underwrites your stock and bond issues. For three generations of America Wall Street has furnished the money to build your railroads and develop your country. Wall Street has paved your streets, built your highways, installed your waterworks and reservoirs, drained your swamps and low-lands, built your irrigation and levee systems, and financed the upbuilding and advancement of every municipality from Maine to Mexico.

Why not be fair with Wall Street?

When default comes in payment of interest and principal of these debts and Wall Street politely asks for the money past due, then Wall Street is Shylock! And Wall Street has been a heavy loser, too.

Now, this is not fair. It is not even decent.

It is what Europe told the United States after the war when we asked for payment of the debts.

I earnestly trust that this stock-market regulation law will not ultimately develop into just another noble experiment.

At the time of the enactment of the eighteenth amendment and the prohibition laws the Congress erred gravely in following the clamor of the people. The Congress should then have been able to apply restraint on a movement that had got out of control and was in a run-away. But the Congress did not apply restraint. Indeed, not! It yielded impotently to the lashings which were being then so vigorously administered by our constituencies. The people were then demanding that we smash the saloon. The cry was "Down with the saloon!" "Smash the saloon!" The saloon was the personal devil on whose trail every man and woman was in hot pursuit.

We smashed it, too. It was the spirit of the times. It was a holy crusade.

The drys carried State after State with smashing majorities and voted dry amendments into State constitutions long before national prohibition came to pass. Since then we have seen the light. We have retraced our steps. There is no law greater than the people.

The innate desire for gain, to trade, to speculate, to try and make some money is as deep-seated in the human heart as is the human appetite.

It is as old as the human race itself. To control it is quite beyond the powers of an act of Congress. The Congress, with all its vast and far-reaching powers, is impotent to cope with such deep-seated human impulses, and its puny efforts to do so will result in disaster, as did that other noble experiment. We cannot break the economic laws. We shall only dash ourselves to pieces against them. Wall Street is now the personal devil on whose trail the country is in hot pursuit. The cry now is, "Down with Wall Street!" "Smash Wall Street!"

To scourge the money changers out of the temple is a fine piece of rhetoric; nothing more. That phrase has lost its virility and its meaning with the ages. It can't be done.

A few years ago a man was bent on destroying Wall Street. He would bring about its ruin even as Tyre and Sidon.

He exploded a huge bomb at the corner of Broad and Wall Streets.

The result was some panes of glass were broken in the New York Stock Exchange, and a famous banking house on that corner and many clerks, stenographers, and bookkeepers were blown to bits. But Wall Street remained.

Wall Street is just another name for the great business organizations and activities of the country. The torrents of commerce and trade not only of America but of the world go roaring through Wall Street. It is a market place, no more.

There may have been dishonest trading and practice in Wall Street. I know of no business that has always been found following the precepts of the Golden Rule.

Why destroy Wall Street? The only way to do it is to strike down the business structure of the country. Do you want to do that? It would be rash, it would be radical to do it. Don't strike down the business.

If the Congress does it more than a billion dollars worth of real estate south of Fulton Street in Manhattan alone will become unproductive and tenantless. More than a hundred thousand people in New York City would be thrown out of employment and into the bread lines. The business of the country would suffer irreparable injury and recovery would be indefinitely retarded, And Wall Street pays taxes.

In 1918 we would make it impossible for any person to get a drink of liquor. Did we do it? We did not.

In 1918 we would abolish the saloon. Did we do it? We did not.

Instead of the saloon came the speakeasy and the bootlegger. Appetite and long-established customs of our people made that law impotent. It was regarded everywhere as a joke.

The revenue that should have gone into our Treasury was dried up and diverted to speak-easy and bootleg channels, and was there used to finance racketeers, highjackers, robbers, and kidnapers. The most successful chain of crime the country has ever seen was financed by this folly of the Congress. But without customers there would have been no bootleggers.

Now, we are not legislating here to reach just a lot of bad boys who can be spanked and put into the corners and told to stay there. We are dealing with the most resolute and resourceful element of our people. We shall find the operators of Wall Street good sportsmen who will always be ready to pay a reasonable tax on its business. Give and take is their gospel. A mayor of New York once tried to put Wall Street in irons. But he did not. He failed.

The Congress will not be able to put Wall Street in irons. When we try to do that Wall Street will go to Canada, where they will be welcomed. Our most prolific source of revenue will be dried up and our business structure reduced to ashes; and again we shall find ourselves the victims of our own folly. Our people will continue to trade and speculate through bootleg channels and the act of Congress to put Wall Street in irons will be just another impotent gesture and of no avail. Then we shall retrace our steps in pathos and humiliation, as we have lately done with prohibiton, and as we have done before a thousand, thousand, times.

Laws are discovered, not made.

And presently the people will compel us to return to the political philosophy and the economics of Adam Smith and John Stuart Mill.

The doctrine and the practice of laissez-faire has not yet perished from the earth. . . .

MR. BRITTEN. . . .Mr. Chairman, one of the interesting features of the debate on this bill has been the denunciation of the first bill, or the first several bills, because of their severity. The distinguished gentleman from New York [Mr. Wadsworth] detailed his many objections to the first bill, and the distinguished chairman of the committee himself, the gentleman from Texas [Mr. Rayburn], than whom there is no more intelligent man in the House, also referred to the objections to the first bill. The chairman of the committee also referred to the lobby that was apparently objecting to the present bill.

Mr. Chairman, why would there not be a lobby? Why would there not be objections when there are 10,000,000 investors in the United States who are affected by this legislation, which in its original form was a monstrosity? That is the reason it has been rewritten, rewritten, and rewritten by the scarlet-fever boys down in the little red house in Georgetown.

Only day before yesterday, when the distinguished chairman was addressing the House, he paid compliment to his visitors in the gallery from the stock exchange. Today I pay compliment to my visitors in the gallery, the youthful legislative wizards from the little red house in Georgetown. They are here to assist in the passage of this important bill, in the drafting of which they have played such an important role. They wrote and rewrote the bills which have been subjected to such merciless criticism from every section of the country. Of course, they should be here following the action of the House on their pet legislative baby.

Everybody is for regulation of the stock market. Nobody would say otherwise; but under the guise of regulation of the stock market these gentlemen have written complicated and very intricate language which will control every industry in the United States direclty or indirectly; and they will control it by rules; Are you gentlemen going to stand for that? Why, of course you are not.

You should not complain because a small number of 10,000,000 investors write us and say, "For God's sake protect my investment." Should we complain? Who has a better right? Each of us has received letters from all over the United States complaining about this bill. Through the operations of the provisions of this bill there can be destroyed if desired any industry in the United States by a rule, or a constantly changing set of rules from which there is practically no appeal.

I have been told that your young leader, Benjamin Victor Cohen, is now on the floor of the House. Why not let him stay? He wrote most of this legislation and should be permitted to remain on the floor during its deliberation. . . .

MR. RAYBURN. I think we might as well settle that now. I shall not object to the gentleman having more time. Frankly, I think the chairmen of committees in times past have been allowed to have an expert sit with them. It was done a year ago when the securities bill was passed. I know the gentleman from Illinois said he would not object.

MR. MARTIN OF MASSACHUSETTS. Mr. Chairman, I may say that in times past it has been customary for one of the legislative counsel only to assist during the consideration of a bill.

MR. RAYBURN. The drafting service always sits in.

MR. MARTIN OF MASSACHUSETTS. He is not a regular drafting clerk, and he is not attached to the committee.

MR. BRITTEN. I am sorry that I started all this, because I truly believe that no one on the floor understands this legislation as does the boyish Mr. Cohen.

MR. RAYBURN. Now that the subject has been brought up, I desire to know whether there is objection?

MR. MARTIN OF MASSACHUSETTS. I am sure there will be objection on the part of four or five over on this side.

MR. BRITTEN. I think the gentleman should be permitted to remain. . . .

I told the chairman of the committee [Mr. Rayburn] a while ago that I would have no objection to Mr. Cohen being on the floor. I think he ought to be here. The language in this bill is very complicated, and the chairman of the committee, one of the most industrious men in Congress or on Capitol Hill, cannot possibly comprehend all of the intricacies carried in this legislation, and for the benefit of the House someone who can interpret the language ought to be permitted to sit here on the floor. I hope the gentlemen on this side will not object to Mr. Cohen being permitted to stay here. . . .

Mr. Chairman, the Rayburn bill for the regulation of securities exchanges which is being considered today was conceived in the little red house in Georgetown and borne to the Capitol on last Friday. It is the fifth and probably the last bill for the regimentation of the country's industries that will come from the youthful intellectuals who have framed most of the so-called "planned legislation" during the present session of Congress. While the popular demand for a rigid regulation of the stock markets is the smoke screen employed by the inexperienced directors of the Government, the real object of the bill is to Russianize everything worth while under the unqualified and unprepared Federal Trade Commission, an act that would make that Commission the most powerful and far-reaching arm of the Federal Government. It could dictate the conduct of officers, directors, and even stockholders of corporations; its requirement for balance sheets, monthly reports, and other accounting data would cost the Nation hundreds of millions of dollars a year, and for no particular purpose; it is given an indirect but very effective control over the investment of all capital by the industries, whether their outstanding securities are registered or not.

The scarlet-fever boys have written into the Rayburn bill an unusual section which in itself is in the nature of an argument for doing the unconstitutional things which the bill itself is intended to circumvent.

The popular demand for stock-exchange regulation has given the Prof. Felix Frankfurter cheer leaders a vehicle to control all credit and corporate practices such as not even Russia can boast of today. The boys in the little red house breathed easier when their child was finally deposited in the congressional hopper by Chairman Rayburn.

I am told that Telford Taylor, a young and recent graduate from Harvard, now in the Interior Department, was the father of the very first Fletcher-Rayburn child, but it was soon kidnaped by Landis (F.T.C.) and Frankfurter (H.U.), who immediately proceeded with the advice of Pecora, Tommy Corcoran (R.F.C.), and Benjamin Cohen (P.W.A.), to put the finishing touches on what was intended to be the second child; too much vodka and too little cream made it too hot for even the red-letter boys, and it was again rewritten only to be drowned in the sea of publicity.

If the present unhappy child should be adopted by Congress, the Federal Trade Commission could restrict the operation of almost every industry in the United States and could regulate it out of existence by the control of credit and other restrictions without having to give its reasons for doing so. Lenin and Trotsky never envisioned such far-reaching possibilities for strangulation. . . .

When the chairman of this very important committee took the floor the other day, followed by the gentleman from New York [Mr. Wadsworth], the speeches of those two gentlemen cost the investment holders of the United States more than $100,000,000 in depreciation that afternoon. Fifteen important stocks reached a new low level that day, and the same situation followed the next day, and they are doing it again today.

The people of the country are desperately afraid of any legislation that may emanate from the little red house in Georgetown, and rightfully so. They are afraid of any commission, particularly the Federal Trade Commission, because it will be dominated by someone who has no kindly interest in the stock exchange. The people know that, and that is what they are afraid of. A man who by rule or regulation can put the industries out of business overnight if he wants to should be a very carefully selected individual. That is the reason the people are afraid, and the complaints that have been received by Members on both sides of the aisle have not come from stock-brokers. They have come from investors who want their little investment protected, and God knows they have been scaled down enough in the last 3 or 4 years, many of them with a few shares of stock in some excellent corporation. The people are concerned about this Commission. . . .

MR. BRITTEN. Mr. Chairman, I move to strike out the last word, and I do so for the purpose of asking the attention of the gentleman from North Carolina [Mr. Bulwinkle]. I should like to say a little more about his proposed amendment for a stock-exchange commission rather than to have the industries and the stock exchanges and everything else controlled by a rule under the Federal Trade Commission. There are many Members on both sides of the aisle who feel as I do—not necessarily as to details, but along that line—and I am wondering if when the gentleman from North Carolina presents his amendment he will do so so that Members on this side can go along with him. Will he provide for a commission composed of 1 member to be recommended by the Federal Trade Commission, 1 member recommended by the Treasury Department, 1 recommended by the Federal Reserve Board, 1 by the Department of Commerce, because of these great regulations of industry under rule and not under law, and the other by the New York Stock Exchange, because of the intricacies of the manipulation of the stock exchange? There may also be one man representing the public.

MR. BULWINKLE. Mr. Chairman, will the gentleman yield?

MR. BRITTEN. Yes.

MR. BULWINKLE. The gentleman evidently does not want the President to name anyone.

MR. BRITTEN. Oh, the President will name all of them. Each department will make the recommendation to the President.

MR. BULWINKLE. I again tell the gentleman that I am not going to offer any amendment of that kind. I am going to offer an amendment that the President appoint three men by and with the advice and consent of the Senate. I do not intend to attempt to tie the hands of the President as to whom he shall name at any time or upon whose recommendation he shall name him. The gentleman knows full well that the President of the United States can be trusted to name the proper man at any time on any commission.

MR. BRITTEN. If the President of the United States had 25 heads and 25 bodies I would trust him any place, but I have no confidence in the men surrounding the President. They are the ones who have thrown this great fear into the populace of the United States. . . .

MR. FISH. . . . I think the gentleman from North Carolina [Mr. Bulwinkle] is correct. I believe, if these appointments to a super agency or commission are to be made, that they should be made directly by the President of the United States. I am sure that he is able and competent to name men well qualified to handle the stock exchange regulations as provided in this bill. The responsibility for this legislation rests with the President and he should have more interest in its proper administration than any other person. He can unquestionably be relied on to select individuals of ability and with special knowledge of market operations and of the New York Stock Exchange. I believe there are many on this side who will support such an amendment giving the President that power, because the Federal Trade Commission already is overburdened with investigations and regulations of thousands of corporations throughout the United States. . . . The Federal Trade Commission . . . is burdened with its work and we should set up a separate committee composed of experts chosen and appointed by the President of the United States. . . .

MR. COX. Due to the close relationship that exists between the pending legislation and the Securities Act, does not the gentleman think that both laws should be administered by the same agency, and does the gentleman not also think that because of the experience which the Federal Trade Commission has had in the administration of the Securities Act and because of the organization it has already built up, if the administration of the pending law should be given to the Commission it could more quickly begin to function effectively, than would be the case in the setting up of a new commission?

MR. FISH. My answer to the distinguished gentleman, who has presented a very logical case, is this: In the first place, the Federal Trade Commission has utterly failed in the administration of the Securities Act. That act has done more to hamper legitimate and honest business in the United States than anything else and to retard recovery.

MR. COX. But is not that the unsupported statement of the gentleman?

MR. FISH. No. No. The Federal Trade Commission has certain powers provided by the Congress of the United States to change the regulations under the Securities Act, and it has failed to do so. It has failed because it has not had time to properly consider the unworkable provisions of the Securities Act, as it has so many other matters to attend to. If I had my way we would liberalize the Securities Act before Congress adjourned and turn it over to a brand-new commission and put both the regulation of the stock exchange and the control of securities under this new agency, to be established by Congress and whose members will be appointed by the President. . . .

MR. COCHRAN OF MISSOURI. Would the gentleman have any objection to enlarging the Federal Trade Commission by three members?

MR. FISH. Now, that is what it is proposed to do. That is exactly what would happen if we enlarged the Committee on Interstate and Foreign Commerce in the House. You would not get any better results. The committee has to meet together. It has to consider other legislation, and it would not accomplish what you are trying to do. I know the Democratic majority can do what it wants to do, because you have the votes. I know in the Senate a special agency or a special commission is proposed, but if the gentleman from North Carolina [Mr. Bulwinkle], a member of the House committee, presents his amendment for a separate agency, I hope there will be plenty of time to discuss it on its merits, and I hope Members will vote on it on its merits, regardless of any kind of partisanship, because there should be no partisanship in it.

I even go further than my distinguished colleague from Illinois [Mr. Britten] about the original bill. The gentleman called it a monstrosity. I call it an abomination of desolation, written by the junior members of the "brain trust." It was nothing but a brain storm of a few young radical lawyers including Mr. Ben Cohen and Thomas Corcoran, aided and abetted by Prof. James M. Landis, Federal Trade Commissioner, and Prof. Felix Frankfurter, of Harvard. Thank goodness we have got a committee in this House and a very able chairman of that committee that took hold of the original destructive proposals that would have hampered and ruined legitimate business, and wrote a constructive measure in the interest of the public [Applause.] There is no question but that the purposes of this bill are to protect the investors, to prevent manipulation of stocks and pool operations, and to prevent destructive and excessive speculation with its disastrous consequences, all of which are sound and in the public interest. The question is whether in some particulars the proposed bill has not gone too far in conferring power to regulate corporations that are only remotely connected with the stock exchange and restricting industry unnecessarily.

There is one statement of the gentleman who is the chairman of the committee, reported in the public press, which I think is unfortunate. It probably was not meant that way, but it was carried in the press that he said he would brand any and all amendments offered on the floor as of Wall Street origin.

MR. RAYBURN. If the gentleman will yield, I did not say any such thing.

MR. FISH. I knew the gentleman did not say it, and I am very glad to hear him say so, because that statement could not have come from the gentleman from Texas.

MR. RAYBURN. I said when the stock-exchange amendments came I was going to so brand them.

MR. FISH. Oh, that is different. Unfortunately, the gentleman is misquoted in an editorial in the New York Tribune.

MR. RAYBURN. I have usually been misquoted about this bill.

MR. FISH. So, then, we can understand that when the gentleman from North Carolina [Mr. Bulwinkle] presents his amendment for a separate agency it will not be designated as originating from Wall Street, and will therefore be considered on its merits, whether it will improve the bill or not?

MR. RAYBURN. I may say to the gentleman from New York that the first suggestion of a separate commission was made by Mr. Whitney.

MR. FISH. After all, who knows more about the stock exchange than the president of the stock exchange?

I am inclined to vote for this bill. I believe some kind of regulation is wise, sound, and necessary. This bill is not perfect; no legislation is perfect; neither are you and I perfect. . . .

MR. McGUGIN. . . .

The country is greatly in need of fair and effective control over stock speculation. Stock speculation has not only swindled the American people out of billions of dollars, but in addition to that it has impoverished millions of people who have never invested a dollar in stock. Stock speculation monopolized and absorbed the banking credit of this country. Throughout the country local banks in the latter part of the twenties closed out sound lines of credit for local business—agricultural, industrial, and commercial. These local banks then took this money and sent it in to New York for call money, where fabulous rates of interest were derived from stock speculation. In the end, this meant that credit was taken away from honest, productive business and given over to speculation.

The orgy of stock speculation in the latter twenties was a swindle upon the people and an economic outrage upon the country. All of this should be corrected, and every right-thinking person in the country favors sound and constructive legislation which will save the people of the United States from a repetition of the ghastly conduct growing out of speculation in the latter twenties.

However, there is a swindle being worked upon the people in 1934 in the name of the stock exchange. That swindle is this bill. Everyone refers to this bill as the stock exchange bill. The people think this is a bill to correct these wrongs which must be corrected. The people have been deceived. The people do not know that that is but a small part of this bill. The people do not know that control over the stock exchange is merely the excuse and title for this bill, while the real reason for this bill is to gain complete governmental control and domination, not alone over speculation in the stock exchange, but over legitimate industry in this country.

The bill itself, upon its face, proves the deception and hypocrisy of the claim that it is a stock-exchange control bill. It contains 61 pages. It does not require 61 pages of law to control speculation. It does require 61 pages insidiously to work into this law complete control and domination over all industry in this country.

The first nine sections of this bill might be accepted as a fairly respectable piece of legislation. Practically all of the remaining 25 sections are insidious, tyrannical control of industry by government. Among the victims of this bill will be the millions of people who are entitled to the opportunity to make a living in industry, but who will be denied that opportunity because this bill, with its control of industry, will only lead to a drying up of the channels of commerce.

I should like to vote for a bill which would control speculation on the stock exchange, but such control as this bill gives over the New York Stock Exchange is a small part of the control which has been written into the bill.

What is more, the 61 pages of this bill will in the end be a small part of the law which will grow out of this bill. Section 10 sets up a commission and authorizes that commission to issue such rules and regulations as it deems necessary or appropriate. In the fullness of time, those regulations will be far more voluminous than these 61 pages of congressional legislation. In the fullness of time those regulations will be the tail which will be wagging the dog. I cannot see where the bill would be materially affected whether this commission is a new commission or the Federal Trade Commission. In any event, it is a commission which will be issuing regulations and rules with the force and effect of criminal law, the violation of which by any citizen will mean that that citizen is on his way to the penitentiary.

Section 32 provides in part:

Any person who willfully violates any provision of this act or any rule or regulation thereunder ... shall, upon conviction, be fined not more than $10,000 or imprisoned not more than 2 years, or both.

Thus, citizens of America will be sent to the penitentiary for the violation of regulations which can only be found in some pamphlets issued by some commission and not in the statutes of the United States. In this respect, this bill bears the same tyranny which is found in much of our so-called "emergency legislation." Russia, Germany, and Italy are not the only countries in which citizens are being imprisoned for the violation of edicts. The United States is such a country under this act and other emergency legislation which has been enacted. Stalin issues the edicts under which Russians are sent to prison, Hitler the edicts under which Germans are sent to prison, Mussolini the edicts under which Italians are sent to prison, Secretary Wallace the regulations under the Agricultural Adjustment Act and Bankhead cotton bill under which American farmers can be sent to prison, and some commission of three men will issue the regulations under this bill under which American citizens will be sent to prison. American citizens under this bill, under the N.R.A., under the A.A.A., and under the Bankhead Act, are to be sent to prison for committing crimes, which crimes have no more been decreed by a representative legislative body of the people than are crimes in Russia, Germany, and Italy prescribed by representative legislative bodies.

I want regulation and honest and effective regulation of speculation and credit, but I will not vote for such tyranny as is found in this bill.

Another fraud which is being perpetrated on the people is the very title of this bill. It is referred to as the Fletcher-Rayburn bill. It is not the Fletcher-Rayburn bill; it is the Corcoran-Cohen bill. These gentlemen are a couple of self-styled intellectuals, a couple of Felix Frankfurter's protégés, a couple of men who do not have and could not obtain the support of any congressional constituency in the United States, yet they can write the bill, sit in the galleries, and watch Congress move while they crack the whip. . . .

Of course, personally, they have no whip to crack. The truth is, Congress detests following their dictation, but Congress does not have the courage to say no and perform its constitutional duty to protect the liberties of the people. The reason Congress has not the courage is because Congress is afraid the President will go on the radio, lead the people to believe that this bill is exclusively a control over the stock exchange, and then lead the people to believe that he who voted against this bill has been the tool of a band of Wall Street pirates. For my part, I am not going to be intimidated by any such political character assassination. I am going to draw about me the cloak of truth and take my chances on that cloak's being a sheet armor of political protection. I am going to vote against this bill unless by amendments it is pared down to the point where it is an honest and exclusive stock-exchange control bill.

As proof that this bill is more nearly the Corcoran-Cohen bill than the Fletcher-Rayburn bill, I cite the incident which occurred in the House yesterday. The chairman of the committee did not feel exactly sure of himself in leading this bill through the House, so he insisted on having by his side Mr. Cohen, the real author of the bill. This bill is not a tariff bill with hundreds of complicated schedules, or a revenue bill with complicated rates. It requires no experts to supply the chairman with the facts. All that it requires is a knowledge of what is in the bill. Of course, the real author of the bill has a better knowledge of what is in it than one who is merely the sponsor of the bill.

MR. RAYBURN. Mr. Chairman, I did not intend to stoop to reply to some things that have been said on this floor, which are a reflection not only upon myself but on the 24 other members of this committee. I thought that on yesterday we had enough of this little red house stuff; and it is stuff. The gentleman from Illinois [Mr. Britten], always alert and alive to what will give him publicity, coined the phrase "the little red house in Georgetown." I did not object to his playing that at all. It is perfectly legitimate and perfectly correct. But every time a Member of this House gets up here and says that he is for legislation for the control of the stock exchanges, he winds up saying that this is not the medicine which the exchange needs.

The same talk was made before our committee by every man who appeared before that committee, who was trying to chisel and defeat stock-exchange legislation. [Applause.] Every man who has written a letter here, who has a reputation to guard, has begun his letter by saying just exactly what the gentleman from Kansas [Mr. McGugin] has said: that he is for stock-exchange regulation; but he always winds up by saying this is not the proper bill. Every member of this committee is convinced that, with the ingenuity of the 25 men upon that committee, we have done our best to bring forward a bill that would be helpful to the American people, to the investors in securities, and not injurious to business. We could not do it without the advice of experts. The members of the committee have done their best, yet the same complaint lodges against the committee, the same chiseling amendments will be offered upon this floor to this bill that would have been offered to the original bill.

Now, our committee sits year in and year out considering the most technical problems of any committee in this House—railroads, transportation of all sorts. We are laymen. We are not experts. We do not arrogate to ourselves all the knowledge in the universe. If we were as able as some people in this country think they are, and as some Members of this House think they are, we would feel so self-sufficient that we would have to call in no experts. We have to sit and listen to men who have specialized in transportation for 40 years; men who have been hired for that time in order to make a case for their people. They are paid salaries for representing them. Special privilege always has counsel in the committees of this House. Now, because we call in Mr. Cohen and Mr. Corcoran, two of the ablest young men that it has ever been my privilege to know—and I think that is the unanimous consent of the other 24 members of the committee—young men who have appeared, not representing institutions that have robbed the investors of this country, but who have appeared there in the capacity of people's counsel; they are held up by men who are really opposed to this bill, but who are not going to have the "guts" to vote against it when the roll is called, as being somebody from Russia or being tainted with socialism or communism. [Applause.]

. . .

It rubs a pretty sore place on us, who have for 9 weeks been charged with this duty, who have considered every proposal from every section and from every person. Republicans and Democrats alike, to have even the gentleman from Illinois, if not even the gentleman from Kansas, come to us, in the face of the statement of the gentleman from Michigan [Mr. Mapes], his own colleague, and the statement of the gentleman from Ohio [Mr. Cooper], and other members of the committee on that side of the

House, and say that even though we listened to those suggestions—and we were glad to have them from any source—it was the duty of the committee to write, and it did write, its own bill.

The committee stands here today practically solidly behind this bill; and we are going to fight down the people who, while saying they stand for legislation to regulate the stock exchanges, yet intend to offer chiseling amendments and make speeches in opposition to the bill.

The first chiseling amendment that was offered was offered by my genial colleague here to my right, my coworker on the committee. In the first instance the bill provided for 60 percent margin requirement. I did not think it was too high myself, because I have seen the lambs shorn for many, many years simply because they got in on a narrow margin and were shaken out sometimes between the hour the stock exchange closed in the afternoon and the hour it opened the following morning. I do not want such a condition to obtain if I can help it. Then in the subcommittee I proposed a 50-percent margin and 50-percent loan value. In order to help the committee along I agreed to a 45-percent margin and a 45-percent original loan value. Had we come in here with a 50-percent margin requirement an amendment would have been offered to reduce it to 45 percent. We have come in with a 45-percent marginal requirement and an amendment has been offered to reduce it to 40 percent; and had our original proposition been 40 percent, an amendment would have been offered to make it 35 percent; and so on down to nothing. So we brought in what we thought was a reasonable provision for the Federal Reserve Board. We made it flexible. We did not fix a rigid margin requirement; but, as I said, in my address the other day, we raised a flag, we drew a white line, and said to the regulatory authority, which is the Federal Reserve Board, that we believed—and it was the expression of congressional will—that somewhere around 45 percent should be the original margin requirement.

Some people said the provision with regard to margin should be flexible. We have set up this standard, this basis; but we have provided that the Federal Reserve may, if it finds it to be in the interests of trade and commerce—I believe that is the expression used—to change that original margin. We go further and say there shall be no rigidity whatever about maintenance and that the Federal Reserve may fix that. Yet we find people who have been so written to and talked to, to whom the provisions of the bill have been so misrepresented, that they say that even this is not flexible enough. . . .

The President of the United States thinks this bill should be passed; and I agree with him.

The margin requirements, so far as I individually am concerned, are not as high as I would have made them, but in order to meet objections I have agreed to a lesser requirement; and we have in the bill a reasonable margin requirement.

If we have safe and definite provisions in this bill to prevent manipulative practices, and then give to the enforcing authority enough power under the legislation to make it effective, we have a good bill. If, however, we adopt amendments that will weaken the margin requirements section, that will weaken the manipulative section, that will rob this board, authority, or whatever you choose to call it, of power to make this law effective, then we might as well strike the enacting clause out of the bill. This bill is 60 pages in length. It has been worked out, we believe, scientifically and sanely. If you begin allowing those who want to chisel this bill, those who at heart—and I do not put my friend from New Jersey in this class—want to weaken this bill, who want to vote against it but many of whom will not vote against it; if you begin adopting amendments offered to tear up the framework of this legislation, you might as well strike out the enacting clause and do nothing about this matter, but let the riots and the disgrace again come as it did in 1929 culminating that orgy of speculation. I trust that friends of this measure, friends of legislation to provide some sort of control of the practices on the stock exchange, will stand behind the members of the committee who are for regulation in voting down these amendments that would draw a knife under the chin of the bill. [Applause.] . . .

MR. COLE. So far as the margin requirement is concerned, with little, if any, strings tied to the Federal Reserve Board, 5 minutes after the passage of the bill if they find the formula prescribed by Congress is not broad enough, they can change it?

MR. RAYBURN. Exactly. I stated in my remarks awhile ago if they found it was in the interest of trade and commerce they could change it at any time they pleased. . . .

MR. BRITTEN. . . .

I am sorry that the distinguished, and always polite, great chairman of this important committee has seen fit to adopt the tactics of Gen. Hugh Johnson in "cracking down" upon Members of Congress and their so-called "chiseling" amendments. The word "chisel" is an old one, but it was made famous by General Johnson when he "cracked down" on the industries of the country.

The amendment before the committee when the distinguished gentleman was speaking was one which provided for a 60-percent credit and a 40-percent margin and had been presented by the gentleman from New Jersey [Mr. Kenney]. What did that amendment provide in money? It provided that upon the purchase of a $10,000 security the buyer put up $4,000 and borrowed $6,000. There is nothing like chiseling in connection with a loan of that kind when you put $4,000 on a $6,000 credit. That is 75 percent.

I hope the gentleman or no other Member of this House will "crack down" on Members of equal standing. Every man is equal to every other man on the floor of this House, and I hope amendments will not be referred to as chiseling amendments and that no Member will be "cracked down" on for offering amendments. We do not deserve that, because we are trying to perfect a bill which has been written by a couple of youngsters—Cohen and Corcoran—who are sitting back here in the gallery—a couple of baby faces. [Laughter.] From here they look like fine, young, upstanding boys of 18 to 21 years of age. . . .

I want the House to know the type of young man that abounds in all of the important departments of the Government. They are brainy; they are good in principle; their character is all right. I have no complaint to make about that, and I had no objection yesterday to Benjamin Victor Cohen sitting on the floor with the chairman of the committee and the other members of the committee to advise them on the technicalities of this bill, which the members themselves did not understand, but which this young boy did.

MR. OLIVER OF NEW YORK. Then why are you always screaming about them?

MR. BRITTEN. I am not screaming about anything.

MR. OLIVER OF NEW YORK. You are always screaming and screaming about them.

MR. BRITTEN. . . .

Every department of this Government is honeycombed, let us say, with fine, young men, like these boys; but they are only boys. They have had no political experience and not the slightest legislative experience. Perhaps they may have an ax to grind. They may not like the stock exchange. They might feel happy if the stock exchange, which is a great medium of business, were closed completely. This might be pleasing to one of them, at least.

But the reason I rose was not particularly to call attention to them—they are undoubtedly very good boys, but they are boys, and I object to having their legislation before us and be refused the privilege to amend that legislation. There are men on the floor of the House who have vast legislative experience in drafting legislation.

These young men happen to have come from the "little red house" in Georgetown. [Laughter.] The distinguished chairman should not object to me because I happened to have referred to the "little red house." It is there that these men gather every night, and I am told by people who go there that they are a very charming set of young men, exceedingly bright, and that one of them tickles the piano keys like nobody's business. [Laughter.]

I like that type of young men, but if they write legislation for the floor of the House, I want the right to amend it or to offer an amendment if I feel that way; and I do not want my very dear friend—and he is a very dear friend of mine—I do not want him to crack down on his old friend Fred Britten because he offers an amendment to improve this revolutionary piece of legislation. [Laughter.]

MR. BULWINKLE. . . . I feel sorry for the gentleman from Illinois, for no matter how much anybody tells him, the gentleman is so obsessed with the idea that Mr. Cohen and Mr. Corcoran are doing this nefarious work that he cannot sleep at night.

MR. BRITTEN. The gentleman never saw me sleeping. [Laughter.]

MR. BULWINKLE. No; I admit that; and am thankful that I have not. But it is pitiful to see the gentleman here talking about the "little red house." Has he ever been there? No; of course he has not. I stated to you yesterday, as well as to other Members of the House, that on the first bill that was drawn they—Mr. Cohen and Mr. Corcoran—did have something to do with it.

I also stated to you that the bill that is before the House now for consideration was drafted by the subcommittee. I do not agree with the subcommittee in all that they have done; but let us be just and let us be fair. It is the most important bill that has passed this session and the most far-reaching of any bill we have ever had before us. It is idle to spend 5 minutes talking about the "little red house" and the two boys.

By the way, I want to tell you that they are about as smart youngsters as you can find anywhere.

MR. BRITTEN. They are too smart.

MR. BULWINKLE. No; they are not. Just right.

MR. BANKHEAD. Will the gentleman yield?

MR. BULWINKLE. I yield.

MR. BANKHEAD. Is not the gentleman of the opinion that the reason the sensitive nerve that has been touched in the gentleman from Illinois is because these gentlemen are so intelligent, so capable, and know so much about the nefarious practices of the New York Stock Exchange, and that they have had brains enough to lay their hands on some of the evils, and capacity enough to suggest a correction of them?

MR. BRITTEN. The gentleman admits that they had hands on the legislation?

MR. BULWINKLE. They have had their hands on the legislation in the first bill, and they know what they are doing.

Let us quit this kind of talk. Let us introduce our amendments to this bill, if we want to, and vote on them and argue the bill; but, in all seriousness, in all candor, it does not make any difference to me now who drafted the bill; let us give very careful consideration to the amendments introduced. The bill is here before us for consideration, and you and I and every Member in this House have a duty to perform in passing upon it; and all I say to the gentleman from Illinois [Mr. Britten] is, do not let your obsessions weigh upon you, because when they become too strong they eventually drive you to a mental illness. . . .

MR. FISH. Mr. Chairman, I offer the following amendment, which I send to the desk.

The Clerk read as follows:

Amendment offered by Mr. Fish: page 42, line 12, after the word "by," strike out the words "rules or regulations" and insert the word "order."

MR. FISH. Mr. Chairman, I trust I may have the attention of the Members of the Committee, because in my humble opinion I believe this to be about the most important amendment that can be considered in the pending bill outside of the Bulwinkle amendment. If the Members will listen to the facts and consider them on their merits, they should support this amendment. As I stated previously, I am inclined to vote for this bill. As I stated, I expect to vote for this bill, and I add that I want to vote for a stock exchange regulation bill, but if this amendment is turned down, it is going to make it very difficult for me, at least, to support the bill. It would be most inconsistent for me to do so, having made the fight on the floor of the House against the cancellation of the air-mail contracts, because the contractors were given no hearing or right to go to court. I merely ask to strike out the words in line 12, page 42, under section 18 (b), "rules or regulations" and insert the word "order." That would permit recourse to the courts by the exchange, whereas under "rules or regulations" the Federal Trade Commission can do about anything it wants to the exchange and its members, even telling them who they are to elect as officers, without the exchange having any recourse whatever to the courts. In the words of Colonel Lindbergh, that is not only unjust but it is un-American. It is an absolutely un-American and an unjust theory. It cannot possibly do any harm to give the members of the exchange recourse to the courts, which is their constitutional right, but it will be exceedingly harmful if the members of an exchange are deprived of this right by any act of Congress.

Let us consider it from another angle. Let us forget the exchange for a minute. At least half the Members of this House are in some kind of business. Most of them are lawyers and take cases when they can get them during the recess of Congress. Suppose the Federal Government should come to Congress and by this sort of bill regulate your business and say to you whom you should elect as your officers, and what you might do with your business and where you could transact it, taking away your personal and property rights, your constitutional rights, without any recourse to the courts.

My amendment simply gives them the right to appeal to the courts. If you apply the same principle of taking away this right to your own business I do not think you would want to do it to any other business. I say that as one who has believed for many years in a sound and firm regulation of the stock exchange, but not in an unfair and un-American regulation.

It is very dangerous for a politician to predict anything, but I predict that if you leave this unlimited power to make rules and regulations you will destroy the purpose of the bill.

... We have built up a Frankenstein. There are sixty-odd pages to this bill. Nine tenths of the provisions are sound, well thought of, and well considered, yet we have built up a legislative Frankenstein that says to us we must not propose any amendment; we must not try to perfect the bill, because it is a reflection on the committee reporting the bill, and the committee is infallible. That is sheer nonsense. We are here to legislate as Members of the House, to try to improve legislation, to try to perfect the bill, to try to make the bill workable. I submit that if you leave this drastic power in, it will not only work a hardship and hinder business recovery and cause a loss of confidence but it will be a target for everybody who is against the bill to say, "This is exactly like the drastic and unworkable provisions of the securities bill." We all know the purpose of the securities bill was excellent. It could not have been improved upon; but that securities bill has already ruined itself by being too drastic. It has prevented business recovery. Everyone of us is interested in trying to get the free flow of capital back into industry. It has prevented that, the very object that we sought. This bill, if you leave it as it is, will prevent the same thing. . . .

MR. MAY. The only fear I have of this bill is the same thing that seems to be in the mind of the gentleman, that there may be too much regulation of business.

MR. FISH. Of course.

MR. MAY. Does the gentleman not think that anyone who is aggrieved by the regulations of the Commission will have the power to go into the courts through an injunction proceeding?

MR. FISH. No. The only power they will have to get into the courts is after they are indicted. As a business man, do you want to be indicted and have your name spread all over the front page, in order to get into court? That is the only recourse they have under this provision.

As the gentleman has raised the question, I should like to make a little comparison. A few days ago the President of the United States said:

We are not in the midst of a revolution.

But he added:

If you take the "r" out, we are in the midst of an evolution.

A quarter of a century ago I went to Harvard University where we were taught about evolution and the Darwinian and monkey theory. The trouble with this bill in this particular section is that there is too much monkey business in it. There is too much monkeying with legitimate business. When you are honestly trying to regulate it, all right, I am with you, particularly in regulating the stock exchange; but when you go as far as to hold a club over their heads and say who their officers are to be and where and how they are to do business and fixing rates of commission, interest, listing, and other charges, it is going beyond the bounds of reason and moderation. It is hard to give you all the facts in a short time. This section is the grab bag. It is the trick in the bill. It is the joker. The Federal Trade Commission takes back all the power in this section that the committee has taken away from it throughout the bill. I can point out section after section that has been rescinded and placed in this grab-bag section 18 (b). The result is that after the committee has done all of its work these young, smart "brain trusters"—and they are smart—these young radicals, visionaries, and dreamers, who know little or nothing about practical business affairs have taken all the power back under this grab-bag section 18 (b). . . .

I just want to point out what this does. What I am trying to do is to strike out "rules and regulations," in order to give the American business man a fair deal. I do not care whether he is on the stock exchange, or whether he is a farmer, or what he is; he is entitled to his constitutional right to appeal to the court.

In the first place, it provides for the methods of election of officers and committees. It controls the election of officers on the stock exchange, the curb, or any other exchange, and the suspension, expulsion, or disciplining of members. It also takes away the powers from the Federal Reserve Board and gives those powers to the Federal Trade Commission. . . .

It takes away the powers from the Federal Reserve Board in two instances and turns them back to the Federal Trade Commission after we have written it in the bill. For instance, on page 43, lines 4 to 6, it controls the question of the time and the method of making settlements, payments, deliveries, and closing of accounts. This was turned over by section 6 to the Federal Reserve Board. The same thing applies as to making minimum deposits on margin accounts. This again is a provision affecting the control of credit, which under the act, is vested in the Federal Reserve Board. There are a number of other instances of that sort. The question we have to decide here, those of us who believe in a regulation bill, is whether we want to perfect the bill or whether we want to pass a new securities act and have it fail and defeat its very purposes, which are to protect investors, the public interest, and to prevent destructive and disastrous overspeculation in the stock market. I hope my amendment, which is in the Senate bill and seeks to provide a court review of any action of the Commission changing the rules of an exchange, will be adopted as a matter of justice, common sense, and fair dealing. The bill as it stands will discourage business, destroy confidence, and be another repetition of the Securities Act and cause loss to hundreds of thousands of small stockholders and prevent the much-needed free flow of capital into industry.

The adoption of this amendment will perfect the bill, make it acceptable and workable, and make it do what it was designed to do. Leaving this language in the bill opens the bill up to the very attacks that everybody in this country has made owing to the blunder of the Postmaster General in canceling the air-mail contracts. There is no recourse to a court of law, and I want to see that provided. I hope you will put partisanship aside. I hope you will consider the amendment on its merits; and I hope you will not pass another securities act simply because you want to stand by the committee.

MR. MAPES. Mr. Chairman, I join the distinguished gentleman from New York in the hope that we may put partisanship aside in the consideration of this amendment.

I think the gentleman from New York in his remarks has demonstrated how easy it is to fall into extravagance of statement in the consideration of this legislation. Speaking of the exchanges—and I think I quote him verbatim—he said:

It will give the Commission authority "even to tell them whom they can elect as officers."

This shows the extreme to which the critics of this legislation go. Had the gentleman read the section carefully, he would have seen that it did no such thing. It authorizes the Commission, if the Commission finds it necessary or appropriate for the protection of investors or to insure fair dealing in securities traded upon such exchanges, or to insure fair administration of the exchanges, by rules and regulations to require the exchanges to alter or amend their rules, not to require them to elect any particular man to office. As far as this particular clause is concerned, it requires them simply to amend their rules as to the classification of members and as to the methods of electing officers and committees. The gentleman may as well say that the Congress of the United States has power to determine who the Members of the House of Representatives shall be, because the Constitution of the United States authorizes Congress to determine the times, places, and manner of holding elections for Senators and Representatives. There would be just as much logic in the argument that Congress could perpetuate itself or its personnel because of this provision of the Constitution as there is in the argument that the Commission can force upon these exchanges any officer that the Commission may choose. . . .

MR. FISH. I know the gentleman wants to be fair. I shall read the language of two or three lines of the bill.

MR. MAPES. I read them.

MR. FISH. No; the gentleman did not finish them at all. I read:

With respect to such matters as the classification of members and the methods of election of officers and committees to insure a fair representation of the membership; the suspension, expulsion, or disciplining of members.

That is very clear language, and anybody can interpret it.

MR. MAPES. I think that is true, Mr. Chairman, that it is clear and that anybody can interpret it. I think the interpretation placed upon it by the gentleman from New York is absurd.

Mr. Chairman, I further call the attention of my Republican colleagues, in particular the gentleman from New York, and others who want to support legislation to regulate stock exchanges, that this particular section relates exclusively to stock exchanges. There is nothing in this section that authorizes the Commission anywhere to control in any way any corporations except stock exchanges; and if we want to regulate stock exchanges, we should leave this provision in the bill. This provision, Mr. Chairman, merely gives the Commission authority to change the rules and regulations of the exchanges, or to require the exchanges to change their own rules in order to guarantee fair dealing on the exchanges. It is a question of policy, Mr. Chairman; it is simply a question as to whether we are going to leave this question of policy to the Commission or whether we are going to delegate it to the courts. . . .

This is the meat of the bill as far as regulation of stock exchanges is concerned, and I repeat that this particular section relates exclusively to the stock exchanges. The question is whether we want to give the Commission some authority over the rules and regulations of the exchanges, whether we want to delegate this power to the Commission or leave it to the courts. A careful reading of this section of the bill shows that the Commission's authority is very limited; it is very closely restricted to certain specific things. I shall not take the time to enumerate these powers, but read the bill and you will find that the Commission is given no power to which anyone could reasonably object. The Commission must have this power if it is adequately to regulate the stock exchanges.

If we are to allow the stock exchanges the right of appeal to the courts from every rule or regulation made by the Commission, we might as well eliminate this section entirely, because it would make the process of enforcing the regulations of the Commission endless. . . .

MR. WADSWORTH. The gentleman from Michigan states that the Commission is confined to certain specific subjects in its power to make regulations.

MR. MAPES. Yes.

MR. WADSWORTH. If the gentleman will notice the language appearing in line 14 of page 43, the gentleman will observe that the Commission can approach any similar matters. This opens the door wide.

MR. MAPES. I think there is some justification for the statement of the gentleman from New York; but, even so, that clause limits the Commission to matters "similar" to those that have been specified in the section. . . .

MR. TRUAX. Mr. Chairman, I think you will all agree with me that the gentleman from Michigan has just made one of the clearest and best statements for passing this bill as it is that can be made.

I want you to remember one thing that the gentleman from New York said, and I challenge his statement. He stated that one half of the Members of this House are in business. Can you imagine what an insidious, what a damnable position that would be to take before the American people, that one half of the Members of this House of 435 Members are in private or legal business for themselves, hence their views, their voices, and their votes should be colored and determined by their own private business rather than by the business of 120,000,000 people of this great country of ours? . . .

MR. FISH. I made no such statement as the gentleman attributes to me, and he has no right to put such words in my mouth.

MR. TRUAX. Mr. Chairman, I refuse to yield. I am quoting the gentleman's own utterances.

Mr. Chairman, we may have some "brain trusters" in this administration. The gentleman likes to impress on this House that he has a fine education. I am glad that he has, but the "brain trusters" of this administration are "brain trusting" for all the people instead of a few racketeers and robbers down on Wall Street, United States of America. That is the difference between Democratic "brain trusters" and Republican "brain trusters." . . .

MR. LEE OF MISSOURI. The gentleman from New York always says that he went to such and such college. Would we know that he went to any college or school unless he said so in his speeches?

MR. TRUAX. The gentleman from New York will have to answer that question himself.

The gentleman speaks about a "grab bag." It means that the thing that is worrying a great many people, and particularly those from the sidewalks of New York, is, that the "grab bag" is about to be taken away from them, the "grab bag" in which they plundered this country of billions of dollars, the "grab bag" in which the brokers of Wall Street made $2,000,000,000, while the investing public, whom they now have the gall to call "suckers" and "fools," lost $65,000,000,000. Why, this game that they play is nothing more than a legalized poker game.

The fellow who runs a poker table has a little kitty. He has a slot in the top of the table, and every time a hand is played the winner drops in a chip or two chips. This is the way the fellows in New York play the game. What they want is violent fluctuations up and down so that regardless of who loses they win. . . .

MR. O'CONNOR. I agree substantially with what the gentleman says, but I am compelled to state to him that New York City is not the only place where they have these stock exchanges.

MR. TRUAX. Oh, no. They have them in Chicago. They have there the Chicago Grain Exchange. They work the same racket. They have fellows there who "bull" the market and who "bear" the market. They sell billions of bushels of wheat, corn, and oats which they never own or never expect to own. There is hardly one of those fellows in Chicago who would recognize a good Ohio cornfield if he met it in the middle of the road. They want to be regulated, too; but they want to do the regulating. They are like the gentleman from New York, who is in favor of regulation as long as he can prescribe the regulations.

The Wall Street brokers say that they favor law and order. Of course they do, so long as they can write the law and issue the orders. . . .

I think a majority of the men and women on the floor of this House—the great majority by and large—are honestly and devotedly giving the best there is in them to give the people of this great country a square deal, something they have not had in decades. I believe that the bill you are debating today is one of the bills that will go down in history as a new declaration of independence, a declaration of independence from the strangling clutch of those long, bony talons of Morgan, Kuhn & Loeb, and the rest of the Wall Street racketeers, who have literally robbed this country of billions and billions of dollars. [Applause.] . . .

MR. SNELL. . . .

Mr. Chairman, I do not intend to try to discuss this bill in detail, but the general intent and purpose of the whole bill, as I get it from reading the bill and the report and the discussion that have been had of the bill on the floor.

I think my good friend, the genial chairman of this committee, was a little severe yesterday when he chastised some of us because we offered and supported some amendments to this bill. I may say to my good friend that in doing this we thought we were just as honest as he was in opposing the amendments.

I may also say that there are some Members of this House who always vote on the floor just exactly as they talk in the cloakrooms and the corridors, and I am one of those who follow this custom. I am not interested to know by whom or where this bill was written, but I am interested in what is in it and how it affects the small business man in this country. I do not want to put any more burdens on him than he is carrying at present.

I have approached the consideration of this bill with an absolutely open mind. As far as any regulation of the stock exchange is concerned, under this bill or any other reasonable bill, I am for it; and if this bill had been confined to that end of the problem or to what is carried in the first part of this bill, I think it would be passed in this House with a 100-percent vote; but, as I understand the bill, it seems to me to go much further than this. It goes so far in regulating and in regimenting individual and private business, small business in the various towns and communities of this country, that I am not willing to support it. Even if these additional regulations were advisable, this is not time to do it. Give the country a rest for a few days. And while I have no disposition to find fault with the committee, in my judgment, at this time you would have done much more to aid recovery if you had proposed some amendments to the present securities act so it would be more workable, rather than put more hurdles to discourage the business which is trying to get capital to make a pay roll and to buy capital goods.

The real crux of this whole bill, as I see it, is whether in the long run you are in favor of continually building up in Washington Federal bureaucratic control, or believe the Federal Government knows more about your own business than you do. I have said publicly and privately a great many times that this is not my idea of the proper function of the Federal Government, and I cannot understand how anyone who thinks as I do along this line can support the latter part of this bill which is really the major part of the whole proposition.

We have spent billions of dollars in trying to change the sentiment of the people and to increase their hope and courage, to help them get on their feet and go forward; but to offset this, Congress is almost continually, day after day, providing new regulations or restrictions and regimentation of business which I honestly believe is taking the hope and the courage which you are trying to create away from the small business man in every part of this country.

He has been so harassed and interfered with he is about ready to throw up his hands, and he is in no condition or frame of mind to have another Federal regulation put on him. . . .

MR. MAPES. Does the gentleman take the position that evils or unfair practices in business should not be corrected?

MR. SNELL. The gentleman has no right to say that I take that position because I never have taken that position in private or in public life, and no man can point to a single act of mine that would lead him to make that insinuation. [Applause.] The gentleman has no right to insinuate such a thing, because I have not made a statement on this floor now or at any time which would give him the right to make such a statement. I say I am opposed to extremes and unnecessary regulation of every small activity of every small business man in this country, and I stand on that statement, and the gentleman from Michigan [Mr. Mapes] can agree with me or not as he sees fit. . . .

MR. SNELL. I think we are making a mistake in placing a new, harassing regulation on business practically every day. The small business man in this country is getting discouraged. He does not have time to recover from the regulation that you put on him yesterday before we put another one on him today. This is the part of the bill I am opposed to.

I shall go just as far as any man on the floor of this House in regulating anything in business that is not right or honest so far as the American people are concerned. I have always followed this in my private business, and I am willing to submit to any reasonable regulation, but there is a limit to the regulations you can provide and have the people do business, and I think this bill goes too far. This is the reason I shall vote against the measure. Let us try for a little while to leave honest business and industry alone; and if we do, I believe they will do their part in aiding recovery and prosperity.

MR. LEA OF CALIFORNIA. Mr. Chairman, the remarks of the gentleman from New York [Mr. Snell] are directed to a general phase of this bill. They have some application to the section to which the amendment of the gentleman from New York [Mr. Fish] is offered.

The bill provides that an exchange shall file an application in which it agrees to abide by the regulations of the Commission. These regulations include the right of the Commission to insist on alterations of the rules and regulations of the stock exchange.

The proposal here is whether there shall be an appeal from the action of the Commission requiring a change in the rules of an exchange.

The section provides that an interested exchange be given a right to a hearing, and after the hearing the Commission by rules and regulations determines whether or not the change in rules shall be made. The practical question is whether or not the exchange shall be given an appeal to a court of law from the ruling of the Commission.

It is important that we shall not give exchanges the right to appeal and go into court from the action of the Commission in making rules and regulations. It would subject the Commission to endless harassment.

There are two types of power delegated to the Commission, and that is true of every regulatory act. The first is a quasi-legislative power, and the other is a quasi-judicial power.

When we give the Commission the right, by rules and regulations to require than an exchange shall have a certain rule governing its functions, that is a quasi-legislative power of Congress. The Commission acts for Congress in establishing such rule or regulation. No one living ever heard of a claim that an interested party should have a right to go into court to restrain the action of Congress in passing laws to regulate the affairs of our country.

There would be a quasi-judicial power, perhaps, if under a rule the Commission should attempt to determine whether or not an alleged guilty man should be penalized or subjected to a fine. That the exercise of quasi-judicial power over the exchange would give it the right to go to court. The exchange would not have the right to claim the attention of the court until it claims to be injured by the action of the Commission. If we want regulation, we must give the Commission power to make its action effective.

We have the same situation in relation to the Interstate Commerce Commission. As members of the Interstate Commerce Committee we have had this policy constantly before us. We have a regulatory system controlling the railroads. I would thoroughly deplore the prospect of Government ownership. As I see it, the problem is between successful regulation or Government ownership. We give the Interstate Commerce Commission full power, because regulation without power to be effective would be a failure. This Commission is given broad powers. I will not deny that. If the Commission does not correctly use those powers, if it is not constructive in its purpose, if it does not act in harmony with the spirit of this bill, its regulation would be a failure. The success of the measure is dependent on the Commission, its ability, common sense, fidelity to duty, courage, yet moderation, in administering its powers. If the spirit and purpose of the bill shall be accepted by the Commission to which its regulations is intrusted, then this measure will be a constructive act and an aid to business. . . .

MR. COX. The gentleman from California [Mr. Lea] was discussing a very interesting question touching the matter of the delegation of power. Of course, the gentleman concedes that there is a limit to the power of Congress to make delegations of power to administrative agencies?

MR. LEA OF CALIFORNIA. That is undoubtedly true.

MR. COX. In every instance where that delegation of power takes the complexion of a power to legislate Congress must lay down standards for the guidance of the administrative agency. Congress cannot delegate to any agency the power to legislate.

MR. LEA OF CALIFORNIA. No; it cannot.

MR. COX. What troubles me is this. I fail to find in the bill in every instance where there is a broad delegation of power a standard prescribed by the Congress for the guidance of the Commission, which brings the delegation within the decisions of the courts construing acts of Congress delegating power. In other words, there is nothing prescribed for the guidance of the agency. You do not lay down a rule which they must follow, but you simply in broad language delegate to them blanket power to adopt regulations having the force of law.

MR. LEA OF CALIFORNIA. There is broad power in the bill, but there are several standards, and in attempting to determine what those standards are the courts have a right to resort to all sections of the bill.

MR. COX. I concede that.

MR. LEA OF CALIFORNIA. The standards of the Commission must be those which are consistent with the purposes of the bill. The establishment of a commission carries ordinary incidental powers to its functioning. This act constantly makes the interest of the investor one of the standards to justify action by the Commission.

MR. COX. What one body might think to the interest of the investor another body might not.

MR. LEA OF CALIFORNIA. A common standard accepted by the courts in the interpretation of the Interstate Commerce Act has been action found to be in the public interest and welfare. Language tantamount to that appears throughout this bill. The committee has been conscious of this situation, and has realized the necessity of setting up standards for the exercise of its powers. We have attempted to establish standards throughout the bill. We believe we have conformed to the requirements of the courts as involved in the interpretation of the interstate commerce and other acts establishing regulatory bodies.

MR. COX. I thank the gentleman.

MR. WADSWORTH. Mr. Chairman, I move to strike out the last three words. May I call the attention of the Committee to the real significance of this section? As has been stated in the discussion that has taken place so far, under this section the Commission may order an exchange to completely revamp its rules. It can do so by the issuance of regulations, and those regulations have to an extent the force of law upon the exchange. A violation of them, of course, subjects the exchange to the penalties of the act. . . .

Yet under this section there is no recourse to the court. The final regulation of the Commission cannot be appealed from, and the amendment offered by the gentleman from New York [Mr. Fish] is merely for the purpose of allowing an exchange, in case of an extreme ruling which threatens to injure its legitimate business and the business of buying and selling securities all over the country, the right of appeal.

I call the attention of the Members to the fact that in various sections of this bill the words "by order" are used, and in order to be consistent the words "by order" should be used in this section. On page 40, line 23, at the bottom of the page, I find this:

After appropriate notice and opportunity for hearing, by order to suspend for a period not exceeding 12 months—

And so forth. There are several other instances of the same thing, in which the Commission may, "by order," suspend or put into effect its regulations. The use of the phrase "by order" automatically gives a person or an exchange thus to be regulated the right to appeal.

Have we come to this point in our consideration of legislation of this drastic kind where we are going to forbid a group of American citizens from appealing to the courts? [Applause.] . . .

MR. SABATH. Mr. Chairman, the small business man is not to be injuriously affected by this legislation. He is going to be protected. This legislation is in his interest. This legislation only attempts to regulate dishonest transactions and manipulations of the New York Stock Exchange and other stock exchanges. The gentleman from New York [Mr. Fish] and others are fearful of governmental regulation in this instance. Do they not know that these stock exchanges are penetrating every section of our country and that during the years 1927, 1928, and 1929 they established offices in the smallest towns in the United States, so that today millions upon millions are being spent on the telegraph service connecting the New York and Chicago institutions with every village and hamlet, for the purpose of encouraging gambling and speculation on the part of the people of the whole United States? The power given to this Commission by this section has been given to every other commission in every act we have ever reported or enacted in this House. It is the power to adopt proper and protective rules and regulations.

There is no man living, there is no committee in existence, that could write in any bill all the desirable regulations for stock exchanges. Consequently, we must delegate this power to the agency we designate to enforce this legislation, namely, the Federal Trade Commission. Personally, I have the utmost confidence in the gentlemen who are given the duty in this bill to administer this legislation. I know they are honest and experienced. I know they are fair, and, because they are honest and because they are fearless, some gentlemen do not want them to have this jurisdiction and power to regulate the stock exchanges.

I repeat, the statements made by some of the gentlemen from New York and others, that this legislation, as well as the legislation which we passed last year and known as the "Securities Act," has retarded business, is unwarranted and not true. Look over the financial pages of the largest Republican newspapers and you will find that we are progressing under Democratic rule. We are improving. You will find that every industry that has made a report within the last few months has shown a gratifying and progressive improvement in business. Where there were losses there are now profits. Carloadings, that dependable barometer, are improving every week. Conditions in the heavy-goods industries, such as iron and steel, are steadily and measurably improving. . . . If some gentlemen here would cease their opposition to this remedial legislation and not permit themselves to unwittingly be the tools of stock-exchange manipulators who are working for the defeat of this good legislation, I feel that the country would make even greater progress. The improvement is in spite of the efforts of some gentlemen here, and it will continue increasingly.

I want to say with confidence that it is absolutely necessary to give to the experienced and trustworthy Federal Trade Commission the duty and the power to prescribe rules and regulations for the conduct of stock exchanges if the clear intent of the Congress is to be properly carried out. As for myself, I should have liked to see some of the restrictive provisions written into the law directly, had that been practicable.

It has been my fervent hope and aim to enact really beneficial legislation that will be full of teeth and which the stock-exchange experts and the stock-exchange corps of attorneys cannot circumvent or evade, so that honest investors of the future would not be at the mercy of these flagitious slickers and confidence men, and that the stock exchange might become an orderly, legitimate market place for the legitimate sale of securities.

In conclusion, though the temptation for me to take the floor to answer some of these reckless statements of opponents of this proposed legislation is great, yet, in the hope that we may pass the bill before adjourning for the day, I shall refrain from doing so.

We had no governmental regulation or interference of any kind between 1920 and 1929—yes; up to March 1933—and what happened! [Applause.]

MR. RAYBURN. Mr. Chairman, I may say in reply to the gentleman from New York [Mr. Wadsworth] that I do not know of any power of Congress—and certainly it could not be exercised under this bill—to deny a man the rights guaranteed to him by the fifth amendment to the Constitution.

I regretted very much to hear my friend the gentleman from New York, the minority leader [Mr. Snell], make the statements he did. I do not try to influence his judgment, so I say only that I regret to hear him say he is going to vote against this bill. I cannot follow the course of reasoning the gentleman pursued in arriving at his conclusion. The gentleman made the statement that from the speeches made on this bill in the House it was demonstrated that it was going to regiment business, and especially small business. I do not think the gentleman from New York heard anybody who understood the bill make such a speech. . . .

MR. SNELL. I think the gentleman misinterpreted my remarks, or else I do not make myself clear. What I said was that I was satisfied from information in my possession, together with a study and examination of the bill, that that would be the outcome and that that was the purport of the bill. I still think so; but I may be wrong.

MR. RAYBURN. I challenged these business men who came to my office. I was interviewed by a man appointed by the business men's committee to contact me. I read to him those sections of this bill which it has been said regimented business, and I told him if he could find ony line in the bill that regimented or tried to run anybody's business, that I would be the first one to strike it out. He said he could not find it. We do call for reports; we do give the Commission power to call for the information that is absolutely necessary in order that it may formulate rules and regulations for the control of the national-securities exchanges.

In my opinion we have a good bill, a fine, reasonable, sane bill; but if we adopt the amendment offered by the gentleman from New York [Mr. Fish], we shall defeat practically everything we have done in the preceding 40 pages.

In my opening statement, and again on yesterday, I said that three features must be contained in this law if there is to be effective control of the stock exchanges: One is a reasonable margin of requirement, the second is a strong antimanipulative section, and the third is to give to the Commission which administers this law the power to make it effective. If you are going to say that the Commission may do this by rules and regulations, that is one thing. If you are going to say that the Commission shall formulate rules and regulations and issue them in the form of orders, that is another thing; and every one of them could be tied up in the courts from 12 to 24 months and thus absolutely negative the very things we have done in the preceding forty-odd pages of this bill.

In my opinion, the question involved in the Fish amendment is whether or not after writing a law you are going to give the administrative body the power to make the law effective and the power to enforce it. [Applause.]

[Here the gavel fell.]

THE CHAIRMAN. The question is on the amendment of the gentleman from New York [Mr. Fish].

The amendment was rejected. . . .

MR. BULWINKLE. Mr. Chairman, I offer an amendment, which I send to the desk.

The Clerk read as follows:

Mr. Bulwinkle moves to strike out subsection (a) of section 31, and the title thereto, beginning at line 15 on page 56, down to and including line 24 on page 59, and insert in lieu thereof, on lines 15 and 16, a new title, and the new section, section 31 (a), to read as follows:

"Members and Employees of the Federal Stock Exchange
Commission

"SEC. 31. (a) There is hereby established a Federal Stock Exchange Commission, to be composed of three members, to be appointed by the President, by and with the advice and consent of the Senate. Not more than two of such appointed Commissioners shall be members of the same 'political party. No appointed Commissioner shall actively engage in any other business, vocation, or employment than that of serving as Commissioner. Each appointed Commissioner shall receive a salary at the rate of $10,000 a year and shall hold office for a term of 6 years, except that (1) any Commissioner appointed to fill a vacancy occurring prior to the expiration of the term for which his predecessor was appointed shall be appointed for the remainder of such term, and (2) the terms of office of the Commissioners first taking office after the date of the enactment of this act shall expire, as designated by the President at the time of nomination, one at the end of 2 years, one at the end of 4 years, and one at the end of 6 years, after the date of enactment of this act."

MR. BULWINKLE. Mr. Chairman, when the Committee on Interstate and Foreign Commerce had under consideration the first so-called "stock exchange bill," which was drafted by Mr. Corcoran, Mr. Cochran, and others, at the close of the hearing, it was apparent that that bill was entirely too vicious, unworkable, and the consequences that would have ensued from its enactment could not be foreseen.

At this time, with the aid of the legislative drafting service, and this alone, I drafted a stock-exchange regulation bill, which I believed then, and believe now, that, if enacted into law, would have been far better for everyone concerned in this country. In that bill I provided for a separate and distinct commission to be appointed by the

President to consist of three members. The amendment that I am offering and that the Clerk has just read follows the lines of that which I proposed originally in the bill. . . .

I am firmly convinced that the fair and just administration of this bill, if it were enacted into law, that a separate commission should be established. We all know that this legislation today is one of the most important that has come before this session of Congress. Everybody in the country is affected by it. It affects credit. It may mean deflation. It may mean on the one hand a partial paralysis of business. All of these things being involved in it, why not let us try to give it the best administration possible?

I am not speaking detrimentally, nor do I know anything against the Federal Trade Commission or any members thereof, but I do know this: that the manifold duties of the Federal Trade Commission are enough for it. I know well enough and you do too, that it is best not to overburden any man or set of men with work. We all know that the Senate bill provides for a separate Commission, and we all know that it has been rumored around here that the only reason to keep the Federal Trade Commission in this bill in the House is to give the conferees ground to trade upon. I do not believe that is either fair or just to the Federal Trade Commission or to the Members of the House.

I ask the members of the committee to adopt my amendment, because I believe that in the long run that it will be better for all concerned. After the adoption or rejection of the amendment that I have offered there is very little else to consider in the few remaining pages of this bill, and it will be passed by an overwhelming majority in the House and sent to the Senate. To a great extent that bill was not considered on its merits in the House. To a great extent, I have noticed that in the debate on the bill and under the 5-minute rule that it was in some of the Members' minds to penalize the stock exchanges for their past misdeeds. We are not here passing ex post facto law. We are here attempting to provide for permanent legislation for the control, regulation, and supervision of the stock exchanges. The idea, through the legislation that we are considering, is to permit and require men in dealing in public securities to do business legitimately, honestly, and under proper supervision and regulation in the interest of the public.

It is unfortunate that no one who offers an amendment could do so without being termed a "chiseler" or being branded as offering a stock-exchange amendment for the purpose of weakening the bill. It is also unfortunate that the bill was not passed upon its merits.

During the course of practicing laws, in many cases, I have seen an attorney representing a client in a case in court who either was not sufficiently acquainted with the law and the facts in his case, or who had a weak case, spending a great deal of the time of the trial not upon the merits of the case but upon a denunciation of the witnesses and others connected with the other side.

I hope and trust that the Senate will amend it in a great many particulars in order that a workable bill may be finally enacted into law. I hope and trust that whatever bill may pass will not in any respect cause any deflation and further restriction of credit to industry. I am vitally interested in all legislation that has for its purpose aiding in employing the unemployed, and I do not want any legislation passed which would in any way retard recovery, and with legislation of this type which we are passing here today that is the great danger that we face. I believe that even now, though it pass in the House, that this bill could, by the Senate and in conference, be made a far better bill.

The second paragraph, which is the argument of its passage, should be omitted. The so-called "section in regard to the margin requirements" should be clarified. The unnecessary burden thrown upon corporations in reporting should be lessened. The multitudinous criminal and penal sections and a great many others could be, to a great extent, done away with. A separate commission should be established. In short, the Roper report should be followed more closely.

We are legislating today for the public interests. We are not legislating to penalize the stock exchanges of the future and the business of the future for what has been done on the stock exchanges in the past.

I trust that this bill, if it should become a law, will do all that the proponents of it think that it will, although I have grave misgivings and doubts. . . .

MR. MAPES. Mr. Chairman, we are approaching the end of the consideration of this bill, and before we conclude I want to say that I have supported this legislation, and that I supported the legislation which resulted in the Securities Act.

I have not been impressed at all with the argument directed against these two pieces of legislation that they will bring about a regimentation of industry. The Securities Act was based upon the theory that anyone who made a false representation of a material fact and benefited by it at the expense of an innocent investor should reimburse the innocent investor whatever he suffered because of that false representation. I stand upon that policy. I think perhaps the Securities Act might be amended to advantage in some particulars, but for one I think the purposes of the legislation were good and that the act itself should not be weakened.

I am supporting this legislation because I believe that if we provide fair and honest market places for the transaction of the purchase and sale of corporate securities in this country, it will be a desirable thing and will be to the benefit of the general public and to the benefit of business.

As I have said, Mr. Chairman, I am not impressed with the argument directed against these two pieces of legislation on the ground that they regiment business. I may say to my Republican colleagues that we have passed act after act based upon the theory which lies behind the pending legislation. A few moments ago I referred to the Congressional Directory to see how many governmental commissions are in existence. I shall mention some of them. I submit that most of them have greater discretionary power over business than this legislation proposes to vest in the Federal Trade Commission with regard to the stock exchanges. Let us start with the Federal Reserve Board. Has any board or agency of the Government power approaching that which this agency has over the banks of the country? I think those familiar with the banking legislation of this country will admit that the Federal Reserve Board exercises a discretionary power so great that by comparison it makes the power conferred upon the Federal Trade Commission by this legislation seem almost insignificant. To continue with governmental boards, we have the War Finance Corporation, the Tariff Commission, the Federal Power Commission, the Radio Commission, the United States Board of Mediation, and the Interstate Commerce Commission, to name only the important ones. All of these agencies have a much greater degree of discretionary power over business than is conferred upon the Federal Trade Commission over stock exchanges by this legislation. . . .

MR. HOLLISTER. How many of those commissions have the right by rules and regulations to make criminal offenses?

MR. MAPES. The Federal Reserve Board and the Comptroller of the Currency have the power to close all the banks of the United States.

MR. HOLLISTER. I did not ask the gentleman that question; I asked the gentleman how many of those boards to which he has referred have the right by rules and regulations to make criminal offenses? This is the great objection to the pending bill.

MR. MAPES. I have heard that argument made many times.

MR. COX. If the gentleman from Michigan will yield, have those boards and commissions not the right to adopt rules and regulations the violation of which constitute a criminal offense?

MR. MAPES. Why, certainly they have.

MR. HOLLISTER. Will the gentleman name those boards which have such power?

MR. MAPES. Mr. Chairman, I decline to yield further. If agencies of the Government have not some power with which to enforce their rules and regulations, what is the sense of giving them any power to make rules and regulations, whether it be with regard to the stock exchange or something else? . . .

MR. COOPER OF OHIO. I wish the gentleman would point out to me any specific provision in the law creating the commissions the gentleman has mentioned, from the Federal Reserve Board down, which gives them the power to adopt a rule or regulation which would send a man to the penitentiary and fine him, if that rule or regulation is not written into the law itself?

MR. MAPES. I may say to the gentleman from Ohio that the Federal Trade Commission is given no such power under this law. . . .

Mr. Chairman, the Federal Trade Commission is given power to prescribe rules and regulations; but it is not given power to punish anyone. The matter must be taken to the courts and a case made out, and then it is left to the judge to determine whether the violator of the rules and regulations shall be punished by sentence of fine or imprisonment. . . .

I think so, but I have not the act before me. Mr. Chairman, may I get to the particular amendment of the gentleman from North Carolina? I expressed myself on this amendment in general debate. I have not considered that it was a matter of first importance whether this act was administered by the Federal Trade Commission or a separate commission, but it seems to me that the organization of the Federal Trade Commission is particularly well adapted to take on the administration of this act. That Commission administers the Securities Act. It is organized for the purpose of maintaining fair practices in business. The Federal Trade Commission will be divided into divisions, as I pointed out in general debate, and one division will be charged with the duty of administering this act.

Anyone who is aggrieved by any order, rule, or regulation of the Commission, may I say to those who are so afraid of the rules and regulations to be promulgated by this Commission, or anyone who is aggrieved by any order of the division of the Federal Commission having this matter in charge has a right to appeal to the full Commission and to have a hearing before the full Commission of 7 members, not by the 2 or 3 making up the division that is centered on this act. In that way he will have the benefit of getting the view of the other members of the Commission as well as those who have the direct administration of the act.

Commissioner Landis, of the Federal Trade Commission, said before our committee in the hearings that the Commission had taken on a personnel of about 65 to administer the Securities Act. A good deal of the same kind of investigation and research work will be required to administer this act as the Securities Act, and it would be a simple duplication of authority if a new commission were established.

May I say further, and I say this without any desire to do anything more than state the facts, I think it may be assumed that everybody who is opposed to this legislation, who wants to see it defeated and who wants to see it fail, will vote for this amendment for a new commission. I think the friends of the legislation should see to it that the amendment does not carry.

MR. MERRITT. Mr. Chairman, I rise in support of the amendment.

Mr. Chairman, I am heartily in favor of the amendment offered by the gentleman from North Carolina [Mr. Bulwinkle], providing for the administration of this act by a commission not connected with the Federal Trade Commission.

The fundamental objection which I have to the bill now before the House is, as I indicated in my minority report, that it goes beyond necessary legislation for stock-exchange regulation and gives the Commission, directly or indirectly, control over securities and therefore the corporate life of practically every corporation in the United States. The amendment proposed by the gentleman from North Carolina will to some extent modify this difficulty, because the commission which would be appointed under his amendment would start with the fundamental idea that they are to control stock-exchange activity, and not business management and business practices. But I go further than the desire to have this amendment of the gentleman from North Carolina adopted, and should like very much to have substituted for the pending bill a bill which he introduced during the discussion of this matter before our committee, which is known as "a bill to establish a Federal Stock Exchange Commission, to provide for the licensing of stock exchanges, and for other purposes," and is numbered 8575. Its main provisions follow:

First. The bill provides first for the establishment of a Federal Stock Exchange Commission, composed of the Secretary of the Treasury, the Governor of the Federal Reserve Board, and three others, to be appointed by the President.

Second. After 6 months no stock exchange can do business without a license. The Commission shall grant the license applied for if it finds that the provisions of the constitution of such exchange reasonably guard against undue speculative activity, manipulative practices, and otherwise afford reasonably adequate protection for investors.

Third. The Commission has power over the future rules and practices of the exchange after a license shall be granted, and to see that the exchange takes such disciplinary measures as are necessary to enforce its rules.

Fourth. The Commission has power to suspend and revoke the licenses of an exchange, to make all necessary inquiries and investigations to see that its rules are carried out, and to summon witnesses, administer oaths, and so forth. It may call for the production of any documentary evidence which may be required from any part of the United States to any designated place of hearing.

Fifth. It provides a penalty for violation of the provisions of the act of a fine not exceeding $10,000, or imprisonment for not more than 5 years. Any person knowingly violating any of the rules or regulations promulgated by the Commission may be fined not more than $1,000, and without any provision for imprisonment.

This bill completely meets the objections which I and a number of other Members of the House have to the present bill and is, as its names implies, a bill strictly for the regulation and government of stock exchanges. It will at the same time carry out the views of President Roosevelt as expressed in his letter of March 26 to Chairman Rayburn:

That the Government be given such definite powers of supervision over exchanges that the Government itself will be able to correct abuses which may arise in the future.

It is perfectly clear from the discussion which has extended for several days in connection with the bill that there is great diversity of opinion in this committee and throughout the country as to the effects of the bill before us. Rightly or wrongly, it engenders great fear and prevents the feeling of security which is necessary to a renewal of business. I submit that whether the bill before us or the bill offered by the gentleman from North Carolina is enacted the efforts of the commission appointed either under one bill or the other must be preliminary work for a large part of the first year, certainly for 6 months. If the Bulwinkle bill is substituted the commission can, during these 6 months, make a full examination of existing stock exchanges and the rules under which they act, and can also provide and insist upon such changes in the rules as will fully protect investors. If they find that additional legislation is needed either to increase their powers or legislation which directly affects the exchanges they can recommend it to the next Congress with fuller knowledge as to the necessity for the legislation and as to its effect.

No possible harm can be brought about by the delay in the enactment of the many specific provisions of the present bill, while their enactment into law may do much present harm and will make any change very difficult. . . .

MR. O'CONNOR. If the gentleman is so enthusiastically in favor of this amendment, I am curious to know why in his minority views on page 32 he wrote these words:

The creation of new commissions having power over business and the creation of new regulations and penalties do not tend to quiet and confidence but to the contrary, and thus retard business.

MR. MERRITT. I was referring, of course, to the present commissions that have the power.

MR. O'CONNOR. The gentleman is advocating a new commission?

MR. MERRITT. Yes; in a way. . . .

MR. COX. Mr. Chairman, I am sure everyone sees the very close and intimate relationship between the Securities Act and this stock-exchange bill. The Securities Act deals primarily with the original distribution of securities, while the Stock Exchange Act deals with trading in outstanding securities. Since this is true it would appear that both acts should be administered by the same agency. If a special commission—as is proposed by the pending amendment—is to be set up to administer the pending bill, then certainly the administration of the Securities Act should be withdrawn from the Federal Trade Commission and put in the hands of the new commission. But, in view of the experience of the Federal Trade Commission in the administration of the Securities Act, and in view of the fact that this Commission has built up an organization made up of the best talent obtainable, I respectfully submit that if the purpose of the Congress is to enact a law which shall be promptly put into effect, its administration should go to the Federal Trade Commission.

This Commission primarily deals with trade and commerce. This bill deals with trade and commerce and I am sure that any Member of the House reading this bill will be impressed with the view that the Federal Trade Commission is the agency to which its administration should be entrusted.

From whence comes the urge for the setting up of a special commission? Does the suggestion come from friends of the bill? Is it something that would make the legislation less objectionable to the exchanges which are to be regulated?

We have proceeded in the consideration of the measure upon the idea that we would follow the committee that wrote the bill, trusting and believing in the committee as friends of the public, and if the committee is to be sustained then I submit it is important to vote down the pending amendment.

By what I have said I do not mean to in any way question the sincerity of the author of the amendment. He invoked the report of the Roper committee or commission in support of the amendment which he offered. In this connection may I direct your attention to the fact that Commissioner Landis was a member of the Roper committee or commission, and the commissioner appeared before the committee sponsoring the legislation and urged very strongly that its administration be put in the hands of that commission. That commission is set up and ready to go, and if you want effective and prompt administration of the law, its administration should be entrusted to this body. [Applause.]

MR. RANKIN. Mr. Chairman, it has been very amusing to me to hear some gentlemen on the floor, especially on the other side, oppose this measure to regulate the stock exchanges, and at the same time say they are strongly in favor of some method of regulating the stock exchanges. When did they get that way? What method do they favor? I wonder where these gentlemen were from 1926 to 1929. "Oh, where was Roderick then?" No blast upon their bugle horns then to warn the American people of the grave dangers that confronted them; no protest came from them at that time against the unjust, dishonest, cruel, and inhuman practices on the stock exchanges.

They talked about prosperity then—Hoover prosperity. The truth is, there was no prosperity. That jamboree on the stock market, fostered by the four M's—Morgan, Mellon, Mills, and Meyer—was simply an artificial stimulation, a drunken orgy, a saturnalia of speculation, graft, fraud, and corruption, the like of which the world has never seen. It wrecked fortunes, blasted hopes, destroyed lives, ruined homes, made beggars of innocent women and children, and thieves of honest men. . . .

Where, then, were these Republican leaders who are now critizing this bill and proclaiming so loudly their desire to regulate the stock exchanges by some other method and at the same time fighting this measure which they know will regulate them? Where were they when these financial buccaneers were unloading onto the American people $2,000,000,000 of Central and South American bonds, selling them to the widows and orphans and to the aged and infirm—bonds that are now scarcely worth the paper they are written on? Their loud professions of a desire to regulate the stock exchanges comes too late. They have sinned away their day of grace.

Let us see what happened at the time when we were going down into the pit of this depression. We find that in 1921 there were in the United States 21 people with incomes of $1,000,000 a year or more. In 1928 it had grown to 511, and in 1929 it reached the peak of 513 individuals with incomes of more than $1,000,000 a year. Where did these millions come from? They came from the American people. Who reaped those fortunes? Did the manufacturers make them? No; they did not. Did the farmers make them? No, indeed. Did the merchants make them? Not on your life. Did they come from our international trade? No, no. Our international trade was already dead. They came from the highway robberies on the stock exchanges, which we are now trying to prevent in the future by the passage of this bill. [Applause.]

Now, Mr. Chairman, I want to say a few words in opposition to this amendment which would take the supervision of the exchanges out of the hands of the Federal Trade Commission.

By all means, this amendment ought to be defeated. In the first place, as the gentleman from Michigan has said, we already have too many commissions. You remember we Democrats used to chide the Republicans because every time they got into trouble they created a new commission. And every time they created a new commission they made it worse. [Laughter.] Let us not fall into that error ourselves. [Applause.]

The Federal Trade Commission is doing some of the greatest work that has ever been done by any agency of the Government. By its investigation of the utilities in the last few years, it has brought relief to the American people through a reduction of utility rates to the ultimate consumers, amounting to $118,000,000. Only yesterday, in the State of Illinois, the Power Trust, seeing the handwriting on the wall, undertook to placate the people of Illinois and reduced their light and power rates to $1,300,000 a year. If they had lowered them to the rates provided by the yardstick of the Tennessee Valley Authority it would have saved the people of Illinois $6,000,000 a year.

It is estimated that this program of the Federal Trade Commission will bring a reduction in utilities to the ultimate consumers of the country in the next 10 years amounting to $1,000,000,000. Yet they have done this work at a cost of less than $2,000,000.

No man can question the efficiency of the Federal Trade Commission. No man can question the effectiveness of its work. No one questions the sincerity of its present membership.

Let us see what it will cost to create another commission, such as this amendment provides. It is estimated that it will add an extra expense of not less than $500,000. You would have to have new quarters. You would have to have new personnel, additional clerks, stenographers, and so forth. You would have to have a library. All this would be additional expenses piled onto the American people, without bringing them any additional relief.

I sincerely trust that the amendment will be voted down and the bill passed as it is written. I congratulate the committee on its efficient work. It is a long step in the right direction—one of the most important that has ever been taken by the Congress of the United States. [Applause.] . . .

MR. O'CONNOR. . . .I sincerely believe that the Federal Trade Commission, from its experience with the Securities Act, and because of the type of the members of that great Commission, possibly augmented in its membership, is well qualified and experienced to administer this act, without setting up another commission and falling into the danger of the "bureaucracy" that helped so much to elect our party to office. . . .

MR. BULWINKLE. I might state that the Senate bill provides for a separate commission. Rumors are that the only reason they want to give this to the Federal Trade Commission is to give them a trading point between the House and Senate. Now, I do not care whether this is carried today or not or whether it is defeated or not. In the end you will come back here from the conference report and vote for a different commission.

MR. O'CONNOR. Of course, the gentleman's prophecy may be correct. In my experience with the recent tax bill, which to my mind was one of the greatest surprises that ever came out of a conference in my experience, we may expect anything to happen in conference if our managers are not adamant. I believe firmly, however, that we should not establish this new commission, at least not now. We should place the powers in the Federal Trade Commission; and as to the bill in main, however, I do believe that if any industry with an unchallenged reputation for unfair practices ever needed regulating, it is those of our stock exchanges, whose unfair practices have been carried on brazenly and defiantly in our country for the last generation, resulting in the loss of billions of dollars to many millions of our people. [Applause.] . . .

MR. RAYBURN. Mr. Chairman, the reason for this amendment and its advocacy, I presume, grow out of the conversation that has been going on around Washington for several years. The Federal Trade Commission has been under fire. It is more under fire right now than it has ever been, because, in response to resolutions of the Senate, it has dug into and found out some things about people in this country who have been violating moral law, if not statutory law.

I echo the sentiments of my distinguished friend from Michigan [Mr. Mapes]. This so-called "Bulwinkle amendment" will get the vote of every man in this House who is opposed to this bill.

Now, the gentleman from North Carolina [Mr. Bulwinkle] offers an amendment to provide for a separate commission of three members to administer this act. It is known, of course, that if a separate commission is provided for, it will have the administration of the Securities Act also.

There has been a great deal said around this Capitol and whispered throughout about Mr. James M. Landis, a so-called "member" of the "brain trust" and present Federal Trade Commissioner. I do not know whether there is a "brain trust" or not, but I say this about Jim Landis—that if there is a "brain trust" in this Government, he is entirely capable of being a member of it. [Applause.] What will happen, therefore, if you want to get away from Landis and Mathers and the other members of the Federal Trade Commission in the administration of this act? If the Securities Act is transferred to this new commission—if there is such a commission, and I hope there never will be—what would the President necessarily and naturally do, being a man of sanity and having appointed two men on the Federal Trade Commission to administer the Securities Act? He would transfer them to this new commission that is provided for under the Bulwinkle amendment, and there would be 2 to 1 in the administration of this act. I hope there will never be any such commission, and whatever has been said around here I am not going to yield on that point in conference unless I have to in order to save the bill at all. . . .

The question involved in the vote upon this amendment and in the vote upon the motion to recommit is whether or not you want effective regulation of the stock exchanges.

If you want effective regulation of the stock exchanges, vote down the [amendment] and send your House conferees into conference with the Senate with a satisfactory, original bill—something upon which they can stand—and bring back to the House a report of real regulation and not a sham or a fraud. [Applause.] . . .

THE CHAIRMAN. The question is on the amendment offered by the gentleman from North Carolina [Mr. Bulwinkle].

The question was taken; and on a division (demanded by Mr. Bulwinkle) there were—ayes 95, noes 143.

MR. BULWINKLE. Mr. Chairman, I ask for tellers.

Tellers were ordered, and the Chair appointed as tellers Mr. Bulwinkle and Mr. Cole.

The Committee again divided; and the tellers reported that there were—ayes 102, noes, 145.

So the amendment was rejected. . . .

THE SPEAKER. The question is on the passage of the bill.

MR. RAYBURN. Mr. Speaker, on that I demand the yeas and nays.

The yeas and nays were ordered.

The question was taken; and there were—yeas 281, nays 84, not voting 66, as follows:

[Roll No. 137]

Yeas—281

Adair	Castellow
Adams	Chapman
Arens	Christianson
Arnold	Church
Auf der Heide	Clark, N.C.
Ayers, Mont.	Cochran, Mo.
Ayres, Kans.	Coffin
Bailey	Colden
Bankhead	Cole
Beam	Collins, Miss.
Beiter	Colmer
Biermann	Condon
Bland	Connery
Blanton	Connolly
Bloom	Cooper, Tenn.
Boehne	Corning
Boileau	Cox
Brennan	Cravens
Brooks	Cross, Tex.
Brown, Ga.	Crosser, Ohio
Brown, Ky.	Crump
Brunner	Cummings
Buchanan	Darden
Buck	Dear
Bulwinkle	Deen
Burch	DeRouen
Busby	Dickinson
Byrns	Dickstein
Caldwell	Dies
Cannon, Mo.	Disney
Cannon, Wis.	Dobbins
Carden, Ky.	Dockweiler
Carmichael	Douglass
Carpenter, Kans.	Dowell
Carpenter, Nebr.	Drewry
Cartwright	Driver
Cary	Duffey

Duncan, Mo.
Dunn
Durgan, Ind.
Eagle
Edmiston
Eicher
Ellenbogen
Ellzey, Miss.
Evans
Faddis
Fernandez
Fiesinger
Fitzgibbons
Fitzpatrick
Flannagan
Fletcher
Ford
Foulkes
Frear
Frey
Fuller
Gambrill
Gasque
Gavagan
Gilchrist
Gillespie
Gillette
Glover
Goldsborough
Granfield
Gray
Green
Greenway
Gregory
Griffin
Haines
Hancock, N.C.
Hart
Harter
Hastings
Healey
Henney
Hildebrandt
Hill, Knute

Hill, Samuel B.
Hoeppel
Hoidale
Hope
Howard
Hughes
Imhoff
Jacobsen
James
Johnson, Minn.
Johnson, Okla.
Johnson, Tex.
Johnson, W. Va.
Jones
Kee
Keller
Kelly, Ill.
Kennedy, Md.
Kerr
Kleberg
Kloeb
Kniffin
Knutson
Kocialkowski
Kopplemann
Kramer
Kvale
Lambertson
Lambeth
Lanham
Lanzetta
Larrabee
Lea, Calif.
Lee, Mo.
Lehr
Lemke
Lesinski
Lewis, Colo.
Lewis, Md.
Lindsay
Lloyd
Lozier
Ludlow
Lundeen

McCarthy	Ramsay
McClintic	Ramspeck
McCormack	Randolph
McDuffie	Rankin
McFarlane	Rayburn
McGrath	Reece
McKeown	Reilly
McReynolds	Richardson
Maloney, Conn.	Robertson
Maloney, La.	Robinson
Mansfield	Rogers, N.H.
Mapes	Romjue
Martin, Colo.	Rudd
Martin, Oreg.	Ruffin
May	Sabath
Meeks	Sadowski
Miller	Sandin
Milligan	Schuetz
Mitchell	Sears
Monaghan, Mont.	Secrest
Montague	Shallenberger
Montet	Shannon
Moran	Sinclair
Morehead	Sirovich
Mott	Sisson
Murdock	Smith, Va.
Musselwhite	Smith, Wash.
Nesbit	Smith, W.Va.
O'Brien	Snyder
O'Connell	Somers, N.Y.
O'Connor	Spence
O'Malley	Steagall
Oliver, N.Y.	Summers, Tex.
Owen	Stubbs
Parker	Sullivan
Parks	Sumners, Tex.
Parsons	Tarver
Patman	Taylor, Colo.
Peavey	Taylor, S.C.
Peterson	Terrell, Tex.
Pettengill	Terry, Ark.
Pierce	Thom
Polk	Thomason
Prall	Thompson, Ill.

Thompson, Tex.
Thurston
Truax
Turner
Umstead
Utterback
Vinson, Ga.
Vinson, Ky.
Wallgren
Warren
Wearin
Weaver
Weideman
Welch
Werner
West, Ohio

West, Tex.
White
Whittington
Wilcox
Willford
Williams
Wilson
Withrow
Wolverton
Wood, Mo.
Woodruff
Woodrum
Young
Zioncheck
The Speaker

Nays—84

Allen
Andrew, Mass.
Andrews, N.Y.
Bacon
Bakewell
Black
Blanchard
Bolton
Britten
Buckbee
Burnham
Cady
Carter, Calif.
Carter, Wyo.
Chase
Claiborne
Cooper, Ohio
Crowther
Darrow
Delaney
Dirksen
Ditter
Dondero
Edmonds
Eltse, Calif.
Englebright

Fish
Foss
Gifford
Goodwin
Goss
Guyer
Hancock, N.Y.
Hartley
Hess
Higgins
Hollister
Holmes
Jenkins, Ohio
Kahn
Kennedy, N.Y.
Kenney
Kinzer
Lehlbach
Luce
McGugin
McLean
McLeod
Marshall
Martin, Mass.
Merritt
Millard

Moynihan, Ill.
Muldowney
Norton
Perkins
Peyser
Plumley
Powers
Ransley
Reed, N.Y.
Reid, Ill.
Rich
Rogers, Mass.
Scrugham
Seger
Simpson
Snell

Stalker
Stokes
Studley
Sutphin
Swick
Taber
Thomas
Tinkham
Tobey
Traeger
Treadway
Wadsworth
Whitley
Wigglesworth
Wolcott
Wolfenden

Not Voting—66

Abernethy
Allgood
Bacharach
Beck
Beedy
Berlin
Boland
Boylan
Brown, Mich.
Browning
Brumm
Burke, Calif.
Burke, Nebr.
Carley, N.Y.
Cavicchia
Celler
Chavez
Clarke, N.Y.
Cochran, Pa.
Collins, Calif.
Crosby
Crowe
Culkin
Cullen
DePriest
Dingell

Doughton
Doutrich
Doxey
Eaton
Farley
Focht
Fulmer
Greenwood
Griswold
Hamilton
Harlan
Hill, Ala.
Huddleston
Jeffers
Jenckes, Ind.
Kelly, Pa.
Kurtz
Lamneck
McFadden
McMillan
McSwain
Marland
Mead
Oliver, Ala.
Palmisano
Richards

Rogers, Okla.	Sweeney
Sanders	Taylor, Tenn.
Schaefer	Turpin
Schulte	Underwood
Shoemaker	Waldron
Strong, Pa.	Walter
Swank	Wood, Ga.

THE SPEAKER. The Clerk will call my name.

The Clerk called Mr. Rainey's name and he voted "yea."

So the bill was passed. . . .

Senate – 73rd Congress, 2d Session
May 7-12, 1934

MR. FLETCHER. I move that the Senate proceed to the consideration of Senate bill 3420, being the bill to regulate securities exchanges, and so forth.

THE VICE PRESIDENT. The question is on the motion of the Senator from Florida.

The motion was agreed to; and the Senate proceeded to consider the bill (S. 3420) to provide for the regulation of securities exchanges and of over-the-counter markets operating in interstate and foreign commerce and through the mails, to prevent inequitable and unfair practices on such exchanges and markets, and for other purposes, which had been reported from the Committee on Banking and Currency without amendment.

MR. FLETCHER. Mr. President, I may be a little tedious in endeavoring to state the case to the Senate regarding a measure which is extremely complicated, difficult, and far-reaching. I shall be as brief as I can, and as fair as I may be in presenting the question of the need for the legislation, the demand for it, and what I concede to be the sound conclusions reached in the form of the bill now presented to the Senate.

On March 2, 1932, a resolution was introduced in this body by the Senator from Delaware [Mr. Townsend], at the request of his colleague [Mr. Hastings], and was approved on the calendar day of March 4, 1932. It provided that the Committee on Banking and Currency or any duly authorized subcommittee thereof was—

Authorized and directed, first, to make a thorough and complete investigation of the practices with respect to the buying and selling and the borrowing and lending of listed securities upon the various stock exchanges, the values of such securities, and the effect of such practices upon interstate and foreign commerce, upon the operation of the national banking system and the Federal Reserve System, and upon the market for securities of the United States Government, and the desirability of the exercise of the taxing power of the United States with respect to any such securities—

And so forth.

Other resolutions were subsequently introduced looking in the same direction, among them being a resolution adopted on April 4, 1933, extending the powers of the committee and providing that the committee——

Shall have authority and hereby is directed——

(1) To make a thorough and complete investigation of the operation by any person, firm, copartnership, company, association, corporation, or other entity, of the business of banking, financing, and extending credit; and of the business of issuing, offering, or selling securities;

(2) To make a thorough and complete investigation of the business conduct and practices of security exchanges and of the members thereof;

(3) To make a thorough and complete investigation of the practices with respect to the buying and selling and the borrowing and lending of securities which are traded in upon the various security exchanges, or on the over-the-counter market, or on any other market; and of the values of such securities; and

(4) To make a thorough and complete investigation of the effect of all such business operations and practices upon interstate and foreign commerce, upon the industrial and commercial credit structure of the United States, upon the operation of the national banking system and the Federal Reserve System, and upon the market for securities of the United States Government, and the desirability of the exercise of the taxing power of the United States——

And so forth.

In pursuance of those resolutions the Committee on Banking and Currency appointed a subcommittee. The subcommittee has been almost continuously engaged in the investigation.

There were a few weeks in 1932, during the summer vacation, and in 1933, when the committee were not holding hearings; but beginning October 3, 1933, practically every day, 4 or 5 days a week, hearings were held by the subcommittee. Every opportunity has been given the stock exchange, investment bankers, holding companies, industrialists, bankers, and what not, everybody interested in the subject, to be heard respecting the bill which was introduced and respecting the matters involved in the investigation. Subsequently there was introduced Senate bill 2693, and hearings were had upon that bill, and all persons interested were given opportunity to present their views to the committee.

Some 21 volumes of hearings have been printed. There probably will be two or three more volumes before we shall finish the final print, including the exhibits. In addition to the printed volumes a cross-reference index is being prepared, and is now practically complete. That will enable Senators to have access to the hearings with more convenience and speed, and will make the volumes all the more usable.

We expect later to make a report covering all the hearings, including the printed documents and the index, and to lay the whole subject before the Senate in response to the resolutions of the Senate.

Considerable results have already been attained. For instance, it may be mentioned that the National Bank Act of 1933 contains provisions based upon the developments before the committee, particularly with reference to the separation of commercial banks from affiliates. Another provision based upon the developments before the committee was the extension of the powers of the Federal Reserve Board so as to enable it to have a greater control over the flow of credit away from agriculture, industry, and commerce into speculation. As I say, that grew out of the hearings.

Another act which Congress passed last year, known as the "Securities Act," is the result of matters brought to light in connection with the hearings.

Now the final stage is reached. This bill, demanded by the country everywhere, is before the Senate. It undertakes to provide a system, plan, or method of Federal supervision of securities exchanges.

The hearings already printed are, of course, available to the Senate. As I stated, they are not entirely complete, because some of the work is now under way in the Government Printing Office. The last volumes of hearings and the index itself will be laid before the Senate shortly, so that all the data may be at the command of the Senate.

It may well be claimed that economic and social problems, and even legal problems, are approached under the influence, more or less, of our political and social philosophy. There is room for a difference of view. It may be conceded that legal principles must form a part of economic and social theories.

Events since the fall of 1929 have shown grievous errors of habits and practices in the past, and established universal demand for corrective measures and new methods. The demand was for a new deal, it being understood that this is a slogan, not a new political system or creed. It is a moral attitude in governmental action. Applying it to the measure now submitted, its cardinal principles I conceive to be, first, restoring as a rule of moral and economic conduct, a sense of fiduciary obligation; and, second, establishing social responsibility, as distinguished from individual gain, as the goal.

The President has three times in public messages and communications recommended legislation of the sort embodied in this bill. He has recognized that the stock exchanges of the country are not only a useful but an essential mechanism in our financial and economic structure, and serve a necessary public purpose. They are not private enterprises, free from a public interest or function.

In the hearings before the committee, representatives of the stock exchanges have conceded the principle of Federal regulation.

The objectives are appreciated by the stock exchanges and the administration.

Mr. Richard Whitney, president of the New York Stock Exchange, the giant among them all, said to our committee:

"It is the purpose of the New York Stock Exchange to assist in every possible way in the prevention of fraudulent practices affecting stock-exchange transactions, excessive speculation, and manipulation of security prices. We should be glad to see a regulatory body, constituted under Federal law, supervise the solution of these grave problems. We suggest in principle, and subject to the requirements of law and the constitutional power of Congress, an authority or board to consist of 7 members, 2 of whom are to be appointed by the President; 2 to be Cabinet officers, who may well be the Secretary of the Treasury and the Secretary of Commerce; and 1 to be appointed by the Open Market Committee of the Federal Reserve System; the 2 remaining members will be representative of stock exchanges, one to be designated by the New York Stock Exchange and the other to be elected by members of exchanges in the United States other than the New York Stock Exchange. Such a body would bring together a personnel which would be properly coordinated with the banking system and in other respects qualified to administer the broad supervisory power which our proposal would give. We suggest the inclusion in the power given to this body of authority to regulate the amount of margin which members of exchanges must require and maintain on customers' accounts; authority to require stock exchanges to adopt rules and regulations designed to prevent dishonest practices and all other practices which unfairly influence the prices of securities or unduly stimulate speculation; authority to fix requirements for listing of securities; authority to control pools, syndicates, and joint accounts and options intended or used to unfairly influence market prices; authority to penalize the circulation of rumors or statements calculated to induce speculative activity, and to control the use of advertising and the employment of customers' men or other employees of brokers who solicit business. This body should also have the power to study and, if need be, to adopt rules governing those instances where the exercise of the function of broker and dealer by the same person may not be compatible with fair dealing, as well as the power to adopt rules in regard to short selling, if the supervisory body should become convinced that such regulation is necessary.

We believe that these regulatory measures will prevent abuses affecting transactions on exchanges, and will at the same time not interfere with the maintenance of free and open markets for securities.

This proposal represents the considered view of the New York Stock Exchange, adopted by its governing committee, which has given me authority to present it to you. I say to you confidently that the exchange will cooperate fully and by all the means in its power to assist in the prevention of unwise or excessive speculation and abuses or bad practices affecting the stock market."

That is a statement by the president of the New York Stock Exchange. . . .

MR. NORRIS. I should like to ask the Senator from Florida the date of the statement made by Mr. Whitney, particularly with reference to the time of taking testimony in the investigation conducted by the committee. Was it near the beginning of the investigation, or did he make the statement at its close?

MR. FLETCHER. Practically at the beginning. My recollection is that it was Mr. Whitney's opening statement to our committee; and it seems to me plainly, inescapably an admission that there are practices on the exchange which are vicious and unjustified and abuses and errors which ought to be corrected. We have not quite conformed to the mechanism of making corrections that Mr. Whitney suggests. In the bill we attempt, however, to accomplish precisely the reforms which he says ought to be accomplished. Every abuse and bad practice set forth in his statement we attempt to correct in the bill.

We do not agree that a commission of seven, such as Mr. Whitney suggests, ought to have the administration of the proposed act. We have provided in the bill now before the Senate for a special commission of five, to be appointed by the President and confirmed by the Senate. The proposed commission is to be similar to that which Mr. Whitney suggests, the original bill which was introduced having provided that the administration of the act should be under the Federal Reserve Board.

The bill has been amended three times, and in the form in which it is now before the Senate, it provides that it shall be administered by a special commission of five, to be selected by the President and confirmed by the Senate.

The bill does not provide that one of the commissioners shall be named by the New York Stock Exchange and one by the other exchanges of the country. What is the use of having a regulatory body controlled by those to be regulated? It provides for a separate commission, an independent commission, to be appointed by the President and confirmed by the Senate, to consist of five members instead of seven. In other respects the recommendations of Mr. Whitney himself are met, in my judgment, by the provisions of the bill. . . .

MR. COSTIGAN. As one member of the Committee on Banking and Currency who prefers using the Federal Trade Commission as a supervising agency, I feel that it might be helpful to the Senate if the able chairman of the committee will state the reasons why he prefers a separate commission.

MR. FLETCHER. Mr. President, frankly, I favored the measure being administered by the Federal Trade Commission and the Federal Reserve Board. I favored the original bill. However, there seemed to be strong demand on the part of the members of our committee for a separate commission, and by a majority vote provision to that end was placed in the bill.

I see no reason why the Federal Trade Commission should not administer the act. I think the Federal Trade Commission have done and are doing splendid work in connection with the Securities Act, and I have every confidence in that Commission; but it was argued before our committee by those representing the exchanges that that is a commission which has had no experience in the handling of securities and that sort of thing, and that this matter ought to be handled by people who have knowledge of transactions involving the distribution and issuance of securities, and so forth. So the committee finally reached the conclusion that it was advisable to have the proposed act administered by a separate commission in connection with the Federal Reserve Board, which has to do with the handling of credit matters. . . .

MR. BARKLEY. It might be added, I think, that one of the reasons which actuated the committee, and also those outside of the committee who felt that an independent commission was preferable, was that, without any sort of reflection upon the good faith or the sincerity of the Federal Trade Commission or its ability to administer the law, necessarily it would have to be done under a subordinate bureau under the Federal Trade Commission; that it would be a sort of a lean-to under the Commission's original activities; while if a separate commission were appointed public attention would always be focused upon that separate commission. It was the theory also that the President could pick five men just as well qualified to administer the law separately as he could pick three additional men to be appointed to the Federal Trade Commission as a sort of a subcommittee of the Federal Trade Commission to administer the law.

I think those considerations had a good deal to do with the amendment substituting an independent commission for the Federal Trade Commission. It ought to be emphasized, however, that it was not done in any way through any lack of faith in the Federal Trade Commission, or any lack of appreciation of the fine work it has done heretofore; but the committee felt that a separate commission, whose duties would be centralized around the stock market and stock securities, would be in a better position to serve the public than a branch of the Federal Trade Commission. . . .

MR. GLASS. The Senator from Kentucky has clearly stated the view of those members of the committee who prefer a separate commission, except that it may be added that to some of us it was inconceivable that either the Federal Trade Commission or the Federal Reserve Board could do the work as effectively as could a separate commission appointed for the purpose, in view of the fact that the Federal Reserve Board and the Federal Trade Commission have important and complex duties which to perform them effectively, now occupy all of their time and their ingenuity. There was no purpose and no word uttered which might be construed into a reflection upon the Federal Trade Commission.

Moreover, the distinguished chairman of the committee will recall that it was not done because at one time the stock exchange wanted a separate commission. The distinguished chairman will remember very well that the commission proposed by the stock exchange was as different from the commission embodied in the bill as day is from night. The stock exchange was to have material representation of its own upon the commission it proposed, and on this commission there is to be no member of the stock exchange, and the members of the commission are textually prohibited from having any connection whatsoever, direct or indirect, with any of the stock exchanges.

Furthermore, the stock exchange did not stay hitched to its own proposal for an independent commission. Its latest proposal was that the whole thing be turned over to the Federal Reserve Board, and there are those of us on the committee who think the Federal Reserve System ought to be kept as far away from the stock-gambling business as it possibly can be gotten, and its facilities denied to those engaged in stock gambling, or, to be rather more polite, in stock speculation.

It was for those as well as other reasons which might be mentioned, that the committee thought a commission picked for the purpose by the President, to be confirmed for the purpose by the Senate, subject to removal at any time, for reason, by the President, could very much more effectively perform these duties, than would be possible if they were divided up between the Federal Reserve Board and the Federal Trade Commission. . . .

MR. COSTIGAN. In fairness should it not be said that much duplication of work will be required if a separate commission shall be established? It has been estimated that approximately half a million dollars a year may be saved if this work is carried on by the Federal Trade Commission. . . .

MR. GLASS. On the contrary, there would be infinite duplication if we adhered to the proposition presented to the committee to divide this work between the Federal Reserve Board and the Federal Trade Commission. In other words, the Federal Reserve Board has immediate and intimate access to all the reports of the Comptroller of the

Currency, who is a member of the Federal Reserve Board. In addition to that, the Federal Reserve Board has its own examiners, supplementing the work of the examiners employed by the Comptroller of the Currency. What could be the sane reason for requiring reports to be made by members of the Federal Reserve Banking System to the Federal Trade Commission, when they are examined by these two sets of examiners, and are required to make reports current and at any time to the Federal Reserve Board?

The Federal Reserve Board should not have anything in the world to do with it except to see to it scrupulously and at all times that Federal Reserve member banks do not lend their facilities for stock-speculating purposes. . . .

MR. COSTIGAN. I fear that there may be some misunderstanding of my suggestion, which was that a separate commission—my inquiry had no reference to the Federal Reserve Board—would necessarily duplicate much work relating to unfair practices and the administration of the Securities Act of 1933 now being carried on by the Federal Trade Commission. It was to the expense of that duplication alone that my remarks were directed.

MR. FLETCHER. Mr. President, in that connection I may say that, while the Federal Trade Commission has done a splendid work in connection with the Securities Act, I see no really serious objection or sound reason for supposing that a special commission, as provided in this bill, should not efficiently and satisfactorily administer the provisions of the Securities Act, and I have offered an amendment, since the bill carries with it the provision that the Securities Act shall be administered by the special commission, providing for the transfer to the commission to be set up under the terms of this bill of the administration of the Securities Act, so there will be no duplication if the Senate shall agree to my amendment.

The Securities Act itself, and the Securities Exchange Act, will be administered by this special commission. Of course, some delay would be involved. It would involve the turning over largely of the personnel and the set-up already established by the Federal Trade Commission, but these two acts, the Securities Act and this Securities Exchange Act, are so intimately connected that it seems to me advisable that they both should be administered by the same authority, and therefore I have provided in the amendment which I have offered, the transfer of the administration of the Securities Act, with all the records and everything pertaining to it, to this Commission. . . .

MR. BARKLEY. In view of the fact that the Securities Act, which has been very admirably administered by the Federal Trade Commission up to date, contemplated regulation with respect only to new securities issued after the passage of that act, and had very little relationship to securities already in existence, and in view of the fact that the bill under consideration sets up a regulation of the stock exchanges in all securities, whether old or new, the combination of the two acts under the administration of one commission would eliminate the duplication to which the Senator from Colorado has already adverted, and inasmuch as they are inseparably related, not only so far as the issue of securities may be concerned but the purchase and sale of those securities on a registered exchange, the logical thing is to have both administered by the same body.

MR. FLETCHER. That is the idea, I think, which was in the minds of the committee, and those who have done the longhand writing of this measure, and devoted weeks and weeks of study to it, and our final solution of it is that the two acts should be administered by the same body, which is provided in the amendment I referred to a moment ago. . . .

We are endeavoring, Mr. President, permanently to correct the evils and abuses which Mr. Whitney mentioned and which he admits should be and may be corrected. We may not fully succeed, but we are making an honest and fair effort in that direction, with every confidence there will result great improvement and real benefit.

We propose by this measure to establish, through Federal regulation of the methods and the mechanical functions and practices of the stock exchange, an efficient, adequate, open, and free market for the purchase and sale of securities; also to correct abuses we know of and others which may exist; to prohibit and prevent, if possible, their recurrence; to restore public confidence in the financial markets of the country; to prevent excessive speculation to the injury of agriculture, commerce, and industry; to outlaw manipulation and unfair practices and combinations by which to exploit the public and misrepresent values, such as pools, wash sales, fictitious transactions, and the like; to oblige disclosure of all material facts respecting securities traded in on the exchanges, which disclosure is essential to give the investor an adequate opportunity to evaluate his investment.

Criticism is made that we are calling upon corporations to make disclosures, and that we are thereby putting them to an enormous expense and trouble, and inquiring into affairs into which we have no business to examine. My suggestion is that if any corporation issues securities which are unfit to be certified because of what is back of them, the securities themselves are unfit to be offered to the public.

What right have brokers to appeal to the public to buy their securities if they are not willing to tell the truth about those securities? That is the whole proposition, and all we ask of them is to tell the truth.

They do not seem to want to tell the truth, in the first place, and, in the next place, they especially complain about liability for material misrepresentations which have misled the public into buying securities. They are willing to expose, to some extent, the facts behind the securities, but they do not want to be liable in case they lie about them. That seems to be the basis of the objection. All we ask in the pending bill and in the Securities Act is that they tell the truth in their registration papers, so the public may know what is behind the securities.

We undertake generally to declare the intention of Congress, and enunciate specific principles as a guide to subsequent administration. That appears particularly in section 2. We lay the foundation for this legislation in section 2 of the bill.

The exchanges themselves, when they complained about our delegation of authority, proposed a bill, and advocated even greater delegation of power in the administrative body than is provided for in the pending bill.

In connection with the propaganda which has been broadcast over the country criticizing and objecting to the provisions of the bill, most of those who criticize say, "We object to the bill in its present form." The language in hundreds of thousands of letters which have come to the Members of Congress is, "We object to the bill in its present form."

This bill has been changed three times. The original bill was revised, and the committee then gave hearings upon the revised bill. The revised bill was introduced in the House. It was never introduced in the Senate, but we considered it in the Senate as a revision of the bill S. 2693. We had hearings on it. Finally that bill was revised. We agreed to certain amendments of that bill, and then the whole question was referred to a subcommittee, and that subcommittee met and considered every word, every line, every sentence in the bill, day after day, week after week, in an honest effort to be fair to all concerned and to eliminate any harsh features that were objected to by those opposing the bill and in endeavoring to satisfy any reasonable demand in connection with the legislation.

Some complained it was too drastic here, some complained it was too drastic there, and we endeavored to straighten that out, and then the subcommittee reported to the full committee a third revision of the bill. The Senate Committee on Banking and Currency unanimously substituted that revision for the original bill, and then by a vote of 11 to 8 ordered a favorable report upon the revised bill, which is the bill S. 3420, now before the Senate.

In the propaganda which was spread all over the country—and we received numerous letters about it—the statement was made: "We understand this bill was prepared by some inexperienced young men in the departments, sometimes called 'brain trusters.' " . . . The question as to who were the authors of this bill is, I think wholly irrelevant, immaterial, and impertinent. . . .

MR. FLETCHER. . . . Upon that subject however, the effort, of course, was to arouse prejudice and discredit at the outset of the work by the allegation that inexperienced young lawyers were the authors of the bill. I would not pay any attention to that suggestion, except that publicly it was declared and announced on several occasions, as if that had anything to do with the merits, which I strongly deny. . . .

Taking up the bill by sections, in a condensed way and without considering its details, it will be found that section 1 simply gives the title.

Section 2 gives an outline of the necessity of and lays the foundation for the bill.

Section 3 gives a definition of the words, terms, and phrases contained in the bill.

Section 4 establishes the Federal exchange commission about which we have been talking, a commission to be composed of five members, selected by the President, and so forth.

Section 5 deals with transactions on unregistered exchanges.

Section 6 deals with the registration of national securities exchanges.

Section 7 deals with margin requirements.

Section 8 deals with restrictions on borrowing by members, brokers, and dealers.

Section 9 imposes a prohibition against manipulation of security prices. That is a very important section.

Section 10 provides for the regulation of the use of manipulative and deceptive devices. That is another very important section.

Section 11 imposes restrictions on floor trading by members.

Section 12 provides registration requirements for securities.

On page 30, line 10, the word "accounts" should be "accountants." We will make that change when we reach it.

Section 13 deals with periodical and other reports.

Section 14 deals with proxies.

Section 15 has to do with over-the-counter markets.

Section 16 relates to directors, officers, and principal stockholders.

Section 17 treats of accounts and records, reports, examinations of exchanges, members, and others.

Section 18 has to do with liability for misleading statements.

Section 19 provides disciplinary powers over exchanges.

Section 20 has reference to the liabilities of controlling persons.

Section 21 has reference to investigations, injunctions, and prosecution of offenses.

Section 22 relates to hearings by the Commission.

Section 23 has reference to the public character of information.

Section 24 provides a court review of orders.

Mr. President, a very comprehensive report, I think, has been submitted by the committee. That report is on the desks of Senators, and I suggest that, if they have not already done so, they read that report, which goes into a very full explanation of the whole bill and analyzes it section by section.

Section 25 has reference to unlawful representations.

Section 26 has to do with the jurisdiction of offenses and suits.

Section 27 refers to the effect on existing law.

Section 28 deals with the validity of contracts.

Section 29 has to do with foreign securities exchanges.

Section 30 provides penalties.

Section 31 has reference to the separability of provisions.

Section 32 provides the effective date.

Mr. President, one of the practices indulged in by the exchanges is intended, as it is claimed, to protect the market for securities at least for a time after the offering, such as pegging the price of the German bonds. . . .

The practice referred to appears to be unfair, unjust, and really fraudulent, misleading the investing public. We endeavor to stop it by this measure.

Evidence before the Senate committee disclosed the case of a specialist who traded for his own account in the stocks in which he was a specialist, bidding it up or down in order to make the market, and thereby a profit to himself. He said that the result of this operation was that he was "murdered." He was a specialist in a certain stock. The theory is that people dealing in a particular stock go to a specialist to make their trades. He had orders to buy and orders to sell. We try to restrain that gentleman from taking advantage of the situation to benefit himself, and to prevent trading in the stocks in which he is a specialist and supposed to represent customers. . . .

Mr. President, it will be remembered that the stock exchange claimed the right to make its own rules and regulations, and insisted that it could prevent abuses and correct errors and was willing to attempt it, and it claimed it had been doing so.

There have been some amendments to the rules and regulations. The officials gave us some assurance that they intended to continue to work out certain reforms and make certain revisions of their rules and regulations which would effect the correction of the abuses to which I have referred.

We appealed to them to do that. We hoped they would inaugurate rules and regulations and establish practices which would overcome what Mr. Whitney so clearly stated existed in connection with the stock exchanges, practices which needed to be reformed. They promised to do that, and they did adopt some amendments to their rules which I think were helpful. But evidently—and I believe this is their own view—they are powerless to accomplish all that should be accomplished. In the first place, they have no jurisdiction except over their own members. They have no jurisdiction over outside people issuing securities. In the next place, they have not the power or authority to accomplish what they would like to see accomplished. There is, therefore, need for some regulatory body with ample power to supervise these conditions.

Mr. President, this shown by the experience, after they had assured us they were amending their rules and were working out reforms, in July and August of last year, in connection with the stocks to which I have referred, showing that these abuses, the formation of pools, the operations of the specialists, and all that sort of thing, were taking place as late as last summer, proving, I think, that the country cannot depend upon the stock exchange to bring about the reforms and the corrections which they themselves admit are necessary in order to correct vicious and unwise practices.

There are some people, of course, who say that the gambling propensity exists in nearly all men, and women as well, and that law should not interfere with its indulgence; in other words, that we cannot prevent people from gambling on the stock exchanges or anywhere else. To a large extent that is true. We cannot by law protect a fool against his folly. We cannot by law do away with gambling propensities. But we can take away the facilities and the attractions and the inducements to people to invest their money in speculative securities and really gamble. We can minimize that sort of thing.

The argument that people must gamble, that they have that impulse which they cannot control, and will gamble, simply leads to a reductio ad absurdum. If it is carried to its full extent, it means that we ought to repeal all laws against gambling in all the States; we ought to establish a lottery in the United States and let people gamble by means of a national lottery, because it is much less harmful than gambling on the stock exchange. . . .

MR. McKELLAR. I was called out today just as the Senator reached the portion of his speech in which he was discussing the question of an independent commission or the Federal Trade Commission as an enforcer of the act. Is it not true that the Federal Trade Commission already has a set-up of experts, and has it not had quite an experience in the handling of other securities, and does not the Senator believe that we would really get a more efficient enforcement of the proposed act by having it administered by the Federal Trade Commission?

MR. FLETCHER. Mr. President, as I stated while the Senator from Tennessee was out of the Chamber, my personal view was expressed in the terms of the original bill,

S. 2693, whereby the administration of the act was reposed in the Federal Trade Commission. I think that Commission has done splendidly in administering the Securities Act. It is a Commission in which I have the fullest confidence, and I have nothing but praise and commendation for what it has already accomplished.

MR. McKELLAR. I feel the same way about it. I think it has done a wonderful work.

MR. FLETCHER. But in view of many objections raised to the Federal Trade Commission administering this proposed act on the ground, as was claimed, that its members were not bankers or financiers or acquainted with the handling of securities and that sort of thing, and that those charged with its administration ought to be specially qualified men, acquainted with such transactions and experienced in stock-exchange matters to a large extent, the prevailing sentiment seemed to be that there ought to be a special commission. That was the claim, and that was the demand—that there should be a commission. Partially, I think, in response to that, but in part independent thereof, there was a large sentiment in our committee in favor of a special commission.

To my mind it does not make very much difference one way or the other. If we shall have a special commission of five, appointed by the President and confirmed by the Senate, I think we will get a very efficient and capable body to administer this act; so we provided for such a commission.

MR. McKELLAR. Mr. President, I have very great doubt about the appointment of experts in that line of business, because I am fearful that their enforcement of the act would not be so good as that of disinterested men, such as the members of the Federal Trade Commission. The House in its bill provided for the Federal Trade Commission as the enforcer of the act, and it seems to me that is a very wise provision to have contained in the bill. I have the greatest confidence in the honesty, the sincerity, and the ability of the Federal Trade Commission. I think it is a wonderful piece of machinery. It has done splendid work. In my judgment, this measure would be better enforced and more equitably enforced, if I may use that expression, in the hands of the Federal Trade Commission than if the enforcement were given over to a new commission. I have very great doubt about a new commission.

MR. FLETCHER. I am not disposed to disagree with the Senator about that. At the same time, a special commission seems to satisfy the demand and meet the approval of most people—at least, some of the critics of the original idea—and I think a special commission named by the President and approved by the Senate undoubtedly would give entire satisfaction.

MR. McKELLAR. What was the vote of the Senate committee on this subject?

MR. FLETCHER. My recollection is that there was a vote of about 2 majority in favor of the special commission. I think the vote was 10 to 8.

I believe the special commission provided for in this bill would give satisfaction to the country and meet some objections; so, accordingly, I have offered an amendment which provides for the transfer of the administration of the Securities Act to the same commission.

MR. LEWIS. Does the Senator mean to the Federal Trade Commission?

MR. FLETCHER. No; to the special commission of five.

It is claimed and it has been argued that this proposed legislation would interfere with business. Business is based on confidence. Credit is the result of confidence. Let us insure confidence by giving securities an acknowledged status and recognition by requiring them to be registered and requiring exchanges where they are dealt in to be registered by a responsible agency. Inevitably that will help business, reassure capital, and increase investments.

It is claimed that pools or trading accounts are formed to stabilize prices and maintain a steady market. This is not what the broker wants. He wishes a gyrating market, because he makes commissions on its active movement up or down. Stabilization is the last thing he wants. He is after making money.

The Securities Act has saved millions of dollars to the people—the public.

This act will save billions of dollars—that is, prevent the loss of billions of dollars. Those whose money will thus be saved are some of the people for whom we are speaking.

It is testified that one out of six may win in stock speculation. These people I should like to serve.

It is said that 93 percent of the odd-lot traders lose.

It has been said this bill will put people out of business; will adversely affect business. What business?

There can be no interference with securities exempted from this bill. What are they? See paragraph 12, page 6, of the bill.

Uncontrolled and arbitrary management of security issues, security markets, speculative pitfalls for the unwary investor, selfish and individual management of large corporations affected with a public interest must come to an end.

The principle of trusteeship in all affairs so affected with the public interest must be made dominant and effective. . . .

I want to warn the people who have flooded this country with propaganda against this bill and against legislation of this kind, misrepresenting the alleged loss to business, the alleged, harmful effect of this proposed legislation on business, the number of people who are going to lose their business, and all that sort of thing, that they will not be able to stem the tide of public opinion demanding this legislation in our country.

It has got to come. They are powerful, but they are not powerful enough to defy Congress. They are strong, but they are not strong enough to obstruct the Government. At least that is my hope and my belief, and I am convinced that unless we pass this proposed legislation now they will take on new strength and double their efforts and we will never pass it.

I feel like warning these gentlemen to this effect, "Continue your opposition and your fight and determination to have your own way, to be free absolutely from any supervision or regulation by anybody; regulate yourselves; I feel that if you persist in that struggle and that determination and that sort of fight and that sort of propaganda, the next movement that will come will be a determined and a successful effort to wipe away margins entirely from stock exchanges." That will take away from the exchanges

40 percent of their business. They will not like to see that; they will not enjoy that; but they are bringing that about, in my judgment, by their attitude respecting this proposed legislation. . . .

MR. STEIWER. Mr. President, this bill summarizes the long effort of the Senate, and its Committee on Banking and Currency, to evolve legislation designed to prevent the abuses which have grown up in stock-market operations in this country.

I regard this proposed legislation as one of the most important measures that Congress has had before it for a very long time.

Senators know that we are not dealing merely with a few brokers. We are not dealing exclusively with a few members of stock exchanges, nor with the stock exchanges themselves, nor with dealers who engage in transactions in securities. We are dealing in a very vital way with enormously large interests. It is said that the corporate wealth represented in securities in this country is more than one third of all the wealth of the people of the Nation. We are dealing with the sources of credit, and with the machinery by which credit is used and enjoyed by the business institutions of the country. We are dealing with the forces which relate directly to recovery and to the maintenance of employment of the people. We are dealing with the hopes and aspirations of institutions to enlarge and to carry on their affairs and expand to meet the new conditions which we believe may come when the day of betterment shall have arrived in the business of the Nation.

In the consideration of legislation so important we are entitled to a correct understanding of the theory and philosophy and purpose of the bill.

As I address the Senate today I am obliged to express some dissent from statements heretofore made in the debate. I express that dissent with some little reluctance. I think the members of the committee probably more than the other Members of the Senate realize what a patient, constructive, able, and persistent effort has been made by the chairman of the committee and by others who have cooperated with him in trying to bring to a close the important enactments involved in this bill. I wish, therefore, that I could agree with the chairman entirely in the statement which he made to the Senate upon yesterday; and in the main I do agree with him.

With some little exception so far as the bill relates to brokers and to dealers, to members of exchanges, and to the exchanges themselves, I am in accord with the work which the committee has done; and yet, in spite of my deep interest in the subject and of the fact that I cooperated with the majority of the committee in most of the important issues that came up in the extended hearings during the last 2 years and supported the employees of the committee in the great effort which they made in order to develop the facts essential to this subject, in spite of my continuing interest when the bill was presented for final consideration before the Committee on Banking and Currency, I was one of the members of the committee who voted against reporting the bill out to the floor of the Senate.

I wish now that the bill could have been retained in the committee. I think a week or two weeks more spent in its consideration would have been of great help in arriving at a proper solution of the many problems involved, and that it would have resulted in a very constructive service to the country. In that my view did not prevail. I make no complaint about it now; and I refer to it merely because I want Senators to know that I am not approaching this subject at this time in a spirit of antagonism toward the legislation, but I do so in the hope that even yet some helpful amendments may be made.

I realize how difficult it is to invite and to command attention to amendments proposed upon the floor of the Senate after one of the great committees has given full and careful consideration to a measure; but I implore Senators to bear with us just a little longer, that we may reveal all the things that are hidden in the bill.

The bill is not alone a stock exchange bill. It is not alone a bill to restrain and regulate brokers and dealers and to control over-the-counter transactions in securities. It is a bill which relates, in addition to the stock exchanges and to the brokers and the over-the-counter markets, to the corporations of the country, and to the internal management of the affairs of those corporations.

It has in it potentialities that may cause some of us to hesitate, regardless of our faith and hope that this kind of legislation will be helpful in protecting American investors against wrongdoing.

The bill has its relation, as I say, to corporations and to their internal management. It affects credit. It affects banking institutions. It provides for formulation of rules and regulations which finally will have their effect and bearing everywhere; not alone upon the stock exchanges, but upon corporations, the stockholders of corporations, upon the officers and directors of corporations, upon investors in corporate securities, upon those who may loan and possibly those who have extended loans to corporations.

Upon yesterday it was said by at least two Senators in the preliminary debate upon this measure that the provisions of the proposed law dealing with corporations were included in the bill merely to require corporations to make truthful disclosure of their business. That statement was reiterated; and even the chairman of the committee—who, I know, wants to be fair, and who has conducted this whole proceeding with a very remarkable showing of even temper and patience, and a very fine disposition to be just to all concerned—even the chairman of the committee yesterday said that the provisions of the bill relating to corporations were for the purpose of requiring them to tell the truth, and that seemingly they did not want to tell the truth, and that that was the reason why they were objecting to the bill. It was stated also that a great propaganda had gone forth, that the propaganda had been misdirected and misconceived, and that under it objections were being made to sections of the bill that had been deleted or changed by committee amendment. It was said that some 3 or 4 different editions of the bill had been printed, and that was true, and that the objections in many cases were laid to the first edition and not to the subsequent editions.

Mr. President, with these statements I am to a considerable extent in disagreement. It is true that some of the objections have been inspired by brokers who have circularized their customers, and it is true that those customers have sent in form letters, and they have sent in series of letters more or less alike, and sometimes identical in purport and meaning; and it is true that in some cases the objections have been made to provisions of the bill that were eliminated by the committee as long as a month ago. It is not true, however, that that character of objection is the only character of objection made by the business institutions of the country. Upon yesterday, or upon the evening before, a statement was made by Mr. Bell, of New York, representing a great group of most responsible business institutions. I have it here and shall read from it one or two very short statements.

Among other things, referring to the group with which he is identified, Mr. Bell said:

It will endeavor to awaken every business man to the fact, apparently little realized, that while ostensibly this legislation is intended only to eliminate recognized speculative abuses from the securities exchanges, actually more than 450,000 firms through the land with no Wall Street connections would be brought under the strangling regulation of a Federal bureau. . . .

MR. COUZENS. I think it would be enlightening to the Senate if the Senator would tell us just in what manner the 450,000 concerns not connected with Wall Street are affected by the bill.

MR. STEIWER. I shall be glad to do that as I go along. I do not know that Mr. Bell is right in his theory that all of them are affected, but very vast numbers are affected; and I am quite certain that if Senators will remain open-minded, even in my humble way and with my poor talents I can convince practically all the Senators in the Chamber that a very vast amount of corporate business in this country is affected by this bill which the people think was written for the regulation and control of Wall Street and of the stock exchanges. . . .

Let me refer to the bill, and, if Senators will be patient, let me call attention to some of the things which I feel justify the criticism I am making. I will omit a discussion of the provisions sections by section and line by line, because presentation of such a discussion would be a very wearying and irksome task.

Section 12 of the bill is the section which provides for the registration of securities upon the national securities exchanges. It is termed in phrase of penalty, as are many other sections of the bill. That is to say, it makes transactions unlawful unless they are done in a certain way.

The particular thing that is made unlawful here is dealing on a national securities exchange by a member or a broker or a dealer in any security which is not exempted, unless the registration of that security has been effected in accordance with the provisions of the act and with rules and regulations made thereunder.

The bill proceeds to outline the steps which are necessary on the part of the corporation in order to make the registration effective. The conditions prescribed by the rules and regulations of the commission must be met or the registration cannot be effected and the corporation may find no lawful market for its securities in the stock exchanges of this country.

The first of the conditions to which I invite attention is paragraph 1 of subsection (b) of section 12. It provides, in effect, that the issuer must furnish to the commission and to the exchange an agreement to comply with the provisions of this measure. I want to interrupt myself there to say that there can be no possible objection to that, and I make none.

It must furnish an agreement to comply with the provisions of this measure and any amendment thereto "and with the rules and regulations made or to be made thereunder." . . .

MR. COUZENS. May I ask the Senator, in that connection, to read the language beginning on line 11 of that page, which considerably modifies the assertion the Senator is making, in my opinion?

MR. STEIWER. I am reading from line 11. That is where I started to read.

MR. COUZENS. The Senator skipped some of it.

MR. STEIWER Does the Senator refer to the language in parentheses, which provides, "which shall not be construed as a waiver of any constitutional right"?

MR. COUZENS. Yes.

MR. STEIWER. I did not read that because I regard it as wholly ineffective and believe it would be of no value to the corporation at all, unless the rule or regulation made at a subsequent time should deprive it of some right, for instance, should deprive it of its property without just compensation, or deprive it of property without due process of law. Unless the rule or regulation effected a deprivation of that kind, there would be no practical protection given to the issuer by the language contained in the parentheses. I assure the Senator that I have given the language very critical and careful attention. I hope Senators will believe me when I say that I would not be making the criticism which I make of this bill unless I were acting quite advisedly. My interest in the measure is such that I should like very much to correct it and make it the kind of a bill I had hoped originally it might be, namely, a bill to regulate effectually the stock exchanges of this country, and dealings in securities, without at the same time imposing blue-sky restrictions upon the corporations, which, in a practical sense, they are going to find great difficulty in meeting.

Mr. President, I am told that some corporations have already indicated that they cannot meet the conditions imposed by the bill. Either their director will not do it, and will restrain the executive officers, or the stockholders will not do it, and will restrain both the executive officers and the directors. Many corporations will be disinclined to permit their officers to sign a contract to meet some condition, which may in the long run be extremely oppressive and extremely costly, without knowing what that condition is to be.

I am asked by a Senator sitting near me if I am referring to the rules and regulations. I am referring, of course, to the provision that corporations are obliged to sign an agreement to comply with provisions of the rules and regulations made or to be made thereunder. I am not particularly concerned about the exaction of an agreement to comply with regulations already made. A corporation can determine, if it is intelligently handled, whether or not it wants to meet conditions which are already known, but this bill creates in the commission an absolute and practically unlimited right to make regulations whenever it may desire to make them, and to change them, or by amendment to extend them, to make them without notice, and to make changes without notice, and to put them into effect forthwith, or to provide that they shall be put into effect at a subsequent time. The executives of corporations can have no way to measure the practical effect of the exaction of an agreement to abide by regulations which are not known and which, in their very nature, cannot be known. . . .

MR. BLACK. I understood the Senator to make the statement that they would have to agree to abide by any regulation which might be made, whatever it might be, whether it was good or bad, whether it was legal or illegal. I do not so read the provision.

MR. STEIWER. If the regulation operates to invade their constitutional rights, they are not bound by it.

MR. BLACK. Or they have a right to contest the validity of any rule or regulation.

The Senator is a lawyer, and let me ask him a question. All that is to be required is an agreement on the part of the corporations to abide by any regulation which does not invade their constitutional rights, and they reserve the right to contest the validity of any rule or regulation. Let us suppose they did not enter into such an agreement. Would we not have the same right to enact a law, and would they not have to obey it? Would they be surrendering anything by signing an agreement? In other words, all they agree to is that they will abide by those regulations which they cannot strike down for their invalidity. They would have to abide by the regulations anyway.

MR. STEIWER. They would have to abide by a change in law if Congress enacted a valid piece of legislation, of course, but that is the risk every business man takes, whether he lists his securities or not, and whether he registers securities upon a stock exchange or not. Business in the United States, I am happy to say, has at least some degree of confidence in Congress, and I do not believe that, generally speaking, business is restrained by fear of oppressive legislation. But we are dealing now with a new instrumentality. We are asked to clothe a commission with enormous powers, and we are told on every hand that business objects to those powers, that they are afraid of what may be done by the commission.

May I say to the Senator that I do not suppose it makes any difference as a practical matter, whether a corporation is actually hurt or whether it merely thinks it is going to be hurt. A state of mind can produce a depression. A state of mind can produce timidity and prevent corporations from taking aggressive steps toward the carrying out of their business enterprises, and their disinclination to go forward from either cause is equally hurtful to the American people.

MR. BLACK. The point I was asking the Senator about was this: I cannot see that it is material whether they make the agreement to abide by the regulation or not. That part of it is immaterial, because they would have to abide by it, anyway, if it were legally and validly enacted. If the Senator is taking the position that we should not vest the commission with the power of issuing regulations, that is quite a different matter. But, as I have read the bill—and this is the reason why I have interrupted the Senator—I cannot see that it is material at all that they agree in advance, either to accept or not to accept the regulations. Is the Senator opposing giving the commission the right to issue regulations, and is he favoring the idea of putting in the statute itself all regulations instead of entrusting any of those powers to the commission?

MR. STEIWER. No, I am not, Mr. President. In the very nature of things the commission must have the authority and the right to issue some rules and regulations.

But both civil and criminal penalties will be exacted under the provisions of the bill for violation of the contract which is required as a condition precedent for the registration of a security. Both civil and criminal penalties are exacted, which therefore brings about a most unusual situation, with unusual penalties, and because they are so unusual in both their civil and criminal aspects, prudent people may not be willing to assume liabilities which they can avoid.

MR. BLACK. Then, if I understand the Senator, he favors giving the Commission the right to issue valid regulations?

MR. STEIWER. I think it is inevitably necessary.

MR. BLACK. Very well. The bill provides that the commission shall have the right to issue valid regulations, and it also requires—why, I confess I cannot see, because I think it is wholly surplusage—the company which puts out its securities to agree to abide by those regulations. Whether the company agrees to abide by those regulations or not is immaterial, if we concede that which the Senator concedes, that we should vest in the commission the prerogative of issuing valid regulations. When those regulations are issued, and they are valid, the company issuing securities must abide by such regulations, whether it desires to do so or not; whether it is agreed in advance to do so or not, because it would be the exercise of a legal privilege vested in the commission by the bill. I cannot see—and that is the reason I am interrogating the Senator in detail on that point—if he agrees that the commission should have the power to issue valid regulations, what difference it makes whether we ask the corporations to agree to abide by them or not, because whether they agree to abide by them or not, if they are valid regulations they must abide by them.

MR. STEIWER. Mr. President, I am not entirely in disagreement with what the Senator is saying, and as proof of that I propose at the proper time to offer an amendment striking from the bill this requirement for agreement, because I can see that every proper authority which the commission needs may be exercised through regulations, and that every proper penalty which should be exacted in order to bring about compliance with this law can be had in the event of violation of the regulations.

This required agreement is entirely unneccesary and is another oppressive provision from which business shrinks.

My argument in this respect, and in others that I shall mention in just a moment, is entirely for the purpose, if I have not made that clear already, of seeking to have the Senate join with me in amending the bill by taking out some of the requirements which are causing responsible business men to worry and to hesitate, and things which will make them reluctant to resort to the facilities provided under the bill.

MR. BLACK. Then if I understand the Senator, he desires to give to the commission the right to issue regulations, and he concedes that if the regulations are valid, the issuing company must abide by them, whether they agree or not. Then what injury can any company suffer from agreeing to do something which it will be obliged to do anyhow?

MR. STEIWER. Because, Mr. President, the contract submits the issuing corporation to penalties, civil and criminal, which would not otherwise exist, and, therefore, will restrain it from attempting to register its securities upon the exchange, and it is important from every standpoint that we make it possible for the corporation to list its securities.

What I am saying goes to the wisdom of this provision. To me it seems most unwise to exact additional penalties, civil and criminal, when it is not necessary to do so, in order to bring about the proper administration of the law.

MR. BLACK. Mr. President I cannot see that any additional penalty is imposed. The Senator from Oregon takes the position that he favors giving the commission the right to issue valid regulations. The agreement is not a penalty. The agreement is simply a statement made by the company that "we will do that which we will have to do anyhow"—which is to abide by valid regulations. Is there any provision of the bill which adds any penalties which are not imposed by the regulations themselves?

MR. STEIWER. I think so, Mr. President.

MR. BLACK. Where?

MR. STEIWER. I should like to come to that in due time. I think that is true. . . .

In section 12, now under discussion, there is a long category of requirements which all relate in one way or the other to the submission of information to the commission concerning the corporation. It is impossible upon even a careful reading of the requirements of this section, to know exactly what information will be required of the corporation. Most of these provisions are more or less permissive. The power vested in the commission is to make rules and regulations which the commission may deem necessary or appropriate in the public interest, or for the protection of investors in respect to a certain listed category of proposals.

The objection was raised before the committee that the commission could require the divulging of trade secrets. The committee provided against that by appropriate language. But there is still in this section an absolutely unrestrained power in the commission to require of corporations information which, although not falling within the definition of trade secrets, is nevertheless very confidential in its character. There is still in this section the complete and full possibility that the commission may at any time require of any corporation disclosure of facts which will be very beneficial to the competitor of that corporation. There is still here the possibility that irreparable damage will be done, and because the corporation never can know what the requirements are going to be, and never can know what the effect of the rules and regulations may be on its particular business, the corporation, in the very nature of the situation, is going to be reluctant to assume this obligation.

Then, Mr. President, there is a third provision that to me is just as important as the other two, and that is the provision pertaining to periodic reports. I refer now to section 13 of the bill, commencing on page 33. For illustration of the kind of information that may be exacted, let me read from the bill. Commencing at line 17, we find this statement as to the information and reports to be furnished:

(1) Such information and documents as the Commission may require to keep reasonably current the information and documents filed pursuant to section 12.

Just what documents, however, are to be filed pursuant to section 12 we do not know; the corporations do not know. They may not know until long after they make their registration. So just what is required of them in order to keep that information current surpasses human imagination and ingenuity. There is no way to know.

So, too, in the next section there is a requirement as to reports. I read now from line 20, on the same page:

(2) Such annual reports as the Commission may prescribe, certified if required by the rules and regulations of the Commission by independent public accountants—

I have no particular objection to that, but listen to what follows:

Such quarterly reports as the Commission may prescribe; and such other reports as the Commission may deem essential in special circumstances.

So, Mr. President, with respect to the question of submitting reports, one may say, just as has been said with respect to the question of information required upon the registration of securities, there is no boundary; there is no little definition; there is no restraint upon the commission; and, what is vastly more hurtful to business, there is no way for a corporation to know in advance what kind of reports are going to be exacted of it. If the corporation is prudently managed, if its officers are conservative and capable, even though the corporation may desire to abide with every law in the land and to conduct the most legitimate and most honorable business possible it may, for competitive reasons or for other reasons, hesitate to attempt to meet the requirements of this section.

The provisions of sections 12 and 13 lay their heavy effect upon the corporation and upon the stockholders of the corporation, but not upon the stock exchange, nor upon the members of the exchanges, nor upon brokers and dealers upon those exchanges. . . .

MR. BARKLEY. Do I understand the Senator from Oregon to object to any except annual reports as provided in the first clause of the provision?

MR. STEIWER. I have not said that.

MR. BARKLEY. The Senator, as I understood, objected to the requirements as to quarterly reports and such other reports.

MR. STEIWER. I have not said that. What I object to is the unlimited uncertainty in the bill and not the requirements as to reports that are clearly and unmistakably defined by its terms.

MR. BARKLEY. The Senator realizes that it is impossible for Congress to know in advance just what information ought to be required of any corporation that lists its securities on the stock exchange and holds them cut to the general public of this country as being worthy of their investment. The Senator also knows that within the period of a year, and frequently within a period of a few months, the financial and economic and responsible conditions of any corporation may change; so that it is in the interest of the investing public that some agency of the Government should have the power to gather such information or require such reports as may keep the investing public advised as to the wisdom of an investment in an offered security; and as between the interest of the whole public, 125,000,000 people, on the one side, and the interest of the corporation that holds its securities out to those 125,000,000 on the other, for fear that some information might leak out that would be of benefit to a competitor, certainly we must not lose sight of the interest of the entire people who would be invited by the mere listing of a stock on an exchange to invest their money in it.

MR. STEIWER. The statement just made by the Senator, in my opinion, is a very excellent argument for leaving the "blue sky" provisions out of this bill in their entirety. If Congress cannot act intelligently with respect to it—

MR. BARKLEY. If what I said is any argument for any such contention as that, then, I was beside my own purpose very widely in making the suggestion.

MR. STEIWER. I will permit the Senator to withdraw his argument, if he wants to do so.

MR. BARKLEY. I will withdraw the Senator's interpretation of it.

MR. STEIWER. If the Congress cannot know what the requirements ought to be, how are we to assume that a commission will know better than we know, and how are we going to assume, even though the information is required, that it will protect the foolhardly or improvident investor? In nearly every State in the Union we have "blue sky" laws and nearly every corporation that has worked a fraud in recent years in this country was organized somewhere under the "blue sky" laws of some State. It has been shown, and demonstrated beyond any question of doubt, that laws of that kind, although intended for the finest purpose in the world, often lull the investor to his injury, to a false sense of security rather than give him the protection the Senator and I would like to give him if we could have our way.

MR. BARKLEY. In that connection, though, it ought to be kept in mind that all the "blue sky" laws, including the national "blue sky" law, apply almost exclusively to the issue of securities initially. They do not require that they shall be followed up from year to year and month to month in order to advise the public of the condition of the company or the stock and the advisability of it as an investment after the issue in the first instance has been approved by the authority of the State. That is why it seems to me to be necessary in any law proposing to regulate a national stock exchange that not only shall the condition of the security and the responsibility of the company, when it issues the security, be supervised, but there shall be some supervision in the way of gathering information from time to time in order that those who may want to buy the security after it has been issued or buy other securities which are not controlled by the Security Act of 1933 may have a medium of obtaining information as to the wisdom of the investment.

MR. STEIWER. The Senator states an ideal, and with his ideal I am thoroughly in agreement, but if in the application of laws intended to effectuate that ideal we drive people from the stock exchange, if we make it impossible to list securities, if we make it essential, in the judgment of the responsible heads of honest institutions, to take their securities elsewhere for sale, what possible gain will there be to the great American public for whom the Senator now speaks? Does not the Senator know that already, under the Securities Act of 1933, there has been a flight from the money centers of this country; that Montreal and other exchanges are offering inducements for Americans to bring their securities there, and already they have gone there in large number? They go to the place where we have no authority at all; the financing is done outside our own country, possibly with American money, but, at the same time, we have a flight of the business in the sale of securities, we have a flight of American money; we lose the whole transaction; we lose the whole control; and we render no service to our people, because when we lay down restrictions that are so stringent that business men will not meet them, then we defeat the object we seek to attain.

MR. BARKLEY. We have heard a good deal about money taking flight from American securities because of the act of 1933, but I have yet to be shown by any proof that would pass in any ordinary court that any corporation has refused to issue securities because of any requirement of the act of 1933.

MR. STEIWER. I think that proof can be had.

MR. BARKLEY. One of the things we required in that act was that dummy directors should not hold their names out to the public to induce men, women, and children to invest their money in securities because they happened to be in the board of directors. There has been a propaganda ever since that law was enacted to repeal or revise that section so that men still might hold themselves out as a window dressing and invite investment without any responsibility on their part for the conduct of the business.

I appreciate that that law, in all probability, is not perfect, and that there ought to be some amendment to it, but I have not very much patience with the idea that men who, in the name of corporations, issue stock or securities and invite the public to invest in them, ought not to let the public know the truth about those stocks and those securities before they invest their money in them. That is all we have done. If the truth is going to make a security unsalable, then the truth ought to be known and the people protected from the investment of their money in unsound securities. . . .

MR. STEIWER. Let me answer my friend from Kentucky in all sincerity by saying that, in my humble judgment, the requirement of truth has never hurt any corporation; I agree with the Senator as to that; it is not the requirement of telling the truth that has prevented the sale of securities under the act of 1933. That act has operated restrictively, however, and it is not because of the requirement of telling the truth nor is it because it excludes the dummy director from the boards, but it has operated restrictively because we have placed liabilities upon the underwriters and upon the directors and other signers of the registration statements that need not have been as severe as they were. We made one man responsible in that act for another man's error, and prudent men would not assume that kind of a liability.

MR. BARKLEY. In other words, we have made the principal responsible for the acts of his agent?

MR. STEIWER. Oh, no; the principal was already responsible for the act of his agent; we have made one agent responsible for another agent's conduct, for they are all agents of the corporation. I had not intended to get into a discussion of the Securities Act of 1933 at this time. I was for that act; I voted for it; I helped to prepare it; and I was just as much interested in that act as I am in this one; but I think it ought to be held up as a horrible example.

Under the guise of writing a perfectly good law for a perfectly fine purpose, we wrote into the law some provisions that were hurtful; and in this bill, under the guise of writing a perfectly good law for a perfectly fine purpose, if we do not watch our step, we are going to permit the enactment of some provisions that will operate against recovery from the depression. I very earnestly suggest this, and urge it upon the Senate, because I think it is perfectly simple to remedy those restrictive provisions and leave the bill to apply to stock exchanges, with possibly some temperate and safe regulation of corporations, so that a great good may be done without injury. Then, as time goes by, if we learn from our experience that we can add further requirement to the law, we may all unite in bringing about proper amendments. I submit that it is better to go not quite far enough and be safe than it is to go too far, as we did with respect to the Securities Act, and then be obliged to retreat after we find that we have worked injury upon our country. . . .

MR. BARKLEY. Coming back to the suggestion made a while ago that the Senator is in favor of a bill regulating the practices of the exchange, but that he doubts the wisdom of going any further than that in the way of regulating the corporations whose stocks might be on the exchange, am I to understand the Senator to mean that he favors simply the enactment of a law regulating the practices and methods of the stock exchange by which stocks are bought and sold, and that he would not require any showing as to the condition of a company whose stocks were bought and sold, or its financial methods or reliability or responsibility?

MR. STEIWER. No; that is not my ultimate object. I think initially we could very well confine ourselves to the control of the exchanges and to the regulation of the procedure and practices upon the exchange and in the over-the-counter markets, with such requirements as to corporations as they can readily meet. At future sessions of the Congress we may supplement these requirements with others. Initially, I would favor a start with a bill that would do good and not do evil.

To answer further the Senator's question, I think we are all at fault. I think the whole Congress of the United States is as fault in that we did not some years ago make a more serious effort to deal with the manipulative and other wrongful practices upon the stock exchange. I think long ago Congress should have dealt with the question of margin requirements and short sales, of wash sales and pools, and all the other abuses that accompanied especially the great boom of 1929. I think we are all subject to some criticism in that we did not recognize our responsibility and make a more vigorous effort to deal with those abuses.

But now, because the whole country is aroused to the nature and extent of those abuses and knows how disastrous was the speculative orgy of 1929 and what injury it did to the country, there is a clamor everywhere for the legislation. In that feeling, of course, we all share. However, the danger of the situation is that while we are endeavoring to deal with the evils, we write a "blue sky" law that goes too far; and because it goes too far it will be hurtful, and instead of bringing to the country unmitigated good it will bring both good and evil at the same time. . . .

THE PRESIDING OFFICER. (Mr. Pope in the chair). Does the Senator from Oregon yield to the Senator from Alabama?

MR. STEIWER. I yield.

MR. BLACK. I have been very much interested in the Senator's discussion. I know the usual care he gives to the consideration of these questions. I have listened carefully to ascertain, if I could, what it is he fears about the report that is to be required. I gather that he would not strike this section from the bill, which requires reports to be made of certain facts. I listened carefully to learn what it is the Senator fears a company might be asked for that would do it injury, because, if there is such a thing, I am frank to say I think it should be excluded.

I have read the itemized statement of things which are to be called for in the reports. I think I am sufficiently familiar with the Senator's political philosophy to believe he will not object to a single one of those items as they are to be called for in the report. May I ask the Senator if he does object to either of paragraphs A, B, C, D, E, or F?

MR. STEIWER. On what page?

MR. BLACK. On page 29. That is the section which the Senator said is too uncertain.

MR. STEIWER. I was discussing section 13.

MR. BLACK. I understand, but the Senator first discussed section 12, and then section 13, which states the documents or details required in a general way under section 12. The Senator in the first place agrees with me and others that the Commission must have authority to prescribe rules and regulations. Therefore he does not intend to have the bill set out specifically every requirement that ought to be imposed. Section 12 sets out certain information which the public ought to have. The first requirement is with reference to the organization, financial structure, nature, operation of business and so forth. I cannot believe the Senator would object to that.

MR. STEIWER. Let us see if the Senator likes that as well as he believes he does. What is the meaning of the requirement of information concerning the "operations of business"?

MR. BLACK. If there is any particular part of the operations the Senator believes ought to be eliminated, I think an amendment should be offered to that effect. I looked at an income-tax report a few days ago. I shall not give any name because I have no right to do so. The man who made the report had sold $1,000,000 worth of the stock of the corporation. He was supposed to put on one side the amount he received for the stock and on the other side the amount he paid for it. The amount stated as paid for it was a "goose egg." The amount he received was $1,000,000. I think that is a part of the operations of the business.

That stock was sold on the stock exchange. The people who paid 100 cents on the dollar for the stock did not know that that man received $1,000,000 worth of stock for nothing. I think, and I believe the Senator agrees with me, that information ought to be reported. That is one of the things that would be included.

MR. STEIWER. I am sorry I am unable to follow the Senator. It seems to me if that stock was worth $1,000,000, it would not make any difference what the trader paid for it when he got it. He set forth the information in his income-tax return. Of course, if he got the stock for nothing and sold it for $1,000,000, he made $1,000,000 profit.

In the consideration of an income-tax return honestly made, I do not see where the public should be interested in the amount paid for the stock.

MR. BLACK. Let us suppose the Senator is one of the untold millions who want to buy some stock. He concludes that he wants to buy some stock in this particular company to which I have been referring. He assumes, when he buys the stock which is sold on the stock exchange, that every other stockholder who had stock issued to him paid hard, honest dollars for it, just as he did. It develops with reference to that particular company that the stock has been issued to the insiders without the payment of a dime by them. The Senator would have no way to find that out unless the parties involved were required to make a report.

I am sure if the Senator were paying money out of his pocket for stock in that company, he would feel that he had the right to know if there had been $20,000,000 worth of that stock out of a total of $55,000,000 issued for nothing—and there was more than that—and which represented no investment.

MR. STEIWER. The Senator pays me too great a compliment when he assumes I might buy $1,000,000 worth of stock.

MR. BLACK. Oh, no; I do not. The Senator could easily buy $1,000,000 worth of stock if he paid nothing for it, like the man did to whom I have referred.

MR. STEIWER. Let us discuss the bill. The language to which the Senator calls attention would not cover the case the Senator has in mind. This language provides that information shall be furnished about the organization, financial structure, nature, and operations of the business; it does not deal with stock manipulation.

MR. BLACK. That is right.

MR. STEIWER. If the issuer corporation were filing its return under section 12 it would file a return of its own operations. The Senator has not disclosed to us how this gentleman got the million dollars' worth of stock.

MR. BLACK. I shall be glad to do so, and to show the Senator that it does affect the interests of the company, and the public ought to have known about it—not only that case, but numerous others. This man came in just as the company did that, put in $1,000, and 2 years later the insiders had stock in the company issued to them at a value that day of $75,000,000. This man came in by the manipulation of certain property at more than its value, and, as a matter of fact, so much more that it did not cost him a nickel.

MR. BARKLEY. Mr. President, will the Senator yield there to the suggestion that the issue of that much stock for nothing, which brings not a dollar into the treasury of the company, materially affects the value of all the stock for which people have paid their money.

MR. BLACK. The Senator is entirely right.

MR. BARKLEY. They are interested in whether or not a company has given away a million dollars' worth of stock for which it received nothing in return.

MR. BLACK. Not only that, but let me call the Senator's attention to the scheme which was adopted in that company and numerous others. I would not refer to one only. They would buy property which had practically no value, and then sell it to the company for a hundred thousand times its then value. If they had been required to report to the public, through the exchange, the organization and financial structure of the company, the prospective stockholder would have known that he was asked to pay a dollar for a dollar's worth of stock, while another man received a million dollars' worth of the same stock for nothing, thereby decreasing the value of the prospective purchaser's holdings.

I think I know enough about the Senator from Oregon to know that he does not want to fail to require any kind of report that would protect the public. I listened carefully to see if the Senator objected to any part of the report that is required. If he did object to any particular clause of it, I fail to hear it; and what I desire to know is which part of the report that is required to be made does the Senator object to? If none, is there something the Senator thinks might be exacted that should be protected? If so, let the Senator offer an amendment to strike that out; but let us not strike down the whole thing on the mere vague statement that it requires an uncertainty.

That is my point. If the Senator has any suggestions, I should be glad to vote for the exceptions that he thinks ought to be made, if I agree with him in his viewpoint; but I do think it is rather a general indictment to say that the measure is uncertain without pointing out which one of these things he objects to.

MR. STEIWER. Evidently I failed to make myself understood by the Senator from Alabama.

I referred first in that section to the subsection commencing upon line 11 of page 28. I objected there because of the necessity of complying with future unknown regulations, and with respect to these others, I made the same objection that they introduce an element of uncertainty that will deter corporations from listing their stock.

I direct the Senator's attention to the fact that on page 29 we find a provision that such information shall be furnished by the issuer—

As the Commission may, by rules and regulations, require as necessary or appropriate in the public interest or for the protection of investors—

In regard to certain things. There is no limitation upon the commission in this bill. They may make rules today. They may change them tomorrow. They may make them at 12 o'clock, and make them effective forthwith, or make them effective at 1 o'clock, as the case may be. Except on the part of the great stock exchanges, who can keep themselves advised currently and up to the moment, there is no way for the ordinary business man to know what the regulations may be today, and there is less opportunity for him to know what they may be next week.

MR. BLACK. Mr. President, will the Senator yield there?

MR. STEIWER. Yes; of course.

MR. BLACK. I understand that what the Senator says is true that the commission can change those regulations from hour to hour, or from week to week, or from month to month; but the Senator has explicitly stated he favors giving to the commission the power to issue regulations. That is the reason why I asked him the question in the beginning.

MR. STEIWER. Mr. President, the Senator has not paid very close attention to my statements.

MR. BLACK. I thought I did.

MR. STEIWER. I do not know that I objected to a single provision upon page 29 to which the Senator now is attaching importance. I did discuss the language on page 28, and then I proceeded to discuss the requirements in the matter of disclosures on page 33; and now, if the Senator will permit me, I desire to go further and discuss the requirements on page 41.

MR. BLACK. Before the Senator gets away from the matter of uncertainty, would he object to pointing out any particular thing that he anticipates might be called for under the bill that would be injurious to the company, and that an amendment should take away from the commission the power to require the company to disclose?

MR. STEIWER. I shall be glad to do so.

Under the guise of getting information concerning the operations of the business the commission may conceivably ask for information which, if published, would absolutely destroy the company, not because the company had done anything wrongful, not because it was a company of the kind to which the Senator referred a little while ago, but because the disclosure would tell a competing company the exact nature of the company's business.

MR. BLACK. What information?

MR. STEIWER. Information concerning its credit status, we will say; information concerning its inventories, concerning its contracts, concerning the people with whom it proposed to do business, or those with whom it had been doing business; every manner of information by which one great institution may profit at the expense of another. Corporations may be wrong in being fearful of the provisions contained in this bill granting wide discretionary powers to the commission. I am not arguing too hard on that particular point. I said a while ago that they might be wrong; but if the effect of the measure is to restrain them, the evil to the country is just as great as if they were right in their judgment with respect to requirements that might be made.

MR. BYRNES. Mr. President—

THE PRESIDING OFFICER. Does the Senator from Oregon yield to the Senator from South Carolina?

MR. BLACK. May I ask the Senator, first, another question?

MR. STEIWER. Certainly.

MR. BLACK. The first thing the Senator anticipated the company might be compelled to divulge is their credit, something they owed somebody. Is not a stockholder entitled to know that?

MR. STEIWER. Oh, the stockholder already knows. This does not affect stockholders.

MR. BLACK. I am talking about prospective purchasers of the company's stock. Suppose, for instance, they had outstanding half a million dollars worth of stock, and owed somebody a million dollars: It might be that their competitor would be glad to know that; but, because their competitor might be glad to know that, should a man be permitted to go ahead and buy stocks blindly, without having that revealed through the exchange when acted as the agent in the sale?

MR. STEIWER. It will be revealed to the exchange, Mr. President. I think those things are usually revealed to the exchange now, without any statute. . . .

MR. BYRNES. Will not the Senator agree that as to the instances referred to by him, section 23 would safeguard the corporation? In that language it is provided that there can be no disclosure of such information unless it is in the public interest, or for the protection of investors, and does not reveal trade secrets. Then it is further provided that if the corporation filing the statement shall make written objections to the disclosure of the information, there must be a private hearing and order, from which order there is provision for an appeal to the courts.

MR. STEIWER. Cannot the Senator see how insecure that kind of a provision is when the statement has just been made by a man having so good a mind as the Senator from Alabama that practically all this information ought to be disclosed for the good of the stockholders and investors? The commission may take the same view that the Senator from Alabama takes; and if the commission takes the same view that the Senator takes in just one instance, there will be no more corporations in America desirous of listing their stock upon any exchange.

MR. BYRNES. Mr. President, if the Senator will yield further, even if it be assumed that the Senator from Alabama, serving upon the commission, held that view, the language of section 23 is that if the Senator from Oregon, for example, held the opposite view, and he were president of the corporation, he could object to the disclosure of the information, demand a hearing, the hearing must be private, an order must be issued, and he has the right of appeal from that order. So if we assume that upon the Commission there might be some member who believed that it would be in the interest of the public to disclose all that information, a remedy is provided under section 23.

MR. STEIWER. I wish I could conclude with the Senator that business institutions would be satisfied and calmed by an assurance of that kind. We are told on every hand that they are not satisfied. We are told in every quarter that they are afraid to place themselves in a position of that kind; and the very fear is going to prevent them from going forward as we should like to see them proceed under this measure.

Mr. President, I desire now to call attention to two paragraphs of section 19 in order to indicate further reasons why corporations will not want to avail themselves of the facilities of this measure.

This section is the one that defines the disciplinary powers over exchanges. One would think, if he did not examine it carefully, that it is a section creating authority in the commission to require of the exchanges a compliance with the provisions of the law. It does that, but it does much more. The first paragraph authorizes the commission—

After appropriate notice and opportunity for hearing, by order to suspend for a period not exceeding 12 months or to withdraw the registration of a national securities exchange if the Commission finds that such exchange has violated any provision of this act or of the rules and regulations thereunder or has failed to enforce, so far as is within its power, compliance therewith by a member or by an issuer of a security registered thereon.

At first thought it would seem that if a stock exchange violated the law or violated the rules and regulations of the Commission it would be very proper to suspend for 12 months, or any other appropriate period, trading upon the exchange. So far as the exchange is concerned, I am entirely in accord with the proposition. In my opinion, the exchange that violates the rule and the regulation is entitled to very little consideration; but let me call attention to a fact which cannot be denied, namely, that when the commission requires the withdrawal of the registration of a national securities exchange and suspends trading upon it, the exchange is not the only sufferer. Primarily the blow falls upon the stock exchange; but ultimately every corporation having its securities listed on the exchange, and every stockholder in every corporation, and every creditor of every corporation, every person having a contractual relationship with the corporation, will feel the force of the blow. So it is that we provide in this bill, under the guise of furnishing a means of disciplining stock exchanges, a provision which would discipline the guilty and then in addition discipline the innocent along with the guilty. . . .

MR. BARKLEY. Does the Senator oppose, then, the granting of disciplinary power with reference to the exchange which violates the rules?

MR. STEIWER. Oh, no. The Senator undoubtedly expected me to answer that question in the negative.

MR. BARKLEY. How can an exchange be closed for a gross violation of the rules and regulations without affecting the stock listed on the exchange? If the Senator can point out how stock can continue to be sold on an exchange after it has been closed, I should like to have him do so. I do not know just how it can be done.

MR. STEIWER. Mr. President, if I had my way, I would not use this theorist method of disciplining exchanges. I would discipline the exchanges by disciplining the officers of the exchanges. I would penalize those who do the wrong. I would penalize them by the severest penalty I could design. I would try to afford an incentive for the officials and officers of the stock exchange to comply with the law and with the rules and regulations. I do not want to make it easy for them. But it does seem to me that, under the guise of punishing them, it is a weak and an indefensible proposition at the same time to punish the innocent man as we would punish the guilty.

Under the same section of the bill, subsection 2, we find this kind of a proposal:

(2) After appropriate notice and opportunity for hearing, by order to suspend for a period not exceeding 12 months or to withdraw the registration of a security if the Commission finds that the issuer of such security has failed to comply with any provision of this act or the rules and regulations thereunder.

Mr. President, I may say, on this subject, much as I did just a moment ago, that if the issuer is guilty of an offense, the issuer should be called to account and penalized for the offense; but the difficulty about a remedy of this kind is that it affects so many persons who are not in any way connected with the offense.

Let us assume the case of a corporation which sold a million shares of its stock, and let us say that after the sale had been effected, the issuer was guilty of some violation of the law, or of the rules and regulations promulgated pursuant to the law. The penalty for the violation is to suspend for a period of not exceeding 12 months, or to withdraw the registration of the security.

The effect of that kind of a penalty is, of course, to punish the issuer, but, in addition to that, the greatest effect of the penalty is to punish every man, woman, and child—every person in the world, who, for one reason or another, has acquired shares of the stock.

It is not necessary in this legislation to punish the innocent with the guilty. I suggest that these two sections be stricken from the bill. I think we can devise a means of punishing those who do wrong by penalizing the wrong-doer in plain and unmistakable language. I think undoubtedly there is a perfectly simple way to provide that those who violate the law or violate the rules and regulations may be indicted and punished as for a crime, and those kinds of penalties will be effective, and they will be effective not only as to the man who transgresses the law, but they will be effective in safeguarding the interests of all innocent persons who may have some relation to the transaction.

The suspension of a stock exchange, or the suspension of a security listed on a stock exchange, or the withdrawal of that security, merely for the purpose of penalizing the person who violated a rule or regulation which may have been made after a registration was effected, and made without the knowledge of the issuer, the penalizing of investors for the offense of another person who possibly did not even have knowledge of the rule or regulation, is a monstrous thing, and, in my judgment, it ought to be avoided.

If we suspend trading upon an exchange in order to punish the issuer of stock, everybody knows the stock is going to be depreciated in the market, and there will be a financial loss to every person who has acquired the stock. If there were no other way of punishing wrongdoing, we might find a justification for legislation of this kind, but, because there are other ways and because we can make the penalty rest upon the man who transgresses the law, let us refrain from punishing the innocent with the guilty.

Mr. President, responsible heads of institutions, knowing of these provisions in the law, and knowing what the consequence may be to their stockholders if they become embroiled in the meshes of these two paragraphs of section 19, may very well hesitate before they permit their securities to be listed upon any stock exchange, and if they are listed, they may very well be justified in seeking to delist the stock in order to protect their stockholders, a great army of innocent people, from the infliction of penalties which are absolutely undeserved under any theory of moral or legal responsibility.

Mr. President, I stated a little while ago that the bill is so constructed that it is intended to prevent any corporation escaping from the commission. I now desire to point out why I made that statement.

Section 15 deals with over-the-counter markets. Some corporations may think that if they cannot meet the oppressive and restrictive provisions of sections 12, 13, and 19, and other sections of the bill which affect corporations and the stockholders of corporations, they will immediately leave the stock exchange, and that upon leaving it, they will be freed from the oppressive requirements of this measure, and will be enabled to sell their securities over the counter. If any such view is entertained, the corporations are seriously in error.

Section 15 provides for regulation of over-the-counter markets, and provides for the making of rules and regulations applying to transactions on such markets, and for the registration with the commission of the dealers and brokers making or creating such markets.

With respect to those various provisions I have no complaint at all. I think operations in the over-the-counter markets should, of course, be regulated, and I see no objection to imposing rules and regulations and requirements of law upon dealers and brokers and others who are professional traders in stock, and who can have knowledge of the rules and regulations and of the law, and who, in good conscience, ought to comply with the law.

Let us see what else the section provides. I read now from line 20. We find there that the rules and regulations to which I have just referred, for the registration with the commission of dealers, of brokers, and others, is extended in this way, "and for the registration of the securities for which they make or create a market."

In other words, Mr. President, the issuers must register upon the stock exchange, if they are to do business there, and if they desire to retreat from the stock exchange and to do business over the counter, they will find that they are required under the rules and regulations of the commission to register there.

But that is not all. Following the language which I have just read, is this statement:

For the purposes of this section the Commission may make special rules and regulations in respect of securities or specified classes thereof listed, or entitled to unlisted trading privileges, upon any exchange on the date of the enactment of this act, which securities are not registered under the provisions of section 12 of this act.

I wonder whether Senators catch the full force and significance of that language. In effect, it means this, that if a security is listed upon a stock exchange at the time of the enactment of this measure, and does not register on a national securities exchange as provided in section 12, and the managers of the corporation attempt to sell its securities over the counter, not only rules and regulations will be made with respect to transactions over the counter, but in addition to that, special rules and regulations may be made by the commission to fit the particular case of the corporation which delisted its securities and took them off the stock exchanges in order to be freed from the oppressive requirements of the sections which deal with those exchanges.

Can it be assumed that the commission will let anybody get away? Does anyone assume for a moment that, with the powers conferred by section 15, the commission will permit anybody to unlist or remain unlisted?

Let us bear in mind that section 4 of the bill provides that the commission may assess stock exchanges for the money necessary to carry on the administration of the act. If the stock exchanges break down, there will be no money. The commission will have killed the goose which laid the golden egg; and I am told unofficially it is the purpose of some of the gentlemen who have been sponsoring this legislation, and of others who are said to be prospective appointees upon the commission, that steps will be taken to drive back to the stock exchanges those corporations which were unwilling to remain there and which attempt to resort to the over-the-counter markets of this country for the sale of their securities.

What justification, I ask, is there for the enactment of legislation which places the business of the United States in a strait-jacket of this kind? Remember that we are not dealing all the time with crooks and with thieves and with outlaws. We are not dealing all the time with institutions which are seeking to defraud somebody. We are dealing with those classes, it is true, but, in addition to them, we are dealing with the great number of institutions in this country which control the industries of the United States and provide labor for the laboring people of the United States. We are dealing with honest enterprise; we are dealing with legitimate investment; and the good with the bad are going to be brought within the strictest requirements of this measure, held down by sections 12, 13, and 19, if they attempt to operate upon the stock exchanges, and then driven back to the stock exchanges by section 15 if they attempt to sell their securities in the markets over the counter.

Mr. President, I do not want to delay longer upon this phase of the bill. There is much to be said about the section requiring proxies. If I had my way, I would either change that section or eliminate it from the bill. The committee was told by men who are experts upon this subject, men like Mr. Untermyer, who, through busy lifetimes, have been engaged in endeavoring to protect the interest of stockholders in great corporations, that this proxy requirement will not help the minority groups; that it will not aid the weak or defenseless; but that probably it will aid those in power, those who control the corporation; that it will operate differently than was contemplated by the committee.

We are told that the administration of this provision will be expensive to the corporations, and there is a very grave feeling in the business world that the requirements made in this section for proxies will be hurtful and not helpful. I am not, however, sufficiently advised concerning the technical workings of the great institutions with respect to the acquisition of proxies to propose a better section. I shall, therefore, pass it by.

Before I conclude I desire to take up a matter which I think is more important than any matter I have discussed until now in this debate. I refer to the penalties provided under the provisions of this bill. I have already said, and Senators fully realize, that the bill is unusual in that it not only clothes the commission with the right to make rules and regulations but it continues the power of the commission to change and alter and amend those rules and regulations. I have said two or three times that there is no provision in the bill requiring the rules and regulations to become effective at some future date. They may, in the judgment of the commission, become effective forthwith. There is no requirement in this bill that the rules and regulations shall be published at any particular time, or that any other effort shall be made to confer notice upon those who might be affected by the rules and regulations.

Throughout the bill there is a rather unusual structure in that acts which are condemned as unlawful in the main are not condemned in every event. There are very few acts in this bill which are condemned outright as unlawful and penalized under the provisions of the bill.

In almost every case the nature of the denunciation, that is, the statement of the crime, is in terms of rules and regulations. One can turn to almost any provision of the bill and find that is true. I have before me section 29 (a) which begins with the words—

It shall be unlawful for any broker or dealer—

And so forth, to do certain acts—

in contravention of such rules and regulations as the Commission may deem necessary or appropriate in the public interest—

And so forth. That kind of structure, Mr. President, is typical of the entire make-up of the bill. Therefore the crimes which are created by this bill are crimes which we do not know today. We could not define them if we wanted to. They are crimes which are yet to be defined by the commission. The nature and extent of those crimes, the conditions and definitions of those crimes, the very elements of the offenses, are unknown to the Congress which is to pass the legislation. These crimes are to be defined by people the identity of whom we do not yet know. They are to be established at different times, and changed and amended at different times in ways which we cannot even imagine in advance, and yet, Mr. President, we are called upon to give our approval to section 30, including section 30 (b), which penalizes violation of rules and regulations.

Permit me to read it so it may appear in this place in my remarks:

(b) Any person who willfully violates any provision of any rule or regulation under this act, or of any agreement made with the Commission and filed under this act, shall upon conviction be fined not more than $10,000, except that if such person is an exchange, a fine not exceeding $100,000 may be imposed.

Mr. President, in order to understand the philosophy of this bill and the theory and purpose of those who prepared and sponsored the bill in the first place, I desire to state to the Senate that when this language came to the committee the penalties in subsection (b) were identical with the penalties in subsection (a), except that there was no jail sentence imposed.

In other words, the fine might be not more than $25,000, and, in case of an exchange, a fine of not more than $500,000. Inasmuch as some of these offenses which might conceivably be committed in violation of the rules and regulations are continuing offenses, and may very well recur day after day, the extent of the penalty may become fairly evident to those who give consideration to this feature of the bill. . . .

MR. BORAH. I am quite in sympathy with the view which the Senator from Oregon expresses with reference to making the violation of these regulations a criminal offense, but we have put that provision in every statute we have passed concerning the relief of agriculture for some time. I think it is an indefensible principle to make the people of the country punishable for the violation of a regulation which may be a regulation tonight and not a regulation tomorrow, but it is in all these laws which we have passed. . . . The thing I am objecting to is the principle of subjecting the citizens of the country to punishment by fine or by imprisonment for the violation of a regulation instead of the violation of a law. . . . What are we going to do about it? Are we going to leave such a penalty in all the provisions of the laws? If things continue, not only will the citizen be tied by a thousand rules issued by some bureau, but if he slips a cog he goes to jail.

MR. STEIWER. . . . Although I can bring myself to a sort of reluctant approval of some penalty for violations of rules and regulations in this bill, I can do that only because it is so essential that the commission have some power to bring about effectual administration of the law. But it seems to me that the vice of this particular provision is that it confuses that which is done with evil purpose from that which is done innocently. It is much like the section I was discussing a while ago in which I pointed out that the innocent investor or stockholder is punished for another man's crime. This is not the case, of course, of the citizen being punished for another man's crime, but there is here the commingling of offenses and the fixing of a penalty for an act done with wrongful purpose and an act done innocently and possibly without knowledge of the rule.

It seems to me that the most insidious thing about this is that the commission may make these rules at will. They may make them without notice. The person charged with the violation may not know there is a rule. He may not know he is violating a rule. It is true that the bill says "willfully," but that may be construed merely to mean "intentionally" as distinguished from "unintentionally" or "voluntarily" as distinguished from "involuntarily."

I have made some little inquiry as to the meaning of the phrase, and I left the subject considerably bewildered, although it may well be that the courts will limit the construction of the provision, because the other construction will be almost monstrous in its nature.

We have no assurance how the court will act with respect to it, and it seems to me that whatever else we do, when dealing with subsection (b) of section 30, we ought to insert after the word "person," the words "with intent to injure and defraud another," so that it would read:

Any person who with intent to injure or defraud another shall willfully –

do the prohibited act, the penalty would follow.

In that way we would be penalizing the purposeful wrongdoer, who, of course, is entitled to no sympathy and no defense. The man who seeks to defraud his neighbor might well be penalized, even though his offense consists of the violation of a rule or regulation. I have no quarrel with that proposal. But when we say that for violation of any provision—I invite attention to that, whether important or unimportant—for violation of any provision, whether known or unknown, or whether with a bad purpose or innocently, a man is to be penalized in the judgment of a court up to a $10,000 fine, I cannot give my consent to it. . . .

MR. FLETCHER. I desire to mention the fact that it was the purpose, and I think that purpose is carried out in the provisions of the bill under section 30, particularly in paragraph (b), to separate penalties for violations of regulations from those for violations of the bill itself. In other words, the bill does not subject to imprisonment a person who violates regulations. He is only subjected to the penalty of a fine in that case. If he violates a rule or regulation willfully and knowingly he is liable to punishment by fine, or if he violates the law itself willfully and knowingly, then he may be subjected to both fine and imprisonment. That distinction is intended in the bill, and I think it is made.

MR. BORAH. I think that is a merciful distinction, but it does not affect the principle which is involved, as I see it.

MR. STEIWER. Let me see if I cannot indicate to the Senator that the proposal here is more far-reaching in its effect and more un-American in principle than anything written in the N.R.A. Act, because when the President approves, he does so by Executive order or proclamation, and all who run may read. So there is a fair chance for people to have some knowledge of what is done and published by the President of the United States.

MR. FESS. Until he undoes it.

MR. STEIWER. Yes, possibly, but I think we will all concede that the President would not act in a whimsical way about a matter of that kind. Under this bill, however, a commission is to be created which does not even need to act by proclamation. It can meet in private, if it wants to, and it is not required to publish anything by proclamation, Executive order, or in any other way. This, in my judgment, is the most unheard-of thing that has yet been presented, and to me, because it is so far beyond the traditional belief of our people, it seems that we ought not to resort to it, because we are not obliged to resort to it. We can provide all the penalties reasonably necessary for the enforcement of this proposed act without putting this unusual un-American penal requirement upon our people. I think it far exceeds even the drastic provisions of the National Recovery Act.

MR. FESS. It is not different in the direction of the step which is taken; but the second step is just a little longer than the first one, and the third step will be longer than the second.

MR. STEIWER. That is true. I yield the floor, Mr. President.

MR. FLETCHER. Mr. President, before the Senator takes his seat, I should like to make a brief statement. In the beginning of the Senator's remarks he referred to an alleged number of 450,000 corporations which are about to be strangled by some of these regulations. I do not quite understand what these corporations may be. Moody's Manual, which is considered something of an authority, and which attempts to give statistical data about all companies in which the public is interested, lists only 34,000 corporations. It seems to be absurd to suppose that this bill affects a great multitude of more than 450,000 corporations throughout the land not connected with Wall Street. This manual lists only 34,000 corporations.

MR. STEIWER. I do not attempt to say that the statement from which I read earlier in the debate is exactly correct as to numbers, but there is information before the committee that there are vastly more than 34,000 corporations in the country. I do not remember the exact figures, but it is vastly more than that.

MR. FLETCHER. Then the Senator made some criticism of the provisions as to the requirement of reports from corporations. The Senator will remember that the president of the New York Stock Exchange has frequently emphasized the necessity for more complete and accurate reports by listed corporations. The members of the stock exchange themselves have complained of that situation, and the president of the New York Stock Exchange last year, in a speech at Cleveland, said:

It is now generally recognized that the lack of complete disclosure of the result of business operations contributed to the inflation of security values which preceded the panic of 1929.

MR. STEIWER. I think the stock exchange is very happy to have some excuse for its own part in the speculative orgy of 1929. It was within its power, in my judgment, at that time to obtain from the issuers of securities all the information that was needed. The fact is it did not get the information. If that be an argument to justify the requirement for further reports, we still have the responsibility of seeing to it that we do not go too far.

Let me call attention, in that regard, to the language on page 34 of the bill, which I did not refer to in my earlier remarks. It is there provided as follows:

(b) The Commission may prescribe, in regard to reports made pursuant to this act, the form or forms in which the required information shall be set forth, the items or details to be shown in the balance sheet and the earning statement, and the methods to be followed in the preparation of reports, in the appraisal or valuation of assets and liabilities, in the determination of depreciation and depletion, in the differentiation recurring and non-recurring income, in the differentiation of investment and operating income, in the preparation, where the Commission deems it necessary or desirable, of separate and/or consolidated balance sheets or income accounts of any person directly or indirectly controlling or controlled by the issuer.

Before the committee the question was raised whether it was advisable for the Congress to supervise the internal affairs of corporations to the extent of controlling their methods of accountancy. It was believed, I think, by a majority of the committee that we should not do that.

In line 6 on page 34 we changed the word "accounts" to "reports," so as to make certain the proposed commission would be requiring reports and not a new and expensive method of accountancy. Yet it seems to me, Mr. President—and I do not want to take a dogmatic position in respect to it, and I confess my interpretation of the language might not be correct—that the committee failed to go far enough in making the corrections necessary in this bill, and that in the language which I just read the committee has left in the measure ample authority on the part of the commission not only to control the kind of reports which are to be made by corporations, but also to control the basic accountancy of corporations. It may be, for one reason or another, that a corporation is compelled to continue its present system of accountancy; and if this be true, as I think it is true, the Commission may require a system of its own; then we will have the spectacle of a Federal agency exacting of business institutions two methods of accountancy, with very great expense to the corporations concerned. In the end the expense will be paid by the stockholders. There is nothing we can provide by the terms of the bill in the way of excessive requirements, the expense of which is to be met exclusively by millionaires. It will in the last analysis be distributed among the American people.

I think the Senator from Florida selected an unfortunate illustration when he referred to the requirement for reports as indicating that the restrictive influences upon corporations will not be great and severe. On the contrary, I think the reporting requirements will be almost devastating, and because of fear that conditions may be even worse than they are, corporations will find it difficult to comply with these provisions of the act. . . .

MR. BARKLEY. I want to ask the Senator a question. The section on page 34 of the bill, to which the Senator has just referred, describes somewhat in detail the power of the commission to exact reports of companies. It does not seem to me it gives the commission any power to impose on a corporation any particular method of book-keeping. Where questions of depreciation, depletion, and valuation enter into the financial statement, which have a great bearing upon the financial condition of the company, does not the Senator think the commission ought to have the power to learn by what method it arrived at the figures which it reports as bearing upon its financial standing? It seems to me that is all the bill does in that regard.

MR. STEIWER. I do not believe the end to be attained justifies the procedure. I think if it involves the requirement of a new system of accountancy, we are not justified in requiring insitutions to set up books to satisfy us as a condition precedent to the listing of their stocks upon the stock exchange.

MR. BARKLEY. It does not require them to adopt a set of books to suit us or the commission. It authorizes the commission to require the company to advise it by what bookkeeping method of its own it has arrived at those conclusions.

MR. STEIWER. With that statement I cannot agree. If the company does not have the information it will have to keep its books in a way to acquire it.

MR. BARKLEY. Any company that does not have the information under its own method of bookkeeping certainly does not deserve very much consideration in the listing of its stock on the exchange.

MR. STEIWER. All honest effort to maintain business and provide employment deserves consideration. The proof of the pudding will be the eating thereof. I am wondering what some of my good friends will be saying 12 months from now if Congress enacts the bill in this form and then finds it is injurious to the business of America and that it causes further unemployment among the laboring people of the United States and retards the recovery for which we are all praying. What excuse can they offer for their action when it is just as easy to make the bill a little more moderate with respect to industry, and start with steps we know are sound, and then add as the necessities may require and in a way that will do injury to no one but will protect the public and American investors against the evil practices which have been permitted in security transactions? . . .

MR. HASTINGS. Mr. President, I have given rather careful consideration to the arguments which have been presented to the Senate during the past few days with respect to the pending proposed legislation. I am frank to admit that during the past year or two I was not very much in sympathy with much which was said about legislation regulating the stock exchange, because I doubted whether it would be possible for the Congress to enact any legislation that would be helpful to the public interest. I am not quite certain that that impression which I entertained did not date back several years.

A great many years ago, in my law practice, I was called upon to defend a stock broker in a transaction growing out of dealings which that broker had with a customer. A suit was brought, and I appeared defending the broker in that action.

Counsel on the other side requested an opportunity to examine the books of the broker. That was readily agreed to by my client, and the examination was made. The examination of the books showed some irregularities of such a character that I could not, in my judgment, defend successfully the action that was brought. A settlement was made. The accountants who had examined the books came from New York. My recollection is they were accountants who were employed from time to time by the New York Stock Exchange.

Shortly thereafter the stock exchange sent accountants again to examine the broker's books and found similar irregularities continuing. As a result, that member of the stock exchange was brought before the governing board and disciplined in a way that seemed to me so effective that there could be no doubt that the stock exchange itself had a very complete control over its members and exercised that control in a way that made it safe for the public to deal with its members. An opportunity was given to the man to sell his seat on the stock exchange, and that necessitated his selling his business. He went out of business and has not been a member of the stock exchange since.

During that examination, I had occasion, the only occasion I ever had, to examine the rules and regulations of the New York Stock Exchange itself. It seemed to me there was in those rules and regulations sufficient control over the members to protect amply everybody who had occasion to deal with stock-exchange members. I got the distinct impression that the safest person with whom a man could deal in the purchase or sale of securities would be a member of the New York Stock Exchange.

Comparatively recently, however, during the examination which has been so carefully made by the Senate Banking and Currency Committee, and in view of the facts there disclosed and the evils which were there exposed, I reached the conclusion that probably my original impression that it was not necessary for Congress to take any action was an erroneous one.

I desire at this point, Mr. President, to read into the Record, from what I conceive to be the very best authority, a statement made by the chairman of the committee having the bill in charge, the distinguished senior Senator from Florida [Mr. Fletcher], appearing at page 8163 of the Record [*supra* p. 2848]. He undertook to state the purpose of the bill. I quote:

"We propose by this measure to establish, through Federal regulation of the methods and the mechanical functions and practices of the stock exchange, an amount adequate, open, and free market for the purchase and sale of securities; also to correct abuses we know of and others which may exist; to prohibit and prevent, if possible, their recurrence; to restore public confidence in the financial markets of the country; to prevent excessive speculation, to the injury of agriculture, commerce, and industry; to outlaw manipulation and unfair practices and combinations by which to exploit the public and misrepresent values, such as pools, wash sales, fictitious transactions, and the like; to oblige disclosure of all material facts respecting securities traded in on the exchanges, which disclosure is essential to give the investor an adequate opportunity to evaluate his investment.

Criticism is made that we are calling upon corporations to make disclosures, and that we are thereby putting them to an enormous expense and trouble, and inquiring into affairs into which we have no business to examine. My suggestion is that if any corporation issues securities which are unfit to be certified because of what is back of them, the securities themselves are unfit to be offered to the public.

What right have brokers to appeal to the public to buy their securities if they are not willing to tell the truth about those securities? That is the whole proposition, and all we ask of them is to tell the truth.

They do not seem to want to tell the truth, in the first place, and, in the next place, they especially complain about liability for material misrepresentations which have misled the public into buying securities. They are willing to expose, to some extent, the facts behind the securities, but they do not want to be liable in case they lie about them. That seems to be the basis of the objection. All we ask in the pending bill and in the Securities Act is that they tell the truth in their registration papers, so the public may know what is behind the securities.

We undertake generally to declare the intention of Congress, and enunciate specific principles as a guide to subsequent administration."

Mr. President, I am quite certain that if the bill were limited to those purposes the distinguished junior Senator from Oregon [Mr. Steiwer], as I know from my talk with him, would have no objection to it at all. Indeed, I think I might safely say that if the bill were confined to the purposes stated by the Senator from Florida there would not be a Member of the body who would oppose its passage. Unfortunately, however, that is not true. The bill involves very much more than the regulation of the stock exchanges. It places a burden upon the corporations of the country which is wholly unnecessary and, in my judgment, not called for.

Somewhere in the argument it was suggested that the complaint about the bill affecting corporations is merely advanced as a blind to protect the stock exchanges themselves. I think I have heard it suggested that it was expected that by putting up such argument the corporations would be thereby compelled to pull from the fire those things in the bill which are objectionable to the stock exchange itself.

In my judgment, in the passage of the bill, we are about to do that which we frequently do when the public is excited and when there is a great prejudice created against a certain institution. I think it is not too much to say that Congress is frequently controlled by public opinion, and oftentimes by the opinion of those who do not know all the facts involved in the controversy about which they form an opinion. . . .

I doubt whether any Member of the Senate will admit, or even believe, that he is being influenced by the outcry of the public with respect to this bill. He believes he is using his own judgment; but it is human nature for persons to be influenced constantly by the cry of the public, and by what the front pages of the newspapers say about matters.

We should bear that in mind as we go along with this proposed legislation. We should bear in mind that the natural course for us to follow is to be persuaded in the direction in which the public is going to be influenced, if you please, as the distinguished chairman of the committee said, by literally bushels of letters which have been sent by the unorganized victims, as they are called, of the stock exchange. I say that we ought, in all fairness to ourselves—and that it is the only point I am making here—to see to it that we are not controlled by mere public clamor; and we ought to see to it that the public secures accurate information by a discussion of this subject upon the floor of the Senate before we act at all. . . .

I mention these facts in order to remind the Senate that there is but one popular side of this question; there is but one popular demand, and that is for the passage of the bill as it came from the committee, except as some persons believe that it might be made more popular by making it even more drastic. . . .

But, Mr. President, if we could approach this subject bearing in mind what the distinguished chairman of the committee declares is desirable and is the real purpose of the bill, with a view of doing as little as possible while still accomplishing that purpose, it seems to me we would write a very different bill, and one that would be very much less objectionable than the bill now pending.

I am one of those who believe that when Congress finds an evil existing, it ought to do no more than to correct the evil as best it can with the least legislation that is necessary to accomplish the result.

In this case we have gone to just the opposite of that proposition. We have not confined it to any such principle as that. We have not confined it, I submit, to any such good sense as that. We have not said that we will do as little as we can, but, on the contrary, we have said here that we will do as much as we possibly can; that we will make this as near perfect as it is possible to make it by correcting not only all the evils we discover but all the evils which we think may possibly occur in the future with respect to stock-exchange transactions.

Mr. President, one of the early prejudices I had against the enactment of this bill was due to my view—which I think must be well founded—that the Congress of the United States cannot enact legislation to protect the "suckers" of the Nation. We heard yesterday about the stock market being merely a gambling place. Some prefer to call it a place where speculation is going on. It is immaterial to me what it is called. I do not believe what goes on there can be stopped by legislative fiat.

I remember the various efforts made by the States of the Union to control the miserable liquor traffic. I remember how they tried local option, how they tried State-wide prohibiton. Ever since I can remember it has been a constant issue in my State and, so far as I know, in communities in every State in the Union. I had much to do with it as a prosecuting officer. I saw crimes committed due to excessive use of alcohol. I saw women and children put into the streets because of husbands and fathers, intelligent enough, and able to earn a good living for a family, would not do so because they could not control their appetites for strong drink.

I believed, with millions of other people of this Nation, that the only way in which we could get rid of it was to make it unlawful all over the country, and to do it by an amendment to the Federal Constitution. I was thoroughly in accord with that. For a year or two I saw what convinced me conclusively that the conditions had improved. Then, as it went along, I became somewhat doubtful about it, and I am not one of those who agree today that the eighteenth amendment ought to have been repealed. I have been in doubt about it for many years and never could reach a definite conclusion, and I have not as yet done so. But the American people did reach a conclusion, and they did so by such an overwhelming vote that there could be no doubt that they did not want to bother any longer with trying to enforce that kind of a law.

In my judgment, what is sought to be done through the pending bill is pretty nearly equal to that. The attempt is to say to people that they cannot do what they please. I do not mean exactly that; I do not mean that people will not be free to do what they please after this measure shall have been enacted, but, in order to protect them from doing what they desire to do, in my judgment, the industries of the Nation and the trading in securities will be loaded down in a way which will greatly retard recovery instead of promoting it.

Mr. President, besides all this, and regardless of whether that argument be reasonable or not, I desire to call attention to the fact that our wish to cure a great evil is leading us a very much greater distance into that new and dangerous path which we have recently begun to tread.

The acts of Congress of the past year or more, with many of which I disagree, and many of which I think are dangerous for the Nation, were enacted under the plea that there was a great emergency, and that relief measures such as those being considered were necessary. No such claim as that is made with respect to the pending bill. It has no relation to the emergency. It has no relation to relief, except as to those persons who voluntarily try to make money on the stock exchange. This is a reform measure; not a relief measure; and, in my judgment, is the definite beginning of the passing of the operation of American business over to the Government upon the excuse that back of it is the popular support of the people of the Nation.

It is impossible to read with any degree of care this entire bill without reaching the definite conclusion that the operation of the stock exchanges of the country would be definitely and positively turned over to the Government of the United States should the bill be enacted.

I shall use the New York Stock Exchange as an example. Though there are 25 other exchanges in the country, apparently the entire discussion and all the evidence relate to the New York Stock Exchange.

The New York Stock Exchange is a voluntary organization, which has been in existence some 150 years. According to the testimony in the record, it has 1,375 members, and the high price for stock-exchange seats has been $600,000, although at the present time it is estimated that the seats are selling for only $190,000. If we figure the seats at $200,000 a piece, there is an investment of $275,000,000.

I suppose the physical property of the exchange is owned by a corporation, and that the interest of the members of the exchange in that corporation is based upon their membership in the stock exchange itself.

Under the bill, the Federal Government would be given the absolute power to destroy everything that association has, except its physical property. The Government control over it would be complete. The matter of the hours of trading by the stock exchange would be under the control of the Government. The time of opening and the time of closing might be fixed by the commission provided for in the bill.

More than that, upon the recommendation of the commission, the stock exchanges of the country might all be closed for a period of 90 days upon the approval of the President of the United States. When that 90 days had expired, the stock exchanges might again open, but, so far as I know, and so far as I can discover from a reading of the bill, the commission, with the approval of the President, could close them before the end of the day for another 90 days.

At the expiration of 181 days, upon the recommendation of the commission and the approval of the President, the stock exchanges might be closed for another 90 days; and upon the expiration of 252 days, on the recommendation of the commission and with the approval of the President, they might be closed for another 90 days. So that, so far as the bill is concerned, so far as the power of the stock exchange itself is concerned, after the bill shall have been enacted, the commission and the President may close every stock exchange in this land, so that they will operate less than 4 days in every year. But that is not all, by any means.

In this bill itself there is the distinct and definite provision that the proposed commission may fix the rate of commission which the stock-exchange members may charge for the service they render. They cannot by rule and regulation govern it any longer. They cannot by rule and regulation fix it at an amount which they believe will return to them a fair amount of money annually, or that will increase their business. They may not use their judgment about it any longer. It passes to the commission.

In addition to that, the rate of interest which they may charge may be fixed by the commission. We heard argument yesterday that we ought to do away with the margin account. We do not need to do that here. We do not need to fix, in the bill, anything with respect to margins. The commission may control the whole thing by fixing the amount of the commission and fixing the amount of interest that may be charged.

Mr. President, I make these statements for the purpose of showing that, in the case of this great institution having today physical assets of $275,000,000, based upon the price of stock-exchange seats, we of the Congress are running ourselves ragged to pass the bill quickly in order that we may protect some person who ought to have known better in the first place than to be trying to guess whether a stock was going up or whether it was going down. . . .

Mr. President, with respect to the control of this business passing to the Federal Government, I insist that what I have said is not in any sense an exaggeration. What I have said is positively true under the pending bill. It can be answered in one way only.

Those who are satisfied with the bill say, "We know that the President never would agree to closing the stock exchange, as you have outlined, and to keeping it closed most of the time, and letting it transact business only 3 or 4 days a year. We cannot conceive of a President's doing that. We know that the present President will appoint capable men on the commission to manage the stock exchange. For that reason we think the alarm which you sound ought not to be responded to in any way, because in actual operation it is a false alarm."

Mr. President, I learned long ago that it is dangerous for any legislative body to pass legislation because a certain individual whom the members of the legislature or the Members of Congress knew and believed in would be the person called upon to administer a particular law. Legislation of every kind ought at all times to be upon such a firm foundation that no person occupying any official position in connection with it could under any circumstances do a wrong under the act itself. In other words, this ought to be, and we have been led to believe that it is, a country which is protected by the Constitution and the laws of the Nation, and that its security does not in any sense depend upon the character of the person who administers the law.

Of course, it is always important to have good administrators of laws. It is important to have good executives, because we always get better results with such executives. We ought not, however, to pass a law which puts into the hands of any man who may not be what we think he ought to be an opportunity to do under the law something that will be hurtful to the people of the Nation. . . .

MR. FLETCHER. Speaking of the power to close the exchange, the Senator has reference, I take it, to paragraph (4), on page 42, which reads:

And if in its opinion the public interest so requires, summarily to suspend trading in any registered security on any national securities exchange for a period not exceeding 10 days, or with the approval of the President, summarily to suspend all trading on any national securities exchange for a period not exceeding 90 days.

I direct attention to the fact that power now exists and is exercised by the stock exchange itself. That is not a new power; but instead of the stock exchange itself exercising the power, the commission is allowed to exercise it in the public interest, with the approval of the President.

That is the first point.

The Senator seems to be apprehensive that the commission will have such power that it will manage and control the exchanges of the country. I think we have carefully guarded against that. Instead of attempting to do that sort of thing, or authorizing the commission to do it, the Senator will find that on page 44, paragraph (c) we provide that—

The Commission is authorized and directed to make a study and investigation of the rules of national securities exchanges with respect to the classification of members, the methods of election of officers and committees to insure a fair representation of the membership, and the suspension, expulsion, and disciplining of members of such exchanges. The Commission shall report to the Congress on or before January 3, 1935, the results of its investigation, together with its recommendations.

The matter is to be investigated by the commission, and it is to report to Congress what it recommends.

MR. HASTINGS. But in the meantime what happens? In the meantime does not the commission have all the control I have suggested?

MR. FLETCHER. No; I do not think so. It has nothing to do with the election of officers or the qualification of members or personnel.

MR. HASTINGS. What will anyone care about the election of officers after this act shall go into effect? The election of officers will become of the least importance to any member of the stock exchange. The kind of rules and regulations that can be made by the members of the stock exchange will amount to nothing to any member of the exchange or to the public after we shall pass this bill.

What the Senator states is true. The Senator says the stock exchange has that power now. Of course it has the power. What I am complaining of, and the only point I make about it, is that we are taking away from the stock exchange the power which it now has and putting the power in the Federal Government. The sole point I have made up to this time in that connection is that we have transferred to the Federal Government this great institution, with $275,000,000 of property, and the control of its operations.

Because of the urgency of the demand for that action, because the public is demanding that something of the kind be done, I have expressed great fear that this is but the beginning of the taking over by the Government of other great institutions in which the public is interested. . . .

MR. FLETCHER. The Senator says that the stock exchange now has the power and authority to adopt rules and regulations and to regulate its own members. I simply desire to mention the fact that the New York Stock Exchange is not the only exchange in the country. It has competition right in New York City. I think there are eight or nine other exchanges in New York City. There is competition there. The control of an exchange extends only to its own membership, however. The non-members, those outside of its own membership, are the people who are giving the exchange trouble, and it cannot control them.

MR. HASTINGS. Mr. President, I desire to call attention to section 2 of this proposed act, in order that we may try to find wherein lies the authority to enact this kind of legislation. Here is what is said in the proposed act itself:

In order to prevent obstruction of the normal flow of interstate commerce and also to preserve and protect the national credit, the Federal taxing power, the national banking and Federal Reserve Systems, and the proper use of the mails and the facilities of interstate commerce, it is imperative that legislation be enacted to regulate and control such transactions.

Mr. President, I suggest that those who had to go to these sources to find authority for this proposed legislation are stretching to the limit the provisions of the Federal Constitution. It never was intended that Congress should interpret the grant of power to control interstate commerce to do such a thing as this. It never was intended that it should prevent the use of the mails except for some improper purpose, and it is undertaken here to make a purpose improper by imposing certain conditions.

However, Mr. President, besides the control of the hours, the days, the rates of commission, the interest, and so on, there is a further provision which ought at least to be shocking to the American people.

Under the provisions of this proposed act there are five commissioners to be selected at a salary of $12,000 a year each. I may say in passing that I think it is a little surprising that this Congress and this administration should suggest any such salary as $12,000 a year for any man when the average income for 1932 was but a little more than $300 for each person. With an administration that is urging upon us the importance of a better distribution of the income of the Nation and with many members of the administration insisting that there must be an equitable distribution of the wealth of the Nation, it is now proposed to give to five men $12,000 a year each in order to administer this proposed law. . . .

MR. LOGAN. Is that an unusual salary for commissioners who perform such important duties as are to be imposed upon these commissioners?

MR. HASTINGS. No.

MR. LOGAN. I will ask the Senator if it is not true that he has voted for bills carrying such a salary during the last 3 or 4 years on several occasions?

MR. HASTINGS. I am not quite certain about that, but I am quite certain that I would have so voted if the occasion had arisen and I believe that it was a reasonable salary.

MR. LOGAN. The Senator is not complaining about the amount of the salary?

MR. HASTINGS. I am not complaining about the amount of the salary, but I am expressing this thought and this thought only: When I read what has been said in this Record and remember what I have heard upon the floor of the Senate during the past year or so and what I have read of the statements made by the President, and by many of his advisers about a better distribution of the income of the Nation and a better distribution of the wealth of the Nation, I merely express surprise that this administration should be urging upon Congress the payment of a salary of $12,000 a year for anybody to do any kind of service and under any kind of circumstances, when it is remembered, as I repeat, that the average income is but a little over $300 a year for every man, woman, and child in America.

MR. LOGAN. As I understand, the Senator was not expressing any personal objection to the amount of the salary—

MR. HASTINGS. Not at all.

MR. LOGAN. But was simply expressing his surprise that some of those whom he has indicated should have proposed such a salary?

MR. HASTINGS. That is correct.

However, Mr. President, there are some things in the pending measure touching that subject to which I do object. I should like to call attention to the powers given under this proposed act to the commission.

(c) The Commission is authorized to appoint and fix the compensation of such officers, attorneys, examiners, and other experts and employees as may be necessary for carrying out its functions under this act, without regard to the provisions of other laws applicable to the employment and compensation of officers and employees of the United States.

There is no limit to that authority. The Congress has nothing to do with it; the President of the United States has nothing to do with it; the Secretary of the Treasury of the United States has nothing to do with it. While the salary paid to the commissioners is fixed in the proposed act, it is the only thing that is fixed, and immediately after the passage of this measure the commission, if it cares to do so, may employ Mr. Pecora at a salary of $100,000 a year, and there will be nobody under the sun who can complain about it. . . .

MR. LOGAN. Are the expenses of the commission to be paid out of the Treasury of the Federal Government or are they to be paid by levying on the various stock exchanges?

MR. HASTINGS. They are to be paid by levying on the stock exchanges. . . .

MR. HASTINGS. I yield.

MR. VANDENBERG. With respect to this staff of employees, I suggest to the Senator that there is another hazard which perhaps could be corrected, but which certainly now stands wide open. Although there are penalties provided in this bill against every man, woman, and child who may be externally related to these transactions in stocks and bonds and other securities, there is not a word in the bill which attaches penalties for the misuse of information on the inside of the commission and its staff. That, it would seem to me, is a tremendous weakness in the bill.

MR. HASTINGS. Is the Senator quite certain about that? It seems to me that somewhere in the bill there is a provision making it unlawful for an employee of the commission to give out certain information. I am not sure that there is any penalty attached, but I remember distinctly that somewhere in this bill there is a prohibition against that.

MR. VANDENBERG. I just canvassed the matter with one of the experts, who was under the impression that such a provision was in the bill, but he could not find it.

MR. HASTINGS. Perhaps he is right.

MR. VANDENBERG. If he is right, the defect ought to be corrected.

MR. HASTINGS. I agree with the Senator.

Mr. President, the salary of the five commissioners is the only thing that is fixed. I take it that every commissioner will be entitled to at least one secretary, and I take it also that the secretary to one of the commissioners will be quite as important as is the secretary to General Johnson who administers the N.R.A. According to the newspapers that particular position now pays $5,600. I doubt very much whether the amount thus paid would be $5,600 if it had been fixed by the Congress of the United States. I doubt whether the commissioners to be appointed under this bill would be able to pay their secretaries anything like that sum if they depended upon Congress for the appropriation and depended upon the Congress to fix the amount; but under this bill they can pay their secretaries and their experts and other employees whatever they please. I care not how much one may speculate upon it, there is nothing under the sun to prevent them from doing as they please except their own conscience.

Who pays the bill? There would be some control over this question if Members of the House and Members of the Senate were charged with the responsibility of making the appropriations for the expenses of the proposed new commission. We would have an opportunity to have the commissioners brought before us and examined as to whether they were paying reasonable or unreasonable salaries. We would have a hearing; we would have an opportunity to discuss the subject in the Senate, because we would be interested. We would know that back in the States where we live there would be somebody complaining about the salary paid, saying that such salary affected the taxes he paid to the Federal Government, and entering complaint about it. No such thing as that can happen here.

O Mr. President, as I read this bill my mind goes back to the Revolution, and the period before the Revolution, when the people in the American Colonies rose in their might and said, "There shall be no taxation without representation." We based the whole theory of our Revolution upon that principle, and here, 150 years afterward, not in the form of emergency legislation but permanent legislation, we find the Congress enacting a measure contrary to that principle, notwithstanding the provision in the Constitution which gives to the Congress alone the right to levy taxes. There is a provision in the Constitution that all legislation involving taxation shall originate in the House, that taxes shall be levied by the Congress, and that they shall be uniform in their nature. All those requirements are written into the Constitution; but, notwithstanding that fact, we find in the year 1934 the Congress rushing headlong to give away this power to a commission created by the Congress, and putting the stock exchanges of the country in a position where they cannot even complain. The commission may be as extravagant as it pleases; it may pay everyone in its employ what it pleases; and then the Congress says to the stock exchanges of the country, "You must pay the bill."

Is there any provision in the bill about the division of the expense? Not at all. The only provision is that it shall be distributed in a way that to the commission seems to be fair and equitable. Is the junior Senator from Ohio [Mr. Buckley], who is much interested in the bill, willing for the two stock exchanges of his State to depend upon equity, as the five commissioners may see it, when it comes to assessing those two stock exchanges out of existence if the commissioners happen to be opposed to them? Is the Senator from Kentucky [Mr. Logan] willing that the stock exchanges in his State shall be dependent upon a commission which may be so prejudiced against the New York Stock Exchange that it will impose the whole burden upon that exchange?

There is no court review; there is no review anywhere after the matter passes out of our hands. We give the power to the commission, without knowing who the commissioners will be, without knowing what their sympathies may be, whether their sympathies will go out to the stock exchange in Detroit or Pittsburgh or New York or California or elsewhere. We have no way of knowing. We are letting this power go from our hands into the hands of five commissioners to say what shall be done with respect to the matter.

Mr. President, the temptation is left with the new taxing authority to be liberal in the matter of the money it deems necessary to carry out the provisions of the bill. When a commission is appointed that is dependent upon Congress for appropriations for its expenses we may naturally expect that commission to use some care with the money it is called upon to expend, because some day it must account to somebody;

but a broad authority is about to be given to this new commission, without any power anywhere to check it, without any responsibility or requirement to respond to those who pay the bills. . . .

MR. LOGAN. I should like to ask the Senator, purely for information if the same broad powers which are found in the bill now before us were granted to the Radio Commission and the Power Commission and possibly some other commissions?

MR. HASTINGS. Am I to understand the question to be whether some such powers have been granted elsewhere?

MR. LOGAN. Is this bill, so far as these provisions are concerned, along the same lines as the provisions in the acts creating the Radio Commission and the Power Commission?

MR. HASTINGS. Not at all. I think I am correct in my answer. The only thing I recall that is comparable at all grows out of the emergency legislative acts we have passed. When we created the Coordinator for the Railroads, a temporary affair to last for a certain number of years, my recollection is there was some provision by the Congress whereby the railroads should pay a certain amount per mile to cover the expenses involved. But there is no such provision with respect to the expenses of the Interstate Commerce Commission itself or the Radio Commission. It might very well be. It is just as applicable to those commissions as to the commission we are about to create. . . .

These cases are not similar to those where organizations, such as the Federal Reserve member banks, are involved. The banks do not have to become member banks. They may do as they please. So far as I know heretofore there has never been any effort to tax the people of the Nation under a plan like this. If this were a scheme set up whereby the stock exchanges wanted to participate in it or not, then it would be perfectly all right to let those who did want to participate bear the expense, and those who did not want to do so to stay outside. But here we are imposing a tax upon people without their consent and through commissions and through code authorities on a basis which I say is un-American and foreign to any ideas we ever had up until the past few months, and which, in my judgment, is exceedingly dangerous. . . .

MR. DAVIS. Can the Senator tell me what it will cost to conduct the business of the commission?

MR. HASTINGS. I have not seen it estimated anywhere. I do not believe anyone has any idea what it will cost. After a while I shall discuss the great task to be imposed upon the commission and let each Senator judge for himself whether or not it will be a huge sum or whether it will be a small sum. I may a little later be able to answer the Senator's question. Of course, a good deal will depend upon whether the commission shall be administered economically or whether the gate shall be thrown wide open and an effort made to be as liberal as possible with the employees of the commission.

Mr. President, before I leave this subject I wish to impress upon the Members of the Senate one further thought. We have on one side a tax, imposed by the commission, uncertain in amount and with nobody daring to estimate what the total will be. On the other side we have the right on the part of the commission to fix the amount of the commissions which may be charged by members of the stock exchanges and the rates of interest that may be charged on the debtor accounts.

If that is not putting stock-exchange members between the two millstones, without any certainty on the part of anybody as to what the result will be, I cannot conceive of anything being true. . . .

MR. FESS. Is not that an unusual set-up? I cannot recall at the moment any other agency where the officers are appointed by the Government to administer a law enacted by the Government and are authorized to assess the cost on some institution outside the Government. Is not that entirely new, unless we might say that some phase of it is involved in the processing tax? It seems to me that we are entering upon a very strange field.

MR. HASTINGS. Mr. President, I will say in that connection that I do not recall that I have had a single protest about that provision. I observed it as I read the bill, and I talked to some members of the committee about it, to see whether that was what was intended. I received from everybody the answer that that was what was intended; and, if you please, that removes one of the objections to the bill. People who are not interested in the stock exchange, people who are not interested in this business at all, might very well say to the Senator and to me, "We see no particular objection to annual salaries of $12,000. It makes no difference to us whether the commission costs $5,000,000 or $10,000,000 or $15,000,000 or $20,000,000 annually. It is no skin off our foreheads. It comes out of the stock exchange." So I suppose one of the purposes in putting this provision in the bill is to get rid of the opposition to it, so that nobody can possibly object to it, because none of the people back home, with the possible exception of a few people interested in stock exchanges, are concerned. . . .

Mr. President, it might be well at this time to call attention to the fact that the beginning of the inquiry into the stock exchange was a resolution which I introduced suggesting that an inquiry be made as to short sales being then made on the stock exchange. I was not responsible for the development into a wider inquiry, but, Mr. President, I have no complaint on that score, and I join in the compliments other Senators on the floor have extended to the committee for their investigation. I think they discovered evils which ought to have been discovered, and that they discovered much that was worth while that does not in any way enter into the bill now before the Senate. I am not complaining about the discoveries made, but I am complaining about trying in one act to remedy all the ills and cure all the injuries being indicted upon people by reason of the transactions taking place at the time the committee began their investigation. . . .

Mr. President, I desire to discuss another phase of the bill. The distinguished junior Senator from Oregon [Mr. Steiwer] the other day pointed out that his principal objection to the bill is to be found in the burden placed upon the corporations of the country. That is the basis of my principal objection. That is found in section 12 (a). The particularly objectionable feature is the one which provides for—

An agreement by the issuer . . . to comply with the provisions of this act and any amendments thereto, and with the rules and regulations made or to be made thereunder.

And so forth.

In the bill as it passed the House that provision has been eliminated. There is no such provision in the House bill. As the Senator from Oregon pointed out, it is particularly important that the issuer shall not be compelled to sign an agreement. It is wholly unnecessary to compel him to sign an agreement. There have been so many safeguards thrown around it in the bill, there is such a heavy penalty imposed upon those who violate any of the rules and regulations when their stock is listed, that it is wholly unnecessary and a useless burden upon the corporations to compel them to sign an agreement to do these things.

Mr. President, I desire to invite attention to what a corporation must do in order to have its stock listed upon any of the exchanges under the terms of the bill.

First. It must sign an agreement.

Mr. President, there are two points to which I particularly desire to call attention. The Senate is familiar with the fact that there must be originally a balance sheet for not more than the 3 preceding fiscal years. I assume that that language is clear enough to let in a corporation that has not been in existence for more than 2 years, although my attention has been called to the fact that it might entirely eliminate a corporation that has been in existence only 2 years; but I think the language is unobjectionable. It might be made a little clearer, but it is not of great importance. To my mind, however, the provision running all through the bill providing for independent public accountants is of the very greatest importance.

Here, let us say, is a corporation which desires to have its stock registered on the exchange. It is required to have a balance sheet for the 3 preceeding fiscal years certified, if required by the rules and regulations of the commission, by independent public accountants.

In the case of a large corporation, for instance, such as the United States Steel Corporation or the du Pont Co.—both of which, I assume, have independent public accountants to examine their books, as most corporations do, at least annually—does that or does it not mean that under the bill it is within the power of the commission to hold that such public accountants are not independent public accountants, because they were employed by the corporation itself, and that independent public accountants, under the bill and under the rules and regulations adopted by the commission, means such public accountants as the commission may select?

If that be the case, that which appears on the face of the matter to be a great burden, namely, the submission of annual and quarterly statements and such other statements as the commission may require, is greatly increased, because corporations cannot be certain that their own independent public accountants whom they have selected will be satisfactory to the commission. It might mean that the public accountants will be selected by the commission themselves, and that all the work will have to be done over.

Mr. President, a casual glance at the bill will indicate that a corporation will have a right to withdraw and have its stock stricken from the stock exchange.

... In that connection I desire to call the attention of the Senate to section 19 (b), to see whether or not my interpretation is correct. Section 19 is the one which gives the broad powers to the commission. Paragraph (b) of that section provides:

The commission is further authorized, if after making appropriate request in writing to a national securities exchange that such change effect on its own behalf specified changes in its rules and practices, and after appropriate notice and opportunity for hearing, the commission determines that such exchange has not made the changes so requested, and that such changes are necessary or appropriate for the protection of investors or to insure fair dealing in securities traded in upon such exchange or to insure fair administration of such exchange, by order to alter or supplement the rules of such exchange.

Of course, everybody must admit that that language, if it means anything, means that the commission is in control, and the stock exchange must do what it is requested to do by the commission; but here are some of the things that are specified that the commission may do if the stock exchange does not do them voluntarily. All of these things are in respect to such matters as—

(1) Safeguards in respect of the financial responsibility of members and adequate provision against the evasion of financial responsibility through the use of corporate forms or special partnerships; (2) the limitation or prohibition of the registration or trading in any security within a specified period after the issuance or primary distribution thereof; (3) the listing or striking from listing of any security—

"The listing or striking from listing of any security."

(4) Hours of trading; (5) the manner, method, and place of soliciting business—

And so forth.
And then, to be certain that everything is covered, the paragraph concludes with:

(13) Similar matters.

Mr. President, I am quite certain that under the provisions of section 19, regardless of what a corporation may want to do, when its securities are once listed on an exchange it cannot withdraw them without the consent of the commission.

Passing from that for a moment, because I do not want to overlook the matter I am about to mention, I desire to call attention to the very extraordinary power given the commission by section 21 of the bill. It provides that:

The commission may, in its discretion, make such investigations as it deems necessary to determine whether any person has violated or is about to violate any provision of this act or any rule or regulation thereunder, and may require or permit any person to file with it a statement in writing, under oath or otherwise as the commission shall determine, as to all the facts and circumstances concerning the matter to be investigated. The commission is authorized, in its discretion, to publish information concerning any such violations, and to investigate any facts, conditions, practices, or matters which it may seem necessary or proper to aid in the enforcement of the provisions of this act, in the prescribing of rules and regulations thereunder.

Listen to the last three lines of that paragraph:

Or in securing information to serve as a basis for recommending further legislation concerning the matters to which this act relates.

If I know anything about what that means, it means passing over to this commission all the things the Committee on Banking and Currency has had the authority to do, and to do the things the committee has been doing for something like a year or more. In other words, the authority to investigate is to be passed over by the Congress, not to some committee of the Senate, but to be passed over to the commission itself, and with authority to punish persons who fail to comply with their requests and appear as witnesses, to furnish books and papers, and what not. They can delve into every corporation, and, so far as I can see, the power extends to corporations which have nothing to do with the stock exchange, and do not care to have anything to do with it, and might disclose, and in many instances would disclose, the most secret formulas of many of the corporations. . . .

Mr. President, much has been said here about all the corporations of the country coming under the provisions of this measure. It is undoubtedly true that the bill in effect grants to the commission control of all the corporations of the country which desire to sell their securities outside the State in which they are incorporated. Section 15 of the bill, under the heading "Over-the-Counter Markets," is a section which has nothing at all to do with the stock exchanges. It is an effort to control the broker or dealer, and it provides that—

It shall be unlawful for any broker or dealer, singly or with any other person or persons, to make use of the mails or any means or instrumentality of interstate commerce for the purpose of making or creating, or enabling another to make or create, a market, otherwise than on a national securities exchange, for both the purchase and sale of any security (other than an exempted security or commercial paper, bankers' acceptances, commercial bills, or other similar obligations) in contravention of such rules and regulations as the commission may prescribe as necessary or appropriate in the public interest and to insure to investors protection comparable to that provided by and under authority of this act in the case of national securities exchanges. Such rules and regulations may provide for the regulation of all transactions on any such market for the registration with the commission of dealers and/or brokers making or creating such a market, and for the registration of the securities for which they make or create a market. For the purposes of this section the commission may make special rules and regulations in respect of securities or specified classes thereof listed, or entitled to unlisted trading privileges, upon any exchange on the date of the enactment of this act, which securities are not registered under the provisions of section 12 of this act.

In other words, if a corporation, at the time this bill becomes effective, concludes that it does not care to go into this agreement with the stock exchange which will make it binding upon the corporation to comply with the forty-odd things prescribed by the bill itself, as well as all the rules and regulations which may be made by the commission, if the corporation concludes that it does not want to take that chance, that it does not want to enter into an agreement to go on the stock exchange when it is uncertain whether it can ever get off, there is no provision made in the bill to let the corporation alone. If it is a corporation of any size, its securities will be scattered throughout many States. That is particularly true if it is a corporation whose stock has been listed upon the prominent exchanges of the country. So what is the corporation to do with respect to that? It cannot escape by saying, "We decline to go on," because no broker or dealer dare have any transaction with that particular stock until the corporation has complied with the provisions of this bill, until it has filed with the commission three annual statements, until it has done all these things.

In other words, there is only one kind of corporation which is not affected by the bill, and that is the corporation whose stock is dealt in by a broker only in the State wherein the particular broker and the particular corporation are located.

Out of the 500,000 corporations [in the country], how many are in such a position as that?

Is it not true that they must comply with the provisions of the bill? Whatever may be said and whatever may be thought about the members of the New York Stock Exchange, is there any reason for and is there any good sense in imposing that kind of obligation upon the corporations of the country? Or is it true, Mr. President, that in the past few months there has developed such a prejudice against capital of all kinds—against capital which is represented by investments in corporations—that we want to destroy them all?

I sometimes wonder whether the suggestion which has been made . . . is, after all, correct, that there are certain persons in this administration, close to the President of the United States, who are deliberately attempting to prevent the country from progressing; who are insisting that the Securities Act of 1933 is a thing that must remain on the statute books without being changed; who insist that we must go further, and strangle other securities by imposing upon them the restrictions contained in this bill, in order that there may be no further progress, and in order that people who have money may find no place to invest it except in the securities of the Government of the United States, and the Government of the United States in return will say, "In view of all these circumstances, in view of the need of these industries to go forward, in order that we may get rid of some of the unemployment, the Government itself must take hold of the industries, and place its own money in them, and place its own officials in charge of them"—in other words, bring all the industries of the Nation, just as they have the farms of the Nation, under the control of some bureau in Washington.

Mr. President, notwithstanding all the prejudices that may have been created against the stock exchange, notwithstanding all the prejudices that may have been created against corporations generally, notwithstanding all the prejudices that have been created against persons of wealth, I am confident in my own mind that unless the Securities Act shall be changed so that capital will be willing to invest in new enterprises, there will be no great progress made in this Nation. At the same time I say, even if we shall do that as is proposed in connection with this bill—amend the Securities Act so as to make it more liberal and attach such amendment to the pending measure—when we pass this proposed act, despite the improvement in the securities law, we shall have made conditions worse than they are at the present time.

I say, in closing, that the majority are proposing to do that which is not necessary to protect the innocent investors of the country. They are taking this action, it seems to me, in order to punish people who they think have done wrong. When they get an opportunity to punish them, they should do it in a way that will be effective; but when they do that, they should at the same time bear in mind that they are doing a great harm to many other people. There are in this country 14,000,000 people holding stocks of corporations to the amount of less than 100 shares each.

Senators must bear in mind that when they destroy corporations, when they destroy the wealth of the Nation, they are destroying the insurance companies which protect me and my family and which protect the families of others. They are destroying the savings banks which, in many instances, have their investments in this kind of securities. They are destroying the widow who has been left a few shares of stock which were once worth a few thousand dollars. They are destroying the very heart of the Nation when they destroy that class of people. This kind of legislation will ultimately do all that; if it shall be persisted in it will retard recovery, and it will be a long time before we get rid of the task of feeding the unemployed of the Nation.

MR. NORRIS. Mr. President, in a few minutes I will be compelled to leave the city to be gone for the balance of the day, and before I go I desire to make a few remarks upon the pending amendment.

The amendment now pending before the Senate is one which would place the control of the operation of the bill, when it shall become a law, in the hands of the Federal Trade Commission, instead of under the special commission proposed to be set up in the bill.

There has been controversy over that matter for some time. It was one of the points of controversy in the committee. The same controversy arose in the House, and the House provided that the control should be in the Federal Trade Commission.

An amendment similar to that now pending was defeated in the Committee on Banking and Currency of the Senate, we are told by the chairman of the committee, by a very small margin. The chairman of the committee himself stated on the floor of the Senate that in the committee he had favored the amendment. He feels, and perhaps some others feel, that since the committee has not seen fit to put the Federal Trade Commission in charge, he should vote against such a proposal now.

Mr. President, to me that argument has but little weight, especially when we realize that very likely it was fully discussed in the committee, and that the committee is almost evenly divided on this question, or was at the time it was voted on in the committee.

The argument is made that since the House provided that the Federal Trade Commission should be in charge of the enforcement of the law, if we insert such provision in the bill now, there will be nothing in conference. That is one reason why I think that if we favor the Federal Trade Commission having charge of the operation of the law, we ought to vote for the amendment, so as to take it out of conference, and therefore settle the matter once and for all.

After all, we are called upon now, in our vote on this amendment, to decide whether we prefer to have the Federal Trade Commission or the special commission to be set up in the Senate bill take charge of the enforcement of the law. That is the test. As I look at it, our votes should not be controlled by the vote in the committee, especially under these circumstances.

Mr. President, I believe the Federal Trade Commission ought to have charge of the enforcement of the law. I regretted exceedingly that the committee, in framing the bill, did not provide that the Federal Trade Commission should be in charge. It seems to me that in the hearings, remarkable as the work of the committee was, they pulled several teeth out of the bill before they reported it, and I think this is one of them. If we put the amendment of the Senator from Colorado [Mr. Costigan] into the bill now, we will be restoring, as I look at it, one very valuable and necessary tooth, which should be in the law in order to aid in its administration. . . .

MR. FLETCHER. I desire to correct one statement from an historical standpoint. The bill as originally introduced in the Senate carried provision that the administration of the law should be in the Federal Trade Commission. The Senator from Virginia offered an amendment to change that so as to provide for a special commission. That was the amendment which by a majority vote the Senate committee adopted. As originally introduced, the bill carried this idea.

MR. NORRIS. I thank the Senator. That only demonstrates the accuracy of what I said, and I am glad to have the Senator's statement.

As I look at it, when the committee took out the provision giving the Federal Trade Commission control and put the control in the special commission they pulled out a good, healthy tooth that was already in the bill. I want to see it go back. . . .

MR. BARKLEY. According to our view, we not only did not pull a tooth, but we established a tooth that will have nothing else to do except to chew on this particular problem.

MR. NORRIS. I understand; the Senator can have his viewpoint, but, as a matter of fact, the country and even the Senate do not look at it that way, and did not look at it that way when that tooth was pulled out. The country was worked up for fear the committee, engaged in pulling teeth out of this bill, would present us with a toothless old woman when they got through. I do not think they did that. As the Senator from Arizona, sitting near me, states, it will be 6 months before "she" can take a bite if they pull many more teeth out. I think there are many teeth in the bill. I do not want to be understood as being opposed to the bill in any respect. With this amendment or without it, I am for the bill, and hope it will be enacted.

Mr. President, in the first place, I am opposed to the establishment, unless it is absolutely necessary, of more bureaus and commissions in our Federal Government. We already have many of them doing good work, it is true; but if we provide for the commission proposed to be set up we are going to duplicate the work, I think. The Federal Trade Commission as now constituted have established offices for the enforcement of the securities law, which will become a part of this work, in different parts of the country. They have the machinery now in operation, practically enough machinery to put this law into operation at once, if it is put on the statute books. They are not inexperienced men who do not understand what this law will be.

It is said, and that is the argument in favor of a special commission, that we shall have specialists in this line on the Commission. I think we can all concede that it should be a commission which is not under the control of the body which we want to govern. The Commission should not be under the control of bankers. It ought to be in the control of independent men. They should, of course, be men who have sufficient ability, wisdom, and courage to carry out the provisions of the bill according to their true meaning. Such are the men now in the Federal Trade Commission. They are able men. They have been engaged in governing business of this kind ever since the establishment of the Commission. They have been dealing with problems which are very much akin to those with which the special commission provided for in the bill will have to deal if the bill becomes a law. We shall then have men already tried to a great extent, and ready to go on with the service.

Another reason why I believe the Federal Trade Commission should be designated is because of what I believe to be the economy of the situation. In the last session of Congress we passed a bill authorizing the President of the United States to bring about economy by the consolidation of bureaus and special offices and departments. If there had been then a separate commission doing this line of work, there is no doubt in my mind that the President, in carrying out the provisions of such a law, would have combined the two Commissions. They ought to be combined. They are very much alike in their operations. Economy will result if we adopt this amendment. We shall thereby save money for the taxpayers.

I think the Federal Trade Commission is more likely to be efficient in administering the law than a new commission. If we have numberless commissions doing all kinds of governmental investigation and work, we shall find that the attention of the country will not be attracted to the different commissions. I feel that if this special commission shall be appointed, it will not be many years before the country will lose track of what it is doing. New appointments may be made; inexperienced, really unqualified men may be put on the commission; and its action will not attract the attention that will be attracted by the addition of the Federal Trade Commission, an outstanding investigating governmental body which has been in the eyes of the people of the country for years, in fact ever since the commission was established during the administration of President Wilson.

If appointments are to be made to another commission which is not in the public eye, it is very likely that appointments will be made and changes will be made in its membership to the detriment of good government without the country ever knowing anything about it. That cannot happen with the Federal Trade Commission.

It is said that the Federal Trade Commission is already overworked. It has done, and is doing, a remarkable work. It is easy to increase its membership if necessary to enable it to do the work entrusted to it. The commission that is designated will be in reality the general for an army of men who will be appointed to go into records more or less of a technical nature and get the facts desired by the Commission. The Commissioners will act finally upon the facts thus assembled.

Here we have a Commission already established, equipped as no other branch of the Government is equipped, prepared to do this kind of work. It does not make any difference whether it investigates a corporation which is selling bonds, or whether it investigates a corporation which is making sewing machines; in either case its purpose is to protect the people of the country against fraud and wrongdoing. . . .

MR. COSTIGAN. No one knows better than the able Senator from Nebraska that the Federal Trade Commission was created in large part to deal with unfair practices.

MR. NORRIS. That is one of the superlative things emphasized at the time of the passage of the original act.

MR. COSTIGAN. Does not that fact and the experience of the Commission in dealing with such practices especially equip it to serve under the bill being considered by the Senate?

MR. NORRIS. I think so. I do not think that can be disputed. The members of the Commission are trained and experienced. The very law that provides for their existence requires that they shall be men of the type qualified to undertake this additional work. They have been engaged in work very similar to this—a part of it, I think, in reality—because the Senator from Florida has announced that if this amendment shall be defeated, and if this task shall be left to a special commission, he will offer another amendment to take away from the Federal Trade Commission authority to operate under the so-called "Securities Act." That act has been in operation for some time, and the Federal Trade Commission has had considerable experience with it.

I called on a member of the Federal Trade Commission for some information about the work they had done under that act. I shall not weary the Senate with any long statistics. I shall simply state that they have had a great many cases, running into the thousands, of little things that have arisen under the Securities Act. Every action they have taken stands at the present time. There has not been a single appeal from any action taken by the Federal Trade Commission under that act.

Let me give the Senate some of the figures. Under that act the Federal Trade Commission has made 144 orders. That is quite a number. Some of them are important. Some of them are of minor importance. Altogether there have been 144 orders. Those were what are called orders of withdrawal. Not a single appeal was taken, although appeal is allowed by law, from any order of withdrawal made by the Commission.

A corporation desiring to issue securities files schedules, and so forth, as provided by law, with the Federal Trade Commission; and in case of adverse action by the Federal Trade Commission an order of withdrawal is made. They do not allow securities to be issued in a particular case where they issue an order of withdrawal. Senators should realize that this is of tremendous importance in saving the investors of America from investing their hard-earned funds in securities that would be considered, if the whole facts were known, to be bad. That is what a withdrawal order means.

Altogether, the Federal Trade Commission has issued 105 of those orders. That means that already there have been 105 cases under the Securities Act in which the Federal Trade Commission has not permitted stocks and bonds to be issued and sold to the public. Of those 105 cases, 39 were stop orders. A stop order requires the corporation to refrain from issuing any stock. From all those orders, as matters stand today, not one appeal has been taken.

I submit that the work already done by the Federal Trade Commission illustrates, and I think practically demonstrates, its equipment for the additional work provided for in this bill.

I said that in carrying out and fulfilling the duties of the Commission it has established offices in different parts of the United States, and has put in employees whose work many times is of a technical nature, whose duty it is to ferret out and assemble the facts before these orders are passed on. So the Commission is already doing a part of this work. It is doing it successfully, I think.

As a matter of fact, Mr. President, I think the work which the bill provides shall be done by this Commission is of tremendous importance. Do not get the idea that the country is not interested in this proposed legislation. People all over the country are watching it. The country, I think, has confidence in the Federal Trade Commission. . . .

MR. FLETCHER. Mr. President, I offer the amendment which I send to the desk. . . .I ask that my amendment may be read.

THE VICE PRESIDENT. The amendment will be read.

THE CHIEF CLERK. On page 57, after line 9, it is proposed to insert the following:

Title II—Amendments to Securities Act of 1933

SECTION 201. (a) That paragraph (1) of section 2 of the Securities Act of 1933 is amended to read as follows:

"The term 'security' means any note, stock, treasury stock, bond, debenture, evidence of indebtedness, certificate of interest or participation in any profit-sharing agreement, collateral trust certificate, preorganization certificate or subscription, transferable share, investment contract, voting-trust certificate, certificate of deposit for a security, fractional undivided interest in oil, gas, or other mineral rights, or, in general, any interest or instrument commonly known as a 'security,' or any certificate of interest or participation in, temporary or interim certificate for, receipt for, or warrant or right to subscribe to or purchase, any of the foregoing."

(b) Paragraph (4) of such section 2 is amended to read as follows:

"(4) The term 'issuer' means every person who issues or proposes to issue any security, except that with respect to certificates of deposit, voting-trust certificates, or collateral-trust certificates, or with respect to certificates of interest or shares in an unincorporated investment trust not having a board of directors (or persons performing similar functions) or of the fixed, restricted management, or unit type, the term 'issuer' means the person performing the acts and assuming the duties of depositor or manager pursuant to the provisions of the trust or other agreement or instrument under which such securities are issued; and except that with respect to equipment-trust certificates or like securities, the term 'issuer' means the person by whom the equipment or property is or is to be used; and except that with respect to fractional undivided interests in oil, gas, or other mineral rights, the term 'issuer' means the owner of any such right or of any interest in such right (whether whole or fractional) who creates fractional interests therein for the purpose of public offering."

(c) Paragraph (10) of such section 2 is amended to read as follows:

"(10) The term 'prospectus' means any prospectus, notice, circular, advertisement, letter, or communication, written or by radio, which offers any security for sale; except that (a) a communication shall not be deemed a prospectus if it is proved that prior to or at the same time with such communication a written prospectus meeting the requirements of section 10 was sent or given to the person to whom the communication was made, by the person making such communication or his principal, and (b) a notice, circular, advertisement, letter, or communication in respect of a security shall not be deemed to be a prospectus if it states from whom a written prospectus meeting the requirements of section 10 may be obtained and, in addition, does no more than identify the security, state the price thereof, and state by whom orders will be executed."

SEC. 202. (a) Paragraph (2) of section 3 (a) of such act is amended to read as follows:

"(2) Any security issued or guaranteed by the United States or any Territory thereof, or by the District of Columbia, or by any State of the United States, or by any political subdivision of a State or Territory, or by any public instrumentality of one or more States or Territories, or by any person controlled or supervised by and acting as an instrumentality of the Government of the United States pursuant to authority granted by the Congress of the United States, or any certificate of deposit for any of the foregoing, or any security issued or guaranteed by any national bank, or by any banking institution organized under the laws of any State or Territory of the District of Columbia, the business of which is substantially confined to banking and is supervised by the State or Territorial banking commission or similar official; or any security issued by or representing an interest in or a direct obligation of a Federal Reserve bank";

(b) Paragraph (4) of such section 3 (a) is amended by striking out "corporation" and inserting in lieu thereof "person."

(c) Such section 3 (a) is further amended by striking out the period at the end of paragraph (8) and inserting in lieu thereof a semicolon, and by inserting immediately after such paragraph (8) the following new paragraphs:

"(9) Any security issued by a person where the issue of which it is a part is exchanged by it with its own security holders exclusively and where no commission or other remuneration is paid or given directly or indirectly for soliciting such exchange;

"(10) Any security which is issued in exchange for one or more bona fide outstanding securities, claims or property interests, or partly in such exchange and partly for cash, where the conditions of such issuance are subject to the supervision of any court, or of any official or agency of the United States authorized to exercise such supervision, or of any State banking or insurance commission or similar authority;

"(11) Any security which is a part of an issue sold only to persons resident within a single State or Territory, where the issuer of such security is a person resident and doing buisness within, or, if a corporation, incorporated by and doing business within, such State or Territory."

SEC. 203. (a) Paragraph (1) of section 4 of such act is amended (1) by striking out "not with or through an underwriter and"; and (2) by striking out "last" and inserting in lieu thereof "first."

(b) Paragraph (3) of such section 4 is hereby repealed.

SEC. 204. Subsection (c) of section 5 of such act is hereby repealed.

SEC. 205. Paragraph (1) of section 10 (b) of such act is amended to read as follows:

"(1) When a prospectus is used more than 13 months after the effective date of the registration statement, the information in the statements contained therein shall be as of a date not more than 12 months prior to such use, so far as such information is known to the user of such prospectus or can be furnished by such user without unreasonable effort or expense."

SEC. 206. (a) Section 11 (a) of such act is amended by adding, after the last line thereof, the following new sentence: "If such person acquired the security after the issuer has made generally available to its security holders an earning statement covering a period of at least 12 months beginning after the effective date of the registration statement, then the right of recovery under this subsection shall be conditioned on proof that such person acquired the security relying upon such untrue statement in the registration statement or relying upon the registration statement and not knowing of such omission, but such reliance may be established without proof of the reading of the registration statement by such person."

(b) Clauses (C) and (D) of paragraph (3) of section 11 (b) of such act are amended to read as follows: "(C) as regards any part of the registration statement purporting to be made on the authority of an expert (other than himself) or purporting to be a copy of or extract from a report or valuation of an expert (other than himself), such part was made by an expert selected after reasonable investigation and with reasonable ground for belief in his ability for such purpose, and he had no reasonable ground to believe and did not believe, at the time such part of the registration statement became effective, that the statements therein were untrue or that there was an omission to state a material fact required to be stated therein or necessary to make the statements therein not misleading, or that such part of the registration statement did not fairly represent the statement of the expert or was not a fair copy or extract from the report or valuation of the expert; and (D) as regards any part of the registration statement purporting to be a statement made by an official person or purporting to be a copy of or extract from a public official document, he had no reasonable ground to believe and did not believe, at the time such part of the registration statement became effective, that the statements therein were untrue or that there was an omission to state a material fact required to be stated therein or necessary to make the statements therein not misleading, or that such part of the registration statement did not fairly represent the statement made by the official person or was not a fair copy of or extract from the public official document."

(c) Subsection (c) of such section 11 is amended to read as follows:

"(c) In determining, for the purpose of paragraph (3) of subsection (b) of this section, what constitutes reasonable investigation and reasonable ground for belief, the standard of reasonableness shall be that required of a prudent man in the management of his own property."

(d) Subsection (e) of such section 11 is amended to read as follows:

"(e) The suit authorized under subsection (a) may be to recover such damages as shall represent the difference between the amount paid for the security (not exceeding the price at which the security was offered to the public) and (1) the value thereof as of the time such suit was brought, or (2) the price at which such security shall have been disposed of in the market before suit, or (3) the price at which such security shall have been disposed of after suit but before judgment if such damages shall be less than the damages representing the difference between the amount paid for the security (not exceeding the price at which the security was offered to the public) and the value thereof as of the time such suit was brought: *Provided*, That if the defendant proves that any portion or all of such damages represents other than the depreciation in value of such security resulting from such part of the registration statement, with respect to which his liability is asserted, not being true or omitting to state a material fact required to be stated therein or necessary to make the statements therein not misleading, such portion of or all such damages shall not be recoverable. In no event shall any underwriter (unless such underwriter shall have received for acting as an underwriter some benefit, directly or indiecty, greater than underwriters similarly situated with reference to the issuer, or other underwriters) be liable in any suit or as a consequence of suits authorized under subsection (a) for damages in excess of the total price at which the securities underwritten by him were offered to the public. In any suit under this or any other section of this title the court may, in its discretion, require an undertaking for the payment of the costs of such suit, including reasonable attorney's fees, and if judgment shall be rendered against a party litigant, upon the motion of the other party litigant, such costs may be assessed in favor of such party litigant (whether or not such undertaking has been required) if the court believes the suit or the defense to have been without merit, in an amount sufficient to reimburse him for the reasonable expenses incurred by him in connection with such suit, such costs to be taxed in the manner usually provided for taxing of costs in the courts in which the suit was heard."

SEC. 207. Section 13 of such act is amended (a) by striking out "2 years" wherever it appears therein and inserting in lieu thereof "1 year"; (b) by striking out "10 years" and inserting in lieu thereof "5 years"; and (c) by inserting immediately before the period at the end thereof a comma and the following: "or under section 12 (2) more than 5 years after the sale."

SEC. 208. Section 15 of such act is amended by inserting immediately before the period at the end thereof a comma and the following: "unless the act for which such controlled person is alleged to be liable under section 11 or 12 was not performed at the direction of the controlling person nor to enable such controlling person to evade liability under said sections."

SEC. 209. (a) The first sentence of subsection (a) of section 19 of such act is amended by striking out the word "accounting" and inserting in lieu thereof the following: "terms deemed by the Commission to be accounting, technical."

(b) Subsection (a) of such section 19 is further amended by adding at the end thereof the following new sentence: "Acts done or omitted in good faith in compliance with the rules and regulations of the Commission authorized by this title shall be deemed, for the purpose of determining any and all liability under this title, to be in compliance with its provisions, notwithstanding the fact that such rules and regulations may, after such act or omission, be amended or rescinded or be determined by judicial or other authority to have been made by the Commission in excess of or contrary to, the authority conferred upon it by the provisions of this title."

SEC. 210. Upon the expiration of 90 days after the date upon which a majority of the members of the Federal Securities Exchange Commission appointed under section 4 of title I of this act have qualified and taken office, all powers, duties, and functions of the Federal Trade Commission under the Securities Act of 1933 shall be transferred to such Commission, together with all property, books, records, and unexpended balances of appropriations used by or available to the Federal Trade Commission for carrying out its functions under the Securities Act of 1933.

On page 1, after line 2, insert:

"Title I—Regulation of Securities Exchanges"

In sections 2 to 30, both inclusive, of the bill, except in section 7 (d), strike out the word "act" wherever it appears and insert in lieu thereof the word "title."

MR. FLETCHER. Mr. President, it will be observed after listening to the reader of this amendment that its purpose is to clarify certain provisions of the present Securities Act to relieve it of some ambiguities and to liberalize it. The effort has been to meet objections and criticisms and complaints which have come to the committee that the present act is too drastic, and is interfering with business. We have tried to meet those objections by this amendment; and, so far as I know, no objection has been raised to the amendment.

I have conferred with a number of Senators, and, so far as I know, the amendment has met with their universal approval. I have heard no objection to it. At any rate, Mr. President, I have not only had the amendment printed, but it has been on the desks of Senators, and I have talked with them about it. There never has been any other purpose than to present the amendment at the proper time.

Last Monday I had inserted in the Record a memorandum explanatory of the amendment, and it has been in the Congressional Record ever since then. I now ask that the clerk read—because he has a better voice than I have —the memorandum which I send to the desk, which will explain the provisions of the amendment.

THE PRESIDING OFFICER. (Mr. Bachman in the chair). Without objection, the memorandum will be read.

The legislative clerk read as follows:

Memorandum Explanatory of Suggested Amendments to the
Securities Act

Amendment to section 2 (1): The purpose of this amendment is to make it clear that certificates of deposit, fractional oil royalties, and similar interests are included within the definition of a security and thus subject to the Securities Act. Some doubt exists whether they are so included under the present language of the act.

Amendment to section 2 (4): The purpose of this amendment are (1) to eliminate a guarantor from the definition of an issuer and (2) to define the issuer of fractional undivided interests in oil, gas, or other mineral rights. The words "or persons" have also been deleted from the definition of an issuer of certificates of deposit, etc. The singular will include the plural where necessary, and the express use of the plural word has caused some doubts about the commission's interpretation that a committee, trust, or other entity, and not the individual member, is the issuer intended by the definition. Putting the status of an issuer of the guaranteed security upon the guarantor raises serious practical difficulties in connection with the filing of registration statements. The act will adequately cover guarantors and the furnishing of information concerning them without this clause. The amendment respecting fractional undivided interests in oil, gas, or other mineral rights is necessary in connection with the amendments to section 2 (1).

Amendment to section 2 (10): The purposes of this amendment are (1) to make clear beyond any doubt the interpretation of the commission that literature accompanying a prospectus as well as literature sent subsequent to the sending of a prospectus shall not be required to conform to the prospectus requirements of section 10 of the act, and (2) to remove from a person required to furnish a prospectus the absolute duty to see that the prospectus is received by the person to whom it is sent. It seems sufficient to require proof of the actual sending of a prospectus without making the sender take a pledge of nondelivery.

Amendment to section 3 (a) (2): The purposes of this amendment are: (1) to put the District of Columbia upon a parity with the States with reference to the exemption of bank stocks issued by banks organized under the laws of the District of Columbia; (2) to exempt municipal bondholders' protective committees; and (3) to extend the scope of the public instrumentality exemption to expanding activities in which governments are indulging. The exemption of municipal bondholders' protective committees is dictated purely by considerations of expediency. These committees have generally had a good record in the past. There is far from the urge present in these cases as contrasted with industrial and real-estate reorganizations for committee members to take responsibility for the sake of profit, so that as a practical matter there is hesitation on the part of committee members to assume even a slight responsibility. The extension of the public instrumentality exemption is dictated by conservative decisions of courts which have refused to regard as "essential governmental functions" such activities as the furnishing of light, transportation, power, and even water.

Amendment to section 3 (a) (4): The purpose of this amendment is to correct an obvious error in the original act which limited this exemption simply to corporate organizations when its extension to unincorporated associations is equally defensible in practice and in theory.

Amendment adding sections 3 (a) (9), (10), and (11): This amendment has several purposes. The primary purpose of the amendment is to make clear that the exemptions accorded by the present sections 4 (3) and 5 (c) of the act extend beyond the particular transactions therein covered, to the security itself. Considerable confusion has existed on this point, and the amendment is merely a confirmation of interpretations of the sections by the Commission. The new section 3 (a) (9) incorporates the first clause of the existing section 4 (3), and makes clear, in accordance with the interpretation of the Commission, that in order that the exemption may be available the entire issue must be exchanged exclusively with existing security holders. This paragraph also effects a change which makes clear that the type of commission or other remuneration the payment of which will remove the exemption is that paid for soliciting an exchange. This conforms to the interpretation of the Commission. The new section 3 (a) (10) incorporates the second clause of the existing section 4 (3) and substantially extends the present provisions in order to cover various forms of readjustments of the rights of holders of outstanding securities, claims, and property interests where the holders will be protected by court supervision of the conditions of the issuance of their new securities. Also, such readjustments under the supervision of State banking, insurance, and similar officials are brought within the exemption. Thus, the amended section will afford an exemption to securities issued in connection with a readjustment of outstanding real estate bond issues, and the exemption will also cover securities issued under the supervision of the Comptroller of the Currency, the Federal Reserve Board, and similar Federal officials, as well as State banking and insurance officials. By the requirement that securities, claims, and property interests must be bona fide outstanding, the new section will provide protection against resort to the exemption for the purpose of evading the registration requirements of the act. The new section 3 (a) (11) incorporates the existing section 5 (c) of the act and further makes clear that the exemption is not limited to the use of the mails. Thus, a person who comes within the purpose of the exemption but happens to use a newspaper for the circulation of his advertising literature, which newspaper is transmitted in interstate commerce, does not thereby lose the benefits of the exemption.

Amendment to section 4(1): The purposes of this amendment are (1) to remove the phrase "not with or through an underwriter" in the second clause of the section; and (2) to correct an error in the third clause of the section, making it clear that the original date of the public offering is the date from which the year is to be calculated during which a dealer is bound to supply his customers with a prospectus. The Commission has recognized by its interpretations that a "public offering" is necessary for "distribution." Therefore, there can be no underwriter within the meaning of the act in the absence of a public offering and the phrase eliminated in the second clause is really superfluous.

Repeal of sections 4 (3) and 5 (c): These are in accordance with the amendment provided by the new sections 3 (a) (9) (10) and (11).

Amendment to section 10 (b) (1): The purpose of this amendment is to place only a reasonable instead of an absolute duty upon the user of a prospectus 13 months after its issuance of keeping the information therein up to date. It was originally conceived that users of prospectuses could protect themselves herein by contract with the issuer, but it appears only too likely that users of the prospectus will not have the forethought, and therefore will be left in a situation where they cannot of their own accord conform with the requirements of the act.

Amendment to section 11 (b) (3): This amendment restates the existing section. It seems that the section as written, though meaning the same thing, has had an unfortunate psychological effect.

Amendment to section 11 (c): This amendment has the same purpose as the preceding amendment. The term "fiduciary relationship" has been terrifyingly portrayed. The amendment substitutes for that language the accepted common-law definition of the duty of a fiduciary.

Amendment to section 11 (e): This amendment is the most important of all. It has three purposes: (1) it permits the defendant in an action under section 11 to reduce the damages so that he will not be liable for damages which he proves had no relation to his misconduct; (2) it provides that an underwriter who does not receive any preferential treatment is permitted to limit his total liability for all suits brought under section 11 to the extent of the public offering price of the securities which he underwrote; and (3) it provides, as a defense against blackmail suits as well as a defense against purely contentious litigation on the part of the defendant, that a court can require a bond for costs and can assess costs against either the plaintiff or the defendant, where the court is convinced either that the plaintiff's suit had no merit or that the defendant's defense had no merit. The suggested amendment seems equitable.

Amendment to section 13: The purpose of this amendment is to reduce the periods of limitations on actions to one half of those at present provided by the section; and also to correct an apparently inadvertent omission by making the 5- (formerly 10-) year period of limitation on actions expressly applicable to section 12 (2).

Amendment to section 15: The purpose of this amendment is to restrict the scope of the section so as more accurately to carry out its real purpose. The mere existence of control is not made a basis for liability unless that control is effectively exercised to bring about the action upon which liability is based.

Amendment to section 19 (a): The purpose of this amendment is to permit the regulations of the Commission, under the powers conferred upon it, adequately to protect persons who rely upon them in good faith. The powers of the Commission are also extended to include the defining of technical as well as trade terms. . . .

MR. FLETCHER. Mr. President, I offer the amendment which I send to the desk. . . .

Mr. President, the amendment has been printed, and I have made no change at all in it. I ask to have it printed in the Record, and that the further reading be dispensed with.

THE PRESIDING OFFICER. Without objection, that order will be made.

Mr. Fletcher's amendment is to insert at the end of the bill the following new sections:

SEC. 211. Section 2 of the Securities Act of 1933 is amended by adding at the end thereof the following new paragraphs:

"(13) The term 'protective committee' means any persons or group of persons who propose or purport to act, or who on the date this paragraph takes effect are acting, for and in behalf of owners or holders of securities for the purpose of protecting, preserving, and/or forwarding the common interests of owners or holders of such securities (A) in connection with a reorganization, rehabilitation, or liquidation of, or composition by, the issuer of the securities, (B) the substitution of other securities therefor, (C) a readjustment or modification of the rights or liabilities evidenced by or embodied in the securities, or (D) the assertion of any such rights other than voting rights; except that such term shall not include any person or group of persons upon whom authority so to act was or is conferred by the instrument under which the securities were originally issued or by any amendment to such instrument.

"(14) The term 'protective committee agreement' means any agreement, consent, authorization, power of attorney, or other instrument, by whatever name called, by which the owners or holders of securities confer upon a protective committee authority to act for and in their behalf.

"(15) The term 'plan of reorganization' means any plan or agreement for reorganization, rehabilitation, liquidation, or composition, or for readjustment or modification of securities, or for the assertion of rights (other than voting rights) evidenced by or embodied in any securities."

SEC. 212. (a) Section 17 of such act is amended by adding after subsection (b) thereof the following new subsections:

"(c) From and after 60 days after this subsection takes effect, it shall be unlawful for any protective committee, directly or indirectly, to make use of any means or instruments of transportation or communication in interstate commerce or of the mails in order to solicit a protective committee agreement or any amendment thereto, or in order to solicit adherence, assent, or consent to any such agreement or amendment for an expression of assent or dissent, or in order to solicit adherence, assent, or consent to any plan of reorganization or any amendment thereto, or in order to submit any such plan or amendment for an expression of assent or dissent, unless—

"(1) a statement concerning such agreement, plan, or amendment, complying with the requirements of subsection (d) shall be in effect;

"(2) at the time of filing of the statement referred to in paragraph (1), such committee shall file with the Commission (A) an undertaking to file monthly thereafter, until this Commission shall determine by appropriate order that the committee has ceased operation, a written report under oath, for the period not covered by previous reports, in such form and containing such information concerning the activities of the committee as the Commission, by rules and regulations, may require as necessary or appropriate for the proper protection of investors, and a list showing the names and the last-known addresses of any persons (other than those listed in any list previously filed) to whom any individual solicitation or submission is proposed to be addressed at the date of the filing of the list, or was addressed during the period since the filing of the last previous list; and (B) an undertaking to file with the Commission copies of any amendments thereafter made to the protective committee agreement or plan or reorganization, and copies of any plan of reorganization thereafter adopted pursuant to the provisions of the protective committee agreement, such filing to be made not later than 10 days after such amendment is made or such plan is adopted;

"(3) at or before the time of solicitation or submission by any such means, the committee shall, (A) in the case of an individual solicitation or submission, send or give to each person to whom the solicitation or submission is addressed a copy of a summary of such of the information contained in the statement required under paragraph (1) as the Commission may by rules and regulations require as necessary or appropriate for the proper protection of investors, or (B) in the case of solicitation or submission by general notice or advertisement, offer to furnish on request a copy of such summary to any member of the group to which the solicitation or submission is addressed; and

"(4) In any case at which the terms of the protective committee agreement, the composition of the protective committee, and/or the qualifications of its members, fail to conform to the recommendations which may be established by the Commission from time to time for various classes of securities and types of situations, all written communications or communications by radio, made by the committee in the course of any solicitation or submission of the character referred to in this subsection, shall contain a clear statement to that effect. In the case of a written communication, such statement shall be in print, type, or writing as legible as that used generally throughout the communication and shall be followed by a brief summary of the provisions or matters in which there is failure to conform to the Commission's recommendations.

"(d) The statement required under subsection (c) (1) shall be filed with the Commission in triplicate, shall be signed by every member of the committee, shall include such information, documents, and exhibits as the Commission by rules and regulations may require as necessary or appropriate for the proper protection of investors, comparable in character to that required in registration statements for certificates of deposit, and shall include specifically a list giving the last-known address of each person known or believed to be the owner or holder of securities to whom any individual solicitation and/or submission is, at the date of filing such statement, proposed to be addressed. A statement with respect to an amendment to a plan of reorganization or a protective committee agreement concerning which a statement has previously been filed, or with respect to a plan of reorganization adopted pursuant to any such agreement, may be filed as an amendment to such previously filed statement. The provisions of section 6 (d) and section 8 with reference to registration statements shall apply to statements required under subsection (c) (1), and the term 'issuer' as used in such sections shall apply to the protective committee. At the time of filing any statement required under such subsection the committee filing the same shall pay to the Commission a fee of $25. The filing of any such statement or of an amendment thereto shall be deemed to have taken place upon the receipt thereof if it is accompanied by a United States postal money order or certified bank check or cash for the amount of the fee required. No such statement shall be filed within the first 30 days after subsection (c) takes effect.

"(e) The provisions of subsection (c) of this section shall not apply to any protective committee which proposes or purports to act for and in behalf of (1) a group of not more than 25 persons; (2) security holders who are all persons resident in, and/or corporations incorporated by and doing business in, the State or Territory in which the members of the committee are all resident; (3) holders of securities of the classes referred to in section 3 (a) (2) or (3); or (4) holders of securities of a value of not more than $100,000, as determined in accordance with the rules and regulations of the Commission, if the committee complies with such terms and conditions as the Commission may by rules and regulations prescribe as necessary or appropriate for the proper protection of investors."

(b) The last subsection of section 17 or such act is amended by striking out "(c)" and inserting in lieu thereof "(f)."

SEC. 213. Section 23 of such act is amended to read as follows:

"SEC. 23. Neither the fact that a registration statement for a security or a statement required under section 17 (c) has been filed or is in effect, nor the fact that a stop order is not in effect with respect thereto, shall be deemed a finding by the Commission that such statement is true and accurate on its face or that it does not contain an untrue statement of fact or omit a material fact, or be held to mean that the Commission has in any way passed upon the merits of, or given approval to, any security, or any protective committee, protective committee agreement, or plan of reorganization. It shall be unlawful to make, or cause to be made, to any person, any representation contrary to the foregoing provisions of this section."

SEC. 214. Section 24 of such act is amended to read as follows:

"SEC. 24. Any person who willfully violates any of the provisions of this title, or the rules and regulations promulgated by the Commission under authority thereof, or any person who willfully fails to carry out the terms of any undertaking filed with the Commission as required by the provisions of this title, or any person who willfully, in a registration statement, or in any statement, list, or report required to be filed under section 17 (c) (1) or (2), or in any summary required to be sent, given, or furnished under section 17 (c) (3), makes any untrue statement of a material fact or omits to state any material fact required to be stated therein or necessary to make the statement therein not misleading, shall upon conviction be fined not more than $5,000 or imprisoned not more than 5 years, or both."

MR. FLETCHER. I have a memorandum explaining the amendment, which I ask to have printed in the Record without reading.

THE PRESIDING OFFICER. Without objection, that order will be made.

The memorandum is as follows:

Memorandum Explanatory of the Attached Proposed Amendments
to the Securities Act of 1933 Offered as Amendments to the
National Securities Exchange Act

SECTION 211: This section adds definitions of the terms "protective committee,"
"protective committee agreement," and "plan of reorganization." The definition of
the term "protective committee" is based upon the definition contained in the Public
Trust Commission Act of Michigan, section 2 (d) (Mich. 1933, Public Act No. 89, as
amended by Act No. 205). The term is so defined as to apply to committees existing
at the time of the passage of the act. It excludes therefrom a trustee under the trust
indenture under which the bonds were originally issued. The term "protective committee agreement" is intended to be drawn broadly enough to include any instrument
by which committees secure power from security holders. In order to avoid the
provisions of the Securities Act, which apply only in case of a sale of securities, many
committees have adopted the device of securing powers of attorney rather than of
issuing certificates of deposit. This definition will subject such committees to the
provisions of section 17 as proposed to be amended.

SECTION 212: This section proposes to amend section 17 of the Securities Act.
Section 17 was chosen because its provisions are left untouched by the proposed
amendment to the Bankruptcy Act (H. R. 5384).

This section adds three new subsections to section 17. Subsection (c) (1) requires of
committees the filing of a statement with the Commission, which, as described by
subsection (d), will correspond to a registration statement now required for non-
exempt certificates of deposit. Paragraph (2) requires an undertaking of each committee to furnish monthly reports on its activities, to furnish supplemental lists of
security holders solicited and copies of plans and of amendments to agreements and
plans later adopted. Paragraph (3) requires each committee to furnish the security
holders it solicits copies of a summary of the statement required by paragraph (1),
which will correspond to the prospectus provided for in section 10 for registered
securities. Paragraph (4) authorizes the Commission to establish recommendations as
to the terms of protective committee agreements and the composition and membership qualifications of protective committees, and requires all literature and broadcasts
of committees to contain statements that there is failure to conform to such recommendations if such is the case. The subsection takes active effect after 60 days.

Subsection (d) describes the statement required under subsection (c). It is to
contain information corresponding to that required in registration statements for
certificates of deposit. The Commission is given the power to issue stop orders against
the effectiveness of any statement, as in the case of registration statements. A filing fee
of $25 is charged. No statements are to be filed for the first 30 days after the
subsection takes effect, so that the Commission may evolve machinery for handling
the new requirements.

Subsection (e) provides exemptions which correspond, in general, to the following
exemptions from registration provided in the act: Section 4 (1), second clause,
exemption for nonpublic offerings; section 5 (c)—or as proposed in the amendments

heretofore submitted, section 3 (a) (11)–exemption for local offerings; section 3 (a) (2) and (3), exemptions for governmental and bank securities, and for short-term obligations, here applied to protective committees acting for such securities; section 3 (b), exemptions for issues of less than $100,000, on conditions established by the Commission.

SECTION 213: This amendment applies the present provisions of section 23 to the statements required under new subsection (c) (1) of section 17.

SECTION 214: The proposed amendment to section 24 imposes criminal liability for violation of the new provisions, including misstatements in the required statements, lists, reports, or summaries, and failures to carry out any agreements required by the new provisions.

It is to be noted that enforcement of the provisions of the new subsection is left to injunction, stop order, and criminal prosecution. No civil liability attaches for any violation thereof.

MR. FLETCHER. I will state that the purpose of the amendment is to place under the jurisdiction of the Federal Trade Commission, so far as the Securities Act goes, bondholders' committees or protective committees. Senators know about them. I need not take the time of the Senate to tell about their operations.

Where bonds are in default, protective committees or bondholders' committees are immediately formed, very often controlled by the people who issued or distributed the bonds. Such committees call for the bonds to be sent in to them, under the representation that they will look after the interests of the bondholders. The bonds are sent in and the committees issue receipts or certificates of some kind against them, and are supposed to endeavor to realize upon the bonds and to take care of the interests of the bondholders.

I have numbers of letters from all parts of the country, from people who have put up their bonds with these committees, in which they say, "We cannot find out anything about our bonds. We understand that a receiver has been appointed, and that receivers' fees and lawyers' fees and other expenses are eating up everything, but we hear nothing as to any interest payments or prospects of realizing anything on the bonds."

Of course, a bondholder may go into court, I take it, and compel an accounting, and reach an adjustment of some kind in that way; but that is too burdensome. It is practically prohibitory, because a bondholder would have to pay out for lawyers' fees and expenses in procuring court action more than his bond would be worth; so that now the bondholders are practically helpless. They are entirely in the hands of the committees; and I think there ought to be some requirement that such committees shall file with the Federal Trade Commission their agreements with the bondholders, and shall be required to make reports there.

The amendment is a rather long one to accomplish that purpose. I thought it might be shortened; but it is very specific and leaves nothing in doubt about what the Federal Trade Commission will do and what it will require of bondholders, or protective committees. Of course, under the amendment the functions of the Federal Trade Commission are transferred to the special commission.

That is the whole proposition. I think there is need for this proposed legislation.

MR. BORAH. Mr. President, do I understand the Senator to say that in view of the fact that the functions of the Federal Trade Commission are transferred to the proposed special commission, such reports will be made to the special commission rather than to the Federal Trade Commission?

MR. FLETCHER. Yes; precisely. All the duties under the Securities Act will go to the new commission if the amendment shall be agreed to.

MR. BORAH. Then this amendment takes that function away from the Federal Trade Commission?

MR. FLETCHER. It puts it under the Securities Act, and the whole matter will now go to the new commission.

MR. BARKLEY. Mr. President, these reports are not now made to anybody. The amendment covers a situation which is not covered at present, so that it is part of the securities situation.

MR. FLETCHER. It is a new provision.

MR. BARKLEY. It will go to whatever commission is finally given jurisdiction.

MR. ROBINSON OF ARKANSAS. Mr. President, if the result of the conference should be that the duties under this act should devolve upon the Federal Trade Commission, jurisdiction would go to the Federal Trade Commission?

MR. FLETCHER. Yes.

MR. BORAH. The amendment, then, would simply send that question to conference?

MR. FLETCHER. Yes.

MR. BONE. Mr. President, as I understand, the amendment simply creates the mechanism and machinery through which the committees would function.

MR. FLETCHER. Yes; it gives an additional duty to the Federal Trade Commission in connection with the Securities Act.

MR. BONE. The amendment adds nothing to the amendment, except the feature as to the machinery under which creditors and security holders can act?

MR. FLETCHER. Yes. . . .

THE PRESIDING OFFICER. The question is on agreeing to the amendment proposed by the Senator from Florida.

The amendment was agreed to.

MR. BYRNES. Mr. President, I have one or two amendments I desire to offer. I send the first amendment to the desk.

THE PRESIDING OFFICER. The clerk will state the amendment.

THE CHIEF CLERK. In section 30, it is proposed to strike out the words "in any material respect" wherever they appear and to insert in lieu thereof the words "with respect to any material fact."

MR. BYRNES. Mr. President, in explanation of the necessity for that amendment, let me say that I find that those words appear in one or two places in the measure other than the places where they were corrected by the amendment of the Senator from Oregon and the amendment is to make the entire bill in accord with the action of the Senate with reference to those words.

THE PRESIDING OFFICER. The question is on agreeing to the amendment offered by the Senator from South Carolina.

The amendment was agreed to.

MR. BYRNES. Mr. President, I send another amendment to the desk and ask that it be agreed to.

THE PRESIDING OFFICER. The clerk will state the amendment.

THE LEGISLATIVE CLERK. On page 21, line 20, it is proposed to strike out the words "party to the transaction."

MR. BYRNES. The necessity for this amendment lies in the fact that in drafting the bill there was a mistake in including the words "party to the transaction," which really is a limitation which was not intended by the committee.

THE PRESIDING OFFICER. The question is on agreeing to the amendment.

The amendment was agreed to.

MR. BYRNES. Mr. President, I offer another amendment.

THE PRESIDING OFFICER. The clerk will state the amendment.

THE LEGISLATIVE CLERK. On page 44, beginning with the comma in line 19, it is proposed to strike out down to the word "action" in line 21, as follows:

unless the controlling person acted in good faith and did not directly or indirectly induce the act or acts constituting the violation or cause of action.

MR. BYRNES. Mr. President, that, too, is a clarifying amendment which it is necessary to adopt.

THE PRESIDING OFFICER. The question is on agreeing to the amendment.

The amendment was agreed to.

MR. BYRNES. Mr. President, I send another amendment to the desk and ask for its adoption.

THE PRESIDING OFFICER. The clerk will state the amendment.

THE LEGISLATIVE CLERK. It is proposed to insert at the end of the bill a new section as follows:

SEC. 215. Section 3 (a) (10) of the Securities Act of 1933 is amended to read as follows:

"(10) Any security which is issued in exchange for one or more bona fide outstanding securities, claims, or property interests, or partly in such exchange and partly for cash, where the conditions of such issuance and exchange (including the fees or remuneration chargeable directly or indirectly to the persons to whom it is proposed to issue securities or to the issuer of such securities, in connection with the preparation or execution of the plan under which such securities are issued) are approved, after a hearing upon the fairness of such conditions of which all persons to whom it is proposed to issue securities in such exchange shall be given reasonable notice and in which all such persons shall be given an opportunity to appear, by any court, or by any official or agency of the United States, or by any State banking or insurance commission or similar authority."

MR. BYRNES. Mr. President, the members of the Federal Trade Commission, charged with the administration of the act, state that if the amendment of the Senator from Florida shall be adopted as to the bondholders' protective situation, which has been explained by the Senator, it will be essential to adopt this amendment in order to correct language which would be inconsistent with the language of the existing law. It is solely to clarify the situation that would arise as a result of the adoption of the amendment of the Senator from Florida.

THE PRESIDING OFFICER. The question is on agreeing to the amendment.

The amendment was agreed to.

MR. FLETCHER. Mr. President, all the amendments now having been agreed to, I ask that the Senate proceed to the consideration of the bill (H. R. 9323) to provide for the regulation of securities exchanges and of over-the-counter markets operating in interstate and foreign commerce and through the mails, to prevent inequitable and unfair practices on such exchanges and markets, and for other purposes.

THE PRESIDING OFFICER. Is there objection?

There being no objection, the Senate proceeded to consider the bill.

MR. FLETCHER. Mr. President, I move to amend the bill now before the Senate by striking out all after the enacting clause and inserting in lieu thereof Senate bill 3420, which has been under consideration in the Senate, as it has been amended. . . .

THE VICE PRESIDENT. . . .

The question is on agreeing to the amendment proposed by the Senator from Florida [Mr. Fletcher], that all after the enacting clause of the House bill now before the Senate be stricken out, and that there be inserted in lieu thereof Senate bill 3420, as it has been amended in the Senate.

The amendment was agreed to. . . .

THE VICE PRESIDENT. The question now is, Shall the bill pass?

MR. ROBINSON OF ARKANSAS. I ask for the yeas and nays.

The yeas and nays were ordered, and the legislative clerk proceeded to call the roll. . . .

The result was announced—yeas 62, nays 13, . . .

Yeas—62

Adams	Coolidge
Ashurst	Couzens
Bachman	Dickinson
Bailey	Dill
Bankhead	Duffy
Barkley	Erickson
Black	Fletcher
Bone	Frazier
Borah	George
Bulkley	Gibson
Bulow	Glass
Byrd	Harrison
Byrnes	Hatch
Capper	Hayden
Clark	Johnson
Connally	King

LaFollette
Lewis
Logan
Lonergan
McCarran
McGill
McKellar
McNary
Murphy
Neely
Norbeck
Norris
Nye
O'Mahoney
Overton

Reynolds
Robinson, Ark.
Schall
Sheppard
Steiwer
Stephens
Thomas, Okla.
Thomas, Utah
Thompson
Tydings
Vandenberg
Van Nuys
Wagner
Walsh
Wheeler

Nays—13

Austin
Barbour
Carey
Fess
Goldsborough
Gore
Hale

Hastings
Hatfield
Hebert
Kean
Metcalf
Patterson

Not Voting—21

Brown
Caraway
Copeland
Costigan
Cutting
Davis
Dieterich
Keyes
Long
McAdoo
Pittman

Pope
Reed
Robinson, Ind.
Russell
Shipstead
Smith
Townsend
Trammell
Walcott
White

So the bill was passed. . . .

Senate—73rd Congress, 2d Session
May 30—June 1, 1934

MR. FLETCHER. I submit a conference report on the securities exchanges bill and ask that it may lie on the table and be printed. . . .

The report is as follows:

The committee of conference on the disagreeing votes of the two Houses on the amendment of the Senate to the bill (H.R. 9323) to provide for the regulation of securities exchanges and of over-the-counter markets operating in interstate and foreign commerce and through the mails, to prevent inequitable and unfair practices on such exchanges and markets, and for other purposes, having met, after full and free conference, have agreed to recommend and do recommend to their respective Houses as follows:

That the House recede from its disagreement to the amendment of the Senate and agree to the same with an amendment as follows:

In lieu of the matter proposed to be inserted by the Senate amendment insert the following: [text of the Securities Exchange Act follows].

And the Senate agree to the same.

Duncan U. Fletcher,
Alben W. Barkley,
James F. Byrnes,
Phillips Lee Goldsborough,
James Couzens,
Managers on the part of the Senate

Sam Rayburn,
George Huddleston,
Clarence F. Lea,
Carl E. Mapes,
Managers on the part of the House

MR. FLETCHER. Mr. President, I move that the Senate proceed to the consideration of the conference report on the securities exchange bill.

MR. HARRISON. Mr. President, will there be any discussion involved?

MR. FLETCHER. I think not. I know of no opposition. I think we can dispose of it in a very few minutes. . . .

MR. HASTINGS. Mr. President, I hope the Senator will not insist upon taking up the conference report now. I should like to have an opportunity to go over the report. I have not had an opportunity yet to do so.

MR. FLETCHER. It has been on the desks of Senators since yesterday. It was reported yesterday, and the report was printed at length in yesterday's proceedings.

MR. HASTINGS. That is not a very long time to consider it.

MR. FLETCHER. We have not a very long time to be here, either. The conference report has to be acted on in the Senate before it can be acted on in the House. It is a unanimous report of the conferees.

THE PRESIDING OFFICER. The motion to consider the report is not debatable. The question is on the motion of the Senator from Florida to proceed to the consideration of the conference report.

The motion was agreed to; and the Senate proceeded to consider the report of the committee of conference on the disagreeing votes of the two Houses on the amendments of the Senate to the bill (H.R. 9323) to provide for the regulation of securities exchanges and of over-the-counter markets operating in interstate and foreign commerce and through the mails, to prevent inequitable and unfair practices on such exchanges and markets, and for other purposes.

MR. FLETCHER. I move the adoption of the report.

THE PRESIDING OFFICER. If there is no objection—

MR. HASTINGS. I object, Mr. President, until I have an opportunity to read the report.

May I inquire of the Senator from Florida whether he does not intend to make any explanation to the Senate of what was agreed upon and why certain amendments were made?

MR. FLETCHER. I have no objection to making any explanation or answering any questions about the report. I do not wish to consume time unnecessarily by reviewing the whole report. It is a pretty extensive report. I can, I think, satisfy the Senate very briefly as to the principal features dealt with by the conferees, and where the principal changes were made in the Senate bill and in the House bill. I do not desire to put myself in the position of understanding or overstating anything, because I do not wish to give an opportunity for some malicious, unscrupulous propagandist to say that I deceived the Senate about something.

The principal features are these:

The Senate receded from its amendment as to section 2, which was the provision with reference to the purpose and object of the bill, and adopted the House provision as to that section.

The House receded from its disagreement to the Senate provision which establishes an independent commission of five, and the Senate provision on that subject was agreed to.

The Senate receded from its disagreement to the House provision with reference to margin requirements, and we agreed to the House provision on that subject, perhaps with an amendment; but, at all events, the report leaves the control of margins as fixed in the House bill and leaves the control of credits in the Federal Reserve Board.

Those were the main features, as I think the Senator will agree. As to some other amendments, the House receded with an amendment here and there through the bill; but not as to very vital or essential provisions.

The House receded from its disagreement to the provision of the Senate bill which transfers to the Commission the administration of the Securities Act, and puts in the hands of the Commission both the administration of this measure and the administration of the Securities Act.

The Senate receded from the provision as to the salaries of the Commissioners. The Senate bill fixed their salaries at $12,000, and the House suggested $10,000; and we agreed on salaries of $10,000.

I think there were some other not so very important provisions—for instance, with reference to the statute of limitations. The bill now provides that any suit for damages brought under the sections of the bill with reference to misleading or false statements as to registration or application must be brought within 1 year after discovery of the facts constituting the cause of action and within 3 years after the cause of action accrued, instead of within 10 years and 5 years, respectively, as I think the other provisions were.

MR. COUZENS. Mr. President, I desire to suggest to the Senator from Florida that one of the important changes made in the bill was as to the question raised particularly by the junior Senator from Oregon [Mr. Steiwer] with respect to having the Commission come under a budgetary plan, rather than to rely upon the fees collected from the stock exchanges.

MR. FLETCHER. Yes. The Senate bill provided that all expenses were to be paid by the exchanges. The House bill provided for a fee of one five-hundredths of 1 percent to be levied on the exchanges when they register; so that the expenses are intended to be taken care of, so far as possible, in that way. In other words, the Senate bill provided that all expenses should be met by the exchanges. The conference report provides for a registration fee of one five-hundredths of 1 percent on the amount of business transacted. . . .

MR. HASTINGS. Mr. President, on yesterday I urged upon the Senate that this conference report go over until today in order that I might at least have an opportunity to read it.

It will be borne in mind that the Senate made some important amendments to the Securities Act of 1933, which amendments were attached to a bill which had passed the House, so that at the time the bill came to the Senate it was not possible to get any idea as to what the House might do with respect to the Securities Act of 1933. That was left solely to the conference committee.

On the day when the bill passed the Senate I offered several amendments to the stock-exchange portion of the bill and one amendment to the securities-act feature. The Chairman of the Committee on Banking and Currency said he saw no objection to the amendment to the securities act which I proposed, and it was therefore accepted by the Senate.

The amendment proposed by me may not to many Senators seem of much importance. Certainly, at the time I offered it, I could not see how there could be any reasonable objection to it, and I assumed the chairman of the committee, and those with whom he consulted, saw no objection. From my point of view it is a very important amendment.

The draft of the bill as passed by the Senate contained this provision, beginning on page 123:

SEC. 203. (a). Paragraph (1) of section 4 of such act is amended (1) by striking out "not with or through an underwriter and"; and (2) by striking out "last" and inserting in lieu thereof "first."

That was an amendment proposed by the committee. Then I suggested that the committee amendment be amended by the addition of the following words—

and (3) by adding after the word "underwriter" the following words "As used in this paragraph, the term 'public offering' shall not be deemed to include an offering made solely to employees of an issuer or of its affiliates in connection with a bona fide plan for the payment of extra compensation or stock-investment plan for the exclusive benefit of such employees."

I do not see why the Federal Government should insist upon having anything to do with the plan of a corporation which decides that, as a part of its policy, it will give certain additional compensation or bonus to its employees. I think that is a matter with which the Government ought not to have anything to do, and there is no public interest involved in the policy of a corporation in adopting such a plan.

For years and years there have been discussions all over this country as to the best method of permitting employees of corporations to share in the profits of the corporations. . . .

MR. COUZENS. I may say, in behalf of the conference, that that matter was given a very great deal of consideration, and one of the controlling factors which caused the elimination of the amendment was the Insull transactions. As a matter of fact, the record shows that literally millions of shares of stock of Insull corporations were sold to their employees merely upon representations of the corporations themselves. We could not find that there was any reason for failing to register those shares, just as any other shares are registered. It would be in no sense governmental interference with a mere plan. It would simply give to the employees of the corporations the same right to have registered the shares which they bought as an outsider would have a right to have the shares he bought registered.

MR. HASTINGS. The Senator does not mean to intimate to the Senate, does he, that the conference on the part of the Senate made that argument to the conference?

MR. COUZENS. No; I am not saying that. I am saying that that was the argument which took place in the committee, and the House conferees were very insistent upon pointing out the evils which have occurred where employees of a number of corporations have been induced to buy shares of the stock of the corporations.

MR. HASTINGS. Of course, the downfall of the Insull companies. I have no doubt, will result in doing many things which will be of great injury to responsible corporations which are conducting a valid business in a valid way. What is now being done is just another illustration of trying to find some means of curbing every kind of fraud which may have been practiced by any and every person and which can be pointed out as having imposed upon someone. We never can pass laws of any kind that will take care of all the evils that are bound to occur. I admit that it is the duty of the Congress and any legislative body to do what they can to protect the innocent people of the country, but I do insist that when that is done it ought to be done with such care as not to destroy the rights and the opportunities which may be offered to other business corporations.

Mr. President, there is nothing that I can do about it. I can cite more than one instance of the great hardship which will result from this legislation, not to the corporation but to the employees of the corporation. This provision of the Securities Act destroys the plan of at least one corporation which has worked perfectly for years and which has never had a word of protest registered against it by any stockholder. The corporation had to abandon its plan when the Securities Act of 1933 was passed. I made an effort here—an honest effort—to relieve that situation by offering what I believed to be a harmless amendment to anybody else but a very helpful amendment to a corporation which desired to carry out that kind of a plan. . . .

MR. FLETCHER. I agree that when the Senator submitted his proposed amendment it struck me as being entirely reasonable, fair, and just. I took it that way. And I can see what he proposes in a favorable light. But when the bill went to conference the House conferees insisted that there was, first, no reason for the amendment. If the Senator will refer to section 4 of the Securities Act, he will find that it provides:

Transactions by any person other than an issuer, underwriter, or dealer, transactions by an issuer—

And so forth—

not involving any public offering.

The contention was, and it seems to me it is almost unanswerable, that an offering to employees solely, as provided in the Senator's amendment, is not a public offering. The argument was made that there was no occasion for this amendment, because under the law there would not be a public offering when the stock was offered simply and solely to employees. That was the effect of the Senator's amendment. His amendment is limited, as will be seen by its language, which is—

The term "public offering" shall not be deemed to include an offering made solely to the employees—

I do not believe under the law it really does.

MR. HASTINGS. May I inquire—and I make this inquiry because it may be helpful in the future—whether the Senator can say that that was the judgment of the conference itself, or is he speaking only for himself?

MR. FLETCHER. Yes; that is the judgment of the conference itself; that there is no reason why employees should not subscribe for stock, and stock be subscribed for by employees under the law as it is. And certainly there is no question in the world that the Commission has the authority to declare that such an offering would not be a public one.

MR. HASTINGS. May I be certain that the Record is clear upon this point, and may I have the Record show that in rejecting the amendment which I had offered and which under the present administration of the law it was necessary to offer the conference was unanimously of the opinion that the amendment was not necessary, because under section 4 of the Securities Act such an offering as that referred to was not believed to be a public offering? Have I overstated it?

MR. FLETCHER. I think not. I do not know that I could be authorized to say that the opinion was unanimous, but certainly a majority thought that way, and there was no objection to that view, as I understood. That was the view. And then there was mention in the argument that there was some danger of abuses arising under the broad language of the Senator's amendment; that some corporations might impose on their employees, might exploit them, and that sort of thing. That was the argument used.

But the opinion of the conferees was that there really was no need for this amendment, because the Senator could accomplish what he desired under the law as it stands now, and that there is no public offering when it is limited solely to employees.

MR. HASTINGS. Mr. President, I desire to thank the Senator from Florida for that contribution, because I think it will be very helpful, and I think, in addition to that, if I may be permitted to say so, it justifies the position I took yesterday in asking that this matter might go over long enough to find out just what was in the conference report. . . .

MR. COUZENS. I desire to add to what the chairman said—that the definition of an employee may vary. In other words, in many pyramidings of corporations by the Insull people there were employees of subsidiaries of a holding company, and vice versa. I may differ with the chairman as to the interpretation of what an employee is. In other words, if a holding company sells shares to a subsidiary employee, it does not necessarily follow that that employee is an employee of the company which issues the shares.

MR. HASTINGS. Mr. President, I shall not detain the Senate longer in the discussion of this matter; but I think what the Senator from Florida has just said will have very much to do with the success of this bill. I am very much opposed to it, because while I think it does very many things and will cure many evils that ought to be cured, I believe that in the net result it will do more harm than it will do good. But, at the same time, I want to say that whether that shall or shall not be true will depend very largely upon the administration of this law. I think there are some provisions in it with which it will be particularly hard for corporations to comply. I think there are so many things of that kind in it that many corporations will feel the necessity of having their stock stricken from the Stock Exchange Board. But the proper administration of this law, with the interest of the country at heart, and at the same time without an effort to put the corporations of the country under the control of this particular Commission, is, in my judgment, the only hope we have for any success under this bill.

MR. STEIWER. Mr. President, I will detain the Senate just long enough to make some inquiry concerning the provisions providing exceptions for certain of the interstate carriers. I am referring to section 13, subsection (b) of the stock exchange bill as it passed the Senate. I think that is the same section and subsection in which the language with respect to carriers is found in the substitute agreed upon in conference. It is contained on page 95 of the bill and on page 15 of the conference report.

Mr. President, when this matter was before the Senate consideration was given to the proposition of exempting rail carriers from the requirements of registration of their securities contained in section 12 and the exemption of certain other carriers from the report requirements of section 13.

The action of the Senate was exemplified by the amendment in subsection (b) of section 13, which reads as follows:

Provided, That carriers subject to the provisions of section 20a of the Interstate Commerce Act, as amended, shall not be subject to the provisions of sections 12 and 13 of this title, except that the Commission may require that such carriers file with it duplicate copies of reports or other documents filed with the Interstate Commerce Commission: *Provided further,* That carriers not subject to the provisions of section 20a of the Interstate Commerce Act, as amended, but subject to section 20 of such act, shall be exempt from the provisions of this section, except that the Commission may require that such carriers file with it duplicate copies of reports or other documents filed with the Interstate Commerce Commission.

The effect of the two provisos just read was to eliminate the railroads entirely from the requirements of section 12 and section 13, and to eliminate the other carriers named in the Interstate Commerce Act, namely, the sleeping-car companies, the telegraph and telephone companies, pipe lines and express companies, from the requirements of section 13 with respect to the filing of periodical reports.

I will not restate the argument upon which that action was taken by the Senate, except to say that the act under which the carriers are controlled already requires more of the railroads with respect to accountancy and with respect to reports than this new Commission under any reasonable conditions conceivably could require of those carriers, both before the issuance of securities and after the issuance of securities. As the Senators know, not only does the Interstate Commerce Commission exercise control over the railroads with respect to the filing of their reports but it also controls the issuance of their securities; it has a veto power under the law, under which no carrier may issue securities except with the consent and approval of the Commission.

The conferees in their treatment of this matter, at page 15, modified the language which I read a minute ago so that the exemption is now stated in this language:

And, in the case of carriers subject to the provisions of section 20 of the Interstate Commerce Act, as amended, or carriers required pursuant to any other act of Congress to make reports of the same general character as those required under such section 20, shall permit such carriers to file with the Commission and the exchange duplicate copies of the reports and other documents filed with the Interstate Commerce Commission, or with the governmental authority administering such other act of Congress, in lieu of the reports, information, and documents required under this section and section 12 in respect of the same subject matter.

The amended language just read to the Senate places the railroads on the same basis as the other carriers mentioned in section 20 of the Interstate Commerce Act. It makes no distinction in favor of the railroads by reason of the unusual and far-reaching requirements of section 20 (a). The effect will be that the railroad carriers, which are already under the control of the Interstate Commerce Commission with respect to the issuance of securities, will be required to register under section 12 of this proposed act, and, although it would appear that the reports which the railroads file with the Interstate Commerce Commission may be filed with the new commission in lieu of the filing of other reports, and that they shall be accepted so far as they go, it still appears that they are required to register.

I merely want to ask the chairman of the committee or some other member of the conference if that was the purpose of the conferees in making that amendment.

MR. BYRNES. Mr. President, if I may answer the question of the Senator from Oregon, it was the thought of the conferees that the railroads should not be required to file reports inconsistent with those required by the Interstate Commerce Commission, but, inasmuch as their securities were dealt in by the public, just as are all other securities, that they should be required to register. The amendment of the Senator from Oregon would have exempted the securities of railroads from registration.

MR. STEIWER. That is true.

MR. BYRNES. I think, as the Senator states, that is the purpose. However, it does not require of them any report differing in any way from those filed with the Interstate Commerce Commission. They are saved the duplication of reports, but are required to register.

MR. STEIWER. On the question suggested by the observation last made, how do the conferees construe the language in the last portion of the section as follows—

Information and documents required under this section and section 12 in respect of the same subject matter.

Does the Senator believe that that will relieve the railroads from the necessity of filing such additional reports as the new commission, in its judgment, may require?

MR. BYRNES. Certainly the intent of the conferees, according to my understanding, was that the railroads should not be required to file reports, differing from those which are now filed by them with the Interstate Commerce Commission.

MR. STEIWER. But would they be required to file additional reports?

MR. FLETCHER. Mr. President, the purpose was to avoid duplicating their work. We did not want them to be required to do the things that are required elsewhere, and if they filed reports pursuant to the Interstate Commerce Act or any other act we did not want to require them to duplicate such reports with the new commission, but merely to file copies.

MR. BYRNES. Mr. President, there is no prohibition against the requirement of information in addition to that which is submitted to the Interstate Commerce Commission. So, answering the question specifically, in this language there is nothing which would prevent a requirement as to supplemental information.

MR. STEIWER. I can only express my deep regret, Mr. President, at that attitude and at that interpretation of the language. I believe the interpretation is justified by the language. I am not quarreling with the Senator from South Carolina in the interpretation he places upon the language. I had most sincerely hoped for a different result from the conference. The language of the House bill with respect to the same subject, found in the House bill in section 12 of its enactment, under subsection (b), was as follows:

Provided, That no additional requirement shall be imposed upon carriers subject to the provisions of section 20-a of the Interstate Commerce Act, as amended.

The effect of that language, of course, would be to leave the entire control and jurisdiction over railroad securities with the Interstate Commerce Commission. I had thought there was abundant reason for doing that, and had hoped that in the final enactment of the bill an effect of that kind could be given to the legislation.

We ought to bear in mind that the Interstate Commerce Commission has more than the power to exact reports; it absolutely controls the accountancy of the railroad carriers; it prescribes the form in which they shall keep their books. It not only does that, but it may, and does, examine their books. It has the power to enforce a complete system of auditing those books. It examines the reports. It sends its field agents to the offices of the railroad companies. But, above that, Mr. President, in many cases it even goes to the extent of requiring monthly reports of the railroad carriers. There is, I think, in the whole country no supervision that is as meticulously detailed as the supervision which the Interstate Commerce Commission exercises over the railroads of this country. That supervision, of course, is costly to the railroad carriers, and the expense is paid by the shippers; it is paid by the people, because those costs are proper items to be taken into consideration in the making of rates which the people must pay. It seems to me that nothing can be gained by increasing that cost or increasing the bill which the people must pay; no advantage possibly can come to the purchaser of securities, because it is inconceivable to me that the Commission can accomplish anything of value which is over and above the requirements presently made by the Interstate Commerce Commission. . . .

MR. BYRNES. It was our thought, in view of the facts referred to by the Senator, that it would be very difficult to conceive of supplemental information which could be required by the commission appointed under this proposed act.

MR. STEIWER. I do not think so at all, Mr. President.

MR. BYRNES. As I think the Senator will see, the language of the conference report is that as to any reports, to which the Senator has referred in detail, that the regulations of the new commission with respect to such reports shall not be inconsistent with the requirements imposed by law, rule, or regulation in respect to the same subject matter. The Senator has said that the reports of the railroads to the Interstate Commerce Commission cover practically every phase of the carrier's business, and there can be no duplication of any of that information.

MR. STEIWER. Oh, Mr. President, I think the requirements that may be made of the railroads will be limited only by the imagination of the clerks who submit the program to this new commission for its approval. There is not any question but that this authority, if it is construed as the Senator construes it—and I regret that I feel he is correct in his construction—will enable the new commission to make very exacting and very expensive requirements of the rail carriers.

To understand fully the effect and consequence of the action taken by the conferees, it must be borne in mind that the Senate amendment not only prohibited additional requirements being made of the railroads but the Senate amendment, in the language which I read a little while ago, provided—

That carriers subject to section 20a—

Namely, the rail carriers—and I again quote—

shall not be subject to the provisions of sections 12 and 13 of this title, except that the commission may require that such carriers file with it duplicate copies of reports or other documents filed with the Interstate Commerce Commission.

Therefore, it would seem to me, if the purpose of the conferees is as stated by the Senator from South Carolina, that the obtaining of the duplicate statements and reports could have been had under the Senate amendment, and the information which he says is all that conceivably could be asked could have been available to the new commission and to all the investors in the land under the provisions of the Senate amendment, and that, therefore, what the conferees must have had in mind, when they changed the language to permit the new commission to exact other information and to prescribe additional requirements of the rail carriers, was that something other or different might be done.

It would be comforting to me if I could know what the conferees had in mind. The only member of the conference committee who expressed himself was content to say merely that he could not conceive of any additional requirement that might be exacted from the rail carriers. To me it is most regrettable, almost pathetic, that our conferees should have permitted a great piece of legislation of this kind to be written in a way that would permit oppressive requirements to be made of the rail carriers at a time when all of them are confronted with financial exactions beyond their ability to meet, at a time when they are barred from borrowing from the Reconstruction Finance Corporation. At a time when we are wondering what we will do with the rail carriers and whether we can leave them in private ownership at all, we find them confronted with these new exactions which, I think, are wholly unnecessary.

This provision in the conference report not only makes the carriers subject to section 12 of the bill requiring registration of securities which are entirely under the control of another Federal agency, but it requires the additional reports to which I have referred. There now remains this consideration: If it was the purpose of the conferees, in placing the railroads back under the registration requirement, to subject the railroads of the country in the issuance of their securities to the requirements of the Exchange Commission, we have an anomalous situation indeed.

I appreciate there is no express requirement here that the issuance of securities shall be subject to the jurisdiction of the Exchange Commission, and yet I can conceive of many circumstances and various ways under and by which the new Commission may absolutely block the issuance of securities, may control, or thwart the effort of a railroad company with respect to the issuance of securities.

I can conceive, moreover, that the Interstate Commerce Commission in the exercise of its jurisdiction may take one attitude with respect to the issuance of securities, and the Exchange Commission take another. In the conflict of authority I am not prepared to say which agency of the Government would be supreme, but it rather seemed to me, because the Exchange Commission actually controls the sale of issues on the exchanges, that the power of the Exchange Commission would become supreme and paramount to the power and jurisdiction of the Interstate Commerce Commission. I very much doubt if Congress, in the enactment of this legislation, intended any such result to follow. . . .

THE VICE PRESIDENT. The question is on agreeing to the conference report.

The report was agreed to.

MR. BYRNES. Mr. President, I desire to make a short statement with reference to the amendments to the Securities Act of 1933 which are contained in the conference report just adopted.

I think it is a fair statement that under the conference report the provisions as to the civil liability of underwriters and of the officers and directors of a corporation are so amended that no honest man need have any fear of the law so long as he is willing to give to the corporation of which he is an officer, and in which he has invested his money, the same reasonable care that he gives to the management of his own property.

Every section of title 2, containing the so-called "Fletcher amendment," liberalizes the provisions of the Securities Act of 1933. The modifications have grown out of the administration of the act during the past 12 months. Some of them seem to be merely administrative changes, but in each case they will be found to liberalize the existing requirements.

The provisions of the Securities Act of 1933 which have caused the greatest complaint are those as to the civil liability of underwriters and of the officers and directors of corporations on account of false statements in the registration statements filed by corporations. Under the existing law, where the registration statement contains a false statement of a material fact, or omits to state a material fact necessary to make the statement not misleading, any person who suffers a loss can sue the underwriters, the officers and the directors of the corporation. The existing law provides, however, among other things, that as regards any part of the statement purporting to be made on the authority of an expert, or to be an extract from the report or valuation of an expert, the defendant shall not be liable if he had reasonable ground to believe and did believe that the statements therein were true. It also provides that a director is not liable if he can establish the same defense as to the statement of an officer.

There can be no doubt that the provisions of the existing law caused many men who were serving as directors of corporations to fear that they might be subjected to so-called "strike suits" as the result of the administration of that law. The existing law defined what constituted reasonable investigation and reasonable ground for belief, and set forth the standard as the care required of a person occupying a fiduciary relationship. That phrase was greatly misunderstood by many officers and directors of corporations.

The amendments which have just been adopted by the Senate change the law in very important and material particulars. These amendments provide that a defendant shall not be liable for any false statement made on the authority of an expert, or purporting to be an extract from the report of an expert, if the defendant can show that he had no reasonable ground to believe, and did not believe, that the statements were untrue; and the law is changed to provide that in determining what constitutes a reasonable investigation and reasonable ground for belief, the standard shall be that required of a prudent man in the management of his own property. No honest man will contend that anything less should be demanded either of an underwriter or of an officer or director of a corporation offering securities for sale to the public.

However, the amendments adopted today give greater assurance to the honest officials of a corporation. Whereas the existing law permits a suit to be brought at any time within 10 years after the filing of the registration, the new law will permit such a suit to be brought only within 3 years. It has been argued heretofore that a director would be uncertain as to the settlement of his estate in case of death because of the liability that would exist for a period of 10 years. Under the new law, a suit must be brought within 3 years.

Under the existing law, the plaintiff is entitled to recover the amount of the loss suffered by him as a result of the purchase and sale of the security. Under the new law, the defendant will have the right to show whether a part of the plaintiff's loss is due to some cause other than the untrue statement, and to such extent will be able to reduce the amount of the recovery by the plaintiff.

Another change in the amendments is as to the requirement that the plaintiff allege or prove that in purchasing the securities he relied upon the statement which was afterward discovered to be false. The new law modifies this requirement. It provides that the plaintiff will not have to allege or prove reliance until the corporation has made available to security holders an earning statement for at least 12 months subsequent to the filing of the registration statement.

After such an earning statement shall be made available, the plaintiff will be required to allege and prove that he relied upon the false statement.

There is justification for the provision that reliance be not required until a 12 months' earning statement is made public. When an issue of securities is proposed, a banking house will investigate the financial statement of the corporation. Based upon the statements contained in the registration statement of the corporation, a banking house will offer the securities at a certain price. Therefore, the market value is fixed by the false statement of the corporation. The individual investor relies upon the investigation made by the banker. It is fair to assume that this situation continues until such time as the corporation makes available a statement showing its earnings for 12 months. Then, the market value is influenced by the statement of actual earnings and not by the statements contained in the registration statement, which deceived the underwriter or banker and the investor. It is entirely different from trading in stocks upon the exchanges, where those who trade have access to statements of earnings constantly filed and published.

An additional assurance to the officers of a corporation is given by the provisions in the new bill aimed at so called "strike suits." Under the new law, the court will have authority to assess costs against the plaintiff; and because it is recognized that the plaintiff who will resort to bringing nuisance suits has, as a rule, no financial responsibility, the court, on motion, can require such plaintiff to give bond to cover the costs of the suit before proceedings with a suit.

I repeat, it is a fair statement to make that when the provisions of the so-called "Fletcher amendments" are analyzed, they give assurance to every honest man who is an official of a corporation that he need have no fear of the Securities Act of 1933 as amended, provided he is willing to give to the corporation in which he has invested his money the same reasonable care that he gives to the management of his own property. . . .

House of Representatives – 73rd Congress, 2d Session
June 1, 1934

Statement

The managers on the part of the House at the conference on the disagreeing votes of the two Houses on the bill (H.R. 9323) to provide for the regulation of securities exchanges and of over-the-counter markets operating in interstate and foreign commerce and through the mails, to prevent inequitable and unfair practices on such exchanges and markets, and for other purposes, submit the following statement in explanation of the effect of the action agreed upon by the conferees and recommended in the accompanying conference report:

The Senate amendment strikes out all of the House bill after the enacting clause. The House recedes from its disagreement to the amendment of the Senate with an amendment which is a substitute for both the House bill and the Senate amendment. The differences between the House bill and the substitute agreed upon by the conferees are noted in the following outline, except for incidental changes made necessary by reason of the agreements reached by the conferees and minor and clarifying changes.

The House bill provides that the administration of the act, other than those provisions to be administered by the Federal Reserve Board, shall be under the Federal Trade Commission, and in section 3 (a) (15) the term "Commission" is defined to mean the "Federal Trade Commission." The Senate amendment defines the term to mean the "Federal Securities Exchange Commission." In view of the action taken by the conferees in placing the administration of the act under a separate commission the term "Commission" is defined in the substitute to mean the "Securities and Exchange Commission."

The House bill (sec. 3 (b)) authorizes the Commission and the Federal Reserve Board to define accounting, technical, and trade terms, and provides that such definitions, insofar as not inconsistent with the provisions of the act, shall have the force of law. The Senate amendment contains a similar provision except that the authority is confined to the Commission, and it is not provided that such definitions shall have the force of law. The substitute retains the House provision except that it is not provided that the definitions "shall have the force of law." This phrase was omitted as unnecessary, since courts commonly give the force of law to administrative interpretations of statutory terms, unless clearly inconsistent with the legislative intent.

The House bill (sec. 4) and the Senate amendment each contain a provision prohibiting the use of the mails or instrumentalities of interstate commerce in using any facility of an exchange unless the exchange is registered under the act or is exempted from registration by the Commission by reason of the limited volume of transactions effected thereon. The House bill contains the further provision that such exemption may be withdrawn by the Commission under specified circumstances. This provision is omitted from the substitute as being unnecessary, since it is thought that the power of the Commission to make the exemption necessarily includes the power to limit the exemption or to withdraw it.

The House bill (sec. 6) and the Senate amendment, in their provisions relating to margin requirements, differ principally in that (1) under the House bill a standard is included for the guidance of the Federal Reserve Board in prescribing its rules and regulations with respect to the amount of credit that may be initially extended on any registered security, subject to the power of the Board to prescribe higher or lower margin requirements in the case of the initial extension of credit if it finds that certain specified conditions prevail to warrant such action, and (2) the House bill places under the Federal Reserve Board the administration of all the margin provisions, whereas the Senate bill places the administration of all such provisions under the Commission except insofar as they relate to member banks of the Federal Reserve System, and to this extent the Senate amendment provides that the margin provisions shall be under the jurisdiction of the Federal Reserve Board. The substitute follows rather closely the provisions of the House bill except that the provision granting authority to the Federal Reserve Board to lower or raise margin requirements in case of the initial extension of credit is applied as well to the maintenance of credit. The House bill gives authority to the Federal Reserve Board to lower or raise margin requirements with respect to "all or specified securities or classes of securities, or classes of transactions." The substitute modifies this provision so that such authority is also given with respect to "specified transactions." The House bill provides that the rules and regulations under the section relating to margin requirements shall not apply on or before January 31, 1939. The Senate amendment fixes the date in the corresponding provision in the Senate amendment at June 30, 1936. The substitute fixes the date at July 1, 1937.

The House bill (sec. 7 (c) and (d)) and the Senate amendment contain similar prohibitions against the hypothecation by members, brokers, and dealers of securities carried for customers' accounts, with the difference, however, that in the Senate bill the prohibitions apply only if the action is in contravention of such rules and regulations as the Commission shall prescribe for the protection of investors. The substitute adopts the Senate provision.

The House bill (sec. 8 (a) (2)) contains a provision prohibiting any series of transactions in a registered security for the purpose of raising or depressing the price of such security. The corresponding provision in the Senate amendment prohibits the manipulation of the price of a registered security by means of any series of trans-actions effected with the specific intent of raising or depressing such price. Both provisions were intended to prohibit pool activities, the rigging, jiggling, or marking up or down of prices by manipulative operations. The substitute, combining the ideas underlying the Senate and the House provisions, prohibits any series of transactions in a registered security creating actual or apparent active trading in such security, or raising or depressing the price of such security, for the purpose of inducing the purchase or sale of such security by others.

The House bill (sec 8 (a) (4)) makes it unlawful for a dealer or broker or other person selling or offering for sale, or purchasing or offering to purchase, a registered security, to induce the purchase or sale of such security by making a statement of any material fact regarding such security which he knows or has reasonable ground to believe is false or misleading. It further provides that any such statement insofar as it is limited to facts set forth in an application, report, or document filed pursuant to the act, shall not be deemed false or misleading unless the person making such statement knew or had reasonable ground to believe that it was false or misleading. The Senate amendment covers substantially the same ground but requires only that the statement be made for the purpose of inducing the purchase or sale of a registered security, and expressly provides that a statement shall be construed to include any omission to state a material fact. The latter provision is omitted from the substitute as surplusage in view of the fact that a statement obviously may be misleading because of a material omission. The Senate amendment also puts the burden of proving good faith in the making of the statement upon the defendant in a civil suit. The substitute provides that it shall be unlawful for a dealer or broker or other person selling or offering for sale, or purchasing or offering to purchase the security, to make regarding any security registered on a national securities exchange, for the purpose of inducing the purchase or sale of such security, any statement which was, at the time and in the light of the circumstances under which it was made, false or misleading in regard to any material fact, and which he knew or had reasonable ground to believe was so false or misleading.

The House bill provision (sec. 8 (a) (6)) which subjects to the regulation of the Commission any series of transactions for the purchase and sale of any registered security for the purpose of pegging, fixing, or stabilizing the price of such security, was accepted with an amendment making it clear that the regulation of such operation extended to a series of transactions for the purchase and/or sale of the security. The substitute provision clarifying the House bill conforms in substance to the Senate amendment.

The House bill (sec 8 (e)) provides that civil suits based upon the violation of the provisions of the act relating to manipulative practices must be brought within a period within 3 years after the violation upon which the action was based. The Senate amendment limits the time within which such suits may be brought to 1 year after the discovery of the facts constituting the violation, and in any case to 5 years after such violation. The substitute requires such suits to be brought within 1 year after discovery of the facts constituting the violation and in any event within 3 years after such violation. The substitute also provides that in the case of any such suit the court may in its discretion require an undertaking for the payment of the costs of such suit, and assess reasonable costs, including reasonable attorney's fees, against either party litigant.

The House bill (sec. 9) and the Senate amendment contain similar provisions regulating the use of manipulative devices, except that the Senate amendment contains a provision prohibiting the use or employment in connection with the purchase or sale of any security of any manipulative or deceptive device or contrivance—

Which the Commission may declare to be detrimental to the interests of investors.

The substitute includes this provision of the Senate amendment with the modification that it is made unlawful to use or employ any such device or contrivance—

In contravention of such rules and regulations as the Commission may prescribe as necessary or appropriate in the public interest or for the protection of investors.

The House bill (sec. 10) contains a prohibition against a specialist disclosing to any person other than a representative of the Commission or a specialist who may be acting for him information in regard to orders placed with him which is not available to all members of the exchange, and authorizes the Commission to require disclosure to all members of all orders placed with specialists. The Senate amendment contains a provision similar to that in the House bill except that it permits specialists to disclose information to an official of the exchange and, instead of authorizing the Commission to provide disclosure, provides that nothing in the section shall be construed to prevent the rules of an exchange requiring disclosure to all members of all orders placed with a specialist. The substitute adopts the House provision, except that it declares that—

It shall be unlawful for a specialist or an official of the exchange to disclose information in regard to orders placed with such specialist which is not available to all members of the exchange, to any person other than an official of the exchange, a representative of the Commission, or a specialist who may be acting for such specialist.

The House bill (sec. 10 (c)) and the Senate amendment each contains a provision authorizing the exemption of any exchange from the provisions of the section because of the limited volume of transactions on the exchange. The House provision gives authority to the Commission to withdraw such exemption in specified circumstances. This provision is omitted from the substitute as unnecessary, since it is thought that the authority to make the exemption necessarily includes the authority to limit the exemption or to withdraw it.

The House bill (sec. 11 (a)) and the Senate amendment both prohibit transactions in any security on a national securities exchange unless a registration is effective as to the security in accordance with the provisions of the act, but in the House bill such prohibition applies to "any person," whereas in the Senate amendment it applies only to a "member, broker, or dealer." The substitute contains the Senate provision.

The House bill (sec. 11 (b))and the Senate amendment impose similar requirements as to information to be filed with an application for the registration of a security on a national securities exchange. The substitute takes some of the provisions from the House bill and some from the Senate amendment. The information which may be required under the substitute which was not required under the House bill is specified in paragraphs (D), (E), (F), (G), and (H), inclusive, of section 12 (b) (1), and includes the following: The underwriters of the security; each security holder of record holding more than 10 percent of any class of any equity security of the issuer (other than any exempted security); the remuneration of underwriters, and the interests of underwriters and such security holders in the securities of, and their material contracts with, the issuer and any person directly or indirectly controlling or controlled by, or under direct or indirect common control with, the issuer; the remuneration to others than directors and officers exceeding $20,000 (the House bill having specified $10,000); bonus and profit-sharing arrangements; and management and service contracts (the House bill having required information as to management and service contracts "of material importance to investors"). The substitute also contains the provision from the Senate amendment authorizing the Commission to require "any further financial statements which the Commission may deem necessary or appropriate for the protection of investors."

The House bill (sec. 11 (f)) and the Senate amendment both authorize the Commission to make a study of trading in unlisted securities upon exchanges and to report to Congress with respect thereto. The date for the making of the report is fixed at January 3, 1935, in the House bill and January 3, 1936, in the Senate amendment. The substitute adopts the Senate amendment.

The House bill (sec. 12 (b)) authorizes the Commission to prescribe, in regard to reports made under the act, in accordance with accepted principles of accounting, the form or forms in which the required information shall be set forth, and the items or details to be shown in the balance sheets and profit-and-loss statements. The Senate amendment contains a similar provision, except that it specifies that the Commission may prescribe the items and details to be shown in the balance sheet and the earning statement, the methods to be followed in the preparation of reports, in the appraisal or valuation of assets and liabilities, in the determination of depreciation and depletion, in the differentiation of recurring and nonrecurring income, in the differentiation of investment and operating income, and in the preparation of separate and/or consolidated balance sheets or income accounts of any person directly or indirectly controlling or controlled by, or any person under direct or indirect common control with, the issuer. The substitute retains the provision of the Senate amendment. In this same subsection the House bill provides that in the case of the reports of any person "whose accounting is subject to the provisions of" any law of the United States or any State, or any rule or regulation thereunder, the rules and regulations of the Commission with respect to reports shall not be inconsistent with the requirements imposed by such law or rule or regulation. The Senate amendment contains a similar provision, except that it does not apply in the case of a person whose accounting is subject only to the provisions of State law or regulations, and only applies where the rules and regulations of the Commission and the requirements under other laws are in respect of the same subject matter. The substitute contains the Senate provision, with the modification that the persons covered are described as those "whose methods of accounting are prescribed under" the provisions of any law of the United States, or any rule or regulation thereunder. The provision of the House bill last referred to above is subject to the exception that it shall not prevent the Commission from imposing such "additional requirements with respect to such reports, within the scope of this section and section 11," as it may deem necessary for the protection of investors. This provision is omitted from the substitute as unnecessary, in view of the limitation imposed by the words "in respect of the same subject matter" contained in the provision above referred to. Another provision in the same subsection of the House bill provides that no additional requirements shall be imposed upon carriers subject to the provisions of section 20 (a) of the Interstate Commerce Act, as amended. The Senate amendment contains a provision that carriers subject to section 20 (a) of the Interstate Commerce Act shall not be subject to the provisions of section 12 and 13 of the Senate bill, except that the Commission may require such carriers to file duplicate copies of reports or other documents filed with the Interstate Commerce Commission; and it further provides that carriers subject to section 20 (but not to sec. 20 (a)) of the Interstate Commerce Act shall be exempt from the provisions of section 13 of the Senate bill, except that the Commission may require the filing of duplicate copies of reports and documents filed with the Interstate Commerce Commission. The substitute provides that in the case of carriers subject to the provisions of section 20 of the Interstate Commerce Act (which will include as well those carriers subject to sec. 20 (a) of such act) the Commission shall permit such carriers to file duplicate copies of the reports and other documents filed with the Interstate Commerce Commission in lieu of the reports, information, and documents required under sections 12 and 13 in respect of the same subject matter. This provision in the substitute also applies to carriers required, pursuant to any other act of Congress, to make reports of the same general character as those required under such section 20. This provision is included because of the anticipated transfer to the proposed Federal Communications Commission of jurisdiction of carriers which are at the present time subject to the provisions of such section 20.

The House bill does not contain a provision corresponding to that contained in subsection (d) of section 13 of the Senate amendment providing that "nothing in this title shall be construed as authorizing the Commission to interfere with the management of the affairs of an issuer." This provision is omitted from the substitute as unnecessary, since it is not believed that the bill is open to misconstruction in this respect.

The House bill (sec. 14) and the Senate amendment contain similar provisions regarding the regulation of over-the-counter markets except that the provision in the House bill applies to any security other than an exempted security, and the Senate amendment specifically includes certain other securities within the exemption. The substitute contains the specific Senate exemptions except that they are modified so as to cover "commercial paper, bankers' acceptances, or commercial bills, or unregistered securities the market in which is predominantly intrastate and which have not been previously registered or listed."

The House bill (sec. 15) requires every person who is directly or indirectly the beneficial owner of more than 5 percent of any class of any equity security (other than an exempted security) which is registered on a national securities exchange, to file information regarding his ownership of securities of such issuer. The Senate provision is almost identical except that it specifies 10 percent. The substitute adopts the Senate provision. The Senate amendment also contains a provision requiring any such beneficial owner, and any director, or officer of the issuer to yield to the issuer any profit realized by him from any purchase and sale, or any sale and purchase, of any equity security of the issuer (other than an exempted security) within a period of less than 6 months, unless the security was acquired in good faith in connection with a debt previously contracted, and authorizes the issuer to recover such profit by suit. The substitute includes the Senate provision but provides that no such suit by the issuer shall be brought more than 2 years after the date the profit was realized. Another provision of the Senate amendment is included in the substitute, providing that the section does not apply to foreign or domestic arbitrage transaction unless they are in contravention of such rules and regulations as the Commission may adopt. This section of the House bill contains a subsection to the effect that the provisions of the section shall not apply if the registration of the equity security has been secured without the consent of the issuer thereof. The provision is omitted from the substitute as being unnecessary in view of the authority of the Commission to make exemptions and in view of the fact that if in any case registration is permitted otherwise than by issuers it will be subject to the control of the Commission.

The House bill (section 17) and the Senate amendment each contains a provision relating to civil liability of any person making a false or misleading statement in any application, report, or document filed pursuant to the act. In the House bill this section is made to apply to "any person (including any director or officer, or any accountant or other expert)." The words in parenthesis are omitted in the substitute as being superfluous. A further difference is that the House bill permits escape from liability by the defendant upon proof that he acted in good faith and did not believe that the statement was false or misleading, while the Senate amendment provides for such escape from liability if the person sued shall prove that he acted in good faith and had no knowledge that such statement was false or misleading. The substitute adopts the Senate amendment. The Senate amendment also expressly provides that a statement shall be construed to include any omission to state a material fact, and this provision is omitted from the substitute as surplusage in view of the fact that a statement obviously may be misleading because of a material omission. The substitute contains a further provision from the Senate amendment which is not contained in the House bill, authorizing the court to require an undertaking for the payment of the costs of the suit, and to assess reasonable costs, including reasonable attorney's fees, against either party litigant. In this same section the House bill provides that no such action shall be maintained unless brought within 3 years after the violation upon which it is based, while the Senate amendment provides that no such action shall be maintained "unless brought within 1 year after discovery of the facts constituting the cause of action, nor unless brought within 5 years after such cause of action accrued." The substitute requires the action to be brought within 1 year after discovery and in any event within 3 years after the cause of action accrued.

The House bill (sec. 18 (a)) authorizes the Commission to suspend registration of a national securities exchange for failure to enforce compliance by its members with the act and rules and regulations thereunder. The Senate amendment also gives such authority to the Commission in any case where the exchange fails to enforce compliance, so far as is within its power, by an issuer of a security registered on such exchange. The substitute includes this Senate provision.

The House bill (sec. 18 (b)) authorizes the Commission, under certain specified circumstances, by rules or regulations to alter or supplement the rules of the exchange in certain respects. The Senate amendment provides that such action of the Commission shall be by order. The substitute provides that such action shall be by rules or regulations or by order. With regard to the matters as to which the Commission may make changes in the rules of the exchange, the substitute includes hours of trading, which is not contained in the House bill, but is contained in the Senate amendment. The substitute omits authority with respect to three matters which are contained in the House bill, but not in the Senate amendment, as follows: Classification of members and methods of election of officers and committees; the suspension, expulsion, or disciplining of members; and the making available of the names and addresses of holders of listed securities. The Senate amendment contains a provision not contained in the House bill authorizing and directing the Commission to make a study and investigation of the rules of national securities exchanges with respect to the classification of members, the methods of selection of officers and committees, and the suspension, expulsion, and disciplining of members, and directing the Commission to report to Congress on or before January 3, 1935. This provision is included in the substitute.

The House bill (sec. 19) makes every person who, directly or indirectly, alone or pursuant to or in connection with any agreement or understanding with one or more persons, controls a person who becomes liable under the act, liable jointly with the controlled person. The Senate amendment does not contain the words "alone or pursuant to or in connection with any agreement or understanding with one or more other persons," and these words are omitted from the substitute as being surplusage.

The House bill (sec. 23) limits the general power of the Commission to give out information by providing that any person filing an application, report, or document may make written objection to the disclosure of information contained therein, and the Commission is authorized to hear objections if it deems it advisable, but in any case the Commission may make the information public despite objection if in its judgment the disclosure is in the public interest; but it is made unlawful for any member, officer, or employee of the Commission to make public any information which, after such objection, is not disclosed. The Senate amendment makes a similar provision but provides that in all cases of objections notice and opportunity for private hearing shall be given the objector. The Senate amendment also makes it unlawful for a member, officer, or employee of the Commission to use for his personal benefit any information not made available to the public. The substitute adopts the provisions of the House bill with the addition of the Senate prohibition on use of information for personal benefit.

The House bill (sec. 28 (b)) provides that every contract made in violation of any provision of the act or of any rule or regulation thereunder, and every contract, including any contract for listing a security on an exchange, heretofore made, the performance of which involves the continuance of any relationship or practice prohibited by the act or any rule or regulation thereunder, shall be void as regards any cause of action arising after the effective date of such provision, rule, or regulation. The Senate amendment limits this provision to contracts made in violation of the act or of any rule or regulation thereunder, and to contracts hereafter made, the performance of which involves the violation of, or the continuance of any relationship or practice in violation of, any provision of the act or of any rule or regulation thereunder. The Senate amendment further restricts the provision by making any such contract void not in toto but only as regards (1) the rights of a person who in violation of the act or regulations thereunder shall have made or engaged in the performance of such contract, and (2) the rights of any person who not being a party to such contract shall have acquired any right thereunder with actual knowledge of the facts by reason of which the making or performance of such contract was in violation of the act or regulation. The substitute follows the language of the Senate amendment except that it treats on the same footing contracts made before or after the act where their performance involves a violation of the act or any regulation thereunder.

The House bill (sec. 32) provides that any person who willfully violates any provision of the act, or any rule or regulation the violation of which is made unlawful under the terms of the act, or any person who willfully and knowingly makes or causes to be made any false or misleading statement in an application, report, or document filed under this act shall be subject to a fine of not more than $10,000 or imprisonment for not more than 2 years or both. The Senate amendment contains substantially the same penalty provision, except with respect to violations of rules and regulations and statements required under rules or regulations, and except that it provides for a fine of not more than $25,000 or imprisonment for not more than 5 years. With respect to violations of rules and regulations, or any false or misleading statement in an application, report, or document required to be filed under a rule or regulation, no imprisonment is provided for and a fine of not more than $10,000 is imposed. The substitute contains substantially the House provision except that it is made clear that it is to apply to violations of rules or regulations the observance of which is required under the terms of title I, and it also provides that "no person shall be subject to imprisonment under this section for the violation of any rule or regulation if he proves that he had no knowledge of such rule or regulation."

The House bill (sec. 34) provides that the act shall become effective upon its enactment, except as to certain sections. The substitute provides that sections 6 and 12 (b), (c), (d), and (e) shall become effective on September 1, 1934, as is provided in the Senate amendment, the House bill having fixed this date as July 1, 1934, and that sections 5, 7, 8, 9 (a) (6), 10, 11, 12 (a), 13, 14, 15, 16, 17, 18, 19, and 30 shall become effective on October 1, 1934, as is provided in the Senate amendment, the House bill having fixed this date as August 1, 1934. The substitute provides that the remainder of the act shall become effective on July 1, 1934.

Title II of the Senate amendment provides for amendments to the Securities Act of 1933. The managers on the part of the House agreed to substantially all of such amendments. The purposes of the amendments agreed upon and of the changes made therein as a result of the conference are noted in the following discussion, except for minor clarifying alterations and such amendments and changes as are of an incidental character made necessary to harmonize various provisions affected by the alterations.

The amendment to section 2 (1) of the act is to make clear what is already a matter of interpretation, that certificates of deposit, fractional oil royalty, or leasehold interests, and interests of a similar character are included within the definition of a security and thus subject to the Securities Act. It is also intended to apply the act to interests commonly known as "securities," whether or not such interests are represented by any document or not. Thus the statute will apply to inscribed shares, and its provisions cannot be evaded by simply refraining from issuing to the subscriber any documentary evidence of his interest. The phrase "certificate of interest in property, tangible or intangible," is stricken out as possibly involving too broad and uncertain application. In conference it was agreed to include guaranties specifically. Their inclusion in section 2 (1) and the omission of specific mention of guarantors in section 2 (4), as proposed by these amendments, will make it clear that guarantors are to be treated as issuers of securities only if the guaranties are incorporated in securities distributed to investors. They will also indicate that the securities of which such guarantors are to be treated as issuers are the guaranties and do not include the securities guaranteed. The result is properly to limit their responsibility under section 11 to the registration statement filed as to the guaranty.

The amendments to section 2 (4) include a definition of the issuer of fractional undivided interests in oil, gas, and other mineral rights. They also provide that the liability of an issuer shall not attach individually to the trustees or members of a trust or committee. The basis for the application of absolute liability under section 11 to the issuer of securities is the principle that one should not retain the fruits of an unfair bargain. In the case of a trust or committee, it is the trust or committee, rather than the trustees or members, which profits from the bargain. Consequently the latter should not have the issuer's liability. The amendment reaches the result attained by the Commission's interpretation that the trusts and committees, recognized as entities by section 2 (2), are themselves the issuers of their securities. In conference the words "or persons" were restored, on the ground that their proposed elimination would not affect the interpretation of the section and the result desired would be accomplished by the amendment last discussed.

The purpose of the amendments to section 2 (10) are (1) to make clear beyond any doubt the interpretation of the commission that literature accompanying a prospectus, as well as literature sent subsequently to the sending of a prospectus, shall not be required to conform to the prospectus requirements of section 10 of the act, and (2) to remove from a person required to furnish a prospectus the absolute duty to see that the prospectus is received by the person to whom it is sent. It seems sufficient to require proof of the actual sending of a prospectus without making the sender take all risk of nondelivery.

The amendments to section 3 (a) (2) have three purposes: (1) To put the District of Columbia upon a parity with the States with reference to the exemption of bank stocks issued by banks organized under the laws of the District of Columbia (2) to exempt municipal bondholders' protective committees; and (3) to extend the scope of the public instrumentality exemption to expanding activities in which governments are engaging.

Section 4 (a) (4) is proposed to be amended to correct an obvious error in the original act which limited this exemption to corporate organizations when its extension to unincorporated associations is equally defensible in practice and theory.

The amendments adding new sections 3 (a) (9), 3 (a) (10), and 3 (a) (11) are based upon sections 4 (3) and 5 (c) of the original act, which are proposed to be repealed. By placing these exemptions under section 3 it is made clear that securities entitled to exemption on original issuance retain their exemption; if the issuer is not obliged to register in order to make the original distribution, dealers within a year are subject to no restriction against dealing in the securities. The result is in line with the Commission's interpretation of the act as it stood before, but the amendment removes all doubt as to its correctness.

Section 3 (a) (9), which is based upon the first clause of old section 4 (3), contains slight verbal changes of a clarifying character, affirming the Commission's interpretation that the type of commission or other remuneration the payment of which will remove the exemption is that paid for soliciting an exchange. The changes to this amendment made in conference are intended only to clarify its meaning.

The new section 3 (a) (10) substantially incorporates the exemption provided by the second clause of the existing section 4 (3), but extends its provisions to cover readjustments of rights of holders of securities, claims, and property interests under court or similar supervision, even though the original issuer of the securities, debtor on the claims, or owner of the property in which interests are held, is not itself in the process of a reorganization. This makes the exemption available in many cases of real-estate reorganizations to which, under the wording of the existing section 4 (3), its application is now denied. The exemption also is made to apply where the supervision is exercised by officials and agencies of the United States, such as the Comptroller of the Currency, the Federal Reserve Board, and the Farm Credit Administration. The supervision of similar State authorities, such as banking and insurance commissioners, will make the exemption available in corresponding cases, such as the reorganization of State banks or insurance companies. A limitation on the exemption has been added by the conferees in the requirement that the approval of the court or official, in order to be effective, must follow a hearing on the fairness of the terms and conditions of the issuance and exchange of the securities at which persons who are to receive such securities shall have a right to appear. Security holders' committees are to be denied the opportunity of obtaining exemptions under this section if they secure and exercise an exclusive right to appear for their depositors at hearings on plans of reorganization.

The new section 3 (a) (11) incorporates the existing section 5 (c) of the act and further makes clear that the exemption is not limited to the use of the mails if sales in the course of the distribution of the issue are limited to residents within a single State or Territory. Thus a person who comes within the purpose of the exemption, but happens to use a newspaper for the circulation of his advertising literature, which newspaper is transmitted in interstate commerce, does not thereby lose the benefits of the exemption.

The purposes of the amendments to section 4 (1) are (1) to remove the phrase "not with or through an underwriter" in the second clause of the section, and (2) to correct an error in the third clause of the section, making it clear that the original date of the public offering is the date from which the year is to be calculated during which a dealer is bound to supply his customers with a prospectus. The Commission has recognized by its interpretations that a "public offering" is necessary for "distribution." Therefore there can be no underwriter within the meaning of the act in the absence of a public offer and the phrase eliminated in the second clause is really superfluous. The conferees eliminated the third proposed amendment to this subsection on the ground that the participants in employees' stock-investment plans may be in as great need of the protection afforded by availability of information concerning the issuer for which they work as are most other members of the public.

The repeal of sections 4 (3) and 5 (c) is in conformity with the purpose of the amendments adding new sections 3 (a) (9), 3 (a) (10), and 3 (a) (11).

The purpose of the amendment to section 10 (b) (1) is to place only a reasonable instead of an absolute duty upon the user of a prospectus 13 months after its issuance of keeping the information therein up to date. It was originally conceived that users of prospectuses could protect themselves by contract with the issuer, but it appears only too likely that users of the prospectus will not exercise this forethought, and therefore will be left in a situation where they cannot of their own accord conform with the requirements of the act.

Section 11 (a) is amended so as to require proof that the purchaser of a security, at the time he acquired the security, relied upon the untrue statement in the registration statement or upon the registration statement and did not know of the omission. But this requirement is imposed only in the case of purchase after a period of 12 months subsequent to the effective registration date, and then only when the issuer shall have published an earning statement to its security holders covering a period of at least 12 months after the registration date. The basis of this provision is that in all likelihood the purchase and price of the security purchased after publication of such an earning statement will be predicated on that statement rather than upon the information disclosed upon registration.

The amendments to section 11 (b) (3) restate the substance of the existing provisions in language calculated more clearly to express the standard of care applicable in these cases. A clause in the amendments proposed by the Senate, continuing a requirement to the defense additional to those in the existing section, was eliminated by agreement in conference.

The amendment to section 11 (c) removes possible uncertainties as to the standard of reasonableness by substituting for the present language the accepted common-law definition of the duty of a fiduciary.

The amendments to section 11 (e) have three purposes: (1) To permit the defendant in an action under section 11 to reduce the damages so that he will not be liable for damages which he proves has no relation to his misconduct; (2) To permit an underwriter who does not knowingly receive preferential treatment to limit his total liability as regards all suits brought under section 11 to the aggregate offering price of that part of the issue underwritten by him and actually distributed; and (3) to provide, as a defense against blackmail suits as well as a defense against purely contentious litigation on the part of the defendant, that a court can require a bond for costs and can assess costs either against the plaintiff if his suit had no merit or against the defendant if his defense had none. The suggested amendments seem equitable. The changes in wording from the Senate amendments, agreed upon in conference, make it clear (1) that the limitation of underwriter's liability is not denied unless the preferential treatment was knowingly received and (2) that the extent of his liability is to be based upon the amount underwritten and distributed.

The amendments to section 13 reduce the periods of limitations on actions from those at present provided by the section. They also correct an apparently inadvertent omission by making the limitation expressly applicable to actions under section 12 (2).

Section 15 is proposed to be amended so as more accurately to carry out its real purpose. The mere existence of control is not made a basis for liability if it is shown that the controlling person had no knowledge of or reasonable ground to believe in the existence of the facts upon which the liability of the controlled person is alleged to be based.

The purpose of the amendments to section 19 (a) is to permit the regulations of the Commission, under the powers conferred upon it, adequately to protect persons who rely upon them in good faith. The powers of the Commission are also extended to include the defining of technical as well as trade and accounting terms.

Section 210 of title II of the substitute transfers the administration of the Securities Act from the Federal Trade Commission to the proposed Securities and Exchange Commission.

Sections 211 to 214 of this title, inclusive, as passed by the Senate, contained several amendments designed to place under requirements comparable to the registration requirement many protective committees which are now enjoying exemption therefrom under section 3 (a) (1), also to require periodical reports from them, and to notify all persons solicited if the composition of the soliciting committee or the terms of its deposit agreement failed to meet the recommendations of the Commission, as established by it by general rules. All these amendments were rejected in conference, on the ground that such changes in the treatment of committees should not be undertaken without more information indicating their advisability. To secure this information, the substitute section 211 agreed upon in conference authorizes and directs the Commission to make a study and investigation of such committees and to submit a report and recommendations on or before January 3, 1936.

Sam Rayburn,
George Huddleston,
Clarence F. Lea,
Carl E. Mapes,
Managers on the part of the House

MR. RAYBURN. Mr. Speaker, I shall make a short statement. I think it might be said that this report of the committee on conference follows very closely the House bill, and also the Senate bill for the reason that in many of the paragraphs of the bill the provisions of the Senate and the House were practically identical.

There were two or three material differences between the bill that the House passed and the bill that the Senate passed. In the first place, the Senate added an amendment which provided for the creation of an independent commission to administer this act, and had a loose margin requirement in their bill. Their bill also provided for a splitting of any margin requirements which might be fixed; that is, that the margin requirement for the Federal Reserve banks should be in the Federal Reserve Board, and that the fixing of any margins for brokers and nonmember banks should be in the Commission. The House Membership thought that that would be a very serious mistake, and we so stated on the floor of the House.

In other words, if you had one body controlling margins, and the Senate bill provided loose margins, that body could fix the margin at anything it pleased. The Federal Reserve Board could fix a margin for a member bank which was on one corner of a street, and the commission, having control of margins for nonmember banks, could fix a different margin for a nonmember bank on another corner of the street, and you might run credit back and forth from one bank to the other, according as to which appeared to be the most favorable market to the prospective borrower. Also, some Members of the Senate shied very much over allowing the Federal Reserve Board, as we had provided in our bill, to fix margins for brokers, thinking they would mix up the Federal Reserve System with the stock exchange. We prevailed in that. We concentrated the margin requirements in the Federal Reserve Board, where we think all credit ought to lie. We also prevailed in the initial margins for borrowings being 45 percent, or a loan value of 55 percent unless the Federal Reserve Board, in its wisdom, made an affirmative finding that in the interest of trade and commerce it should be made higher or lower.

The House conferees prevailed on those two points, which we thought very vital; the House conferees yielded on the independent commission. As far as I am individually concerned, I still think it would have been better all the way around if the administration of the Securities Act had remained in the Federal Trade Commission and if the administration of this act had gone to the Federal Trade Commission, and for this reason: I think it is of great importance that the people who are going to be controlled and regulated by and under this law should know what the rules and regulations are to be at the earliest possible date, and I think, as other members of the House conference think, that it would bring about the rules and regulations at an earlier date if left to the Federal Trade Commission, but we finally yielded, and the law will be administered by a commission of five members, and the Federal Securities Act of 1933 by this conference-report agreement is transferred to this new commission, where I thought all the time it ought to be.

The Senate added a new section to the bill with reference to these protective committees, and we were not opposed to that in principle, but there are at least 13,000 of these protective committees in the United States, and to thrust this matter upon this new commission when it was organizing we thought would be too much, and that it might not result in any good. So in lieu of that we provided that this commission should study this matter of protective committees and report back to Congress by the 1st of January 1936.

Our bill provided the act should go into effect upon its passage. It was thought when setting out this new commission it might be better to change the date to July 1, 1934, and that was done.

Mr. Speaker, those are the material matters that I think are in the bill. That was the one point upon which we yielded, and the others run along practically with what the House bill had in it. I think that is all I desire to state. . . .

MR. SABATH. Has any change been made in the bill relative to short selling?

MR. RAYBURN. No; it is practically the same as the House provision.

MR. SABATH. That leaves it up to the board or commission to pass upon?

MR. RAYBURN. Yes.

MR. COLE. In the consideration of the bill in the House there were no changes made in the Securities Act of 1933?

MR. RAYBURN. Yes. I forgot about that.

MR. COLE. There were some amendments added to the stock-exchange bill in the Senate?

MR. RAYBURN. Yes.

MR. COLE. Does the conference report change the Senate amendments of the Securities Act of 1933 in any respect?

MR. RAYBURN. It does not change them in any respect except to revise them and take them over, not make any additions to.

Before I yield the floor I may say there were some amendments to the Securities Act of 1933 put on in the Senate. As I said in my statement on the floor, some people have gone out and unnecessarily frightened prospective issuers of securities with reference to the provisions of the Securities Act of 1933. I am frank to say that I had seen those amendments before they were offered in the Senate. It was thought that there were at least some psychological amendments that might go in, some clarifying amendments, and perhaps one or two material amendments. There has been a question ever since the adoption of the Securities Act of 1933 with reference to the underwriter. We make it clear in these amendments that hereafter under no circumstances shall an underwriter be held responsible for any more of the issue than he himself personally underwrites.

In other words, if there is an issue of securities of $500,000 and an underwriter assumes the responsibility of putting upon the market $100,000, in no way can that be mixed with the other $400,000, and he can in no way be held responsible for any statement that anyone else makes.

Another rather material amendment goes to the responsibilities of directors and officers of corporations making these issues. It has been argued by many, and was argued during the consideration of the act of 1933, that before a purchaser of a security could recover from an issuer for a false or misleading statement, he should prove that he absolutely relied upon this false or misleading statement that was made.

There is one thing certain, if that kind of section were put into the bill it would defeat action in 99 cases out of 100. But we did agree to an amendment put on by the Senate which provides that after the first financial statement of the issuer is made, then the man who buys a security in commerce after that must prove that he relied upon the statement and that he was deceived by the false and misleading statement. Up until the year or 23 months before some corporations makes a financial statement, the law remains the same as to the liability of officers and directors for false and misleading statements.

Those were the main amendments in the Securities Act. There are some clarifying amendments, but they are more psychological, I think, than material.

Does the gentleman from Michigan [Mr. Mapes] desire some time?

MR. MAPES. Mr. Speaker, I had not intended to discuss the conference report, and I do not care to do so now. The gentleman from Texas [Mr. Rayburn] has called attention to the high points in the report. I joined in signing the report of the conferees. The bill is not materially different as reported by the conference committee from what it was when it was passed by the House of Representatives. In my judgment, the chief difference is the establishment of a new commission to administer the act and the Securities Act, instead of the Federal Trade Commission, as provided in the House bill. It is my judgment, too, that those who are responsible for and who were the proponents of this change will live to rue the day that the change was made. It seems to me it would be preferable to leave the administration of this act with the Federal Trade Commission and to have the broad general policies of the act determined by that Commission as a body, some members of which will not be absorbed entirely in the administration of the act and would, therefore, bring to bear upon the questions of policy perhaps a broader viewpoint for that reason.

As the gentleman from Texas [Mr. Rayburn] has explained, the Senate conferees insisted upon this new commission, and the House conferees yielded on that point, on the theory that, after all, it was not a major provision of the bill.

Personally I think this is very desirable and wholesome legislation. No one knows just how a law of this kind will work out in practice, but I have confidence that it will prove to be very much in the interest of the general public and the country. . . .

MR. COOPER OF OHIO. Mr. Speaker, when this bill was before the House, I voiced my objections to certain provisions of the bill. I was in hope that when we went into conference they could be modified or eliminated altogether. The Committee on Interstate and Foreign Commerce, especially the conferees, have worked hard to put this measure together. There is no one, except the members of the committee, who knows what a great problem this has been for us during the last 10 or 12 weeks. I want to commend the Chairman of the Committee on Interstate and Foreign Commerce for his fairness, for the manner in which he has conducted the hearings as chairman of the committee, and also the proceedings of the conference; also all the other members of the committee, and especially those who were members of the conference committee.

The provisions of the bill to which I objected when it was before the House are still in the measure, and I think it is only fair for me to say at this time that it would be rather inconsistent for me to change my attitude now and vote for the measure. Therefore, I shall vote against the conference report. . . .

MR. FISH. Mr. Speaker, I voted against this bill, somewhat reluctantly, when it came before the House, because I believed that some regulation of the stock exchange was necessary. I believed at the time there were a number of rather drastic provisions in the bill. Therefore, when it came to a final vote, I voted against it, with the hope that when the conferees met they would bring back a workable, better, and more acceptable bill by eliminating some of the drastic provisions.

I am glad today not only to go on record as favoring the conference report but I also hope to vote for it. I commend the chairman of the committee and the conferees for the ability they displayed and their fairness in yielding on the Bulwinkle amendment for a separate commission and for including modifications of the Securities Act which I believe will be beneficial to business and help the flow of capital into industry. They partially accepted the amendment I proposed, to put in the word "order" alongside "regulations" so as to protect private-property rights. I hope the chairman of the committee will ask for a roll call. I believe that there are a score or more of Republicans who did not vote for the bill originally who, if given an opportunity, today will vote for it because they believe the conference report is much fairer and that the measure is greatly improved and in the public interest.

There is only one provision which, in my judgment, is in dispute, and that is the question of margins. I, frankly, do not know enough about it to know whether the provision in regard to margin in the conference report is workable. Time alone will tell. Members of the stock exchange tell us that it will ruin their business. The members of the committee who heard the witnesses at the hearings state that it is the proper thing to do in order to protect the American public. We do not know ourselves as Members of Congress which is correct; only actual trial will tell, and if we are wrong, we will have to formulate new legislation. But in the meanwhile it is evident that most of the rest of the provisions of the bill are workable. We started to pass a bill to regulate the exchange, and the committee taking the radical and socialistic concoctions of the junior "brain trust," amounting almost to economic and financial atrocities, has written perhaps what is as fair a bill as could be passed at this session to regulate the exchanges in order to prevent a recurrence of excessive speculation and to safeguard, as far as possible, marginal gambling which has caused financial panics and enormous financial losses and ruin to millions of industrious Americans. . . .

MR. SABATH. Mr. Speaker, ladies, and gentlemen, when in 1929 it became generally known that the deposits, as well as other available cash, were being withdrawn from legitimate channels for speculative and gambling purposes, I realized the danger that confronted the country and endeavored in my humble way to arrest the vicious and dangerous wave of speculation then engulfing the Nation by appealing to President Hoover, the Federal Reserve, and to the controlling stock-exchange officials, but they paid no heed to my warning.

Therefore, Mr. Speaker, in December of that fateful year I introduced my first resolution to investigate the stock exchanges and also several other bills, one to tax short selling and one to prevent short selling, believing that short selling is a crime, because in the end it brings about the complete destruction of the value of all stocks as well as bonds.

I shall not detain you today with a recital of all the activities and work of the committee during 4½ years, but permit me to say that I am immensely pleased that the committee have been able to agree on a bill. They did not go perhaps as far as I wish they had gone, but I am immensely pleased with the results that have been accomplished and shall support the conference report. I am firmly convinced that this bill will bring about control of the greatest gambling institution in the world. [Applause.]

Mr. Speaker, ladies, and gentlemen, it is my opinion that of all the legislation enacted during my 28 years' service—yes, from the inception of the Government—none was of greater importance or will be more beneficial to the American people than this stock-exchange regulation bill of 1934, provided, of course, it is sanely and efficiently enforced.

I very much deplore that the Federal Reserve Board, which is more or less controlled by the banking institutions, not only of this country but also of England, has been given in this act the power to determine marginal requirements. I had hoped that the responsibility and enforcement would not be divided.

As many of you know, since December 9, 1929, I have made many speeches on this subject, and 2 months before that I started what I believed to be a righteous crusade against the palpable, vicious practices that were tolerated and practiced on all the stock exchanges; therefore I hesitate to address the House at this late date on this subject, important though it be; but I feel that I owe it to the country and to myself to set forth in permanent form the motives that have ever actuated me, with modest ability, in trying to eliminate the obnoxious and nefarious abuses that caused the catastrophic, economic, and financial hurricane which, by the way, was not a providential act, but the act of a few greedy, avaricious, modern Herods, malefactors, most of whom had by most questionable methods acquired great wealth and assumed high social and business positions. I refer, or course, to that unenviable class that has never honestly produced or created any portion of its wealth.

Mr. Speaker, when, in the fall of 1928 and early in 1929, bank deposits were being withdrawn, especially from small banks, I persistently and insistently and continuously urged officers of these institutions to ascertain for what purpose those withdrawals were being made. Shortly thereafter I was, unfortunately, confirmed in my suspicion that these withdrawals were being made for the purpose of investing in stocks and bonds; but no amount of suasion or argument by officials of these banks could deter the depositors from so doing.

Vividly remembering the conditions that brought about the panic of 1893 and the panic of 1907, I felt it to be my duty to urge strenuously that people desist from such dubious investments and adventurous speculations, but, unfortunately, the press of the country, encouraged and prodded by President Coolidge, President Hoover, Secretary Mellon, Assistant Secretary Mills, the House of Morgan, and other large financiers, together with many of the officials of the largest corporations, made the people believe that we were on the verge of still greater prosperity, which would continue forever.

But, Mr. Speaker, ladies, and gentlemen, reading the financial reports and other news of our economic status as of that date, I could easily discern that we could not possibly maintain that unprecedented activity, and that sooner or later we would be engulfed in the maelstrom of our own folly. In that belief I was also, unfortunately, confirmed. In June and July, when the directors of most of the large corporations started in an astute and clever manner to unload gradually their holdings and securities, when call money started to rise and reached 15, 18, and 20 percent, and the small bankers all over the Nation were being urged to send their available cash to Wall Street, I urged the directors of several small banks not to yield to the temptation of gambling, and thereby deprive legitimate business of necessary and proper credit.

But, as was shown later, the temptation was too great to resist the clarion calls of the Wall Street musicians and the balances of cash in assets used by individuals for this were withdrawn from every section of our land, so that not only the employees and people in private life but also the small manufacturers and small business men all over the United States were inveigled into parting with their hard-earned and accumulated savings, and in that way the country was milked dry of nearly all available cash, which found its eternal resting place in the coffers of the Wall Street manipulators.

Realizing that the value of stocks had been driven to such an unreasonable height, in many instances 10 or 20 times their value, and that the banks, as well as many of the insurance companies, in their greed and lust for great profits had loaned at a high rate of interest millions and millions of the people's money in connection with these fictitious prices of stock, I feared the awful crash that later came.

It was not until then that we heard a word of warning from the Federal Reserve Board; and that is the reason I am unwilling to give that recreant institution that so inexcusably and untenably failed in its plain, unmistakable duty to safeguard the credit of the Nation the power that is being given it in this bill.

Sensing the approaching danger and the catastrophic hurricane that ensued, long before the storm broke with such great fury, I urged minimizing or an actual suspension of the activities of the stock exchanges, and I especially urged the immediate cessation of all short selling of stocks.

Feeling that the professional manipulators who were responsible for this criminal inflation would at the first chance take the other side and start a forced selling campaign by those who had purchased on their advice on margins, and thereby effect a demoralization if not a complete destruction of prices, I appealed by letters and telegrams to President Hoover, to the Federal Reserve Board, to the Secretary of the Treasury, to the blessed House of Morgan, and to the responsible officers of the stock exchanges.

I am reminded by copies of many telegrams and letters in my files that I pleaded earnestly with these rascals of the stock exchanges that they should, if not for the country's sake, then for their own ultimate sake, immediately stop these malignant practices that were even then so unerringly pointing to destruction. I called timely attention to the effect these practices would have if these unscrupulous, soulless Herods were permitted to continue that ruthless program of annihilation.

On December 9, 1929, the first day of the Seventy-second Congress, I took the floor of this House and though the storm had then almost completely engulfed us, made a plea that there was still time within which to save the Nation and the millions of honest investors from complete ruin, but my appeals and warnings received about as much thoughtful attention as does the wave that hits yonder shore, because the answer was, "Let the liquidation take its course." No effort was made to minimize the effect of that soul-stirring catastrophe.

During the entire 3 years, 1930, 1931, and 1932, not a single effort was made by the powerful, predatory banking interests or the spineless Hoover administration to soften the blow or arrest the progress of this raging financial storm; but I did not desist. Early in 1930 and 1931 I pleaded with the Federal Reserve Board with the emphasis of hand upon heart to accept for rediscount the Reconstruction Finance Corporation paper, short-term municipal paper, and mortgages on the homes of American citizens; and through the Federal Reserve Board had ample power to rediscount Reconstruction Finance Corporation paper to the extent of two billions, which would have strenthened, if not saved, the credit of the Nation, yet the Federal Reserve Board supinely refused to act, while the indefensible practices on the stock exchanges continued to force the sale of millions upon millions of securities held by the various banks and like institutions, until late in 1932 there was an average loss on all investments of our country of more than 83 percent. Many securities even became absolutely valueless. During these trying and heart-rending times of complete despair the gentlemen of the stock exchanges through their hundreds of new branches established in every village and hamlet in the United States continued to reap a harvest by circulating false and misleading rumors through a subsidized press and their own representatives in all parts of the country.

I charge again today that the authors of that great Nation-wide crash were the stock exchanges, the criminal inflation, the unpardonable, shameful manipulation of stocks, the unwarranted issuance of millions and millions of new shares of stocks, the overcapitalization of companies and corporations, the merger of corporations, all for the purpose of giving them additional new worthless issues to unload at 10 times their value upon a gullible and credulous public.

As will be recalled, six, yes, as many as ten million shares a day were traded on the New York Exchange, the curb, and other exchanges throughout the United States. Iniquitous gambling pools to sell short were being organized and everything possible was being done to destroy the last vestige of worth in any of these issues. During these trying days I pleaded and pleaded and urged and urged and appealed and appealed to the New York Stock Exchange to arrest and to stop this damnable procedure, to stop the short selling, to stop the pool operations and many other baneful abuses practiced there, for all the one purpose and it alone, namely, to make profits for themselves regardless of the cost to the country. Instead of complying with my appeals and supplications and exhortations the stock exchanges engaged in publicity directed by the greatest experts in that field. They directed radiobroadcasts and issued thousands and thousands of bulletins and press notices to disparage me and my efforts in opposing their vile machinations.

Naturally, I am gratified, after 4 1/2 years of trial, to see a remedial and just law going upon the statutes, which law, I hope, may forever prevent such panics as those of 1893, 1907, and the archcrime of 1929. When I say crime, Mr. Speaker, I mean crime. That was the greatest crime perpetrated against a nation of 130,000,000 freedmen in the history of the world. True, from time to time the multitudes have suffered from war, from devastation of their country by foreign enemies, by pestilence, by floods, by great conflagrations, but these were understandable acts of Providence. Not so, however, as to the ruthless and indelible destruction of 1929 which caused more suffering, which caused untold deaths among men and women and children through malnutrition, which filled thousands of cemeteries with unmerited suicides, and made thousands upon thousands homeless, and deprived 16,000,000 men of employment with which to earn their bread. These were not providential visitations but were due solely to the unchecked greed of stock gamblers.

Millions upon millions of willing men and women, stalwart American citizens, lost their farms, their homes, their self-respect, their all. Millions of depositors lost the savings that they had calculated to allow them to spend the declining years of life in earned happiness and peace after storm-tossed careers. Not even old men and old women and orphans escaped this scourge. The thirst for the lifeblood of society was so strong that nothing could prevail against it. I am told that even blind men and women were robbed without mercy or conscience. Over 16,000,000 men and women, willing workers all were, through no fault of their own, deprived of the means of livelihood and were reduced to the deplorable necessity of asking their Government, their cities, and their municipalities for aid, which aid has bankrupted many States and municipalities and caused an enormous increase in the public debt of the National Government. These are the unpardonable crimes these shameless racketeers, these flagitious buccaneers, these cold-blooded murderers will have to meet before the bar of history.

All this was brought about by a few designing men who continued to live in luxury in their palatial homes here and abroad and on their expensive yachts, living shamelessly upon the ill-gotten profits garnered from the misery of millions of suffering human beings. And, as if to add insult to injury, these criminals yet have the temerity, the gall, the audacity, the impudence, and the effrontery to say to us representatives of 130,000,000 free people, "You must not go too far to abbreviate our privileges, we have an institution that is needed as a legitimate agency of business, as a legitimate exchange."

Mr. Speaker and ladies and gentlemen, I fully recognize that we need a legitimate exchange, but we should unmistakably put an end to the illegitimate, dishonest, vicious trespasses and excesses of this or any other similar institution in the United States.

Again, I very much deplore that we have in the United States many intelligent, well-meaning men who permit themselves to be used by this dastardly institution, which has admitted, under the compulsion of an official oath, that it has expended more than a billion dollars in propaganda to prevent this wholesome legislation.

I am today more proud of my associates than I have ever been. Undeniably real representatives of a free electorate, you have done a great work for a great people. I have always maintained that the vast majority of public officials, especially of the Congress, are not only honest and of splendid ability, but they desire faithfully to serve the people. The vote on this legislation proves unmistakably that any attempt on the part of the unrighteous to browbeat is always doomed to failure. I admit that here and there we find a man in public life who forgets his duty, his oath of office, and who permits his name, his character, his intellect, to be used by the vested interests behind such as the stock exchanges; but what, I ask, makes men dishonest; who, I ask, is it that is responsible for men going wrong? It is the temptation, it is the bribes, in one way or another, left-handed and right-handed, that are forthcoming from these greedy, avaricious degenerates who have tempted and who will continue to tempt deserving men.

If I personally had the necessary power, I would utilize it all, and the entire remainder of my life, in trying to devise legislation whereby, not those who accept bribes but those who give them would be punished.

In conclusion, I cannot refrain from stating that I am glad that I have been in a position to in some degree bring about this remedial legislation. I hope with all my heart this legislation may prevent a repetition of the unprecedented crime of 1929 by the stock exchanges of the United States; and though the important Committee on Interstate and Foreign Commerce of the House is entitled to great credit in this connection, yet the real credit for this very good work belongs and must go to that intrepid, splendid, courageous, determined, forward-looking, sincere leader of leaders in the betterment of humankind, who had the best interests of the masses at heart, and whose only aim in the world is to improve the conditions of the masses, the greatest of all the great Presidents, Franklin Delano Roosevelt. . . .

MR. DIRKSEN. The gentleman will remember that in the discussion when the bill was under consideration in the House I voiced some apprehension about the small corporate entities whose securities were unregistered, that they might be placed under undue restrictions with respect to the over-the-counter markets. I understand the bill has been amended and an excpetion has been made in their favor.

MR. RAYBURN. An exception is made in unregistered securities of companies predominantly intrastate in character.

Mr. Speaker, I move the previous question.

The question was taken; and the Speaker announced that the ayes seemed to have it.

MR. FISH. Mr. Speaker, I ask for the yeas and nays.

The yeas and nays were refused.

So the conference report was agreed to. . . .

NATIONAL LABOR RELATIONS BOARD

NATIONAL LABOR RELATIONS ACT
1935

NATIONAL LABOR RELATIONS ACT
1935

Commentary

The legislative history of the National Labor Relations Act is contained in the volume *Statutory History of the United States: Labor Organization* (1970) edited by Robert F. Koretz. Here only those portions of the Act and its legislative history dealing with the establishment of the National Labor Relations Board and its position as an independent regulatory agency are reproduced.

There is surprisingly little in the legislative history of the Labor Act on the setting up of the NLRB as an independent regulatory body. Certainly there was no discussion in either house remotely comparable to that which took place before the Federal Trade Commission (the closest counterpart of the NLRB in the federal regulatory process) was created. The relative lack of discussion in the 1935 debates may be explained by the fact that no one disputed the need for setting up the new regulatory agency as an independent body. No one proposed setting it up as a bureau within an existing department. There was, however, debate over whether the NLRB should be completely independent like the FTC or be set up as an independent board in the Department of Labor. This debate occurred in the House. The Senate bill provided for FTC-type independence and all Senator Robert F. Wagner [Dem., N.Y.] felt it necessary to state, in presenting the bill, was that it was modeled in this respect on the FTC Act and the Interstate Commerce Act.

In the House, Congressman Thomas L. Blanton [Dem., Tex.] attacked the merger of powers in the Board, with it "made judge, jury, bailiff, prosecutor, and executioner." But the only real discussion on the position of the Board took place on the House Commerce Committee's proposed amendment to place the agency "in the Department of Labor." The opposing speeches of Congressman Robert C. Work Ramspeck [Dem., Ga.] and Vito Marcantonio [Rep., N.Y.] (repeating, in large part, the latter's minority committee report, *infra* p. 2966) discuss the position of the NLRB and the need for independence. Marcantonio's speech contains a good statement of the need to have such a quasi-judicial agency vested with independent status. The committee amendment was defeated and the bill as passed by the House set up the Board "as an independent agency in the executive branch of the Government." In conference committee, after the *Humphrey* decision (*supra* p. 1811), the quoted phrase was eliminated. As the House conference managers statement (*infra* p. 2978) puts it, why, in the light of the Court's decision, should the statute declare an independent agency to be "in the executive branch"?

NATIONAL LABOR RELATIONS ACT
July 5, 1935

Be it enacted by the Senate and House of Representatives of the United States of America in Congress assembled, . . .

National Labor Relations Board

SEC. 3. (a) There is hereby created a board, to be known as the "National Labor Relations Board" (hereinafter referred to as the "Board"), which shall be composed of three members, who shall be appointed by the President, by and with the advice and consent of the Senate. One of the original members shall be appointed for a term of one year, one for a term of three years, and one for a term of five years, but their successors shall be appointed for terms of five years each, except that any individual chosen to fill a vacancy shall be appointed only for the unexpired term of the member whom he shall succeed. The President shall designate one member to serve as chairman of the Board. Any member of the Board may be removed by the President, upon notice and hearing, for neglect of duty or malfeasance in office, but for no other cause.

(b) A vacancy in the Board shall not impair the right of the remaining members to exercise all the powers of the Board, and two members of the Board shall, at all times, constitute a quorum. The Board shall have an official seal which shall be judicially noticed.

(c) The Board shall at the close of each fiscal year make a report in writing to Congress and to the President stating in detail the cases it has heard, the decisions it has rendered, the names, salaries, and duties of all employees and officers in the employ or under the supervision of the Board, and an account of all moneys it has disbursed.

SEC. 4. (a) Each member of the Board shall receive a salary of $10,000 a year, shall be eligible for reappointment, and shall not engage in any other business, vocation, or employment. The Board shall appoint, without regard for the provisions of the civil-service laws but subject to the Classification Act of 1923, as amended, an executive secretary, and such attorneys, examiners, and regional directors, and shall appoint such other employees with regard to existing laws applicable to the employment and compensation of officers and employees of the United States, as it may from time to time find necessary for the proper performance of its duties and as may be from time to time appropriated for by Congress. The Board may establish or utilize such regional, local, or other agencies, and utilize such voluntary and uncompensated services, as may from time to time be needed. Attorneys appointed under this section may, at the direction of the Board, appear for and represent the Board in any case in court. Nothing in this Act shall be construed to authorize the Board to appoint individuals for the purpose of conciliation or mediation (or for statistical work), where such service may be obtained from the Department of Labor.

(b) Upon the appointment of the three original members of the Board and the designation of its chairman, the old Board shall cease to exist. All employees of the old Board shall be transferred to and become employees of the Board with salaries under the Classification Act of 1923, as amended, without acquiring by such transfer a permanent or civil service status. All records, papers, and property of the old Board shall become records, papers, and property of the Board, and all unexpended funds and appropriations for the use and maintenance of the old Board shall become funds and appropriations available to be expended by the Board in the exercise of the powers, authority, and duties conferred on it by this Act.

(c) All of the expenses of the Board, including all necessary traveling and subsistence expenses outside the District of Columbia incurred by the members or employees of the Board under its orders, shall be allowed and paid on the presentation of itemized vouchers therefor approved by the Board or by any individual it designates for that purpose.

SEC. 5. The principal office of the Board shall be in the District of Columbia, but it may meet and exercise any or all of its powers at any other place. The Board may, by one or more of its members or by such agents or agencies as it may designate, prosecute any inquiry necessary to its functions in any part of the United States. A member who participates in such an inquiry shall not be disqualified from subsequently participating in a decision of the Board in the same case.

SEC. 6. (a) The Board shall have authority from time to time to make, amend, and rescind such rules and regulations as may be necessary to carry out the provisions of this Act. Such rules and regulations shall be effective upon publication in the manner which the Board shall prescribe. . . .

Prevention of Unfair Labor Practices

SEC. 10. (a) The Board is empowered, as hereinafter provided, to prevent any person from engaging in any unfair labor practice (listed in section 8) affecting commerce. This power shall be exclusive, and shall not be affected by any other means of adjustment or prevention that has been or may be established by agreement, code, law, or otherwise.

(b) Whenever it is charged that any person has engaged in or is engaging in any such unfair labor practice, the Board, or any agent or agency designated by the Board for such purposes, shall have power to issue and cause to be served upon such person a complaint stating the charges in that respect, and containing a notice of hearing before the Board or a member thereof, or before a designated agent or agency, at a place therein fixed, not less than five days after the serving of said complaint. Any such complaint may be amended by the member, agent, or agency conducting the hearing or the Board in its discretion at any time prior to the issuance of an order based thereon. The person so complained of shall have the right to file an answer to the original or amended complaint and to appear in person or otherwise and give testimony at the place and time fixed in the complaint. In the discretion of the member, agent or agency conducting the hearing or the Board, any other person may be allowed to intervene in the said proceeding and to present testimony. In any such proceeding the rules of evidence prevailing in courts of law or equity shall not be controlling.

(c) The testimony taken by such member, agent or agency or the Board shall be reduced to writing and filed with the Board. Thereafter, in its discretion, the Board upon notice may take further testimony or hear argument. If upon all the testimony taken the Board shall be of the opinion that any person named in the complaint has engaged in or is engaging in any such unfair labor practice, then the Board shall state its findings of fact and shall issue and cause to be served on such person an order requiring such person to cease and desist from such unfair labor practice, and to take such affirmative action, including reinstatement of employees with or without back pay, as will effectuate the policies of this Act. Such order may further require such person to make reports from time to time showing the extent to which it has complied with the order. If upon all the testimony taken the Board shall be of the opinion that no person named in the complaint has engaged in or is engaging in any such unfair labor practice, then the Board shall state its findings of fact and shall issue an order dismissing the said complaint.

(d) Until a transcript of the record in a case shall have been filed in a court, as hereinafter provided, the Board may at any time, upon reasonable notice and in such manner as it shall deem proper, modify or set aside, in whole or in part, any finding or order made or issued by it.

(e) The Board shall have power to petition any circuit court of appeals of the United States (including the Court of Appeals of the District of Columbia), or if all the circuit courts of appeals to which application may be made are in vacation, any district court of the United States (including the Supreme Court of the District of Columbia), within any circuit or district, respectively, wherein the unfair labor practice in question occurred or wherein such person resides or transacts business, for the enforcement of such order and for appropriate temporary relief or restraining order, and shall certify and file in the court a transcript of the entire record in the proceeding, including the pleadings and testimony upon which such order was entered and the findings and order of the Board. Upon such filing, the court shall cause notice thereof to be served upon such person, and thereupon shall have jurisdiction of the proceeding and of the question determined therein, and shall have power to grant such temporary relief or restraining order as it deems just and proper, and to make and enter upon the pleadings, testimony, and proceedings set forth in such transcript a decree enforcing, modifying, and enforcing as so modified, or setting aside in whole or in part the order of the Board. No objection that has not been urged before the Board, its member, agent or agency, shall be considered by the court, unless the failure or neglect to urge such objection shall be excused because of extraordinary circumstances. The findings of the Board as to the facts, if supported by evidence, shall be conclusive. If either party shall apply to the court for leave to adduce additional evidence and shall show to the satisfaction of the court that such additional evidence is material and that there were reasonable grounds for the failure to adduce such evidence in the hearing before the Board, its member, agent, or agency, the court may order such additional evidence to be taken before the Board, its member, agent, or agency, and to be made a part of the transcript. The Board may modify its findings as to the facts, or make new findings, by reason of additional evidence so taken and filed, and it shall file such modified or new findings, which, if supported by evidence, shall be conclusive, and shall file its recommendations, if any, for the modification or setting aside of its original order. The jurisdiction of the court shall be exclusive and its judgment and decree shall be final, except that the same shall be subject to review by the appropriate circuit court of appeals if application was made to the district court as hereinabove provided, and by the Supreme Court of the United States upon writ of certiorari or certification as provided in sections 239 and 240 of the Judicial Code, as amended (U.S.C., title 28, secs. 346 and 347).

(f) Any person aggrieved by a final order of the Board granting or denying in whole or in part the relief sought may obtain a review of such order in any circuit court of appeals of the United States in the circuit wherein the unfair labor practice in question was alleged to have been engaged in or wherein such person resides or transacts business, or in the Court of Appeals of the District of Columbia, by filing in such court a written petition praying that the order of the Board be modified or set aside. A copy of such petition shall be forthwith served upon the Board, and thereupon the aggrieved party shall file in the court a transcript of the entire record in the proceeding, certified by the Board, including the pleading and testimony upon which the order complained of was entered and the findings and order of the Board. Upon such filing, the court shall proceed in the same manner as in the case of an application by the Board under subsection (e), and shall have the same exclusive jurisdiction to grant to the Board such temporary relief or restraining order as it deems just and proper, and in like manner to make and enter a decree enforcing, modifying, and enforcing as so modified, or setting aside in whole or in part the order of the Board; and the findings of the Board as to the facts, if supported by evidence, shall in like manner be conclusive.

(g) The commencement of proceedings under subsection (e) or (f) of this section shall not, unless specifically ordered by the court, operate as a stay of the Board's order.

(h) When granting appropriate temporary relief or a restraining order, or making and entering a decree enforcing, modifying, and enforcing as so modified or setting aside in whole or in part an order of the Board, as provided in his section, the jurisdiction of courts sitting in equity shall not be limited by the Act entitled "An Act to amend the Judicial Code and to define and limit the jurisdiction of courts sitting in equity, and for other purposes," approved March 23, 1932 (U.S.C., Supp. VII, title 29, secs. 101-115).

(i) Petitions filed under this Act shall be heard expeditiously, and if possible within ten days after they have been docketed.

Investigatory Powers

SEC. 11. For the purpose of all hearings and investigations, which, in the opinion of the Board, are necessary and proper for the exercise of the powers vested in it by section 9 and section 10—

(1) The Board, or its duly authorized agents or agencies, shall at all reasonable times have access to, for the purpose of examination, and the right to copy any evidence of any person being investigated or proceeded against that relates to any matter under investigation or in question. Any member of the Board shall have power

to issue subpenas requiring the attendance and testimony of witnesses and the production of any evidence that relates to any matter under investigation or in question, before the Board, its member, agent, or agency conducting the hearing or investigation. Any member of the Board, or any agent or agency designated by the Board for such purposes, may administer oaths and affirmations, examine witnesses, and receive evidence. Such attendance of witnesses and the production of such evidence may be required from any place in the United States or any Territory or possession thereof, at any designated place of hearing.

(2) In case of contumacy or refusal to obey a subpena issued to any person, any District Court of the United States or the United States courts of any Territory or possession, or the Supreme Court of the District of Columbia, within the jurisdiction of which the inquiry is carried on or within the jurisdiction of which said person guilty of contumacy or refusal to obey is found or resides or transacts business, upon application by the Board shall have jurisdiction to issue to such person an order requiring such person to appear before the Board, its member, agent, or agency, there to produce evidence if so ordered, or there to give testimony touching the matter under investigation or in question; and any failure to obey such order of the court may be punished by said court as a contempt thereof.

(3) No person shall be excused from attending and testifying or from producing books, records, correspondence, documents, or other evidence in obedience to the subpena of the Board, on the ground that the testimony or evidence required of him may tend to incriminate him or subject him to a penalty or forfeiture; but no individual shall be prosecuted or subjected to any penalty or forfeiture for or on account of any transaction, matter, or thing concerning which he is compelled, after having claimed his privilege against self-incrimination, to testify or produce evidence, except that such individual so testifying shall not be exempt from prosecution and punishment for perjury committed in so testifying.

(4) Complaints, orders, and other process and papers of the Board, its member, agent, or agency, may be served either personally or by registered mail or by telegraph or by leaving a copy thereof at the principal office or place of business of the person required to be served. The verified return by the individual so serving the same setting forth the manner of such service shall be proof of the same, and the return post office receipt or telegraph receipt therefor when registered and mailed or telegraphed as aforesaid shall be proof of service of the same. Witnesses summoned before the Board, its member, agent, or agency, shall be paid the same fees and mileage that are paid witnesses in the courts of the United States, and witnesses whose depositions are taken and the persons taking the same shall severally be entitled to the same fees as are paid for like services in the courts of the United States.

(5) All process of any court to which application may be made under this Act may be served in the judicial district wherein the defendant or other person required to be served resides or may be found.

(6) The several departments and agencies of the Government, when directed by the President, shall furnish the Board, upon its request, all records, papers, and information in their possession relating to any matter before the Board. . . .

THE ORIGINS

REPORT OF THE SENATE LABOR AND EDUCATION COMMITTEE
May 1 (calendar day, May 2), 1935

Mr. Walsh, from the Committee on Education and Labor, submitted the following

REPORT
[To accompany S. 1958]

The Committee on Education and Labor, to whom was referred the bill (S. 1958) to promote equality of bargaining power between employers and employees, to diminish the causes of labor disputes, to create a National Labor Board, and for other purposes, after holding hearings and giving consideration to the bill, report the same with amendments and recommend the passage of the bill as amended. . . .

Section 3. National Labor Relations Board. —This section creates as an independent agency in the executive branch of the Government, a board to be known as the National Labor Relations Board. The Board shall be composed of three members, appointed for 5-year terms by the President by and with the advice and consent of the Senate.

Section 4. Organization of the Board. —This section provides that members of the Board shall receive salaries of $10,000 a year each. It also provides for the appointment of employees, for the transfer to the Board of the cases, records, and employees of the present National Labor Relations Board, and for the method of paying the expenses of the Board. These provisions are all in accordance with commonly accepted practice in setting up administrative agencies.

It is of special import that the National Labor Relations Board is not empowered to engage in conciliation of wage and hour disputes insofar as that activity can be carried on by the Department of Labor. Duplication of services is thus avoided, and in addition the Board is left free to engage in quasi-judicial work that is essentially different from conciliation or mediation of wage and hour controversies. And of course the binding effect of the provisions of this bill forbidding unfair labor practices are not subject for mediation or conciliation.

The committee does not believe that the Board should serve as an arbitration agency. Such work, like conciliation, might impair its standing as an interpreter of the law. In addition, there is at present no dearth of arbitration agencies in this country. If arbitration lags, it is only because parties are not ready to submit to it. And compulsory arbitration has not received the sanction of the American people.

Section 5. Prosecution of inquiry. —This section follows the customary policy of allowing the Board or its agencies to move to the scene of action, rather than compelling all parties at all times to come to Washington.

Section 6. Rules and regulations.—This section follows the customary policy of giving the Board the power to make and amend rules and regulations. Such rules and regulations become effective only upon publication and there are no criminal penalties attached to their breach. . . .

REPORT OF THE HOUSE LABOR COMMITTEE (WITH A MINORITY VIEW)
June 10, 1935

Mr. Connery, from the Committee on Labor, submitted the following

REPORT
[To accompany S. 1958]

The Committee on Labor, to whom was referred the bill (S. 1958) to promote equality of bargaining power between employers and employees, to diminish the causes of labor disputes, to create a National Labor Relations Board, and for other purposes, having had the same under consideration, report it back to the House with amendments and recommended that the bill, as amended, do pass. . . .

National Labor Relations Board

Section 3: This section establishes a nonpartisan board of three members appointed by the President by and with the advice and consent of the Senate. The committee has departed from S. 1958, as it passed the Senate, by providing that the Board shall be "created in the Department of Labor" instead of being established "as an independent agency in the executive branch of the Government."

The committee does not intend, by this change, to subject the Board to the jurisdiction of the Secretary of Labor in respect of its decisions, policies, budget, or personnel. An amendment offered by the Secretary of Labor, requiring that the Board's appointments of employees shall be subject to the approval of the Secretary, was not accepted by the committee. We recognize the necessity of establishing a board with independence and dignity, in order that men of high caliber may be persuaded to serve upon it, and in order to give it a national prestige adequate to the important functions conferred upon it. While it is convenient to locate the Board in the Department which deals wtih labor problems, this nominal connection will not impair the independence of the Board, which will be free to administer the statute without accountability except to Congress and the courts.

For the information of the House, we insert letters from the Secretary of Labor and the Chairman of the National Labor Relations Board, expressing their respective views on this point.

Labor Department
Washington, May 13, 1935

Hon. William P. Connery, Jr.
House of Representatives, Washington, D.C.

My Dear Mr. Congressman: I have your letter of May 10 enclosing a copy of H. R. 7978, your bill "to promote equality of bargaining power between employers and employees, to diminish the cause of labor disputes, to create a National Labor Relations Board, and for other purposes." As you know, I am deeply interested in the success of this legislation, and therefore, was very pleased to learn that the House Committee on Labor had voted to report the bill favorably.

The bill which your committee has approved embodies the principles of the measure introduced by you earlier in the session, the principal objectives of which I commended in my testimony before your committee. Briefly summed up, it proposes to write into the statute law of the United States the legal right of collective bargaining to clarify that right by precise definition, and to provide machinery for its enforcement by creating a new National Labor Relations Board, vested with quasi-judicial powers.

I am very grateful to your committee for the careful consideration which it accorded to my testimony when I appeared before it, and I note that several of the suggestions I made at that time have been incorporated in the present text of the bill. One of the most important of these changes has been the revision of section 3 (a), so that in its present form it makes the National Labor Relations Board a part of the Department of Labor. Although I believe that the judicial independence of the Board should be insured, by making its decisions subject to review only in the courts, I think it would have been unwise to have recommended a bill creating the Board as an entirely separate agency dissociated from all the permanent executive departments.

Your bill recognizes the importance of constant integration of the problems of collective bargaining with other labor problems, which is essential if the Department and the Board are to have the greatest possible understanding of the ramifications of their decisions in the field of industrial relations. Despite any restrictions which legislation might define, there would always be pressure upon a labor board to engage in conciliation and research. If the Board was separate this would mean an unnecessary duplication of functions already performed by the Department of Labor. Moreover, your bill, by providing for a unified administrative structure, guards against the confusion produced in the public mind by an increase in governmental agencies, and brings the Board more closely within the sphere of the problems of Government which ordinarily comes to the attention of the President and Cabinet.

Moreover, it seems to me that your bill tends to make the proposed Board more judicial in character than would be possible were it an independent agency whose attention would be subject to distraction from specific cases by the temptation to strengthen its prestige through educational and administrative activities. A court is free from such temptation because the groove of its activity is so well defined that it can ignore all propaganda in an administration and devote its entire time to the quiet unimpassioned performance of the judicial processes. Anyone interested in making the proposed labor board as much as possible like a court should favor provisions restricting the scope of its activities to actual cases rather than to encourage it to enter the disconcerting tasks of administration. I am not sure that your bill goes as far as it might in relieving the Board of administrative responsibilities, for it charges the Board with the duty of making all the appointments to its own staff without the advice and consent of the head of the Department (sec. 4 (a)), and the task of reporting directly each year to the President and Congress (sec. 3 (c)). It would seem to me that these duties are possibly administrative in character and might consistently be given to the Secretary of Labor.

The other changes which your committee has made in the original draft also impress me favorably, particularly the omission of the section giving Federal district courts jurisdiction of unfair labor practices. I am glad that you concur with me in thinking that this section would have been productive of a welter of conflicting decisions, and that greater promise of uniform interpretation of the law will result from confining original jurisdiction to the Board or its subordinate agencies. I also feel that section 10 (c), defining the Board's procedure, considerably clarifies the phraseology of the original section. The redrafting of section 9 (a) dealing with the troublesome question of majority rule and the rights of minority groups also strengthens the bill by preventing any questions of minority representation being raised. The original wording was not altogether clear on this point.

Sincerely yours,

Frances Perkins

National Labor Relations Board
Washington, D.C., May 17, 1935

Hon. William P. Connery, Jr.
House Office Building, Washington, D.C.

My Dear Mr. Congressman: In answer to your favor of the 10th, enclosing a copy of H. R. 7978, National Labor Relations bill, I note that this bill is identical with Senator Wagner's bill as it came out of the Senate Committee on Education and Labor, with the exception of section 3 (a) of the House bill. The language in the Senate bill is: "There is hereby created as an independent agency in the executive branch of the Government." The language of the House bill reads: "There is hereby created in the Department of Labor." Otherwise the two bills are identical.

We are of opinion that the amendment proposed by your committee is distinctly harmful to the general purposes of the bill. It may be a matter of doubt what are the implications of the unexplained phrase "created in the Department of Labor." Were it not for the fact that your committee declined to accept one of the amendments proposed by the Secretary of Labor specifically subjecting to the approval of the Secretary the Board's appointment of employees, it might have been assumed that putting the Board "in the Department of Labor" carried with it automatic control by the Secretary over personnel. The phrase "created in the Department of Labor" might also carry the implication of budgetary control, which inevitably, though indirectly, enables the Secretary to influence the policy of the Board. Believing as we do that the independence of the Board should be established upon an unquestionable basis, we favor the unequivocal Senate version creating the Board "as an independent agency in the executive branch of the Government."

The value and success of any quasi-judicial board dealing with labor relations lies first and foremost in its independence and impartiality. After all, although the bill deals with the rights of labor, for the success of the machinery contemplated by the act it must in the long run have the confidence of industry and of the public at large. In our view it is in derogation of such independence and such impartiality to attach the Board to any department in the executive branch of the Government, and particularly to a department whose function in fact and in the public view is to look after the interests of labor.

The Board is to administer an act of Congress laying down a specific policy. If the Board is subject to the control of the Secretary of Labor as to personnel and budget, there will be an inevitable tendency to conform the administrative policies of the Board to the policies of the particular administration in power.

Where Congress has defined a policy and created an administrative board to carry out that policy, it has with marked consistency recognized that the board so created should be appointed for comparatively long terms of office and be free of control by the executive departments or by any particular administration. The arguments advanced for putting the Board in the Department of Labor would, if accepted by the Congress, have resulted in putting the Interstate Commerce Commission, the Federal Trade Commission, the Communications Commission in the Department of Commerce, and the Reconstruction Finance Corporation in the Treasury Department, instead of their being given an independent status. A similar observation may be made with reference to the Securities Exchange Commission and the National Mediation Board. It is of profound significance that the four outstanding permanent administrative agencies created by the last Congress to effectuate declared congressional policies were established as independent agencies; these are the Securities Exchange Commission, the Communications Commission, the Federal Housing Administration, and the National Mediation Board. Considering the specific quasi-judicial functions of the proposed National Labor Relations Board, there are even stronger reasons why it should have the prestige of independent status, than there were for establishing the National Mediation Board, to quote the words of its organic act, "as an independent agency in the executive branch of the Government."

It may be further observed that the multiplication of the functions of Cabinet officers has already proceeded to such a point that the practical supervision of any further agencies set up by the Congress, if entrusted to the departments, would necessarily be exercised by subordinates, themselves often overworked, and often not intimately acquainted with the special problems.

We wish to emphasize the essential difference between mediation and conciliation in adjusting disputes over wage and hour demands, and the work of the National Labor Relations Board in handling 7 (a) cases under the present law, or the work of the proposed new Board in handling complaints that an employer has been guilty of unfair labor practices under the pending legislation. Wages and hours, apart from minimum standards prescribed by the codes, are a matter of give and take, in which conciliation serves a useful function. But the rights of labor under section 7 (a), or under the Wagner-Connery bill, are written into the law to be enforced, not to be bargained about or compromised. When a complaint of law violation is presented to the National Labor Relations Board or one of its regional boards, it is the function of the Board to see that the law is vindicated. Compliance with the law is often obtained without the necessity of formal hearings, or after hearing and before enforcement processes are involved; but obtaining such compliance is quite different from the mediation which is the function of the Conciliation Service of the Department in settling disputes about wages and working conditions.

As Senator Wagner said in his testimony before the Senate Committee on Education and Labor:

"The atmosphere of compromise and adaptation is perfectly suited to the settlement of disputes concerning hours and wages where shifting scales are fitting to particular conditions. But it is unsuited to section 7 (a) which Congress intended for universal application, not universal modification. The practical effect of letting each disputant bargain and haggle about what section 7 (a) means is that the weakest groups which need its basic protection most receive it the least."

The National Labor Relations Board, as set up by Executive order of June 29, 1934, though it was directed to make its report to the President through the Secretary of Labor, and directed not to duplicate the mediatory and statistical work of the Department, has nevertheless been, in its administration of section 7 (a) and in its control of its own personnel and expenditures, an agency independent of the Department. This independence has not resulted in the duplication of work which the Secretary fears as likely to result from the bill as it passed the Senate. The Board has taken pains not to encroach upon the work of the conciliation service of the Department.

It has proceeded under a harmonious working arrangement with the Department, specifying the respective functions of the board and the Department. It has found no difficulty, indeed has had the warmest cooperation of the Department, in the matter of making use of the Department's statistical and research agencies and other facilities. To make it abundantly clear that there shall be no duplication of work, the Senate committee inserted an amendment, which was entirely agreeable to the board, forbidding the board to appoint persons to engage in mediation, conciliation, or statistical work when the services of such persons may be obtained from the Department of Labor. That provision also appears in section 4 of H. R. 7978. A similar provision in section 1 (b) of the Executive order under which the board now operates has proven entirely satisfactory.

The fact that the administrative and quasi-judicial functions of the board should be kept distinct from the work of mediation and conciliation is an added reason why its functions should not be transferred to the jurisdiction of the Secretary of Labor. The tendency toward confusion of the two functions is enhanced by confiding them both to the Labor Department.

We conclude that every consideration of congressional precedent in like cases of efficiency, of giving the board an assured independence in its judicial and administrative work, requires that the board be established as an independent agency in the executive branch of the Government.

With this one exception noted, the National Labor Relations Board heartily endorses H. R. 7978 as a statesmanlike contribution to healthy labor relations and industrial peace.

Sincerely yours

Francis Biddle, Chairman

The other amendment to this section is merely clarifying. It provides that the decision of the Supreme Court in the recent *Humphreys case* shall be embodied in this statute so as not to leave the matter open to further litigation. The Court held that a Federal Trade Commissioner could not be removed by the President except for neglect of duty. There was considerable language in the opinion indicating that a quasi-judicial body would stand a better chance of favorable treatment if it were divorced from the executive branch of the Government.

Section 4: This section deals with matters such as the appointment and salaries of members of the Board, the appointment of personnel by the Board, the transfer of the personnel and records of the old Board established on June 29, 1934, by Executive Order No. 6763, pursuant to Public Resolution No. 44. It is also made clear that orders and proceedings in the courts pursuant to the public resolution, to which the old Board is a party, shall be continued by the Board in its discretion, in order that the important questions of law therein involved may be brought to final determination in the highest courts. In connection with this section, the committee wishes to emphasize two points.

First, there is no conflict with or duplication of the functions of the Department of Labor in its statistical and conciliation work. The bill expressly provides that:

> Nothing in this act shall be construed to authorize the Board to appoint individuals for the purpose of conciliation or mediation (or for statistical work), where such service may be obtained from the Department of Labor.

Conciliation or mediation is desirable in disputes or differences as to wages and hours or conditions of work, where friendly adjustment requires give and take and the compromising of conflicting views.

The work of the Board and its agents or agencies, on the other hand, is quasi-judicial in character, dealing with the investigation and determination of charges of unfair labor practices as defined in the bill, and questions of representation for the purposes of collective bargaining. This of course does not preclude securing compliance, either by a stipulation procedure or otherwise, prior to formal hearing or application to the courts. But the Board and its agents or agencies are required to carry out the declared will of Congress as provided in this definite legislation; the law must have application in all cases, and must not be haggled about or compromised because of the exigency of a particular situation or the weakness of a particular employee group as against a more powerful employer. Under the bill it is contemplated that the Board, its agents or agencies, will not confuse the quasi-judicial nature of their function by intruding upon the regular work of the Conciliation Service of the Department of Labor.

Second, the section authorizes the Board to appoint regional directors and to establish such regional, local, or other agencies as may from time to time be needed. The Board itself cannot be expected in the ordinary case to travel to the scene of dispute; nor can it be expected that the parties or their witnessess must be brought before the Board at the center of government in Washington. Upon the efficiency of permanently established, compensated regional officers and regional agencies operating under the direction of the Board at the source of dispute, will thus depend in an important measure the effective administration of the law.

The effect of the first amendment to subsection (b) is merely to strike out the provision that proceedings in cases of the present National Labor Relations Board shall be conducted by the new Board. Since the President through the Attorney General has already ordered the discontinuance of these cases, the old language in the bill providing for their continuance should certainly be deleted.

The purpose of the second amendment to subsection (b) is to give a permanent civil-service status to those employees transferred from the old Board who are required to be under the civil service by section 4 (a) of the bill.

Section 5: This is a provision commonly incorporated in similar statutes. The importance of holding inquiries necessary to the functions of the Board at places convenient to their proper and expeditious handling, has already been pointed out above.

Section 6: This is a common provision authorizing the Board to make, amend, and rescind such rules and regulations as may be found necessary to implement and carry out the provisions of the bill. It is important to note that the rules will be effective only upon due publication, so that there may be no claims of doubt or ignorance as to their content. . . .

MINORITY VIEW

At the very outset I want to make my position clear. I am wholeheartedly in favor of this bill. I believe it to be a great step for the protection of the rights of organized labor of the United States; and irrespective of whether or not the following suggestions are adopted I shall vote for the bill.

I find myself unable to agree with the decision of the committee to affiliate the National Labor Relations Board with the Department of Labor. It is clearly immaterial whether this affiliation is accomplished merely by providing generally that the Board shall be located in the Department of Labor, or by providing in detail that the Secretary of Labor shall control the personnel, the regional agencies, and the budget of the Board. Regardless of variations in language, if the Board is placed within the Department, the Secretary of Labor will control the purse strings, and that control will be the decisive factor in determining the extent and the character of the personnel, the nature of the work done, and the administrative set-up of the Board, both in Washington and throughout the country. This in turn will be determinative of the major policies of the Board, as I shall presently discuss. On this issue there can be no compromise; either the Board must be completely independent or it must be reduced to the level of a departmental bureau.

I should have thought that even without regard for the past history of the National Labor Relations Board and the testimony before this committee, both of which seem to me compelling upon this point, precedent alone would have induced the establishment of the Board as an independent agency. The Board is to be solely a quasi-judicial body with clearly defined and limited powers. Its policies are marked out precisely by the law. That such an agency should be free from any other executive branch of the Government has been the recognized policy of Congress. Ready examples are the Interstate Commerce Commission, the Federal Trade Commission, the Communications Commission, the Securities and Exchange Commission, the National Mediation Board, and agencies that are even less judicial in character, such as the Federal Housing Administration and the Reconstruction Finance Corporation. It seems strange that this committee, which has built up so fine a record in the interests of labor, should be grudgingly unwilling to establish for the protection of labor's most basic rights an agency as dignified and independent, and as likely to attain the prestige that flows from such independence, as those which have been established to protect the interests of other groups.

The vital need for the complete independence of a quasi-judicial board that must enforce the law has been best illustrated by the collapse of section 7 (a) of the Recovery Act. That famous section broke down, not so much because the Recovery Act into which it was written did not contain adequate enforcement provisions, but because the actual enforcement of 7 (a) was tied up with the wrong agencies. The Labor Board, it is true, could make "decisions"; but actual enforcement rested with the National Recovery Administration and the Department of Justice. Since the N.R.A. had other functions, such as code making, etc. which required constant cultivation of friendly and conciliatory feelings between the N.R.A. and those with whom it had to deal, the N.R.A. has been forced repeatedly to compromise and bargain away the specific rights guaranteed by section 7 (a). And the Department of Justice likewise has been reluctant to act upon this touchy subject, because of entirely extrinsic consideration of government policy that should have had nothing to do with section 7 (a). The complete frustration of the present National Labor Relations Board has resulted from this very simple failure to maintain the traditional and tested division between quasi-judicial bodies on the one hand and the general work of executive departments tied up with the governmental policy of a particular administration, on the other.

This anomalous situation would be perpetuated by placing the National Labor Relations Board in the Department of Labor. The Department is an executive arm of the Government. The Secretary of Labor is an officer of a particular administration, and I say this from a long-range point of view, and with due regard for the abilities of the present Secretary. The Department is thus quickly susceptible to political repercussions, and it is charged with many administrative duties involving constant compromise between industry and government. Thus the Board would quickly be swallowed up in the general policies of the Department of Labor.

These difficulties are not answered at all by insisting that the judicial decisions of the National Labor Relations Board would not be subject to review by the Secretary of Labor or by any officer in the executive branch of the Government. If in fact the Board were to be independent in its actions, there would be no reason for anyone wanting to set it up in the Department of Labor. But that is not the case; the final "judicial decisions" are only a small part of the work of such a Board, and by control over other stages in the enforcement process the Department of Labor would be the final arbiter of the policies of the Board.

For example, to be effective in enforcement, the Board must control complaints of unfair labor practices from their very inception. Yet this would not be the case were the Board in the Department. It is quite true that the proponents of placing the Board in the Department insist that there should be no mediation or conciliation done by the Board. But that does not preclude the possibility of mediation of an unfair labor practice by the Conciliation Service of the Department before the Board would act. And in the long run, that would inevitably result from locating the Board in the Department, while its advent would be hastened by an administration unsympathetic toward labor. This is the very worst kind of confusion of conciliation and quasi-judicial work, not in that the Board will do both but that both will be used at successive stages in attempting to enforce the law.

What will result from such a procedure? Conciliation at the source will not build up the kind of records that the Board might later refer to the courts for enforcement. Compromise of the law at the outset will constantly plague the Government when the time comes to vindicate the law. A wide variety of interpretations without any centralizing force will create uncertainty and distrust. The National Labor Relations Board will be called into operation only where there has been a record of failure rather than success; only when the prestige of the Government has already been impaired by the failure of its agencies. Moreover, the duplication of effort and the long delay before complaints of unfair practices finally reach the Board will wreak havoc upon workers' rights. The worker who is wronged must get help quickly if at all. The injury of the long delay can never be redressed. The occasion to protest by his own collective action, once let past, can never be recalled. These are not fancied evils; they are present now because of the very policies which I do not wish to see continued.

To prevent unfair labor practices, the National Labor Relations Board must have control of enforcement not at the end of the trail but from the very beginning. It must follow the procedure that is followed by the Federal Trade Commission in preventing unfair trade practices. No one would suggest, when there is a claim of an unfair trade practice, that there should first be mediation by the Department of Commerce and then action by the Commission in the event of failure.

In addition, if the Department of Labor is to control the first steps in regard to the prevention of unfair practices, it will have the discretion to cut enforcement off its sources. "Judicial independence" will do the Board no good as to cases that never reach it.

Thus the issue raised is a very narrow one. If the purpose of placing the National Labor Relations Board in the Department of Labor is that the Department and the Board shall function jointly to protect the rights guaranteed by section 7 (a), then the whole enforcement mechanism will collapse because of dispersion of responsibility and because of an overlapping of conciliation and judicial work. And if the Board should operate independently of the Department, it is unfair to make it subject to departmental control over budget and personnel.

In view of these major considerations, which have proved controlling in every other case where the Government has set up a quasi-judicial body, the point that there might be some overlapping of statistical work by the Board and the Department of Labor is trivial and unrealistic. In fact, it is entirely appropriate to amend the bill, as has been done, to provide that the Board should not do any statistical work, mediation, or conciliation, when such services are available in the Department of Labor.

It should be repeated that the National Labor Relations Board is to be purely a quasi-judicial commission. Its prestige and efficacy must be grounded fundamentally in public approval and in equal confidence in its impartiality by Labor and Industry. If the Board is placed in the Department it will suffer ab initio from the suspicion that it is not a court, but an organ devoted solely to the interests of laboring groups. Far from helping labor, this will impair the work of the Board and render more difficult the sustaining of its supposedly impartial decisions by the Federal courts.

Finally, let me emphasize the paramount consideration that the inclusion of the Board in the Department of Labor will injure not only the Board, but the Department itself, and through it the interests of labor. The Department was not established to handle all the industrial relation problems of the Government. It was not established to covet impartial or quasi-judicial functions, or to interpret laws of Congress. It was founded, as is too often forgotten now, as a department for labor, and to "foster, promote, and develop the welfare of the wage earners of the United States, to improve their working conditions, and to advance their opportunities for profitable employment." There is more work of this type to be done than ever before and the Department is in no danger of lapsing into disuse if it is aware of its duties. I believe that labor would have fared better under the codes if the Department had remained true to its function as a militant organ for working people, rather than attempting to appear as a labor relations bureau of the Federal Government, representing all interests alike, and overzealous to guard itself against supposed encroachments. The efforts to secure control over an impartial quasi-judicial board is a definite step by the Department away from those activities which can make it most useful to the working people of America.

The Senate bill very wisely has made the Board an independent agency. The House should follow the Senate on this very vital matter.

I also find myself unable to agree with the committee in its exclusion of agricultural workers. It is a matter of plain fact that the worst conditions in the United States are the conditions among the agricultural workers. They have been brought to the public attention many times, for example, by the investigations of the National Child Labor Committee into the horrible conditions, especially as affecting children, in the beet-sugar fields. The complete denial of civil liberty and the reign of terror in the Imperial Valley have been the subject of investigation by Government agents. Last summer saw a protracted and heroic strike by the terribly exploited union workers in the fertile fields of Hardin County, Ohio, against their employers. These workers were organized in a federal local of the A.F. of L. They were victims of the usual type of oppression which was called to public attention in the press.

However, the most conclusive proof that there must be Federal action to protect the right of agricultural workers to organize is to be found in the situation in Arkansas. In that State, within the last year, there has come into being an admirable union of agricultural workers, the Southern Tenant Farmers Union. It has been incorporated under the laws of the State. Its immediate demands are entirely reasonable and its methods have been extraordinarily peaceful. Yet that union is at present holding no meetings on advice of its counsel who says that it cannot be protected from terroristic attacks. Armed planters have patrolled the roads looking for the principal organizers of the union. The president of the union, a former rural school teacher, was driven out of the county by threats of lynching. Members of the union have been beaten up. Some of them have been cast in jail from which they were ultimately delivered but only in one or two cases after they had been confined on trumped charges for 45 days. Meetings have been forcibly broken up. The lawyer for the union is C.T. Carpenter, one of the outstanding lawyers of the State of Arkansas. He was waited on by an armed mob one night in his own home. He met them at the door with a pistol in his hand. The mob left but not without firing shots at the house.

THE DEBATE

MR. WAGNER. . . . The present bill cures the defects in existing law. It clarifies and amplifies the provisions of section 7 (a), and it centralizes in a single permanent National Labor Relations Board the duty to protect the collective-bargaining rights of employees. The Board will, of course, have regional agencies throughout the country to handle violations initially at their source, and will be empowered to designate any existing industrial board for such purposes. In all cases, however, the findings and recommendations of these agencies will be transferred to the National Labor Relations Board for final action. After these appropriate hearings the Board will be empowered to issue orders forbidding violations of the law and making restitution to those who have been injured thereby. All such orders will be fully reviewable at the instance of any aggrieved party in the Federal courts.

The procedure set forth in this bill is so closely modeled upon other statutes, such as the Federal Trade Commission Act and the Interstate Commerce Act, that one is astounded to hear the charges circulated to the effect that this measure would sweep aside the courts and endow a new and queer kind of agency with dictatorial or arbitrary powers. . . .

Board Made Judge, Jury, Bailiff, Prosecutor, and Executioner

MR. BLANTON. . . . I quote the following from section 10 of the bill:

PREVENTION OF UNFAIR LABOR PRACTICES

SEC. 10(a) The Board is empowered, as hereinafter provided, to prevent any person from engaging in any unfair labor practice (listed in sec. 8) affecting commerce. . . .

(b) Whenever it is charged that any person has engaged in or is engaging in any such unfair labor practice, the Board, or any agent or agency designated by the Board for such purposes, shall have power to issue and cause to be served upon such person a complaint stating the charges in that respect, and containing a notice of hearing before the Board or a member thereof, or before a designated agent or agency, at a place therein fixed, not less than 5 days after the serving of said complaint.

Under the above provision, any one of our constituents engaged in business could be summoned to appear before some agent anywhere in the United States, and to answer any kind of ridiculous charges, and would be forced to the great expense of employing high-salaried attorneys, and paying the expenses of his attorney, his witness, and his own far distant from his home for a period that could extend into weeks. This bill is going to cause more men to go out of business and more long-established businesses to close up, and more employees to lose good-paying jobs in which they are now well satisfied, than anything that has been done by Congress before in half a century. . . .

The Clerk read as follows:

NATIONAL LABOR RELATIONS BOARD

SEC. 3 (a) There is hereby created as an independent agency in the executive branch of the Government a board, to be known as the "National Labor Relations Board" (hereinafter referred to as the "Board"), which shall be composed of three members, who shall be appointed by the President, by and with the advice and consent of the Senate. One of the original members shall be appointed for a term of 1 year, 1 for a term of 3 years, and 1 for a term of 5 years, but their successors shall be appointed for terms of 5 years each, except that any individual chosen to fill a vacancy shall be appointed only for the unexpired term of the member whom he shall succeed. The President shall designate one member to serve as chairman of the Board.

(b) A vacancy in the Board shall not impair the right of the remaining members to exercise all the powers of the Board, and two members of the Board shall, at all time, constitute a quorum. The Board shall have an official seal which shall be judicially noticed.

(c) The Board shall at the close of each fiscal year make a report in writing to Congress and to the President stating in detail the cases it has heard, the decisions it has rendered, the names, salaries, and duties of all employees and officers in the employ or under the supervision of the Board, and an account of all moneys it has disbursed.

With the following committee amendment:

Page 7, line 24, after the word "created," strike out: "as an independent agency in the executive branch of the Government" and insert in lieu thereof: "in the Department of Labor."

MR. RAMSPECK. Mr. Chairman, I rise in opposition to the amendment.

Mr. Chairman, I think the question involved in this amendment is the most important one involved in the bill. The question of whether or not the agency set up to administer this law shall be an independent agency of the Government or under one of the executive departments is, in my opinion, the most important provision in the bill.

I regret that I cannot agree about this particular question with the chairman of my committee, for whom I have the highest regard, or with the Secretary of Labor, for whom also I have a very high regard.

In addition to the matter of policy I call the attention of the members of the committee to the fact that making this an independent agency will strengthen the reception given this law when it reaches the Supreme Court. The decision of the Court in the Schechter case indicates that one of the troubles with that case was the delegation of power to the executive department. The decision of the same Court rendered on the same day holding that the President had no authority to remove Commissioner Humphreys from the Federal Trade Commission gives even more evidence of the fact that if we make this an independent agency it will have more strength when it reaches a test in the Supreme Court. In 5 minutes' time I shall not be able to read references from the decision, but I do want to read one paragraph from that decision. In referring to the Federal Trade Commission the Supreme Court said:

To make this possible Congress set up a special procedure, a Commission, a quasi-judicial body was created, provision was made for formal complaint, for notice and hearing, for appropriate findings of fact supported by adequate evidence, and for judicial review to give assurance that the action of the Commission is done within its statutory authority.

Further on in the decision the Court referred to the fact that the Members of this body, the Federal Trade Commission, are free from any influence in the executive department and free from all political influence except in the matter of appointment.

If this committee amendment is voted down I expect to offer an amendment to strike out, on page 3, in line 24, after the word "created," the words "as an independent agency in the executive branch of the Government," so that we simply create a board that is not in any other agency of the Government, not a part of the executive branch of the Government at all. I submit, as a friend of the bill, that if this law is to succeed it must succeed through the support of public opinion.

MR. CONNERY. Mr. Chairman, this question was fully debated in the committee. Mr. Biddle, the Chairman of the National Labor Relations Board, and Senator Wagner are in favor of making it an independent Board, appeared before our committee and so testified. The Secretary of Labor appeared before the committee and wanted the Board established under the Department of Labor. President Green, of the American Federation of Labor, appeared before the committee and wanted the Board placed under the Department of Labor. Their reasons were that it had taken many years to create a Department of Labor, to create a Cabinet position for Labor, and that any independent board set up away from the Department of Labor would be a weakening of the Department.

I consulted with the President at the White House in reference to this. After that conference I returned to my committee and reported its result, and the committee decided to put the Board under the Department of Labor.

MR. MARCANTONIO. . . .Mr. Chairman, as the gentleman from Georgia has pointed out, this is the most important question over which the committee disagreed.

I find myself unable to agree with the decision of the committee to affiliate the National Labor Relations Board with the Department of labor. It is clearly immaterial whether this affiliation is accomplished merely by providing generally that the Board shall be located in the Department of Labor, or by providing in detail that the Secretary of Labor shall control the personnel, the regional agencies, and the budget of the Board. Regardless of variations in language, if the Board is placed within the Department, the Secretary of Labor will control the purse strings, and that control will be the decisive factor in determining the extent and the character of the personnel, the nature of the work done, and the administrative set-up of the Board, both in Washington and throughout the country. This in turn will be determinative of the major policies of the Board, as I shall presently discuss. On this issue there can be no compromise—either the

Board must be completely independent or it must be reduced to the level of a departmental bureau.

I should have thought that even without regard for the past history of the National Labor Relations Board and the testimony before this committee, both of which seem to me compelling upon this point, precedent alone would have induced the establishment of the Board as an independent agency. The Board is to be solely a quasi-judicial body with clearly defined and limited powers. Its policies are marked out precisely by the law. That such an agency should be free from any other executive branch of the Government has been the recognized policy of Congress. Ready examples are the Interstate Commerce Commission, the Federal Trade Commission, the Communications Commission, the Securities and Exchange Commission, the National Mediation Board, and agencies that are even less judicial in character, such as the Federal Housing Administration and the Reconstruction Finance Corporation. It seems strange that this committee, which has built up so fine a record in the interests of labor, should be grudgingly unwilling to establish for the protection of labor's most basic rights an agency as dignified and independent, and as likely to attain the prestige that flows from such independence, as those which have been established to protect the interests of other groups.

The vital need for the complete independence of a quasi-judicial board that must enforce the law has been best illustrated by the collapse of section 7 (a) of the Recovery Act. That famous section broke down, not so much because the Recovery Act into which it was written did not contain adequate enforcement provisions, but because the actual enforcement of 7 (a) was tied up with the wrong agencies. The Labor Board, it is true, could make decisions, but actual enforcement rested with the National Recovery Administration and the Department of Justice. Since the N.R.A. had other functions, such as code making, and so forth, which required constant cultivation of friendly and conciliatory feelings between the N.R.A. and those with whom it had to deal, the N.R.A. has been forced repeatedly to compromise and bargain away the specific rights guaranteed by section 7 (a). And the Department of Justice likewise has been reluctant to act upon this touchy subject, because of entirely extrinsic consideration of government policy that should have had nothing to do with section 7 (a). The complete frustration of the present National Labor Relations Board has resulted from this very simple failure to maintain the traditional and tested division between quasi-judicial bodies on the one hand and the general work of executive departments tied up with the governmental policy of a particular administration, on the other.

This anomalous situation would be perpetuated by placing the National Labor Relations Board in the Department of Labor. The Department is an executive arm of the Government. The Secretary of Labor is an officer of a particular administration, and I say this from the long-range point of view, and with due regard for the abilities of the present Secretary. The Department is thus quickly susceptible to political repercussions, and it is charged with many administrative duties involving constant compromise between industry and government. Thus the Board would quickly be swallowed up in the general policies of the Department of Labor.

These difficulties are not answered at all by insisting that the judicial decisions of the National Labor Relations Board would not be subject to review by the Secretary of Labor or by any officer in the executive branch of the Government. If in fact the Board were to be independent in its actions, there would be no reason for anyone wanting to set it up in the Department of Labor. But that is not the case; the final judicial decisions are only a small part of the work of such a Board, and by control over other stages in the enforcement process the Department of Labor would be the final arbiter of the policies of the Board.

For example, to be effective in enforcement, the Board must control complaints of unfair labor practices from their very inception. Yet this would not be the case were the Board in the Department. It is quite true that the proponents of placing the Board in the Department insist that there should be no mediation or conciliation done by the Board. But that does not preclude the possibility of mediation of an unfair labor practice by the Conciliation Service of the Department before the Board would act. And in the long run, that would inevitably result from locating the Board in the Department, while its advent would be hastened by an administration unsympathetic toward labor. This is the very worst kind of confusion of conciliation and quasi-judicial work, not in that the Board will do both but that both will be used at successive stages in attempting to enforce the law.

What will result from such a procedure? Conciliation at the source will not build up the kind of records that the Board might later refer to the courts for enforcement. Compromise of the law at the outset will constantly plague the Government when the time comes to vindicate the law. A wide variety of interpretations without any centralizing force will create uncertainty and distrust. The National Labor Relations Board will be called into operation only where there has been a record of failure rather than success; only when the prestige of the Government has already been impaired by the failure of its agencies. Moreover, the duplication of effort and the long delay before complaints of unfair practices finally reach the Board will wreak havoc upon workers' rights. The worker who is wronged must get help quickly if at all. The injury of the long delay can never been redressed. The occasion to protest by his own collective action, once let past, can never be recalled. These are not fancied evils; they are present now because of the very policies which I do not wish to see continued.

To prevent unfair labor practices, the National Labor Relations Board must have control of enforcement not at the end of the trail but from the very beginning. It must follow the prcedure that is followed by the Federal Trade Commission in preventing unfair trade practices. No one would suggest, when there is a claim of an unfair trade practice, that there should first be mediation by the Department of Commerce and then action by the Commission in the event of failure.

In addition, if the Department of Labor is to control the first steps in regard to the prevention of unfair practices, it will have the discretion to cut enforcement off its sources. "Judicial independence" will do the Board no good as to cases that never reach it.

Thus the issue raised is a very narrow one. If the purpose of placing the National Labor Relations Board in the Department of Labor is that the Department and the

Board shall function jointly to protect the rights guaranteed by section 7 (a), then the whole enforcement mechanism will collapse because of dispersion of responsibility and because of an overlapping of conciliation and judicial work. And if the Board should operate independently of the Department, it is unfair to make it subject to departmental control over budget and personnel.

In view of these major considerations, which have proved controlling in every other case where the Government has set up a quasi-judicial body, the point that there might be some overlapping of statistical work by the Board and the Department of Labor is trivial and unrealistic. In fact, it is entirely appropriate to amend the bill, as has been done, to provide that the Board should not do any statistical work, mediation, or conciliation, when such services are available in the Department of Labor.

It should be repeated that the National Labor Relations Board is to be purely a quasi-judicial commission. Its prestige and efficacy must be grounded fundamentally in public approval and in equal confidence in its impartiality by labor and industry. If the Board is placed in the Department it will suffer ab initio from the suspicion that it is not a court, but an organ devoted solely to the interests of laboring groups. Far from helping labor, this will impair the work of the Board and render more difficult the sustaining of its supposedly impartial decisions by the Federal court.

Finally, let me emphasize the paramount consideration that the inclusion of the Board in the Department of Labor will injure not only the Board, but the Department itself, and through it the interests of labor. The Department was not established to handle all the industrial relation problems of the Government. It was not established to covet impartial or quasi-judicial functions, or to interpret laws of Congress. It was founded, as is too often forgotten now, as a department for labor, and to "foster, promote, and develop the welfare of the wage earners of the United States, to improve their working conditions, and to advance their opportunities for profitable employment." There is more work of this type to be done than ever before and the Department is in no danger of lapsing into disuse if it is aware of its duties. I believe that labor would have fared better under the codes if the Department had remained true to its function as a militant organ for working people, rather than attempted to appear as a labor relations bureau of the Federal Government, representing all interests alike, and overzealous to guard itself against supposed encroachments. The efforts to secure control over an impartial quasi-judicial board is a definite step by the Department away from those activities which can make it most useful to the working people of America.

The Senate bill very wisely has made the Board an independent agency. The House should follow the Senate on this very vital matter. . . .

MR. CONNERY. The gentleman knows, and I think the House should know, that in this amendment all we did was to put the Board under the Department of Labor.

MR. MARCANTONIO. The answer is that while it is claimed that only nominally do we place the Board under the Department of Labor, nevertheless once it is placed there the Department of Labor and the Secretary of Labor are given budgetary control over the Board.

Once you have budgetary control over that Board, the Board must naturally become susceptible to the policies of the Department of Labor. . . .

MR. CONNERY. The Supreme Court of the United States is under the Attorney General. They cannot hire a janitor without that item appearing in the budget of the Attorney General. Now, no one would say that the Supreme Court is not an independent body.

MR. MARCANTONIO. We are not dealing with the Supreme Court here. Those gentlemen are appointed for life. . . .

In a letter to the House Committee on Labor, set forth in the committee's report on the Wagner-Connery bill, Chairman Biddle, of the National Labor Relations Board, set forth the various reasons why the proposed board should be an independent agency rather than in the Department of Labor. These reasons are powerfully reinforced by the decision of the Supreme Court in the Schechter case and in Rathbun against the United States.

One of the main points in the Schechter decision was that section 3 of the National Industrial Recovery Act, authorizing the President to promulgate codes of fair competition, constituted an invalid delegation of legislative power in that it permitted the President, without the guidance of adequate standards fixed by Congress, "to exercise an unfettered discretion to make whatever laws he thinks may be needed or advisable for the rehabilitation and expansion of trade or industry." The Court contrasted the delegation of legislative power and the executive procedure provided in the National Industrial Recovery Act with the laying down by Congress of a specific policy to be administered by boards, with procedure of a quasi-judicial nature. Thus the Court referred to the Federal Trade Commission Act, which declared unlawful "unfair methods of competition," a phrase which the Court said "does not admit of precise definition, its scope being left to judicial determination as controversies arise." The following is quoted from the decision in the Schechter case:

What are "unfair methods of competition" are thus to be determined in particular instances, upon evidence, in the light of particular competitive conditions and of what is found to be a specific and substantial public interest. . . .

To make this possible, Congress set up a special procedure. A commission, a quasi-judicial body, was created. Provision was made for formal complaint, for notice and hearing, for appropriate findings of fact supported by adequate evidence, and for judicial review to give assurance that the action of the Commission is taken within its statutory authority. . . .

In providing for codes, the National Industrial Recovery Act dispenses with this administrative procedure and with any administrative procedure of an analogous character.

To enforce the prohibition of the unfair labor practices described in section 8, the Wagner-Connery bill contemplates the creation of a tribunal whose procedure and functions are modeled closely after the Federal Trade Commission. To assure that the proposed National Labor Relations Board will be accorded a similar standing by the courts, it is important that nothing appear in the act indicating that Congress regards the Board merely as a bureau or agency of one of the executive departments.

The nature of boards like the Federal Trade Commission, the Interstate Commerce Commission, and the proposed National Labor Relations Board is again clearly set forth by the Supreme Court in the case of Rathbun against United States, decided May 27 [*Humprey's Executor* v. *United States, supra* p. 1811] ....

It is to be noted that though the House Committee on Labor voted to establish a National Labor Relations Board "in the Department of Labor," the committee report states:

> The committee does not intend by this change to subject the Board to the jurisdiction of the Secretary of Labor in respect of its decisions, policies, budget, or personnel. An amendment offered by the Secretary of Labor requiring that the Board's appointments of employees shall be subject to the approval of the Secretary was not accepted by the committee. We recognize the necessity of establishing a board with independence and dignity, in order that men of high caliber may be persuaded to serve upon it, and in order to give it a national prestige adequate to the important functions conferred upon it. While it is convenient to locate the Board in the Department which deals with labor problems, this nominal connection will not impair the independence of the Board, which will be free to administer the statute without accountability except to Congress and the courts.

This being the purpose of the committee, is it not the part of prudence to put the matter beyond doubt and establish the Board as a wholly independent agency? The phrase in the bill "in the Department of Labor" standing alone might carry an implication that the Board is a bureau of the Department of Labor and hence automatically subject to the control of the Secretary in the matter of budget and personnel, and invites the risk that under the Myers case [*supra* p. 1808] the President might have the unrestrained power of removal of the members of the Board during their statutory terms of office, contrary to the intent of Congress.

Therefore the committee amendment should be defeated and the Board should be left independent. ...

Conference Report (With Statement of the Managers on the Part of the House)
June 26, 1935

Mr. Connery, from the committee of conference, submitted the following

CONFERENCE REPORT
[TO ACCOMPANY S. 1958]

Statement of the Managers on the Part of the House

The managers on the part of the House at the conference on the disagreeing votes of the two Houses on the bill (S. 1958) to create a National Labor Relations Board, and for other purposes, submit the following statement of the effect of the action agreed upon by the conferees and recommended in the accompanying conference report. . . .

Section 3 (a) of the Senate bill provided:

There is hereby created as an independent agency in the executive branch of the Government a board, to be known as the "National Labor Relations Board."

House amendment no. 6 strikes out the phrase "as an independent agency in the executive branch of the Government." The Board as contemplated in the bill is in no sense to be an agency of the executive branch of the Government. It is to have a status similar to that of the Federal Trade Commission, which, as the Supreme Court pointed out in the *Schechter case,* is a quasi-judicial and quasi-legislative body. The conference agreement accepts this amendment

The conference agreement accepts House amendment no. 7, stating specifically the circumstances under which a member of the Board may be removed. This amendment is desirable in the light of the decision of the Supreme Court in *Rathpun* v. *U.S.,* decided May 27, 1935, involving the removal by the President of Commissioner Humphreys of the Federal Trade Commission. If Congress in creating the Board vests the appointing power in the President it might be implied that it is intended to vest also in the President a general power of removal as an incident to the power to appoint. This inference is negatived by an express provision stating the conditions under which a member of the Board may be removed. Similar provisions are found in the Railway Labor Act of 1934 and the Federal Trade Commission Act. . . .

William P. Connery, Jr.
Richard J. Welch
Glenn Griswold
Robert Ramspeck
W. P. Lambertson
Managers on the part of the House

CIVIL AERONAUTICS BOARD

CIVIL AERONAUTICS ACT
1938

CIVIL AERONAUTICS ACT
1938

Commentary

The last of the important regulatory commissions to be created was the Civil Aeronautics Board, set up (as the Civil Aeronautics Authority) under the Civil Aeronautics Act of 1938. There had been a need for governmental regulation of the aviation industry some years earlier. The first pressing problem had been that of safety, and an Act of 1926 gave the Secretary of Commerce broad authority to provide for air safety. Just as important, however, was the need for economic regulation. Disagreements among proponents of such regulation as to the details of the regulatory scheme (particularly as to what governmental body should exercise the regulatory powers) were not resolved until 1938. At that time comprehensive regulation of the public-utility type was provided, to be administered by an independent agency.

The Act of 1938 created the Civil Aeronautics Authority, an independent five-man agency, to exercise regulatory powers over civil aviation. By a presidential reorganization plan of 1940, most of these powers were transferred to the Civil Aeronautics Board. This is the agency which has since exercised the main regulatory authority over aviation, though certain functions were vested by the 1938 Act in the Administrator. The fact that the CAB, unlike the other "big six" agencies, is called a "board" rather than a "commission" has no legal consequences, though it does prevent its members from being entitled to the more pretentious title of "commissioners."

The 1938 Act confers upon the CAB two principal regulatory functions:
1) regulation of the economic aspects of air carrier operations;
2) investigation and analysis of aircraft accidents.

As far as economic regulation is concerned, the Act gives the board both licensing and rate-making authority. No American air carrier can engage in any domestic or international operation without a license from the CAB. This gives the board a life-and-death power over the airlines similar to that exercised by the FCC over the networks and other broadcasters. In addition, the CAB has the authority to prescribe the rates charged by air carriers and (a matter of vital importance to the economic health of the airlines) to determine the mail rates and amounts of subsidy received by carriers from the government. It has powers (analogous to those vested in the ICC over the railroads) over improper practices on the part of airlines, over their corporate and financial structure, and consolidations and mergers.

The legislative history of the Civil Aeronautics Act starts with a bill introduced in 1934 by Senator Patrick McCarran [Dem., Nev.], under which there was to be economic regulation of civil aviation by an independent commission. During the next few years there were several official studies. The Federal Aviation Commission in 1935 recommended an independent air commerce commission. President Roosevelt urged that air regulation be given to the Interstate Commerce Commission. Bills to accomplish this were introduced in both houses; although lengthy hearings were held, no legislative action was taken. The President then created an interdepartmental committee on aviation to study the matter. The committee held hearings in 1937 and drafted a bill providing for unified regulation of aviation, with regard to economic matters and safety. Regulation was to be administered by a three-member Civil Aeronautics Board. The Civil Aeronautics Act was introduced in the two houses, to give effect to the committee's recommendations, by Congressman Clarence F. Lea [Dem., Calif.] and Senator McCarran.

The congressional debate on the Civil Aeronautics Act began in the House on May 7, 1938. Over the objection of the minority, the House voted to limit debate to two hours. Congressman Edward E. Cox [Dem., Ga.], for the majority, stated that the majority and minority on the Commerce Committee had both conceded the need for legislation on the subject. The difference was only as to the agency set up to administer the law. Congressman Carl E. Mapes [Rep., Mich.], the ranking minority committee member, objected to consideration of the matter on a Saturday, when most committee members were away; he and Congressman Bertrand H. Snell [Rep., N.Y.] criticized the rush to enact the measure toward the end of the session. Yet, as Mapes recognized, "We are at the mercy of the majority as to what the procedure will be." The Democratic leadership was easily able to secure passage of the resolution limiting debate.

The House then resolved itself into Committee of the Whole House for detailed consideration of the bill (or at least as detailed as possible in two hours). The fundamental issue (as Mr. Mapes had pointed out in the debate on the Cox resolution) was "whether or not another governmental agency shall be created to regulate air commerce or whether additional authority shall be given to the Interstate Commerce Commission to do the job." Mr. Lea, who had introduced the bill in the House, began the Committee of the Whole debate by giving the background of the bill, emphasizing the need for the legislation, and summarized its provisions. He stressed the independence of the three-man authority to be created and its performance of quasi-judicial and quasi-legislative functions. Lea explained why the committee had opted in favor of a new commission, instead of the earlier proposal to vest the authority in the ICC. The ICC, he stressed, was unable to handle the additional job of regulating aviation. Though it was theoretically desirable to unify all regulation of transportation, the ICC was already overburdened, and would have to be completely overhauled to be able to take on the task. This theme of need for ICC reorganization was also stressed by other speakers. It was, indeed, urged that this bill could serve as the catalyst for ICC reorganization which would make it possible to vest air regulation in that commission in a few years. Yet, as Congressman James W. Wadsworth, Jr. [Rep., N.Y.] put it in opposing the bill, that was "taking a big chance"—"once you establish a commission . . . , you have the devil's own time passing any act abolishing it."

The key issue in the debate was focused by the Mapes amendment to substitute "Commission" (meaning the ICC) for "Authority" (meaning the CAA) and motion to recommit with instructions to provide for ICC instead of CAA regulation. Speakers repeated the theme on one side of need for a new agency because of the overburdened state of the ICC, as well as the need for expertise in aviation, and, on the other, of the desirability of unifying transportation regulation in the ICC. On May 18, the House debate ended with rejection of the Mapes motion to recommit, by 214 to 94, and passage of the Lea bill, without a roll call. As a technical matter, the House had to substitute the House bill for the Senate bill, for the upper house had passed its bill two days earlier.

The debate in the Senate began on May 11, 1938. The situation was confused by the existence of three bills. The situation in this respect was discussed at the very outset of the debate. S.3845, which became the Civil Aeronautics Act, had been introduced by Senator McCarran, and was known popularly as the McCarran Act. McCarran had for years advocated an independent commission to regulate aviation and had introduced bills for the purpose since 1934. As he himself tells us during the debate, McCarran had been called to the White House at the beginning of the session and asked to draft a bill, together with Congressman Lea. The result was introduced in the Senate in March, 1938. Later that month, separate bills were introduced by Senator Royal S. Copeland [Dem., N.Y.], Chairman of the Commerce Committee, and Senator Harry S. Truman [Dem., Mo.], then head of the subcommittee which considered the aviation legislation. McCarran then revised his bill and reintroduced it as S.3845. The chief difference between the McCarran bill and those of Truman and Copeland related to the independence of the regulatory agency. The Truman and Copeland bills provided for different types of presidential control, particularly with regard to the removal power.

There was less discussion than in the House on the issue of the new regulatory agency versus the ICC. Senator William H. King [Dem., Utah] declaimed against "creating a new Federal agency at enormous cost." Senator McCarran, while giving the background of the legislation, was asked by Senator James P. Pope [Dem., Idaho] why he had changed his mind from the previous session, when he had backed the ICC as the regulatory authority. McCarran answered by referring to the overburdened state of the ICC and the need for men trained in aviation to regulate the new field. But, on the whole, as Senator Warren R. Austin [Rep., Vt.] pointed out, "there is pretty general agreement" in the Senate on a new commission to handle aviation and the issue did not give rise to the sharp debate that had occurred in the House.

In the Senate debate itself, notice should be taken of the colloquy on the proper number for the new agency (three in the House bill versus five in the Senate), the discussion on the qualification of members, that on the bill's grandfather clause, and the debate on the antitrust provisions.

The key issue in the Senate debate was that over the chief difference between the McCarran and Truman bills, namely that over CAA independence from presidential control. Truman himself gives his version of the various bills and their history, including a detailed statement of the differences between his bill and S.3659 (the original McCarran bill) and S.3845 (the McCarran bill in its revised form then before the Senate). The chief difference, as it turned out, was over presidential removal power. So great was the difference here that McCarran himself stated that if the bill did not limit the President's removal power, "then I do not want my name on the bill."

The controversy was really one over the question of independence that has been crucial in the history of the regulatory agency. It was crystallized in the Senate debate by the Truman amendment to strike from the bill the provision giving the President the power to remove Authority members for "inefficiency, neglect of duty, or malfeasance in office." Under the *Humphrey* decision, (*supra* p. 1811), such a provision limits the President's power to removal only for the causes specified. The Truman amendment was intended to eliminate the limitation—to give the President the same unrestricted power to remove that he has in the case of cabinet members. As McCarran put it, the amendment would destroy the independence of the agency. He was doubtless right as the law then stood, for he could not be expected to anticipate the decision in *Wiener* v. *United States*, 357 U.S. 349 (1958), holding that the limitation on presidential removal power over an agency vested with quasi-judicial powers did not depend on the existence of a provision like that which the Truman amendment sought to strike out.

The lengthy debate on the Truman amendment is most pertinent to the student of the regulatory agency, since it focused on the essential element of independence from presidential control. McCarran and his supporters emphasized the need for independence in the new agency. The fight for the amendment was led by Senator Sherman Minton [Dem., Ind.] (later a member of the Supreme Court). He and his supporters argued that the CAA was an executive agency; they denied that the agency was given legislative powers, and, even if it was, Congress could not tie up presidential power over executive agencies by giving it legislative functions as well. McCarran answered that the new agency was like the ICC, exercising blended legislative, executive, and judicial powers; though not a court (note the confused colloquy on this between Senators Austin and Thomas Connally [Dem., Tex.]), it exercised tripartite functions. Much of the discussion was on the Supreme Court decisions, notably the *Myers* and *Humphrey* cases. The debate ended with Senator Henry Schwartz's [Dem., Wyo.] plea for trust in the President. There was no need, he said, to guard the people against the President. He believed that the industry would control the CAA and there would be a need for presidential power as a balance, since, after all, "The President represents the public." The Truman amendment then carried 34 to 28 and, on May 16, the bill was passed without a roll call.

On May 23 Mr. Truman tried unsuccessfully to persuade the Senate to adopt the House bill, without a conference, though it had the provision on removal which his amendment had stricken from the Senate bill. The House bill separated the executive functions (vesting them in an Administrator) from the quasi-legislative and quasi-judicial functions left in the CAA. This, said Truman, fully meets the problem. The Truman speech foreshadowed the approach of the conference committee.

The conference report is explained in the statement of the House managers, (*infra* p. 3203). The conference adopted the House structure of a division of functions between an Administrator and an Authority (though it accepts the Senate membership of five). Mr. Lea states that the division had originated with Congressman Alfred L. Bulwinkle [Dem., N.C.]; in actuality, others had thought along those lines, particularly the President's Committee on Administrative Management, which had reported the year before.

There was little debate in either House on the conference report. It was agreed to by the House on June 11 and the Senate on June 13—in both cases without a roll call. The bill became law when the President signed it on June 23, 1938.

CIVIL AERONAUTICS ACT
June 23, 1938

Be it enacted by the Senate and House of Representatives of the United States of America in Congress assembled, That this Act, divided into titles and sections according to the following table of contents, may be cited as the "Civil Aeronautics Act of 1938":

TABLE OF CONTENTS

Title I—General Provisions

Title II—Organization of Authority

Title V—Nationality and Ownership of Aircraft

Title VI—Civil Aeronautics Safety Regulation

SEC. 602. Airman certificates.
(a) Power to issue certificate.
(b) Issuance of certificate.
(c) Form and recording of certificate.
SEC. 603. Aircraft certificates.
(a) Type certificates.
(b) Production certificate.
(c) Airworthiness certificate.
SEC. 604. Air carrier operating certificates.
(a) Power to issue.
(b) Issuance.
SEC. 605. Maintenance of equipment in air transportation.
(a) Duty of carriers and airmen.
(b) Inspection.
SEC. 606. Air navigation facility rating.
SEC. 607. Air agency rating.
SEC. 608. Form of applications.
SEC. 609. Amendment, suspension, and revocation of certificates.
SEC. 610. Prohibitions.
(a) Violations of title.
(b) Exemption of foreign aircraft and airmen.

Title VII—Air Safety Board

SEC. 701. Creation and organization of board.
(a) Appointment of board.
(b) Personnel.
(c) Temporary personnel.
(d) Authorization of expenditures.
(e), Preservation of records and reports.
SEC. 702. Duties of the board.
(a) General duties.
(b) Manner of performance.
(c) Conduct of investigations.
(d) Aircraft.

Title VIII—Other Administrative Agencies

SEC. 801. The President of the United States.
SEC. 802. The Department of State.
SEC. 803. Weather Bureau.

Title IX—Penalties

SEC. 901. Civil penalties.
(a) Safety and postal offenses.
(b) Liens.
 SEC. 902. Criminal penalties.
(a) General.
(b) Forgery of certificates.
(c) Interference with air navigation.
(d) Granting rebates.
(e) Failure to file reports; falsification of records.
(f) Divulging information.
(g) Refusal to testify.
 SEC. 903. Venue and prosecution of offenses.
(a) Venue.
(b) Procedure in respect of civil penalties.

Title X—Procedure

 SEC. 1001. Conduct of proceedings.
 SEC. 1002. Complaints to and investigations by the Authority.
(a) Filing of complaints authorized.
(b) Investigations on initiative of Authority.
(c) Entry of orders for compliance with Act.
(d) Power to prescribe rates and practices of air carriers.
(e) Rule of rate making.
(f) Removal of discrimination in foreign air transportation.
(g) Suspension of rates.
(h) Power to prescribe divisions of rates.
(i) Power to establish through air transportation service.
 SEC. 1003. Joint boards.
(a) Designation of boards.
(b) Through service and joint rates.
(c) Jurisdiction of boards.
(d) Power of boards.
(e) Judicial enforcement and review.
 SEC. 1004. Evidence.
(a) Power to take evidence.
(b) Power to issue subpena.
(c) Enforcement of subpena.
(d) Contempt.

Title XI—Miscellaneous

TITLE I—GENERAL PROVISIONS

Definitions

SECTION 1. As used in this Act, unless the context otherwise requires—

(1) "Aeronautics" means the science and art of flight.

(2) "Air carrier" means any citizen of the United States who undertakes, whether directly or indirectly or by a lease or any other arrangement, to engage in air transportation: *Provided,* That the Authority may by order relieve air carriers who are not directly engaged in the operation of aircraft in air transportation from the provisions of this Act to the extent and for such periods as may be in the public interest.

(3) "Air commerce" means interstate, overseas, or foreign air commerce or the transportation of mail by aircraft or any operation or navigation of aircraft within the limits of any civil airway or any operation or navigation of aircraft which directly affects, or which may endanger safety in, interstate, overseas, or foreign air commerce.

(4) "Aircraft" means any contrivance now known or hereafter invented, used, or designed for navigation of or flight in the air.

(5) "Aircraft engine" means an engine used, or intended to be used, for propulsion of aircraft and includes all parts, appurtenances, and accessories thereof other than propellers.

(6) "Airman" means any individual who engages, as the person in command or as pilot, mechanic, or member of the crew, in the navigation of aircraft while under way; and (except to the extent the Authority may otherwise provide with respect to individuals employed outside the United States) any individual who is directly in charge of the inspection, maintenance, overhauling, or repair of aircraft, aircraft engines, propellers, or appliances; and any individual who serves in the capacity of aircraft dispatcher of air-traffic control-tower operator.

(7) "Air navigation facility" means any facility used in, available for use in, or designed for use in, aid of air navigation, including landing areas, lights, any apparatus or equipment for disseminating weather information, for signaling, for radio-directional finding, or for radio or other electrical communication, and any other structure or mechanism having a similar purpose for guiding or controlling flight in the air or the landing and take-off of aircraft.

(8) "Airport" means a landing area used regularly by aircraft for receiving or discharging passengers or cargo.

(9) "Air-space reservation" means air space, identified by an area on the surface of the earth, in which the flight of aircraft is prohibited or restricted.

(10) "Air transportation" means interstate, overseas, or foreign air transportation or the transportation of mail by aircraft.

(11) "Appliances" means instruments, equipment, apparatus, parts, appurtenances, or accessories, of whatever description, which are used, or are capable of being or intended to be used, in the navigation, operation, or control of aircraft in flight

(including parachutes and including communication equipment and any other mechanism or mechanisms installed in or attached to aircraft during flight), and which are not a part or parts of aircraft, aircraft engines, or propellers.

(12) "Authority" means the Civil Aeronautics Authority.

(13) "Citizen of the United States" means (a) an individual who is a citizen of the United States or of one of its possessions, or (b) a partnership of which each member is such an individual, or (c) a corporation or association created or organized under the laws of the United States or of any State, Territory, or possession of the United States, of which the president and two-thirds or more of the board of directors and other managing officers thereof are such individuals and in which at least 75 per centum of the voting interest is owned or controlled by persons who are citizens of the United States or of one of its possessions.

(14) "Civil aircraft" means any aircraft other than a public aircraft.

(15) "Civil aircraft of the United States" means any aircraft registered as provided in this Act.

(16) "Civil airway" means a path through the navigable air space of the United States, identified by an area on the surface of the earth, designated or approved by the Administrator as suitable for interstate, overseas, or foreign air commerce.

(17) "Conditional sale" means (a) any contract for the sale of an aircraft or portion thereof under which possession is delivered to the buyer and the property is to vest in the buyer at a subsequent time upon the payment of part or all of the price, or upon the performance of any other condition or the happening of any contingency; or (b) any contract for the bailment or leasing of an aircraft or portion thereof by which the bailee or lessee contracts to pay as compensation a sum substantially equivalent to the value thereof, and by which it is agreed that the bailee or lessee is bound to become, or has the option of becoming, the owner thereof, upon full compliance with the terms of the contract. The buyer, bailee, or lessee shall be deemed to be the person by whom any such contract is made or given.

(18) "Conveyance" means a bill of sale, contract of conditional sale, mortgage, assignment of mortgage, or other instrument affecting title to, or interest in, property.

(19) "Foreign air carrier" means any person, not a citizen of the United States, who undertakes, whether directly or indirectly or by a lease or any other arrangement, to engage in foreign air transportation.

(20) "Interstate air commerce," "overseas air commerce," and "foreign air commerce," respectively, mean the carriage by aircraft of persons or property for compensation or hire, or the carriage of mail by aircraft, or the operation or navigation of aircraft in the conduct or furtherance of a business or vocation, in commerce between, respectively—

(a)   a place in any State of the United States, or the District of Columbia, and a place in any other State of the United States, or the District of Columbia; or between places in the same State of the United States through the air space over any place outside thereof; or between places in the same Territory or possession (except the Philippine Islands) of the United States, or the District of Columbia;

(b)　a place in any State of the United States, or the District of Columbia, and any place in a Territory or possession of the United States; or between a place in a Territory or possession of the United States, and a place in any other Territory or possession of the United States; and

(c)　a place in the United States and any place outside thereof, whether such commerce moves wholly by aircraft or partly by aircraft and partly by other forms of transportation.

(21) "Interstate air transportation," "overseas air transportation," and "foreign air transportation," respectively, mean the carriage by aircraft of persons or property as a common carrier for compensation or hire or the carriage of mail by aircraft, in commerce between, respectively—

(a)　a place in any State of the United States, or the District of Columbia, and a place in any other State of the United States, or the District of Columbia; or between places in the same State of the United States through the air space over any place outside thereof; or between places in the same Territory or possession (except the Philippine Islands) of the United States, or the District of Columbia;

(b)　a place in any State of the United States, or the District of Columbia, and any place in a Territory or possession of the United States; or between a place in a Territory or possession of the United States, and a place in any other Territory or possession of the United States; and

(c)　a place in the United States and any place outside thereof, whether such commerce moves wholly by aircraft or partly by aircraft and partly by other forms of transportation.

(22) "Landing area" means any locality, either of land or water, including airports and intermediate landing fields, which is used, or intended to be used, for the landing and take-off of aircraft, whether or not facilities are provided for the shelter, servicing, or repair of aircraft, or for receiving or discharging passengers or cargo.

(23) "Mail" means United States mail and foreign-transit mail.

(24) "Navigable air space" means air space above the minimum altitudes of flight prescribed by regulations issued under this Act.

(25) "Navigation of aircraft" or "navigate aircraft" includes the piloting of aircraft.

(26) "Operation of aircraft" or "operate aircraft" means the use of aircraft, for the purpose of air navigation and includes the navigation of aircraft. Any person who causes or authorizes the operation of aircraft, whether with or without the right of legal control (in the capacity of owner, lessee, or otherwise) of the aircraft, shall be deemed to be engaged in the operation of aircraft within the meaning of this Act.

(27) "Person" means any individual, firm, copartnership, corporation, company, association, joint-stock association, or body politic; and includes any trustee, receiver, assignee, or other similar representative thereof.

(28) "Propeller" includes all parts, appurtenances, and accessories thereof.

(29) "Possessions of the United States" means (a) Puerto Rico, notwithstanding the provisions of the Act of March 2, 1917, entitled "An Act to provide a civil government for Porto Rico," and any other Act or Acts which are inconsistent with the provisions of this Act; (b) the Canal Zone, but nothing herein shall impair or affect the

jurisdiction which has heretofore been, or may hereafter, be, granted to the President in respect of air navigation in the Canal Zone; (c) the Philippine Islands, except that the operation of civil aircraft within the jurisdiction of the Philippine Islands shall be governed by laws enacted by the legislature of the islands and by executive regulations designating air-space reservations or other prohibited areas; and (d) all other possessions of the United States.

(30) "Public aircraft" means an aircraft used exclusively in the service of any government or of any political subdivision thereof, including the government of any State, Territory, or possession of the United States, or the District of Columbia, but not including any government-owned aircraft engaged in carrying persons or property for commercial purposes.

(31) "United States" means the several States, the District of Columbia, and the several Territories and possessions of the United States, including the Territorial waters and the overlying air space thereof.

Declaration of Policy

SEC. 2. In the exercise and performance of its powers and duties under this Act, the Authority shall consider the following, among other things, as being in the public interest, and in accordance with the public convenience and necessity—

(a) The encouragement and development of an air-transportation system properly adapted to the present and future needs of the foreign and domestic commerce of the United States, of the Postal Service, and of the national defense;

(b) The regulation of air transportation in such manner as to recognize and preserve the inherent advantages of, assure the highest degree of safety in, and foster sound economic conditions in, such transportation, and to improve the relations between, and coordinate transportation by, air carriers;

(c) The promotion of adequate, economical, and efficient service by air carriers at reasonable charges, without unjust discriminations, undue preferences or advantages, or unfair or destructive competitive practices;

(d) Competition to the extent necessary to assure the sound development of an air-transportation system properly adapted to the needs of the foreign and domestic commerce of the United States, of the Postal Service, and of the national defense;

(e) The regulation of air commerce in such manner as to best promote its development and safety; and

(f) The encouragement and development of civil aeronautics.

Public Right of Transit

SEC. 3. There is hereby recognized and declared to exist in behalf of any citizen of the United States a public right of freedom of transit in air commerce through the navigable air space of the United States.

TITLE II–ORGANIZATION OF AUTHORITY

Creation of Authority

Appointment of Members of Authority

SEC. 201. (a) An agency is created and established to be known as the "Civil Aeronautics Authority" which shall be composed of five members who shall be appointed by the President, by and with the advice and consent of the Senate, as soon as practicable after the passage of this Act, and who shall continue in office as designated by the President at the time of nomination through the last day of the second, third, fourth, fifth, and sixth calendar years, respectively, following the passage of this Act. The President shall designate annually one of the members of the Authority as chairman and one of the members as vice chairman who shall act as chairman in the absence or incapacity of the chairman. The successors of the members shall be appointed for terms of six years in the same manner as the members originally appointed under this Act, except that any person appointed to fill a vacancy occurring prior to the expiration of the term for which his predecessor was appointed shall be appointed only for the remainder of such term. The members of the Authority may be removed by the President for inefficiency, neglect of duty, or malfeasance in office. No more than three of the members shall be appointed from the same political party. Each member of the Authority shall receive a salary at the rate of $12,000 per annum.

Administrator

(b) There shall be in the Authority an Administrator who shall be appointed by the President by and with the advice and consent of the Senate, and who shall receive a salary at the rate of $12,000 per annum.

Qualifications of Members

(c) The members of the Authority shall be appointed with due regard to their fitness for the efficient dispatch of the powers and duties vested in and imposed upon the Authority by this Act. Each member of the Authority, and the Administrator shall be a citizen of the United States, and no member of the Authority, or the Administrator, shall have any pecuniary interest in or own any stock in or bonds of any civil aeronautics enterprise. No member of the Authority, or the Administrator, shall engage in any other business, vocation, or employment.

Quorum, Principal Office, and Seal

(d) Three of the members shall constitute a quorum of the Authority. The principal office of the Authority shall be in the District of Columbia where its general sessions shall be held, but whenever the convenience of the public or of the parties may be promoted, or delay or expense may be prevented, the Authority may hold hearings or other proceedings at any other place. The Authority shall have an official seal which shall be judicially noticed and which shall be preserved in the custody of the secretary of the Authority.

Organization of Authority

Officers and Employees

SEC. 202. (a) The Authority shall, without regard to the civil-service laws, appoint and prescribe the duties of a secretary of the Authority and a secretary for each member, and, subject to such noncompetitive tests of fitness as the Civil Service Commission may prescribe, appoint and prescribe the duties of a general counsel, a director for each Bureau, and such assistant directors and heads of divisions or sections as may be necessary. Subject to the provisions of the civil-service laws, the Authority shall employ such other officers and employees as it shall deem necessary in exercising and performing its powers and duties. The Administrator shall, without regard to the civil-service laws, appoint and prescribe the duties of a secretary, and, subject to the civil-service laws, appoint and prescribe the duties of such other officers and employees as he shall deem necessary in exercising and performing his powers and duties. The compensation of all officers and employees appointed by the Authority or by the Administrator under this subsection shall be fixed in accordance with the Classification Act of 1923, as amended.

Temporary Personnel

(b) The Authority, and the Administrator, may, from time to time, without regard to the provisions of the civil-service laws, engage for temporary service such duly qualified consulting engineers or agencies, or other qualified persons as are necessary in the exercise and performance of the powers and duties of each, and fix the compensation of such engineers, agencies, or persons without regard to the Classification Act of 1923, as amended, and the expenses of such employment shall be paid out of the appropriation for the administration of this Act.

Personnel, Property, and Appropriations

Personnel and Property

SEC. 203. (a) Such officers and employees of the Bureau of Air Mail of the Interstate Commerce Commission and of the Bureau of Air Commerce of the Department of Commerce, and such property (including office equipment and official records), as the President shall determine to have been employed by the Secretary of Commerce in the exercise and performance of the powers and duties vested in and imposed upon him by the Air Commerce Act of 1926, as amended (44 Stat. 568; U. S. C., 1934 ed., title 49, sec. 171 et seq.), and by the Secretary of Commerce and the Interstate Commerce Commission in the exercise and performance of the powers and duties vested in and imposed upon them by the Air Mail Act of 1934, approved June 12, 1934, as amended (48 Stat. 933; U. S. C., 1934 ed., Supp. II, title 39, sec. 469 et seq.), are transferred to the Authority upon such date or dates as the President shall specify by Executive order: *Provided,* That the transfer of such personnel shall be without reduction in classification or compensation, except that this requirement shall not operate after the end of the fiscal year during which such transfer is made to prevent the adjustment of classification or compensation to conform to the duties to which such transferred personnel may be assigned: *Provided further,* That such of the personnel so transferred as do not already possess a classified civil-service status shall not acquire such status by reason of such transfer except (1) upon recommendation of the Authority within one year after such personnel have been so transferred and certification within such period by the Authority to the Civil Service Commission that such personnel have served with merit for not less than six months prior to the transfer, and (2) upon passing such suitable noncompetitive examinations as the Civil Service Commission may prescribe: *And provided further,* That no officer or employee taking such examination shall be discharged or reduced in grade or compensation pending the result thereof, except for cause in the manner provided by law.

Appropriations

(b) Such of the unexpended balances of appropriations available for use by the Secretary of Commerce in the exercise and performance of the powers and duties vested in and imposed upon him by the Air Commerce Act of 1926, as amended, and by the Secretary of Commerce and the Interstate Commerce Commission in the exercise and performance of the powers and duties vested in and imposed upon them by the Air Mail Act of 1934, approved June 12, 1934, as amended, as the President shall deem necessary and specify by Executive order, are transferred to the Authority upon such date or dates as the President shall specify by Executive order, and shall be available for use in connection with the exercise and performance of the powers and duties vested in and imposed upon the Authority, the Administrator, and the Air Safety Board by this Act.

Authorization of Expenditures and Travel

General Authority

SEC. 204. (a) The Authority is empowered to make such expenditures at the seat of government and elsewhere as may be necessary for the exercise and performance of the powers and duties vested in and imposed upon the Authority, the Administrator, and the Air Safety Board by law, and as from time to time may be appropriated for by Congress, including expenditures for (1) rent and personal services at the seat of government and elsewhere; (2) travel expenses; (3) office furniture, equipment and supplies, lawbooks, newspapers, periodicals, and books of reference (inluding the exchange thereof); (4) printing and binding; (5) membership in and cooperation with such organizations as are related to, or are part of, the civil-aeronautics industry or the art of aeronautics in the United States or in any foreign country; (6) attendance at meetings and conventions when in the public interest; (7) making investigations and conducting studies in matters pertaining to aeronautics; and (8) acquisition (including exchange), operation, and maintenance of passenger-carrying automobiles and aircraft, and such other property as is necessary in the exercise and performance of the powers and duties of the Authority, the Administrator, and the Air Safety Board: *Provided,* That no aircraft or motor vehicle, purchased under the provisions of this section, shall be used otherwise than for official business. The Authority may include, among expenditures for travel, reasonable expenditures for transportation between airports and centers of population whether or not such transportation is incidental to travel by aircraft.

Purchase of Aircraft

(b) The Authority, within the limits of appropriations made available by Congress, may purchase and exchange modern aircraft, completely equipped in such manner that such aircraft can be used in testing and checking every phase of flight operation; and may purchase and exchange for the use of the Administrator and the Air Safety Board modern aircraft similar to aircraft used or suitable for use in air transportation, completely equipped in such manner that they can be used in testing and checking every phase of flight operation encountered in air transportation. The Authority is authorized to obtain necessary space, facilities, and personnel for the storage, maintenance, operation, and navigation of such aircraft.

Travel

(c) Travel by personnel of the United States Government on commercial aircraft, domestic or foreign, including travel between airports and centers of population or posts of duty when incidental to travel on commercial aircraft, shall be allowed at public expense when authorized or approved by competent authority, and transportation requests for such travel may be issued upon such authorizations. Such expense shall be allowed without regard to comparative costs of transportation by aircraft with other modes of transportation.

General Powers and Duties of the Authority

General Powers

SEC. 205. (a) The Authority is empowered to perform such acts, to conduct such investigations, to issue and amend such orders, and to make and amend such general or special rules, regulations, and procedure, pursuant to and consistent with the provisions of this Act, as it shall deem necessary to carry out such provisions and to exercise and perform its powers and duties under this Act.

Cooperation With State Aeronautical Agencies

(b) The Authority is empowered to confer with or to hold joint hearings with any State aeronautical agency, or other State agency, in connection with any matter arising under this Act, and to avail itself of the cooperation, services, records, and facilities of such State agencies as fully as may be practicable in the administration and enforcement of this Act.

Exchange of Information

(c) The Authority is empowered to exchange with foreign governments, through appropriate agencies of the United States, information pertaining to aeronautics.

Publications

(d) Except as may be otherwise provided in this Act, the Authority shall make a report in writing in all proceedings and investigations under this Act in which formal hearings have been held, and shall state in such report its conclusions together with its decision, order, or requirement in the premises. All such reports shall be entered of record and a copy thereof shall be furnished to all parties to the proceeding or investigation. The Authority shall provide for the publication of such reports, and all other reports, orders, decisions, rules, and regulations issued by it under this Act in such form and manner as may be best adapted for public information and use. Publications purporting to be published by the Authority shall be competent evidence of the orders, decisions, rules, regulations, and reports of the Authority therein contained in all courts of the United States, and of the several States, Territories, and possessions thereof, and the District of Columbia, without further proof or authentication thereof.

Annual Report

SEC. 206. The Authority shall make an annual report to the Congress, copies of which shall be distributed as are other reports transmitted to Congress. Such report shall contain in addition to a report of the work performed under this Act, such information and data collected by the Authority, the Administrator, and the Air Safety Board as may be considered of value in the determination of questions connected with the development and regulation of civil aeronautics, together with such recommendations as to additional legislation relating thereto as the Authority may deem necessary. The Authority may also transmit recommendations as to such additional legislation more frequently.

TITLE III—POWERS AND DUTIES OF ADMINISTRATOR

Fostering of Air Commerce

SEC. 301. The Administrator is empowered and directed to encourage and foster the development of civil aeronautics and air commerce in the United States, and abroad, and to encourage the establishment of civil airways, landing areas, and other air navigation facilities. The Administrator and the Air Safety Board shall cooperate with the Authority in the administration and enforcement of this Act.

Civil Airways and Facilities

General

SEC. 302. (a) The Administrator is empowered to designate and establish civil airways and, within the limits of available appropriations made by the Congress, (1) to acquire, establish, operate, and maintain along such airways all necessary air navigation facilities; (2) to chart such airways and arrange for the publication of maps of such airways, utilizing the facilities and assistance of existing agencies of the Government so far as practicable; (3) to acquire, establish, operate, and maintain, in whole or in part, air navigation facilities at and upon any municipally owned or other landing area approved for such installation, operation, or maintenance by the Administrator; and (4) to provide necessary facilities and personnel for the regulation and protection of air traffic moving in air commerce: *Provided,* That the Administrator shall not acquire any airport by purchase or condemnation. The Administrator is empowered to approve the establishment of such civil airways, not designated or established by the Administrator, as may be required in the interest of the public. No exclusive rights shall be granted for the use of any civil airway, landing area, or other air navigation facility.

Method of Establishment

(b) The Administrator shall insofar as practicable designate and establish civil airways with relation to visual, mechanical, electrical, radio, or other like aids along the ground for air navigation, and in such manner that not more than one airway shall embrace the same air space, except to the extent necessary for intersection of airways at landing areas or elsewhere, or except when such action is necessary in the interest of safety or efficient operation of aircraft, or when the operation of aircraft over one airway will not interfere with the operation of aircraft over another airway embracing the same air space: *Provided,* That nothing herein shall be construed to affect the promulgation or enforcement of any rules and regulations under this Act for the control of traffic.

Airport Survey

(c) The Authority shall, through the Administrator, make a field survey of the existing system of airports and shall present to the Congress not later than February 1, 1939, definite recommendations (1) as to whether the Federal Government should participate in the construction, improvement, development, operation, or maintenance of a national system of airports, and (2) if Federal participation is recommended, the extent to which, and the manner in which, the Federal Government shall so participate.

Expenditure of Federal Funds

SEC. 303. No Federal funds, other than those expended under this Act, shall be expended, other than for military purposes (whether or not in cooperation with State or other local governmental agencies), for the acquisition, establishment, construction, alteration, repair, maintenance, or operation of any landing area, or for the acquisition, establishment, construction, maintenance, or operation of air navigation facilities thereon, except upon written recommendation and certification by the Administrator, made after consultation with the Authority, that such landing area, or facility is reasonably necessary for use in air commerce or in the interests of national defense. Any interested person may apply to the Administrator, under regulations prescribed by him, for such recommendation and certification with respect to any landing area or air navigation facility proposed to be established, constructed, altered, repaired, maintained, or operated by, or in the interests of, such person. There shall be no exclusive right for the use of any landing area or air navigation facility upon which Federal funds have been expended.

Meteorological Service

SEC. 304. The Administrator is empowered and directed to make recommendations to the Secretary of Agriculture for providing meteorological service necessary for the safe and efficient movement of aircraft in air commerce.

Development of Facilities

SEC. 305. The Administrator is empowered to undertake or supervise such developmental work and service testing as tends to the creation of improved air navigation facilities, aircraft, aircraft engines, propellers, and appliances. For such purpose, the Administrator is empowered, subject to the approval of the Authority, to make purchases (including exchange) by negotiation or otherwise of experimental aircraft, aircraft engines, propellers, appliances, air navigation facilities, and radio apparatus, which seem to offer special advantages to aeronautics.

Collection and Dissemination of Information

SEC. 306. The Administrator is empowered and directed to collect and disseminate information relative to civil aeronautics (other than information collected and disseminated by the Authority under titles IV and VI of this Act and by the Air Safety Board); to study the possibilities of the development of air commerce and the aeronautical industry; and to exchange with foreign governments, through appropriate governmental channels, information pertaining to civil aeronautics.

Development Planning

SEC. 307. The Administrator is empowered and directed to make plans for such orderly development and location of landing areas, airways, and all other aids and facilities for air navigation, as will best meet the needs of, and serve the interest of safety in, civil aeronautics.

Other Duties of Administrator

SEC. 308. The Administrator shall exercise and perform the powers and duties vested in and imposed upon him by this Act, and such powers and duties vested in and imposed upon the Authority by this Act (except the powers under sections 202, 203, 204, and 206, and the powers and duties under titles IV and VI) as may, from time to time, be assigned to him by the Authority; and shall so exercise and perform his powers and duties as best to effectuate the policies declared in, and the purposes of, this Act. The Authority may request the Administrator to make reports to it of his work under this Act.

TITLE IV—AIR CARRIER ECONOMIC REGULATION

Certificate of Public Convenience and Necessity

Certificate Required

SEC. 401. (a) No air carrier shall engage in any air transportation unless there is in force a certificate issued by the Authority authorizing such air carrier to engage in such transportation: *Provided,* That if an air carrier is engaged in such transportation on the date of the enactment of this Act, such air carrier may continue so to engage between the same terminal and intermediate points for one hundred and twenty days after said date, and thereafter until such time as the Authority shall pass upon an application for a certificate for such transportation if within said one hundred and twenty days such air carrier files such application as provided herein.

Application for Certificate

(b) Application for a certificate shall be made in writing to the Authority and shall be so verified, shall be in such form and contain such information, and shall be accompanied by such proof of service upon such interested persons, as the Authority shall by regulation require.

Notice of Application

(c) Upon the filing of any such application, the Authority shall give due notice thereof to the public by posting a notice of such application in the office of the secretary of the Authority and to such other persons as the Authority may by regulation determine. Any interested person may file with the Authority a protest or memorandum of opposition to or in support of the issuance of a certificate. Such application shall be set for public hearing, and the Authority shall dispose of such application as speedily as possible.

Issuance of Certificate

(d) (1) The Authority shall issue a certificate authorizing the whole or any part of the transportation covered by the application, if it finds that the applicant is fit, willing, and able to perform such transportation properly, and to conform to the provisions of this Act and the rules, regulations, and requirements of the Authority hereunder, and that such transportation is required by the public convenience and necessity; otherwise such application shall be denied.   (2) In the case of an application for a certificate to engage in temporary air transportation, the Authority may issue a certificate authorizing the whole or any part thereof for such limited periods as may be required by the public convenience and necessity, if it finds that the applicant is fit, willing, and able properly to perform such transportation and to conform to the provisions of this Act and the rules, regulations, and requirements of the Authority hereunder.

Existing Air Carriers

(e) (1) If any applicant who makes application for a certificate within one hundred and twenty days after the date of enactment of this Act shall show that, from May 14,

1938, until the effective date of this section, it, or its predecessor in interest, was an air carrier, continuously operating as such (except as to interruptions of service over which the applicant or its predecessor in interest had no control), the Authority, upon proof of such fact only, shall, unless the service rendered by such applicant for such period was inadequate and inefficient, issue a certificate or certificates, authorizing such applicant to engage in air transportation (A) with respect to all classes of traffic for which authorization is sought, except mail, between the terminal and intermediate points between which it, or its predecessor, so continuously operated between May 18, 1938, and the effective date of this section; and (B) with respect to mail and all other classes of traffic for which authorization is sought, between the terminal and intermediate points between which the applicant or its predecessor was authorized by the Postmaster General prior to the effective date of this section, to engage in the transportation of mail: *Provided,* That no applicant holding an air-mail contract shall receive a certificate authorizing it to serve any point not named in such contract as awarded to it and not served by it prior to April 1, 1938, if any other air carrier competitively serving the same point under authority of a contract as awarded to such air carrier shall prove that it is adversely affected thereby, and if the Authority shall also find that transportation by the applicant to and from such point is not required by the public convenience and necessity.

(2) If paragraph (1) of this subsection does not authorize the issuance of a certificate authorizing the transportation of mail between each of the points between which air-mail service was provided for by the Act of Congress making appropriations for the Treasury Department and the Post Office Department, approved March 28, 1938, the Authority shall, notwithstanding any other provision of this Act, issue certificates authorizing the transportation of mail, and all other classes of traffic for which authorization is sought, between such points, namely, (A) from Wichita, Kansas, to Pueblo, Colorado, via intermediate cities; (B) from Bismarck, North Dakota, to Minot, North Dakota; (C) from Detroit, Michigan, to Sault Sainte Marie, Michigan, via intermediate cities; (D) from Brownsville, Texas, via Corpus Christi, to Houston to San Antonio, Texas; (E) from Phoenix, Arizona, to Las Vegas, Nevada, via intermediate cities; (F) from Jacksonville, Florida, to New Orleans, Louisiana, via intermediate cities; (G) from Tampa, Florida, to Atlanta, Georgia, via intermediate cities (which projects have been advertised); and (H) by extension from Yakima, Washington, to Portland, Oregon; and (I) by extension from Grand Rapids, Michigan, to Chicago, Illinois.

Terms and Conditions of Certificate

(f) Each certificate issued under this section shall specify the terminal points and intermediate points, if any, between which the air carrier is authorized to engage in air transportation and the service to be rendered; and there shall be attached to the exercise of the privileges granted by the certificate, or amendment thereto, such reasonable terms, conditions, and limitations as the public interest may require. A certificate issued under this section to engage in foreign air transportation shall, insofar as the operation is to take place without the United States, designate the terminal and intermediate points only insofar as the Authority shall deem practicable, and otherwise shall designate only the general route or routes to be followed. Any air carrier holding a certificate for foreign air transportation shall be authorized to handle and transport mail of countries other than the United States. No term, condition, or limitation of a certificate shall restrict the right of an air carrier to add to or change schedules, equipment, accommodations, and facilities for performing the authorized transportation and service as the development of the business and the demands of the public shall require. No air carrier shall be deemed to have violated any term, condition, or limitation of its certificate by landing or taking off during an emergency at a point not named in its certificate or by operating in an emergency, under regulations which may be prescribed by the Authority, between terminal and intermediate points other than those specified in its certificate. Any air carrier may make charter trips to perform any other special service, without regard to the points named in its certificate, under regulations prescribed by the Authority.

Effective Date and Duration of Certificate

(g) Each certificate shall be effective from the date specified therein, and shall continue in effect until suspended or revoked as hereinafter provided, or until the Authority shall certify that operation thereunder had ceased, or, if issued for a limited period of time under subsection (d) (2) of this section, shall continue in effect until the expiration thereof, unless, prior to the date of expiration, such certificate shall be suspended or revoked as provided herein, or the Authority shall certify that operations thereunder have ceased: *Provided,* That if any service authorized by a certificate is not inaugurated within such period, not less than ninety days, after the date of the authorization as shall be fixed by the Authority, or if, for a period of ninety days or such period as may be designated by the Authority, any such service is not operated, the Authority may by order, entered after notice and hearing, direct that such certificate shall thereupon cease to be effective to the extent of such service.

Authority to Modify, Suspend, or Revoke

(h) The Authority, upon petition or complaint or upon its own initiative, after notice and hearing, may alter, amend, modify, or suspend any such certificate, in whole or in part, if the public convenience and necessity so require, or may revoke any such certificate in whole or in part, for intentional failure to comply with any provision of this title or any order, rule, or regulation issued hereunder or any term, condition, or limitation of such certificate: *Provided,* That no such certificate shall be revoked unless the holder thereof fails to comply, within a reasonable time to be fixed by the Authority, with an order of the Authority commanding obedience to the provision, or to the order (other than an order issued in accordance with this proviso), rule, regulation, term, condition, or limitation found by the Authority to have been violated. Any interested person may file with the Authority a protest or memorandum in support of or in opposition to the alteration, amendment, modification, suspension, or revocation of a certificate.

Transfer of Certificate

(i) No certificate may be transferred unless such transfer is approved by the Authority as being consistent with the public interest.

Certain Rights Not Conferred by Certificate

(j) No certificate shall confer any proprietary, property, or exclusive right in the use of any air space, civil airway, landing area, or air-navigation facility.

Application for Abandonment

(k) No air carrier shall abandon any route, or part thereof, for which a certificate has been issued by the Authority, unless, upon the application of such air carrier, after notice and hearing, the Authority shall find such abandonment to be in the public interest. Any interested person may file with the Authority a protest or memorandum of opposition to or in support of any such abandonment. The Authority may, by regulations or otherwise, authorize such temporary suspension of service as may be in the public interest.

Compliance With Labor Legislation

(l) (1) Every air carrier shall maintain rates of compensation, maximum hours, and other working conditions and relations of all of its pilots and copilots who are engaged in interstate air transportation within the continental United States (not including Alaska) so as to conform with decision numbered 83 made by the National Labor Board on May 10, 1934, notwithstanding any limitation therein as to the period of its effectiveness.

(2) Every air carrier shall maintain rates of compensation for all of its pilots and copilots who are engaged in overseas or foreign air transportation or air transportation wholly within a Territory or possession of the United States, the minimum of which shall be not less, upon an annual basis, than the compensation required to be paid under said decision 83 for comparable service to pilots and copilots engaged in interstate air transportation within the continental United States (not including Alaska).

(3) Nothin herein contained shall be construed as restricting the right of any such pilots or copilots, or other employees, of any such air carrier to obtain by collective bargaining higher rates of compensation or more favorable working conditions or relations.

(4) It shall be a condition upon the holding of a certificate by any air carrier that such carrier shall comply with title II of the Railway Labor Act, as amended.

(5) The term "pilot" as used in this subsection shall mean an employee who is responsible for the manipulation of or who manipulates the flight controls of an aircraft while under way including take-off and landing of such aircraft, and the term "copilot" as used in this subsection shall mean an employee any part of whose duty is to assist or relieve the pilot in such manipulation, and who is properly qualified to serve as, and holds a currently effective airman certificate authorizing him to serve as, such pilot or copilot.

Requirement as to Carriage of Mail

(m) Whenever so authorized by its certificate, any air carrier shall provide necessary and adequate facilities and service for the transportation of mail, and shall transport mail whenever required by the Postmaster General. Such air carrier shall be entitled to receive reasonable compensation therefor as hereinafter provided.

Application for New Mail Service

(n) Whenever, from time to time, the Postmaster General shall find that the needs of the Postal Service require the transportation of mail by aircraft between any points within the United States or between the United States and foreign countries, in addition to the transportation of mail authorized in certificates then currently effective, the Postmaster General shall certify such finding to the Authority and file therewith a statement showing such additional service and the facilities necessary in connection therewith, and a copy of such certification and statement shall be posted for at least twenty days in the office of the secretary of the Authority. The Authority shall, after notice and hearing, and if found by it to be required by the public convenience and necessity, make provision for such additional service, and the facilities necessary in connection therewith, by issuing a new certificate or certificates or by amending an existing certificate or certificates in accordance with the provisions of this section.

Permits to Foreign Air Carriers

Permit Required

SEC. 402. (a) No foreign air carrier shall engage in foreign air transportation unless there is in force a permit issued by the Authority authorizing such carrier so to engage:

Provided, That if any foreign air carrier is engaged in such transportation on the date of the enactment of this Act, such carrier may continue so to engage between the same terminal and intermediate points for one hundred and twenty days after said date, and thereafter until such time as the Authority shall pass upon an application for a permit for such transportation if within said one hundred and twenty days such carrier files such applications as provided in this section.

Issuance of Permit

(b) The Authority is empowered to issue such a permit if it finds that such carrier is fit, willing, and able properly to perform such air transportation and to conform to the provisions of this Act and the rules, regulations, and requirements of the Authority hereunder, and that such transportation will be in the public interest.

Existing Permits

(c) Any such carrier who holds a permit issued by the Secretary of Commerce under section 6 of the Air Commerce Act of 1926, as amended, which was in effect on May 14, 1938, and which authorizes such carrier to operate between any foreign country and the United States, shall be entitled to receive a permit under this section upon proof of that fact only.

Application for Permit

(d) Application for a permit shall be made in writing to the Authority, shall be so verified, shall be in such form and contain such information, and shall be accompanied by such proof of service upon such interested persons, as the Authority shall by regulation require.

Notice of Application

(e) Upon the filing of an application for a permit the Authority shall give due notice thereof to the public by posting a notice of such application in the office of the secretary of the Authority and to such other persons as the Authority may be regulation determine. Any interested person may file with the Authority a protest or memorandum of opposition to or in support of the issuance of a permit. Such application shall be set for public hearing and the Authority shall dispose of such applications as speedily as possible.

Terms and Conditions of Permit

(f) The Authority may prescribe the duration of any permit and may attach to such permit such reasonable terms, conditions, or limitations as, in its judgment, the public interest may require.

Authority to Modify, Suspend, or Revoke

(g) Any permit issued under the provisions of this section may, after notice and hearing, be altered, modified, amended, suspended, canceled, or revoked by the Authority whenever it finds such action to be in the public interest. Any interested person may file with the Authority a protest or memorandum in support of or in opposition to the alteration, modification, amendment, suspension, cancelation, or revocation of a permit.

Transfer of Permit

(h) No permit may be transferred unless such transfer is approved by the Authority as being in the public interest.

Tariffs of Air Carriers

Filing of Tariffs Required

SEC. 403. (a) Every air carrier and every foreign air carrier shall file with the Authority, and print, and keep open to public inspection, tariffs showing all rates, fares, and charges for air transportation between points served by it, and between points served by it and points served by any other air carrier or foreign air carrier when through service and through rates shall have been established, and showing to the extent required by regulations of the Authority, all classifications, rules, regulations, practices, and services in connection with such air transportation. Tariffs shall be filed, posted, and published in such form and manner, and shall contain such information, as the Authority shall by regulation prescribe; and the Authority is empowered to reject any tariff so filed which is not consistent with this section and such regulations. Any tariff so rejected shall be void. The rates, fares, and charges shown in any tariff shall be stated in terms of lawful money of the United States, but such tariffs may also state rates, fares, and charges in terms of currencies other than lawful money of the United States, and may, in the case of foreign air transportation, contain such information as may be required under the laws of any country in or to which an air carrier or foreign air carrier is authorized to operate.

Observance of Tariffs; Rebating Prohibited

(b) No air carrier or foreign air carrier shall charge or demand or collect or receive a greater or less or different compensation for air transportation, or for any service in connection therewith, than the rates, fares, and charges specified in its currently effective tariffs; and no air carrier or foreign air carrier shall, in any manner or by any device, directly or indirectly, or through any agent or broker, or otherwise, refund or remit any portion of the rates, fares, or charges so specified, or extend to any person any privileges or facilities, with respect to matters required by the Authority to be specified in such tariffs, except those specified therein. Nothing in this Act shall prohibit such air carriers or foreign air carriers, under such terms and conditions as the Authority may prescribe, from issuing or interchanging tickets or passes for free or reduced-rate transportation to their directors, officers, and employees and their immediate families; witnesses and attorneys attending any legal investigation in which any such air carrier is interested; persons injured in aircraft accidents and physicians and nurses attending such persons; and any person or property with the object of providing relief in cases of general epidemic, pestilence, or other calamitous visitation; and, in the case of overseas or foreign air transportation, to such other persons and under such other circumstances as the Authority may by regulations prescribe.

Notice of Tariff Change

(c) No change shall be made in any rate, fare, or charge, or any classification, rule, regulation, or practice affecting such rate, fare, or charge, or the value of the service thereunder, specified in any effective tariff of any air carrier or foreign air carrier, except after thirty days' notice of the proposed change filed, posted, and published in accordance with subsection (a) of this section. Such notice shall plainly state the change proposed to be made and the time such change will take effect. The Authority may in the public interest, by regulation or otherwise, allow such change upon notice less than that herein specified, or modify the requirements of this section with respect to filing and posting of tariffs, either in particular instances or by general order applicable to special or peculiar circumstances or conditions.

Filing of Divisions of Rates and Charges Required

(d) Every air carrier or foreign air carrier shall keep currently on file with the Authority, if the Authority so requires, the established divisions of all joint rates, fares, and charges for air transportation in which such air carrier or foreign air carrier participates.

Rates for Carriage of Persons and Property

Carrier's Duty to Provide Service, Rates, and Divisions

SEC. 404. (a) It shall be the duty of every air carrier to provide and furnish interstate and overseas air transportation, as authorized by its certificate, upon reasonable request therefor and to provide reasonable through service in such air transportation in connection with other air carriers; to provide safe and adequate service, equipment, and facilities in connection with such transportation; to establish, observe, and enforce just and reasonable individual and joint rates, fares, and charges, and just and reasonable classifications, rules, regulations, and practices relating to such air transportation; and, in case of such joint rates, fares, and charges, to establish just, reasonable, and equitable divisions thereof as between air carriers participating therein which shall not unduly prefer or prejudice any of such participating air carriers.

Discrimination

(b) No air carrier or foreign air carrier shall make, give, or cause any undue or unreasonable preference or advantage to any particular person, port, locality, or description of traffic in air transportation in any respect whatsoever or subject any particular person, port, locality, or description of traffic in air transportation to any unjust discrimination or any undue or unreasonable prejudice or disadvantage in and respect whatsoever.

Foreign Rate Study

(c) The Authority is empowered and directed to investigate and report to the Congress within one year from the effective date of this section, to what extent, if any, the Federal Government should further regulate the rates, fares, and charges of air carriers engaged in foreign air transportation, and the classifications, rules, regulations, and practices affecting such rates, fares, or charges.

Transportation of Mail

Continuation and Termination of Mail Contracts

SEC. 405. (a) Each contract between the United States and any person for the carriage of mail, entered into or continued under the provisions of the Air Mail Act of 1934, as amended, and each contract for the carriage of mail by aircraft in Alaska, shall be continued in effect until canceled in accordance with this subsection. Each such contract shall be canceled upon the issuance to the holder of such contract of a certificate of public convenience and necessity authorizing the transportation of mail by aircraft between the points covered by such contract, or upon the failure of the holder of such contract to apply for such certificate within one hundred and twenty days after the date of enactment of this act, or upon a determination by the Authority that such certificate should not be issued. Until the Authority fixes rates under section 406 of this Act, the Postmaster General shall pay compensation for the transportation of mail by aircraft at the rates provided by each such contract or, where rates have been heretofore or shall hereafter be fixed by orders of the Interstate Commerce Commission, pursuant to proceedings instituted prior to the date of enactment of this Act, shall pay compensation for such transportation in accordance with such orders as if this Act had not been enacted.

Continuation and Termination of Foreign Mail Contracts

(b) Each contract between the United States and any person heretofore entered into under the provisions of the Act of March 8, 1928, as amended (45 Stat. 248), shall be continued in effect until canceled in accordance with this subsection. Each such contract shall be canceled upon the issuance of a certificate of public convenience and necessity to the holder of such contract authorizing the transportation of mail by aircraft between the points covered by such contract, or upon the effective date of any order of the Authority hereunder fixing a fair and reasonable rate of compensation for the transportation of mail by aircraft between the points covered by such contract, whichever is later, or upon the failure of the holder of such contract to apply for such certificate within one hundred and twenty days after the data of enactment of this Act, or upon a determination by the Authority that such certificate should not be issued.

Termination of Bonds

(c) Upon the cancelation, pursuant to the provisions of this Act, of any contract for the transportation of mail by aircraft, the bond or bonds required from the holder thereof shall terminate and cease to be effective, and such holder and his or its surety or sureties thereon shall be released and discharged from all obligations thereunder, and all securities deposited with such bond or bonds shall forthwith be returned to such holder: *Provided,* That the foregoing provision shall not be construed to terminate or make ineffective any bond or bonds of such holder, or to release or discharge from any obligation thereunder such holder or his or its surety or sureties thereon, in respect of any matter arising prior to the date of the cancelation of such contract, and such holder or his or its surety or sureties thereon shall not be released or discharged prior to disposition of any such matter: *Provided further,* That nothing in this Act shall be construed to affect any right which may have accrued to any air carrier prior to the date of the cancelation, pursuant to the provisions of this Act, of any contract for the transportation of mail by aircraft.

Rules and Regulations

(d) The Postmaster General is authorized to make such rules and regulations, not inconsistent with the provisions of this Act, or any order, rule, or regulation made by the Authority thereunder, as may be necessary for the safe and expeditious carriage of mail by aircraft.

Mail Schedules

(e) Each air carrier shall, from time to time, file with the Authority and the Postmaster General a statement showing the points between which such air carrier is authorized to engage in air transportation, and all schedules, and all changes therein, of aircraft regularly operated by the carrier between such points, setting forth in respect of each such schedule the points served thereby and the time of arrival and departure at each such point. The Postmaster General may designate any such schedule for the transportation of mail between the points between which the air carrier is authorized by its certificate to transport mail, and may, by order, require the air carrier to establish additional schedules for the transportation of mail between such points. No change shall be made in any schedules designated or ordered to be established by the Postmaster General except upon ten days' notice thereof filed as herein provided. The Postmaster General may by order disapprove any such change or alter, amend, or modify any such schedule or change. No order of the Postmaster General under this subsection shall become effective until ten days after its issuance. Any person who would be aggrieved by any such order of the Postmaster General under this subsection may, before the expiration of such ten-day period, apply to the Authority, under such regulations as it may prescribe, for a review of such order. The Authority may review, and, if the public convenience and necessity so require, amend, revise, suspend, or cancel such order; and, pending such review and the determination thereof, may postpone the effective date of such order. The Authority shall give preference to proceedings under this subsection over all proceedings pending before it. No air carrier shall transport mail in accordance with any schedule other than a schedule designated or ordered to be established under this subsection for the transportation of mail.

Maximum Mail Load

(f) The Authority may fix the maximum mail load for any schedule or for any aircraft or any type of aircraft; but, in the event that mail in excess of the maximum load is tendered by the Postmaster General for transportation by any carrier in accordance with any schedule designated or ordered to be established by the Postmaster General under subsection (e) of this section for the transportation of mail, such air carrier shall, to the extent such air carrier is reasonably able as determined by the Authority, furnish facilities sufficient to transport, and shall transport, such mail as nearly in accordance with such schedule as the Authority shall determine to be possible.

Tender of Mail

(g) From and after the issuance of any certificate authorizing the transportation of mail by aircraft, the Postmaster General shall tender mail to the holder thereof, to the extent required by the Postal Service, for transportation between the points named in such certificate for the transportation of mail, and such mail shall be transported by the air carrier holding such certificate in accordance with such rules, regulations, and requirements as may be promulgated by the Postmaster General under this section.

Foreign Postal Arrangements

(h) (1) Nothing in this Act shall be deemed to abrogate or affect any arrangement made by the United States with the postal administration of any foreign country with respect to transportation of mail by aircraft, or to impair the authority of the Postmaster General to enter into any such arrangement with the postal administration of any foreign country.

(2) The Postmaster General may, in any case where service may be necessary by a person not a citizen of the United States who may not be obligated to transport the mail for a foreign country, make arrangements, without advertising, with such person for transporting mail by aircraft to or within any foreign country.

Transportation of Foreign Mail

(i) (1) Any air carrier holding a certificate to engage in foreign air transportation and transporting mails of foreign countries shall transport such mails subject to control and regulation by the United States. The Postmaster General shall from time to time fix the rates of compensation that shall be charged the respective foreign countries for the transportation of their mails by such air carriers, and such rates shall be put into effect by the Postmaster General in accordance with the provisions of the postal convention regulating the postal relations between the United States and the respective foreign countries, or as provided hereinafter in this subsection. In any case where the Postmaster General deems such action to be in the public interest, he may approve rates provided in arrangements between any such air carrier and any foreign country covering the transportation of mails of such country, under which mails of such country have been carried on scheduled operations prior to January 1, 1938, or in extensions or modifications of such arrangements, and may permit any such air carrier to enter into arrangements with any foreign country for the transportation of its mails at rates fixed by the Postmaster General in advance of the making of any such arrangement. The Postmaster General may authorize any such air carrier, under such limitations as the Postmaster General may prescribe, to change the rates to be charged any foreign country for the transportation of its mails by such air carrier within that country or between that country and another foreign country.

(2) In any case where such air carrier has an arrangement with any foreign country for transporting its mails, made or approved in accordance with the provisions of subdivision (1) of this subsection, it shall collect its compensation from the foreign country under its arrangement, and in case of the absence of any arrangement between the air carrier and the foreign country consistent with this subsection, the collections made from the foreign country by the United States shall be for the account of such air carrier: *Provided,* That no such air carrier shall be entitled to receive compensation both from such foreign country and from the United States in respect of the transportation of the same mail or the same mails of foreign countries.

(3) In the case of any air carrier holding a contract under the provisions of the Act of March 8, 1928, as amended (45 Stat. 248), providing for the carriage of mails of foreign countries for the account of the United States, this subsection shall apply only upon the cancelation of such contract as provided in this section.

Evidence of Performance of Mail Service

(j) Air carriers transporting or handling United States mail shall submit, under oath, when and in such form as may be required by the Postmaster General, evidence of the performance of mail service; and air carriers transporting or handling mails of foreign countries shall submit, under oath, when and in such form as may be required by the Postmaster General, evidence of the amount of such mails transported or handled, and the compensation payable and received therefor.

Emergency Mail Service

(k) In the event of emergency caused by flood, fire, or other calamitous visitation, the Postmaster General is authorized to contract, without advertising, for the transportation by aircraft of any or all classes of mail to or from localities affected by such calamity, where available facilities of persons authorized to transport mail to or from such localities are inadequate to meet the requirements of the Postal Service during such emergency. Such contracts may be only for such periods as may be necessitated, for the maintenance of mail service, by the inadequacy of such other facilities. No operation pursuant to any such contract, for such period, shall be air transportation within the purview of this Act. Payment of compensation for service performed under such contracts shall be made, at rates provided in such contracts, from appropriations for the transportation of mail by the means normally used for transporting the mail transported under such contracts.

Experimental Air-Mail Service

(l) Nothing contained in this Act shall be construed to repeal in whole or in part the provisions of sections 1, 2, and 6 of the Act entitled "An Act to provide for experimental air-mail service, to further develop safety, efficiency, economy, and for other purposes," approved April 15, 1938 (Public, Numbered 486, Seventy-fifth Congress; chapter 157, third session). The transportation of mail under contracts entered into under such sections shall not, except for sections 401 (1) and 416 (b), be deemed to be "air transportation" as used in this Act and the rates of compensation for such transportation of mail shall not be fixed under this Act. Such Act of April 15, 1938, is amended by striking out so much of the first section as reads "the Secretary of Commerce shall prescribe in accordance with the authority vested in him under the Air Commerce Act of 1926, as amended" and inserting in lieu thereof the following: "May be prescribed in accordance with the Civil Aeronautics Act of 1938."

Free Travel for Postal Employees

(m) Every air carrier carrying the mails shall carry on any plane that it operates and without charge therefor, the persons in charge of the mails when on duty, and such duly accredited agents and officers of the Post Office Department, and post office inspectors, while traveling on official business relating to the transportation of mail by aircraft, as the Authority may by regulation prescribe, upon the exhibition of their credentials.

Rates for Transportation of Mail

Authority to Fix Rates

SEC. 406. (a) The Authority is empowered and directed, upon its own initiative or upon petition of the Postmaster General or an air carrier, (1) to fix and determine from time to time, after notice and hearing, the fair and reasonable rates of compensation for the transportation of mail by aircraft, the facilities used and useful therefor, and the services connected therewith (including the transportation of mail by an air carrier by other means than aircraft whenever such transportation is incidental to the transportation of mail by aircraft or is made necessary by conditions of emergency arising from aircraft operation), by each holder of a certificate authorizing the transportation of mail by aircraft, and to make such rates effective from such date as it shall determine to be proper; (2) to prescribe the method or methods, by aircraft-mile, pound-mile, weight, space, or any combination thereof, or otherwise, for ascertaining such rates of compensation for each air carrier or class of air carriers; and (3) to publish the same; and the rates so fixed and determined shall be paid by the Postmaster General from appropriations for the transportation of mail by aircraft.

Rate-Making Elements

(b) In fixing and determining fair and reasonable rates of compensation under this section, the Authority, considering the conditions peculiar to transportation by aircraft and to the particular air carrier or class of air carriers, may fix different rates for different air carriers or classes or air carriers, and different classes of service. In determining the rate in each case, the Authority shall take into consideration, among other factors, the condition that such air carriers may hold and operate under certificates authorizing the carriage of mail only by providing necessary and adequate facilities and service for the transportation of mail; such standards respecting the character and quality of service to be rendered by air carriers as may be prescribed by or pursuant to law; and the need of each such air carrier for compensation for the transportation of mail sufficient to insure the performance of such service, and, together with all other revenue of the air carrier, to enable such air carrier under honest, economical, and efficient management, to maintain and continue the development of air transportation to the extent and of the character and quality required for the commerce of the United States, the Postal Service, and the national defense.

Statement of Postmaster General and Carrier

(c) Any petition for the fixing of fair and reasonable rates of compensation under this section shall include a statement of the rate the petitioner believes to be fair and reasonable. The Postmaster General shall introduce as part of the record in all proceedings under this section a comprehensive statement of all service to be required of the air carrier and such other information in his possession as may be deemed by the Authority to be material to the inquiry.

Weighing of Mail

(d) The Postmaster General may weigh the mail transported by aircraft and make such computations for statistical and administrative purposes as may be required in the interest of the mail service. The Postmaster General is authorized to employ such clerical and other assistance as may be required in connection with proceedings under this Act. If the Authority shall determine that it is necessary or advisable, in order to carry out the provisions of this Act, to have additional and more frequent weighing of the mails, the Postmaster General, upon request of the Authority, shall provide therefor in like manner, but such weighing need not be for continuous periods of more than thirty days.

Availability of Appropriations

(e) Except as otherwise provided in section 405 (k), the unexpended balances of all appropriations for the transportation of mail by aircraft pursuant to contracts entered into under the Air Mail Act of 1934, as amended, and the unexpended balances of all appropriations available for the transportation of mail by aircraft in Alaska, shall be available, in addition to the purposes stated in such appropriations, for the payment of compensation by the Postmaster General, as provided in this Act, for the transportation of mail by aircraft, the facilities used and useful therefor, and the services connected therewith, between points in the continental United States or between points in Hawaii or in Alaska or between points in the continental United States and points in Canada within one hundred and fifty miles of the international boundary line. Except as otherwise provided in section 405 (k), the unexpended balances of all appropriations for the transportation of mail by aircraft pursuant to contracts entered into under the Act of March 8, 1928, as amended, shall be available in addition to the purposes stated in such appropriations, for payment to be made by the Postmaster General, as provided by this Act, in respect of the transportation of mail by aircraft, the facilities used and useful therefor, and the services connected therewith, between points in the United States and points outside thereof, or between points in the continental United States and Territories or possessions of the United States, or between Territories or possessions of the United States.

Payments to Foreign Air Carriers

(f) In any case where air transportation is performed between the United States and any foreign country, both by aircraft owned or operated by one or more air carriers holding a certificate under this title and by aircraft owned or operated by one or more foreign air carriers, the Postmaster General shall not pay to or for the account of any such foreign air carrier a rate of compensation for transporting mail by aircraft between the United States and such foreign country, which, in his opinion, will result (over such reasonable period as the Postmaster General may determine, taking account of exchange fluctuations and other factors) in such foreign air carrier receiving a higher rate of compensation for transporting such mail than such foreign country pays to air carriers for transporting its mail by aircraft between such foreign country and the United States, or receiving a higher rate of compensation for transporting such mail than a rate determined by the Postmaster General to be comparable to the rate such foreign country pays to air carriers for transporting its mail by aircraft between such foreign country and an intermediate country on the route of such air carrier between such foreign country and the United States.

Accounts, Records, and Reports

Filing of Reports

SEC. 407. (a) The Authority is empowered to require annual, monthly, periodical, and special reports from any air carrier; to prescribe the manner and form in which such reports shall be made; and to require from any air carrier specific answers to all questions upon which the Authority may deem information to be necessary. Such reports shall be under oath whenever the Authority so requires. The Authority may also require any air carrier to file with it a true copy of each or any contract, agreement, understanding, or arrangement, between such air carrier and any other carrier or person, in relation to any traffic affected by the provisions of this Act.

Disclosure of Stock Ownership

(b) Each air carrier shall submit annually, and at such other times as the Authority shall require, a list showing the names of each of its stockholders or members holding more than 5 per centum of the entire capital stock or capital, as the case may be, of such air carrier, together with the name of any person for whose account, if other than the holder, such stock is held; and a report setting forth a description of the shares of stock, or other interests, held by such air carrier, or for its account, in persons other than itself.

Disclosure of Stock Ownership by Officer or Director

(c) Each officer and director of an air carrier shall annually and at such other times as the Authority shall require transmit to the Authority a report describing the shares of stock or other interests held by him in any air carrier, any person engaged in any phase of aeronautics, or any common carrier, and in any person whose principal business, in purpose or in fact, is the holding of stock in, or control of, air carriers, other persons engaged in any phase of aeronautics, or common carriers.

Form of Accounts

(d) The Authority shall prescribe the forms of any and all accounts, records, and memoranda to be kept by air carriers, including the accounts, records, and memoranda of the movement of traffic, as well as of the receipts and expenditures of money, and the length of time such accounts, records, and memoranda shall be preserved; and it shall be unlawful for air carriers to keep any accounts, records, or memoranda other than those prescribed or approved by the Authority: *Provided,* That any air carrier may keep additional accounts, records, or memoranda if they do not impair the integrity of the accounts, records, or memoranda prescribed or approved by the Authority and do not constitute an undue financial burden on such air carrier.

Inspection of Accounts and Property

(e) The Authority shall at all times have access to all lands, buildings, and equipment of any carrier and to all accounts, records, and memoranda, including all documents, papers, and correspondence, now or hereafter existing, and kept or required to be kept by air carriers; and it may employ special agents or auditors, who shall have authority under the orders of the Authority to inspect and examine any and all such lands, buildings, equipment, accounts, records, and memoranda. The provisions of this section shall apply, to the extent found by the Authority to be reasonably necessary for the administration of this Act, to persons having control over any air carrier, or affiliated with any air carrier within the meaning of section 5 (8) of the Interstate Commerce Act, as amended.

Consolidation, Merger, and Acquisition of Control

Acts Prohibited

SEC. 408. (a) It shall be unlawful, unless approved by order of the Authority as provided in this section—

(1) For two or more air carriers, or for any air carrier and any other common carrier or any person engaged in any other phase of aeronautics, to consolidate or merge their properties, or any part thereof, into one person for the ownership, management or operation of the properties theretofore in separate ownerships;

(2) For any air carrier, any person controlling an air carrier, any other common carrier, or any person engaged in any other phase of aeronautics, to purchase, lease, or contract to operate the properties, or any substantial part thereof, of any air carrier;

(3) For any air carrier or person controlling an air carrier to purchase, lease, or contract to operate the properties, or any substantial part thereof, of any person engaged in any phase of aeronautics otherwise than as an air carrier;

(4) For any foreign air carrier or person controlling a foreign air carrier to acquire control, in any manner whatsoever, of any citizen of the United States engaged in any phase of aeronautics;

(5) For any air carrier or person controlling an air carrier, any other common carrier, or any person engaged in any other phase of aeronautics, to acquire control of any air carrier in any manner whatsoever;

(6) For any air carrier or person controlling an air carrier to acquire control, in any manner whatsoever, of any person engaged in any phase of aeronautics otherwise than as an air carrier; or

(7) For any person to continue to maintain any relationship established in violation of any of the foregoing subdivisions of this subsection.

Power of Authority

(b) Any person seeking approval of a consolidation, merger, purchase, lease, operating contract, or acquisition of control, specified in subsection (a) of this section, shall present an application to the Authority, and thereupon the Authority shall notify the persons involved in the consolidation, merger, purchase, lease, operating contract, or acquisition of control, and other persons known to have a substantial interest in the proceeding, of the time and place of a public hearing. Unless, after such hearing, the Authority finds that the consolidation, merger, purchase, lease, operating contract, or acquisiton of control will not be consistent with the public interest or that the conditions of this section will not be fulfilled, it shall by order, approve such consolidation, merger, purchase, lease, operating contract, or acquisition of control, upon such terms and conditions as it shall find to be just and reasonable and with such modifications as it may prescribe: *Provided further,* That the Authority shall not approve any consolidation, merger, purchase, lease, operating contract, or acquisition of control which would result in creating a monopoly or monopolies and thereby restrain competition or jeopardize another air carrier not a party to the consolidation, merger, purchase, lease, operating contract, or acquisition of control: *Provided further,* That if the applicant is a carrier other than an air carrier, or a person controlled by a carrier other than an air carrier or affiliated therewith within the meaning of section 5 (8) of the Interstate Commerce Act, as amended, such applicant shall for the purposes of this section be considered an air carrier and the Authority shall not enter such an order of approval unless it finds that the transaction proposed will promote the public interest by enabling such carrier other than an air carrier to use aircraft to public advantage in its operation and will not restrain competition.

Interests in Ground Facilities

(c) The provisions of this section and section 409 shall not apply with respect to the acquisition or holding by any air carrier, or any officer or director thereof, of (1) any interest in any ticket office, landing area, hangar, or other ground facility reasonably incidental to the performance by such air carrier of any of its services, or (2) any stock or other interest or any office or directorship in any person whose principal business is the maintenance or operation of any such ticket office, landing area, hangar, or other ground facility.

Jurisdiction of Accounts of Noncarriers

(d) Whenever, after the effective date of this section, a person, not an air carrier, is authorized, pursuant to this section, to acquire control of an air carrier, such person thereafter shall, to the extent found by the Authority to be reasonably necessary for the administration of this Act, be subject, in the same manner as if such person were an air carrier, to the provisions of this Act relating to accounts, records, and reports, and the inspection of facilities and records, including the penalties applicable in the case of violations thereof.

Investigation of Violations

(e) The Authority is empowered, upon complaint or upon its own initiative, to investigate and, after notice and hearing, to determine whether any person is violating any provision of subsection (a) of this section. If the Authority finds after such hearing that such person is violating any provision of such subsection, it shall by order require such person to take such action, consistent with the provisions of this Act, as may be necessary, in the opinion of the Authority, to prevent further violation of such provision.

Prohibited Interests

Interlocking Relationships

SEC. 409. (a) After one hundred and eighty days after the effective date of this section, it shall be unlawful, unless such relationship shall have been approved by order of the Authority upon due showing, in the form and manner prescribed by the Authority, that the public interest will not be adversely affected thereby—

(1) For any air carrier to have and retain an officer or director who is an officer, director, or member, or who as a stockholder holds a controlling interest, in any other person who is a common carrier or is engaged in any phase of aeronautics.

(2) For any air carrier, knowingly and willfully, to have and retain an officer or director who has a representative or nominee who represents such officer or director as an officer, director, or member, or as a stockholder holding a controlling interest, in any other person who is a common carrier or is engaged in any phase of aeronautics.

(3) For any person who is an officer or director of an air carrier to hold the position of officer, director, or member, or to be a stockholder holding a controlling interest, or to have a representative or nominee who represents such person as an officer, director, or member, or as a stockholder holding a controlling interest, in any other person who is a common carrier or is engaged in any phase of aeronautics.

(4) For any air carrier to have and retain an officer or director who is an officer, director, or member, or who as a stockholder holds a controlling interest, in any person whose principal business, in purpose or in fact, is the holding of stock in, or control of, any other person engaged in any phase of aeronautics.

(5) For any air carrier, knowingly and willfully, to have and retain an officer or director who has a representative or nominee who represents such officer or director as an officer, director, or member, or as a stockholder holding a controlling interest, in any person on whose principal business, in purpose or in fact, is the holding of stock in, or control of, any other person engaged in any phase of aeronautics.

(6) For any person who is an officer or director of an air carrier to hold the position of officer, director, or member, or to be a stockholder holding a controlling interest, or to have a representative or nominee who represents such person as an officer, director, or member, or as a stockholder holding a controlling interest, in any person whose principal business, in purpose or in fact, is the holding of stock in, or control of, any other person engaged in any phase of aeronautics.

Profit from Transfer of Securities

(b) After this section takes effect it shall be unlawful for any officer or director of any air carrier to receive for his own benefit, directly or indirectly, any money or thing of value in respect of negotiation, hypothecation, or sale of any securities issued or to be issued by such carrier, or to share in any of the proceeds thereof.

Loans and Financial Aid

SEC. 410. The Authority is empowered to approve or disapprove, in whole or in part, any and all applications made after the effective date of this section for or in connection with any loan or other financial aid from the United States or any agency thereof to, or for the benefit of, any air carrier. No such loan or financial aid shall be made or given without such approval, and the terms and conditions upon which such loan or financial aid is provided shall be prescribed by the Authority.

Methods of Competition

SEC. 411. The Authority may, upon its own initiative or upon complaint by any air carrier or foreign air carrier, if it considers that such action by it would be in the interest of the public, investigate and determine whether any air carrier or foreign air carrier has been or is engaged in unfair or deceptive practices or unfair methods of competition in air transportation. If the Authority shall find, after notice and hearing, that such air carrier or foreign air carrier is engaged in such unfair or deceptive practices or unfair methods of competition, it shall order such air carrier or foreign air carrier to cease and desist from such practices or methods of competition.

Pooling and Other Agreements

Filing of Agreements Required

SEC. 412. (a) Every air carrier shall file with the Authority a true copy, or, if oral, a true and complete memorandum, of every contract or agreement (whether enforceable by provisions for liquidated damages, penalties, bonds, or otherwise) affecting air transportation and in force on the effective date of this section or hereafter entered into, or any modification or cancelation thereof, between such air carrier and any other air carrier, foreign air carrier, or other carrier for pooling or apportioning earnings, losses, traffic, service, or equipment, or relating to the establishment of transportation rates, fares, charges, or classifications, or for preserving and improving safety, economy, and efficiency of operation, or for controlling, regulating, preventing, or otherwise eliminating destructive, oppressive, or wasteful competition, or for regulating stops, schedules, and character of service, or for other cooperative working arrangements.

Approval by Authority

(b) The Authority shall by order disapprove any such contract or agreement, whether or not previously approved by it, that it finds to be adverse to the public interest, or in violation of this Act, and shall by order approve any such contract or agreement, or any modification or cancelation thereof, that it does not find to be adverse to the public interest, or in violation of this Act.

Form of Control

SEC. 413. For the purposes of this title, whenever reference is made to control, it is immaterial whether such control is direct or indirect.

Legal Restraints

SEC. 414. Any person affected by any order made under sections 408, 409, or 412 of this Act shall be, and is hereby, relieved from the operations of the "antitrust laws," as designated in section 1 of the Act entitled "An Act to supplement existing laws against unlawful restraints and monopolies, and for other purposes," approved

October 15, 1914, and of all other restraints or prohibitions made by, or imposed under, authority of law, insofar as may be necessary to enable such person to do anything authorized, approved, or required by such order.

Inquiry into Air Carrier Management

SEC. 415. For the purpose of exercising and performing its powers and duties under this Act, the Authority is empowered to inquire into the management of the business of any air carrier and, to the extent reasonably necessary for any such inquiry, to obtain from such carrier, and from any person controlling or controlled by, or under common control with, such air carrier, full and complete reports and other information.

Classification and Exemptions of Carriers

Classification

SEC. 416. (a) The Authority may from time to time establish such just and reasonable classifications or groups of air carriers for the purposes of this title as the nature of the services performed by such air carriers shall require; and such just and reasonable rules, and regulations, pursuant to and consistent with the provisions of this title, to be observed by each such class or group, as the Authority finds necessary in the public interest.

Exemptions

(b) (1) The Authority, from time to time and to the extent necessary, may (except as provided in paragraph (2) of this subsection) exempt from the requirements of this title or any provision thereof, or any rule, regulation, term, condition, or limitation prescribed thereunder, any air carrier or class of air carriers, if it finds that the enforcement of this title or such provision, or such rule, regulation, term, condition, or limitation is or would be an undue burden on such air carrier or class of air carriers by reason of the limited extent of, or unusual circumstances affecting, the operations of such air carrier or class of air carriers and is not in the public interest.

(2) The Authority shall not exempt any air carrier from any provision of subsection (1) of section 401 of this title, except that (A) any air carrier is not engaged in scheduled air transportation, and (B), to the extent that the operations of such air carrier are conducted during daylight hours, any air carrier engaged in scheduled air transportation, may be exempted from the provisions of paragraphs (1) and (2) of such subsection if the Authority finds, after notice and hearing, that, by reason of the limited extent of, or unusual circumstances affecting, the operations of any such air

carrier, the enforcement of such paragraphs is or would be such an undue burden on such air carrier as to obstruct its development and prevent it from beginning or continuing operations, and that the exemption of such air carrier from such paragraphs would not adversely affect the public interest: *Provided,* That nothing in this subsection shall be deemed to authorize the Authority to exempt any air carrier from any requirement of this title, or any provision thereof, or any rule, regulation, term, condition, or limitation prescribed thereunder which provides for maximum flying hours for pilots or copilots.

TITLE V—NATIONALITY AND OWNERSHIP OF AIRCRAFT

Registration of Aircraft Nationality

Registration Required

SEC. 501. (a) It shall be unlawful for any person to operate or navigate any aircraft eligible for registration if such aircraft is not registered by its owner as provided in this section, or (except as provided in section 6 of the Air Commerce Act of 1926, as amended) to operate or navigate within the United States any aircraft not eligible for registration: *Provided,* That aircraft of the national defense forces of the United States may be operated and navigated without being so registered if such aircraft are identified, by the agency having jurisdiction over them, in a manner satisfactory to the Authority. The Authority may, by regulation, permit the operation and navigation of aircraft without registration by the owner for such reasonable periods after transfer of ownership thereof as the Authority may prescribe.

Eligibility for Registration

(b) An aircraft shall be eligible for registraion if, but only if—

(1) It is owned by a citizen of the United States and is not registered under the laws of any foreign country; or

(2) It is an aircraft of the Federal Government, or of a State, Territory, or possession of the United States, or the District of Columbia, or of a political subdivision thereof.

Issuance of Certificate

(c) Upon request of the owner of any aircraft eligible for registration, such aircraft shall be registered by the Authority and the Authority shall issue to the owner thereof a certificate of registration.

Applications

(d) Applications for such certificates shall be in such form, be filed in such manner, and contain such information as the Authority may require.

Suspension or Revocation

(e) Any such certificate may be suspended or revoked by the Authority for any cause which renders the aircraft ineligible for registration.

Effect of Registration

(f) Such certificate shall be conclusive evidence of nationality for international purposes, but not in any proceeding under the laws of the United States. Registration shall not be evidence of ownership of aircraft in any proceeding in which such ownership by a particular person is, or may be, in issue.

Registration of Engines, Propellers, and Appliances

SEC. 502. The Authority may establish reasonable rules and regulations for registration and identification of aircraft engines, propellers, and appliances, in the interest of safety, and no aircraft engine, propeller, or appliance shall be used in violation of any such rule or regulation.

Recordation of Aircraft Ownership

Establishment of Recording System

SEC. 503. (a) The Authority shall establish and maintain a system for recording all conveyances affecting the title to, or interest in, any civil aircraft of the United States.

Conveyances to be Recorded

(b) No conveyance made or given on or after the effective date of this section, which affects the title to, or interest in, any civil aircraft of the United States, or any portion thereof, shall be valid in respect of such aircraft or portion thereof against any person other than the person by whom the conveyance is made or given, his heir or devisee, and any person having actual notice thereof, until such conveyance is recorded in the office of the secretary of the Authority. Every such conveyance so recorded in the office of the secretary of the Authority shall be valid as to all persons without further recordation. Any instrument, recordation of which is required by the provisions of this section, shall take effect from the date of its recordation, and not from the date of its execution.

Form of Conveyance

(c) No conveyance shall be recorded unless it states the interest in the aircraft of the person by whom such conveyance is made or given or, in the case of a contract of conditional sale, the interest of the vendor, and states the interest transferred by the conveyance, and unless it shall have been acknowledged before a notary public or other officer authorized by law of the United States, or of a State, Territory, or possession thereof, or the District of Columbia, to take acknowledgement of deeds.

Index of Conveyances

(d) The Authority shall record conveyances delivered to it in the order of their reception, in files to be kept for that purpose, and indexed to show—
   (1) the identifying description of the aircraft;
   (2) the names of the parties to the conveyance;
   (3) the time and date of reception of the instrument and the time and date of recordation thereof;
   (4) the interest in the aircraft transferred by the conveyance; and
   (5) if such conveyance is made as security for indebtedness, the amount and date of maturity of such indebtedness.

Regulations

(e) The Authority is authorized to provide by regulation for the endorsement upon certificates of registration, or aircraft certificates, of information with respect to the ownership of the aircraft for which each certificate is issued, for the recording of discharges and satisfactions of recorded instruments and other transactions affecting title to, or interest in, aircraft, and for such other records, proceedings, and details as may be necessary to facilitate the determination of the rights of parties dealing with civil aircraft of the United States.

Previously Unrecorded Ownership

(f) The person applying for the issuance or renewal of an airworthiness certificate for an aircraft with respect to which there has been no recordation of ownership as provided in this section shall present with his application such information with respect to the ownership of the aircraft as the Authority shall deem necessary to show the persons who are holders of property interests in such aircraft and the nature and extent of such interests.

TITLE VI—CIVIL AERONAUTICS SAFETY REGULATION

General Safety Powers and Duties

Minimum Standards; Rules and Regulations

SEC. 601. (a) The Authority is empowered, and it shall be its duty to promote safety of flight in air commerce by prescribing and revising from time to time—

(1) Such minimum standards governing the design, materials, workmanship, construction, and performance of aircraft, aircraft engines, and propellers as may be required in the interest of safety;

(2) Such minimum standards governing appliances as may be required in the interest of safety;

(3) Reasonable rules and regulations and minimum standards governing, in the interests of safety, (A) the inspection, servicing, and overhaul of aircraft, aircraft engines, propellers, and appliances; (B) the equipment and facilities for such inspection, servicing, and overhaul; and (C) in the discretion of the Authority, the periods for, and the manner in, which such inspection, servicing, and overhaul shall be made, including provision for examinations and reports by properly qualified private persons whose examinations or reports the Authority may accept in lieu of those made by its officers and employees;

(4) Reasonable rules and regulations governing the reserve supply of aircraft, aircraft engines, propellers, appliances, and aircraft fuel and oil, required in the interest of safety, including the reserve supply of aircraft fuel and oil which shall be carried in flight;

(5) Reasonable rules and regulations governing, in the interest of safety, the maximum hours or periods of service of airmen, and other employees, of air carriers;

(6) Such reasonable rules and regulations, or minimum standards, governing other practices, methods, and procedure, as the Authority may find necessary to provide adequately for safety in air commerce; and

(7) Air traffic rules governing the flight of, and for the navigation, protection, and identification of, aircraft, including rules as to safe altitudes of flight and rules for the prevention of collisions between aircraft, and between aircraft and land or water vehicles.

Needs of Service to Be Considered; Classifications of Standards, and so Forth

(b) In prescribing standards, rules, and regulations, and in issuing certificates under this title, the Authority shall give full consideration to the duty resting upon air carriers to perform their services with the highest possible degree of safety in the public interest and to any differences between air transportation and other air commerce; and it shall make classifications of such standards, rules, and regulations, and certificates appropriate to the differences between air transportation and other air commerce. The Authority may authorize any aircraft, aircraft engine, propeller, or appliance, for which an aircraft certificate authorizing use thereof in air transportation has been issued, to be used in other air commerce without the issuance of a further certificate. The Authority shall exercise and perform its powers and duties under this Act in such manner as will best tend to reduce or eliminate the possibility of, or recurrence of, accidents in air transportation, but shall not deem itself required to give preference to either air transportation or other air commerce in the administration and enforcement of this title.

Airman Certificates

Power to Issue Certificate

SEC. 602. (a) The Authority is empowered to issue airman certificates specifying the capacity in which the holders thereof are authorized to serve as airmen in connection with aircraft.

Issuance of Certificate

(b) Any person may file with the Authority an application for an airman certificate. If the Authority finds, after investigation, that such person possesses proper qualifications for, and is physically able to perform the duties pertaining to, the position for which the airman certificate is sought, it shall issue such certificate, containing such terms, conditions, and limitations as to duration thereof, periodic or special examinations, tests of physical fitness, and other matters as the Authority may determine to be necessary to assure safety in air commerce. Any person whose application for the issuance or renewal of an airman certificate is denied may file with the Authority a petition for reconsideration, and the Authority shall thereupon assign such application for hearing at a place convenient to the applicant's place of residence or employment: *Provided,* That the Authority may, in its discretion, prohibit or restrict the issuance of airman certificates to aliens, or may make such issuance dependent on the terms of reciprocal agreements entered into with foreign governments.

Form and Recording of Certificate

(c) Each certificate shall be numbered and recorded by the Authority; shall state the name and address of, and contain a description of, the person to whom the certificate is issued; and shall be entitled with the designation of the class covered thereby. Certificates issued to all pilots serving in scheduled air transportation shall be designated "airline transport pilot" of the proper class.

Aircraft Certificates

Type Certificates

SEC. 603. (a) (1) The Authority is empowered to issue type certificates for aircraft, aircraft engines, and propellers; to specify in regulations for appliances for which the issuance of type certificates is reasonably required in the interest of safety; and to issue such certificates for appliances so specified.

(2) Any interested person may file with the Authority an application for a type certificate for an aircraft, aircraft engine, propeller, or appliance specified in regulations under paragraph (1) of this subsection. Upon receipt of an application, the Authority shall make an investigation thereof and may hold hearings thereon. The Authority shall make, or require the applicant to make, such tests during manufacture and upon completion as the Authority deems reasonably necessary in the interest of safety, including flight tests and tests of raw materials or any part of appurtenance of such aircraft, aircraft engine, propeller, or appliance. If the Authority finds that such aircraft, aircraft engine, propeller, or appliance is of proper design, material, specification, construction, and performance for safe operation, and meets the minimum standards, rules, and regulations prescribed by the Authority, it shall issue a type certificate therefor. The Authority may prescribe in any such certificate the duration thereof and such other terms, conditions, and limitations as are required in the interest of safety. The Authority may record upon any certificate issued for aircraft, aircraft engines, or propellers, a numerical determination of all of the essential factors relative to the performance of the aircraft, aircraft engine, or propeller for which the certificate is issued.

Production Certificate

(b) Upon application, and if it satisfactorily appears to the Authority that duplicates of any aircraft, aircraft engine, propeller, or appliance for which a type certificate has been issued will conform to such certificate, the Authority shall issue a production certificate authorizing the production of duplicates of such aircraft, aircraft engines, propellers, or appliances. The Authority shall make such inspection and may require such tests of any aircraft, aircraft engine, propeller, or appliance manufactured under a production certificate as may be necessary to assure manufacture of each unit in conformity with the type certificate or any amendment or modification thereof. The Authority may prescribe in any such production certificate the duration thereof and such other terms, conditions, and limitations as are required in the interest of safety.

Airworthiness Certificate

(c) The registered owner of any aircraft may file with the Authority an application for an airworthiness certificate for such aircraft. If the Authority finds that the aircraft conforms to the type certificate therefor, and, after inspection, that the aircraft is in condition for safe operation, it shall issue an airworthiness certificate. The Authority may prescribe in such certificate the duration of such certificate, the type of service for which the aircraft may be used, and such other terms, conditions, and limitations as are required in the interest of safety. Each such certificate shall be registered by the Authority and shall set forth such information as the Authority may deem advisable. The certificate number, or such other individual designation as may be required by the Authority, shall be displayed upon each aircraft in accordance with regulations prescribed by the Authority.

Air Carrier Operating Certificates

Power to Issue

SEC. 604. (a) The Authority is empowered to issue air carrier operating certificates and to establish minimum safety standards for the operation of the air carrier to whom any such certificate is issued.

Issuance

(b) Any person desiring to operate as an air carrier may file with the Authority an application for an air carrier operating certificate. If the Authority finds, after investigation, that such person is properly and adequately equipped and able to conduct a safe operation in accordance with the requirements of this Act and the rules, regulations, and standards prescribed thereunder, it shall issue an air carrier operating certificate to such person. Each air carrier operating certificate shall prescribe such terms, conditions, and limitations as are reasonably necessary to assure safety in air transportation, and shall specify the points to and from which, and the civil airways over which, such person is authorized to operate as an air carrier under an air carrier operating certificate.

Maintenance of Equipment in Air Transportation

Duty of Carriers and Airmen

SEC. 605. (a) It shall be the duty of each air carrier to make, or cause to be made, such inspection, maintenance, overhaul, and repair of all equipment used in air transportation as may be required by this Act, or the orders, rules, and regulations of the Authority issued thereunder. And it shall be the duty of every person engaged in operating, inspecting, maintaining, or overhauling equipment to observe and comply with the requirements of this Act relating thereto, and the orders, rules, and regulations issued thereunder.

Inspection

(b) The Authority shall employ inspectors who shall be charged with the duty (1) of making such inspections of aircraft, aircraft engines, propellers, and appliances designed for use in air transportation, during manufacture, and while used by an air carrier in air transportation, as may be necessary to enable the Authority to determine that such aircraft, aircraft engines, propellers, and appliances are in safe condition and are properly maintained for operation in air transportation; and (2) of advising and cooperating with each air carrier in the inspection and maintenance thereof by the air carrier. Whenever any inspector shall, in the performance of his duty, find that any aircraft, aircraft engine, propeller, or appliance used or intended to be used by any air carrier in air transportation, is not in condition for safe operation, he shall so notify the carrier, in such form and manner as the Authority may prescribe; and, for a period of five days thereafter, such aircraft, aircraft engine, propeller, or appliance shall not be used in air transportation, or in such manner as to endanger air transportation, unless found by the Authority or its inspector to be in condition for safe operation.

Air Navigation Facility Rating

SEC. 606. The Authority is empowered to inspect, classify, and rate any air navigation facility available for the use of civil aircraft of the United States, as to its suitability for such use. The Authority is empowered to issue a certificate for any such air navigation facility.

Air Agency Rating

SEC. 607. The Authority is empowered to provide for the examination and rating of (1) civilian schools giving instruction in flying or in the repair, alteration, maintenance, and overhaul of aircraft, aircraft engines, propellers, and appliances, as to the adequacy of the course of instruction, the suitability and airworthiness of the equipment, and the competency of the instructors; (2) repair stations or shops for the repair, alteration, maintenance, and overhaul of aircraft, aircraft engines, propellers, or appliances, as to the adequacy and suitability of the equipment, facilities, and materials for, and methods of, repair, alteration, maintenance, and overhaul of aircraft, aircraft engines, propellers, and appliances, and the competency of those engaged in the work or giving any instruction therein; and (3) such other air agencies as may, in its opinion, be necessary in the interest of the public. The Authority is empowered to issue certificates for such schools, repair stations, and other agencies.

Form of Applications

SEC. 608. Applications for certificates under this title shall be in such form, contain such information, and be filed and served in such manner as the Authority may prescribe, and shall be under oath whenever the Authority so requires.

Amendment, Suspension, and Revocation of Certificates

SEC. 609. The Authority may, from time to time, reinspect any aircraft, aircraft engine, propeller, appliance, air navigation facility, or air agency, may reexamine any airman, and, after investigation, and upon notice and hearing, may alter, amend, modify, or suspend, in whole or in part, any type certificate, production certificate, airworthiness certificate, airman certificate, air carrier operating certificate, air navigation facility certificate, or air agency certificate if the interest of the public so requires, or may revoke, in whole or in part, any such certificate for any cause which, at the time of revocation, would justify the Authority in refusing to issue to the holder of such certificate a like certificate. In cases of emergency, any such certificate may be suspended, in whole or in part, for a period not in excess of thirty days without regard to any requirement as to notice and hearing. The Authority shall immediately give notice of such suspension to the holder of such certificate and shall enter upon a hearing which shall be disposed of as speedily as possible. During the pendency of the proceeding the Authority may further suspend such certificate, in whole or in part, for an additional period not in excess of thirty days.

Prohibitions

Violations of Title

SEC. 610. (a) It shall be unlawful—

(1) For any person to operate in air commerce any civil aircraft for which there is not currently in effect an airworthiness certificate, or in violation of the terms of any such certificate;

(2) For any person to serve in any capacity as an airman in connection with any civil aircraft used in air commerce without an airman certificate authorizing him to serve in such capacity, or in violation of the terms of any such certificate;

(3) For any person to employ for service in connection with any civil aircraft used in air commerce an airman who does not have an airman certificate authorizing him to serve in the capacity for which he is employed;

(4) For any person to operate as an air carrier without an air carrier operating certificate, or in violation of the terms of any such certificate; and

(5) For any person to operate aircraft in air commerce in violation of any other rule, regulation, or certificate of the Authority under this title.

Exemption of Foreign Aircraft and Airmen

(b) Foreign aircraft and airmen serving in connection therewith may, except with respect to the observance by such airmen of the air traffic rules, be exempted from the provisions of subsection (a) of this section, to the extent, and upon such terms and conditions, as may be prescribed by the Authority as being in the interest of the public.

TITLE VII—AIR SAFETY BOARD

Creation and Organization of Board

Appointment of Board

SEC. 701. (a) There is created and established within the Authority an Air Safety Board. Such Board shall consist of three members to be appointed by the President by and with the advice and consent of the Senate. One of the members shall, at the time of his nomination, be an active airline pilot and shall have flown not less than three thousand hours in scheduled air transportation. Each member of the Board shall be a citizen of the United States, and shall continue in office as designated by the President at the time of nomination until the last day of the second, fourth, and sixth calendar years, respectively, following the passage of this Act, but their successors shall be appointed for terms of six years, except that any person appointed to fill a vacancy occurring prior to the expiration of the term for which his predecessor was appointed shall be appointed only for the remainder of such term. Any member of the Board may be appointed to succeed himself. The Board shall annually elect one of its members as chairman of the Board. Each member of the Board shall receive a salary of $7,500 per annum. No member of the Board shall have any pecuniary interest in or own any stock in or bonds of any civil aeronautics enterprise.

Personnel

(b) Subject to the provisions of the civil-service laws and the Classification Act of 1923, as amended, the Board shall appoint, fix the salaries, and prescribe the duties, of such assistants and other employees as it shall deem necessary in exercising and performing its powers and duties under this Act. Such of the personnel transferred to the Authority from the Department of Commerce under section 203 of this Act as were regularly employed in the investigation and analysis of accidents in air commerce prior to such transfer may, upon request of the Board, be transferred to the Board.

Temporary Personnel

(c) The Board may, without regard to the civil-service laws, engage, for temporary service in the investigation of any accident involving aircraft, persons other than officers or employees of the United States and may fix their compensation without regard to the Classification Act of 1923, as amended; and may, with the consent of the head of the executive department or independent establishment under whose jurisdiction the officer or employee is serving, secure for such service any officer or employee of the United States.

Authorization of Expenditures

(d) All expenses incurred by the Board in the investigation of accidents, or for the maintenance or operation of aircraft acquired for the use of the Board, shall be allowed upon vouchers approved by the chairman of the Board. The members and assistants of the Board are authorized to travel in the same manner as employees of the Authority.

Preservation of Records and Reports

(e) The records and reports of the Board shall be preserved in the custody of the secretary of the Authority in the same manner and subject to the same provisions respecting publication as the records and reports of the Authority, except that any publication thereof shall be styled "Air Safety Board of the Civil Aeronautics Authority," and that no part of any report or reports of the Board or the Authority relating to any accident, or the investigation thereof, shall be admitted as evidence or used in any suit or action for damages growing out of any matter mentioned in such report or reports.

Duties of the Board

General Duties

SEC. 702. (a) It shall be the duty of the Board to—
(1) Make rules and regulations, subject to the approval of the Authority, governing notification and report of accidents involving aircraft;

(2) Investigate such accidents and report to the Authority the facts, conditions, and circumstances relating to each accident and the probable cause thereof;

(3) Make such recommendations to the Authority as, in its opinion, will tend to prevent similar accidents in the future;

(4) Make such reports and recommendations public in such form and manner as may be deemed by it to be in the public interest; and

(5) Assist the Authority in ascertaining what will best tend to reduce or eliminate the possibility of, or recurrence of, accidents by investigating such complaints filed with the Authority or the Board, and by conducting such special studies and investigations, on matters pertaining to safety in air navigation and the prevention of accidents, as may be requested or approved by the Authority.

Manner of Performance

(b) The Board shall exercise and perform its powers and duties independently of the Authority and shall not be assigned any duties in, or in connection with, any other section or unit of the Authority.

Conduct of Investigations

(c) In conducting any hearing or investigation, any member of the Board or any other officer or employee of the Board or any other person engaged or secured under subsection (c) of section 701 shall have the same powers as the examiners or other employees of the Authority have with respect to hearings or investigations conducted by the Authority.

Aircraft

(d) Any aircraft, aircraft engine, propeller, or appliance affected by, or involved in, an accident in air commerce shall be preserved in accordance with, and shall not be moved except in accordance with, regulations prescribed by the Board.

TITLE VIII—OTHER ADMINISTRATIVE AGENCIES

The President of the United States

SEC. 801. The issuance, denial, transfer, amendment, cancelation, suspension, or revocation of, and the terms, conditions, and limitations contained in, any certificate authorizing an air carrier to engage in overseas or foreign air transportation, or air transportation between places in the same Territory or possession, or any permit issuable to any foreign air carrier under section 402, shall be subject to the approval of the President. Copies of all applications in respect of such certificates and permits shall be transmitted to the President by the Authority before hearing thereon, and all decisions thereon by the Authority shall be submitted to the President before publication thereof. This section shall not apply to the issuance or denial of any certificate issuable under section 401 (e) or any permit issuable under section 402 (c) or to the original terms, conditions, or limitations of any such certificate or permit.

The Department of State

SEC. 802. The Secretary of State shall advise the Authority of, and consult with the Authority concerning, the negotiation of any agreements with foreign governments for the establishment or development of air navigation, including air routes and services.

Weather Bureau

SEC. 803. In order to promote the safety and efficiency of aircraft to the highest possible degree, the Chief of the Weather Bureau, under the direction of the Secretary of Agriculture, shall, in addition to any other functions or duties pertaining to weather information for other purposes, (1) make such observations, measurements, investigations, and studies of atmospheric phenomena, and establish such meteorological offices and stations, as are necessary or best suited for ascertaining, in advance, information concerning probable weather conditions; (2) furnish such reports, forecasts, warnings, and advices to the Authority, and to such air carriers and other persons engaged in civil aeronautics as may be designated by the Authority, and to such other persons as the Chief of the Weather Bureau may determine, and such reports shall be made in such manner and with such frequency as will best result in safety in air navigation; (3) cooperate with any person employed by air carriers in meteorological service; and (4) detail annually not to exceed ten members of the Weather Bureau personnel for training at Government expense, either at civilian institutions or otherwise, in advanced methods of meteorological science: *Provided,* That no such member shall lose his individual status or seniority rating in the Bureau merely by reason of absence due to such training.

TITLE IX—PENALTIES

Civil Penalties

Safety and Postal Offenses

SEC. 901. (a) Any person who violates (1) any provision of titles V, VI, and VII of this Act, or any provision of subsection (a) (1) of section 11 of the Air Commerce Act of 1926, as amended, or (2) any rule or regulation issued by the Postmaster General under this Act, shall be subject to a civil penalty of not to exceed $1,000 for each such violation. Any such penalty may be compromised by the Authority or the Postmaster General, as the case may be. The amount of such penalty, when finally determined, or the amount agreed upon in compromise, may be deducted from any sums owing by the United States to the person charged.

Liens

(b) In case an aircraft is involved in such violation and the violation is by the owner or person in command of the aircraft, such aircraft shall be subject to lien for the penalty: *Provided,* That this subsection shall not apply to a violation of a rule or regulation of the Postmaster General.

Criminal Penalties

General

SEC. 902. (a) Any person who knowingly and willfully violates any provision of this Act (except titles V, VI, and VII), or any order, rule, or regulation issued under any such provision or any term, condition, or limitation of any certificate or permit issued under title IV, for which no penalty is otherwise herein provided, shall be deemed guilty of a misdemeanor and upon conviction thereof shall be subject for the first offense to a fine of not more than $500, and for any subsequent offense to a fine of not more than $2,000. If such violation is a continuing one, each day of such violation shall constitute a separate offense.

Forgery of Certificates

(b) Any person who knowingly and willfully forges, counterfeits, alters, or falsely makes any certificate authorized to be issued under this Act, or knowingly uses or attempts to use any such fraudulent certificate, shall be deemed guilty of a misdemenor and upon conviction thereof shall be subject to a fine of not exceeding $1,000 or to imprisonment not exceeding three years, or to both such fine and imprisonment.

Interference With Air Navigation

(c) A person shall be subject to a fine of not exceeding $5,000 or to imprisonment not exceeding five years, or to both such fine and imprisonment, who—

(1) with intent to interfere with air navigation within the United States, exhibits within the United States any light or signal at such place or in such manner that it is likely to be mistaken for a true light or signal in connection with an airport or other air navigation facility; or

(2) after due warning by the Administrator, continues to maintain any misleading light or signal; or

(3) knowingly removes, extinguishes, or interferes with the operation of any such true light or signal.

Granting Rebates

(d) Any air carrier or foreign air carrier, or any officer, agent, employee, or representative thereof, who shall, knowingly and willfully, offer, grant, or give, or cause to be offered, granted, or given, any rebate or other concession in violation of the provisions of this Act, or who, by any device or means, shall, knowingly and willfully, assist, or shall willingly suffer or permit, any person to obtain transportation or services subject to this Act at less than the rates, fares, or charges lawfully in effect, shall be deemed guilty of a misdemeanor and, upon conviction thereof, shall be subject for each offense to a fine of not less than $100 and not more than $5,000.

Failure to File Reports; Falsification of Records

(e) Any air carrier, or any officer, agent, employee, or representative thereof, who shall, knowingly and willfully, fail or refuse to make a report to the Authority as required by this Act, or to keep or preserve accounts, records, and memoranda in the form and manner prescribed or approved by the Authority, or shall, knowingly and willfully, falsify, mutilate, or alter any such report, account, record, or memorandum, or shall knowingly and willfully file any false report, account, record, or memorandum, shall be deemed guilty of a misdemeanor and, upon conviction thereof, be subject for each offense to a fine of not less than $100 and not more than $5,000.

Divulging Information

(f) If any member of the Authority or the Air Safety Board, or the Administrator, or any officer or employee of any of them, shall knowingly and willfully divulge any fact or information which may come to his knowledge during the course of an examination of the accounts, records, and memoranda of any air carrier, or which is withheld from public disclosure under section 1104, except as he may be directed by the Authority, or the Air Safety Board in the case of information ordered to be withheld by it, or by a court of competent jurisdiction or a judge thereof, he shall upon conviction thereof be subject for each offense to a fine of not more than $5,000 or imprisonment for not more than two years, or both.

Refusal to Testify

(g) Any person who shall neglect or refuse to attend and testify, or to answer any lawful inquiry, or to produce books, papers, or documents, if in his power to do so, in obedience to the subpena or lawful requirement of the Authority or the Air Safety Board, shall be guilty of a misdemeanor and, upon conviction thereof, shall be subject to a fine of not less than $100 nor more than $5,000, or imprisonment for not more than one year, or both.

Venue and Prosecution of Offenses

Venue

SEC. 903. (a) The trial of any offense under this Act shall be in the district in which such offense is committed; or if the offense is committed upon the high seas, or out of the jurisdiction of any particular State or district, the trial shall be in the district where the offender may be found or into which he shall be first brought. Whenever the offense is begun in one jurisdiction and completed in another it may be dealt with, inquired of, tried, determined, and punished in either jurisdiction in the same manner as if the offense had been actually and wholly committed therein.

Procedure in Respect of Civil Penalties

(b) (1) Any civil penalty imposed under this Act may be collected by proceedings in personam against the person subject to the penalty and, in case the penalty is a lien, by proceedings in rem against the aircraft, or by either method alone. Such proceedings shall conform as nearly as may be to civil suits in admiralty, except that either party may demand trial by jury of any issue of fact, if the value in controversy exceeds $20, and the facts so tried shall not be reexamined other than in accordance with the rules of the common law. The fact that in a libel in rem the seizure is made at a place not upon the high seas or navigable waters of the United States shall not not be held in any way to limit the requirement of the conformity of the proceedings to civil suits in rem in admiralty.

(2) Any aircraft subject to such lien may be summarily seized by and placed in the custody of such persons as the Authority may by regulation prescribe, and a report of the cause shall thereupon be transmitted to the United States attorney for the judicial district in which the seizure is made. The United States attorney shall promptly institute proceedings for the enforcement of the lien or notify the Authority of his failure so to act.

(3) The aircraft shall be released from such custody upon payment of the penalty or the amount agreed upon in compromise; or seizure in pursuance of process of any court in proceedings in rem for enforcement of the lien, or notification by the United States attorney of failure to institute such proceedings; or deposit of a bond in such amount and with such sureties as the Authority may prescribe, conditioned upon the payment of the penalty or the amount agreed upon in compromise.

(4) The Supreme Court of the United States, and under its direction other courts of the United States, may prescribe rules regulating such proceedings in any particular not provided by law.

TITLE X–PROCEDURE

Conduct of Proceedings

SEC. 1001. The Authority may conduct its proceedings in such manner as will be conducive to the proper dispatch of business and to the ends of justice. No member of the Authority shall participate in any hearing or proceedings in which he has a pecuniary interest. Any person may appear before the Authority and be heard in person or by attorney. Every vote and official act of the Authority shall be entered of record, and its proceedings shall be open to the public upon the request of any interested party unless the Authority determines that secrecy is requisite on grounds of national defense.

Complaints to and Investigations by the Authority

Filing of Complaints Authorized

SEC. 1002. (a) Any person may file with the Authority a complaint in writing with respect to anything done or omitted to be done by any person in contravention of any provision of this Act, or of any requirement established pursuant thereto. If the person complained against shall not satisfy the complaint and there shall appear to be any reasonable ground for investigating the complaint, it shall be the duty of the Authority to investigate the matters complained of. Whenever the Authority is of the opinion that any complaint does not state facts which warrant an investigation or action on its part, it may dismiss such complaint without hearing.

Investigations on Initiative of Authority

(b) The Authority is empowered at any time to institute an investigation, on its own initiative, in any case and as to any matter or thing concerning which complaint is authorized to be made to or before the Authority by any provision of this Act, or concerning which any question may arise under any of the provisions of this Act, or relating to the enforcement of any of the provisions of this Act. The Authority shall have the same power to proceed with any investigation instituted on its own motion as though it had been appealed to by complaint.

Entry of Orders for Compliance With Act

(c) If the Authority finds, after notice and hearing, in any investigation instituted upon complaint or upon its own initiative, that any person has failed to comply with any provision of this Act or any requirement established pursuant thereto, the Authority shall issue an appropriate order to compel such person to comply therewith.

Power to Prescribe Rates and Practices of Air Carriers

(d) Whenever, after notice and hearing, upon complaint, or upon its own initiative, the Authority shall be of the opinion that any individual or joint rate, fare, or charge demanded, charged, collected or received by any air carrier for interstate or overseas air transportation, or any classification, rule, regulation, or practice affecting such rate, fare, or charge, or the value of the service thereunder, is or will be unjust or unreasonable, or unjustly discriminatory, or unduly preferential, or unduly prejudicial, the Authority shall determine and prescribe the lawful rate, fare, or charge (or the maximum or minimum, or the maximum and minimum thereof) thereafter to be demanded, charged, collected, or received, or the lawful classification, rule, regulation, or practice thereafter to be made effective: *Provided,* That as to rates, fares, and charges for overseas air transportation, the Authority shall determine and prescribe only a just and reasonable maximum or minimum or maximum and minimum rate, fare, or charge.

Rule of Rate Making

(e) In exercising and performing its powers and duties with respect to the determination of rates for the carriage of persons or property, the Authority shall take into consideration, among other factors—

(1) The effect of such rates upon the movement of traffic;

(2) The need in the public interest of adequate and efficient transportation of persons and property by air carriers at the lowest cost consistent with the furnishing of such service;

(3) Such standard respecting the character and quality of service to be rendered by air carriers as may be prescribed by or pursuant to law;

(4) The inherent advantages of transportation by aircraft; and

(5) The need of each air carrier for revenue sufficient to enable such air carrier, under honest, economical, and efficient management, to provide adequate and efficient air carrier service.

Removal of Discrimination in Foreign Air Transportation

(f) Whenever, after notice and hearing, upon complaint, or upon its own initiative, the Authority shall be of the opinion that any individual or joint rate, fare, or charge demanded, charged, collected, or received by any air carrier or foreign air carrier for foreign air transportation, or any classification, rule, regulation, or practice affecting such rate, fare, or charge or the value of the service thereunder, is or will be unjustly discriminatory, or unduly preferential, or unduly prejudicial, the Authority may alter the same to the extent necessary to correct such discrimination, preference, or prejudice and make an order that the air carrier or foreign air carrier shall discontinue demanding, charging, collecting, or receiving any such discriminatory, preferential, or prejudicial rate, fare, or charge, or enforcing any such discriminatory, preferential, or prejudicial classification, rule, regulation, or practice.

Suspension of Rates

(g) Whenever any air carrier shall file with the Authority a tariff stating a new individual or joint (between air carriers) rate, fare, or charge for interstate or overseas air transportation or any classification, rule, regulation, or practice affecting such rate, fare, or charge, or the value of the service thereunder, the Authority is empowered, upon complaint or upon its own initiative, at once, and, if it so orders, without answer or other formal pleading by the air carrier, but upon reasonable notice, to enter upon a hearing concerning the lawfulness of such rate, fare, or charge, or such classification, rule, regulation, or practice; and pending such hearing and the decision thereon, the Authority, by filing with such tariff, and delivering to the air carrier affected thereby, a statement in writing of its reasons for such suspension, may suspend the operation of such tariff and defer the use of such rate, fare, or charge, or such classification, rule, regulation, or practice, for a period of ninety days, and, if the proceeding has not been concluded and a final order made within such period, the Authority may, from time to time, extend the period of suspension, but not for a longer period in the aggregate than one hundred and eighty days beyond the time when such tariff would otherwise go into effect; and, after hearing, whether completed before or after the rate, fare, charge, classification, rule, regulation, or practice goes into effect, the Authority may make such order with reference thereto as would be proper in a proceeding instituted after such rate, fare, charge, classification, rule, regulation, or practice had become effective. If the proceeding has not been concluded and an order made within the period of suspension, the proposed rate, fare, charge, classification, rule, regulation, or practice shall go into effect at the end of such period: *Provided,* That this subsection shall not apply to any initial tariff filed by any air carrier.

Power to Prescribe Divisions of Rates

(h) Whenever, after notice and hearing, upon complaint or upon its own initiative, the Authority is of the opinion that the divisions of joint rates, fares, or charges for air transportation are or will be unjust, unreasonable, inequitable, or unduly preferential or prejudicial as between the air carriers or foreign air carriers parties thereto, the Authority shall prescribe the just, reasonable, and equitable divisions thereof to be received by the several air carriers. The Authority may require the adjustment of divisions between such air carriers from the date of filing the complaint or entry of order of investigation, or such other date subsequent thereto as the Authority finds to be just, reasonable, and equitable.

Power to Establish Through Air Transportation Service

(i) The Authority shall, whenever required by the public convenience and necessity, after notice and hearing, upon complaint or upon its own initiative, establish through service and joint rates, fares, or charges (or the maxima or minima, or the maxima and minima thereof) for interstate or overseas air transportation, or the classifications, rules, regulations, or practices affecting such rates, fares, or charges, or the value of the service thereunder, and the terms and conditions under which such through service shall be operated: *Provided,* That as to joint rates, fares, and charges for overseas air transportation the Authority shall determine and prescribe only just and reasonable maximum or minimum or maximum and minimum joint rates, fares, or charges.

Joint Boards

Designation of Boards

SEC. 1003. (a) The Authority and the Interstate Commerce Commission shall direct their respective chairmen to designate, from time to time, a like number of members of each to act as a joint board to consider and pass upon matters referred to such board as provided in subsection (c) of this section.

Through Service and Joint Rates

(b) Air carriers may establish reasonable through service and joint rates, fares, and charges with other common carriers. In case of through service by air carriers and common carriers subject to the Interstate Commerce Act or the Motor Carrier Act, 1935, it shall be the duty of the carriers parties thereto to establish just and reasonable joint rates, fares, or charges and just and reasonable classifications, rules, regulations, and practices affecting such joint rates, fares, or charges, or the value of the service thereunder, and just, reasonable, and equitable divisions of such joint rates, fares, or charges as between the carriers participating therein. Any air carrier, and any common carrier subject to the Interstate Commerce Act or the Motor Carrier Act, 1935, which is participating in such through service and joint rates, fares, or charges, shall include in its tariffs, filed with the Authority or the Interstate Commerce Commission, as the case may be, a statement showing such through service and joint rates, fares, or charges.

Jurisdiction of Boards

(c) Matters relating to such through service and joint rates, fares, or charges may be referred by the Authority or the Interstate Commerce Commission, upon complaint or upon its own initiative, to a joint board created as provided in subsection (a). Complaints may be made to the Interstate Commerce Commission or the Authority with respect to any matter which may be referred to a joint board under this subsection.

Power of Boards

(d) With respect to matters referred to any joint board as provided in subsection (c), if such board finds, after notice and hearing, that any such joint rate, fare, or charge, or classification, rule, regulation, or practice, affecting such joint rate, fare, or charge or the value of the service thereunder is or will be unjust, unreasonable, unjustly discriminatory, or unduly preferential or prejudicial, or that any division of any such joint rate, fare, or charge, is or will be unjust, unreasonable, inequitable, or unduly preferential or prejudicial as between the carriers parties thereto, it is authorized and directed to take the same action with respect thereto as the Authority is empowered to take with respect to any joint rate, fare, or charge, between air carriers, or any divisions thereof, or any classification, rule, regulation, or practice affecting such joint rate, fare, or charge or the value of the service thereunder.

Judicial Enforcement and Review

(e) Orders of the joint boards shall be enforceable and reviewable as provided in this Act with respect to orders of the Authority.

Evidence

Power to Take Evidence

SEC. 1004. (a) Any member or examiner of the Authority, when duly designated by the Authority for such purpose, may hold hearings, sign and issue subpenas, administer oaths, examine witnesses, and receive evidence at any place in the United States designated by the Authority. In all cases heard by an examiner or a single member the Authority shall hear or receive argument on request of either party.

Power to Issue Subpena

(b) For the purposes of this Act the Authority shall have the power to require by subpena the attendance and testimony of witnesses and the production of all books, papers, and documents relating to any matter under investigation. Witnesses summoned before the Authority shall be paid the same fees and mileage that are paid witnesses in the courts of the United States.

Enforcement of Subpena

(c) The attendance of witnesses, and the production of books, papers, and documents, may be required from any place in the United States, at any designated place of hearing. In case of disobedience to a subpena, the Authority, or any party to a proceeding before the Authority, may invoke the aid of any court of the United States in requiring attendance and testimony of witnesses and the production of such books, papers, and documents under the provisions of this section.

Contempt

(d) Any court of the United States within the jurisdiction of which an inquiry is carried on may, in case of contumacy or refusal to obey a subpena issued to any person, issue an order requiring such person to appear before the Authority (and produce books, papers, or documents if so ordered) and give evidence touching the matter in question; and any failure to obey such order of the court may be punished by such court as a contempt thereof.

Deposition

(e) The Authority may order testimony to be taken by deposition in any proceeding or investigation pending before it, at any stage of such proceeding or investigation. Such depositions may be taken before any person designated by the Authority and having power to administer oaths. Reasonable notice must first be given in writing by the party or his attorney proposing to take such deposition to the opposite party or his attorney of record, which notice shall state the name of the witness and the time and place of the taking of his deposition. Any person may be compelled to appear and depose, and to produce books, papers, or documents, in the same manner as witnesses may be compelled to appear and testify and produce like documentary evidence before the Authority, as hereinbefore provided.

Method of Taking Depositions

(f) Every person deposing as herein provided shall be cautioned and shall be required to swear (or affirm, if he so request) to testify the whole truth, and shall be carefully examined. His testimony shall be reduced to writing by the person taking the deposition, or under his direction, and shall, after it has been reduced to writing, be subscribed by the deponent. All depositions shall be promptly filed with the Authority.

Foreign Depositions

(g) If a witness whose testimony may be desired to be taken by deposition be in a foreign country, the deposition may be taken, provided the laws of the foreign country so permit, by a consular officer or other person commissioned by the Authority, or agreed upon by the parties by stipulation in writing to be filed with the Authority, or may be taken under letter rogatory issued by a court of competent jurisdiction at the request of the Authority.

Fees

(h) Witnesses whose depositions are taken as authorized in this Act, and the persons taking the same, shall severally be entitled to the same fees as are paid for like services in the courts of the United States: *Provided,* That with respect to commissions or letters rogatory issued at the initiative of the Authority, executed in foreign countries, the Authority shall pay such fees, charges, or expenses incidental thereto as may be found necessary, in accordance with regulations on the subject to be prescribed by the Authority.

Compelling Testimony

(i) No person shall be excused from attending and testifying, or from producing books, papers, or documents before the Authority, or in obedience to the subpena of the Authority, or in any cause or proceeding, criminal or otherwise, based upon or growing out of any alleged violation of this Act, or of any rule, regulation, requirement, or order thereunder, or any term, condition, or limitation of any certificate or permit, on the ground, or for the reason, that the testimony or evidence, documentary or otherwise, required of him may tend to incriminate him or subject him to a penalty or forfeiture; but no individual shall be prosecuted or subjected to any penalty or forfeiture for or on account of any transaction, matter, or thing concerning which he is compelled, after having claimed his privilege against self-incrimination, to testify or produce evidence, documentary or otherwise, except that any individual so testifying shall not be exempt from prosecution and punishment for perjury committed in so testifying.

Orders, Notices, and Service

Effective Date of Orders; Emergency Orders

SEC. 1005. (a) Except as otherwise provided in this Act, all orders, rules, and regulations of the Authority shall take effect within such reasonable time as the Authority may prescribe, and shall continue in force until its further order, rule, or regulation, or for a specified period of time, as shall be prescribed in the order, rule, or regulation: *Provided*, That whenever the Authority is of the opinion that an emergency requiring immediate action exists in respect of safety in air commerce, the Authority is authorized, either upon complaint or upon its own initiative without complaint, at once, if it so orders, without answer or other form of pleading by the interested person or persons, and with or without notice, hearing, or the making or filing of a report, to make such just and reasonable orders, rules, or regulations, as may be essential in the interest of safety in air commerce to meet such emergency: *Provided further,* That the Authority shall immediately initiate proceedings relating to the matters embraced in any such order, rule, or regulation, and shall, insofar as practicable, give preference to such proceedings over all others under this Act.

Designation of Agent for Service

(b) It shall be the duty of every air carrier and foreign air carrier within sixty days after the effective date of this section to designate in writing an agent upon whom service of all notices and process and all orders, decisions, and requirements of the Authority may be made for and on behalf of said carrier, and to file such designation in the office of the secretary of the Authority, which designation may from time to time be changed by like writing similarly filed. Service of all notices and process and orders, decisions, and requirements of the Authority may be made upon such carrier by service upon such designated agent at his office or usual place of residence with like effect as if made personally upon such carrier, and in default of such designation of such agent, service of any notice or other process in any proceeding before said Authority, or of any order, decision, or requirement of the Authority, may be made by posting such notice, process, order, requirement, or decision in the office of the secretary of the Authority.

Other Methods of Service

(c) Service of notices, processes, orders, rules, and regulations upon any person may be made by personal service, or upon an agent designated in writing for the purpose, or by registered mail addressed to such person or agent. Whenever service is made by registered mail, the date of mailing shall be considered as the time when service is made.

Suspension or Modification of Order

(d) Except as otherwise provided in this Act, the Authority is empowered to suspend or modify its orders upon such notice and in such manner as it shall deem proper.

Compliance With Order Required

(e) It shall be the duty of every person subject to this Act, and its agents and employees, to observe and comply with any order, rule, regulation, or certificate issued by the Authority under this Act affecting such person so long as the same shall remain in effect.

Form and Service of Orders

(f) Every order of the Authority shall set forth the findings of fact upon which it is based, and shall be served upon the parties to the proceeding and the persons affected by such order.

Judicial Review of Authority's Orders

Orders of Authority Subject to Review

SEC. 1006. (a) Any order, affirmative or negative, issued by the Authority under this Act, except any order in respect of any foreign air carrier subject to the approval of the President as provided in section 801 of this Act, shall be subject to review by the circuit courts of appeals of the United States or the United States Court of Appeals for the District of Columbia upon petition, filed within sixty days after the entry of such order, by any person disclosing a substantial interest in such order. After the expiration of said sixty days a petition may be filed only by leave of court upon a showing of reasonable grounds for failure to file the petition theretofore.

Venue

(b) A petition under this section shall be filed in the court for the circuit wherein the petitioner resides or has his principal place of business or in the United States Court of Appeals for the District of Columbia.

Notice of Authority; Filing of Transcript

(c) A copy of the petition shall, upon filing, be forthwith transmitted to the Authority by the clerk of the court; and the Authority shall thereupon certify and file in the court a transcript of the record, if any, upon which the order complained of was entered.

Power of Court

(d) Upon transmittal of the petition to the Authority, the court shall have exclusive jurisdiction to affirm, modify, or set aside the order complained of, in whole or in part, and if need be, to order further proceedings by the Authority. Upon good cause shown, interlocutory relief may be granted by stay of the order or by such mandatory or other relief as may be appropriate: *Provided,* That no interlocutory relief may be granted except upon at least five days' notice to the Authority.

Findings of Fact by Authority Conclusive

(e) The findings of facts by the Authority, if supported by substantial evidence, shall be conclusive. No objection to an order of the Authority shall be considered by the court unless such objection shall have been urged before the Authority or, if it was not so urged, unless there were reasonable grounds for failure to do so.

Certification or Certiorari

(f) The judgment and decree of the court affirming, modifying, or setting aside any such order of the Authority shall be subject only to review by the Supreme Court of the United States upon certification or certiorari as provided in sections 239 and 240 of the Judicial Code.

Judicial Enforcement

Jurisdiction of Court

SEC. 1007. (a) If any person violates any provision of this Act, or any rule, regulation, requirement, or order thereunder, or any term, condition, or limitation of any certificate or permit issued under this Act, the Authority, its duly authorized agent, or, in the case of a violation of section 401 (a) of this Act, any party in interest, may apply to the district court of the United States, for any district wherein such person carries on his business or wherein the violation occurred, for the enforcement of such provision of this Act, or of such rule, regulation, requirement, order, term, condition, or limitation; and such court shall have jurisdiction to enforce obedience thereto by a writ of injunction or other process, mandatory or otherwise, restraining such person, his officers, agents, employees, and representatives, from further violation of such provision of this Act or of such rule, regulation, requirement, order, term, condition, or limitation, and enjoining upon them obedience thereto.

Application for Enforcement

(b) Upon the request of the Authority, it shall be the duty of any district attorney of the United States to whom the Authority may apply to institute in the proper court and to prosecute under the direction of the Attorney General all necessary proceedings for the enforcement of the provisions of this Act or any rule, regulation, requirement, or order thereunder, or any term, condition, or limitation of any certificate or permit, and for the punishment of all violations thereof, and the costs and expenses of such prosecutions shall be paid out of the appropriations for the expenses of the courts of the United States.

Participation by Authority in Court Proceedings

SEC. 1008. Upon request of the Attorney General, the Authority shall have the right to participate in any proceeding in court under the provisions of this Act.

Joinder of Parties

SEC. 1009. In any proceeding for the enforcement of the provisions of this Act, or any rule, regulation, requirement, or order thereunder, or any term, condition, or limitation of any certificate or permit, whether such proceedings be instituted before the Authority or be begun originally in any court of the United States, it shall be lawful to include as parties, or to permit the intervention of, all persons interested in or affected by the matter under consideration; and inquiries, investigations, orders, and decrees may be made with reference to all such parties in the same manner, to the same extent, and subject to the same provisions of law, as they may be made with respect to the persons primarily concerned.

TITLE XI–MISCELLANEOUS

Hazards to Air Commerce

SEC. 1101. The Authority shall, by rules and regulations, or by order where necessary, require all persons to give adequate public notice, in the form and manner prescribed by the Authority, of the construction or alteration, or of the proposed construction or alteration, of any structure along or near the civil airways where notice will promote safety in air commerce.

International Agreements

SEC. 1102. In exercising and performing its powers and duties under this Act, the Authority shall do so consistently with any obligation assumed by the United States in any treaty, convention, or agreement that may be in force between the United States and any foreign country or foreign countries, shall take into consideration any applicable laws and requirements of foreign countries and shall not, in exercising and performing its powers and duties with respect to certificates of convenience and necessity, restrict compliance by any air carrier with any obligation, duty, or liability imposed by any foreign country: *Provided,* That this section shall not apply to any obligation, duty, or liability arising out of a contract or other agreement, heretofore or hereafter entered into between an air carrier, or any officer or representative thereof, and any foreign country, if such contract or agreement is disapproved by the Authority as being contrary to the public interest.

Nature and Use of Documents Filed

SEC. 1103. The copies of tariffs, and of all contracts, agreements, understandings, and arrangements filed with the Authority as herein provided, and the statistics, tables, and figures contained in the annual or other reports of air carriers and other persons made to the Authority as required under the provisions of this Act shall be preserved as public records (except as otherwise provided in this Act) in the custody of the secretary of the Authority, and shall be received as prima facie evidence of what they purport to be for the purpose of investigations by the Authority and in all judicial proceedings; and copies of, and extracts from, any of such tariffs, contracts, agreements, understandings, arrangements, or reports, certified by the secretary of the Authority, under the seal of the Authority, shall be received in evidence with like effect as the originals.

Withholding of Information

SEC. 1104. Any person may make written objection to the public disclosure of information contained in any application, report, or document filed pursuant to the provisions of this Act or of information obtained by the Authority, the Administrator, or the Air Safety Board pursuant to the provisions of this Act, stating the grounds for such objection. Whenever such objection is made, the Authority, or the Air Safety Board if the information was obtained by it, shall order such information withheld from public disclosure when, in its judgment, a disclosure of such information would adversely affect the interests of such person and is not required in the interest of the public. The Authority is authorized to withhold publication of records containing secret information affecting national defense.

Cooperation With Government Agencies

SEC. 1105. The Authority, the Administrator, and the Air Safety Board may avail themselves of the assistance of the National Advisory Committee for Aeronautics and any research or technical agency of the United States on matters relating to aircraft fuel and oil and to the design, materials, workmanship, construction, performance, maintenance, and operation of aircraft, aircraft engines, propellers, appliances, and air navigation facilities. Each such agency is authorized to conduct such scientific and technical researches, investigations, and tests as may be necessary to aid the Authority, the Administrator, and the Air Safety Board in the exercise and performance of their powers and duties. Nothing contained in this Act shall be construed to authorize the duplication of the laboratory research activities of any existing governmental agency.

Remedies not Exclusive

SEC. 1106. Nothing contained in this Act shall in any way abridge or alter the remedies now existing at common law or by statute, but the provisions of this Act are in addition to such remedies.

Amendments and Repeals

SEC. 1107. (a) Section 3964 of the Revised Statutes is hereby amended by adding "and all air routes," after the words "or parts of railroads."

(b) The Act of May 24, 1928, as amended (45 Stat. 728), is further amended by striking out the words "Secretary of Commerce" wherever they appear and inserting in lieu thereof the words "Civil Aeronautics Authority."

(c) The Independent Offices Appropriations Act, 1934, as amended (48 Stat. 283), is further amended by striking out in section 6 thereof the words "any air mail contract or."

(d) The Act approved February 21, 1925 (43 Stat. 960), as amended by the Act approved August 24, 1935 (45 Stat. 744), and the Act approved August 29, 1937 (50 Stat. 725), is further amended by striking out the words"; and he is authorized, in his discretion, to contract, after advertisement in accordance with law, for the carriage of all classes of mail to, from or within the Territory of Alaska, by airplane, payment therefor to be made from the appropriation for star-route service in Alaska."

(e) The ninth paragraph of the Act approved March 3, 1915 (38 Stat. 930), as amended by the Act of March 2, 1929 (45 Stat. 1451; U.S.C., 1934 ed., title 50, sec. 151), is further amended by inserting after the words "naval aeronautics;" in that paragraph the following: "two members from the Civil Aeronautics Authority;", by striking out the word "eight" in that paragraph and inserting in lieu thereof the word "six," and by striking out the colon after the words "allied sciences" and inserting in lie thereof a period and the following: "The members of the National Advisory Committee for Aeronautics, not representing governmental agencies, in office on the date of enactment of the Civil Aeronautics Act of 1938, shall continue to serve as members of the Committee until the effective date of section 1107 of the Civil Aeronautics Act of 1938. Upon the expiration of their terms of office, the President is authorized to appoint successors to six of such members for terms of office to expire, as designated by the President at the time of appointment, two at the end of one year, two at the end of three years, and two at the end of five years from December 1, 1938. Successors to those first appointed shall be appointed by the President for terms of five years from the date of the expiration of the terms of the members whom they succeed, except that any such successor, appointed to fill a vacancy occurring prior to the expiration of a term, shall be appointed only for the unexpired term of the member whom he succeeds: . "

(f) Section 5 (a) of the Federal Trade Commission Act, approved September 26, 1914, as amended (38 Stat. 719; U.S.C., 1934 ed., title 15, sec. 41), is further amended by inserting before the words "and persons" the following: "air carriers and foreign air carriers subject to the Civil Aeronautics Act of 1938, . "

(g) Section 11 of the Act of October 15, 1914, as amended (38 Stat. 734; U.S.C., 1934 ed., title 15, sec. 21), is amended by inserting after the word "energy;" the following: "in the Civil Aeronautics Authority where applicable to air carriers and foreign air carriers subject to the Civil Aeronautics Act of 1938;" and by inserting after the word "commission" wherever it appears in that section a comma and the word "authority, . "

(h) The Department of Commerce Appropriation Act, 1939, is amended by striking out the words "Secretary of Commerce," wherever they appear in the second paragraph under the heading "Bureau of Air Commerce," and inserting in lieu thereof the words "Administrator in the Civil Aeronautics Authority, with the approval of the Civil Aeronautics Authority."

(i) The Air Commerce Act of 1926, as amended, is further amended—

(1) By striking out the words "Secretary of Commerce" wherever they appear (except in section 7 and section 11 (a), (b), and (c)) and inserting in lieu thereof in section 6 (c) and section 10 the words "Civil Aeronautics Authority" and in sections 5 (f), 9(j), and 11 (e) the words "Administrator in the Civil Aeronautics Authority."

(2) By inserting after the word "Act" in the first line of subsection (f) of section 5 the words "or the Civil Aeronautics Act of 1938."

(3) By striking out the first sentence of section 6 and inserting in lieu thereof the following: "The United States of America is hereby declared to possess and exercise complete and exclusive national sovereignty in the air space above the United States, including the air space above all inland waters and the air space above those portions of the adjacent marginal high seas, bays, and lakes, over which by international law or treaty or convention the United States exercises national jurisdiction."

(4) By striking out so much of subsection (b) of section 6 as reads "; and if so authorized, such aircraft and airmen serving in connection therewith, shall be subject to the requirements of section 3, unless exempt under subdivision (c) of this section."

(5) By striking out so much of subsection (c) of section 6 as reads ", and may by regulation exempt such aircraft, and/or airmen serving in connection therewith, from the requirements of section 3, other than the air traffic rules; but no foreign aircraft shall engage in interstate or intrastate air commerce. , " and by inserting in lieu thereof a period and the following: "No foreign aircraft shall engage in air commerce otherwise than between any State, Territory, or possession of the United States (including the Phillipine Islands) or the District of Columbia, and a foreign country."

(6) By striking out "51 per centum" in subsection (a) of section 9 thereof and inserting in lieu thereof "75 per centum."

(7) By inserting after the word "Act" in subsection (f) of section 9 the words "or the Civil Aeronautics Act of 1938."

(8) By striking out so much of section 10 as reads "under section three,"

(9) By striking out so much of subsection (b) of section 11 as reads "any provision of subdivision (a) of this section or any entry or clearance regulation made under section 7 (b)" and inserting in lieu thereof "any entry or clearance regulation made under section 7 (c)."

(j) Section 203 (b) of the Motor Carrier Act, 1935, is amended by inserting after the words "(7) motor vehicles used exclusively in the distribution of newspapers" a semicolon and the following: "or (7a) the transportation of persons or property by motor vehicle when incidental to transportation by aircraft."

(k) Sections 2 (b) (2) and (3), 3, 4, 5, 6, 7, 9, 10, 11, 12, 13, 14, 15, 16, 17, 18, 19, 20, and 21, and so much of section 8 as reads "; and any person not ineligible under the terms of this Act who qualified under the other requirements of this Act, shall be eligible to contract for carrying air mail, notwithstanding the provisions of section 3950 of the Revised Statutes (Act of June 8, 1872)", of the Act of June 12, 1934, as amended (48 Stat. 933); the joint resolution of June 26, 1934 (48 Stat. 1243); the Act of March 8, 1928 (45 Stat. 248), as amended; sections 2, 3, and 3a, subsections (a), (b), (e), and (g) of section 5, the second sentence of section 8, and paragraphs (2), (3), (4), and (5) of subsection (a) of section 11 of the Air Commerce Act of 1926, as amended (44 Stat. 568; U.S.C., 1934 ed., title 49, sec. 177); and all other Acts or parts of Acts inconsistent with any provision of this Act are hereby repealed.

Effect of Transfers, Repeals, and Amendments

Effectiveness of Existing Orders, Regulations, and So Forth

SEC. 1108. (a) All orders, determinations, rules, regulations, permits, contracts, certificates, licenses, and privileges which have been issued, made, or granted by the Interstate Commerce Commission, the Department of Commerce, or the Postmaster General, or any court of competent jurisdiction, under any provision of law repealed or amended by this Act, or in the exercise of duties, powers, or functions transferred to the Authority by this Act, and which are in effect at the time this section takes effect, shall continue in effect until modified, terminated, superseded, set aside, or repealed by the Authority, or by any court of competent jurisdiction, or by operation of law.

Pending Administrative Proceedings

(b) The provisions of this Act shall not affect any proceedings pending before the Secretary of Commerce or the Postmaster General, or proceedings pending before the Interstate Commerce Commission for the determination of rates for the transportation of air mail by aircraft, on the date of the enactment of this Act; but any such proceedings shall be continued, orders therein issued, appeals therefrom taken, and payments made by the Postmaster General pursuant to such orders, as if this Act had not been enacted; and orders issued in any such proceeding shall continue in effect until modified, terminated, superseded, or repealed by the Authority or by operation of law: *Provided,* That the rates determined by the Interstate Commerce Commission shall be determined without regard to that portion of section 6 (e) of the Air Mail Act approved June 12, 1934, which provides as follows: "which, in connection with the rates fixed by it for all other routes, shall be designed to keep the aggregate cost of the transportation of air mail on and after July 1, 1938, within the limits of the anticipated postal revenue therefrom."

Pending Judicial Proceedings

(c) The provisions of this Act shall not affect suits commenced prior to the date of the organization of the Authority; and all such suits shall be continued, proceedings therein had, appeals therein taken, and judgments therein rendered, in the same manner and with the same effect as if this Act had not been passed. No suit, action, or other proceeding lawfully commenced by or against any agency or officer of the United States, in relation to the discharge of official duties, shall abate by reason of any transfer of authority, power, or duties from such agency or officer to the Authority under the provisions of this Act, but the court, upon motion or supplemental petition filed at any time within twelve months after such transfer, showing the necessity for a survival of such suit, action, or other proceeding to obtain a settlement of the questions involved, may allow the same to be maintained by or against the Authority.

Records Transferred to Authority

(d) All records transferred to the Authority under this Act shall be available for use by the Authority to the same extent as if such records were originally records of the Authority.

Separability

SEC. 1109. If any provision of this Act or the application thereof to any person or circumstance is held invalid, the remainder of the Act and the application of such provision to other persons or circumstances shall not be affected thereby.

Effective Date

SEC. 1110. The provisions of this Act, except this section, title II, and section 408, shall become effective sixty days after enactment: *Provided,* That the Authority shall, if it finds such action necessary or desirable in the public interest, by general or special order, postpone the effective date of any provision of this Act, except this section, title II, and section 408, to such time as the Authority shall prescribe, but not beyond the one hundred and eightieth day following the enactment of this Act.

Approved, June 23, 1938.

THE ORIGINS

COPELAND REPORT ON THE CIVIL
AERONAUTICS ACT
April 20, 1938

Mr. Copeland, from the Committee on Commerce, submitted the following

REPORT
[To accompany S. 3845]

The Committee on Commerce, to whom was referred the bill (S. 3845) to create a Civil Aeronautics Authority, to provide for the regulation of civil aeronautics and for other purposes, having considered the same, report the bill back favorably with the recommendation that it be passed at this session.

The Committee on Commerce, on June 7, 1935, were directed by resolution (S. Res. 146, 74th Cong., 1st sess.) to investigate certain airplane accidents in interstate air commerce and to make suitable recommendations thereon.

The resolution placed upon the committee the responsibility of determining "What legislation, if any, shall be adopted in the interest of safety of life and property transported in interstate air commerce, and what legislation, if any, shall be adopted to prevent accidents in the air and to provide appropriate safeguards for their prevention."

On March 30, 1938, the committee submitted to the Senate its third report (S. Rept. 185, pt. 2). This third report concerned legislation which the committee considered fundamental to safety and progress in aeronautics for, without economic stability, there can be no safety.

In its third report, the committee recommended the enactment, at this session of the Congress, of legislation intended to create an independent Authority over all civil aeronautics and urged instant action "for the safety and good of the public" and in the interest of America's air commerce, the Postal Service, and the national defense.

Legislation of the character contemplated by S. 3760 has the approval of six executive departments of the Government (State, Treasury, War, Navy, Commerce, and Post Office) after months of study intended to recommend legislation of a permanent character, destined to last for a long period into the future. In principle, S. 3845 confirms the report of the President's Aviation Commission which was created by the Air Mail Act of 1934, the report of which was transmitted to the Congress by the President as of January 31, 1935. Committees of Congress have labored for years in the hope of permanent legislation intended to meet the needs of our country's civil aeronautics. The present bill reflects the coordination of thought of important Senate and House committees in a general recognition of the dependence of safety in the air upon the need for permanent economic legislation, and consequent economic stability, in the air-carrier industry. (See pp. 27 and 28 of S. Rept. 185, 75th Cong.)

The bill provides for the usual system of economic regulation of air-transportation companies and applies to all air carriers, who operate as common carriers or who transport mail by air. The legislation is adapted to the special characteristics of transportation by air and is, at present, carried no further than is necessary in the interests of the public and of civil aeronautics.

In recent years there has been an extraordinary growth of civil aeronautics, including common-carrier transportation by air—17,681 licensed civil pilots fly 7,300 licensed civil airplanes and utilize 2,327 airports. The air lines cover the country, transporting over a million and a quarter passengers and over 8 million pounds of express annually and approximately 1 billion and a quarter pound-miles of air mail per month. Competition among air carriers is being carried to an extreme, which tends to jeopardize the financial status of the air carriers and to jeopardize and render unsafe a transportation service appropriate to the needs of commerce and required in the public interest, in the interests of the Postal Service, and of the national defense. Aviation in America today, under present laws, is unsatisfactory to investors, labor, and the air carriers themselves.

The technological advance of recent years, together with the increase in the volume of business done by the air-transport industry, have altered air carriers from the status of air-mail contractors to that of common carriers. As all present economic legislation is directed solely to conditions pertaining to the carriage of air mail, it is clearly seen that the present laws are both inadequate and obsolete. The recognized and accepted principles of the regulation of public utilities, as applied to other forms of transportation, have been incorporated in S. 3845. The committee feels that this bill will not only promote an orderly development of our Nation's civil aeronautics, but by its immediate enactment prevent the spread of bad practices and of destructive and wasteful tactics resulting from the intense competition now existing within the air-carrier industry.

The immediate enactment of S. 3845 is in the public interest as well as in the interest of the civil aeronautics industry itself.

LEA REPORT ON THE CIVIL
AERONAUTICS BILL
April 28, 1938

Mr. Lea, from the Committee on Interstate and Foreign Commerce, submitted the following

REPORT
[To accompany H. R. 9738]

The Committee on Interstate and Foreign Commerce, to whom was referred the bill (H. R. 9738) to create a Civil Aeronautics Authority, to provide for the regulation of civil aeronautics, and for other purposes, having had the same under consideration, report it back to the House with an amendment and recommend that the bill do pass.

Need for Legislation

It is the purpose of this legislation to coordinate in a single independent agency all of the existing functions of the Federal Government with respect to civil aeronautics, and, in addition, to authorize the new agency to perform certain new regulatory functions which are designed to stabilize the air-transportation industry in the United States.

Under existing law three separate agencies of the Government have control over vital phases of civil-aeronautics regulation: The Bureau of Air Commerce of the Department of Commerce regulates safety, and exercises certain promotional functions, in civil aeronautics; the Post Office Department through the letting of air-mail contracts exerts substantial economic control over the air lines; and the Interstate Commerce Commission through its authority to fix rates for the carriage of mail and to exercise certain regulatory functions exerts further economic control over the air lines. The result of this divided jurisdiction over civil aeronautics has been a lack of coordination in the efforts of the Government to regulate, foster, and develop the air-transportation industry and miscellaneous flying. This has proved a burden upon the air carriers and private flyers and has increased the work and detracted from the efficiency of the Government itself in this field.

Under existing law there is little economic regulation of air carriers. Routes are awarded not upon the basis of the ability of the particular air carrier to perform the service or the requirements of the public convenience and necessity, but upon the letting of air-mail contracts to the lowest responsible bidders. This system has completely broken down in recent months, because the air carriers, in their desire to secure the right to carry the mail over a new route, have made absurdly low bids, indeed, have virtually evinced a willingness to pay for the privilege of carrying the mail over a particular route. A route once secured, however, under the existing system of air-mail contracts does not protect the air carrier operating that route from possible cutthroat competition, for air carriers are not required to secure a certificate or other authorization from the Government before beginning operations, other than one based upon safety requirements. Nor, is there any authority in the Federal Government under existing law to prevent competing carriers from engaging in rate wars which would be disastrous to all concerned.

The result of this chaotic situation of the air carriers has been to shake the faith of the investing public in their financial stability and to prevent the flow of funds into the industry. Col. Edgar S. Gorrell, president of the Air Transport Association, representing substantially all of the scheduled American-flag air lines, testified before your committee during the public hearings on H. R. 9738 that $120,000,000 of private capital has been invested in the present air-transport system and that 50 percent of this investment has been lost. He further testified that unless legislation is enacted which would give the carriers reasonable assurance of the permanency of their operation and would protect them from cutthroat competition, a number of the air lines would soon be in serious financial trouble.

Character of Legislation

H. R. 9738 would prohibit any person from operating as a common carrier by aircraft unless such person holds a certificate of convenience and necessity, and provides that the rates, regulations, and practices of such air carriers shall be subject to regulation. Thus, if this legislation is enacted, the air carriers will be able to operate on a stable basis, their routes secured by a certificate of convenience and necessity, which may be revoked only for cause, and their rates regulated so as to eliminate cutthroat competition among themselves. Moreover, the existing system of carrying mail under contracts with the Postmaster General would be abolished and any air carrier holding a certificate authorizing it to carry mail would be permitted to do so. Provision is also made for requiring air carriers to cease and desist from engaging in unfair competition and unfair or deceptive practices.

The existing methods of safety regulation are permitted to remain virtually as they are under existing law but an additional means which will be discussed below has been provided for securing impartial and efficient investigation of accidents.

H. R. 9738 would provide for the establishment of a three-member independent agency, to be known as the Civil Aeronautics Authority. The members would be appointed by the President and confirmed by the Senate for 6-year staggered terms and would be removable only for cause. In this agency would be vested all of the regulatory functions now exercised by the Federal Government over civil aeronautics and, in addition, the Authority would be vested with the new regulatory power over the economic phases of air transportation. It would have the power to issue certificates of public convenience and necessity, to fix rates for the carriage of passengers, property, and mail, and to regulate interrelationships among air carriers and between air carriers and other branches of the aeronautical industry. The Authority would also have power to promulgate all air traffic rules and to issue aircraft safety certificates, airman certificates, and air carrier operating certificates. Thus, the new agency would regulate safety not only in commercial air transportation but also in miscellaneous flying.

The bill also provides for the establishment of a Safety Division within the Authority, headed by a Director, who would be appointed by the President and confirmed by the Senate. The duty of this Division would be to investigate accidents in air commerce, to report to the Authority concerning such accidents and to recommend to the Authority possible means of eliminating such accidents in the future. The Division would exercise its functions independently of the Authority but would, upon the request of the Authority, carry on investigations and studies in safety matters.

The bill would also create within the Authority the office of Administrator, who would be appointed by the President and confirmed by the Senate. It would be his duty to establish airways and construct, operate, and maintain air-navigation facilities and landing areas on such airways. He would also perform such routine administrative duties as the Authority might assign to him.

The reason for so organizing this new agency, i.e., for giving the Authority the power to exercise the regulatory functions, the Administrator the power to perform the administrative work, and the Director of the Safety Division the power to investigate and report on accidents in air navigation, is to permit the new agency to exercise its functions smoothly and efficiently. It was believed by your committee that the Authority, if burdened with the necessity of performing functions which are in their nature routine and administrative, could not properly carry out its regulatory duties. On the other hand, it was believed that the establishment of airways and the construction of air-navigation facilities and landing areas could be supervised by one man more efficiently than this could be done by a quasi-judicial board of three.

As to the investigation of accidents, with which the Director of the Safety Division is charged, it was felt by your committee that this function should be exercised by one as independent as possible of those whom he is investigating. For example, in many cases, a structural failure in the aircraft will be found to be the cause of an accident. In such cases, the person investigating the accident might be called upon to place the blame upon the Authority for issuing an aircraft certificate for the aircraft. As a further example, faulty air-navigation facilities might be found to be the cause of an accident and the person investigating the accident would be called upon to place the blame upon the Administrator. Thus, it is necessary that accident investigations be carried on by a person who is not subject to control by either the Authority or the Administrator so that such investigations may be completely impartial.

Need for an Independent Agency

Careful consideration was given by your committee to the question as to the desirability of creating an independent agency to regulate civil aeronautics. Due to the unique character of the regulatory problem presented by civil aeronautics, it was concluded by your committee that for the present the most efficient and advantageous regulation, both from the standpoint of the public interest and from that of the industry to be regulated, could be secured by the coordination of all governmental functions relating to civil aeronautics in a newly created independent agency.

The regulatory problem presented by civil aeronautics is unique because the Federal Government in the Air Commerce Act of 1926 established the policy of not merely regulating common-carrier operations by air carriers but also of regulating the design, manufacture, and operation of every aircraft flying in interstate or foreign commerce, of prescribing the qualifications for every airman, and of promulgating the air-traffic rules to be observed by every person operating an aircraft. Moreover, the Federal Government has established the policy of constructing airways, air-navigation facilities, and emergency landing fields to serve the public traveling by air.

These differences which exist between the scope of the regulatory control of the Federal Government over operations by aircraft and those by any other mode of transportation require the establishment of a new independent agency for the present. The economic and safety regulation of common-carrier operations by air carriers, the safety regulation of miscellaneous flying, and the building of airways, air-navigation facilities, and emergency landing fields are so closely interrelated as to defy successful separation. To divide them among separate agencies would be extremely costly and would lead to inefficiency and duplication of effort.

For example, if the economic and safety regulation of air-carrier operations were to be vested in the Interstate Commerce Commission, leaving with the Department of Commerce the safety regulation of private flying and the building of airways, air-navigation facilities, and intermediate landing fields, duplication of effort could not be prevented. The Department of Commerce would require a corps of inspectors and other employees to inspect private aircraft, and the Interstate Commerce Commission would require an equal number to inspect air-carrier aircraft, despite the fact that they are built in the same factory and many times it is not known until they are completed whether they will eventually become air-carrier aircraft or private aircraft. As to the building of airways, the Interstate Commerce Commission could not authorize operations over a particular route until the Department of Commerce has been convinced that air-navigation facilities should be established over that route.

It is the view of your committee that the functions of the Federal Government relating to transportation should be consolidated in a single agency as soon as possible. However, it appears at this time that it is impossible to secure a proper coordination of all of the functions relating to civil aeronautics in one agency otherwise than by reorganizing the Interstate Commerce Commission or by creating a new agency for that purpose. The Interstate Commerce Commission, the only available existing agency, would unquestionably be over-burdened by undertaking the establishment, operation, and maintenance of all airways, air-navigation facilities, and landing areas, the safety regulation of both air-carrier operation and private flying, and the economic regulation of air-carrier operations. Moreover such functions, except for the latter, are entirely unlike any functions now performed by that agency.

Since the consolidation of all the transportation functions of the Federal Government in a single agency will require extended study and since the aviation industry is desperately in need of this legislation at once, your committee recommends that an independent establishment be created to perform the functions relating to aeronautics.

In order to have a unified, efficient regulation of competing means of transportation the powers of such agency must be distributed according to the different functions performed. We now have no such agency.

This legislation has the approval of the aeronautical industry, the private flyers, and the executive departments which deal with civil aeronautics, i.e., the Departments of Commerce, Post Office, State, Navy, War, and Treasury.

SECTION BY SECTION ANALYSIS

Title I—General Provisions

SECTION 1: *Definitions.*—This section contains the definitions of the important terms used in the bill. The most important terms defined in this section are "air carrier" and "air transportation." These terms delimit the persons to whom the act applies.

SECTION 2: *Public right of transit.*—This section declares that any citizen of the United States has the right of freedom of transit through the navigable air space of the United States in interstate, overseas, and foreign air commerce. A similar provision has been in the Air Commerce Act of 1926 since the enactment of that act.

Title II—Organization of Authority

SECTION 201: *Creation of Civil Aeronautics Authority.*—This section provides for the creation of a Civil Aeronautics Authority to be composed of three persons appointed by the President and confirmed by the Senate for 6-year staggered terms. The section also provides for the appointment by the President, by and with the advise and consent of the Senate, of an Administrator within the Authority. This section further prescribes the qualifications of the members of the Authority and the Administrator, and fixes their salaries at $10,000 per year.

SECTION 202: *Officers and employees.*—This section empowers the Authority to appoint such officers and employees as it shall deem necessary to carry out its powers and duties and those of the Administrator.

SECTION 203: *Personnel, property, and appropriations.*—This section transfers to the Authority such personnel, property, and appropriations of the Department of Commerce and the Interstate Commerce Commission as are employed in the exercise of functions which, if this legislation is enacted, will be performed by the Authority.

SECTION 204: *Expenditures.*—This section empowers the Authority to make such expenditures as are required in the performance of its duties, those of the Administrator, and those of the Director of the Safety Division. Under this section the Authority is specifically empowered to purchase aircraft.

SECTION 205: *Travel.*—This section provides that the cost of travel by aircraft by any officer or employee of the United States on official business shall be paid as travel expense by the United States. Under existing law officers and employees of the United States may only be reimbursed for the cost of travel by aircraft when there exists an emergency justifying the speedier means of transportation. It is the purpose of this section to permit officers and employees of the United States to travel by commercial aircraft and be reimbursed therefor without regard to the existence of an emergency and upon the same terms and conditions that such officers and employees now travel by rail.

Title III—Fostering of Civil Aeronautics

SECTION 301: *Fostering of air commerce.*—This section directs the Administrator to foster the development of air commerce and civil aeronautics.

SECTION 302: *Civil airways and facilities.*—This section empowers the Administrator to designate, establish, and chart civil airways and to establish and operate necessary air-navigation facilities on such airways. This section also requires the Authority to investigate, through the Administrator, the existing system of airports in the United States and to recommend to the Congress a definite policy to be followed with respect to Federal participation in the building of airports.

SECTION 303: *Meteorological service.*—This section directs the Administrator to make recommendations to the Secretary of Agriculture with respect to meteorological service.

SECTION 304: *Development of facilities.*—This section empowers the Administrator to undertake developmental work and service testing of experimental aircraft, aircraft engines, propellors, appliances, air-navigation facilities, and radio apparatus. This section will not permit the Administrator to engage in laboratory research work of the type now carried on by the National Advisory Committee for Aeronautics.

SECTION 305: *Other duties of Administrator.*—This section provides that the Administrator shall perform the duties specifically vested in him by the act and such other duties as may be assigned to him by the Authority. The Administrator is specifically vested with duties relating to the designation of airways, the construction, operation, and maintenance of air-navigation facilities and duties having as their purpose the control and assistance of traffic on the airways. This section is designed to authorize him to perform, subject to the direction of the Authority, other duties of an administrative character which are incidental to the duties of the Authority.

Title IV—Air Carrier Economic Regulation

SECTION 401: *Declaration of policy.*—This section sets forth the congressional policy to guide the Authority in performing its duties.

SECTION 402: *Certificates of public convenience and necessity.*—This section prohibits any air carrier from engaging in interstate, overseas, or foreign air transportation, or the transportation of mail by aircraft, unless the carrier holds a certificate issued by the Authority authorizing it to do so. Unless the Authority finds that the service of a particular air carrier has been inadequate and inefficient, the Authority is required to issue a certificate to any air carrier who operated continuously from December 1, 1937, until the effective date of the section, authorizing the carrier to operate over the routes over which it operated continuously between April 15, 1938, and the effective date of the section or was authorized by the Postmaster General to operate on April 15, 1938.

Whenever an air carrier is authorized by its certificate to transport mail, it is required to furnish adequate facilities therefor, and it must transport mail whenever required by the Postmaster General. Any air carrier is prohibited from abandoning any route for which it has a certificate unless the Authority finds that the abandonment is in the public interest. However, the Authority is empowered to authorize temporary suspension of service.

The Authority is empowered to modify or suspend any certificate if the public convenience and necessity so require and to revoke any certificate for violation of the act, any order or regulation issued thereunder, or any term of the certificate. This section also empowers the Authority to fix the maximum mail load for any schedule or for any aircraft or type of aircraft, thus avoiding unsafe weight and also permitting the carriers to maintain necessary passenger space; however, no order of the Authority fixing the maximum mail load can relieve the carriers of their obligation to furnish additional facilities for transporting the mail in the event that mail in excess of the maximum load is tendered. All air carriers are required by the section to maintain certain minimum wages for, and differentials between, pilots and copilots, and maximum flying hours are imposed for pilots and copilots engaged in interstate air transportation.

SECTION 403: *Foreign air-carrier permits.*—This section prohibits any foreign air carrier from operating to the United States unless it holds a permit issued by the Authority empowering it to do so. The issuance of any such permit, other than one to an existing carrier, would be subject to the approval of the President.

SECTION 404: *Tariffs of air carriers.*—Every air carrier and foreign air carrier is required to file with the Authority its tariffs showing its rates, regulations, and practices, is required to adhere to its tariffs, and is forbidden to charge discriminatory rates or enforce discriminatory regulations.

SECTION 405: *Standards as to rates.*—This section sets forth the congressional policy to guide the Authority in determining rates for the carriage of persons or property.

SECTION 406: *Rates for the carriage of persons and property.*—This section imposes a duty upon air carriers to provide interstate or overseas air transportation upon request, to provide adequate service in interstate or overseas air transportation, and to enforce just and reasonable rates, regulations and practices, and establish just and reasonable divisions of joint rates for interstate or overseas air transportation. The section empowers the Authority to change rates, regulations, or practices for interstate and overseas air transportation which it finds to be unreasonable by fixing the exact rate in the case of interstate air transportation and by fixing maximum and minimum rates for overseas air transportation. The section further empowers the Authority to establish through service and joint rates for interstate or overseas air transportation between air carriers and to require just and equitable divisions of such joint rates. The Authority is also empowered to adjust discriminatory rates for foreign air transportation and is required to investigate and determine whether it should be given additional rate-making power in foreign air transportation.

SECTION 407: *Joint boards.*—This section requires the chairman of the Authority and the Interstate Commerce Commission, respectively, to designate, from time to time, one or more members of the Authority and a like number of members of the

Interstate Commerce Commission to constitute a joint board to coordinate transportation between air carriers and common carriers subject to the jurisdiction of the Interstate Commerce Commission. Air carriers are permitted to establish through service and joint rates with such other common carriers, and, when such through service and joint rates have been established, the joint boards will have the authority to regulate the joint rates and the divisions of such rates. A case can be brought before a joint board upon the initiative of either the Interstate Commerce Commission or the Authority, or upon complaint filed with either the Interstate Commerce Commission or the Authority.

SECTION 408: *Rates for the carriage of mail.*—This section empowers the Authority to fix mail rates and sets forth the congressional policy to guide the Authority in fixing such rates and enables the Authority to adjust rates so that the policy of Congress may be properly carried out in the case of each carrier or class of carriers according to the needs of the particular case.

SECTION 409: *Transportation of mail.*—This section provides for the cancelation of existing mail contracts and sets forth the conditions under which foreign mail may be carried by American air carriers. Subsection (e) of this section provides that air carriers shall fix the schedules of their aircraft carrying mail in the first instance and empowers the Postmaster General to alter any such schedule. Persons aggrieved by orders of the Postmaster General altering such schedules, may appeal to the Authority. The Authority is authorized to revise or revoke the orders of the Postmaster General if the public interest requires.

SECTION 410: *Consolidation, merger, and acquisition of control.*—This section prohibits consolidations, mergers, or interlocking relationships between air carriers and between air carriers and certain other types of companies unless approved by the Authority. This section also requires all air carriers to file with the Authority all pooling or other operating arrangements entered into by them and prescribes the conditions under which the Authority may approve them.

SECTION 411: *Interlocking directorates.*—This section prohibits interlocking directorates between air carriers and between air carriers and certain other types of companies unless approved by the Authority.

SECTION 412: *Exemption from antitrust provisions.*—This section exempts from the antitrust laws any person affected by an order of the Authority approving a consolidation, merger, interlocking relationship, or operating contract to the extent necessary to permit such person to do anything authorized, approved, or required by the order.

SECTION 413: *Unfair competition.*—This section empowers the Authority to order any air carrier or foreign air carrier to cease and desist from engaging in unfair practices or unfair methods of competition in air transportation.

SECTION 414: *Accounts, records, and reports.*—This section empowers the Authority to require reports from air carriers and prescribe the forms of the air-carriers' accounts.

SECTION 415: *Inquiry into air-carrier management.*—This section empowers the Authority, for the purpose of performing its duties, to inquire into the management of the business of any air carrier.

SECTION 416: *Financial air.*—This section requires all loans or other financial aid granted to an air carrier by any agency of the United States to be approved by the Authority and requires the terms and conditions upon which such aid is given to be prescribed by the Authority.

Title V—Nationality and Ownership of Aircraft

SECTION 501: *Registration of aircraft nationality.*—This section prohibits any person from operating any aircraft eligible for registration unless such aircraft is registered as provided in the section, and prohibits the operation of foreign aircraft within the United States unless such operation is authorized by the Authority or the Secretary of State, as the case may be, under section 6 of the Air Commerce Act of 1926. Any civil aircraft of the United States, not registered in a foreign country, and any public aircraft of the United States, is made eligible for registration.

SECTION 502: *Effect of registration.*—This section declares that registration shall be conclusive evidence of the nationality of the aircraft for international purposes.

SECTION 503: *Recording of transfer of aircraft ownership.*—This section requires the recordation with the Authority of every transfer made after July 1, 1939, of any interest in a civil aircraft of the United States. It further provides that no such transfer shall be valid against any person, other than the person by whom the conveyance was made or given, his heirs or devisees, and any person having actual notice thereof, until the transfer is recorded but upon recording it shall be valid as to all persons without further recordation of any sort with any governmental agency.

Title VI—Civil Aeronautics Safety Regulation

SECTION 601: *General safety powers and duties.*—This section requires the Authority to regulate the operation of aircraft in interstate, overseas, and foreign air commerce in the interest of safety and to impose minimum safety standards for aircraft, air-navigation facilities, and airports.

SECTION 602: *Aircraft certificates.*—This section empowers the Authority to issue various types of safety certificates for aircraft. These certificates are (1) type certificates, based upon the adequacy of the design, materials, and construction of aircraft, aircraft engines, propellers, or appliances, (2) production certificates, issued for the purpose of certifying that the production of duplicates of aircraft, aircraft engines, propellers, or appliances for which type certificates have been issued will conform to the type certificate, and (3) airworthiness certificates, issued from time to time for the purpose of certifying that the aircraft is in condition for safe operation.

SECTION 603: *Airman certificates.*—This section empowers the Authority to issue to any properly qualified person an appropriate airman certificate authorizing such person to operate, inspect, service, or overhaul aircraft. However, the Authority is empowered to restrict or condition the issuance of such certificates to aliens.

SECTION 604: *Air-carrier-operating certificates.*—This section empowers the Authority to issue an operating certificate to an air carrier if it finds that such air carrier is prepared to operate safely.

SECTION 605: *Air-navigation-facility rating.*—This section empowers the Authority to inspect and rate air-navigation facilities as to their suitability for use.

SECTION 606: *Air agency rating.*—This section empowers the Authority to examine and rate schools giving flying instructions, aircraft repair stations, and similar agencies.

SECTION 607: *Amendment, suspension, and revocation of certificates.*—This section provides that the Authority may amend, suspend, or revoke, in whole or in part, any type certificate, production certificate, airworthiness certificate, airman certificate, air-carrier-operating certificate, air-navigation-facility certificate, or air-agency certificate, in the interests of safety.

SECTION 608: *Prohibitions.*—This section makes it unlawful for any person (1) to operate in interstate, overseas, or foreign air commerce an aircraft for which an airworthiness certificate is not in effect, (2) to serve as an airman in connection with a civil aircraft used in interstate, overseas, or foreign air commerce without an appropriate airman certificate, or to employ any such airman for service in connection with such aircraft, (3) to operate as an air carrier without an air-carrier-operating certificate, or (4) to operate aircraft in interstate, overseas, or foreign air commerce in violation of the regulations prescribed by the Authority under section 601.

Title VII—Safety Division

SECTION 701: *Organization and duties of Division.*—This section provides for the establishment within the Authority of a Safety Division which would be headed by a Director appointed by the President by and with the advice and consent of the Senate. The Director would receive a salary of $6,000 per year. It would be the duty of the Director and his assistants in the Safety Division to investigate accidents, to report to the Authority the probable cause of each accident, and to recommend to the Authority possible means of eliminating such accidents in the future. The Director would also, at the request of the Authority, make studies and other investigations of safety matters. The Director would exercise his functions independently of the Authority, would appoint his own personnel, and would be empowered to secure persons outside the Government service and persons in other executive departments or independent establishments of the Government to assist him in the investigation of accidents. The purpose of the Safety Division is to insure the impartial investigation of accidents and the careful analysis of the results of such investigations.

Title VIII—Other Administration Agencies

SECTION 801: *The President of the United States.*—This section provides that any action of the Authority with respect to a permit authorizing a foreign air carrier to operate to this country, or a certificate authorizing an American air carrier to operate in overseas or foreign air transportation or between places in the same Territory or possession, shall be subject to the approval of the President. This section does not apply, however, to the issuance or denial or the original terms and conditions of a certificate or permit issuable to an existing line.

SECTION 802: *Department of State.*—This section authorizes the negotiation by the State Department of agreements with foreign governments for the establishment of air routes and services between the United States and such foreign countries. These agreements are subject to the approval of the Authority and the President before they take effect.

SECTION 803: *The Post Office Department.*—This section confers upon the Postmaster General authority to make rules and regulations regarding the transportation of mail by aircraft and authorizes him to apply to the Authority for new mail service. The section also contains a limitation upon the amount that the Postmaster General may pay a foreign air carrier for carrying United States mail and requires the Postmaster General to tender mail to the holder of a certificate authorizing the carriage of mail to the extent required by the Postal Service. The emergency carriage of mail into areas affected by flood, fire, or other calamity is also provided for.

Title IX—Penalties

This title prescribes the penalties for violations of the act.

Title X—Procedure

This title prescribes the procedure to be followed by the Authority in carrying out its duties and sets out the method of appeal from, and enforcement of, the orders and requirements of the Authority. The orders of the Authority would be enforced in the district courts but judicial review of an order of the Authority would be had in the circuit courts of appeals. Negative as well as affirmative orders would be reviewable. The doctrine of *Procter and Gamble* v. *United States* (225 U.S. 282), and similar cases will not be applicable under the judicial review provision of this title. This doctrine has proved burdensome and unfair both to the carrier and the public (*II Sharfman, Interstate Commerce Commission*, 406-417). The judicial review provision also enables the court either to stay an order or to require some affirmative act by the Authority, where necessary to give interlocutory protection to a petitioner. Upon final decree the courts of appeals can take whatever action may be appropriate to the case within their constitutional powers by ordering further proceedings or otherwise. Such final decrees would be subject to review by the Supreme Court.

Title XI—Miscellaneous

SECTION 1101: *Regulation and classification.*—This section empowers the Authority to classify air carriers and perform all acts, issue all orders, and make all regulations necessary to carry out the act.

SECTION 1102: *International agreements.*—This section requires the Authority to act in accordance with the international obligations of the United States, and to take into consideration applicable laws of foreign countries. The section also forbids the Authority to restrict compliance by any air carrier with any obligation imposed upon it by a foreign country, unless such obligation arises out of a contract between the carrier and a foreign country which is disapproved by the Authority.

SECTION 1103: *Publications.*—This section requires the Authority to provide for the publication of official documents.

SECTION 1104: *Annual report.*—This section requires the Authority to make an annual report to Congress.

SECTION 1105: *Nature and use of documents filed.*This section provides that copies of all documents filed with the Authority shall be preserved as public records except those withheld from publication as confidential.

SECTION 1106: *Collection and dissemination of information.*—This section empowers the Authority to conduct studies and disseminate information relative to the development of civil aeronautics.

SECTION 1107: *Cooperation with Government agencies.*—This section provides that the Authority may avail itself of the assistance of research and technical agencies of the United States.

SECTION 1108: *Amendments and repeals.*—This section contains the statutes amended or repealed by the act.

SECTION 1109: *Effect of transfers, repeals, and amendments.*—This section contains saving provisions with respect to orders, regulations, contracts, and certificates in force, and administrative and judicial proceedings pending, on the effective date of the act.

SECTION 1110: *Separability.*—This section is the customary separability clause.

SECTION 1111: *Effective date.*—Under this section the act would become effective 60 days after enactment except title II and section 410, which would become effective immediately. However, the Authority is given power to extend the effective date of any section for not more than 180 days after enactment. . . .

MAPES REPORT WITH A MINORITY VIEW ON THE CIVIL AERONAUTICS BILL
May 5, 1958

Mr. Mapes, from the Committee on Interstate and Foreign Commerce, submitted the following

MINORITY VIEWS
[To accompany H. R. 9738]

The undersigned members of the Committee on Interstate and Foreign Commerce submit the following minority views with respect to the fundamental issue involved in the bill; that is, whether or not another commission or bureau, designated in the bill as recommended by the majority of the committee as the "Civil Aeronautics Authority," shall be created to regulate air commerce, or whether the Interstate Commerce Commission shall be clothed with authority to do the job.

The undersigned believe that it is totally unnecessary to create a new governmental agency for the purpose. To do so is not only an extravagant and useless expenditure of public funds but will actually retard and weaken the proper regulation of this industry, which all agree is urgent. It will mean setting up an entirely new and inexperienced organization with all that that means, when the Interstate Commerce Commission already has an experienced and expert organization in existence.

As was well stated by David L. Behncke, president, Air Line Pilots Association, in testifying before the committee:

> We believe that all forms of transportation should be coordinated into a single agency. We believe there is a great advantage to having air transportation regulated by an experienced body such as the Interstate Commerce Commission where the rules and practices are known and the effects can be reasonably predicted. Any new agency must necessarily be an unknown quantity until it has gone through a character-building period during which time practically all of its rules, procedures, practices, and so forth must be worked out by trial and error, and after many years they will probably be on the same footing with an agency such as the Interstate Commerce Commission insofar as actual results are concerned. In other words, a new agency will have to go through a long period before it becomes stabilized in the same way and to the same extent as the Interstate Commerce Commission practices are stabilized today."

The action of the majority of the committee in reporting the bill providing for this new Authority is a complete reversal of the unanimous action of the committee during the first session of this Congress. The committee reported H. R. 7273, now on the calendar, without a dissenting vote. It has been on the calendar since May 28, 1937. It proposes to amend the Interstate Commerce Act by providing for the regulation of the transportation of passengers and property by air carriers in interstate, overseas, and foreign commerce by the Interstate Commerce Commission. No action has been taken on that bill since it was reported by the committee nearly a year ago.

In its report on H. R. 7273 last year the committee stated that—

> The fundamental purpose of this proposed legislation is to extend to the Interstate Commerce Commission regulatory powers over air transportation, generally similar, so far as applicable, to the powers it now exercises over rail and motor transportation.
>
> The Interstate Commerce Act, as amended, including parts I and II, governs the regulation of steam railroads, electric railways, express companies, sleeping-car companies, pipe lines, steamship lines controlled by railroads, water lines engaged in joint operation with rail lines, and motor carriers. This bill would continue the established policy of the Congress in coordinating under the jurisdiction of the Interstate Commerce Commission, all interstate transportation. The regulation is adapted to the special characteristics of transportation by air and is carried no further than is necessary in the interest of the public.
>
> This bill follows the program recommended by the President in messages to the Congress. The ultimate purpose of the program is the coordination of the transportation of the Nation, thus serving the needs of interstate and foreign commerce and the national defense.

No adequate reason has been assigned to justify this complete reversal of form on the part of a majority of the committee. The same reasons exist today for clothing the Interstate Commerce Commission with authority to regulate air commerce as existed 1 year ago.

The present action of the majority of the committee is not only contrary to the unanimous action of the committee 1 year ago, but it is contrary to the recommendations of the President as submitted to Congress on two separate occasions. The majority report says that certain executive departments approved of the present bill, but it makes no reference to the attitude of the President toward it. There is nothing in the report to indicate that he has changed his position.

The undersigned believe that it is bad public policy to create different commissions to regulate different phases of transportation. It cannot help but create conflict, overlapping of authority, duplication of work, and unnecessary expenditure of public funds. It is against the public interest from every standpoint. There should be unified control of all phases of transportation.

In submitting the report of the Federal Aviation Commission to Congress in January 1935, the President said:

I believe that we should avoid the multiplication of separate regulatory agencies in the field of transportation. Therefore, in the interim before a permanent consolidated agency is created or designated over the transportation as a whole, a division of the Interstate Commerce Commission can well serve the needs of air transportation. In the granting of powers and duties by the Congress orderly government calls for the administration of executive functions by those administrative departments or agencies which have functioned satisfactorily in the past and, on the other hand, calls for the vesting of judicial functions in agencies already accustomed to such powers. It is this principle that should be followed in all the various aspects of transportation legislation.

And, as recently as April 11, 1938, in his message to Congress relating to relief for railroads, the President said:

From the point of view of business efficiency, such as a private corporation would seek, it would seem to be the part of common sense to place all executive functions relating to all transportation in one Federal department—such as the Department of Commerce, the Department of the Interior, or some other old or new department. At the same time all quasi-judicial and quasi-legislative matters relating to all transportation could properly be placed under an independent commission—a reorganized Interstate Commerce Commission.

The present bill does not adhere to the recommendations of the President in either one of these respects.

Commissioner Eastman, of the Interstate Commerce Commission, during the hearings on H. R. 7273, speaking of his experience as Coordinator of Railroads, testified:

I also reached the conclusion that the transportation problem is, after all, a single problem and not a series of problems, because all of these forms of transportation are interrelated in at least two different ways: They are either interrelated by competition or they are interrelated by the opportunities for cooperation and coordination between them or by both. Therefore, it seems highly desirable to concentrate regulation in a single body instead of spreading it over a number of separate bodies. That is necessary not only in the interest of proper coordination between these various forms of transportation but to insure fair and impartial treatment of them all by a body, which has not greater or different responsibility with respect to any one of them than to any of the others.

All students of the transportation question agree with the position taken by the President and Commissioner Eastman on the desirability of unified control of the transportation systems of the country.

As stated by Prof. Emery R. Johnson, of the Wharton School of Finance and Commerce of the University of Pennsylvania, in a new work on Government Regulation of Transportation:

> The task to be performed by the Government is the regulation of transportation as a whole and in the general public interest. This involves the regulation of all the agencies of transportation by applying to each of them like principles of regulation for the accomplishment of a common purpose—that of enabling each agency to function advantageously and appropriately as a part of a national transportation system.

We recognize the need of additional legislation for the regulation of agencies engaged in transportation in air commerce. We favor the passage of the bill on the calendar reported unanimously by the Committee on Interstate and Foreign Commerce giving the Interstate Commerce Commission additional authority for that purpose. We are opposed to the pending bill for the reasons above stated.

Carl E. Mapes
Chas. A. Wolverton
James Wolfenden
Pehr G. Holmes
Carroll Reece
James W. Wadsworth
Charles A. Halleck
Gardner R. Withrow